Portrait of

America

CONTENTS

millionaires. Yet he also acted on his own self-proclaimed sense of duty and gave away most of his huge fortune during his lifetime.

Smith takes us on a vivid journey through the plants, railroads, steel mills, oil fields, and coal mines of the Gilded Age, reminding us that the robber barons amassed their fortunes at the expense of the men, women, and children they employed. The working conditions Smith describes reminds us of the terrible human toll the United States paid for industrialization.

Boroff's picture of the Jewish immigrants who landed in New York is so graphic that readers can see them, hear them speak, and smell the food they ate. He not only captures the immigrant experience but explains the influence of the Jewish immigrants on the United States and the country's influence on them.

Burns recounts the story of the Populist crusade without bogging his narrative down in dense details of economics. What energized populism, he believes, was the notion of liberty as self-fulfillment through cooperative action. Burns's account is sensitive to the farmers' plight in industrial America and to the important role that women played in launching the Populist movement.

The authors show how American involvement in the Filipino insurrection of 1898–1902 grew out of the Spanish-American War and the U.S. bid for empire. They also draw significant parallels between the Filipino war and the war in Vietnam six decades later.

Teddy Roosevelt's personality was similar to his dessert plate, which, says Edmund Morris, was filled with "so many peaches that the cream spilled over the sides." TR's Pulitzer Prize-winning biographer uses that personality to point out the importance of personal qualities in shaping the conduct and careers of historical figures.

witnessed the events he describes. Allen credits the impact of the
First World War and "the growing independence of the American
woman" with the youth rebellion of the 1920s, and he points to the
significant cultural change it brought about.

XV   TOWARD THE TWENTY-FIRST CENTURY 449

PREFACE

Like its predecessors, the Sixth Edition of this anthology stresses the human side of history, suggesting how the interaction of people and events shaped the course of the American past. As I compiled selections for *Portrait of America*, my primary criteria were that they be well written and suffused with human interest and insight. I chose essays, narratives, and biographical portraits that humanize American history, portraying it as the story of real people who actually lived, who struggled, enjoyed triumphs, suffered failures and anxieties, just like people in our own time. I hope that the anthology is an example of humanistic history at its best, the kind that combines scrupulous and engaging scholarship with a compelling narrative style. My feeling is that, since college survey audiences are not professional ones, they might enjoy reading history if it presents the past in an exciting and readable form.

There is another reason why students will find *Portrait of America* edifying: it showcases the writings of some of America's most eminent historians. The prizes their work has won testifies to their important places in the galaxy of American letters. Eric Foner's extraordinary new study of Reconstruction received the Bancroft Prize and the Francis Parkman Prize of the Society of American Historians. Arthur M. Schlesinger, Jr., has won two Pulitzer Prizes, two National Book Awards, the Gold Medal Award of the American Institute of Arts and Letters, the Francis Parkman Prize, and the Bancroft Prize. James Mac-Gregor Burns has received the Pulitzer Prize, plus the National Book Award and the Francis Parkman Prize. Page Smith and Eric Goldman have each won the Bancroft Prize; Goldman also won an Emmy Award from the National Academy of Television Arts and Sciences. William H. Chafe has won the Robert F. Kennedy Memorial Book Award, and William Manchester has won the Washington Irving Award and the Sarah Josepha Hale Award. Many of the other contributors have also received significant literary and scholarly awards. Thus *Portrait of America* offers readers a unique opportunity to learn from a lineup of nationally recognized historians and writers.

The Sixth Edition of Volume II has been extensively revised and has fourteen new selections. Some of them—Robert M. Utley's account of Sitting Bull and the Sioux resistance, Alonzo L. Hamby's discussion of Franklin D. Roosevelt and the New Deal, Otto Friedrich's gripping account of the genesis and execution of the Japanese air attack against Pearl Harbor, Sara M. Evans's essay on the contributions of American women during the Second World War, Lawrence B. Goodheart's assessment of Malcolm X, Allen J. Matusow's survey of the origins and high points of the 1960s counterculture, and Karl Zinsmeister's evaluation of the Reagan era—replace and improve upon earlier selections on similar subjects. Other new selections focus on topics not previously covered—Eric Foner's discussion of the birth of the modern black community during Reconstruction, Miriam Horn's report on how a new generation of historians has assailed the old interpretations and myths of the frontier, James MacGregor Burns's account of the momentous Populist crusade, David R. Kohler and James W. Wensyel's discussion of America's first Southeast Asian War (in the Philippines), Lerone Bennett's account of the black river of protest during the Progressive era, Nicholas Lemann's reassessment of the 1970s, and Arthur M. Schlesinger's analysis of the end of the Cold War and its lessons for furure generations.

Although the Sixth Edition retains the best and most popular selections of the previous edition, I have rewritten the introductions to most of them. I hope that *Portrait of America* remains as balanced as ever, for it offers samplings of virtually every kind of history—men's and women's, black and white, social and cultural, political and military, urban and economic, national and local—so that students can appreciate the rich diversity of the American experience.

The Sixth Edition offers an important new feature. Each selection is preceded by a glossary, designed to help readers identify important individuals, events, and concepts that appear in the reading. Introductions set the selections in proper context and suggest ways to approach studying them. They also tie all the selections together so that they can be read more or less as connected episodes. Study questions following the selections raise significant issues and encourage students to make comparisons and contrasts between the selections. The questions also help students review the readings and suggest points for class discussion.

The anthology is intended for use largely in college survey courses. It could be utilized as a supplement to a textbook or to a list of paperback readings. Or it could serve as the basic text. The book is organized into fifteen parts according to periods or themes; each part contains two or three related selections. This organization allows readers to make comparisons and contrasts between different events or viewpoints.

In preparing the Sixth Edition, I drew on the expertise of many enthusiastic colleagues across the country. I owe a special thanks to Professor Charles J. Errico of Northern Virginia Community College, who has provided constructive critiques of both volumes through many editions. I am indebted to my research assistant, Anne-Marie Taylor, for writing the study questions to the new selections and offering excellent critical advice. Dr. Karen Smith and Professor Betty L. Mitchell of the University of Massachusetts, Dartmouth, wrote the study questions for the other selections and gave me helpful suggestions about readings on women's and social history. Professor Joyce Berkman of the University of Massachusetts, Amherst, also counseled me on women's history. I want to thank the following professors for reviewing one or both volumes:

Glenn C. Altschuler
Cornell University

James F. Cook
Floyd College

Jean E. Friedman
University of Georgia

James W. Hill
Riverside Community College

Robert Ireland
University of Kentucky

Monroe H. Little, Jr.
Indiana University–Purdue

Lessing H. Nohl
American River College

My gratitude, too, to Rebecca Watson, who brought me countless articles and books, photocopied materials, and performed many other indispensable tasks. Finally, I am grateful to the many students who have offered praise and suggestions for *Portrait of America*, for they are invaluable arbiters of how effectively it teaches them about the past.

S.B.O.

Portrait of

America

A Troubled Peace

From Slavery to Freedom:
The Birth of the Modern Black Community

ERIC FONER

For African Americans in North and South alike, the Civil War had profound religious meaning from the beginning. Hundreds of thousands, writes Vincent Harding, "believed unwaveringly that their God moved in history to deliver his people, and they had been looking eagerly, praying hourly, waiting desperately for the glory of the coming of the Lord. For them, all the raucous, roaring guns of Charleston Harbor and Bull Run, of Antietam and Fort Pillow, of Shiloh and Murfreesboro and Richmond were the certain voice of God, announcing his judgment across the bloody stretches of the South, returning blood for blood to the black river." During the course of that war, African Americans believed, God did deliver them. He drove out the rebels and slaveholders, just as he had once driven out the Hittites and Canaanites. With the Confederacy's collapse, as one song went, "slavery chain done broke at last."

> *Slavery chain done broke at last!*
> *Broke at last! Broke at last!*
> *Slavery chain done broke at last!*
> *Gonna praise God till I die!*

Some reacted to their liberation with cautious elation. When a young Virginia woman heard her former masters weeping over the capture of Jefferson Davis, she went down to a spring alone and cried out, "Glory, glory, hallelujah to Jesus! I's free! I's free!" Suddenly afraid, she looked about. What if the white folks heard her? But seeing no one, she fell to the ground and kissed it, thanking "Master Jesus" over and over. For her, freedom meant hope — hope that she could find her husband and four children who had been sold to a slave trader.

Others celebrated their liberation in public. In Athens, Georgia, they danced around a liberty pole; in Charleston, they paraded through the streets. Many African Americans, however, were wary and uncertain. "You're joking me," one man said when the master told him he was free. He asked some neighbors if they were free also. "I couldn't believe we was all free alike," he said. Some African Americans, out of feelings of obligation or compassion, remained on the home place to help their former masters. But others were hostile. When a woman named Cady heard that the war was over, she decided to protest the cruel treatment she had suffered as a slave. She threw down her hoe, marched up to the big house, found the mistress, and flipped her dress up. She told the white woman, "Kiss my ass!"

For Cady, for the young black woman, for hosts of other African Americans, freedom meant an end to the manifold evils of slavery; it meant the right to say what they felt and go where they wanted. But what else did freedom mean? In this selection, Eric Foner, today's leading Reconstruction scholar, describes how the former slaves in the first critical year or so of Reconstruction defined and exercised freedom for themselves. Above all, they wanted independence from their former masters, wanted control of their families, churches, and schools. And they wanted their own land, too, and mules to work it. As they set about expanding, consolidating, and strengthening their traditional institutions and forging their own political culture, African Americans in Reconstruction formed the modern black community, one "whose roots lay deep in slavery but whose structure and values reflected the consequences of emancipation."

It is an inspiring story, and Foner relates it with great insight. Instead of being passive and undeserving recipients of freedom (as an earlier generation of histories portrayed them), the former slaves in Foner's telling reached out and seized control of their destinies. As they sought independence from white control, Foner says, the former slaves actively sought inclusion in the body politic. Across the South, they held political conventions in which they demanded their "equal rights as citizens." They would not gain the right to vote and to hold public office until 1867, when the Republican-controlled Congress assumed control of southern restoration, in what became known as Radical Reconstruction. But "the seeds that flowered then," as Foner notes, "were planted in the first years of freedom." What happened to African American dreams of economic independence and full citizenship after the Radicals took over is treated in the next selection, "Reconstruction: The Revolution That Failed."

GLOSSARY

FREEDMEN'S BUREAU Established by congressional statute in March 1865, the Bureau of Freedmen, Refugees, and Abandoned Lands was supposed to provide food and schools for the former slaves, help them secure jobs, and make certain they received fair wages.

LAND DISTRIBUTION Had the federal government seized the estates of ex–Confederates and distributed the land among the former slaves, it "would have had profound consequences for Southern society, weakening the land-based economic and political power of the old ruling class, offering blacks a measure of choice as to whether, when, and under what circumstances to enter the labor market, and affecting the former slaves' conception of themselves." In the next selection, you will see what happened to the idea of land distribution.

LYNCH, JAMES D. African American who served as Mississippi's secretary of state during Reconstruction.

PEARCE, REV. CHARLES H. "Preachers played a central role in Reconstruction black politics," Foner writes. The Reverend Pearce held "several Reconstruction offices in Florida."

RAPIER, JAMES T. African American member of Congress from Alabama during Reconstruction.

SHARECROPPING System of renting land by which a tenant farmer paid the landowner a share of the tenant's crop as rent.

F reedom came in different ways to different parts of the South. In large areas, slavery had disintegrated long before Lee's surrender, but elsewhere, far from the presence of federal troops, blacks did not learn of its irrevocable end until the spring of 1865. Despite the many disappointments that followed, this generation of blacks would always regard the moment when "de freedom sun shine out" as the great watershed of their lives. Houston H. Holloway, who had been sold three times before he reached the age of twenty in 1865, later recalled with vivid clarity the day emancipation came to his section of Georgia: "I felt like a bird out of a cage. Amen. Amen. Amen. I could hardly ask to feel any better than I did that day. . . . The week passed off in a blaze of glory."

"Freedom," said a black minister, "burned in the black heart long before freedom was born." But what did "freedom" mean? "It is necessary to define that word," Freedmen's Bureau Commissioner O. O. Howard told a black audience in 1865, "for it is most apt to be misunderstood." Howard assumed a straightforward definition existed. But "freedom" itself became a terrain of conflict, its substance open to different and sometimes contradictory interpretations, its content changing for whites as well as blacks in the aftermath of the Civil War.

Blacks carried out of bondage an understanding of their new condition shaped both by their experience as slaves and by observation of the free society around them. What one planter called their "wild notions of rights and freedom" encompassed, first of all, an end to the myriad injustices associated with slavery. Some, like black minister Henry M. Turner, stressed that freedom meant the enjoyment of "our rights in common with other men." "If I cannot do like a white man I am not free," Henry Adams told his former

From *A Short History of Reconstruction* by Eric Foner (New York: Harper & Row, 1990), 35–52.

Former slaves pose in front of the ruins of Richmond, Virginia, after the cruel war was over. African Americans like these, writes Eric Foner, formed the modern black community, by expanding, consoli- *dating, and strengthening their traditional institutions and forging their own political culture. (Library of Congress)*

master in 1865. "I see how the poor white people do. I ought to do so too, or else I am a slave."

But underpinning the specific aspirations lay a broader theme: a desire for independence from white control, for autonomy both as individuals and as members of a community being transformed by emancipation. Before the war, free blacks had created churches, schools, and mutual benefit societies, while slaves had forged a culture centered on the family and church. With freedom, these institutions were consolidated, expanded, and liberated from white supervision, and new ones — particularly political organizations — joined them as focal points of black life. In stabilizing their families, seizing control of their churches, greatly expanding their schools and benevolent societies, staking a claim to economic independence, and forging a political culture, blacks during Reconstruction laid the foundation for the modern black community, whose roots lay deep in slavery but whose structure and values reflected the consequences of emancipation.

☆

FROM SLAVERY TO FREEDOM

Long after the end of the Civil War, the experience of bondage remained deeply etched in blacks' collective memory. The freedmen resented not only the brutal incidents of slavery but the fact of having been held as slaves at all. During a visit to Richmond, Scottish minister David Macrae was surprised to hear a former slave complain of past mistreatment, while acknowledging he had never been whipped. "How were you cruelly treated then?" asked Macrae. "I was cruelly treated," answered the freedman, "because I was kept in slavery."

In countless ways, the newly freed slaves sought to overturn the real and symbolic authority whites had exercised over every aspect of their lives. Blacks relished opportunities to flaunt their liberation from the innumerable regulations, significant and trivial, associated with slavery. Freedmen held mass meetings and religious services unrestrained by white surveillance, acquired previously forbidden dogs, guns, and liquor, and refused to yield the sidewalks to whites. They dressed as they pleased, black women sometimes wearing gaudy finery, carrying parasols, and replacing the slave kerchief with colorful hats and veils. Whites complained of "insolence" and "insubordination" among the freedmen, by which they meant any departure from the deference and obedience expected under slavery. On the Bradford plantation in Florida, one untoward incident followed another. First, the family cook told Mrs. Bradford "if she want any dinner she kin cook it herself." Then the former slaves went off to a meeting with Northern soldiers to discuss "our freedom." Told that she and her daughter could not attend, one woman replied "they were now free and if she saw fit to take her daughter into that crowd it was nobody's business." "Never before had I a word of impudence from any of our black folk," recorded nineteen-year-old Susan Bradford, "but they are not ours any longer."

Among the most resented of slavery's restrictions was the rule, enforced by patrols, that no black could travel without a pass. With emancipation, it seemed that half the South's black population took to the roads. Southern towns and cities experienced an especially large influx of freedmen during and immedi-

ately after the Civil War. In the cities, many blacks believed, "freedom was free-er." Here were schools, churches, and fraternal societies, as well as the army (including, in 1865, black soldiers) and the Freedmen's Bureau, offering protection from the violence so pervasive in much of the rural South. Between 1865 and 1870, the black population of the South's ten largest cities doubled, while the number of white residents rose by only ten percent. Smaller towns, from which blacks had often been excluded as slaves, experienced even more dramatic increases.

Black migrants who hoped to find urban employment often encountered severe disappointment. The influx from the countryside flooded the labor market, consigning most urban blacks to low-wage, menial employment. Unable to obtain decent housing, black migrants lived in squalid shantytowns on the outskirts of Southern cities, where the incidence of disease and death far exceeded that among white city dwellers. The result was a striking change in Southern urban living patterns. Before the war, blacks and whites had lived scattered throughout Southern cities. Reconstruction witnessed the rise of a new, segregated, urban geography.

No aspect of black mobility was more poignant than the effort to reunite families separated during slavery. "In their eyes," wrote a Freedmen's Bureau agent, "the work of emancipation was incomplete until the families which had been dispersed by slavery were reunited." One freedman, writing from Texas, asked the Bureau's aid in locating "my own dearest relatives," providing a long list of sisters, nieces, nephews, uncles, and in-laws, none of whom he had seen since his sale in Virginia twenty-four years before. A typical plea for help appeared in the Nashville *Colored Tennessean*:

During the year 1849, Thomas Sample carried away from this city, as his slaves, our daughter, Polly, and son. . . . We will give $100 each for them to any person who will assist them . . . to get to Nashville, or get word to us of their whereabouts.

Although vulnerable to disruption, strong family ties had existed under slavery. Emancipation allowed blacks to solidify their family connections, and most freedmen seized the opportunity. Many families, in addition, adopted the children of deceased relatives and friends rather than see them apprenticed to white masters or placed in Freedmen's Bureau orphanages. By 1870, a large majority of blacks lived in two-parent households.

But while emancipation strengthened the preexisting black family, it also transformed the roles of its members and relations among them. One common, significant change was that slave families, separated because their members belonged to different owners, could now live together. More widely noticed by white observers in early Reconstruction was the withdrawal of black women from field labor.

Beginning in 1865, and for years thereafter, Southern whites throughout the South complained of the difficulty of obtaining female field laborers. Planters, Freedmen's Bureau officials, and Northern visitors all ridiculed the black "female aristocracy" for "acting the *lady*" or mimicking the family patterns of middle-class whites. White employers also resented their inability to force black children to labor in the fields, especially after the spread of schools in rural areas. Contemporaries appeared uncertain whether black women, black men, or both were responsible for the withdrawal of females from agricultural labor. There is no question that many black men considered it manly to have their wives work at home and believed that, as head of the family, the male should decide how its labor was organized. But many black women desired to devote more time than under slavery to caring for their children and to domestic responsibilities like cooking, sewing, and laundering.

The shift of black female labor from the fields to the home proved a temporary phenomenon. The rise of renting and sharecropping, which made each family responsible for its own plot of land, placed a premium on the labor of all family members. The dire poverty of many black families, deepened by the de-pression of the 1870s, made it essential for both women and men to contribute to the family's income. Throughout this period, a far higher percentage of black than white women and children worked for wages outside their homes. Where women continued to concentrate on domestic tasks, and children attended school, they frequently engaged in seasonal field labor. Thus, emancipation did not eliminate labor outside the home by black women and children, but it fundamentally altered control over their labor. Now blacks themselves, rather than a white owner or overseer, decided where and when black women and children worked.

For blacks, liberating their families from the authority of whites was an indispensable element of freedom. But the family itself was in some ways transformed by emancipation. Although historians no longer view the slave family as matriarchal, it is true that slave men did not function as economic breadwinners and that their masters wielded authority within the household. In a sense, slavery had imposed on black men and women the rough "equality" of powerlessness. With freedom came developments that strengthened patriarchy within the black family and consigned men and women to separate spheres.

Outside events strongly influenced this development. Service in the Union Army enabled black men to participate more directly than women in the struggle for freedom. The Freedmen's Bureau designated the husband as head of the black household, insisting that men sign contracts for the labor of their entire families and establishing lower wage scales for women. After 1867 black men could serve on juries, vote, hold office, and rise to leadership in the Republican party, while black women, like their white counterparts, could not. And black preachers, editors, and politicians emphasized women's responsibility for making the home "a place of peace and comfort" for men and urged them to submit to their husbands' authority.

Not all black women placidly accepted the increasingly patriarchal quality of black family life. Indeed, many proved more than willing to bring family disputes before public authorities. The records of the Freedmen's Bureau contain hundreds of complaints by black women of beatings, infidelity, and lack of child support. Some black women objected to their husbands' signing labor contracts for them, demanded separate payment of their wages, and refused to be liable for their husbands' debts at country stores. Yet if emancipation not only institutionalized the black family but also spawned tensions within it, black men and women shared a passionate commitment to the stability of family life as the solid foundation upon which a new black community could flourish.

☆

BUILDING THE BLACK COMMUNITY

Second only to the family as a focal point of black life stood the church. And, as in the case of the family, Reconstruction was a time of consolidation and transformation for black religion. With the death of slavery, urban blacks seized control of their own churches, while the "invisible institution" of the rural slave church emerged into the light of day. The creation of an independent black religious life proved to be a momentous and irreversible consequence of emancipation.

In antebellum Southern Protestant congregations, slaves and free blacks had enjoyed a kind of associate membership. Subject to the same rules and discipline as whites, they were required to sit in the back of the church or in the gallery during services and were excluded from Sabbath schools and a role in church governance. In the larger cities, the number of black members often justified the organization of wholly black congregations and the construction of separate churches, although these were legally required to have white pastors. In the aftermath of emancipation, the wholesale withdrawal of blacks from biracial congregations redrew the religious map of the South. Two causes combined to produce the independent

black church: the refusal of whites to offer blacks an equal place within their congregations and the black quest for self-determination.

Throughout the South, blacks emerging from slavery pooled their resources to purchase land and erect their own churches. Before the buildings were completed, they held services in structures as diverse as a railroad boxcar, where Atlanta's First Baptist Church gathered, or an outdoor "bush arbor," where the First Baptist Church of Memphis congregated in 1865. The first new building to rise amid Charleston's ruins was a black church on Calhoun Street; by 1866 ten more had been constructed. In the countryside, a community would often build a single church, used in rotation by the various black denominations. By the end of Reconstruction in 1877, the vast majority of Southern blacks had withdrawn from churches dominated by whites. On the eve of the war, 42,000 black Methodists worshipped in biracial South Carolina churches; by the 1870s, only 600 remained.

The church was "the first social institution fully controlled by black men in America," and its multiple functions testified to its centrality in the black community. Churches housed schools, social events, and political gatherings. In rural areas, church picnics, festivals, and excursions often provided the only opportunity for fellowship and recreation. The church served as an "Ecclesiastical Court House," promoting moral values, adjudicating family disputes, and disciplining individuals for adultery and other illicit behavior. In every black community, ministers were among the most respected individuals, esteemed for their speaking ability, organizational talents, and good judgment on matters both public and private.

Inevitably, too, preachers played a central role in Reconstruction black politics. Many agreed with Rev. Charles H. Pearce, who held several Reconstruction offices in Florida, that it was "impossible" to separate religion and politics: "A man in this State cannot do his whole duty as a minister except he looks out for the political interests of his people." Even those preachers who lacked ambition for political position sometimes found it thrust upon them. Often among the few literate blacks in a community, they were called on to serve as election registrars and candidates for office. Over 100 black ministers, hailing from North and South, from free and slave backgrounds, and from every black denomination from African Methodist Episcopal to Primitive Baptist, would be elected to legislative seats during Reconstruction.

Throughout Reconstruction, religious convictions shaped blacks' understanding of the momentous events around them, the language in which they voiced aspirations for justice and autonomy. Blacks inherited from slavery a distinctive version of Christian faith, in which Jesus appeared as a personal redeemer offering solace in the face of misfortune, while the Old Testament suggested that they were a chosen people, analogous to the Jews in Egypt, whom God, in the fullness of time, would deliver from bondage. "There is no part of the Bible with which they are so familiar as the story of the deliverance of the Children of Israel," a white army chaplain reported in 1866.

Emancipation and the defeat of the Confederacy strongly reinforced this messianic vision of history. Even nonclerics used secular and religious vocabulary interchangeably, as in one 1867 speech recorded by a North Carolina justice of the peace:

He said it was not now like it used to be, that . . . the negro was about to get his equal rights. . . . That the negroes owed their freedom to the courage of the negro soldiers and to God. . . . He made frequent references to the II and IV chapters of Joshua for a full accomplishment of the principles and destiny of the race. It was concluded that the race have a destiny in view similar to the Children of Israel.

The rise of the independent black church was accompanied by the creation of a host of fraternal, benevolent, and mutual aid societies. In early Reconstruction, blacks created literally thousands of such organizations; a partial list includes burial societies, debating clubs, Masonic lodges, fire companies, drama societies, trade associations, temperance clubs, and equal rights leagues. Offering social fellowship, sickness and funeral benefits, and, most of all, a chance to manage their own affairs, these voluntary associations embodied a spirit of collective self-improvement. Robert G. Fitzgerald, who had been born free in Delaware, served in both the U.S. Army and Navy, and came to Virginia to teach in 1866, was delighted to see rural blacks establishing churches, lyceums, and schools. "They tell me," he recorded in his diary, "before Mr. Lincoln made them free they had nothing to work for, to look up to, now they have everything, and will, by God's help, make the best of it." Moreover, the spirit of mutual self-help extended outward from the societies to embrace destitute nonmembers. In 1865 and 1866, blacks in Nashville, Jackson, New Orleans, and Atlanta, as well as in many rural areas, raised money to establish orphanages, soup kitchens, employment agencies, and poor relief funds.

Perhaps the most striking illustration of the freedmen's quest for self-improvement was their seemingly unquenchable thirst for education. Before the war, every Southern state except Tennessee had prohibited the instruction of slaves, and although many free blacks had attended school and a number of slaves became literate through their own efforts or the aid of sympathetic masters, over ninety percent of the South's adult black population was illiterate in 1860. Access to education for themselves and their children was, for blacks, central to the meaning of freedom, and white contemporaries were astonished by their "avidity for learning." Adults as well as children thronged the schools. A Northern teacher in Florida reported how one sixty-year-old woman, "just beginning to spell, seems as if she could not think of any thing but her book, says she spells her lesson all the evening, then she dreams about it, and wakes up thinking about it."

Northern benevolent societies, the Freedmen's Bureau, and, after 1868, state governments provided most of the funding for black education during

A class at the Zion School for Colored Children in Charleston, South Carolina. During Reconstruction, the Freedmen's Bureau, a federal agency, established African American schools like this one throughout the conquered South. (The Granger Collection, New York)

Reconstruction. But the initiative often lay with blacks themselves. Urban blacks took immediate steps to set up schools, sometimes holding classes temporarily in abandoned warehouses, billiards rooms, or, in New Orleans and Savannah, former slave markets. In rural areas, Freedmen's Bureau officials repeatedly expressed surprise at discovering classes organized by blacks already meeting in churches, basements, or private homes. And everywhere there were children teaching their parents the alphabet at home, laborers on lunch breaks "poring over the elementary pages," and the "wayside schools" described by a Bureau officer:

A negro riding on a loaded wagon, or sitting on a hack waiting for a train, or by the cabin door, is often seen, book in hand delving after the rudiments of knowledge. A group on the platform of a depot, after carefully conning an old spelling book, resolves itself into a class.

Throughout the South, blacks in 1865 and 1866 raised money to purchase land, build schoolhouses, and pay teachers' salaries. Some communities voluntarily taxed themselves; in others black schools charged tuition, while allowing a number of the poorest families to enroll their children free of charge. Black artisans donated their labor to construct schoolhouses, and black families offered room and board to teachers to supplement their salaries. By 1870, blacks had expended over $1 million on education, a fact that long remained a point of collective pride. "Whoever may hereafter lay claim to the honor of 'establishing' . . . schools," wrote a black resident of Selma in 1867, "I trust the fact will never be ignored that Miss Lucy Lee, one of the emancipated, was the pioneer teacher of the colored children, . . . without the aid of Northern societies."

Inevitably, the first black teachers appeared incompetent in Northern eyes, for a smattering of education might place an individual in front of a class. One poignantly explained, "I never had the chance of goen to school for I was a slave until freedom. . . . I am the only teacher because we can not doe better now." Yet even an imperfect literacy, coupled with the courage often required to establish a rural school in the face of local white opposition, marked these teachers as community leaders. Black teachers played numerous roles apart from education, assisting freedmen in contract disputes, engaging in church work, and drafting petitions to the Freedmen's Bureau, state officials, and Congress. Like the ministry, teaching frequently became a springboard to political office. At least seventy black teachers served in state legislatures during Reconstruction. And many black politicians were linked in other ways to the quest for learning, like Alabama Congressman Benjamin S. Turner, an ex-slave "destitute of education," who financed a Selma school.

Not surprisingly, the majority of black teachers who held political office during Reconstruction had been free before the Civil War. Indeed the schools, like the entire institutional structure established by blacks during Reconstruction, symbolized the emergence of a community that united the free and the freed, and Northern and Southern blacks. The process occurred most smoothly in the Upper South, where the cultural and economic gap between free blacks and slaves had always been less pronounced than in the urban Deep South. While generally lighter in color than slaves, most Upper South free blacks were poor urban workers or farm laborers, often tied to the slave community through marriage and church membership. In cities like New Orleans, Mobile, Savan-

nah, and Charleston, however, affluent mulatto elites responded with deep ambivalence to the new situation created by emancipation. Even in New Orleans, where politically conscious free blacks had already moved to make common cause with the freedmen, a sense of exclusivity survived the end of slavery. The Freedmen's Bureau found many free blacks reluctant to send their children to school with former slaves.

After New Orleans, the South's largest and wealthiest community of free blacks resided in Charleston, although the free elite there was neither as rich nor as culturally distinct as its Louisiana counterpart. Arriving in Charleston in November 1865, Northern journalist John R. Dennett found some members of the free elite cultivating their old exclusiveness. Others, however, took the lead in organizing assistance for destitute freedmen and in teaching the former slaves. Sons and daughters of prominent free families, mostly young people in their twenties, fanned out into the South Carolina countryside as teachers and missionaries. Several thereby acquired positions of local political leadership and later returned to Charleston as constitutional convention delegates and legislators. Thus the children of the Charleston elite cast their lot with the freedmen, bringing, as they saw it, modern culture to the former slaves. This encounter was not without its tensions. But in the long run it hastened the emergence of a black community stratified by class rather than color, in which the former free elite took its place as one element of a new black bourgeoisie, instead of existing as a separate caste as in the antebellum port cities.

In the severing of ties that had bound black and white families and churches to one another under slavery, the coming together of blacks in an explosion of institution building, and the political and cultural fusion of former free blacks and former slaves, Reconstruction witnessed the birth of the modern black community. All in all, the months following the end of the Civil War were a period of remarkable accomplishment for Southern blacks. Looking back in January 1866, the Philadelphia-born black missionary

Jonathan C. Gibbs could only exclaim: "we have progressed a century in a year."

☆

THE ECONOMICS OF FREEDOM

Nowhere were blacks' efforts to define their freedom more explosive for the entire society than in the economy. Freedmen brought out of slavery a conception of themselves as a "Working Class of People" who had been unjustly deprived of the fruits of their labor. To white predictions that they would not work, blacks responded that if any class could be characterized as lazy, it was the planters, who had "lived in idleness all their lives on stolen labor." It is certainly true that many blacks expected to labor less as free men and women than they had as slaves, an understandable aim considering the conditions they had previously known. "Whence comes the assertion that the 'nigger won't work'?" asked an Alabama freedman. "It comes from this fact: . . . the freedman refuses to be driven out into the field two hours before day, and work until 9 or 10 o'clock in the night, as was the case in the days of slavery."

Yet freedom meant more than shorter hours and payment of wages. Freedmen sought to control the conditions under which they labored, end their subordination to white authority, and carve out the greatest measure of economic autonomy. These aims led them to prefer tenancy to wage labor, and leasing land for a fixed rent to sharecropping. Above all, they inspired the quest for land. Owning land, the freedmen believed, would "complete their independence."

To those familiar with the experience of other postemancipation societies, blacks' "mania for owning a small piece of land" did not appear surprising. Freedmen in Haiti, the British and Spanish Caribbean, and Brazil all saw ownership of land as crucial to economic independence, and everywhere former slaves sought to avoid returning to plantation labor.

Unlike freedmen in other countries, however, American blacks emerged from slavery convinced that the federal government had committed itself to land distribution. Belief in an imminent division of land was most pervasive in the South Carolina and Georgia lowcountry, but the idea was shared in other parts of the South as well, including counties that had never been occupied by federal troops. Blacks insisted that their past labor entitled them to at least a portion of their owners' estates. As an Alabama black convention put it: "The property which they hold was nearly all earned by the sweat of *our* brows."

In some parts of the South, blacks in 1865 did more than argue the merits of their case. Hundreds of freedmen refused either to sign labor contracts or to leave the plantations, insisting that the land belonged to them. On the property of a Tennessee planter, former slaves not only claimed to be "joint heirs" to the estate but, the owner complained, abandoned the slave quarters and took up residence "in the rooms of my house." Few freedmen were able to maintain control of land seized in this manner. A small number did, however, obtain property through other means, squatting on unoccupied land in sparsely populated states like Florida and Texas, buying tiny city plots, or cooperatively purchasing farms and plantations. Most blacks, however, emerged from slavery unable to purchase land even at the depressed prices of early Reconstruction and confronted by a white community unwilling to advance credit or sell them property. Thus, they entered the world of free labor as wage or share workers on land owned by whites. The adjustment to a new social order in which their persons were removed from the market but their labor was bought and sold like any other commodity proved in many respects difficult. For it required them to adapt to the logic of the economic market, where the impersonal laws of supply and demand and the balance of power between employer and employee determine a laborer's material circumstances.

Most freedmen welcomed the demise of the paternalism and mutual obligations of slavery and embraced many aspects of the free market. They patronized the stores that sprang up throughout the rural South, purchasing "luxuries" ranging from sardines, cheese, and sugar to new clothing. They saved money to build and support churches and educate their children. And they quickly learned to use and influence the market for their own ends. The early years of Reconstruction witnessed strikes or petitions for higher wages by black urban laborers, including Richmond factory workers, Jackson washerwomen, New Orleans and Savannah stevedores, and mechanics in Columbus, Georgia. In rural areas, too, plantation freedmen sometimes bargained collectively over contract terms, organized strikes, and occasionally even attempted to establish wage schedules for an entire area. Blacks exploited competition between planters and nonagricultural employers, seeking work on railroad construction crews and at turpentine mills and other enterprises offering pay far higher than on the plantations.

Slavery, however, did not produce workers fully socialized to the virtues of economic accumulation. Despite the profits possible in early postwar cotton farming, many freedmen strongly resisted growing the "slave crop." "If ole massa want to grow cotton," said one Georgia freedman, "let him plant it himself." Many freedmen preferred to concentrate on food crops and only secondarily on cotton or other staples to obtain ready cash. Rather than choose irrevocably between self-sufficiency and market farming, they hoped to avoid a complete dependence on either while taking advantage of the opportunities each could offer. As A. Warren Kelsey, a representative of Northern cotton manufacturers, shrewdly observed:

The sole ambition of the freedman at the present time appears to be to become the owner of a little piece of land, there to erect a humble home, and to dwell in peace and security at his own free will and pleasure. If he wishes, to cultivate the ground in cotton on his own account, to be able to do so without anyone to dictate to him hours or system of labor, if he wishes instead to plant corn or sweet potatoes — to be able to do *that* free from any outside control. . . . That is their idea, their desire and their hope.

Historical experience and modern scholarship suggest that acquiring small plots of land would hardly, by itself, have solved the economic plight of black families. Without control of credit and access to markets, land reform can often be a hollow victory. And where political power rests in hostile hands, small landowners often find themselves subjected to oppressive taxation and other state policies that severely limit their economic prospects. In such circumstances, the autonomy offered by land ownership tends to be defensive, rather than the springboard for sustained economic advancement. Yet while hardly an economic panacea, land redistribution would have had profound consequences for Southern society, weakening the land-based economic and political power of the old ruling class, offering blacks a measure of choice as to whether, when, and under what circumstances to enter the labor market, and affecting the former slaves' conception of themselves.

Blacks' quest for economic independence not only threatened the foundations of the Southern political economy, it put the freedmen at odds with both former owners seeking to restore plantation labor discipline and Northerners committed to reinvigorating staple crop production. But as part of the broad quest for individual and collective autonomy, it remained central to the black community's effort to define the meaning of freedom. Indeed, the fulfillment of other aspirations, from family autonomy to the creation of schools and churches, all greatly depended on success in winning control of their working lives and gaining access to the economic resources of the South.

☆

ORIGINS OF BLACK POLITICS

If the goal of autonomy inspired blacks to withdraw from religious and social institutions controlled by whites and to attempt to work out their economic destinies for themselves, in the polity, "freedom" meant inclusion rather than separation. Recognition of their equal rights as citizens quickly emerged as the animating impulse of Reconstruction black politics. In the spring and summer of 1865, blacks organized a seemingly unending series of mass meetings, parades, and petitions demanding civil equality and suffrage as indispensable corollaries of emancipation. By midsummer, "secret political Radical Associations" had been formed in Virginia's major cities. Richmond blacks first organized politically to protest the army's rounding up of "vagrants" for plantation labor, but soon expanded their demands to include the right to vote and the removal of the "Rebel-controlled" local government.

Statewide conventions held throughout the South in 1865 and early 1866 offered the most visible evidence of black political organization. Several hundred delegates attended these gatherings, some selected by local meetings, others by churches, fraternal societies, Union Leagues, and black army units, still others simply appointed by themselves. The delegates "ranged all colors and apparently all conditions," but urban free mulattoes took the most prominent roles, and former slaves were almost entirely absent from leadership positions. But other groups also came to the fore in 1865. In Mississippi, a state with few free blacks before the war, ex-slave army veterans and their relatives comprised the majority of the delegates. Alabama and Georgia had a heavy representation of black ministers, and all the conventions included numerous skilled artisans.

The prominence of free blacks, ministers, artisans, and former soldiers in these early conventions foreshadowed black politics for much of Reconstruction. From among these delegates emerged such prominent officeholders as Alabama Congressman James T. Rapier and Mississippi Secretary of State James D. Lynch. In general, however, what is striking is how few of these early leaders went on to positions of

prominence. In most states, political mobilization had advanced far more rapidly in cities and in rural areas occupied by federal troops during the war than in the bulk of the plantation counties, where the majority of the former slaves lived. The free blacks of Louisiana and South Carolina who stepped to the fore in 1865 remained at the helm of black politics throughout Reconstruction; elsewhere, however, a new group of leaders, many of them freedmen from the black belt, soon superseded those who took the lead in 1865.

The debates at these conventions illuminated conflicting currents of black public life in the immediate aftermath of emancipation. Tensions within the black community occasionally rose to the surface. One delegate voiced resentment that a Northern black had been chosen president of North Carolina's convention. By and large, however, the proceedings proved harmonious, the delegates devoting most of their time to issues that united blacks rather than divided them. South Carolina's convention demanded access to all the opportunities and privileges enjoyed by whites, from education to the right to bear arms, serve on juries, establish newspapers, assemble peacefully, and "enter upon all the avenues of agriculture, commerce, [and] trade."

The delegates' central preoccupation, however, was equality before the law and the suffrage. In justifying their demand for the vote, the delegates invoked America's republican traditions, especially the Declaration of Independence — "the broadest, the deepest, the most comprehensive and truthful definition of human freedom that was ever given to the world." The North Carolina freedmen's convention portrayed the Civil War and emancipation as chapters in the onward march of "progressive civilization," embodiments of "the fundamental truths laid down in the great charter of Republican liberty, the Declaration of Independence." Such language was not confined to the convention delegates. Eleven Alabama blacks, who complained of contract frauds, injustice before the courts, and other abuses, concluded their petition with a revealing masterpiece of understatement: "This is not the pursuit of happiness."

Like their Northern counterparts during the Civil War, Southern blacks proclaimed their identification with the nation's history, destiny, and political system. The abundance of letters and petitions addressed by black gatherings and ordinary freedmen to military officials, the Freedmen's Bureau, and state and federal authorities, as well as the decision of a number of conventions to send representatives to Washington to lobby for black rights, revealed a belief that the political order was at least partially open to their influence. "We are Americans," declared a meeting of Norfolk blacks, "we know no other country, we love the land of our birth." Their address reminded white Virginians that in 1619, "our fathers as well as yours were toiling in the plantations on James River" and that a black man, Crispus Attucks, had shed "the first blood" in the American Revolution. And, of course, blacks had fought and died to save the Union. America, resolved one meeting, was "now *our* country — made emphatically so by the blood of our brethren."

Despite the insistence on equal rights, the convention resolutions and public addresses generally adopted a moderate tone, offering "the right hand of fellowship" to Southern whites. Even the South Carolina convention, forthright in claiming civil and political equality and in identifying its demand with "the cause of millions of oppressed men" throughout the world, took pains to assure the state's white minority of blacks' "spirit of meekness," their consciousness of "your wealth and greatness, and our poverty and weakness."

To some extent, this cautious tone reflected a realistic assessment of the political situation at a time when Southern whites had been restored to local power by President Johnson and Congress had not yet launched its own Reconstruction policy. But the blend of radicalism and conciliation also mirrored the indecision of an emerging black political leadership still finding its own voice in 1865 and 1866 and dom-

inated by urban free blacks, ministers, and others who had in the past enjoyed harmonious relations with at least some local whites and did not always feel the bitter resentments of rural freedmen.

Nor did a coherent economic program emerge from these assemblies. Demands for land did surface at local meetings that chose convention delegates. Yet such views were rarely expressed among the conventions' leadership. By and large, economic concerns figured only marginally in the proceedings, and the addresses and resolutions offered no economic program apart from stressing the "mutual interest" of capital and labor and urging self-improvement as the route to personal advancement. The ferment rippling through the Southern countryside found little echo at the state conventions of 1865, reflecting the paucity of representation from plantation counties and the prominence of political leaders more attuned to political equality and self-help formulas than to rural freedmen's thirst for land.

Nonetheless, these early black conventions both reflected and advanced the process of political mobilization. Some Tennessee delegates, for example, took to heart their convention's instruction to "look after the welfare" of their constituents. After returning home, they actively promoted black education, protested to civil authorities and the Freedmen's Bureau about violence and contract frauds, and struggled against unequal odds to secure blacks a modicum of justice in local courts. Chapters of the Georgia Equal Rights and Educational Association, established at the state's January 1866 convention, became "schools in which the colored citizens learn their rights." Spreading into fifty counties by the end of the year, the Association's local meetings attracted as many as 2,000 freedmen, who listened to speeches on issues of the day and readings from Republican newspapers.

All in all, the most striking characteristic of this initial phase of black political mobilization was unevenness. In some states, organization proceeded steadily in 1865 and 1866; in others, such as Mississippi, little activity occurred between an initial flurry in the summer of 1865 and the advent of black suffrage two years later. Large parts of the black belt remained untouched by organized politics, but many blacks were aware of Congressional debates on Reconstruction policy and quickly employed on their own behalf the Civil Rights Act of 1866. "The negro of today," remarked a correspondent of the New Orleans *Tribune* in September 1866, "is not the same as he was six years ago. . . . He has been told of his rights, which have long been robbed." Only in 1867 would blacks enter the "political nation," but in organization, leadership, and an ideology that drew on America's republican heritage to demand an equal place as citizens, the seeds that flowered then were planted in the first years of freedom.

QUESTIONS TO CONSIDER

1. What effects did emancipation have on the status and importance of the southern black family and on its various members? What changes occurred in the lives of African American women? How did southern whites react to those changes?

2. What do changes in African American churches after 1865 reveal about what their members most desired from freedom? What kinds of roles did the church and ministers play in the community? Why?

3. Describe what education meant to African Americans at the time of emancipation and why. What accomplishments did they achieve in this domain?

4. In what ways did the economic status of African Americans change as a result of emancipation, and how did they see themselves in economic terms? Why was their "quest for land" so intense? Did African Americans differ in this from freed slaves in other countries, and how does Eric Foner judge the importance of land redistribution?

5. What were the principal political goals of African Americans and their delegates at the statewide conventions of 1865 and 1866? On what did they base these goals, and how did they feel about the United States?

2

Reconstruction:
The Revolution That Failed

JAMES MACGREGOR BURNS

For defeated southern whites, the loss of the Civil War was a monumental calamity. By turns, they were angry, helpless, vindictive, resigned, and heartsick. Their cherished South was not just defeated; it was annihilated. Some 260,000 rebel soldiers, the flower of southern manhood, were dead and thousands more were maimed and crippled for life. The South's major cities were in ruins, railroads and industry desolated, commerce paralyzed, and two-thirds of the assessed wealth, including billions of dollars in slaves, destroyed. As James MacGregor Burns says in The Workshop of Democracy *(1985), from which the following selection is excerpted, "Many [white southerners] were already grieving over sons, plantations, and fortunes taken by war; losing their blacks was the final blow." Some masters shot or hanged African Americans who proclaimed their freedom. That was a harbinger of the years of Reconstruction, for most white southerners were certain that their cause had been just and were entirely unrepentant about fighting against the Union. A popular ballad captured the current mood in conquered Dixie:*

> *Oh, I'm a good ole Rebel, now that's just what I am*
> *For this fair land of freedom I do not care a damn,*
> *I'm glad I fit against it, I only wish't we'd won*
> *And I don't want no pardon for nothin' what I done. . . .*
>
> *I hates the Yankee nation and everything they do*
> *I hates the Declaration of Independence too*

I hates the glorious Union, 'tis dripping with our blood
And I hate the striped banner, I fit it all I could. . . .

I can't take up my musket and fight 'em now no mo'
But I ain't gonna love 'em and that is certain sho'
And I don't want no pardon for what I was and am
And I won't be reconstructed and I don't care a damn.

In Washington, Republican leaders were jubilant in victory and determined to deal firmly with southern whites in order to preserve the fruits of the war. But what about the new president, Andrew Johnson? A profane, hard-drinking Tennessee Democrat who bragged about his plebeian origins, Johnson had been the only southern senator to oppose secession openly. He had sided with the Union, served as war governor of Tennessee, and become Lincoln's running mate in 1864, on a Union ticket comprising both Republicans and War Democrats. As a result of the assassination of Lincoln, Johnson was now president, and he faced one of the most difficult tasks ever to confront an American chief executive: how to bind the nation's wounds, preserve African American freedom, and restore the southern states to their proper places in the Union.

Lincoln had contemplated an army of occupation for the South, thinking that military force might be necessary to protect the former slaves and prevent the old southern leadership from returning to power. Now there was such an army in the South: some 200,000 Union troops had moved in to restore order there and to perform whatever reconstruction duties Johnson might ask of them.

Initially, Republican leaders were hopeful about Johnson, for in talking about his native region he seemed tough, even uncompromising. But as he set about restoring defeated Dixie, Johnson alarmed and then enraged congressional Republicans by adopting a soft, conciliatory reconstruction policy. The President not only opposed granting blacks the right to vote but allowed former Confederates to return to power in the southern states. He stood by as they adopted black codes that reduced blacks to a virtual condition of peonage, and he hotly opposed congressional interference in the reconstruction process. He even urged southern states to reject the Fourteenth Amendment, pushed through Congress by the Republicans, which would protect southern blacks. The amendment would prevent the states from enacting laws that abridged "the privileges or immunities of citizens of the United States." It would also bar the states from depriving "any person of life, liberty, or property, without due process of law," or from denying any person the "equal protection of the law." Johnson did more than just oppose the amendment; he damned Republican leaders like Charles Sumner of Massachusetts and Thaddeus Stevens of Pennsylvania, calling them tyrants and traitors. He even campaigned against the Republican party in the 1866 off-year elections. As a consequence, he alienated moderate as well as radical Republicans, who soon united against him. When the 1866 elections gave the Republicans *huge majorities in both houses of Congress, they set out to take control of Reconstruction and to reform the South themselves.*

This sets the scene for Burns's account of Republican Reconstruction. Burns believes that it was a revolutionary experiment that failed. He does not, of course, subscribe to the outmoded interpretation of Reconstruction as a misguided attempt to "put the colored people on top" in the South and turn the region over to hordes of beady-eyed carpetbaggers and roguish scalawags intent on "stealing the South blind." In the old view, Reconstruction was "a blackout of honest government," a time when the "Southern people were put to the torch," a period so rife with "political rancor, and social violence and disorder," that nothing good came out of it. Since the 1930s, modern scholarship has systematically rejected this interpretation and the bigotry that underlay it. Drawing on modern studies of the period, Burns argues that the Republican Congress did go too far in trying to centralize power in the legislative branch. But he is sympathetic to Republican efforts to bring southern blacks into the American mainstream, to grant them political, social, and educational opportunities for self-advancement. On this score, however, the Republicans did not go far enough, for they failed to provide blacks with the economic security they needed to be truly free in America. Alas, that failure was to plague black Americans for generations to come.

GLOSSARY

CARPETBAGGER   A northern white who migrated to the South and became politically active as a Republican.

ENFORCEMENT ACT OF 1870   Enacted in response to mob violence in the South, it prohibited the use of force, intimidation, and bribery to inhibit African American voting in local and state elections.

FIFTEENTH AMENDMENT   The right of United States citizens to vote could not be denied or abridged, the amendment said, "on account of race, color, or previous condition of servitude." Many white feminists pressed Congress to include "regardless of sex" in the amendment; this would have enfranchised women as well as black men. But Congress refused on the ground that the amendment was already controversial enough and would never be ratified if it enfranchised women, too. It was ratified in 1870.

GRANT, ULYSSES S.   Northern war hero elected president in 1868.

JOHNSON, ANDREW   United States president, 1865–1869; because he defied and obstructed congressional reconstruction measures, the Republican-controlled House of Representatives impeached him, but the Senate failed to convict him by just one vote; it was the first and last attempt to impeach an American president for political reasons.

KU KLUX KLAN   Southern white supremacist group organized in response to the Fifteenth Amendment; dressed in white sheets and hoods, Klansmen tried to prevent African Americans from voting by mob violence and other means of intimidation.

RECONSTRUCTION ACTS OF 1867   "The heart of congressional strategy to democratize the South," the measures divided the South into five military districts under army commanders and empowered them "to suppress disorder, protect life and property, remove civil officeholders [and] to initiate political reconstruction by enrolling qualified voters including blacks, and excluding the disloyal."

SCALAWAG   Native southern white who became a Republican during Reconstruction.

For a brief fleeting moment in history — from late 1866 to almost the end of the decade — radical senators and congressmen led the Republican party in an audacious venture in both the organization and the goals of political power. To a degree that would have astonished the constitution-makers of earlier years, they converted the eighty-year-old system of checks and balances into a highly centralized, majoritarian system that elevated the legislative branch, subordinated the executive and judicial branches, and suspended federalism and "states' rights" in the South. They turned the Constitution on its head. The aims of these leaders were indeed revolutionary — to reverse age-old human and class relationships in the South and to raise millions of people to a much higher level of economic, political, social, and educational self-fulfillment. That such potent means could not in the end produce such humane and democratic ends was the ultimate tragedy of this revolutionary experiment.

This heroic effort was not conducted by men on white horses, but rather by quarrelsome parliamentarians — by a Congress that seemed to one of its members as never "more querulous, distracted, incoherent and ignoble." In the Senate, [Charles] Sumner had good reason to be distracted, for he had married a woman half his age shortly before the [1866] election and was preoccupied first by marital bliss and very soon by marital distress as he and his wife found themselves hopelessly incompatible. His colleagues found him more remote and unpredictable than ever. In the House, [Thaddeus] Stevens worked closely with his Radical allies, but he was now desperately anxious to move swiftly ahead, for he knew that time was running out for him and perhaps for his cause. Rising on the House floor, he now presented the countenance of death, with his dourly twisted mouth,

From *The Workshop of Democracy* by James MacGregor Burns. Copyright © 1981 by James MacGregor Burns. Reprinted by permission of Alfred A. Knopf, Inc.

deeply sunken eyes, parchment skin, and a body so wasted that he often conducted business from a couch just outside the chamber. But the old man never lost his ferocious drive to dominate; as he spoke, his eyes lighted up in a fierce gleam and his croaking voice turned thunderous, while he stretched his bony arm out in a wide sweep and punctuated his arguments with sudden thrusts of his long yellow forefinger.

The strength of the Republican party lay in the advanced positions of these two men but even more in the quality and commitment of other party leaders in both houses. Some of these men — John Sherman, James A. Garfield, James G. Blaine — would gain fame in the decades ahead. Others . . . would fade into the mists of history. Occupying almost every hue on the party rainbow, these men differed sharply and disputed mightily, but they felt they had a clear election mandate to establish civil and other rights in the South; they had a strong sense of party solidarity; and they had the backing of rank-and-file senators and representatives and of party organizations throughout the North.

They also had a common adversary in Andrew Johnson. The President stewed over his election defeat, but he would make no fundamental change in his political and legislative strategy. Setbacks seemed only to mire him more deeply in his own resentments. . . . He received little independent advice from his Cabinet, which appeared to believe that the beleaguered President needed above all their loyalty. [Secretary of War Edwin] Stanton dissented on occasion but, characteristically, Johnson did not wholly trust him. As the President stuck to the disintegrating political center and the Republicans moved toward a radical posture, the legislative stage was set for drama and conflict.

The upshot was a burst of legislative creativity in the "hundred days" of winter 1866–67:

December 14, 1866: Congress enacts black suffrage for the District of Columbia, later reenacts it over Johnson's veto. *January 7, 1867:* the House adopts [James M.] Ashley's resolution instructing the Judi-

ciary Committee to "inquire into the conduct of Andrew Johnson." *January 22:* Congress grants itself authority to call itself into special session, a right recognized until now as belonging only to the President. *March 2:* all on the same day, Congress passes a basic act laying out its general plan of political reconstruction; in effect deprives the President of command of the army; and enacts the Tenure of Office Act barring the Chief Executive from removing officials appointed by and with the advice of the Senate, without Senate approval. *March 23:* Congress passes a supplementary Reconstruction Act requiring military commanders to start registering "loyal" voters.

The heart of congressional strategy to democratize the South lay in the first Reconstruction Act of March 2, 1867, as clarified, strengthened, and implemented in later acts. With the ostensible purpose of restoring social order and republican government in the South, and on the premise that the existing "Johnson" state regimes there could not realize these ends or even protect life or property, the South was divided into five military districts subject to martial law. The commanders were empowered not only to govern — to suppress disorder, protect life and property, remove civil officeholders — but to initiate political reconstruction by enrolling qualified voters including blacks, and excluding the disloyal. To be restored to the Union, the Southern states must call new constitutional conventions that, elected under universal manhood suffrage, in turn must establish new state governments that would guarantee black suffrage and ratify the Fourteenth Amendment. These states would be eligibile for representation in the national legislature only after Congress had approved their state constitutions and after the Fourteenth Amendment had become part of the Constitution.

It was a radical's dream, a centralist's heaven — and a states'-righter's nightmare. Congress held all the governmental strings in its hands. No more exquisite punishment could have been devised for secessionists than to make them conform to national standards in reconstructing their own state governments and gaining restor..tion to the Union. Congress did not stop with upsetting the division of powers between nation and states; it overturned the separation of powers [between the executive and legislative branches of the national government. In 1868, congressional Republicans sought to remove Johnson by a method never before used against an American president. The Republican-controlled House impeached Johnson on various partisan charges, including his defiance of the Tenure of Office Act and his efforts to undermine the Reconstruction Act, but the Senate failed to convict him by just one vote short of the two-thirds required for removal. Thus ended the first and last attempt to impeach an American president for political reasons. Even so, Johnson's presidency was irreparably damaged; he served out his last year in office, as truculent as ever. The Republicans, meanwhile, nominated war hero Ulysses S. Grant as their candidate in the 1868 presidential election. Because Grant had maintained ties with congressional Republicans and seemed genuinely militant in his stance on reconstruction, congressional Republicans were certain that he would cooperate with them. That November, Grant defeated Democratic candidate Horatio Seymour by winning all but three Northern states and polling 52.7 percent of the popular vote.]

Some Radical Republicans now were more optimistic than ever. Grant's election, they felt, provided a supreme and perhaps final opportunity to reconstruct the South. Now the Republicans had their own men in the White House; they still controlled both houses of Congress; they had established their supremacy over the Supreme Court; they had considerable influence over the federal military and civilian bureaucracy in the South. They still had the power to discipline the Southern states, by admitting them to the Union or expelling them. The Republicans had pushed through the Thirteenth and Fourteenth Amendments. They still possessed the ablest, most experienced political leadership in the nation. Stevens had died during the campaign, but Sumner had been handsomely reelected in Massachusetts. "So at last I have conquered; after a life of struggle," the senator said.

Other Radicals were less sanguine. They knew that far more than Andrew Johnson had thwarted Reconstruction. The national commitment to black equality was weak, the mechanisms of government faulty, and even with the best of intentions and machinery, the connecting line between a decision in Washington and an actual outcome affecting a black family in Virginia or Mississippi was long and fragile. Time and again, voters had opposed black wrongs without favoring black rights. Before the war, they had fought the extension of slavery but not slavery where it existed. During the war, they had come to approve emancipation only after Lincoln issued his proclamation. After the war, in a number of state elections — especially those of 1867 — Northerners had shown that they favored black suffrage in the South but not at home.

Spurred by effective leaders, Americans were moving toward racial justice, but the journey was agonizingly slow and meandering. "It took America three-quarters of a century of agitation and four years of war to learn the meaning of the word 'Liberty,'" the *American Freedman* editorialized. "God grant to teach us by easier lessons the meaning of the words 'equal rights.'" How quickly and firmly Americans moved ahead on black rights could turn significantly on continuing moral and political leadership.

The crucial issue after Grant's election was the right of blacks to vote. Republican leaders in Congress quickly pushed ahead with the Fifteenth Amendment, which declared in its final form that the "right of the citizens of the United States to vote shall not be denied or abridged by the United States or by any State on account of race, color, or previous condition of servitude." It was a noble sentiment that had emerged out of a set of highly mixed motives. Democrats charged, with some reason, that the majority party was far less interested in legalizing the freedman's vote in the South than in winning the black vote in the North. But the Republican leadership, knowing that countless whites in the North opposed black voting there, were responding to the demands of morality as well as practicality. Senator Henry Wilson reminded his colleagues that the "whole struggle in this country to give equal rights and equal privileges to all citizens of the United States has been an unpopular one; that we have been forced to struggle against passions and prejudices engendered by generations of wrong and oppression." He estimated that the struggle had cost his party a quarter of a million votes. Another Republican senator, however, contended that in the long run adherence to "equality of rights among men" had been not a source of party weakness but of its strength and power. . . .

If political morality in the long run meant political practicality, the Fifteenth Amendment nevertheless bore all the markings of compromise. To gain the two-thirds support constitutionally required in each chamber, the sponsors were compelled to jettison clauses that would have outlawed property qualifications and literacy tests. The amendment provided only that Congress and the states could not deny the vote, rather than requiring them to take positive action to secure black suffrage; nor was there any provision against denial of vote by mobs or other private groups. And of course the amendment did not provide for female voting — and so the National Woman Suffrage Association opposed it.

Still, radicals in and out of Congress were elated when the Fifteenth cleared Congress, elated even more when the measure became part of the Constitution in March 1870, after Republican state parties helped drive it through the required number of legislatures. . . .

The legal right of blacks to vote soon produced a phenomenon in Southern politics — black legislators, judges, superintendents of education, lieutenant governors and other state officials, members of Congress, and even two United States senators. These, however, made up only a fraction of Southern officeholders: in none of the legislatures did blacks hold a majority, except briefly in South Carolina's lower house.

Usually black leaders shared power with "carpetbaggers" — white Northerners who came south and became active in politics as Republicans — and "scalawags" — white Southerners who cooperated with Republicans and blacks. While many black leaders were men of "ability and integrity," in [historian] Kenneth Stampp's view, the whites and blacks together comprised a mixed lot of the corrupt and the incorruptible, moderate and extreme, opportunistic and principled, competent and ignorant. The quality of state government under such leadership also was mixed, but on the whole probably no worse than that of many state and local governments of the time. The state governments in the South bore unusually heavy burdens, moreover — demoralization and poverty in the wake of a devastating war, the need to build or rebuild public services throughout the region, the corrupting influence of contractors, speculators, and promoters seeking subsidies, grants, contracts, franchises, and land.

Far more important than the reality of black-and-white rule in the South was the perverted image of it refracted through the distorted lenses of Southern eyes. It was not easy for the white leadership to see newly freed men . . . occupy positions of prestige and power; and it was perhaps inevitable that they would caricature the new rulers to the world. A picture emerged of insolent boors indulging in legislative license, lording it over downtrodden whites, looting the public treasury, bankrupting the state, threatening white traditions, womanhood, and purity. . . .

The worst fear of the old white leadership — that black-and-white rule would produce a social revolution — turned out to be the least warranted of all. The mixed rule of blacks, scalawags, and carpetbaggers produced a few symbolic and actual changes: rhetoric drawn directly from the Declaration of Independence proclaiming liberty, "equality of all persons before the law," various civil and political rights; a mild effort in two or three states to integrate certain educational institutions; a feeble effort at land reform. [Southern state] constitutions were made somewhat more democratic, legislative apportionment less discriminatory, more offices elective; "rights of women were enlarged, tax systems were made more equitable, penal codes were reformed, and the number of crimes punishable by death was reduced," in Stampp's summation. The constitution of South Carolina — the state that had served as the South's political and ideological heartland, and the state that now paradoxically had elevated the most blacks to leadership positions — was converted almost into a model state charter, with provisions for manhood suffrage, public education, extension of women's rights, and even the state's first divorce law. . . .

But what the black-and-white leadership failed to do was of far more profound consequence than what it did. Both radicals and moderates understood that education was a fundamental need for Southern blacks, but the obstacles were formidable and progress slow. Even the best educational system could hardly have compensated for decades of illiteracy and ignorance. "The children," James McPherson noted, "came from a cultural environment almost entirely devoid of intellectual stimulus. Many of them had never heard of the alphabet, geography, or arithmetic when they first came to school. Few of them knew their right hand from their left, or could tell the date of their birth. Most of them realized only vaguely that there was a world outside their own plantation or town." In the early years, teachers sponsored by "Freedmen's Aid" and missionary groups met the challenge, often finding to their surprise that black children had a passion to learn, could be taught to read as quickly as white children, and might be found laboriously teaching their own parents the alphabet and the multiplication table.

These private educational efforts were never adequate, however, to teach more than a fraction of the South's black children. The question was whether the reconstructed black-and-white state governments would take over the task in a comprehensive way, and here they failed. The difficulties were at least as great as ever: inadequate facilities, insufficient money, lack

of teachers, inadequate student motivation, discipline problems (black teachers tended to be the harsher disciplinarians). But the biggest hurdle was the constant, pervasive, and continuing hostility of many Southern whites to schooling for blacks. "I have seen many an absurdity in my lifetime," said a Louisiana legislator on observing black pupils for the first time, "but this is the climax of absurdities." A Southern white woman warned a teacher that "you might as well try to teach your horse or mule to read, as to teach these niggers. They *can't* learn."

Behind these white Southern attitudes toward schooling for black children lay a host of fears. One was their old worry that blacks would be educated above their station and out of the labor supply. "To talk about educating this drudge," opined the Paducah (Kentucky) *Herald,* "is to talk without thinking. Either to 'educate,' or to teach him merely to read and write, is to ruin him as a laborer. Thousands of them have already been ruined by it." Even more pervasive was the white fear of integration, although most black leaders made it clear that their main interest was education, whether segregated or not. Southern fears often took the form of harassing and humiliating teachers or, more ingeniously, depriving them of white housing so that some teachers lived with blacks — and hence could be arrested as vagrants. Defending the arrest of a freedmen's teacher, the mayor of Enterprise, Mississippi, said that the teacher had been "living on terms of equality with negroes, living in their houses, boarding with them, and at one time gave a party at which there were no persons present (except himself) but negroes, all of which are offenses against the laws of the state and declared acts of vagrancy." Black-and-white governments could not overcome such deep-seated attitudes.

To many blacks, even more important than education was land — "forty acres and a mule." During the war, when workers on a South Carolina plantation had rejected a wage offer from their master, one of them had said, "I mean to own my own manhood, and I'm goin' on to my own land, just as soon as when I git dis crop in. . . ." Declared a black preacher in Florida to a group of field hands: "It's de white man's turn ter labor now. He ain't got nothin' lef' but his lan', an' de lan' won't be his'n long, fur de Guverment is gwine ter gie ter ev'ry Nigger forty acres of lan' an' a mule." Black hopes for their own plots had dwindled sharply after the war, when Johnson's amnesty proclamation restored property as well as civil rights to most former rebels who would take an oath of allegiance. His expectations dashed, a Virginia black said now that he would ask for only a single acre of land — "ef you make it de acre dat Marsa's house sets on."

Black hopes for land soared again after the congressional Republicans took control of Reconstruction in the late 1860s, only to collapse when Republican moderates — and even some radicals — refused to support a program of land confiscation. Black hopes rose still again when black-and-white regimes took over state governments; some freedmen heard rumors that they need only go to the polls and vote and they would return home with a mule and a deed to a forty-acre lot. But, curiously, "radical" rule in no state produced systematic effort at land redistribution. Some delegates to the Louisiana constitutional convention proposed that purchases of more than 150 acres be prohibited when planters sold their estates, and the South Carolina convention authorized the creation of a commission to buy land for sale to blacks, but little came of these efforts. One reason was clear: Southern whites who had resisted black voting and black education would have reacted with even greater fury to as radical a program as land redistribution, with all its implications for white pride, white property — and the white labor supply.

Black leaders themselves were wary of the freedmen's lust for "forty acres and a mule." In part, this caution may have been due to the class divisions between the black Southern masses and their leaders, many of whom had been artisans or ministers, had been free before the war, and had never experienced plantation life and closeness to the soil. Some of these leaders were, indeed, virtually middle-class in their attitudes toward property, frugality, "negative" liberty, and hard work, and in their fear that radical blacks might infuriate white power elites by talking "confiscation." Such leaders preferred to bargain with the white power structure rather than threaten its control over land and other property. Prizing liberal values of individual liberty, the need for schooling, and above all the right to vote, they played down the economic and social needs of the blacks. And they based their whole strategy on the suffrage, arguing that all the other rights that blacks claimed — land, education, homes — were dependent on their using the potential power inherent in their right to vote.

Would black voting make the crucial difference? Of the three prongs of black advance in the South — schools, land, and the vote — the limited success of the first and the essential failure of the second left black suffrage as the great battlefield of Southern reform. Certainly Southern whites realized this and, as the Republican commitment faltered during the Grant Administration, they stepped up their efforts to thwart black voting. They used a battery of stratagems: opening polling places late or closing them early or changing their location; gerrymandering districts in order to neutralize the black vote; requiring the payment of a poll tax to vote; "losing" or disregarding black ballots; counting Democratic ballots more than once; making local offices appointive rather than elective; plying blacks with liquor. These devices had long been used against white Americans, and by no means did all Southern whites use them now, but fraud and trickery were especially effective against inexperienced and unlettered blacks.

When nonviolent methods failed, many Southern whites turned to other weapons against voting: intimidation, harassment, and terror. Mobs drove blacks away from the polls. Whites blocked polling entrances or crowded around ballot boxes so blacks could not vote. Rowdies with guns or whips followed black voters away from the polling place. When a group of black voters in Gibson County,

Tennessee, returned the fire of a band of masked men, the authorities put the blacks in jail, from which an armed mob took them by force to a nearby riverbank and shot them down. Fifty-three defendants were arrested by federal authorities and tried, none convicted.

Some of this violence erupted spontaneously as young firebrands, emboldened by liquor, rode into polling areas with their guns blazing. But as the stakes of voting rose, terrorists organized themselves. Most notable was the Ku Klux Klan, with its white robes and hoods, sheeted horses, and its weird hierarchies of wizards, genii, dragons, hydras, ghouls, and cyclopes. Proclaiming its devotion to "Chivalry, Humanity, Mercy, and Patriotism," the Klan proposed to protect the "weak, the innocent, and the defenseless" — and the "Constitution of the United States." The Klan had allies in the Knights of the White Camelia, the White Brotherhood, and other secret societies.

Incensed by mob violence, the Republicans in Washington tried to counter it with legislation. The Enforcement Act of May 1870 outlawed the use of force, bribery, or intimidation that hindered the right to vote because of race in state and local elections. Two more enforcement acts during the next twelve months extended and tightened enforcement machinery, and in April 1871 Congress in effect outlawed the Klan and similar groups. But actual enforcement in the thousands of far-flung polling places required an enormous number of marshals and soldiers. As army garrisons in the South thinned out, enforcement appropriations dwindled, and the number of both prosecutions by white prosecutors and convictions by white juries dropped, black voting was more and more choked off.

After his election to a second term Grant tried vigorously though spasmodically to support black rights for the sake of both Republican principle and Republican victories. In a final effort, the Republicans were able to push through the Civil Rights Act of 1875, designed to guarantee equal rights for blacks in public places, but the act was weak in coverage and enforce-ment, and later would be struck down by the Supreme Court.

By the mid-seventies Republicanism, Reconstruction, and reform were all running out of steam. Southern Democrats were extending their grip over political machinery; the Republican leadership was shaken by an economic panic in 1873, and the party lost badly in the 1874 midterm elections. The *coup de grâce* for Reconstruction came after Rutherford Hayes's razor-thin electoral-college victory in 1876 over [Democrat] Samuel J. Tilden. Awarded the office as a result of Republican control over three Southern states where voting returns were in doubt, and as a result, too, of a Republican majority on the Electoral Commission, Hayes bolstered his position by offering assurances about future treatment of the South. While these were in the soft political currency of veiled promises and delphic utterances, the currency was hard enough for the Democrats — and for Hayes as well. Within two months of his inauguration, he ordered the last federal troops out of the South and turned over political control of Louisiana, South Carolina, and Florida to the Southern [Democrats].

*   *   *

And what of the objects of this long political struggle — the black people of the South? The vast majority were in the same socioeconomic situation as ten years before, at the end of the war. They had gained certain personal liberties, such as the right to marry, and a modicum of legal and civil and political rights, including the right to vote in certain areas; but their everyday lot was much the same as before. Most still lacked land, property, money, capital; they were still dependent on the planters, sometimes the same old "massa." It was not a black man but a prominent white Georgian who said of the freedman late in 1865: "The negro's first want is, not the ballot, but a chance to live, — yes, sir, *a chance to live*. Why, he can't even live without the consent of the white man!

When the war ended, most of the former slaves owned little more than the skin on their backs. To secure their liberty, they needed their own land, schools, and the right to vote. During Reconstruction, they did gain such personal liberties as the right to marry and a modicum of political, civil, and legal rights. But their everyday lot improved *little. When Reconstruction ended, as James MacGregor Burns says, most African Americans in the South "still lacked land, property, money, capital; they were still dependent on the planters, sometimes the same old 'massa.' " (Collection of William Gladstone)*

He has no land; he can make no crops except the white man gives him a chance. He hasn't any timber; he can't get a stick of wood without leave from a white man. We crowd him into the fewest possible employments, and then he can scarcely get work anywhere but in the rice-fields and cotton plantations of a white man who has owned him and given up slavery only at the point of the bayonet. . . . What sort of freedom is that?"

Many a freedman had exchanged bondage for a kind of bargaining relationship with employers, but his bargaining position was woefully weak. If he held out for better terms, he could be evicted; if he left, he might be denied work elsewhere and arrested for va-

grancy; if he struck, he had no unions or money to sustain him. So the "bargains" were usually one-sided; contracts sometimes literally required "perfect obedience" from employees. Some blacks had had the worst of both worlds — they had left the security of old age and sickness in bondage, under masters who cared for them because they were valuable property, for a strange "free-market" world in which they developed new dependencies on old masters.

Could Reconstruction have turned out differently? Many have concluded that the impotence of the blacks was too deeply rooted, the white intransigence too powerful, the institutions of change too faulty, and the human mind too limited to begin to meet the requirements of a genuine Reconstruction. Yet the human mind had already conducted a stupendous social revolution with the blacks. For a hundred years and more, Southern planters, assisted by slave recruiters in Africa, masters of slaving ships, various middlemen, auctioneers, and drivers, had been uprooting blacks by the hundreds of thousands out of far-off tribal civilizations, bringing most of them safely across broad expanses of water, establishing them in a new and very different culture, and converting them into productive and profit-creating slaves. Somehow the human mind seemed wholly capable of malign "social engineering," incapable of benign.

Yet there were some Americans who did understand the kind of broad social planning and governmental action that was needed to reconstruct genuine democracy in the South and truly to liberate the freed people. [Abolitionist] Wendell Phillips understood the depth of the problem, the need for a "social revolution." He said: "You must plant at the South the elements which make a different society. You cannot enact four millions of slaves, ignorant, down-trodden, and despised, into personal equals of the old leaders of the South." He wanted to "give the negroes land, ballot and education and to hold the arm of the Federal government over the whole Southern Territory until these seeds have begun to bear fruit beyond any possibility of blighting." We must see to it, said Senator Henry Wilson, that "the man made free by the Constitution is a freeman indeed; that he can go where he pleases, work when and for whom he pleases; that he can sue and be sued; that he can lease and buy and sell and own property, real and personal; that he can go into the schools and educate himself and his children. . . ." [Black leader Frederick] Douglass and Stevens and Sumner took similar positions.

These men were not typical of Republicans or even of Radical Republicans, but many other radicals and moderates recognized that the freed people needed an array of economic, political, social, and legal supports, and that these were interrelated. Congressman George Hoar lamented that blacks had been given universal suffrage without universal education. Some radicals believed that voting was the black's first need and others that land or sustenance came first, but most recognized that no single "solution" was adequate. Antislavery men, said Phillips, "will believe the negro safe when we see him with 40 acres under his feet, a schoolhouse behind him, a ballot in his right hand, the sceptre of the Federal Government over his head, and no State Government to interfere with him, until more than one-half of the white men of the Southern States are in their graves." . . .

The critical failure of Reconstruction probably lay . . . in the realm of leadership — especially that of opinion-makers. Editors, ministers, and others preached liberty and equality without always comprehending the full dimensions of these values and the means necessary — in the South of the 1870s — to accomplish such ends. The radicals "seemed to have little conception," according to Stampp, "of what might be called the sociology of freedom, the ease with which mere laws can be flouted when they alone support an economically dependent class, especially a minority group against whom is directed an intense racial prejudice." Reconstruction could have succeeded only through use of strategy employed in a number of successful postwar reconstructions of a comprehensive nature — a strategy of combining ideological, economic, political, educational, and institutional forces in such a firm and coordinated way as truly to transform the social environment in which Southerners, both black and white, were trying to remake their lives after the Civil War. And such a strategy, it should be noted, would have imposed heavy intellectual, economic, and psychological burdens on the North as well.

Not only would such a strategy have called for rare political leadership — especially for a leader, in William Gillette's words, able to "fashion a means and then persevere in it, bending men to his purpose by vigorous initiative, skillful influence, and masterful policy." Even more it called for a rare kind of *intellectual* leadership — political thinkers who could translate the component elements of values such as liberty and equality into policy priorities and operational guidelines. But aside from a few radicals such as Phillips, most of the liberals and many of the radicals had a stunted view of the necessary role of public authority in achieving libertarian and egalitarian purposes. *The Nation,* the most influential liberal weekly in the postwar period, under Edwin L. Godkin shrank from using the only means — government — that could have marshaled the resources necessary for genuine reconstruction. "To Govern Well," *The Nation* proclaimed, "Govern Little." A decisive number of otherwise liberal-minded and generously inclined intellectual leaders held similar views. . . . There were many reasons for the failure of Reconstruction, but the decisive one — because it occurred in people's conceptualizing and analyzing processes and not merely in ineluctable social and economic circumstances — took place in the liberal mind. Most of the liberals were effective transactional leaders, or brokers; few displayed transforming leadership.

That liberal mind seemed to have closed itself off even to the results of practical experimentation. During the war, General Sherman had set aside for freedmen several hundred thousand acres on the Sea Islands south of Charleston and on the abandoned rice lands inland for thirty miles along the coast. Each black family was to receive its forty acres until Congress should rule on their final disposition. Federal officials helped settle 40,000 blacks on these lands. When the whole enterprise was terminated by Johnson's pardon and amnesty program, and land turned back to former owners, the black farmers were incredulous. Some had to be driven off their land by force. The program had lasted long enough, however, to demonstrate that freed people could make a success of independent farming, and that "forty acres and a mule" could serve as the foundation of Reconstruction. But the lesson seemed lost

on Northerners who shuddered at the thought of "land confiscation."

Thus the great majority of black people were left in a condition of dependency, a decade after war's end, that was not decisively different, in terms of everyday existence, from their prewar status. They were still landless farm laborers, lacking schooling, the suffrage, and self-respect. They achieved certain civil and legal rights, but their expectations had been greatly raised too, so the Golden Shore for many seemed more distant than ever. Said a black woman: "De slaves, where I lived, knowed after de war dat they had abundance of dat somethin' called freedom, what they could not eat, wear, and sleep in. Yes, sir, they soon found out dat freedom ain't nothin', 'less you is got somethin' to live on and a place to call home. Dis livin' on liberty is lak young folks livin' on love after they gits married. It just don't work."

Or as an Alabama freedman said more tersely when asked what price tag he bore — and perhaps with two meanings of the word in mind:

"I'se free. Ain't wuf nuffin."

QUESTIONS TO CONSIDER

1. Why does Burns call Reconstruction a revolution? Why does he consider the actions of federal officials, especially members of Congress, to be revolutionary? What happened to the Constitution during Reconstruction? Why was Reconstruction "a radical's dream, a centralist's heaven, and a states'-righter's nightmare"?

2. What compromises and weaknesses vitiated the strength of the Fifteenth (voting rights) Amendment?

3. Reconstructionists recognized that African Americans needed education, land, and the vote if equality was to become a reality in the South. What fundamental fears and racist attitudes in both the South and the North kept these goals from being realized? What practical steps does Burns feel ought to

have been taken to ensure the success of Reconstruction policies? Do you see any potential problems in aggressive governmental policies temporarily adopted to make Reconstruction work? Or do you think the Constitution is strong enough to protect us from government excesses?

4.   Discuss Burns's contention that the failure of liberal intellectual leaders to shape public opinion was responsible for the failure of Reconstruction. Were the leaders more to blame than the weak enforcement policies of the federal government or the repressive, sometimes violent reactions of white southerners?

5.   Selections 13 and 25 in this book deal with the harsh legacy of the Civil War and failed Reconstruction. Imagine for a moment that Reconstruction had been a success, that African Americans in the late nineteenth century had achieved lives founded on a sound economic and legal base, with equal access to land, education, and the franchise. How would the United States be different today? Would the nation have elected an African American president by now? How might other issues of social justice, such as women's rights, have been affected?

II

CONQUEST OF THE WEST

3

Sitting Bull and the Sioux Resistance

ROBERT M. UTLEY

In the forty years after the Civil War, American pioneers conquered and exploited an immense inner frontier that lay between California and the Mississippi River. It was an area as diverse as it was expansive, a region of windy prairies, towering mountains, painted deserts, and awesome canyons. Heading east out of California or west from the Mississippi, Americans by the thousands poured into this great heartland, laying out cattle ranches and farms, building towns and mining camps, and creating a variety of local and state governments. People moved to the frontier for various reasons: to start a new life, seek glory and adventure, strike it rich in a single, fabulous windfall, and prevail over the West's challenging environment.

Still, the winning of the West was not all romance. Driven by the aggressive, exploitive imperatives of their culture, American pioneers — especially whites — infiltrated Indian lands and hunting grounds, and conflicts between settlers and Indians broke out all across the frontier line, thus opening a gruesome chapter in the westward movement after the Civil War. The fact was that white-dominated America tended to regard the Indians as savages who deserved violent treatment. If these "ignorant nomads" blocked the advance of Christian civilization across the West, they should be "removed." And so, terrible fights erupted whenever whites and Indians came into contact. Trying to reduce the violence, the government sent out additional federal troops, including several African American regiments; instead of enforcing existing treaties, the soldiers usually defended whites who violated the pacts, which only provoked the Indians all the more.

In 1867, the federal government decided to confine the Indians to small, remote reservations in areas of the West spurned by United States settlers. Herein lies a paradox, for the whites' handling of the Indians in the late 1860s contrasted sharply with the way they treated southern blacks. The Congress that approved the small reservation policy, with its philosophy of strict segregation and inequality for western Indians, was the same Congress that attempted to give African American men in the South political rights equal to those of white men.

But many Indian bands refused to surrender their ancient hunting grounds, refused to be herded onto reservations and made to "walk the white man's road," and they fought back tenaciously. None did so with more resolve than the warrior elements of the proud, buffalo-hunting Lakota (or Sioux) of the northern Plains, who united behind Sitting Bull and vowed to throw the white invaders out of Lakota country. Sitting Bull, the great holy man and war chief of the Hunkpapa Lakota, is the subject of the selection by Robert M. Utley, a distinguished historian and biographer of the American West. Based on his newly published biography, The Lance and the Shield: The Life and Times of Sitting Bull (1993), Utley's essay affords rare insight into Lakota culture and what happened to it when it collided with a rapacious, acquisitive invader whose superior military power, forked tongue, and deadly diseases brought doom to Native Americans everywhere.

As Utley points out, the government's small reservation policy, which was implemented by treaties in 1868, split the Lakota into two camps. The agency Indians, under the leadership of Red Cloud of the Oglala Sioux, accepted reservation life and tried to adapt to it. The nonreservation Indians, headed by Sitting Bull, elected to fight the United States Army in a desperate attempt to save "the free life of old." Indeed, rising to the unprecedented position of head chief of all the Lakota, Sitting Bull assembled the most formidable Indian force in the West, one that on a hot June day in 1876 massacred George Armstrong Custer and 262 men of the United States Seventh Cavalry in the Battle of the Little Bighorn in Montana. But it was a Pyrrhic victory for the Lakota and their Cheyenne allies: in the fall, the army trapped them and compelled them to surrender. Sitting Bull escaped to Canada, and his followers ended up in out-of-the way reservations in the Dakota Territory.

The other western tribes met the same fate. Overwhelmed by superior firepower and faced with starvation, because whites were exterminating the buffalo, the Indians' "commissary," the Native Americans had no choice but to abandon their way of life and submit to segregation on small reservations in the Dakotas, Oklahoma, New Mexico, Oregon, Idaho, and Montana. The federal government systematically obliterated Indian culture and tribal organization, placed the Indians on individual plots of land, and ordered them to become farmers and accept the culture of their conquerors. By 1890, thanks to generations of bloodletting and sickness, scarcely 200,000 Indians remained in the United States, compared with the 2 million Indians in North America at the time of the European discovery.

Meanwhile, Sitting Bull himself returned from Canada and surrendered to the military, which placed him on the Standing Rock Reservation as a prisoner of war. Here, as Utley says, the Indian agent — a petty tyrant — attempted to destroy Sitting Bull's reputation among his incarcerated people. Yet the great Lakota war chief and holy man remained indomitable: he accepted schooling for his offspring but rejected all other government efforts to make Indians into "imitation whites."

Defeated and broken in spirit, many reservation Indians turned to religion for comfort in a hostile world. First the Indians of Nevada, then the Lakota and other Plains Indians took up the Ghost Dance, a sacred ritual that reaffirmed tribal unity and prophesied the return of the old days, when the buffalo would be plentiful again and the Indians would be free of the white invaders. Intimidated by such a "frightful conglomeration of rituals and customs," as one white put it, the United States government outlawed the Ghost Dance. But Sitting Bull and his people kept on dancing. Indeed, Sitting Bull became "the high priest of the religion at Standing Rock," which put him on a collision course with the Indian agent and his Lakota police. Utley recounts the violent, ironic climax to Sitting Bull's life and goes on to observe that he lost his struggle with white Americans, not because of any personal failing but because of "impersonal forces beyond his control or even his understanding." As you study Sitting Bull's life, the evolution of his three distinct personalities, and his tragic end, you might want to consider this question: Which do you think was the better way for the Indians to deal with the white invaders — the appeasement of Red Cloud, or the uncompromising resistance of Sitting Bull?

GLOSSARY

ARROW CREEK (battle, August 13, 1872)   Here Sitting Bull performed a feat of bravery that awed his followers: he seated himself and calmly smoked his pipe within range of the soldiers' guns.

BLACK HILLS (SOUTH DAKOTA)   Sacred Lakota domain called Paha Sapa; gold miners invading the Black Hills helped ignite the Great Sioux War of 1876.

BROTHERTON, MAJOR DAVID H. Accepted Sitting Bull's surrender in 1881.

CRAZY HORSE   An Oglala Lakota and the greatest of all the Sioux war chiefs, he also fought to drive the white invaders away and save the old ways.

CROW FOOT   Sitting Bull's favorite son who died with him in the confrontation with Indian police in 1890.

CROWS   Plains Indian tribe and traditional enemy of the Lakota.

FORT LARAMIE TREATY (1868)   Set aside all of present-day South Dakota west of the Missouri River as the Great Sioux Reservation.

FOUR HORNS   Sitting Bull's uncle who was wounded in the battle of Killdeer Mountain.

GHOST DANCE RELIGION   Begun by a Paiute messiah named Wovoca, the Ghost Dance movement swept the Plains Indians incarcerated on reservations; it prophesied the end of the white invaders and the return of the buffalo and all previous generations of Indians.

HUNKPAPA   Sitting Bull's division of the Lakota; the other six divisions were Miniconjou, Sans Arc, Two Kettle, Bruele, Oglala, and Blackfeet Sioux (not to be confused with the Blackfeet tribe that lived and hunted northwest of the Lakota).

KILLDEER MOUNTAIN (battle, July 28, 1864) A "calamitous" defeat for the Lakota that pointed up the futility of the Indians' fighting an open battle with well-armed soldiers.

LONG KNIVES   Indian name for white soldiers armed with rifles and bayonets.

MCLAUGHLIN, JAMES   Agent of the Standing Rock Lakota Reservation who tried to shape the Indians into "imitation whites" and to destroy Sitting Bull's reputation.

SULLY, GENERAL ALFRED   Commanded United States Army forces in the Battle of Killdeer Mountain.

SUN DANCE   The central ceremony in the sacred life of the Lakota; in it the dancers engaged in self-sacrifice and self-torture in order to gain the favor of the Great Mysterious and ensure a successful buffalo hunt.

WAKANTANKA   Lakota word for the Great Mystery.

WICHASHA WAKAN   Lakota term for a holy man such as Sitting Bull.

S itting Bull's fighting days ended on July 20, 1881, when he led his little band of faithful headmen into the cramped office of the commanding officer at Fort Buford, Dakota Territory. All were shabbily dressed and gaunt from the hunger of their Canadian exile. Sitting Bull, once the mightiest chief of the Lakota Sioux, wore a threadbare calico shirt and black leggings; a tattered, dirty blanket was loosely draped around his waist. Suffering a severe eye infection, he had tied a kerchief turbanlike around his head and drawn it partly across his eyes. Beneath, his dark seamed face with jutting nose and chin and perpetually downturned mouth registered both resignation and despair.

His men grouped behind him, the Sioux chief sat next to the blue-clad soldier chief. Placing his Winchester rifle beneath the chair, Sitting Bull drew to him his five-year-old son Crow Foot. Major David H. Brotherton opened the council by setting forth the terms on which the surrender would be received. In fact, they were no terms at all, since the U.S. government's adamant insistence on unconditional surrender had put off this day until starvation left no other recourse.

After the officer ceased speaking, Sitting Bull slumped in his chair, silent and glum. Brotherton invited him to speak. He sat motionless for five minutes — as if in a trance, thought one witness. He said a few words to his men, then gestured to Crow Foot, who picked up his father's rifle and handed it to the army officer. Then Sitting Bull spoke in words that the interpreter translated:

I surrender this rifle to you through my young son, whom I now desire to teach in this manner that he has become a friend of the Americans. I wish him to learn the habits of the whites and to be educated as their sons are educated. I wish it to be remembered that I was the last man of my tribe to

From Robert M. Utley, "Sitting Bull and the Sioux Resistance," *MHQ: The Quarterly Journal of Military History*, 5(4) (summer 1993), 48–53, 56–59. Reprinted by permission.

surrender my rifle. This boy has given it to you, and he now wants to know how he is going to make a living.

The ceremony at Fort Buford marked the end, at age fifty, of Sitting Bull's career as a warrior, war leader, and tribal war chief, a career that had begun at the age of fourteen, when he counted his first coup on a Crow Indian. He had achieved power and distinction in other fields, too — as a *wichasha wakan,* a holy man; as a band chief; and finally, a post unique in Sioux history, as supreme chief of all the Lakota tribes. His war honors and trophies, however, provided his greatest satisfaction. That he understood the tragic symbolism of giving up his rifle he betrayed in a song composed to connect what had been to what would be: A warrior / I have been / Now / It is all over / A hard time / I have.

What "had been" began in 1831 with Sitting Bull's birth into a distinguished family of the Hunkpapa tribe, one of the seven tribes of Teton or Lakota Sioux. A nomadic people, the Lakotas occupied the high plains between the Missouri River and the Bighorn Mountains while ranging north to the British possessions and south as far as the Platte and Republican rivers. Together, they numbered between 15,000 and 20,000 people. Other Sioux lived to the east — Yanktons and Yanktonais east of the Missouri River, and Dakotas, or Santees, in Minnesota.

At the age of fourteen, his name was not yet Sitting Bull but Jumping Badger, although his deliberate and willful ways had earned him the nickname Hunkesni, or "Slow." Much against his parents' counsel, Slow insisted on accompanying a war party of ten men striking westward from the Powder River in search of horses and scalps of the enemy Crow tribe. Unproven lads often tagged along on such expeditions as errand boys. They learned the ways of war without actually fighting.

On the third day out, crossing a divide, the party spotted a dozen mounted Crows gathered in conference beside a creek. Whooping and shouting, the Lakotas raced down the slope in a headlong charge.

Startled, the Crows spread out to receive the attack. But one Crow spurred his horse to escape. Slow, mounted on a sturdy gray horse his father had given him, his naked body painted yellow from head to foot and hung with colorful strands of beads, shrieked a war cry and galloped in pursuit. The powerful gray swiftly overtook the quarry. Pulling abreast, Slow smashed his adversary with a tomahawk and knocked him from his mount. Another warrior hurried in to finish the act and count second coup. In fierce fighting, the Sioux killed all but four of the Crows, who fled the field.

In a jubilant ceremony at the home village, Slow donned his first white eagle feather, emblem of a first coup, and entered one of the world's most highly developed warrior societies. His mother presented him with the beaded, feathered lance that became his favorite offensive weapon. His father presented a shield bearing a sacred design that appeared to him in a dream. From his father also came his own name, to replace Slow and resonate in the history of not only the Sioux but their enemies as well: Tatanka-Iyotanka, Sitting Bull.

As Sitting Bull's adolescent years fell behind in the 1840s, he took on his adult build. With a heavy, muscular frame, a big chest, and a large head, he impressed people as short and stocky, although he stood five feet ten inches tall. His dark hair reached to his shoulders, often braided with otter fur on one side, hanging loose on the other. A severe part at the center of the scalp glistened with a heavy streak of crimson paint. A low forehead surmounted piercing eyes, a broad nose, and thin lips. Although dexterous afoot and superbly agile mounted, he was thought by some to be awkward and even clumsy.

In adulthood Sitting Bull developed into the Hunkpapa incarnate, the admired epitome of the four cardinal virtues of the Lakotas: bravery, fortitude, generosity, and wisdom. "There was something in Sitting Bull that everybody liked," one of his tribesmen recalled. "Children liked him because he was kind, the women because he was kind to the family and liked to settle family troubles. Men liked him be-cause he was brave. Medicine men liked him because they knew he was a man they could consider a leader."

Sitting Bull evolved three distinct personalities. One was the superlative warrior and huntsman, adept at all the techniques of war and the hunt, boastful of his deeds, laden with honors and ambitious for more, celebrated and rewarded with high rank by his peo-ple. Another personality was the holy man, suffused with reverence and mysticism, communing con-stantly with Wakantanka, the Great Mysterious, dreaming sacred dreams and carrying out the rites and ceremonies they mandated, entreating for the welfare of his people, offering sacrifices ranging from a buffalo carcass to his own flesh. A third was the good tribes-man, a man of kindness, generosity, and humility, un-ostentatious in dress and bearing, composer and singer of songs, a friend of children and old people, peace-maker, sportsman, gentle humorist, wise counselor, and leader. That he excelled in all three realms testi-fied to uncommon merit.

The Lakota culture was hardly a generation old at the time of Sitting Bull's birth. Only around the be-ginning of the nineteenth century did the Lakotas be-come fully mounted on horses and begin to acquire guns. Horses and guns enabled them to seize and de-fend their rich hunting grounds, to follow the great migrating herds of buffalo that shaped their distinctive way of life, and by the middle of the nineteenth cen-tury to evolve into the proud and powerful monarchs of the northern Great Plains. Ironically, by furnishing the horses and guns, white people made possible the Lakota way of life; then, in less than a century, they destroyed it.

In the years of Sitting Bull's youth, the Hunkpapas had little conception of the white world. The only whites they knew were traders based at posts along the Missouri River. From them, or other tribes acting as intermediaries, came the horses and guns, along with other useful manufactures. Whites in substantial

numbers lived 500 miles to the southeast; the Hunkpapas sensed no threat from them. Their hostil-ity was reserved for enemy tribes such as the Crows, Flatheads, Assiniboines, and Arikaras.

By Sitting Bull's thirtieth birthday, however, the white world had begun to intrude alarmingly on the Hunkpapas. Treaty makers, government agents, and soldiers had begun to appear along the upper Missouri in the 1850s, and by the 1860s the menace had grown distressingly clear. Settlers fingered up the river valleys to the south. Emigrants bound for the gold mines of western Montana killed the buffalo and grazed their livestock on the choice grasses. The voracious boilers of the steamboats consumed the timber stands in the river valleys. The Hunkpapas began to add the whites to their list of enemies.

By this time Sitting Bull had participated in many war expeditions. These were usually limited both in objectives and in scale, though large-scale expeditions and pitched battles sometimes occurred. He had per-formed many feats of bravery that won the applause of his people and membership in the men's societies that played a major part in Lakota life. He became a war chief of the Hunkpapa tribe. His very name struck terror in the hearts of enemy warriors. Observing this effect, his comrades sometimes disconcerted an oppo-nent by shouting, "Tatanka-Iyotanka tahoksila!" — "We are Sitting Bull's boys!"

Sitting Bull and his "boys" fought for a variety of motives. Where their range overlapped with that of others, they fought for control of hunting grounds. They fought in defense against the aggressions of oth-ers; for plunder, chiefly the horses that constituted the prime measure of wealth; for revenge of injuries real and fancied; for glory and the strictly prescribed war honors that determined prestige and leadership.

In any battle, whatever the scale, the Hunkpapas, like all Plains Indians, fought in time-honored fash-ion. Singly and in knots they galloped back and forth, firing arrows or musket balls at the enemy. Sometimes they gathered in bunches for a thrust aimed at over-running their foes. Each man indulged in a variety of

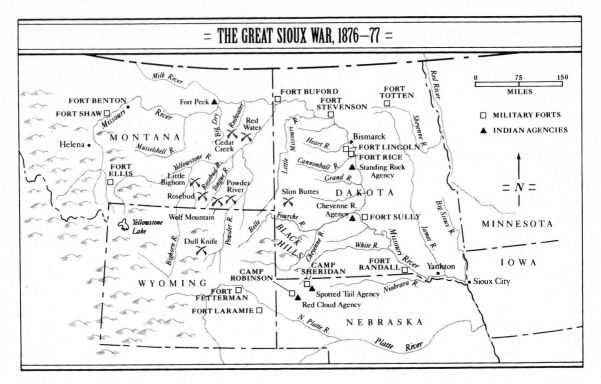

= THE GREAT SIOUX WAR, 1876—77 =

(From The Lance and the Shield by Robert M. Utley. Maps by Jeffrey L. Ward. Copyright © 1993 by Jeffrey L. Ward. Reprinted by permission of Henry Holt and Company, Inc.)

flashy escapades to display bravery; he followed a leader only when it suited his convenience or inclination. In any such encounter, Sitting Bull's role was chiefly, through exhortation and example, to inspire men to exhibit ever greater personal daring and to join with him in whatever tactical move circumstances seemed to dictate. Neither he nor any other chief "commanded," as whites used the term.

Typifying this mode of combat and Sitting Bull's part in it was the Lakotas' most memorable fight with an enemy tribe. This occurred in the winter of 1869–70, and they remembered it as the Thirty-Crows-Killed battle.

Sitting Bull's band wintered that year in Montana, along the Missouri River and Big Dry Creek. In the middle of the winter, amid bitter cold and deep snow, two Hunkpapa boys were returning from a day of hunting when a party of thirty Crows cut their trail in the snow. Except for two men mounted on one pony, the Crows were afoot. The two hurried to overtake the boys and succeeded in killing one. Wounded, the other escaped to carry word to the Hunkpapa village.

At once Sitting Bull organized a revenge expedition of about 100 warriors. Guided by the surviving boy, the men found their enemies posted behind rock breastworks at the head of Big Dry Creek. As dawn broke, the Hunkpapas attacked. A few on each side had firearms, but most had only bow and arrows. The Hunkpapas fought in the usual fashion, each man for himself, each striving for deeds of bravery and the coups that added to war honors. Although outnumbered more than three to one, the Crows enjoyed the advantages of defense from a fortified position. Steady in their own bravery, they sold their lives dearly. But as the morning hours slipped by, the Hunkpapas gradually took their toll on the Crows.

Like his warriors, Sitting Bull charged as chance presented and retreated when the fire grew too hot. Once he darted to the breastworks and reached across with his bow to count three coups. Finally, as noon approached, he and his comrades surged forward, leaped the walls, and in desperate hand-to-hand fighting killed the last of the Crows. Hunkpapa casualties were much lighter: Thirteen died and seventeen limped off with serious wounds.

This style of combat worked well enough against an enemy practicing the same style, as Crows, Assiniboines, and other Plains tribes did. Pursued in battles with white people, especially white soldiers, it had severe drawbacks.

Sitting Bull's Hunkpapas and other Lakotas of the upper Missouri had their first combat with United States troops in 1863–64. In two summer campaigns, Generals Henry H. Sibley and Alfred Sully led formidable expeditions to the Dakota plains, at first to round up Santee Sioux fugitives from the Minnesota uprising of 1862, then to punish Lakotas who had interfered with the migration to the newly discovered Montana mines.

Almost certainly, Sitting Bull fought in the battles of Dead Buffalo Lake and Stony Lake, July 26 and 28, 1863. He may have been at Whitestone Hill on September 3, 1863. He unquestionably played a leading part in the battles of Killdeer Mountain and the Badlands, July 28 and August 7–9, 1864. In all these fights, the Indians relied on their traditional techniques, and in all they suffered severe to calamitous defeats.

Killdeer Mountain should have shown the Sioux the perils of trying to take on the soldiers in open battle. As many as 1,400 lodges representing four Lakota tribes traced the southern edge of a low range of rugged, wooded mountains falling away on the north to the Little Missouri badlands. A series of buttes and

ridges, separated by deep gorges, rose stairlike to the dominating mountain mass. In this natural fortress, emboldened by a force exceeding 2,000 warriors, the Sioux felt confident of routing the approaching army of General Sully.

With 2,200 cavalry and artillery, Sully advanced across the parched plains from the south. Judging the terrain too broken for mounted action, he dismounted and pushed forward on a broad front of skirmishers. Horseholders, then wagons and artillery, brought up the rear.

The Indians came out to meet him. Resplendent in paint and war costume, they sat their ponies in little clusters on every hill and ridge facing the blue lines and curling around their flanks. When within range, the two forces opened fire.

For five miles the fighting roiled northward toward the village at the foot of Killdeer Mountain, the Lakotas attacking in typical fashion. Despite their numbers, however, they could not slow the steady advance of the soldiers.

Mounted on a fast sorrel and armed with musket and bow and arrows, Sitting Bull fought with his usual bravery. As the soldiers launched a final assault aimed at the village itself, he saw a bullet slam into the back of his revered uncle, Chief Four Horns. "I am shot," yelled Four Horns, clinging grimly to his mount.

Sitting Bull dashed to the rescue, seized the horse's bridle, and, as his young nephew White Bull steadied the injured man, led the way into a sheltering thicket. There Sitting Bull gave Four Horns water to drink, applied medicine to the wound, and bandaged it. The bullet remained inside, Four Horns said; he could feel it and it hurt. (Later he recovered and explained that the bullet had dropped into his stomach and never bothered him again.)

While Sitting Bull doctored his uncle, the soldiers won final victory, scattering men, women, and children into the mountains and seizing the village. The next day they methodically destroyed everything that could benefit the Indians. Lodges, meat, robes, utensils — all went up in flames. The troops counted more than a hundred Sioux bodies left on the battlefield; how many dead and wounded were carried away is not known. By contrast, Sully reported casualties of two killed and ten wounded.

The Sibley-Sully campaigns, especially Killdeer Mountain, gave Sitting Bull his first taste of battle with the Long Knives. They did not, he discovered, fight like Indians. Instead they fought in organized formations, obedient to commands of their officers, and brought overwhelming firepower to bear. Their rifled muskets claimed greater range, accuracy, and hitting force than the feeble smoothbore trade muskets of the Indians. The soldiers' cannon in particular were frightening and deadly.

The lessons were clear: Acquire better firearms, and avoid open battle with the Long Knives, relying instead on the hit-and-run tactics at which the Sioux excelled. Sitting Bull's record suggests that he fully grasped the first lesson, only partly the second. Not surprisingly in view of the dictates of culture, neither he nor any other chief ever thought to fight in disciplined formations maneuvered by a hierarchy of command.

The Battle of Killdeer Mountain heralded two decades of conflict with the Long Knives. As whites edged onto the northern Great Plains, soldiers came to protect them. Their "war houses" on the Missouri River, along with the steamboats that carried people and merchandise to the Montana mines, infuriated the Sioux. No chief took a more uncomplicated or inflexible view of this invasion than Sitting Bull. Except for traders, he held, the whites must all get out of Lakota domain and quit traveling through it. If they would not go peaceably, they would be driven out.

It now fell to Sitting Bull to embody the spirit of Lakota resistance to the white threat. Throughout the late 1860s he led the Hunkpapa offensive against the whites. In this aggressive war, he wielded his favorite attack weapon, the lance, which symbolized his role as the offensive arm of the Hunkpapa tribe.

Principal objectives of the offensive were the military posts of the upper Missouri: Forts Rice, Stevenson, Totten, and Buford. Permanent abodes of the detested Long Knives, the forts stood for the resolve of the whites to possess Lakota territory. The campaign took the form mainly of raids near the forts. Logging details, stock herders, mail riders, and travelers bound for the mines periodically ran afoul of nearby war parties.

Sioux usually regarded direct assaults as risks not worth the prospective gain, but twice they launched such attacks, in each instance with Sitting Bull in the lead. The first occurred at Fort Rice on July 28, 1865. In four hours of desperate fighting, the garrison of "Galvanized Yankees" — Confederate prisoners enlisted for Indian duty — held the defenses and drove off the assailants with well-directed rifle and artillery fire. The second clash occurred on December 24, 1866, when Sitting Bull and his warriors seized the outbuildings of Fort Buford and battled their foes until routed by artillery and charging infantry.

Sitting Bull's offensive on the upper Missouri paralleled an even more determined one to the west, in the Powder River country, over the same issues. Spearheaded by Red Cloud's Oglala tribe, Lakotas fought to close the Bozeman Trail to the Montana mines and get rid of the three forts the army had built to guard travelers. Unlike Sitting Bull, Red Cloud won his war. In the Fort Laramie Treaty of 1868, the United States yielded the three forts and agreed to regard the Powder River country as "unceded Indian country." There the Sioux could live so long as the buffalo sustained their way of life.

The Treaty of 1868 profoundly shaped the destiny of both Red Cloud and Sitting Bull. Besides the unceded territory, it defined a Great Sioux Reservation — all the present state of South Dakota west of the Missouri — and bound all Sioux to settle there eventually. Within a few years Red Cloud and many of his followers had settled there, launching him on a career as mediator between his people and government authorities.

For his part, Sitting Bull scorned the treaty, the res-

Sitting Bull in 1885, four years after his surrender. The great Lakota was both a holy man and a war chief who embodied the four cardinal virtues of his people: bravery, fortitude, generosity, and wisdom. The crucifix he wears in this photograph was supposedly presented to him by a Jesuit missionary in the council of 1868. (Library of Congress)

personalized two powerful magnetic poles of leadership. Red Cloud emerged as the principal chief of the agency Lakotas, those who chose to live within the Great Sioux Reservation and accept government dole. Sitting Bull emerged as the principal chief of the nonreservation Lakotas, who ranged the plains country in the free life of old. Indeed, he had his followers proclaim him supreme chief of all the Lakotas. Such a post had never existed, but his force of personality gave it substance.

The Sitting Bull bands, the "northern Indians," the "hunting bands," or simply the "hostiles," in the white lexicon, numbered about 450 lodges, about 4,000 people including about 800 fighting men. Ranging the valleys of the Yellowstone River and its southern tributaries, many bands came together in the summer for the annual sun dance and perhaps a communal buffalo hunt and a big war expedition against an enemy tribe. In the winter they scattered to remote valleys to sit out the cold, hungry months. In the warm season their numbers swelled with reservation kin out for a summer's lark. In the frigid season their numbers dwindled as rations at the agencies beckoned.

In the aftermath of the Treaty of 1868, with the Lakotas increasingly divided into reservation and nonreservation factions, Sitting Bull called off his offensive against the Missouri River forts. From now on he would fight the white people only in defense of his homeland — the Powder and Yellowstone country that roughly coincided with the unceded territory of the treaty. Sitting Bull's last raid on Fort Buford occurred in September 1870. Now the shield instead of the lance symbolized his role among Lakotas.

Staunchly backing Sitting Bull in his new defense posture was the greatest of all Lakota war leaders — Crazy Horse of the Oglalas. He shared Sitting Bull's aversion to the reservation and the ways of the white people. To the hunting bands, he was a chief second in stature only to Sitting Bull.

Of more ambiguous conviction was another war chief, Gall of the Hunkpapas. Close to Sitting Bull

ervation, and everything else associated with the whites (except trade goods, especially arms and ammunition). He had not signed this or any other treaty, and never would. He intended to live as always, following the buffalo, raiding Crows and Assiniboines, and defending his homeland. "You are fools," he had lectured some agency Indians, "to make yourselves slaves to a piece of fat bacon, some hard-tack, and a little sugar and coffee."

In Red Cloud and Sitting Bull, the Treaty of 1868

since childhood, Gall tended to take counsel in expediency. Sometimes he even slipped into the Hunkpapa agency at Grand River to sample government rations.

The defensive policy expressed itself most forcibly in the opposition of the hunting bands to the Northern Pacific Railroad. In the summers of 1872 and 1873, they fought army units escorting company surveyors marking out a rail route in the Yellowstone Valley. This was the heart of Lakota hunting grounds and the more valuable to them because only recently wrested from the Crows at great cost in blood.

At the Battle of Arrow Creek on August 13, 1872, Sitting Bull performed one of his most memorable feats of bravery. Urged on by Sitting Bull and Crazy Horse, Lakota and Cheyenne warriors struck engineers and their cavalry guardians in the bend of a dry streambed in the upper Yellowstone Valley.

As the sun rose on the battlefield, all eyes turned in wonder to Sitting Bull, who staged a spectacle of bravery so imaginative that it surpassed all others that day. Getting his pipe and tobacco pouch from his horse, he walked from the bluffs out into the open valley to within enemy range. Seating himself on the ground, he shouted, "Who other Indians wish to smoke with me come." As Sitting Bull calmly and with studied deliberation filled the bowl with tobacco, his nephew White Bull, Gets-the-Best-Of, and two Cheyennes ventured into the open and seated themselves beside the chief.

The "smoking party," as White Bull termed it, was a terrifying experience. After kindling the tobacco, Sitting Bull puffed placidly, then passed the pipe to his companions. With pounding hearts, each puffed vigorously and passed it quickly down the line. Throughout he said nothing, just looked around and smoked quietly as bullets kicked up dirt and sang through the air. When all the tobacco had burned, Sitting Bull picked up a stick, thoroughly cleaned the bowl, and stowed the pipe in its pouch. He rose and slowly walked back to the admiring knots of fellow tribesmen. The other smokers ran back.

This ingenious exhibition, so captivating to people who placed great emphasis on daring, added to Sitting Bull's long list of valorous deeds. It reinforced his reputation for bravery and answered those who, in the worsening factionalism of the early 1870s, mocked his pretensions. It was, White Bull remembered, "the bravest deed possible."

After 1873 the Northern Pacific faded from the Lakotas' list of grievances. In four inconclusive battles and a few skirmishes, they had expressed their violent opposition, but they had not stopped the railroad. The Panic of 1873 did that, and the railhead rested at Bismarck, on the Missouri, until after other events had neutralized the Sioux.

Although furious, the Sitting Bull bands offered no violent opposition to a far more blatant assault on their territory. Blazing the "Thieves' Road" into the Black Hills, the Custer Expedition of 1874 saw only a few Lakotas and fought none. But the discovery of gold set off a rush that doomed the Indians' possession of the hills.

It also confronted the administration of President Ulysses S. Grant with a hard dilemma. The Black Hills lay within the Great Sioux Reservation, inarguably guaranteed the Indians by the Treaty of 1868. Yet miners flocked to the hills, and the electorate demanded that the government legalize the invasion. In part because of intimidation by the Sitting Bull bands, however, the reservation chiefs refused to sell. Not until the independent bands yielded to government control, federal officials concluded, could they buy the Black Hills.

A rationale was necessary to force the hunting bands onto the Great Sioux Reservation. They had not interfered with the gold rush, and although they had not signed the Treaty of 1868, it sanctioned their residence in the unceded territory. The defensive policy of Sitting Bull and Crazy Horse, furthermore, left only the thinnest pretext for military force. But their young men had raided Crows, Assiniboines, and Arikaras, as they had always done. They had also terrorized whites on the upper Yellowstone, more in fear of what might happen than of what had happened. In these treaty violations by people who had never subscribed to a treaty, the government found its excuse to order the Sitting Bull bands to the reservation or face military action. Such were the origins of the Great Sioux War of 1876.

Even when confronted with the government's ultimatum in their winter villages, Sitting Bull and his fellow chiefs did not understand that a war was brewing. They were minding their own business and had no plans to fight the white soldiers. Then, on March 17, 1876, cavalry stormed through a village on Powder River, killing two and wounding several others; now the hunting bands knew the Long Knives had declared war.

Sitting Bull drew the winter camps together for self-defense. As spring gave way to summer, reservation Indians began to make their way westward, to join in the defense. By late June his village had swollen from 3,000 to 7,000 people, from 800 to 1,800 warriors.

Now forty-five, Sitting Bull no longer took the lead on the battlefield. He was the "old man chief" and holy man whose judgment and counsel guided the policies and decisions of the allied tribes. Crazy Horse, Gall, and other fighters set the example in combat.

At a sun dance early in June, in supplication to Wakantanka, Sitting Bull gave 100 pieces of flesh from his arms. He also fasted and danced while gazing at the sun. Just below the sun he saw soldiers and horses bearing down on an Indian village. They rode upside down, their feet to the sky, their heads to the earth with hats falling off. A voice proclaimed: "These soldiers do not possess ears. They are to die." The vision and prophecy thrilled his people.

Soldiers were coming — three armies from three directions. They were led by General Alfred H. Terry, Colonel John Gibbon, and "Three Stars," George Crook. With Terry rode "Long Hair," George Armstrong Custer. On June 17, 1876, Sitting Bull's warriors confronted General Crook on the upper reaches of Rosebud Creek. Shoshone and Crow auxiliaries broke the Sioux charge and saved Crook's force from being overrun. Sitting Bull, his arms cut and useless from the sun-dance sacrifice, ranged the lines, exhorting the warriors. Crook limped back to his supply base.

The Battle of the Rosebud did not fulfill Sitting Bull's prophecy. Crook's soldiers had not fallen into the Sioux camp and died. But a week later, Long Hair Custer and his cavalrymen fell into the Sioux camp. It sprawled sleepily in the Little Bighorn Valley on that hot Sunday of June 25, 1876. As depicted in the sun-dance vision, many soldiers died.

A stunned white world gave Sitting Bull all the credit. The "Napoleon of the Sioux," the *New York Herald* labeled him two weeks later, and in subsequent issues self-appointed experts explained how such a catastrophe had happened. One of them declared that the famed Jesuit missionary Father Pierre-Jean De Smet had taught Sitting Bull to speak and read French; the chief had then studied French histories of the Napoleonic Wars and "modeled his generalship after the little Corsican corporal." An army officer, who should have known better, wrote, "The tactics of Sitting Bull seem to have been those pursued by the great Napoleon in his famous campaign of 1814, and were the same practiced by General Lee at Richmond in 1864–65." Soon the nation would be told that Sitting Bull, in a youthful guise, had attended West Point.

In such fantasies a dazed public and a mortified army sought explanations for the disaster that had befallen a supposedly elite regiment and its valiant commander. They wanted to believe that Custer's 7th Cavalry had been overwhelmed by superior numbers commanded by a military genius, the Napoleon of the Sioux.

The truth, of course, was that, as at Killdeer Mountain and all other encounters with Plains tribes, there had been no Indian general at the Little Bighorn. As one of his followers pointed out, "The chief might give orders to fight but he does not direct how to proceed."

The Indians did not win the battle because of generalship or even leadership. They won because they outnumbered the enemy three to one, because they were united, confident, and angry, and above all because the threat to their women and children fired every man with determination to save his family. The Indians won, too, because their foes let themselves be beaten in fragments. Both in the valley and on the battle ridge where the "last stand" occurred, command and control collapsed, discipline evaporated, and men panicked, which left the initiative to the Indians.

If whites ascribed Napoleonic genius to Sitting Bull in 1876, in less than a decade they had produced another interpretation. On the reservation, abetted by Indians currying favor with the Great Father, white officials now said Sitting Bull had not participated in the battle at all; he had remained in his tipi making medicine, or fled to the hills in terror, even abandoning his family, or skulked somewhere else safely out of danger.

In truth, at the Battle of the Little Bighorn, Sitting Bull was a chief several times over whose bravery no one questioned. He was far more valuable as a counselor than as a fighting man. Leave that to the young warriors striving for glory. Chiefs were expected to fight only to protect noncombatants, and that is what he did when soldiers led by Major Marcus Reno threatened the women and children at the upper end of the village.

After that threat receded, he could have withdrawn with honor. Instead he continued to fire at the soldiers and shout encouragement to the warriors, hovering on the edge of the fighting until everyone left to confront Custer downstream. Then he posted himself at the village's northern end, where many women and children had collected. More than enough men swarmed on the battle ridge to wipe out Long Hair, which they did in less than an hour.

Sitting Bull's significance at the Little Bighorn lay not in flaunting bravery, or directing the movements of warriors, or even inspiring them to fight. It lay instead in leadership so wise and powerful that it drew together and held together a muscular coalition of tribes, one so infused with his defiant cast of mind that it could rout Three Stars Crook at the Rosebud and rub out Long Hair Custer at the Little Bighorn. Never had the Sioux triumphed so spectacularly — and they never would again. For that triumph, more than any other chief they could thank Sitting Bull.

But the triumph contained the seeds of defeat. A stunned nation lashed back, and the Sioux country swarmed with regiments of "Custer avengers." By the spring of 1877, most of the hunting bands had surrendered and gone to the reservation, setting the stage for the government to seize the Black Hills and legalize the invasion.

Sitting Bull could not stomach such humiliation. With a die-hard following he crossed the "medicine road" into the land of the Grandmother. There he got along famously with the queen's redcoats, the North-West Mounted Police, and formed his first close ties to white men. But the buffalo were disappearing in Canada as they were in the United States, and "Bear Coat" — General Nelson A. Miles — watched the boundary like a hawk. After four years of hardship, starvation overcame humiliation, and young Crow Foot handed his father's rifle to Major Brotherton.

The final decade was one of despair. After nearly two years as a prisoner of war, Sitting Bull went to the reservation. At Standing Rock Agency, Agent James McLaughlin's goal was to transform his charges into imitation whites. He sought to make them into tillers of the soil embracing Christianity, Americanism, and the customs and values of the white people. Sitting Bull refused to be made over. He accepted what he thought would be beneficial, such as schooling for his children and grandchildren, and rejected the rest. Finding him unpliable, McLaughlin launched the campaign of ridicule and derision that included the imputation of cowardice at the Little Bighorn.

Hunger, disease, a decade of cultural breakdown,

and another land grab made the Sioux reservations fertile ground for the Ghost Dance religion that took root in 1890. It promised a new world, without whites, peopled by all the generations of Indians that had gone before, and stocked with an abundance of buffalo and other game. Whether Sitting Bull truly believed, he functioned as the high priest of the religion at Standing Rock. The government decided to remove him to a distant military post.

Irony and tragedy stalked Sitting Bull's final days. Not the Long Knives of old, but *ceska maza,* "metal breasts" (for their police badges) of his own tribe, closed in on their former leader. At dawn on December 15, 1890, a platoon of Indian policemen forced their way into his cabin on Grand River and placed him under arrest. Excited Ghost Dancers crowded around the cabin, and his own son Crow Foot, now fourteen, taunted him for giving up. The volatile confrontation blew up in a paroxysm of gunfire and hand-to-hand fighting. Sitting Bull went down, shot at close range in the chest and the back of the head by *ceska maza.* Crow Foot died too, beaten and shot by enraged policemen.

The Hunkpapas, even those who had forsaken the old ways, knew McLaughlin's portrait of Sitting Bull to be grotesquely flawed. They well remembered he had been a magnificent warrior, an inspiring war chief, a statesman and political leader of vast wisdom, a holy man of marvelous power, and to his last day a leader of compelling force.

The world remembers Sitting Bull not for what he achieved in his own culture but for his battle against the westward movement of the American people. It is this battle that gives him nearly universal name recognition beyond his own culture. In this struggle, as both lance and shield, his inflexibility served him well. He acted on faultless reasoning: The land of the Lakotas belonged to the Lakotas, and no whites had any right to be there. He fought to keep them out, and when that failed, he fought to defend his people and his territory from invasion. He lost not because of failings of leadership or, given his cultural outlook, failings of judgment, but because of impersonal forces beyond his control or even his understanding.

QUESTIONS TO CONSIDER

1.   How did Lakota culture change during the nineteenth century? What effect did white settlers have on that culture throughout the century?

2.   What was the traditional Lakota manner of fighting, and what were the values that it highlighted? Why did this style of warfare not work against white troops, and what lessons does Robert Utley think Sitting Bull should have learned from this?

3.   Describe Sitting Bull and his three "personalities." Discuss the stance he took toward whites and compare it to that taken by Red Cloud. Which one of them do you think was right and why?

4.   What were the principal interests of Americans in Sioux territory, and how did Americans generally react to Sitting Bull's effort at resistance? How did the United States government deal with the Lakota Sioux? How and on what pretext did they finally break the resistance of Sitting Bull's people?

5.   Describe life on the reservation. What was the principal purpose of the reservation from the American point of view? What is the significance of the Ghost Dance religion and of Sitting Bull's tragic death? How do you feel about Utley's conclusion that Sitting Bull lost, not because of any personal or cultural failings but because of forces beyond his control?

4

How the West Was Really Won

Miriam Horn

With the Indians out of the way, Americans were free at last to conquer the vast Great Plains that reached from Texas to the Canadian border in the center of the country. Westering farmers had stopped at the edge of this enormous grassland, because its arid climate and shallow topsoil seemed unsuited to agricultural techniques devised in the East. But after the Civil War came the development of new farming techniques and new machinery such as the windmill, the chilled-iron plow, and the combine, all of which made agriculture feasible on the windy prairies. As a consequence, farmers from east of the Mississippi swarmed there during the postwar years, some claiming 160 acres free under the 1862 Homestead Act, most buying their land from speculators or the railroads. In the 1880s alone, more than 1 million people poured onto the Great Plains from the Great Lakes states. Meanwhile, after the failure of Reconstruction, African Americans headed west as well; they were sodbusters, cowboys, speculators, miners, lawmen, desperadoes, and cavalrymen. Asian and Mexican Americans were present, too, all contributing to the drama of frontier conquest. The pioneers lived in all manner of homes — from dugouts to sod houses — battling tornadoes, hail, dust storms, blizzards, prairie fires, and grasshopper plagues in an endless struggle to make new lives for themselves on the nation's last frontier.

In 1890, the United States Census Bureau reported that the frontier was now settled. What had the frontier experience meant? How had it affected the national character? In 1893, a young history professor named Frederick Jackson Turner answered that question in a seminal essay, "The Significance of the Frontier in American History." The Turner thesis, as it would be known, argued that the American was a unique national type made that way by the frontier experience. According to Turner, a new society had sprung up in

America, one that borrowed from the Old World but was distinctly different because of its inexorable march westward. A significant consequence of that march was "the formation of a composite nationality," as the "crucible of the frontier" Americanized wave after wave of immigrants. Turner asserted, "To the frontier, the American intellect owes its striking characteristics. That coarseness and strength combined with acuteness and inquisitiveness; that practical, inventive turn of mind, quick to find expedients; that masterful grasp of material things, lacking in the artistic but powerful to effect great ends; that restless, nervous energy, that dominant individualism, working for good and for evil, and withal that buoyancy and exuberance which come with freedom — these are traits of the frontier, or traits called out elsewhere because of the existence of the frontier." As the country marched west, frontier types emerged, all of them, in the Turner pantheon, men: the explorer, the trapper, the trader, the soldier, the rancher, the farmer, and finally the town builder, each contributing in his distinct way to "the advance of civilization." Not only did the frontier produce "rugged individualism," the prime trait of Turner's all-American man, but it also carved democracy itself out of a virgin wilderness, producing the free political institutions that made America unique.

The Turner thesis had the force of myth, and its staying power in American popular culture may be attributed to its mythic quality. By myth, we do not mean some preposterous story. We mean the wishful, grandiose way a culture views its past. "Myths tell us of the exploits of the gods," says X. J. Kennedy, "all on a scale of magnificence larger than our life. We envy their freedom and power; they enact our wishes and dreams." Our wishes and dreams, projected onto the history of the West, reveal our deepest longing as a people.

If the Turner thesis, popularized in novels and motion pictures, has captured the popular imagination, it has also been the subject of heated controversy, especially in academe. While western historians such as Ray Allen Billington and Martin Ridge accepted Turner's basic argument and refined and updated it, others disputed his theory as romantic nonsense and fraught with error. Never, however, has the Turner argument been more assailed than today, what with the emergence of a younger generation of western historians who have placed the Turner hypothesis under siege. For them, as Miriam Horn says, "the West was not some rough-hewn egalitarian democracy, where every man had a piece of land and the promise of prosperity, but a world quickly dominated by big money and big government." The new western historians take Turner to task, too, for ignoring America's brutal treatment of the Indians and for the greed and destruction that characterized so much of the westering experience. They chastise Turner for omitting women, blacks, Asians, and Mexican Americans from the frontier equation. Disputing the notion of westerners as self-sufficient individualists, the new historians point out that the frontier in fact gave birth to the welfare state, thanks to federal irrigation projects, crop subsidies, and drought aid. Indeed, the example of supreme rugged individualism, the cattleman, enjoyed a huge *federal subsidy in the form of free range on government land. But perhaps the worst aspect of the westward movement, the new historians believe, was the ecological devastation that accompanied it. "The settlement of the Great Plains," one of them asserted, "was a world-class environmental catastrophe," the effects of which are still being felt.*

In the selection that follows, Miriam Horn summarizes the findings of the new western historians and reflects on what their work has done to our cherished western myths. Note, in particular, how these historians, using the techniques of the new social history, which focuses on everyday life, have shed new light on the role and experience of women on the frontier. Note, too, the western experiences of African, Asian, and Mexican Americans. If the new western historians sometimes overstate their case, concentrating too much on the negative side of the frontier story and its "legacy of conquest," they have forced us to reconsider that story, to acknowledge and benefit from its mistakes and its tragedies. As you study this selection, ask yourself how much you agree with the new western historians. Do you think that they have created a countermyth of the West, born of their disillusionment over Vietnam and the anti-imperialist views of the sixties? Why do you think the old myths of the West — which constitute America's only national mythology — have had such enduring appeal?

GLOSSARY

BECKWOURTH, JIM   African American fur trapper.

DAWES ACT (1887)   Broke up Indian reservations into individually owned plots of land; its goal was to make the Indians into "imitation white" farmers.

CROCKETT, DAVY   Legendary hero of the Alamo, the famous "last stand" in Texas's war for independence against Mexico (1836); historian Dan Kilgore stirred up a storm of protest when he suggested that Crockett might not have died as mythology claims.

GOETZ, BERNHARD   Manhattan citizen who in 1984 shot four African American teenagers in a New York City subway when they asked him for money; Goetz said that he packed a pistol in self-defense — he had been mugged in New York City in 1981; he was acquitted of homicide but was sentenced to five months in jail for carrying an unlicensed gun.

LAMAR, HOWARD   Yale historian who regards the near-extermination of the buffalo "as one of the biggest ecological changes in North American history."

LIMERICK, PATRICIA   Her book, *The Legacy of Conquest,* is "the most comprehensive summary of the new view" of western history.

NORTH, OLIVER   American army colonel who was involved in the Iran-Contra scandal of the second Reagan administration (see selection 31); segments of the American public celebrated him as a hero, although he admitted to having lied to Congress and destroying incriminating documents; in 1994, he ran for the U.S. Senate.

PICKETT, BILL   African American cowboy who felled steers by biting them on the lip and forcing them to the ground.

I t is our Book of Genesis. Our legend of Romulus and Remus. The story of the frontier is America's myth of creation. In those rolling prairies and gold-rich mountains, a new, freer man was born, unhindered by tradition, restless and independent, endlessly optimistic, hard-working and unafraid. Living on the "hither edge" of wilderness, in historian Frederick Jackson Turner's phrase, the pioneer had "broken the cake of custom" to forge the headstrong young nation that would become America.

Or so we were told by generations of historians. But the Turnerian view of the West is falling apart these days, dismantled by a group of young scholars raised on the disillusionments of Vietnam and the anti-imperialist rhetoric of the '60s. Turner himself understood that "each age writes the history of the past anew with reference to the conditions uppermost in its own time." So this new group of historians sifts through the evidence with an eye toward race, gender and class. They are turning away from Great Men and Great Events to ordinary people and daily life, poring over diaries and letters and the evidence left in the land itself.

Read the new studies, and you discover that the West was not some rough-hewn egalitarian democracy, where every man had a piece of land and the promise of prosperity, but a world quickly dominated by big money and big government. It was not Walt Whitman's "newer garden of creation," where the sodbuster might dwell in sweet harmony with nature, but a nearly unmitigated environmental catastrophe. Nor was the pioneer family, so often invoked by nostalgic politicians urging a return to fundamental American values, a close-knit little household facing down hardship. Often, it was torn apart by the great desert emptiness of the West.

Frederick Jackson Turner was right to locate the

From Miriam Horn, "How the West Was Really Won," *U.S. News & World Report,* May 21, 1990, 57–65. Copyright © U.S. News & World Report.

roots of the American character on the frontier. But that legacy, say the new historians, is one of rapaciousness and environmental plunder, of fragmented families, racial strife, vast disparities between rich and poor. Though the frontier was "closed" 100 years ago, when the 1890 census showed settlement from sea to sea, that date did not mark a decisive break in history, as Turner and his followers argued. The new historians see a continuous story, with the issues that consumed the old West remaining central concerns in America today.

Still, these historians struggle to be taken seriously. Their more traditional colleagues are mildly critical, charging that they sometimes overstate their case. "Not all of their work is necessarily so new," says Martin Ridge, author with Ray Billington of the pre-eminent college text on Western history, *Westward Expansion.* "But they are without question innovative and committed scholars, and everybody welcomes new approaches to the region's history." A respectful hearing outside the field is more elusive. University of Colorado Prof. Patricia Limerick, author of the most comprehensive summary of the new view, *The Legacy of Conquest,* likens the "stereotypes of noble savages and noble pioneers struggling quaintly in the wilderness" to the aura of moonlight and magnolias that long shrouded Southern history, handicapping scholars in their efforts to excavate the realities of slavery and Reconstruction. With the mountain man and cowboy "the domain of mass entertainment and lighthearted national escapism," says Limerick, Western historians are relegated to a quaint regionalism.

They must also do battle with a deep ideological attachment to the fantasies of the frontier. In 1985, Ronald Reagan spoke of the men of the Alamo calling out encouragement to one another, the settler pushing west and singing his song: "It is the American sound: Hopeful, bighearted, idealistic; daring, decent and fair. That's our heritage . . . there is always a better tomorrow. We believed then and now there are no limits to growth." That faith in limitless bounty,

Homesteaders on the plains, with their sod house in the background. "Most homesteaders," writes Miriam Horn, "went broke when their fields dried up, and were forced to sell to the handful of landowners lucky enough to have water." (The Bettmann Archive)

say these historians, has been nothing but trouble for the American West.

Economic success was the ordained lot of frontier settlers; men and women had only to apply themselves to achieve wealth and an elevated social status. . . . The wide dispersal of land ownership mitigated against control by the few or the distant. If people fell by the wayside they had only themselves to blame.

— BILLINGTON AND RIDGE,
Westward Expansion, 1949

The idea of the self-sufficient individual is the most elevated tenet in the American gospel, codified by none other than Thomas Jefferson. With a vast conti-

nent before him, Jefferson foresaw a nation of yeoman farmers, each in possession of 160 acres carved out of the wilderness or liberated from indolent natives to be made productive by the sweat of the American brow. [Jefferson's vision was incorporated in the 1862 Homestead Act, which offered adult citizens and aliens alike, regardless of their sex or race, free 160-acre tracts of government land in the West; they would receive final titles to their farms after they had lived on them for five years and paid nominal fees.]

Unfortunately, what worked in the lush valleys of Virginia was doomed to fail in the arid reaches of the Far West. This was a land of deserts that were fiercely hot and fiercely cold, streams that flooded a few weeks each year and went dry the rest, grasshopper plagues, hail followed by drought followed by hail, sterile salt beds and relentless winds. A rancher might survive with 2,500 acres to run his livestock, but expecting a farmer to make it on 160 acres, wrote Ian Frazier in *Great Plains,* published last year [1989], "was like expecting a fisherman to survive on a little square of ocean." Most homesteaders went broke when their fields dried up, and were forced to sell to the handful of landowners lucky enough to have water.

Those men accumulated massive holdings, sometimes exceeding a million acres, despite feeble legal efforts to constrain their empire building. According to Marc Reisner, whose 1987 *Cadillac Desert* examines the role of federal and urban bureaucracies in the competition for water, the West presented endless opportunities for fraud. A speculator might meet the requirement for a domicile on each section, for instance, by scattering birdhouses across his land. Consequently, by the 1890s, seven eighths of the farmland west of the Mississippi was owned by nonfarmers, and agribusiness was born. Organized around large-scale water management, the West had become a "land of authority and restraint, of class and exploitation, and ultimately of imperial power," says University of Kansas historian Donald Worster, author of *Rivers of Empire.*

Monopoly enterprise came quickly to ranching and mining, as well, turning the "rugged individualist" into an impoverished wage laborer. In 1855, 157 Eastern-based corporations ran cattle in Colorado, and the Scotland-based Prairie Land & Cattle Company owned a strip 50 miles wide from the Arkansas River to New Mexico. The cowboy, that icon of freedom, wrote Wallace Stegner in 1987, "was and is an overworked, underpaid hireling, almost as homeless and dispossessed as a modern crop worker." Prospectors, too, soon exhausted the surface gold in the mountains and became virtually indentured to the Eastern financiers who owned the machines, mills and smelters necessary for underground mining.

Ironically, notes Limerick, the myth of self-suffi-

ciency deprived miners of recourse. Compensation for injury was typically denied by courts, which deemed the individual responsible for his own safety. Despite lung-clogging dust and temperatures often exceeding 120 degrees, unionization was long blocked on the ground that it would compromise the independence of the solitary miner.

And it was in the ostensibly self-reliant West, say the new historians, that the modern welfare state was born, beginning with mass federal irrigation projects in 1902 and evolving to include the crop subsidies and drought assistance of modern times. Though he had been lured to barren land by politicians and railroad marketeers, still the farmer was flogged for requiring aid. In the 1870s, Governor Pillsbury of Minnesota warned that assistance to farmers would "sap and destroy the vital energies of self-reliance."

Oh, faith rewarded! Now no idle dream,
The long-sought Canaan before him lies;
He floods the desert with the mountain stream,
And Lo! It leaps transformed to paradise.

— TRADITIONAL MORMON HYMN

The Romantic sensibility of the 19th century was fertile ground for the idea of "Natural Man" — an innocent fleeing dark, corrupted cities to settle in the promised land and bring forth its God-given bounty. In fact, says Worster, "the settlement of the Great Plains was a world-class environmental catastrophe, one we still refuse to admit, given our pride in our agricultural expertise."

Historians are now tapping geologists, biologists, botanists and environmental scientists to perform an autopsy on the land. Where alder trees have replaced Douglas fir, it means there was clearcutting and the land was burned over several times. An abundance of sage and juniper indicates overgrazing well in the past. The damage is vast: Ground water contaminated or depleted; plowed-up topsoil lost to drought and the merciless winds; entire species destroyed.

Yale historian Howard Lamar, who taught many of

the new historians and laid the foundation for their work with his *Reader's Encyclopedia of the American West,* describes the slaughter of the buffalo as one of the biggest ecological changes in North American history. In just 30 years, some 60 million animals were destroyed and replaced by cattle, disrupting the native ecology and leaving the land overgrazed and exhausted. "The rancher is a man who supplants the native grasses with tumbleweed, snakeweed, mud, dust and flies," wrote environmental activist and novelist Edward Abbey. "He drives off elk and antelope, shoots eagles, bears and cougars on sight. And then leans back and grins at the TV cameras and talks about how much he loves the American West." The problem has always been greed, argues Worster. The 1880s were a veritable free-for-all on the grasslands. Cattle barons eager to get rich quick built their herds to untenable size, leading finally to the collapse of the cattle kingdom. Miners, too, gutted the countryside to get out the minerals as fast as possible, heedless of the wasted land they left behind.

Cow country was man's country, but a cowboy was obliged to protect decent Christian women. Sometimes he would get a hankerin' to hit town, where he would spend his cash on liquor, gambling and women of ill repute. The ranch boss knew the cowboy had worked hard, felt isolated, built up tension and needed a binge.

— ROBERT HEIDE AND JOHN GILMAN. *Box Office Buckaroos,* 1990

Until recently, Western history has been by and about men. Now, as scholars reconstruct the lives of frontier women and children, they dismantle nostalgic notions of the prairie family. Again, individualism emerges as a decidedly mixed blessing. "Our national celebration of separation and autonomy has given us the justification for taking families apart," says historian Lillian Schissel, co-author of *Far from Home; Families of the Westward Journey.*

Drawing on diaries, letters and reminiscences, Schissel traces the sagas of pioneer families. A family

of Colorado prospectors buries all but one of seven children. A widow on an Oregon homestead is abandoned by her only son and must contend on her own with a failing farm, one daughter gone mad and another whose husband threatens to cut her throat. In South Dakota, two families of Russian immigrants live their first winter on the plains with all 12 people crowded into a boxcar "worse than a coyote hole" and so little food the children howl constantly with hunger.

The private records of this misery are richer than any fiction. One of the Russian men writes: "We were so lacking in tools for changing the rugged prairies into productive farmland that when I think back to our first year on that coyote land, I can hardly keep from crying." Things got better the second year, but "my wife Sophie, with seven children and all sleeping in a shanty that became a pond when it rained, loathed everything about America. It is odd we even slept together, but we had no other choice."

Given high mortality rates and the economic advantages of having numerous children, frontier women were nearly always pregnant and worked even in their ninth month hauling buckets of mud or armfuls of wheat to the threshing floor. The men were often drunk and occasionally violent. One frontier ditty advised: "A woman, a dog, a hickory tree, The more you beat them the better they be." Worst of all was the endless isolation. Tied to their homes and often miles from the nearest neighbor, says Schissel, the women would walk down to the tracks to catch a glimpse of human faces when the train passed by. Some went mad in their loneliness, listening to nothing but the incessant wailing of the wind. One prairie daughter recalled often "finding my mother crying, and wondering whether she cried of fatigue, craving a word of recognition, gratitude or praise."

Children, too, worked as soon as they were able. In *Growing up with the Country: Childhood on the Far Western Frontier,* historian Elliott West unearths a Kansas farmer's letter home about his son: "Little Baz

Backbreaking toil was the lot of women and men on the frontier. "Worst of all was the isolation. Tied to their homes and often miles from the nearest neighbor, women would walk down to the tracks to *catch a glimpse of human faces when the train passed by." (The Bettman Archive)*

can fetch up cows out of the stock fields, or oxen, carry in stove wood and climb in the corn crib and feed the hogs and go on errands down to his grandma's." At the time, Little Baz was just over 2 years old. Another boy, at age 11, was breaking horses for 50 cents apiece. "His father tied him to the horse, and tied his hat to his head, and after the kid had flopped around for a bit he got to be an expert," says West.

In the positive view he takes of frontier childhood, West is unusual among the new historians. He emphasizes the youngsters' closeness to the land, a sense of home never fully achieved by their displaced parents. Though to some degree perplexed by their wild prairie children, says West, these parents were extremely loving, if for no other reason than that they couldn't afford to have their children run away. That benign view is disputed by Schissel and others, who argue that frontier children were often emotionally neglected and physically abused. These more pessimistic historians stress the torments of childhood, the bedbugs and pinworms and cholera and fevers, the filth and starvation and death.

Anglo-American pioneers were uniquely equipped to capitalize on frontier opportunity for self-betterment.

— BILLINGTON AND RIDGE

For decades, Western history was not only male but white. The Indian was an object for Western heroism: A savage to be conquered or a noble primitive waiting to be civilized. The Hispanic was the enemy — remember the Alamo. Blacks and Chinese were simply left out. "The migration from the East was only one of many in the 19th century," says University of Utah historian Richard White, who [was in 1990] writing a text to replace Billington and Ridge. "There were also large migrations from the South and from Asia, both of which were periodically blocked and both of which continue to this day."

The approach of the 500th anniversary of the landing of Columbus . . . spurred extensive scholarship on the southern migration, much of it aimed at reclaiming Spain's status as the first to settle the American West. Coronado was already exploring western North America in 1539, hundreds of years before Anglos arrived there. In 1598, Don Juan de Onate led 400 colonists across the Rio Grande, and on April 30, they formally claimed the land for Spain. Last month [April 1990], the Texas House of Representatives passed a resolution declaring that day the first Thanksgiving in America, and asked Massachusetts to concede defeat.

Even before 1821, the year Mexico won independence, trappers and prospectors had begun encroaching on Mexican land. They were the "illegal aliens" of their day, says Limerick, but were tolerated and assimilated into Mexican culture. By the 1830s, however, distinguished Anglo writers were championing the notion of "the white man's burden" to civilize the more savage races and lamenting the waste of such rich territory. "In the hands of an enterprising people, what a country this might be," wrote Richard Dana in *Two Years Before the Mast* (1840). Historian Francis Parkman, touring the Rockies and Plains in 1846, described Hispanics as "slavish-looking, stupid, squalid, miserable and mean." That same year, America went to war [against Mexico]. Mexico lost half its territory. And though the Treaty of Guadalupe Hidalgo guaranteed Hispanics rights to their land, says Limerick, 80 percent ultimately went to American lawyers and settlers. As the final blow, in 1850 California passed the Foreign Miners' Tax, driving Hispanics out of the mines.

Writing Hispanic-American history is tricky business: The issues of the 19th century — bilingualism, cultural assimilation, immigration and labor competition — remain so volatile today that accounts of the past are inevitably highly politicized. Black Western history suffers an additional handicap — an acute lack of sources. In the few accounts that have been written, some remarkable heroes emerge, men like Jim Beckwourth, a fur trapper who lived with the Crow Indians; Britt Johnson, who rode alone hundreds of miles beyond the frontier to retrieve his wife and two children from their Kiowa captors, and cowboy Bill Pickett, who could drop a steer by biting its front lip and dragging it to the ground.

The first historians of the black West found in the frontier the seeds of racial equality. "Americans need to remember that the Wyoming pioneers desegregated their first school; that the West once approached the democracy they are still striving to achieve," wrote Philip Durham in *The Negro Cowboys* (1965). But the current crop of historians tells a more sorrowful story.

They write, for instance, of the migration of 40,000 blacks to Kansas in the 1870s, lured by the railroads to a false paradise. Homeless and jobless, they set up shantytowns and began to die at the rate of 50 a day. Within a few years, two thirds were dead or gone. Other states put provisions in their constitutions excluding free blacks: Blacks would intermarry with Indians, explained Oregon's delegate to Congress, and "led on by the Negro, these savages would become much more formidable. The fruits of their commingling would be long and bloody wars."

The new Asian historians tell equally bleak tales. The internment of the Japanese during World War II and the current increase in anti-Asian violence, they say, have their roots in the murderous attacks on Chinese railroad workers in the 1870s and in the chilling denial of civil rights in the California Constitution: "No native of China, no idiot or insane person . . . shall ever exercise the privileges of an elector."

We made this country. We found it and we made it.
RUFE, in *Shane,* 1953

Once it was clear in the early part of this century that the conquest of the Native American was complete, it became fashionable to lament the beautiful tragedy of nature's wise child. "White people love to watch Indians die," says Ian Frazier. "They love to stand around and say things like 'the red man joins his ancestors' or talk about the 'end of the trail' for the noble brave. The problem is that the real end of the trail was usually smallpox or murder then and alcoholism or car accidents or diabetes now."

The noble-savage mythology has been terribly destructive. Settlers convinced of the natives' barbarism were mistrustful and aggressive, provoking violent confrontation that might have been avoided. The myth of the Indian's primitive purity has been equally destructive: When a tribe adapts to modern life, it is branded as "inauthentic" and therefore unworthy of the rights guaranteed by treaty.

But most damaging for the Indian has been the cult of individualism. Early 20th-century reformers saw Indian loyalty to the tribe as un-American, even socialist. One supporter of the 1887 Dawes Act, aimed at breaking up reservations into individually owned tracts of land, suggested the Indian needed to be "touched by the wings of the divine angel of discontent . . . to get the Indian out of the blanket and into trousers, trousers with a pocket that ached to be filled with dollars."

The new historians borrow the methods of anthropology to trace the evolution of the many Indian cultures. They are finding, says White, that many tribes were in fact the creation of European settlers, who herded disparate groups onto a reservation and required them to act as a single people. The Utes, as well as the Navajos, were originally scattered over a huge area with vastly divergent cultures. The Cheyenne were a group of autonomous bands brought together out of necessity as clan members fell to smallpox. These groups often shared no previous political affiliation, and in some cases didn't even speak the same language, but "the whites needed to invent a tribe so someone could sign the treaties," says White.

Surprisingly, the picture of Indian history now emerging is quite positive, focusing on the ability of the Indian, against all odds, to maintain semisovereign status. America's founders felt a deep moral obligation to treat Indians fairly, explains White, and chose treaty negotiations over genocide, the favored solution in Argentina and Chile, or the denial of all legal rights, as in Guatemala and Peru. For a century, the treaties were violated in every way possible: Tribal landholdings were broken up, Indians were denied the right to practice their religion, children were removed from their families to assimilationist schools. But the last two decades [since the 1970s] have seen a resurgence of Indian power in the courts and legislatures, and as severe water shortages have developed in the West, tribal leaders have begun to make use of the "mortgage on Western development" their water rights represent. Historian Vine Deloria, a member of the Sioux tribe, makes the highly controversial argument that "American Indians have actually been treated considerably better than any other aboriginal group on any continent."

A fiery horse with the speed of light, a cloud of dust and a hearty hi-ho Silver!
Introduction to "The Lone Ranger"

Times are tough for the classic hero of the American West. Howard Lamar brands General Custer "a foolish general who got himself into a spot where he was roundly defeated," and objects to "turning that defeat into a kind of moral victory or martyrdom." Frazier describes the William Edwards biography of "the gun-nut" Col. Samuel Colt "as stupider than any biography of Lenin," and notes that the heroes of Dodge City were all kingpins in gambling, prostitution and alcohol. In the words of Wallace Stegner, "Our principal folk hero, the frontiersman, was an antisocial loner, impatient of responsibility and law, ferocious, coarse, selfish, ready to violence."

Such hero-bashing can have nasty consequences. In 1978, historian Dan Kilgore published an essay — "How Did Davy Die?" — that disputed the heroic account of Davy Crockett's defense of the Alamo (he was supposed to have died with dozens of the enemy at his feet). Drawing on a diary of one of Gen. Santa Anna's officers, Kilgore revealed that Crockett hid during the battle, possibly under a mattress. When discovered, he claimed to be a tourist who had taken refuge in the Alamo on the approach of the Mexican Army. Texans were furious. One newspaper branded Kilgore's essay a "Communist plan to degrade our heroes." And in a remarkable display of the power of myth over reality, *People* ran a photo of diary translator Carmen Perry alongside one of John Wayne — as Crockett in the 1960 movie *The Alamo* — and invited the public to decide who was more credible.

The mythic West, it appears, has a tenacious hold on the national imagination. "America has always thought of the West as an escape from history," says Donald Worster, "an escape from Europe, corruption, evil, greed, failure, lust, tragedy." No such escape was possible, then or now, and the legacy of the frontier past remains fully alive today. The welfare state persists in the growing Western dependency on federal aid — farm supports, military installations, defense contracts, public land management and water projects. Right alongside it persists the dream of the self-reliant individual, the sage-brush rebel shaking his fist at Eastern corporations and politicians. The idea of a nation without limits endures in the unchecked growth of cities like Denver and Los Angeles. Both continue to import water from politically weaker agricultural areas, and both have lately begun effectively exporting their pollution by relying on power sources outside the state. "We persist in the fantasy," says White, "that we can transform a desert into a garden."

Most enduring is the idea of the lone ranger, the solitary hero, mistrustful of authorities and ready to take matters in his own hands. Oliver North was nicknamed a cowboy by his admirers, and subway vigilante Bernhard Goetz was cheered as a hero in the mold of Billy the Kid. Perhaps America isn't yet ready to give up its frontier vision — of a world where you can always tell the good guys from the bad guys, a world where complexity gives way to blissful simplicity.

QUESTIONS TO CONSIDER

1. Miriam Horn says that according to the new western historians the "faith in limitless bounty . . . has been nothing but trouble for the American West." How do they show the idea of individual self-sufficiency to have been harmful for western settlers? How was the idea that the "Great American Desert" could be made to bloom harmful to both settlers and the land?

2. How do the new historians differ from other historians in their view of the effect of westward migration on the family? Do the new historians agree with one another?

3. There has been much emphasis by the new historians on nonwhite settlers of the West — African, Mexican, and Asian Americans. How have evaluations of the experiences of these groups changed over time? How do the new historians evaluate the effect of European settlement of the West on the Indians and its consequences up to the present? How does this fit with the view given in selection 3?

4. Why has the myth of the taming of the American West been so enduring? How was it created, and is it the view Americans have always held of the West? What are some of the legacies of this myth, according to Miriam Horn? Do you think there are others? Why have the new histories often been badly received?

5. Frederick Jackson Turner said that "each age writes the history of the past anew with reference to the conditions uppermost in its own time." What conditions have influenced the new western historians? How might this influence your evaluation of these historians? Can there ever be such a thing as "the definitive history" of any subject?

III

THE NEW
INDUSTRIAL ORDER

5

The Master of Steel: Andrew Carnegie

ROBERT L. HEILBRONER

From the 1820s on, the United States industrialized at an impressive rate. But the real boost came during the Civil War, when the United States Congress created a national currency and banking system, enacted homestead legislation, and appropriated federal aid for a transcontinental railroad. Such measures, argues historian James M. McPherson, provided "the blueprint for modern America." From the crucible of civil war emerged a new America of big business, heavy industry, and commercial farming that became by 1880 "the foremost industrial nation" in the world. The federal government played a crucial role in the postwar boom. One Republican administration after another not only maintained a protective tariff to minimize foreign competition but gave away millions of dollars' worth of public land to railroad companies, adopted a hard money policy that pleased big business, and — except for the Interstate Commerce and Sherman Anti-trust acts, both adopted because of popular unrest — cheerfully refused to regulate or restrict the consolidation of America's new industrial order.

It was during the Gilded Age (as Mark Twain called it), an era between Robert E. Lee's surrender at Appomattox and the turn of the century, that American capitalism, growing for decades now, produced mighty combinations that controlled most of the nation's wealth. The leaders of the new industrial order comprised a complex gallery of individuals popularly known as the robber barons. There had, of course, been many rich Americans before the Gilded Age, people who made fortunes from traffic in lands and goods. But the post–Civil War robber barons were a different breed, for they controlled the essential tools of the booming industrial economy itself: railroads (the nation's basic transportation system), banking, and manufacturing. They eliminated competition, set prices, exploited workers, and commanded the awe or fear of an entire generation. Enough of them were rags-to-riches individuals, the kind celebrated in the novels of Horatio Alger, to encourage the notion of the American dream at work, a dream that in the United States all who were capable could rise to the top. Some of the tycoons were gaudy vulgarians such as one H. A. W. Tabor. Finding a portrait of Shakespeare hanging in a Denver opera house that he had built, Tabor demanded that the portrait be replaced with his own, storming, "What the hell has Shakespeare done for Denver?" Others were industrial pirates such as Jay Gould, a consumptive rascal who made his money by various nefarious means.

But other entrepreneurs fit a different pattern: like the rapacious capitalist played by Michael Douglas in the movie Wall Street, they were obsessed with the power that wealth brought them. An example was Cornelius "Commodore" Vanderbilt, who began his career as a ferryboatman, rose to ownership of riverboats (hence his nickname), and went on to become a railroad magnate who owned a transportation empire worth $80 million and lived in splendor in a Manhattan mansion. This rowdy, profane man loved to win in any way he could, once proclaiming, "Law? What do I care about the law. H'ain't I got the power?"

Then there was John D. Rockefeller, a quiet, penny-pinching millionaire whose Standard Oil Company became one of the nation's most powerful monopolies. Indeed, Rockefeller's business methods, stressing the virtues of order, organization, and planning, set the example of modern business organization. Unlike other Gilded Age entrepreneurs, however, Rockefeller had little interest in money for money's sake. At the end of his life, through foundations named after him, he donated millions of dollars to religious activities, medical research, and higher education.

And then there was steel magnate Andrew Carnegie, the subject of the insightful portrait that follows. Another self-made man, Carnegie was at one time the richest person in the world. Perhaps more than any other tycoon, he embodied the spirit of the age, a man who not only created but advocated and celebrated industrial power. He defended democracy, capitalism, and the Anglo-Saxon race, and he even argued that evolution produced millionaires such as he, ignoring the fact that such folk enjoyed generous government benefits, not to mention the help of federal troops serving as strikebreakers. Yet Carnegie also acted on his own self-proclaimed sense of duty: having amassed a prodigious fortune, he proceeded to give almost all of it away during his lifetime. In him, Robert L. Heilbroner sees both the failures and the integrity of Gilded Age America.

GLOSSARY

CARNEGIE CORPORATION OF NEW YORK   After making his fortune, Andrew Carnegie established this "first great modern" philanthropic foundation.

CARNEGIE, McCANDLESS & COMPANY   Andrew Carnegie's British-American steel company and the nucleaus of his steel empire.

FRICK, HENRY   Self-made millionaire who amalgamated his coke empire and Andrew Carnegie's steelworks and assumed "the active management of the whole." Frick, Captain William Jones, and Charles Schwab constituted "the vital energy" of the Carnegie empire.

GOSPEL OF WEALTH   Andrew Carnegie's philosophy (in a book of that title) that the millionaire had a duty to distribute wealth while still alive.

JONES, CAPTAIN WILLIAM   One of a "brilliant assemblage" of men around Andrew Carnegie, "a kind of Paul Bunyon of steel," who was inventive in handling machinery and talented at dealing with people.

MORGAN, J. P.   Wealthy banker who purchased the Carnegie steel empire in 1901 for $492 million; it became the core of the United States Steel Company.

PULLMAN, GEORGE   Developed the Pullman railroad sleeping car and joined forces with Andrew Carnegie to form the Pullman Palace Car Company.

SCHWAB, CHARLES   Assistant manager of Andrew Carnegie's Braddock plant and another of the brilliant men surrounding Carnegie.

SCOTT, THOMAS A.   Superintendent of the Pennsylvania Railroad and Andrew Carnegie's boss who first encouraged him to invest in stock.

UNITED STATES STEEL COMPANY   J. P. Morgan merged the Carnegie empire with other interests to create this huge corporation, which controlled more than 60 percent of America's steel production.

WOODRUFF, T. T.   When Andrew Carnegie bought a one-eighth interest in Woodruff's company, Woodruff began production of the first sleeping car for trains.

Toward the end of his days, at the close of World War I, Andrew Carnegie was already a kind of national legend. His meteoric rise, the scandals and successes of his industrial generalship — all this was blurred into nostalgic memory. What was left was a small, rather feeble man with a white beard and pale, penetrating eyes, who could occasionally be seen puttering around his mansion on upper Fifth Avenue, a benevolent old gentleman who still rated an annual birthday interview but was even then a venerable relic of a fast-disappearing era. Carnegie himself looked back on his career with a certain savored incredulity. "How much did you say I had given away, Poynton?" he would inquire of his private secretary; "$324,657,399" was the answer. "Good Heaven!" Carnegie would exclaim. "Where did I ever get all that money?"

Where he *had* got all that money was indeed a legendary story, for even in an age known for its acquisitive triumphs, Carnegie's touch had been an extraordinary one. He had begun, in true Horatio Alger fashion, at the bottom; he had ended, in a manner that put the wildest of Alger's novels to shame, at the very pinnacle of success. At the close of his great deal with J. P. Morgan in 1901, when the Carnegie steel empire was sold to form the core of the new United States Steel Company, the banker had extended his hand and delivered the ultimate encomium of the times: "Mr. Carnegie," he said, "I want to congratulate you on being the richest man in the world."

It was certainly as "the richest man in the world" that Carnegie attracted the attention of his contemporaries. Yet this is hardly why we look back on him with interest today. As an enormous money-maker Carnegie was a flashy, but hardly a profound, hero of the times; and the attitudes of Earnestness and Self-Assurance, so engaging in the young immigrant, become irritating when they are congealed in the millionaire. But what lifts Carnegie's life above the rut of a one-dimensional success story is an aspect of which his contemporaries were relatively unaware.

Going through his papers after his death, Carnegie's executors came across a memorandum that he had written to himself fifty years before, carefully preserved in a little yellow box of keepsakes and mementos. It brings us back to December, 1868, when Carnegie, a young man flushed with the first taste of great success, retired to his suite in the opulent Hotel St. Nicholas in New York, to tot up his profits for the year. It had been a tremendous year and the calculation must have been extremely pleasurable. Yet this is what he wrote as he reflected on the figures:

Thirty-three and an income of $50,000 per annum! By this time two years I can so arrange all my business as to secure at least $50,000 per annum. Beyond this never earn — make no effort to increase fortune, but spend the surplus each year for benevolent purposes. Cast aside business forever, except for others.

Settle in Oxford and get a thorough education, making the acquaintance of literary men — this will take three years of active work — pay especial attention to speaking in public. Settle then in London and purchase a controlling interest in some newspaper or live review and give the general management of it attention, taking part in public matters, especially those connected with education and improvement of the poorer classes.

Man must have an idol — the amassing of wealth is one of the worst species of idolatry — no idol more debasing than the worship of money. Whatever I engage in I must push inordinately; therefore should I be careful to choose that life which will be the most elevating in its character. To continue much longer overwhelmed by business cares and with most of my thoughts wholly upon the way to make more money in the shortest time, must degrade me beyond hope of permanent recovery. I will resign business at thirty-five, but during the ensuing two years I wish to spend the afternoons in receiving instruction and in reading systematically.

Reprinted from *American Heritage,* August 1960, pp. 4–9, 107–111, by permission of the author.

It is a document which in more ways than one is Carnegie to the very life: brash, incredibly self-confident, chockablock with self-conscious virtue — and more than a little hypocritical. For the program so nobly outlined went largely unrealized. Instead of retiring in two years, Carnegie went on for thirty-three more; even then it was with considerable difficulty that he was persuaded to quit. Far from shunning further money-making, he proceeded to roll up his fortune with an uninhibited drive that led one unfriendly biographer to characterize him as "the greediest little gentleman ever created." Certainly he was one of the most aggressive profit seekers of his time. Typically, when an associate jubilantly cabled: "No. 8 furnace broke all records today," Carnegie coldly replied, "What were the other furnaces doing?"

It is this contrast between his hopes and his performance that makes Carnegie interesting. For when we review his life, what we see is more than the career of another nineteenth-century acquisitor. We see the unequal struggle between a man who loved money — loved making it, having it, spending it — and a man who, at bottom, was ashamed of himself for his acquisitive desires. All during his lifetime, the money-maker seemed to win. But what lifts Carnegie's story out of the ordinary is that the other Carnegie ultimately triumphed. At his death public speculation placed the size of his estate at about five hundred million dollars. In fact it came to $22,881,575. Carnegie *had* become the richest man in the world — but something had also driven him to give away ninety per cent of his wealth.

Actually, his contemporaries knew of Carnegie's inquietude about money. In 1889, before he was world-famous, he had written an article for the *North American Review* entitled "The Gospel of Wealth" — an article that contained the startling phrase: "The man who dies thus rich dies disgraced." It was hardly surprising, however, if the world took these sentiments at a liberal discount: homiletic millionaires who preached the virtues of austerity were no novelty; Carnegie himself, returning in 1879 from a trip to the

Andrew Carnegie, in his mid-twenties when photographed here in 1861, was the son of Scottish working-class radicals and the product of a stern religious upbringing. In his younger days, he thought that the amassing of wealth was "one of the worst species of idolatry." However, he abandoned his plans to retire at thirty-five in order to devote his energies to self-improvement and benevolent enterprises. Instead, he became one of the richest men the world had ever known. (Courtesy, Carnegie Corporation of New York)

miseries of India, had been able to write with perfect sincerity, "How very little the millionaire has beyond the peasant, and how very often his additions tend not to happiness but to misery."

What the world may well have underestimated, however, was a concern more deeply rooted than these pieties revealed. For, unlike so many of his self-made peers, who also rose from poverty, Carnegie was the product of a *radical* environment. The village of Dunfermline, Scotland, when he was born there in 1835, was renowned as a center of revolutionary ferment, and Carnegie's family was itself caught up in the radical movement of the times. His father was a regular speaker at the Chartist rallies, which were an almost daily occurrence in Dunfermline in the 1840's, and his uncle was an impassioned orator for the rights of the working class to vote and strike. All this made an indelible impression on Carnegie's childhood.

"I remember as if it were yesterday," he wrote seventy years later, "being awakened during the night by a tap at the back window by men who had come to inform my parents that my uncle, Bailie Morrison, had been thrown in jail because he dared to hold a meeting which had been forbidden . . . It is not to be wondered at that, nursed amid such surroundings, I developed into a violent young Republican whose motto was 'death to privilege.'"

From another uncle, George Lauder, Carnegie absorbed a second passion that was also to reveal itself in his later career. This was his love of poetry, first that of the poet Burns, with its overtones of romantic egalitarianism, and then later, of Shakespeare. Immense quantities of both were not only committed to memory, but made into an integral — indeed, sometimes an embarrassingly evident — part of his life: on first visiting the Doge's palace in Venice he thrust a companion in the ducal throne and held him pinioned there while he orated the appropriate speeches from *Othello*. Once, seeing Vanderbilt walking on Fifth Avenue, Carnegie smugly remarked, "I would not exchange his millions for my knowledge of Shakespeare."

But it was more than just a love of poetry that remained with Carnegie. Virtually alone among his fellow acquisitors, he was driven by a genuine respect for the power of thought to seek answers for questions that never even occurred to them. Later, when he "discovered" Herbert Spencer, the English sociologist, Carnegie wrote to him, addressing him as "Master," and it was as "Master" that Spencer remained, even after Carnegie's lavishness had left Spencer very much in his debt.

But Carnegie's early life was shaped by currents more material than intellectual. The grinding process of industrial change had begun slowly but ineluctably to undermine the cottage weaving that was the traditional means of employment in Dunfermline. The Industrial Revolution, in the shape of new steam mills, was forcing out the hand weavers, and one by one the looms which constituted the entire capital of the Carnegie family had to be sold. Carnegie never forgot the shock of his father returning home to tell him, in despair, "Andra, I can get nae mair work."

A family council of war was held, and it was decided that there was only one possible course — they must try their luck in America, to which two sisters of Carnegie's mother, Margaret, had already emigrated. With the aid of a few friends the money for the crossing was scraped together, and at thirteen Andrew found himself transported to the only country in which his career would have been possible.

It hardly got off to an auspicious start, however. The family made their way to Allegheny, Pennsylvania, a raw and bustling town where Carnegie's father again sought work as an independent weaver. But it was as hopeless to compete against the great mills in America as in Scotland, and soon father and son were forced to seek work in the local cotton mills. There Andrew worked from six in the morning until six at night, making $1.20 as a bobbin boy.

After a while his father quit — factory work was impossible for the traditional small enterprise — and Andrew got a "better" job with a new firm, tending an engine deep in a dungeon cellar and dipping newly made cotton spools in a vat of oil. Even the raise to $3 a week — and desperately conjured visions of Wallace and the Bruce — could not overcome the horrors of that lonely and foul-smelling basement. It was perhaps the only time in Carnegie's life when his self-assurance deserted him: to the end of his days the merest whiff of oil could make him deathly sick.

Yet he was certain, as he wrote home at sixteen, that "anyone could get along in this Country," and the rags-to-riches saga shortly began. The telegraph had just come to Pittsburgh, and one evening over a game of checkers, the manager of the local office informed Andrew's uncle that he was looking for a messenger. Andy got the job and, in true Alger fashion, set out to excel in it. Within a few weeks he had carefully memorized the names and the locations, not only of the main streets in Pittsburgh, but of the main firms, so that he was the quickest of all the messenger boys.

He came early and stayed late, watched the telegraphers at work, and at home at night learned the Morse code. As a result he was soon the head of the growing messenger service, and a skilled telegrapher himself. One day he dazzled the office by taking a message "by ear" instead of by the commonly used tape printer, and since he was then only the third operator in the country able to turn the trick, citizens used to drop into the office to watch Andy take down the words "hot from the wire."

One such citizen who was especially impressed with young Carnegie's determination was Thomas A. Scott, in time to become one of the colorful railway magnates of the West, but then the local superintendent of the Pennsylvania Railroad. Soon thereafter Carnegie became "Scott's Andy" — telegrapher, secretary, and general factotum — at thirty-five dollars a month. In his *Autobiography* Carnegie recalls an instance which enabled him to begin the next stage of his career.

One morning I reached the office and found that a serious accident on the Eastern Division had delayed the express passenger train westward, and that the passenger train eastward was proceeding with a flagman in advance at every curve. The freight trains in both directions were standing on the sidings. Mr. Scott was not to be found. Finally I could not resist the temptation to plunge in, take the responsibility, give "train orders" and set matters going. "Death or Westminster Abbey" flashed across my mind. I knew it was dismissal, disgrace, perhaps criminal punishment for me if I erred. On the other hand, I could bring in the wearied freight train men who had lain out all night. I knew I could. I knew just what to do, and so I began.

Signing Scott's name to the orders, Carnegie flashed out the necessary instructions to bring order out of the tangle. The trains moved; there were no mishaps. When Scott reached the office Carnegie told him what he had done. Scott said not a word but looked carefully over all that had taken place. After a little he moved away from Carnegie's desk to his own, and that was the end of it. "But I noticed," Carnegie concluded good-humoredly, "that he came in very regularly and in good time for some mornings after that."

It is hardly to be wondered at that Carnegie became Scott's favorite, his "white-haired Scotch devil." Impetuous but not rash, full of enthusiasm and good-natured charm, the small lad with his blunt, open features and his slight Scottish burr was every executive's dream of an assistant. Soon Scott repaid Andy for his services by introducing him to a new and very different kind of opportunity. He gave Carnegie the chance to subscribe to five hundred dollars' worth of Adams Express stock, a company which Scott assured Andy would prosper mightily.

Carnegie had not fifty dollars saved, much less five hundred, but it was a chance he could ill afford to miss. He reported the offer to his mother, and that pillar of the family unhesitatingly mortgaged their home to raise the necessary money. When the first dividend check came in, with its ornate Spencerian flourishes, Carnegie had something like a revelation. "I shall remember that check as long as I live," he subsequently wrote. "It gave me the first penny of revenue from capital — something that I had not worked for with the sweat of my brow. 'Eureka!' I cried, 'Here's the goose that lays the golden eggs.'" He was right; within a few years his investment in the Adams Express Company was paying annual dividends of $1,400.

It was not long thereafter that an even more propitious chance presented itself. Carnegie was riding on the Pennsylvania line one day when he was approached by a "farmer-looking" man carrying a small green bag in his hand. The other introduced himself as T. T. Woodruff and quite frankly said that he wanted a chance to talk with someone connected with the railroad. Whereupon he opened his bag and took out a small model of the first sleeping car.

Carnegie was immediately impressed with its possibilities, and he quickly arranged for Woodruff to meet Scott. When the latter agreed to give the cars a trial, Woodruff in appreciation offered Carnegie a chance to subscribe to a one-eighth interest in the new company. A local banker agreed to lend Andy the few hundred dollars needed for the initial payment — the rest being financed from dividends. Once again Andy had made a shrewd investment: within two years the Woodruff Palace Car Company was paying him a return of more than $5,000 a year.

Investments now began to play an increasingly important role in Carnegie's career. Through his railroad contacts he came to recognize the possibilities in manufacturing the heavy equipment needed by the rapidly expanding lines, and soon he was instrumental in organizing companies to meet these needs. One of them, the Keystone Bridge Company, was the first successful manufacturer of iron railway bridges. Another, the Pittsburgh Locomotive Works, made engines. And most important of all, an interest in a local iron works run by an irascible German named Andrew Kloman brought Carnegie into actual contact with the manufacture of iron itself.

None of these new ventures required any substantial outlay of cash. His interest in the Keystone Bridge Company, for instance, which was to earn him $15,000 in 1868, came to him "in return for services rendered in its promotion" — services which Carnegie, as a young railroad executive, was then in a highly strategic position to deliver. Similarly the interest in the Kloman works reflected no contribution on Carnegie's part except that of being the human catalyst and buffer between some highly excitable participants.

By 1865 his "side" activities had become so important that he decided to leave the Pennsylvania Railroad. He was by then superintendent, Scott having moved up to a vice presidency, but his salary of $2,400 was already vastly overshadowed by his income from various ventures. One purchase alone — the Storey farm in Pennsylvania oil country, which Carnegie and a few associates picked up for $40,000 — was eventually to pay the group a million dollars in dividends in *one* year. About this time a friend dropped in on Carnegie and asked him how he was doing. "Oh, I'm rich, I'm rich!" he exclaimed.

He was indeed embarked on the road to riches, and determined, as he later wrote in his *Autobiography,* that "nothing could be allowed to interfere for a moment with my business career." Hence it comes as a surprise to note that it was at this very point that Carnegie retired to his suite to write his curiously introspective and troubled thoughts about the pursuit of wealth. But the momentum of events was to prove far too strong for these moralistic doubts. Moving his headquarters to New York to promote his various interests, he soon found himself swept along by a succession of irresistible opportunities for money-making.

One of these took place quite by chance. Carnegie was trying to sell the Woodruff sleeping car at the same time that a formidable rival named George Pullman was also seeking to land contracts for his sleeping car, and the railroads were naturally taking advantage of the competitive situation. One summer evening in 1869 Carnegie found himself mounting the resplendent marble stairway of the St. Nicholas Hotel side by side with his competitor.

"Good evening, Mr. Pullman," said Carnegie in his ebullient manner. Pullman was barely cordial.

"How strange we should meet here," Carnegie went on, to which the other replied nothing at all.

"Mr. Pullman," said Carnegie, after an embarrassing pause, "don't you think we are making nice fools of ourselves?" At this Pullman evinced a glimmer of interest: "What do you mean?" he inquired. Carnegie quickly pointed out that competition between the two companies was helping no one but the railroads. "Well," said Pullman, "what do you suggest we do?"

"Unite!" said Carnegie. "Let's make a joint proposition to the Union Pacific, your company and mine. Why not organize a new company to do it?" "What would you call it?" asked Pullman suspiciously. "The Pullman Palace Car Company," said Carnegie and with this shrewd psychological stroke won his point. A new company was formed, and in time Carnegie became its largest stockholder.

Meanwhile, events pushed Carnegie into yet another lucrative field. To finance the proliferating railway systems of America, British capital was badly needed, and with his Scottish ancestry, his verve, and his excellent railroad connections Carnegie was the natural choice for a go-between. His brief case stuffed with bonds and prospectuses, Carnegie became a transatlantic commuter, soon developing intimate relations both with great bankers like Junius Morgan (the father of J. P. Morgan), and with the heads of most of the great American roads. These trips earned him not only large commissions — exceeding on occasion $100,000 for a single turn — but even more important, established connections that were later to be of immense value. He himself later testified candidly on their benefits before a group of respectfully awed senators:

For instance, I want a great contract for rails. Sidney Dillon of the Union Pacific was a personal friend of mine. Huntington was a friend. Dear Butler Duncan, that called on me the other day, was a friend. Those and other men were presidents of railroads . . . Take Huntington; you know C. P. Huntington. He was hard up very often. He was a great man, but he had a great deal of paper out. I knew his things were good. When he wanted credit I gave it to him. If you help a man that way, what chance has any paid agent going to these men? It was absurd.

But his trips to England brought Carnegie something still more valuable. They gave him steel. It is fair to say that as late as 1872 Carnegie did not see the future that awaited him as the Steel King of the world. The still modest conglomeration of foundries and mills he was gradually assembling in the Allegheny and Monongahela valleys was but one of many business interests, and not one for which he envisioned any extraordinary future. Indeed, to repeated pleas that he lead the way in developing a steel indus-

68

try for America by substituting steel for iron rails, his reply was succinct: "Pioneering don't pay."

What made him change his mind? The story goes that he was awe-struck by the volcanic, spectacular eruption of a Bessemer converter, which he saw for the first time during a visit to a British mill. It was precisely the sort of display that would have appealed to Carnegie's mind — a wild, demonic, physical process miraculously contained and controlled by the dwarfed figures of the steel men themselves. At any rate, overnight Carnegie became the perfervid prophet of steel. Jumping on the first available steamer, he rushed home with the cry, "The day of iron has passed!" To the consternation of his colleagues, the hitherto reluctant pioneer became an advocate of the most daring technological and business expansion; he joined them enthusiastically in forming Carnegie, McCandless & Company, which was the nucleus of the empire that the next thirty years would bring forth.

The actual process of growth involved every aspect of successful business enterprise of the times: acquisition and merger, pools and commercial piracy, and even, on one occasion, an outright fraud in selling the United States government overpriced and underdone steel armor plate. But it would be as foolish to maintain that the Carnegie empire grew by trickery as to deny that sharp practice had its place. Essentially what lay behind the spectacular expansion were three facts.

The first of these was the sheer economic expansion of the industry in the first days of burgeoning steel use. Everywhere steel replaced iron or found new uses — and not only in railroads but in ships, buildings, bridges, machinery of all sorts. As Henry Frick himself once remarked, if the Carnegie group had not filled the need for steel another would have. But it must be admitted that Carnegie's company did its job superlatively well. In 1885 Great Britain led the world in the production of steel. Fourteen years later her total output was 695,000 tons less than the output of the Carnegie Steel Company alone.

Second was the brilliant assemblage of personal talent with which Carnegie surrounded himself. Among them, three in particular stood out. One was Captain William Jones, a Homeric figure who lumbered through the glowing fires and clanging machinery of the works like a kind of Paul Bunyan of steel, skilled at handling men, inventive in handling equipment, and enough of a natural artist to produce papers for the British Iron and Steel Institute that earned him a literary as well as a technical reputation. Then there was Henry Frick, himself a self-made millionaire, whose coke empire naturally complemented Carnegie's steelworks. When the two were amalgamated, Frick took over the active management of the whole, and under his forceful hand the annual output of the Carnegie works rose tenfold. Yet another was Charles Schwab, who came out of the tiny monastic town of Loretto, Pennsylvania, to take a job as a stake driver. Six months later he had been promoted by Jones into the assistant managership of the Braddock plant.

These men, and a score like them, constituted the vital energy of the Carnegie works. As Carnegie himself said, "Take away all our money, our great works, ore mines and coke ovens, but leave our organization, and in four years I shall have re-established myself."

But the third factor in the growth of the empire was Carnegie himself. A master salesman and a skilled diplomat of business at its highest levels, Carnegie was also a ruthless driver of his men. He pitted his associates and subordinates in competition with one another until a feverish atmosphere pervaded the whole organization. "You cannot imagine the abounding sense of freedom and relief I experience as soon as I get on board a steamer and sail past Sandy Hook," he once said to Captain Jones. "My God!" replied Jones. "Think of the relief to us!"

But Carnegie could win loyalties as well. All his promising young men were given gratis ownership participations — minuscule fractions of one per cent, which were enough, however, to make them millionaires in their own right. Deeply grateful to Jones, Carnegie once offered him a similar participation. Jones hemmed and hawed and finally refused; he would be unable to work effectively with the men, he said, once he was a partner. Carnegie insisted that his contribution be recognized and asked Jones what he wanted. "Well," said the latter, "you might pay me a hell of a big salary." "We'll do it!" said Carnegie. "From this time forth you shall receive the same salary as the President of the United States." "Ah, Andy, that's the kind of talk," said Captain Bill.

Within three decades, on the flood tide of economic expansion, propelled by brilliant executive work and relentless pressure from Carnegie, the company made immense strides. "Such a magnificent aggregation of industrial power has never before been under the domination of a single man," reported a biographer in 1902, describing the Gargantuan structure of steel and coke and ore and transport. Had the writer known of the profits earned by this aggregation he might have been even more impressed: three and a half million dollars in 1889, seven million in 1897, twenty-one million in 1899, and an immense forty million in 1900. "Where is there such a business!" Carnegie had exulted, and no wonder — the majority share of all these earnings, without hindrance of income tax, went directly into his pockets.

Nevertheless, with enormous success came problems. One of these was the restiveness of certain partners, under the "Iron-Clad" agreement, which prevented any of them from selling their shares to anyone but the company itself — an arrangement which meant, of course, that the far higher valuation of an outside purchaser could not be realized. Particularly chagrined was Frick, when, as the culmination of other disagreements between them, Carnegie sought to buy him out "at the value appearing on the books." Another problem was a looming competitive struggle in the steel industry itself that presaged a period of bitter industrial warfare ahead. And last was Carnegie's own growing desire to "get out."

Already he was spending half of each year abroad, first traveling, and then, after his late marriage, in residence in the great Skibo Castle he built for his wife on Dornoch Firth, Scotland. There he ran his business enterprises with one hand while he courted the literary and creative world with the other, entertaining Kipling and Matthew Arnold, Paderewski and Lloyd

George, Woodrow Wilson and Theodore Roosevelt, Gladstone, and of course, Herbert Spencer, the Master. But even his career as "Laird" of Skibo could not remove him from the worries — and triumphs — of his business: a steady flow of cables and correspondence intruded on the "serious" side of life.

It was Schwab who cut the knot. Having risen to the very summit of the Carnegie concern he was invited in December, 1900, to give a speech on the future of the steel industry at the University Club in New York. There, before eighty of the nation's top business leaders he painted a glowing picture of what could be done if a super-company of steel were formed, integrated from top to bottom, self-sufficient with regard to its raw materials, balanced in its array of final products. One of the guests was the imperious J. P. Morgan, and as the speech progressed it was noticed that his concentration grew more and more intense. After dinner Morgan rose and took the young steel man by the elbow and engaged him in private conversation for half an hour while he plied him with rapid and penetrating questions; then a few weeks later he invited him to a private meeting in the great library of his home. They talked from nine o'clock in the evening until dawn. As the sun began to stream in through the library windows, the banker finally rose. "Well," he said to Schwab, "if Andy wants to sell, I'll buy. Go and find his price."

Carnegie at first did not wish to sell. Faced with the actual prospect of a withdrawal from the business he had built into the mightiest single industrial empire in the world, he was frightened and dismayed. He sat silent before Schwab's report, brooding, loath to inquire into details. But soon his enthusiasm returned. No such opportunity was likely to present itself again. In short order a figure of $492,000,000 was agreed on for the entire enterprise, of which Carnegie himself was to receive $300,000,000 in five per cent gold bonds and preferred stock. Carnegie jotted down the terms of the transaction on a slip of paper and told Schwab to bring it to Morgan. The banker glanced only briefly at the paper. "I accept," he said.

In his late years, Carnegie turned again toward the idealism of his youth. Declaring that his riches had come to him as a "sacred trust" to administer for the good of humanity, he endowed numerous philanthropies and managed to give away 90 percent of his wealth before he died. (Carnegie Corporation of New York)

After the formalities were in due course completed, Carnegie was in a euphoric mood. "Now, Pierpont, I am the happiest man in the world," he said. Morgan was by no means unhappy himself: his own banking company had made a direct profit of $12,500,000 in the underwriting transaction, and this was but a prelude to a stream of lucrative financings under Morgan's aegis, by which the total capitalization was rapidly raised to $1,400,000,000. A few years later, Morgan and Carnegie found themselves aboard the same steamer en route to Europe. They fell into talk and Carnegie confessed, "I made one mistake, Pierpont, when I sold out to you."

"What was that?" asked the banker.

"I should have asked you for $100,000,000 more than I did."

Morgan grinned. "Well," he said, "you would have got it if you had."

Thus was written *finis* to one stage of Carnegie's career. Now it would be seen to what extent his "radical pronouncements" were serious. For in the *Gospel of Wealth* — the famous article combined with others in book form — Carnegie had proclaimed the duty of the millionaire to administer and distribute his wealth *during his lifetime*. Though he might have "proved" his worth by his fortune, his heirs had shown no such evidence of their fitness. Carnegie bluntly concluded: "By taxing estates heavily at his death, the State marks its condemnation of the selfish millionaire's unworthy life."

Coming from the leading millionaire of the day, these had been startling sentiments. So also were his views on the "labor question" which, if patronizing, were nonetheless humane and advanced for their day. The trouble was, of course, that the sentiments were somewhat difficult to credit. As one commentator of the day remarked, "His vision of what might be done with wealth had beauty and breadth and thus serenely overlooked the means by which wealth had been acquired."

For example, the novelist Hamlin Garland visited the steel towns from which the Carnegie millions came and bore away a description of work that was ugly, brutal, and exhausting: he contrasted the lavish care expended on the plants with the callous disregard of the pigsty homes: "the streets were horrible; the buildings poor; the sidewalks sunken and full of holes. . . . Everywhere the yellow mud of the streets lay kneaded into sticky masses through which groups of pale, lean men slouched in faded garments. . . ." When the famous Homestead strike erupted in 1892, with its private army of Pinkerton detectives virtually at war with the workers, the Carnegie benevolence seemed revealed as shabby fakery. At Skibo Carnegie stood firmly behind the company's iron determination to break the strike. As a result, public sentiment swung sharply and suddenly against him; the St. Louis *Post-Dispatch* wrote: "Three months ago Andrew Car-

negie was a man to be envied. Today he is an object of mingled pity and contempt. In the estimation of nine-tenths of the thinking people on both sides of the ocean he has . . . confessed himself a moral coward."

In an important sense the newspaper was right. For though Carnegie continued to fight against "privilege," he saw privilege only in its fading aristocratic vestments and not in the new hierarchies of wealth and power to which he himself belonged. In Skibo Castle he now played the role of the benign autocrat, awakening to the skirling of his private bagpiper and proceeding to breakfast to the sonorous accompaniment of the castle organ.

Meanwhile there had also come fame and honors in which Carnegie wallowed unashamedly. He counted the "freedoms" bestowed on him by grateful or hopeful cities and crowed, "I have fifty-two and Gladstone has only seventeen." He entertained the King of England and told him that democracy was better than monarchy, and met the German Kaiser: "Oh, yes, yes," said the latter worthy on being introduced. "I have read your books. You do not like kings." But Mark Twain, on hearing of this, was not fooled. "He says he is a scorner of kings and emperors and dukes," he wrote, "whereas he is like the rest of the human race: a slight attention from one of these can make him drunk for a week. . . ."

And yet it is not enough to conclude that Carnegie was in fact a smaller man than he conceived himself. For this judgment overlooks one immense and irrefutable fact. He did, in the end, abide by his self-imposed duty. He did give nearly all of his gigantic fortune away.

As one would suspect, the quality of the philanthropy reflected the man himself. There was, for example, a huge and sentimentally administered private pension fund to which access was to be had on the most trivial as well as the most worthy grounds: if it included a number of writers, statesmen, scientists, it also made room for two maiden ladies with whom Carnegie had once danced as a young man, a boyhood acquaintance who had once held Carnegie's books while he ran a race, a merchant to whom he had once delivered a telegram and who had subsequently fallen on hard times. And then, as one would expect, there was a benevolent autocracy in the administration of the larger philanthropies as well. "Now everybody vote Aye," was the way Carnegie typically determined the policies of the philanthropic "foundations" he established.

Yet if these flaws bore the stamp of one side of Carnegie's personality, there was also the other side — the side that, however crudely, asked important questions and however piously, concerned itself with great ideals. Of this the range and purpose of the main philanthropies gave unimpeachable testimony. There were the famous libraries — three thousand of them costing nearly sixty million dollars; there were the Carnegie institutes in Pittsburgh and Washington, Carnegie Hall in New York, the Hague Peace Palace, the Carnegie Endowment for International Peace, and the precedent-making Carnegie Corporation of New York, with its original enormous endowment of $125,000,000. In his instructions to the trustees of this first great modern foundation, couched in the simplified spelling of which he was an ardent advocate, we see Carnegie at his very best:

Conditions on erth [sic] inevitably change; hence, no wise man will bind Trustees forever to certain paths, causes, or institutions. I disclaim any intention of doing so . . . My chief happiness, as I write these lines lies in the thot [sic] that, even after I pass away, the welth [sic] that came to me to administer as a sacred trust for the good of my fellow men is to continue to benefit humanity . . .

If these sentiments move us — if Carnegie himself in retrospect moves us at last to grudging respect — it is not because his was the triumph of a saint or a philosopher. It is because it was the much more difficult triumph of a very human and fallible man struggling to retain his convictions in an age, and in the face of a career, which subjected them to impossible tempta-

tions. Carnegie is something of America writ large; his is the story of the Horatio Alger hero *after* he has made his million dollars. In the failures of Andrew Carnegie we see many of the failures of America itself. In his curious triumph, we see what we hope is our own steadfast core of integrity.

QUESTIONS TO CONSIDER

1. Robert L. Heilbroner suggests that Andrew Carnegie was interesting because of the contrasts in his character: the conflict between his Calvinist simplicity and his overpowering urge to accumulate wealth. What are the sources of Carnegie's contradictory character?

2. Describe Carnegie's personal "gospel of wealth." Did he live up to his own ideals? Why do you think he was attracted to the teachings of his "master," evolutionist Herbert Spencer?

3. All his life, Carnegie insisted upon his hatred of aristocratic privilege, yet he lived a life of magnificence in his Scottish castle, and he courted the acquaintance of famous politicians, scholars, and royal personages. How did he justify his actions? Did he see himself as a different sort of aristocrat? Why did he go back to Britain to live?

4. Carnegie left a rich legacy of philanthropies, most notably the vast network of libraries that has developed into our present public library system. How was the money to fund these philanthropies obtained in the first place? Why do you think Carnegie — and many others — failed to see the contrast between the good money could do and the way it was made? How might wealthy people in the Gilded Age have viewed the lives of the working poor?

5. How does what Heilbroner calls the "failure" of Andrew Carnegie reflect the failure of America in the Gilded Age? What were the social and economic consequences of the *Gospel of Wealth* and of huge concentrations of capital in late nineteenth-century America?

6

How the Other Side Lived

Page Smith

Since the colonial era, a shortage of labor in America had kept wage levels higher here than overseas. Even so, the American worker had a miserable time of it in the grim industrial age. The expansion and mechanization of the factory system, which took place at an incredible rate after the Civil War, forced workers to make painful adjustments that reduced their status and independence.

Before industrialization, as C. Vann Woodward has said, skilled artisans who owned their own tools were likely to take pride in their craft and enjoy a strong bargaining position. The new factory system, Woodward points out, lowered the workers' status, forcing them to surrender their tools, a good deal of their bargaining power, and almost all the pride they took in their product. Under the employ of people they never knew and probably never saw, they operated a machine that made their craftsmanship insignificant, because their place at the machine could be taken by an unskilled worker. Their relationship to their work and to the boss became increasingly impersonal. With the factory growing ever larger, workers felt a dispiriting loss of identity, security, and meaning in the value of labor.

To make matters worse, the mass of statutes that protects factory workers today had not been enacted in the Gilded Age. This meant that laborers, including women and children, were at the mercy of the industrial bosses. In "company towns," employers owned all the houses, stores, and services and often bossed and harassed workers to the point of tyranny. With little to restrain them beyond their own consciences and the weak protest of labor, employers were likely to cut costs by slashing wages. Throughout the 1890s, wages remained at an average of $9 a week; farm workers received far less than that.

Despite how bad things were, workers in industrial America were slow to organize. Part of the problem was the bitter opposition of the industrial leaders, who broke strikes with hired thugs and associated organized labor with socialism and anarchy. But another difficulty was the fragmentation of the work force, which was divided by color and race, sex and age, as well as by national origin, geography, philosophy, and styles of protest. The utopian Knights of Labor, founded in 1869, did attempt to unite the disparate working population, appealing to both skilled and unskilled workers regardless of race, color, or nationality. The Knights understood clearly that the consolidation of industry made the consolidation of labor imperative. Rejecting strikes as a useful weapon, the organization sought political as well as economic objectives, demanding equal pay for both sexes, an eight-hour workday, and the abolition of child labor. But the union was only marginally successful: at its peak, the Knights of Labor could claim little more than 700,000 members. When labor conditions became intolerable, workers in specific areas ignored the Knights of Labor and resorted to spontaneous strikes to protest their lot, only to meet with adamant hostility on the part of police, business and government leaders, and the public itself.

The other major union of the period was the conservative American Federation of Labor (AFL), a loose coalition of craft unions founded under Samuel Gompers in 1881. From the outset, the AFL shunned government intervention in management labor relations and rejected political goals in favor of specific economic benefits for skilled workers alone. It had little quarrel with industrial consolidation, and it ignored the mass of unskilled laborers across the land.

Let us accompany historian Page Smith on a journey through the plants, railroads, steel mills, oil fields, and coal mines of the Gilded Age and examine the lives and working conditions of the men, women, and children employed by industrial captains such as Andrew Carnegie. As Smith makes clear, American workers in the iron age of industry toiled in conditions almost inconceivable to us today. Smith's account reminds us that, necessary though industrialization was for the United States, it came at a terrible human cost.

GLOSSARY

ALGER, HORATIO   Gilded Age author whose heroes rose from poverty to greatness and thus fulfilled the "American Dream."

JONES, MARY "MOTHER"   Legendary champion of the rights of miners and the author of a graphic "account of a miner's life."

MARX, ELEANOR, AND EDWARD AVELING   The daughter of Karl Marx and her husband toured the United States in 1886, surveying labor conditions there and talking with socialists and labor leaders; the Avelings concluded that the conditon of working men and women in America was as bad as that of Britain's laboring class.

PHILLIPS, WENDELL   Former abolitionist who raised his voice on behalf of the American worker; he demanded higher wages and shorter working hours and urged organization and group efforts to challenge "the organization of capital."

THE SHANTY BOY   A kind of documentary about the brutal and dangerous conditions in American lumber camps.

In 1886 Karl Marx's daughter Eleanor Marx Aveling and her husband, Edward, visited the United States to make a general survey of labor conditions and to talk with socialists and labor leaders around the country. They were struck by the activity in the labor movement generally, both in unionization and in radical political action on the part of various socialist and anarchist groups. In their opinion, the condition of workingmen and women in the United States was in every important respect as bad as that of the British working class. In addition, unionization in America was twenty or thirty years behind that in Britain. On the other hand, there were far more labor newspapers and journals in the United States than in Britain. The Avelings counted ninety-seven, including one entitled the *Woman's World* and excluding most of the foreign-language socialist and labor journals. Wherever the Avelings went they addressed large crowds of working-class people with a substantial admixture of middle- and upper-class reformers. In a twelve-week tour they visited thirty-five cities and towns as far west as Kansas. The meetings were, the Avelings wrote, "with the very rarest exceptions, largely attended. In many places hundreds of people were unable to gain admission. . . . We have never spoken to any audiences like the American audiences for patience, fairness, anxiety to get at the meaning of the speaker," they added. The Avelings found an enormous curiosity about the doctrines of socialism, which heretofore had been preached largely by Germans for German immigrants. "And in every town we met, both in private and in public, the leading men and women in the various working-class organizations."

In the view of the Avelings, British laborers still believed that "there is a community of interests between them and their employers. . . . But in America this mutual deception is nearly at an end. The workingmen and the capitalists in the majority of cases quite understand that each, as a class, is the deadly and inexorable foe of the other. . . ." The capitalists believed the struggle must end "in the subjugation of the working class," while the workingmen were equally convinced it would end "in the abolition of all classes."

. . . The Avelings were also struck by the degree to which the labor commissioners of the various states in their statistical reports revealed a profound sympathy for the workingmen and women of their states. The report of the Massachusetts commissioners on conditions in Fall River, for example, noted that "every mill in the city is making money . . . but the operatives travel in the same old path — sickness, suffering, and small pay. . . . There is a state of things that should make men blush for shame."

In state after state the testimony of workers in different industrial crafts was monotonously the same. Things were getting worse with each passing year. "Times are harder now than I ever knew them before," a laborer in Kansas declared, while another said, "The condition of the laboring classes is too bad for utterance, and is rapidly growing worse." The testimony was also uniformly to the effect that "the rich and poor are further apart than ever before." A coal miner reported that he had had to move five times during the year to find employment. In Michigan a worker in a shoe factory testified: "Labor to-day is poorer paid than ever before; more discontent exists, more men in despair, and if a change is not soon devised, trouble must come. . . ."

The Avelings were convinced by their reading of the reports of the state labor commissioners and their own observations that, hours and wages aside, the physical demands placed by American employers on their workers were much more severe than those prevailing in Britain. American laborers started to work at an earlier age than their British counterparts, worked more strenuously, and died, on the average, almost a decade earlier. Thus the life expectancy of a British iron molder was fifty years and eleven months, while "the American moulder dies before he reaches the age of forty. . . ."

Employers and foremen practiced innumerable small deceits: short measures in the cloth mills; short weights in the mines; fines for the mildest infractions of innumerable restrictive rules governing every action of the worker. Blacklists and intimidation were common. Many workers reported to the Avelings that they were afraid to be seen talking to them for fear of losing their jobs and being thereafter blacklisted as troublemakers, radicals, or union sympathizers. Workers were threatened with loss of their jobs simply for voting for political candidates antithetical to their employers. It was common practice for newly employed workers to be required to take an "ironclad oath" to belong to no working-class organization. Even subscription to a labor journal or newspaper could be cause for dismissal. Western Union, for example, required an oath which read, "I, —— —— —— , . . . hereby promise and agree . . . that I will forthwith abandon any and all membership, connection, or affiliation with any organization or society, whether secret or open, which in any wise attempts to regulate the conditions of my services or the payment therefor. . . ." The Knights of Labor, which became the first major union in the country, was often specifically proscribed. The employees of the Warren Foundry were required immediately to "free [themselves] from a combination in hostility to the company. . . . If they are not willing to do so, we request them to leave our premises. . . ."

Employers often required their workers to accept in whole or in part company script in lieu of money, which script, needless to say, could be redeemed only at the company store. Companies commonly deducted from their employees' pay — in addition to advances from the company store — money for the salary of a doctor or nurse, rent for a company house, and coal given out by the company on credit. Thus it was not unusual for workers at the end of the year to

find themselves actually in debt to the company that employed them. The reports of the New Jersey labor commissioners in 1884 contained numerous instances of workers who ended a year of labor in debt to the company. A worker in Paterson reported, "My actual earnings last year were but 100 dollars, while the cost of living was 400." A silk worker in the same town reported a 50 percent reduction in wages over a three-year period. A railroad employee told the Kansas commissioners: "A man . . . has to wait 50 days before he receives a cent of wages, and then only gets paid for 30 days, leaving the proceeds of 20 days' labor in the company's hands until he quits their employ."

Of a sample of 520 Michigan workers, 146 were paid weekly, 32 biweekly, 177 monthly, and 28 on demand, while 137 had no regular payday. Of the 137 with no regular payday, a number reported waiting 60 to 90 days for their pay. Only two-fifths of Michigan's factory employees were paid weekly, while two-fifths were paid monthly. As for hours, of 65,627 mill and factory "hands" in the state, 76 percent worked 60 hours a week or more. Moreover, 12 percent of the men, 22 percent of the women, and 34 percent of the children worked more than 10 hours daily.

Ironically, the men, better organized, worked on the average fewer hours than the women and children (the last worked longest of all). Tram drivers in Fall River, Massachusetts, worked an average of 15 hours a day, while for streetcar conductors in Kansas, 16 and 17 were standard. In New York bakers averaged 16 ⅔ hours, six days a week. In the Pennsylvania coal mines 14 to 18 hours a day were typical, and one witness before the labor commissioners reported, "I know that some [men] go into the mines on Sunday, trying to make a living and cannot, while their employers own Sunday-schools, churches, preachers, Government bonds . . . with yachts, steamboats, orange plantations, and are very rich."

Along with low pay and long, long hours, workers in most trades and industries had to contend with extended periods of unemployment. In Topeka, Kansas, in 1885, of 660 skilled workmen, 156 worked part-time and 108 had no work at all. During the year 1 out of 5 skilled and unskilled workers was unemployed.

A constant complaint voiced to the Avelings on their tour in 1886 was that hundreds of thousands of men had been displaced by machines, a fact confirmed by one Philadelphia manufacturer, who told the Avelings that in a thirty-year period "machinery has displaced 6 times the amount of hand labor formerly required." In carpets, weaving, spinning ten to twenty times fewer workers were required; in spinning alone seventy-five times fewer. In the milling of flour one person did the work done by four a few decades earlier, while in machine tooling "one boy can produce as much as was formerly produced by 10 skilled men." In mining the story was similar. In the Hocking Valley of Ohio, improved machines enabled 160 men to do the work of 500.

The housing conditions of working-class men and women had deteriorated to an alarming degree. In New York City in 1883 there were 25,000 tenement buildings containing 1,000,000 inhabitants. Some 19,000 tenements accommodated 50 or more persons each, and families of 6 to 8 people living in a single room were not uncommon. The New York labor commissioners noted that the tenants "cook, eat, and sleep in the same room, men, women, and children together. Refuse of every description makes the floors damp and slimy, and the puny, half-naked children crawl or slide about it."

At Fall River sixteen houses occupied by more than 500 human beings used the same privy, and the odor was hardly to be endured in summer. In Lowell "the tenants of a single block had to carry their refuse of all kinds, and human excrements . . . into Austin Avenue for deposit." In another block in Lowell, commissioners counted thirty-six tenements containing thirty-six families and 396 persons. Such "excessively filthy," "unsanitary," "foul," wretched, and dirty lodgings were the property of the millowners, whose workers were often required to live in them as a condition of employment.

In cigarmaking operations, often carried on at home, "I see women," one witness reported to the New York labor commissioners, "surrounded by filth with children waddling in it, and having sores on their hands and faces and various parts of the body. . . . They are all the time handling this tobacco they make into cigars." Every industry had its own peculiar health hazards. "Sewing machine girls are subject to diseases of the womb," a report noted, "and when married mostly have miscarriages. In tobacco factories women are mostly affected with nervous and hysterical complaints, consumption and chest ailments. . . ."

"We have lived in English factory towns," the Avelings wrote, "and know something of English factory hands; but we may fairly say we have never in the English Manchester seen women so worn out and degraded, such famine in their cheeks, such need and oppression, starving in their eyes, as in the women we saw trudging to their work in the New Hampshire Manchester. What must the children born of such women be?" A consequence of the starvation wages paid women workers and the uncertainty of their employment was that many of them were driven to part-time prostitution or, as the New York labor commissioners' report put it, "*quasi* prostitution. . . . When out of work they cohabit with one or two men, but when work was obtained dropped such associations." In addition, many women complained to the commissioners that they were taken advantage of sexually by their bosses or employers. In Kansas City and Indianapolis two clergymen told the Avelings "of the fearful state of women forced to choose between starvation and prostitution" in those "flourishing towns."

It was also evident to the Avelings that wherever possible men were replaced as factory operatives by women and children, who were paid far lower wages. The criterion in replacing a man with a woman or child was simply whether the latter had the strength to operate a particular machine.

The New Jersey labor commissioners noted: "Woman and child labor is much lower priced than that of men . . . the hours of labor are longer and the rate of wages less, women never agitate, they merely 'toil and scrimp, and bear.'" However, those women who joined the Knights of Labor received the same wages as the men. Tens of thousands of women worked in what later came to be called sweatshops as seamstresses paid by piecework. The New York labor bureau report for 1885 noted that an expert at crocheting shawls could make no more than 12 to 15 cents a day. Seamstresses, in addition, were required to pay for the machine and for the thread they used. A sewer earned $1.50 per dozen for trousers. Vests were 15 cents apiece; gloves, 90 cents a dozen. An experienced "tailoress" earned no more than $3 or $4 a week. Less skilled millinery workers made 12 cents a day and were paid every two weeks. While the law required that chairs be provided for women workers, they were frequently not allowed to sit down. Of 1,322 women studied in a survey of the New York clothing industry, 27 earned $6 per week and 534 earned $1 a week. Fines were exacted, such as 25 cents for being five minutes late (two days' wages for a millinery worker); $1 for eating at the loom; 25 cents for washing hands; for imperfect work, for sitting down, for taking a drink of water, and so on.

The rooms in which women worked were foul, poorly ventilated, dirty, and badly lighted. It was a common practice to lock the workers in their rooms, thereby risking lives in case of fire. "One hundred women and small girls work in a cellar without ventilation, and electric light burning all day," the New York commissioners reported. Workers often suffered crippling injuries and sometimes incurable diseases. A woman who made artificial flowers found that her hands had been "poisoned" by the coloring she used. When she could not work, she was discharged, and the labor commissioners had to bring suit against her employer to collect 50 cents in back wages.

Increasingly child labor competed with schooling. A report of the New Jersey labor commissioners of 1885 noted that of an estimated 343,897 children of school age in the state, 89,254 attended no school,

and of these, the majority worked in factories or in mines. In New York, out of 1,685,000 children and young people between the ages of five and twenty-one, only 1,041,089 were listed as enrolled in the "common schools," and average daily attendance was 583,142. In other words, on any given day an average of 1,101,958 children were *absent from school*. Even allowing for a number educated in private schools, the figure seemed to the commissioners "almost incredible." They declared: "An army of uneducated and undisciplined children is growing up among us."

Each year saw an increase in the numbers of children laboring. In Michigan statistics indicated that seventy-one "establishments" — factories and businesses — in forty-six towns and cities employed 350 boys and girls between eight and fourteen years of age. In New Jersey there were twice as many children employed in factories in 1880 as there had been ten years earlier, while the increase of women was 142 percent in the same time. In Detroit in 1885, ninety-two businesses employed 372 boys and girls at 50 cents a day for the boys and 31 cents for the girls. In Connecticut, out of a factory labor force of 70,000, 5,000 were children under fifteen.

In the mills of Yorkville, in New York City, children under fourteen worked an eleven-hour day, while in the cigar factories, which employed many children, the workday was ten hours. "In the smaller bakeries," the Avelings reported, "children of from 9 to 13 start work at eleven at night and go on until 4 in the morning."

The Pennsylvania mines were dangerous places for boys. Thousands were killed or maimed each year without compensation or aid of any kind except that which might be provided by some local charitable group. The *Luzerne Union* reported in January, 1876: "During the past week nearly one boy a day has been killed, and the public has become so familiar with these calamities, that no attention is given them after the first announcement through a newspaper or a neighbor." A Sunday school convention that met in Scranton in 1874 was taken on a tour of the nearby

Fully a third of these Massillon, Ohio, iron-mill workers were children. On the average, children in nineteenth-century mines and factories worked ten hours a day, often in dangerous conditions, and were paid at the bottom of the wage scale. Frequently, child labor competed with schooling. In one city alone, on any given day, two-thirds of the school-age children were absent from school. Labor commissioners feared that the country was raising "an army of uneducated and undisciplined children." (Massillon Museum)

mines, where they saw the "bare-footed, black-faced urchins . . . picking slate from the dusty diamonds" and then heard a lecture on the "wonders of the Great Creator" — that was to say, on fossils.

A Fall River textile worker named Thomas O'Donnell told a Senate Committee on Labor-Capital Relations in 1883: "I have a brother who has four children besides his wife and himself. All he earns is $1.50 a day. He works in the iron works at Fall River. He only works nine months out of twelve. There is generally three months of stoppage . . . and his wife and family all have to be supported for a year out of the wages of nine months — $1.50 a day for

nine months to support six of them. It does not stand to reason that those children and he himself can have natural food and be naturally dressed. His children are often sick, and he has to call in doctors." O'Donnel himself earned $133 a year with which to feed a family of four. He dug clams and scavenged wood and coal.

Two seven-story factory buildings in Rochester, New York, one employing 150 and the other about 270 women, had only one stairway each. An Ohio fire inspector, describing similar conditions, wrote that "it is somewhat difficult to speak with calmness of men who, while liberally insuring their property against fire, so that in case of such a visitation — a danger always imminent — their pockets shall not suffer, will not spend a dollar for the security of the lives of those by whose labor they profit."

A Massachusetts labor commissioner sounded more like a reformer than a bureaucrat when he wrote at the end of a report describing the conditions of child labor in that state: "I plead for the little ones. . . . In these days of legislative interference, when the shield of the State protects the dumb beast from the merciless blows of his driver; when the over-worked horse is remembered and released from his work . . . it would seem pitiable if childhood's want of leisure for rest of body and education should be denied them. Massachusetts . . . goes on regardless of the consequences, protecting the strong, forgetting the weak and poor . . . under the false plea of non-interference with the liberty of the people. The children have rights that the State is bound to respect. Their right is to play and make merry; to be at school, to be players not workers."

Quite by accident the Avelings discovered one of the most exploited groups in the United States: cowboys. Taken by their hosts in Kansas City to a Wild West show, they got into conversation with a handsome, blue-eyed cowboy named Broncho John, who, with encouragement from the Avelings, described vividly the manner in which ranchers exploited their hands. "To our great astonishment," the Avelings wrote, "he plunged at once into a denunciation of capitalists in general and of ranchowners in particular. Broncho John estimated that there were at least 10,000 cowboys" — the Avelings believed there were many more — and "no class is harder worked . . . none so poorly paid for their services" because "they have no organization back of them" while their employers had "one of the strongest and most systematic and, at the same time, despotic unions that was ever formed to awe and dictate to labor." Listening to Broncho John, the Avelings, confident that "a Cowboy Assembly of the Knights of Labor or a Cowboy Union is sure to be started in the near future," de-

voted a whole chapter in their study *The Working-Class Movement in America* to the hardships of the cowboy.

Mary ("Mother") Jones, whose labors on behalf of miners made her a legendary figure among those who labored in the earth, wrote a vivid account of a coal miner's life: "Mining at best is wretched work, and the life and surroundings of the miner are hard and ugly. His work is down in the black depths of the earth. He works alone in a drift. There can be little friendly companionship as there is in the factory; as there is among men who build bridges and houses, working together in groups. The work is dirty. Coal dust grinds itself into the skin, never to be removed. The miner must stoop as he works in the drift. He becomes bent like a gnome. His work is utterly fatiguing. Muscles and bones ache. His lungs breathe coal dust and the strange, damp air of places that are never filled with sunlight. His house is a poor make-shift and there is little to encourage him to make it attractive. . . . Around his house is mud and slush. Great mounds of culm, black and sullen, surround him. His children are perpetually grimy from play on the culm mounds. The wife struggles with dirt, with inadequate water supply, with small wages, with overcrowded shacks."

The breaker boys, who picked flint and rocks out of the coal, Mary Jones wrote, "did men's work and they had men's ways, men's vices and men's pleasures. They fought and spit tobacco and told stories out on the culm piles of a Sunday. They joined the breaker boys union and beat up scabs." Mother Jones lamented to her death that there was "still too little joy and beauty in the miner's life"; the end of the "long, long struggle" was not yet.

Lumbering was akin to mining in the type of man it attracted and the arduous and highly hazardous nature of the work involved. John W. Fitzmaurice, who worked in lumber camps, told the story of them in *The Shanty Boy,* a kind of documentary which painted a vivid picture of the cruelly hard and dangerous conditions. He quoted the foreman of one such camp as declaring, "It's saw-logs we're after out here," and Fitzmaurice added, "it is saw logs men are after in the woods, and in the rush, push and crush to get them, God help the sick or wounded!" The men were pitted against each other in merciless competition for the number of logs cut in a day. At the end of each day the tally was made. "As each speaks the others listen nervously, and with ill-concealed jealousy, to the men with the big figures. . . . This hurry and rush brings to the surface the 'survival of the fittest,' and the weakling or debauched fall out by the way. Consequently, the hospital business never lags." The larger camps had bars and prostitutes as standard adjuncts.

In every industry the story was monotonously the same: paupers' wages; the constant fear of dismissal; wretched and unsanitary working conditions; ten-, twelve-, and even fourteen-hour days (sixteen for bakers); six- and sometimes seven-day weeks; erratic pay; little or no compensation for injuries or fatalities; a constant increase in the number of women and children employed under such conditions; and, worst of all, the widespread conviction that workingmen and women (not to mention children) had been losing ground ever since the end of the Civil War.

Under such circumstances it is hardly surprising that the number of strikes increased year by year following the Great Strikes of 1877. In 1881 there were 471 strikes affecting 2,928 companies and 129,521 employees. Five years later the number of strikes had risen to 1,411, involving 9,861 companies and almost half a million employees. Roughly half (46 percent) of the struck companies acquiesced in the principal demands of the strikers. Over 3,000 more strikes were partially successful, and 40 percent of the strikes, involving 50 percent of the strikers, were judged "failures."

But the formation of unions was dishearteningly slow. The fierce competition between mine operators was one factor impeding effective unions. Marginal operators, struggling, especially in depression years, to stay solvent or at least existent, saw unions as dangerous enemies. Even more significant was the constant

Mill "girls" came in all ages; many were married, and many were immigrants and the daughters of immigrants. All of them received lower wages than their male coworkers. Before the advent of protective legislation, most worked longer hours than men, too. Although wretchedly paid, these textile workers may have been better off than their sisters in city sweatshops, who were paid by piecework and frequently earned no more than $1 a week. Despite their hard lives and soiled clothing, the women seem proud to be photographed on the job. (Museum of American Textile History)

turnover of workers themselves. In such circumstances it was difficult for able leadership to emerge and to develop loyalty among a transient population. Every mining village had a nucleus of professional men, storekeepers, mine officials, and a few "old families," but the workers themselves came and went through the middle years of the century with bewildering rapidity. Rather than endure the rigors of long strikes, miners would simply decamp. The mine-owners suffered from this phenomenon almost as much as the workers themselves. One deplored the fact that "the best men have of course gone," while the least enterprising and capable remained. In the Pennsylvania coal fields the widely varying national origins of the workers were another deterrent to common action. Welsh, Irish, English, and Germans had provided the initial cadres. During and more dramatically after the Civil War, Italians, Poles, and Slovaks began to come in increasing numbers. Italians were especially in demand as strikebreakers in the bituminous coal fields of Pennsylvania. Race wars were common. Particular traits were attributed by employers to each ethnic group. The Welsh, for example, were described by one mineowner as "a little tricky, & [apt] to lie a little more or less gently, as it suited their purposes," and as "bearing malice, and . . . being clannish." The larger towns where different ethnic groups lived were divided into sections or neighborhoods called by such names as "Scotch Hill, Welshtown, Shanty Mill or Cork Lane or Paddy's Land, Nigger Hill, Dutch Hollow, . . . Little Italy, Hungarian Hill, Polander Street." Each ethnic group had its own social customs, from the exuberant Polish wedding to the Welsh eisteddfod and the German *Turnverein* or *Sängerfest*. The different nationalities often could not even converse with each other, let alone work together to improve conditions.

When the Sage Foundation put out a report on the conditions in the Carnegie steel mills, it emphasized the role of immigrant labor. Slavs and Italians were given preference in employment, the report stated, "because of their docility, their habit of silent submission . . . and their willingness to work long hours and overtime without a murmur. Foreigners as a rule earn the lowest wages and work the full stint of hours. . . .

"Many work in intense heat, the din of machinery and the noise of escaping steam. The congested conditions of most of the plants in Pittsburgh add to the physical discomfort . . . while their ignorance of the language and of modern machinery increases the risk. How many of the Slavs, Lithuanians and Italians are injured in Pittsburgh in one year is unknown. No reliable statistics are compiled. . . . When I mentioned a plant that had a bad reputation to a priest he said: 'Oh, that is the slaughter-house; they kill them there every day.' . . . It is undoubtedly true, that exaggerated though the reports may be, the waste in life and limb is great, and if it all fell upon the native-born a cry would long since have gone up which would have stayed the slaughter."

With the slaves freed, [former abolitionist] Wendell Phillips . . . devoted a portion of his reformist energies to the plight of the Indian, but he had more than enough left for the workingman. He had watched the postwar business and financial interests, the growth of the railroads, and the first stirrings of modern industrialism with growing alarm. In October, 1871, at the Boston Music Hall, he expressed his indignation with the "capitalists." A few months later, addressing the International Grand Lodge of the Knights of St. Crispin, Phillips urged his listeners to "get hold of the great question of labor, and having hold of it, grapple with it, rip it open, invest it with light, gathering the facts, piercing the brains about them . . . then I know, sure as fate, though I may not live to see it, that *they will certainly conquer this nation in twenty years*. It is impossible that they should not." Phillips stressed the importance of organization. "I welcome organization," he declared. "I do not care whether it calls itself trades-union, Crispin, international, or commune; any thing that masses up a unit in order that they may put in a united force to face the organization of capital; anything that does that, I say amen to it. One hundred thousand men [the number of members claimed by the Knights of St. Crispin]. It is an immense army. I do not care whether it considers chiefly the industrial or the political question; it can control the land if it is in earnest." The abolitionists had been only a handful, but they "knew what they wanted, and were determined to have it. Therefore they got it." It was the same with the struggle of workingmen for decent conditions and decent wages.

Phillips offered his listeners a larger vision than simply higher pay and shorter hours. When he looked "out upon Christendom, with its 300,000,000 of people," he saw that a third of them did not have enough to eat. "Now, I say," he declared, "that the social civilization which condemns every third man in it to be below the average in the nourishment God prepared for them" was ordained from below, by greedy and sinful men, rather than from above. "Now I say that the civilization that has produced this state of things in nearly the hundredth year of the American Revolution did not come from above." Long hours, poor food, and hard work brutalized a man and crowded him "down to mere animal life, . . . eclipsed his aspirations, dulled his senses, stunted his intellect, and made him a mere tool to work. . . . That is why I say, lift a man; give him life; let him work eight hours a day; give him the school; develop his taste for music; give him a garden; give him beautiful things to see and good books to read. . . . Unless there is power in your movement, industrially and politically, the last knell of democratic liberty in this Union is struck; for, as I said, there is no power in the State to resist such a giant as the Pennsylvania road. . . . From Boston to New Orleans, from Mobile to Rochester, from Baltimore to St. Louis, we have now but one purpose, and that is, having driven all other political questions out of the arena, the only question left is labor — the relations of capital and labor."

Those relations, however, became increasingly strained. In 1886, labor militancy reached a climax when the rhetoric of solidarity resulted in spontaneous strikes, sympathetic work stoppages, and even boycotts and political demonstrations nationwide. In Chicago's Haymarket Square, labor militancy turned violent. During an anarchist demonstration against police brutality, someone hurled a bomb that killed a police officer and fatally injured five other people. Although the bomb thrower was never identified, a jury convicted eight anarchists, four of whom died on the gallows. The episode was a terrible reversal for the incipient labor movement, as courts and police clamped down and unions became associ-
ated in the public mind with disorder and violence. The Knights of Labor suffered an irreversible decline in membership; by 1893, it was dead.

That left only the American Federation of Labor, the conservative union of exclusively skilled workers, which by 1905 had a membership of more than 1.5 million. As America entered the twentieth century, the vast majority of American workers — 30 million men and 8 million women — remained unorganized, underpaid, and overworked. In 1909, for example, a laborer in a manufacturing plant toiled fifty-nine hours a week for less than $10. Not until Woodrow Wilson's presidency did the federal government abolish child labor and grant railroad workers an eight-hour workday.

QUESTIONS TO CONSIDER

1. Who were Eleanor and Edward Aveling, and what was their political bias? What were they looking for in America? What useful comparisons could the Avelings supply to highlight their picture of working-class America? Why does Page Smith use the Avelings' journey around working America to structure his article?

2. What effect did the arrival of ever-increasing waves of immigrants have on America's workingclass populations? How did the owners of industry use immigrant labor? What problems did the isolation of individual ethnic groups present for labor organizers? What was the effect of mechanization on workers?

3. Drawing on what you have read here, describe a typical American industrial town in the late nineteenth century. Where would people live in the town? How would they live? Describe a typical working day for a man, a woman, a child. What would a mining town look like? What was the significance of the company store?

4. Where was the United States government in relation to all the misery and squalor of the urban and industrial working classes? What was the role of the

state labor commissions and private foundations such as the Sage Foundation? Was there any sympathy for the plight of laboring people? What essential philosophies associated with democracy and capitalism made government slow to pass protective legislation? Why might the workers themselves have resented some aspects of protective legislation?

5. "The formation of unions was dishearteningly slow," says Page Smith. The Avelings found labor organization in America twenty or thirty years behind that in England. Discuss the obstacles that stood in the way of American labor organization, particularly among miners and unskilled laborers.

7

A Little Milk, a Little Honey:
Jewish Immigrants
in America

DAVID BOROFF

The Gilded Age witnessed an enormous surge of immigration from Europe, as the roman-
tic lure of America seemed to draw more people than ever. For Europeans, as one historian
has noted, "America was rich, America was good, America was hope, America was the
future." They came over by the millions, crowding into American cities and swelling the
bottom ranks of American labor. Between 1850 and 1910, some 22,800,000 immi-
grants arrived in the United States, more than three-fourths of them after 1881. There
was also a significant shift in the source of immigration. The "old" immigrants were from
western and northern Europe — Britain, Ireland, Germany, and the Scandinavian coun-
tries. But in the 1890s, most immigrants were from eastern and southern Europe —
Russia, Serbia, Austria-Hungary, and Italy — and most were Jewish or Catholic. When
these people arrived in America's northeastern cities, they invariably antagonized native-
born Protestants, who unfairly blamed them for America's growing urban problems.

   The major gateway of the new immigration was New York City, where the population
swelled from 1.5 million in 1870 to a spectacular 5 million by 1915. The constant
stream of new arrivals made New York the largest and most ethnically diverse city in
America. In fact, by 1900, more than three-fourths of New York's citizenry was foreign
born. Among them were several hundred thousand east European Jews, most of whom

settled in the crowded and tumultuous Lower East Side, where they lived in conditions that contrasted sharply with the dream of America that had brought them here.

David Boroff provides a vivid picture of the Jewish immigrants, who first began arriving in New Amsterdam (later New York) in 1654. His focus, however, is on the period after 1880, when Jewish immigration was, as he puts it, "in flood tide." Boroff's lively narrative not only captures the immigrant experience but points out the influence of the Jewish immigrants on the United States and America's influence on them.

In significant ways, the Jewish immigrant experience mirrored that of other ethnic groups newly arrived in America. Italians, Poles, Slovaks, Greeks, and Irish also congregated in "immigrant ghettos" in which they tended to recreate the features of the Old World societies they had left behind. While the ghetto had its bleak side, it nevertheless afforded ethnic groups "a sense of belonging," of "cultural cohesiveness," that assuaged the pain of leaving their homelands and starting over in a strange, often overwhelming, new land.

GLOSSARY

AUSWANDERERHALLEN   Emigrant building.

CASTLE GARDEN   Huge building, situated at the foot of Manhattan, where immigrants were cleaned and interrogated after their arrival.

CHEDERS   Hebrew schools.

COFFEE HOUSE   The most popular cultural institution in the Jewish ghetto.

GEHENNA   Hell.

GENTILE   People who are not Jewish.

GREENHORN, OR GREENER   Pejorative term for newly arrived immigrants.

JEWISH DAILY FORWARD   Socialistic Yiddish newspaper, edited by Abraham Cahan.

MAX HOCHSTIM ASSOCIATION Energetically recruited girls to work as prostitutes.

NEW YORK INDEPENDENT BENEVOLENT ASSOCIATION   An organization of pimps.

ORTHODOX JEW   One who adheres faithfully to traditional Judaism, who is devoted to the study of the Torah, attends synagogue daily, and takes care to observe the sabbath, Jewish holy days, dietary laws, and religious festivals.

"PIG MARKET"   Functioned as the labor exchange on the Lower East Side.

POGROM   Organized massacre of Jews.

SHTETL   Typical small Jewish town in Europe.

WHITE PLAGUE   Immigrants' term for tuberculosis.

YIDDISH   The Hebrew-German dialect and the main vehicle for a Jewish cultural renaissance between 1890 and World War I.

ZHID   Yiddish word for leave.

It started with a trickle and ended in a flood. The first to come were twenty-three Jews from Brazil who landed in New Amsterdam in 1654, in flight from a country no longer hospitable to them. They were, in origin, Spanish and Portuguese Jews (many with grandiloquent Iberian names) whose families had been wandering for a century and a half. New Amsterdam provided a chilly reception. Governor Peter Stuyvesant at first asked them to leave, but kinder hearts in the Dutch West India Company granted them the right to stay, "provided the poor among them . . . be supported by their own nation." By the end of the century, there were perhaps one hundred Jews; by the middle of the eighteenth century, there were about three hundred in New York, and smaller communities in Newport, Philadelphia, and Charleston.

Because of their literacy, zeal, and overseas connections, colonial Jews prospered as merchants, though there were artisans and laborers among them. The Jewish community was tightly knit, but there was a serious shortage of trained religious functionaries. There wasn't a single American rabbi, for example, until the nineteenth century. Jews were well regarded, particularly in New England. Puritan culture leaned heavily on the Old Testament, and Harvard students learned Hebrew; indeed, during the American Revolution, the suggestion was advanced that Hebrew replace English as the official language of the new country. The absence of an established national religion made it possible for Judaism to be regarded as merely another religion in a pluralistic society. The early days of the new republic were thus a happy time for Jews. Prosperous and productive, they were admitted to American communal life with few restrictions. It is little wonder that a Jewish spokesman asked rhetorically in 1820: "On what spot in this habitable Globe does an Israelite enjoy more blessings, more privileges?"

The second wave of immigration during the nineteenth century is often described as German, but that is misleading. Actually, there were many East European Jews among the immigrants who came in the half century before 1870. However, the German influence was strong, and there was a powerful undercurrent of Western enlightenment at work. These Jews came because economic depression and the Industrial Revolution had made their lot as artisans and small merchants intolerable. For some there was also the threatening backwash of the failure of the Revolution of 1848. Moreover, in Germany at this time Jews were largely disfranchised and discriminated against. During this period, between 200,000 and 400,000 Jews emigrated to this country, and the Jewish population had risen to about half a million by 1870.

This was the colorful era of the peddler and his pack. Peddling was an easy way to get started — it required little capital — and it often rewarded enterprise and daring. Jewish peddlers fanned out through the young country into farmland and mining camp, frontier and Indian territory. The more successful peddlers ultimately settled in one place as storekeepers. (Some proud businesses . . . made their start this way.) Feeling somewhat alienated from the older, settled Jews, who had a reputation for declining piety, the new immigrants organized their own synagogues and community facilities, such as cemeteries and hospitals. In general, these immigrants were amiably received by native Americans, who, unsophisticated about differences that were crucial to the immigrants themselves, regarded all Central Europeans as "Germans."

Essentially, the emigration route was the same between 1820 and 1870 as it would be in the post–1880 exodus. The travellers stayed in emigration inns while awaiting their ship, and since they had all their resources with them, they were in danger of being robbed. The journey itself was hazardous and, in the

From David Boroff, "A Little Milk, A Little Honey," *American Heritage,* October/November 1966, Vol. 17, No. 6. © 1961 by Forbes, Inc. Reprinted by permission of *American Heritage* Magazine, a division of Forbes, Inc.

days of the sailing vessels when a good wind was indispensable, almost interminable. Nor were the appointments very comfortable even for the relatively well to do. A German Jew who made the journey in 1856 reported that his cabin, little more than six feet by six feet, housed six passengers in triple-decker bunks. When a storm raged, the passengers had to retire to their cabins lest they be washed off the deck by waves. "Deprived of air," he wrote, "it soon became unbearable in the cabins in which six sea-sick persons breathed." On this particular journey, sea water began to trickle into the cabins, and the planks had to be retarred.

Still, the emigration experience was a good deal easier than it would be later. For one thing, the immigrants were better educated and better acquainted with modern political and social attitudes than the oppressed and bewildered East European multitudes who came after 1880. Fewer in number, they were treated courteously by ships' captains. (On a journey in 1839, described by David Mayer, the ship's captain turned over his own cabin to the Jewish passengers for their prayers and regularly visited those Jews who were ill.) Moreover, there was still the bloom of adventure about the overseas voyage. Ships left Europe amid the booming of cannon, while on shore ladies enthusiastically waved their handkerchiefs. On the way over, there was a holiday atmosphere despite the hazards, and there was great jubilation when land was sighted.

There were, however, rude shocks when the voyagers arrived in this country. The anguish of Castle Garden and Ellis Island was well in the future when immigration first began to swell. But New York seemed inhospitable, its pace frantic, the outlook not entirely hopeful. Isaac M. Wise, a distinguished rabbi who made the journey in 1846, was appalled. "The whole city appeared to me like a large shop," he wrote, "where everyone buys or sells, cheats or is cheated. I had never before seen a city so bare of all art and of every trace of good taste; likewise I had never witnessed anywhere such rushing, hurrying, chasing, running. . . . Everything seemed so pitifully small and paltry; and I had had so exalted an idea of the land of freedom." Moreover, he no sooner landed in New York than he was abused by a German drayman whose services he had declined. "Aha! thought I," he later wrote, "you have left home and kindred in order to get away from the disgusting Judaeo-phobia and here the first German greeting that sounds in your ears is hep! hep!" (The expletive was a Central European equivalent of "Kike.") Another German Jew who worked as a clothing salesman was affronted by the way customers were to be "lured" into buying ("I did not think this occupation corresponded in any way to my views of a merchant's dignity").

After 1880, Jewish immigration into the United States was in flood tide. And the source was principally East Europe, where by 1880 three-quarters of the world's 7.7 million Jews were living. In all, over two million Jews came to these shores in little more than three decades — about one-third of Europe's Jewry. Some of them came, as their predecessors had come, because of shrinking economic opportunities. In Russia and in the Austro-Hungarian empire, the growth of large-scale agriculture squeezed out Jewish middlemen as it destroyed the independent peasantry, while in the cities the development of manufacturing reduced the need for Jewish artisans. Vast numbers of Jews became petty tradesmen or even *luftmenschen* (men without visible means of support who drifted from one thing to another). In Galicia, around 1900, there was a Jewish trader for every ten peasants, and the average value of his stock came to only twenty dollars.

Savage discrimination and pogroms also incited Jews to emigrate. The Barefoot Brigades — bands of marauding Russian peasants — brought devastation and bloodshed to Jewish towns and cities. On a higher social level, there was the "cold pogrom," a government policy calculated to destroy Jewish life. The official hope was that one third of Russia's Jews would die out, one third would emigrate, and one third would be converted to the Orthodox Church.

Crushing restrictions were imposed. Jews were required to live within the Pale of Settlement in western Russia, they could not Russify their names, and they were subjected to rigorous quotas for schooling and professional training. Nor could general studies be included in the curriculum of Jewish religious schools. It was a life of poverty and fear.

Nevertheless, the *shtetl,* the typical small Jewish town, was a triumph of endurance and spiritual integrity. It was a place where degradation and squalor could not wipe out dignity, where learning flourished in the face of hopelessness, and where a tough, sardonic humor provided catharsis for the tribulations of an existence that was barely endurable. The abrasions and humiliations of everyday life were healed by a rich heritage of custom and ceremony. And there was always Sabbath — "The Bride of the Sabbath," as the Jews called the day of rest — to bring repose and exaltation to a life always sorely tried.

To be sure, even this world showed signs of disintegration. Secular learning, long resisted by East European Jews and officially denied to them, began to make inroads. Piety gave way to revolutionary fervor, and Jews began to play a heroic role in Czarist Russia's bloody history of insurrection and suppression.

This was the bleak, airless milieu from which the emigrants came. A typical expression of the Jewish attitude towards emigration from Russia — both its hopefulness and the absence of remorse — was provided by Dr. George Price, who had come to this country in one of the waves of East European emigration:

Should this Jewish emigrant regret his leave-taking of his native land which fails to appreciate him? No! A thousand times no! He must not regret fleeing the clutches of the blood-thirsty crocodile. Sympathy for this country? How ironical it sounds! Am I not despised? Am I not urged to leave? Do I not hear the word *Zhid* constantly? . . . Be thou cursed forever my wicked homeland, because you remind me of the Inquisition. . . . May you rue the day when you exiled the people who worked for your welfare.

After 1880, going to America — no other country really lured — became the great drama of redemption for the masses of East European Jews. (For some, of course, Palestine had that role even in the late nineteenth century, but these were an undaunted Zionist cadre prepared to endure the severest hardships.) The assassination of Czar Alexander II in 1881, and the subsequent pogrom, marked the beginning of the new influx. By the end of the century, 700,000 Jews had arrived, about one quarter of them totally illiterate, almost all of them impoverished. Throughout East Europe, Jews talked longingly about America as the "goldene medinah" (the golden province), and biblical imagery — "the land of milk and honey" — came easily to their lips. Those who could write were kept busy composing letters to distant kin — or even to husbands — in America. (Much of the time, the husband went first, and by abstemious living saved enough to fetch wife and children from the old country.) Children played at "emigrating games," and for the entire *shtetl* it was an exciting moment when the mail-carrier announced how many letters had arrived from America.

German steamship companies assiduously advertised the glories of the new land and provided a one-price rate from *shtetl* to New York. Emigration inns were established in Brody (in the Ukraine) and in the port cities of Bremen and Hamburg, where emigrants would gather for the trip. There were rumors that groups of prosperous German Jews would underwrite their migration to America; and in fact such people often did help their co-religionists when they were stranded without funds in the port cities of Germany. Within Russia itself, the government after 1880 more or less acquiesced in the emigration of Jews, and connived in the vast business of "stealing the border" (smuggling emigrants across). After 1892, emigration was legal — except for those of draft age — but large numbers left with forged papers, because that proved to be far easier than getting tangled in the red tape of the Czarist bureaucracy. Forged documents, to be sure, were expensive — they cost twenty-five rubles, for many Jews the equivalent of five weeks' wages. Nor was the departure from home entirely a happy event. There were the uncertainties of the new life, the fear that in America "one became a gentile." Given the Jewish aptitude for lugubriousness, a family's departure was often like a funeral, lachrymose and anguished, with the neighbors carting off the furniture that would no longer be needed.

For people who had rarely ventured beyond the boundaries of their own village, going to America was an epic adventure. They travelled with pitifully little money; the average immigrant arrived in New York with only about twenty dollars. With their domestic impedimenta — bedding, brass candlesticks, samovars — they would proceed to the port cities by rail, cart, and even on foot. At the emigration inns, they had to wait their turn. Thousands milled around, entreating officials for departure cards. There were scenes of near chaos — mothers shrieking, children crying; battered wicker trunks, bedding, utensils in wild disarray. At Hamburg, arriving emigrants were put in the "unclean" section of the *Auswandererhallen* until examined by physicians who decided whether their clothing and baggage had to be disinfected. After examination, Jews could not leave the center; other emigrants could.

The ocean voyage provided little respite. (Some elected to sail by way of Liverpool at a reduction of nine dollars from the usual rate of thirty-four dollars.) Immigrants long remembered the "smell of ship," a distillation of many putrescences. Those who went in steerage slept on mattresses filled with straw and kept their clothes on to keep warm. The berth itself was generally six feet long, two feet wide, and two and a half feet high, and it had to accommodate the passenger's luggage. Food was another problem. Many Orthodox Jews subsisted on herring, black bread, and tea which they brought because they did not trust the dietary purity of the ship's food. Some ships actually maintained a separate galley for kosher food, which was coveted by non-Jewish passengers because it was allegedly better.

Unsophisticated about travel and faced by genuine dangers, Jewish emigrants found the overseas trip a long and terrifying experience. But when land was finally sighted, the passengers often began to cheer and shout. "I looked up at the sky," an immigrant wrote years later. "It seemed much bluer and the sun much brighter than in the old country. It reminded me on [*sic*] the Garden of Eden."

Unhappily, the friendly reception that most immigrants envisioned in the new land rarely materialized. Castle Garden in the Battery, at the foot of Manhattan — and later Ellis Island in New York Harbor — proved to be almost as traumatic as the journey itself. "Castle Garden," an immigrant wrote, "is a large building, a Gehenna, through which all Jewish arrivals must pass to be cleansed before they are considered worthy of breathing freely the air of the land of the almighty dollar. . . . If in Brody, thousands crowded about, here tens of thousands thronged about; if there they were starving, here they were dying; if there they were crushed, here they were simply beaten."

One must make allowances for the impassioned hyperbole of the suffering immigrant, but there is little doubt that the immigration officials were harassed, overworked, and often unsympathetic. Authorized to pass on the admissibility of the newcomers, immigration officers struck terror into their hearts by asking questions designed to reveal their literacy and social attitudes. "How much is six times six?" an inspector asked a woman in the grip of nervousness, then casually asked the next man, "Have you ever been in jail?"

There were, of course, representatives of Jewish defense groups present, especially from the Hebrew Immigrant Aid Society. But by this time, the immigrants, out of patience and exhausted, tended to view them somewhat balefully. The Jewish officials tended to be highhanded, and the temporary barracks which they administered on Ward's Island for those not yet settled soon became notorious. Discontent culminated in a riot over food; one day the director —

called The Father — had to swim ashore for his life, and the police were hastily summoned.

Most immigrants went directly from Castle Garden or Ellis Island to the teeming streets of Manhattan, where they sought relatives or *landsleit* (fellow townsmen) who had gone before them. Easy marks for hucksters and swindlers, they were overcharged by draymen for carrying their paltry possessions, engaged as strikebreakers, or hired at shamelessly low wages.

"Greenhorn" or "greener" was their common name. A term of vilification, the source of a thousand cruel jokes, it was their shame and their destiny. On top of everything else, the immigrants had to abide the contempt of their co-religionists who had preceded them to America by forty or fifty years. By the time the heavy East European immigration set in, German Jews had achieved high mercantile status and an uneasy integration into American society. They did not want to be reminded of their kinship with these uncouth and impoverished Jews who were regarded vaguely as a kind of Oriental influx. There was a good deal of sentiment against "aiding such paupers to emigrate to these shores." One charitable organization declared: "Organized immigration from Russia, Roumania, and other semi-barbarous countries is a mistake and has proved to be a failure. It is no relief to the Jews of Russia, Poland, etc., and it jeopardizes the well-being of the American Jews."

A genuine uptown-downtown split soon developed, with condescension on one side and resentment on the other. The German Jews objected as bitterly to the rigid, old-world Orthodoxy of the immigrants as they did to their new involvement in trade unions. They were fearful, too, of the competition they would offer in the needle trades. (Indeed, the East Europeans ultimately forced the uptown Jews out of the industry.) On the other side of the barricades, Russian Jews complained that at the hands of their uptown brethren, "every man is questioned like a criminal, is looked down upon . . . just as if he were standing before a Russian official." Nevertheless,

many German Jews responded to the call of conscience by providing funds for needy immigrants and setting up preparatory schools for immigrant children for whom no room was yet available in the hopelessly overcrowded public schools.

Many comfortably settled German Jews saw dispersion as the answer to the problem. Efforts were made to divert immigrants to small towns in other parts of the country, but these were largely ineffective. There were also some gallant adventures with farming in such remote places as South Dakota, Oregon, and Louisiana. Though the Jewish pioneers were brave and idealistic, drought, disease, and ineptitude conspired against them. (In Oregon, for example, they tried to raise corn in cattle country, while in Louisiana they found themselves in malarial terrain.) Only chicken farming in New Jersey proved to be successful to any great degree. Farm jobs for Jews were available, but as one immigrant said: "I have no desire to be a farm hand to an ignorant Yankee at the end of the world. I would rather work here at half the price in a factory; for then I would at least be able to spend my free evenings with my friends."

It was in New York, then, that the bulk of the immigrants settled — in the swarming, tumultuous Lower East Side — with smaller concentrations in Boston, Philadelphia, and Chicago. Far less adaptable than the German Jews who were now lording it over them, disoriented and frightened, the East European immigrants constituted a vast and exploited proletariat. According to a survey in 1890, sixty per cent of all immigrant Jews worked in the needle trades. This industry had gone through a process of decentralization in which contractors carried out the bulk of production, receiving merely the cut goods from the manufacturer. Contracting establishments were everywhere in the Lower East Side, including the contractors' homes, where pressers warmed their irons on the very stove on which the boss's wife was preparing supper. The contractors also gave out "section" work to families and *landsleit* who would struggle to meet the quotas at home. The bondage of the sewing machine was therefore extended into the tenements, with entire families enslaved by the machine's voracious demands. The Hester Street "pig market," where one could buy anything, became the labor exchange; there tailors, operators, finishers, basters, and pressers would congregate on Saturday in the hope of being hired by contractors.

Life in the sweatshops of the Lower East Side was hard, but it made immigrants employable from the start, and a weekly wage of five dollars — the equivalent of ten rubles — looked good in immigrant eyes. Moreover they were among their own kin and kind, and the sweatshops, noisome as they were, were still the scene of lively political and even literary discussions. (In some cigar-making shops, in fact, the bosses hired "readers" to keep the minds of the workers occupied with classic and Yiddish literature as they performed their repetitive chores.) East European Jews, near the end of the century, made up a large part of the skilled labor force in New York, ranking first in twenty-six out of forty-seven trades, and serving, for example, as bakers, building-trade workers, painters, furriers, jewellers, and tinsmiths.

Almost one quarter of all the immigrants tried their hands as tradesmen — largely as peddlers or as push-cart vendors in the madhouse bazaar of the Lower East Side. For some it was an apprenticeship in low-toned commerce that would lead to more elegant careers. For others it was merely a martyrdom that enabled them to subsist. It was a modest enough investment — five dollars for a license, one dollar for a basket, and four dollars for wares. They stocked up on pins and needles, shoe laces, polish, and handkerchiefs, learned some basic expressions ("You wanna buy somethin'?"), and were on their hapless way.

It was the professions, of course, that exerted the keenest attraction to Jews, with their reverence for learning. For most of them it was too late; they had to reconcile themselves to more humble callings. But it was not too late for their children, and between 1897 and 1907, the number of Jewish physicians in Man-hattan rose from 450 to 1,000. Of all the professions it was medicine that excited the greatest veneration. (Some of this veneration spilled over into pharmacy, and "druggists" were highly respected figures who were called upon to prescribe for minor — and even major — ills, and to serve as scribes for the letters that the immigrants were unable to read and write themselves.) There were Jewish lawyers on the Lower East Side and by 1901 over 140 Jewish policemen, recruited in part by Theodore Roosevelt, who, as police commissioner, had issued a call for "the Maccabee or fighting Jewish type."

The Lower East Side was the American counterpart of the ghetto for Jewish immigrants, as well as their glittering capital. At its peak, around 1910, it packed over 350,000 people into a comparatively small area — roughly from Canal Street to Fourteenth Street — with as many as 523 people per acre, so that Arnold Bennett was moved to remark that "the architecture seemed to sweat humanity at every window and door." The most densely populated part of the city, it held one sixth of Manhattan's population and most of New York's office buildings and factories. "Uptowners" used to delight in visiting it (as a later generation would visit Harlem) to taste its exotic flavor. But the great mass of Jews lived there because the living was cheap, and there was a vital Jewish community that gave solace to the lonely and comfort to the pious.

A single man could find lodgings of a sort, including coffee morning and night, for three dollars a month. For a family, rent was about ten dollars a month, milk was four cents a quart, kosher meat twelve cents a pound, herring a penny or two. A kitchen table could be bought for a dollar, chairs at thirty-five cents each. One managed, but the life was oppressive. Most families lived in the notorious "dumbbell" flats of old-law tenements (built prior to 1901). Congested, often dirty and unsanitary, these tenements were six or seven stories high and had four apartments on each floor. Only one room in each three or four room apartment received direct air and sunlight, and the families on each floor shared a toilet in the hall.

Many families not only used their flats as workshops but also took in boarders to make ends meet. [Journalist and reformer] Jacob Riis tells of a two-room apartment on Allen Street which housed parents, six children, and six boarders. "Two daughters sewed clothes at home. The elevated railway passed by the window. The cantor rehearses, a train passes, the shoemaker bangs, ten brats run around like goats, the wife putters. . . . At night we all try to get some sleep in the stifling, roach-infested two rooms." In the summer, the tenants spilled out into fire escapes and rooftops, which were converted into bedrooms.

Nevertheless, life on the Lower East Side had surprising vitality. Despite the highest population density in the city, the Tenth Ward had one of the lowest death rates. In part, this was because of the strenuous personal cleanliness of Jews, dictated by their religion. Though only eight per cent of the East European Jews had baths, bathhouses and steam rooms on the Lower East Side did a booming business. There was, of course, a heavy incidence of tuberculosis — "the white plague." Those who were afflicted could be heard crying out, "*Luft! Gib mir luft!*" ("Air! Give me air!"). It was, in fact, this terror of "consumption" that impelled some East Side Jews to become farmers in the Catskills at the turn of the century, thus forerunning the gaudy career of the Catskill Borscht Belt resort hotels. The same fear impelled Jews on the Lower East Side to move to Washington Heights and the Bronx, where the altitude was higher, the air presumably purer.

Alcoholism, a prime affliction of most immigrant groups, was almost unknown among Jews. They drank ritualistically on holidays but almost never to excess. They were, instead, addicted to seltzer or soda water . . . which they viewed as "the worker's champagne." The suicide rate was relatively low, though higher than in the *shtetl,* and there was always a shud-der of sympathy when the Yiddish press announced that someone had *genumen di ges* (taken gas).

The Lower East Side was from the start the scene of considerable crime. But its inhabitants became concerned when the crime rate among the young people seemed to rise steeply around 1910. There was a good deal of prostitution. The dancing academies, which achieved popularity early in this century, became recruiting centers for prostitutes. In 1908–9, of 581 foreign women arrested for prostitution, 225 were Jewish. There was the notorious Max Hochstim Association, which actively recruited girls, while the New York Independent Benevolent Association — an organization of pimps — provided sick benefits, burial privileges, bail, and protection money for prostitutes. The membership was even summoned to funerals with a two-dollar fine imposed on those who did not attend. Prostitution was so taken for granted that Canal Street had stores on one side featuring sacerdotal articles, while brothels were housed on the other.

Family life on the Lower East Side was cohesive and warm, though there was an edge of shrillness and hysteria to it. Marriages were not always happy, but if wives were viewed as an affliction, children were regarded as a blessing. The kitchen was the center of the household, and food was almost always being served to either family or visitors. No matter how poor they were, Jewish families ate well — even to excess — and mothers considered their children woefully underweight unless they were well cushioned with fat.

It was a life with few conventional graces. Handkerchiefs were barely known, and the Yiddish newspapers had to propagandize for their use. Old men smelled of snuff, and in spite of bathing, children often had lice in their hair and were sent home from school by the visiting nurse for a kerosene bath. Bedbugs were considered an inevitability, and pajamas were viewed as an upper-class affectation. Parents quarrelled bitterly — with passionate and resourceful invective — in the presence of their children. Telephones were virtually unknown, and a telegram surely meant disaster from afar.

The zeal of the immigrants on behalf of their children was no less than awe-inspiring. Parents yearned for lofty careers for their offspring, with medicine at the pinnacle. In better-off homes, there was always a piano ("solid mahogany"), and parents often spent their precious reserves to arrange a "concert" for their precocious youngsters, often followed by a ball in one of the Lower East Side's many halls.

To be sure, the children inspired a full measure of anxiety in their parents. "Amerikane kinder" was the rueful plaint of the elders, who could not fathom the baffling new ways of the young. Parents were nervous about their daughters' chastity, and younger brothers — often six or seven years old — would be dispatched as chaperones when the girls met their boy friends. There was uneasiness about Jewish street gangs and the growing problem of delinquency. The old folks were vexed by the new tides of secularism and political radicalism that were weaning their children from traditional pieties. But most of all, they feared that their sons would not achieve the success that would redeem their own efforts, humiliations, and failures in the harsh new land. Pressure on their children was relentless. But on the whole the children did well, astonishingly well. "The ease and rapidity with which they learn," Jacob Riis wrote, "is equalled only by their good behavior and close attention while in school. There is no whispering and no rioting at these desks." Samuel Chotzinoff, the music critic, tells a story which reveals the attitude of the Jewish schoolboy. When an altercation threatened between Chotzinoff and a classmate, his antagonist's reaction was to challenge him to spell "combustible."

The Lower East Side was a striking demonstration that financial want does not necessarily mean cultural poverty. The immigrant Jews were nearly always poor and often illiterate, but they were not culturally deprived. In fact, between 1890 and World War I,

the Jewish community provides a remarkable chapter in American cultural history. Liberated from the constrictions of European captivity, immigrant Jews experienced a great surge of intellectual vitality. Yiddish, the Hebrew-German dialect which some people had casually dismissed as a barbarous "jargon," became the vehicle of this cultural renascence. Between 1885 and 1914, over 150 publications of all kinds made their appearance. But the new Yiddish journalism reached its apogee with the *Jewish Daily Forward* under the long editorial reign of Abraham Cahan. The *Forward* was humanitarian, pro-labor, and socialistic. But it was also an instrument for acclimatizing immigrants in the new environment. It provided practical hints on how to deal with the new world, letters from the troubled (*Bintel Brief*), and even, at one time, a primer on baseball ("explained to nonsports"). The *Forward* also published and fostered an enormous amount of literature in Yiddish — both original works by writers of considerable talent, and translations of classic writers.

In this cultural ferment, immigrants studied English in dozens of night schools and ransacked the resources of the Aguilar Free Library on East Broadway. "When I had [a] book in my hand," an immigrant wrote, "I pressed it to my heart and wanted to kiss it." The Educational Alliance, also on East Broadway, had a rich program designed to make immigrant Jews more American and their sons more Jewish. And there were scores of settlement houses, debating clubs, ethical societies, and literary circles which attracted the young. In fact, courtships were carried on in a rarefied atmosphere full of lofty talk about art, politics, and philosophy. And though there was much venturesome palaver about sexual freedom, actual behavior tended to be quite strait-laced.

But the most popular cultural institution was the café or coffee house, which served as the Jewish saloon. There were about 250 of them, each with its own following. Here the litterateurs sat for hours over steaming glasses of tea; revolutionaries and Bohemians

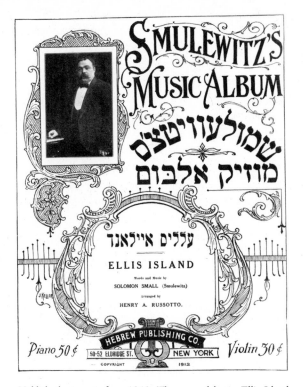

Yiddish sheet music from 1912. The song celebrates Ellis Island, which had replaced Castle Garden in 1892 as the point of entry for immigrants. A culture within a culture, Jewish New York had its own schools, newspapers, publishing houses, literary and musical circles, and a thriving Yiddish theater. (Sheet Music Collection, The John Hay Library, Brown University)

Elizabethan England. Tickets were cheap — twenty-five cents to one dollar — and theatergoing was universal. It was a raucous, robust, and communal experience. Mothers brought their babies (except in some of the "swellest" theaters, which forbade it), and peddlers hawked their wares between the acts. There were theater parties for trade unions and *landsmanschaften* (societies of fellow townsmen), and the audience milled around and renewed old friendships or argued the merits of the play. The stage curtain had bold advertisements of stores or blown-up portraits of stars.

There was an intense cult of personality in the Yiddish theater and a system of claques not unlike that which exists in grand opera today. The undisputed monarch was Boris Thomashefsky, and a theater program of his day offered this panegyric:

Tomashefsky! Artist great!
No praise is good enough for you!
Of all the stars you remain the king
You seek no tricks, no false quibbles;
One sees truth itself playing.
Your appearance is godly to us
Every movement is full of grace
Pleasing is your every gesture
Sugar sweet your every turn
You remain the king of the stage
Everything falls to your feet.

gathered to make their pronouncements or raise money for causes; actors and playwrights came to hold court. For immigrant Jews, talk was the breath of life itself. The passion for music and theater knew no bounds. When Beethoven's Ninth Symphony was performed one summer night in 1915, mounted police had to be summoned to keep order outside Lewisohn Stadium, so heavy was the press of crowds eager for the twenty-five-cent stone seats. Theater (in Yiddish) was to the Jewish immigrants what Shakespeare and Marlowe had been to the groundlings in

Many of the plays were sentimental trash — heroic "operas" on historical themes, "greenhorn" melodramas full of cruel abandonments and tearful reunions, romantic musicals, and even topical dramas dealing with such immediate events as the Homestead Strike, the Johnstown Flood, and the Kishinev Pogrom of 1903. Adaptability and a talent for facile plagiarism were the essence of the playwright's art in those days, and "Professor" Moses Horwitz wrote 167 plays, most of them adaptations of old operas and melodramas. The plays were so predictable that an actor once admitted he didn't even have to learn his lines; he merely had to have a sense of the general situation and then adapt lines from other plays.

There was, of course, a serious Yiddish drama, introduced principally by Jacob Gordin, who adapted classical and modernist drama to the Yiddish stage. Jewish intellectuals were jubilant at this development. But the process of acculturation had its amusing and grotesque aspects. Shakespeare was a great favorite but *"verbessert and vergrossert"* (improved and enlarged). There was the Jewish *King Lear* in which Cordelia becomes Goldele. (The theme of filial ingratitude was a "natural" on the Lower East Side, where parents constantly made heroic sacrifices.) *Hamlet* was also given a Jewish coloration, the prince becoming a rabbinical student who returns from the seminary to discover treachery at home. And *A Doll's House* by Ibsen was transformed into *Minna,* in which a sensitive and intelligent young woman, married to an ignorant laborer, falls in love with her boarder and ultimately commits suicide.

Related to the Jewish love of theater was the immigrant's adoration of the cantor, a profession which evoked as much flamboyance and egotistical preening as acting did. (In fact, actors would sometimes grow beards before the high holydays and find jobs as cantors.) Synagogues vied with each other for celebrated cantors, sometimes as a way of getting out of debt, since tickets were sold for the high-holyday services.

The Lower East Side was a vibrant community, full of color and gusto, in which the Jewish immigrant felt marvelously at home, safe from the terrors of the alien city. But it was a setting too for fierce conflict and enervating strain. There were three major influences at work, each pulling in a separate direction: Jewish Orthodoxy, assimilationism, and the new socialist gospel. The immigrants were Orthodox, but their children tended to break away. *Cheders* (Hebrew schools) were everywhere, in basements and stores and tenements, and the old custom of giving a child a taste of honey when he was beginning to learn to read

— as symbolic of the sweetness of study — persisted. But the young, eager to be accepted into American society, despised the old ways and their "greenhorn" teachers. Fathers began to view their sons as "freethinkers," a term that was anathema to them. Observance of the Law declined, and the Saturday Sabbath was ignored by many Jews. A virulent antireligious tendency developed among many "enlightened" Jews, who would hold profane balls on the most sacred evening of the year — Yom Kippur — at which they would dance and eat nonkosher food. (Yom Kippur is a fast day.) And the trade-union movement also generated uneasiness among the pious elders of the Lower East Side. "Do you want us to bow down to your archaic God?" a radical newspaper asked. "Each era has its new Torah. Ours is one of freedom and justice."

But for many immigrants the basic discontent was with their American experience itself. The golden province turned out to be a place of tenements and sweatshops. A familiar cry was *"a klug of Columbus!"* ("a curse on Columbus") or, "Who ever asked him, Columbus, to discover America?" Ellis Island was called *Tremindzl* (Island of Tears), and Abraham Cahan, in his initial reaction to the horrors of immigration, thundered: "Be cursed, immigration! Cursed by those conditions which have brought you into being. How many souls have you broken, how many courageous and mighty souls have you shattered." The fact remains that most Jewish immigrants, in the long run, made a happy adjustment to their new land.

After 1910, the Lower East Side went into a decline. Its strange glory was over. New areas of Jewish settlement opened up in Brooklyn, the Bronx, and in upper Manhattan. By the mid-twenties, less than ten per cent of New York's Jews lived on the Lower East Side, although it still remained the heartland to which one returned to shop, to see Yiddish theater, and to renew old ties. By 1924 Jewish immigration into the United States was severely reduced by new immigration laws, and the saga of mass immigration was done. But the intensities of the Jewish immigrant experience had already made an indelible mark on American culture and history that would endure for many years.

QUESTIONS TO CONSIDER

1.   Compare the migration experience of Jewish emigrants to America in the periods before and after 1880. In what ways did the experience become easier or more difficult? How did the emigrants themselves change?

2.   For some Jewish immigrants, America was "the land of milk and honey," whereas others cursed Columbus and called Ellis Island the "Island of Tears." Discuss the reality of the Jewish immigrant experience hidden behind both images of America.

3.   Analyze the reasons for the ambivalent feelings and divisions that developed between newer eastern European Jewish immigrants and those Jews, usually of German origin, who had been settled in the United States for several generations.

4.   The lure of land in the New World brought generations of Europeans to America. Why did the bulk of eastern European Jewish immigrants choose to remain in urban industrial centers such as New York City? Was there anything about their *shtetl* experience that made Jews more adaptable to city life?

5.   Boroff says, "The immigrant Jews were nearly always poor and often illiterate, but they were not culturally deprived." What evidence is there to support this statement?

IV

REFORM AND EXPANSION

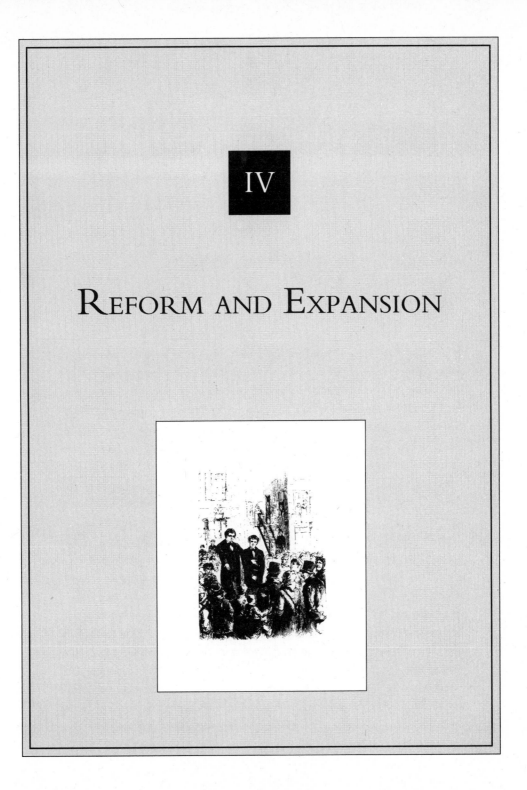

8

The Populist Protest

James MacGregor Burns

In the Gilded Age, politics became a big business, too, as the big industrialists poured money into government circles at an unprecedented rate. Men now entered politics for the same reason they went into business: to make their fortunes. The new politics even derived much of its vocabulary from the world of industry. "A political party," contended American statesman William H. Seward, "is in one sense a joint stock company in which those who contribute the most direct the action and management of the concern." The United States Senate became known as the Millionaires' Club, because only the rich and powerful seemed able to get in. A sizable portion of both major parties not only vigorously defended the industrial barons but were as eager to accept their campaign contributions as the barons were ready to give them. A number of politicians shamelessly took bribes as well.

In the 1880s, the two national parties—the Republicans and Democrats — had a monopoly on American politics, and neither was responsive to the grassroots of America. The industrial consolidation had left many victims in its wake — workers, farmers, consumers, and small or aspiring business and professional people who wanted their share of opportunity and wealth. Among the most devastated victims of the new industrial order were one-crop family farmers in the Midwest, Texas, and the South. By the 1880s, faced with ruinous farm prices and the advent of mechanized, diversified, commercial agriculture, southern and midwestern small farmers and southern sharecroppers, black and white alike, were in desperate straits and yet had no place to turn for help. American agrarians, it seemed, had no choice but to organize cooperative action among themselves. They had tried this in the Grange movement of the previous decade, but that movement had faded when prosperity returned in the late 1870s. But by the mid-1880s, as Bernard Weisberger has written, farmers everywhere suffered "from a long, deflationary squeeze between falling agricultural prices, on the one hand, and, on the other, rising interest rates, freight charges, and production costs that they argued were artificially boosted by the trusts and the tariff." To make matters worse, the farmers saw big business — the "money power" — buying off politicians in exchange for favorable legislation. As a consequence, first in Texas and then across the South and Midwest, American farmers organized alliances to protect themselves against the rich and powerful who ran America. The Alliance movement was an effort at cooperative agriculture to free farmers from "the furnishing merchants," banks, trusts, and railroads. The alliances, in turn, led to political organization, first in the People's Party of Kansas (which drew men and women alike to its banners) and ultimately in the national People's Party, or the Populist Party, which was formed in Omaha, Nebraska, in 1892. According to Lawrence Goodwyn, author of Democratic Promise (1976) and The Populist Moment (1978), the agrarian revolt that culminated in the Populist crusade constituted "the largest democratic mass movement in American history." And the objective of that mass movement was to restore government to the people.

In the selection that follows, James MacGregor Burns recounts the story of the Populist crusade, pointing out how it broke down racial barriers in the South and attracted a cadre of talented women orators and activists in Kansas. Burns stresses that "the idea of liberty" was populism's energizing force. The word liberty meant different things to different Americans in that period, but to the Populists it meant more than individual freedom, more than freedom from interference and exploitation. To Populist farmers and their middle-class leaders, liberty meant self-fulfillment through cooperative action. Thus, as Burns concludes, the Populists moved closer than any other American group to the third of the great concepts of the Enlightenment. The first two were liberty and equality. The third was "fraternity, or comradeship."

GLOSSARY

DIGGS, ANNIE   Journalist and lay preacher in the Unitarian church who wrote for the Populist cause and became associate editor of the Populist newspaper, the Topeka *Advocate*.

FARMERS' ALLIANCE OF TEXAS   "Built firmly on a network of suballiances," or neighborhood chapters, this organization was the prototype for farmers' alliances in other states.

GREENBACKERS   Pressed Washington to issue inflationary paper money — greenbacks — that would make it easier for debtors to pay what they owed.

JUTE BAGGING   Jute is a strong, rough fiber used to make gunny and burlap bagging.

LAMB, WILLIAM   First state lecturer for the Texas Alliance and one of its most creative and radical leaders.

LEASE, MARY   One of the first woman lawyers in Kansas and indefatigable activist in numerous causes, Lease was a stemwinding lecturer for the Kansas Populists.

LEWELLING, LORENZO   First Populist governor of Kansas who headed the "first People's party government on earth" in that prairie state.

McCORMICK, FANNY   Assistant state lecturer and noted leader of the Kansas Populists.

MACUNE, CHARLES   Texas Alliance leader who envisioned a national network of state Alliance Exchanges, which would collectively buy equipment and supplies and market cotton; he became the first president of the National Farmers' Alliance and Cooperative Union.

SIMPSON, "SOCKLESS JERRY"   Kansas Populist who won a seat in Congress in 1890 and promoted the Alliance program there.

SINGLE-TAX MOVEMENT   Contending that monopolists grew rich because of rising land values, the proponents of the movement advocated a single tax on land in place of all other taxes; such a tax, they believed, would destroy monopolies, lead to a more equitable distribution of wealth, and end poverty.

SUBTREASURY PLAN   Charles Macune's plan for "providing treasury notes to farmers, as a means of financing cooperatives with public rather than private credit and thus enlisting the government in the struggle to raise agricultural prices."

WATSON, TOM   Southern reformer who helped promote the Alliance platform in Congress and forged a biracial Populist coalition in Georgia.

WEAVER, JAMES B.   Populist party candidate for president in 1892.

*S*omewhere in central Texas, sometime in the late eighties: In the twilight splendor of the Plains, men and women march along dusty trails toward the glow of a campfire in the distance. Some walk; some ride horses or burros; some — whole families — jolt along on covered wagons or buckboards. With their creased, careworn faces, their poor gingham clothes, they might seem to be one more trek in the great western movement of American homesteaders. But not so. These people walk with hope and pride — even with exhilaration as they reach a hillcrest and see stretching for miles ahead and behind thousands of people marching with them, hundreds of wagons emblazoned with crude signs and banners. Soon they reach their encampment, not to settle down for the night but, in company with five or ten thousand comrades, to hear fiery speeches late into the evening.

These people will be part of an arresting venture in popular grass-roots democracy, part of the "flowering of the largest democratic mass movement in American history," in Lawrence Goodwyn's judgment. Ultimately they will fail — but not until they have given the nation an experiment in democratic ideas, creative leadership and followership, and comradely cooperation.

At first on the Texas frontier but soon in the South and Midwest, farmers in the mid-1880s collectively sensed that something was terribly wrong. In the South, farmers white and black were shackled by the crop lien system and the plummeting price of cotton. In the West, homesteaders were losing their mortgaged homes. Grain prices fell so low that Kansas farm families burned corn for heat. Everywhere farmers suffered from a contracting currency, heavy taxation, and gouging by railroads and other monopolies. As farmers perceived the "money power" buying elections and public officials in order to pass class

From James MacGregor Burns, *The American Experiment*, Vol. 2: *The Workshop of Democracy*, 180–191. Copyright © 1985 by James MacGregor Burns. Reprinted by permission of Alfred A. Knopf, Inc.

legislation, some agrarian leaders and editors wondered if the farm areas trembled on the brink of revolution.

The crop lien system, tight money, and the rest of the farmers' ills — these seemed remote and impersonal to many an eastern city dweller. But for countless Southern cotton farmers "crop lien" set the conditions of their existence.

It meant walking into the store of the "furnishing merchant," approaching the counter with head down and perhaps hat in hand, and murmuring a list of needs. It meant paying "the man" no money but watching him list items and figures in a big ledger. It meant returning month after month for these mumbled exchanges, as the list of debts grew longer. It meant . . . that the farmer brought in the produce from his long year's hard labor, watched his cotton weighed and sold, and then learned that the figures in the ledger, often with enormously inflated interest, added up to more than his crop was worth — but that the merchant would carry him into the next year if he signed a note mortgaging his next year's crop to the merchant. It meant returning home for another year's toil, knowing that he might lose his spread and join the army of landless tenant farmers. From start to finish it meant fear, self-abasing deference, hatred of self and others.

Above all, the system meant loss of liberty, as the farmer became shackled to one crop and one merchant — loss of liberty for men and women raised in the Jeffersonian tradition of individual freedom in a decentralized agrarian republic, in the Jacksonian tradition of equality of opportunity in a land free of usurious banks and grasping monopolies. Their forefathers had fought for independence; was a second American revolution needed to overthrow a new, an economic, monarchy? "Laboring men of America," proclaimed a tract, the voices of 1776 "ring down through the corridors of time and tell you to strike" against the "monopolies and combinations that are eating out the heart of the Nation." But strike how? "Not with glittering musket, flaming sword and deadly cannon," the pamphlet exhorted, "but with the silent, potent and all-powerful ballot, the only vestige of liberty left."

One course seemed clear — people must organize themselves as powerfully against the trusts as the trusts were organized against them. But organize how? Economically or politically? Experience did not make for easy answers. Farmers had plunged into politics with Greenbackers and laborites and ended up on the short end of the ballot counts. The answer of the recently founded Farmers' Alliance in Texas was to try both economic and political structures, but more intensively and comprehensively than ever before. Built firmly on a network of "suballiances" — neighborhood chapters of several dozen members meeting once or twice a month to pray, sing, conduct rituals, debate issues, and do organizational business — the state Alliance experimented with several types of grass-roots cooperatives, including stores, county trade committees to bargain with merchants, and county-wide "bulking" of cotton.

The key to Alliance power was not organization, though, but leadership — and not the leadership merely of a few persons at the top but of dozens, then hundreds, of men and women who were specially hired and trained to journey across the state visiting suballiances, helping to form new ones, and above all teaching members graphically and in detail about the complex political and economic issues of the day, both national issues like money and finance and local ones like the building and expanding of co-ops. These were the famed "lecturers," who in turn were responsible to a state lecturer. The Alliance's first state lecturer was William Lamb, a rugged, red-haired, thirty-four-year-old farmer. Born in Tennessee, he had traveled alone at sixteen to the Texas frontier, where he lived in a log hut until he could build a house, raise children with his wife, and learn to read and write at night.

Lamb soon emerged as one of the most creative and radical of Alliance leaders. When the Great Southwest Strike erupted against Jay Gould's railroad early in 1886, Lamb defied the more conservative Alliance leaders by demanding that the Alliance back a Knights of Labor boycott. Though suballiances gave food and money to striking railroad workers, the strike collapsed. The Knights continued on their downward slide, but the Texas Alliance continued its phenomenal growth, with perhaps 2,000 suballiances and 100,000 members by the summer of that year.

Lamb and other lecturers also took leadership on another critical issue facing the Alliance. Wracked by scorching drought, crop failures, and increasing tenantry, Texas farmers by 1886 were meeting in schoolhouses and clamoring for a new strategy — *political* action. They were impatient with the old shibboleth that the Alliance must steer clear of politics because politics would kill it. The decisive turning point in the agrarian revolt came at the Alliance state convention in Cleburne in early August 1886. A majority of the disgruntled, rustic-looking delegates from eighty-four counties "demanded" of the state and federal governments "such legislation as shall secure to our people freedom from the onerous and shameful abuses that the industrial classes are now suffering at the hands of arrogant capitalists and arrogant corporations" — legislation including an interstate commerce law and land reform measures. A conservative minority, opposing a proposal for greenbacks that defied the Democratic party, rejected the demands, absconded with the treasury, and formed a strictly "nonpartisan" Alliance.

At this critical moment Charles Macune, another leader fresh from the grass roots, stepped into the fray. Settled on the Texas frontier at nineteen after early years of poverty and wanderings, Macune had married, studied law and medicine, and practiced both. Developing into a skillful writer, compelling speaker, and innovative thinker, Macune had become well versed in farming matters and active in his county Alliance. And now this tall, magnetic physician-lawyer-farmer, buoyed by the rising militance of the delegates, proposed an ingenious compromise that was also a creative act of leadership.

Persuading the conservatives to give up their rival Alliance and the radicals to tone down their drive toward partisan politics, he proposed an expansion that was both geographic and functional. In his dazzling vision, a national network of state Alliance "Exchanges," starting in Texas, would collectively market cotton and buy supplies and farm equipment. This giant farmers' cooperative would not only achieve higher, more stable prices, but would provide the credit to free all farmers from the furnishing merchant and mortgage company. Thus, he proclaimed, mortgage-burdened farmers could "assert their freedom from the tyranny of organized capital." At a statewide meeting at Waco in January 1887 the farmer delegates enthusiastically adopted Macune's grand strategy, decided on merger with the Louisiana Farmers' Union, and chose Macune as first president of the National Farmers' Alliance and Cooperative Union. The state Alliance built a huge headquarters in Dallas even while doubling its membership and preparing a small army of lecturers to proselytize the South during mid-1887.

Even that army of enthusiasts seemed astonished by the response. "The farmers seemed like unto ripe fruit," one reported from North Carolina. "You can garner them by a gentle shake of the bush." He had held twenty-seven meetings in one county and left twenty-seven suballiances in his wake. With cotton down to eight cents a pound, farmers were desperate for relief. Together they and the lecturers set up trade committees, cotton yards, and warehouses in hundreds of counties, along with state exchanges. Georgia, with its big state exchange and its cooperative stores, gins, and warehouses, was the most successful. When manufacturers of the commonly used jute bagging organized a trust and doubled the price, the Georgia Alliance — and later other state groups — successfully boycotted the "jute trust," using cotton or pine straw instead, while protesting farmers donned cotton bagging and even witnessed a double wedding in which both brides and both grooms were decked out in that finery.

The idea of farm cooperation swept into the Midwest. The Alliance came to be most deeply rooted in the corn and wheat fields of Kansas, where a great boom had busted in 1887 amid mounting debts and foreclosures. When political efforts failed the next year, farm leaders visited Texas and returned full of missionary zeal. The formation of suballiances and the building of cooperatives proceeded feverishly until the entire state boasted of over 3,000 local units. When the "twine trust" hiked by 50 percent the price of the twine used to bind wheat, the Alliance staged a boycott. The trust lowered its price.

As early as 1889, however, Alliance leaders in Kansas were concluding that education and cooperation were not enough, that electoral political action was necessary too. The question was not whether to engage in politics but how — independent political action versus third-party efforts versus working through a major party; lobbying and pressuring established parties versus direct action to take power. The existing political landscape was barren. The Republican and Democratic parties both were sectional entities, appealing to lingering Civil War hatreds to win elections. Farmers who actually shared common conditions and needs were polarized by politicians who waved the bloody shirt. Though most farm leaders in Kansas spurned "partisan politics" at every turn, what they actually rejected was the familiar brand of party politics animated by sectionalism and penetrated by railroad and other monopolies. Many envisioned not just an alternative party, but an alternative *kind* of party that would overcome racial and sectional hatred and respond to grass-roots needs.

A county "people's convention" that nominated — and elected — a "people's ticket" for county offices against the trusts inspired Alliance leaders in Kansas to raise their sights to state action. A convention of industrial organizations in Topeka, with delegates from the Knights of Labor and the "single tax" movement as well as from Alliance groups, assembled in Representative Hall in the statehouse, formally set up the People's Party of Kansas, and called a state convention to choose statewide candidates and adopt the first People's Party platform.

Once again new leaders emerged out of this agitation and conflict. In the "Big Seventh" congressional district in southwest Kansas, a Medicine Lodge rancher and town marshal named Jerry Simpson quickly emerged as the most noted Kansas Populist. A sailor on the Great Lakes and later an Illinois soldier in the Civil War, Simpson had run a farm and sawmill in northeastern Kansas before turning to cattle-raising. After the harsh winter of 1887 killed his cattle and destroyed his life's savings, he turned to the Alliance and the new political insurgency.

Simpson won his imperishable title as "Sockless Jerry" during his campaign in 1890 against Colonel James Hallowell. "I tried to get hold of the crowd," Simpson recalled. "I referred to the fact that my opponent was known as a 'Prince.' Princes, I said, wear silk socks. I don't wear any." Hallowell, he went on, boasted that he had been to Topeka and had made laws. Picking up a book, Simpson recalled, he tapped on a page with his finger. "I said, here is one of Hal's laws. I find that it is a law to tax dogs, but I see that Hal proposes to charge two dollars for a bitch and only one dollar for a son of a bitch. Now the party I belong to believes in equal and exact justice to all."

Women leaders in Kansas attracted even more attention than the men. "Women who never dreamed of becoming public speakers," wrote Annie Diggs, "grew eloquent in their zeal and fervor. Josh Billings' saying that 'wimmin is everywhere,' was literally true in that wonderful picknicking, speech-making Alliance summer of 1890." While most Alliance women did rather mundane tasks, a good number of them emerged as compelling leaders and stump speakers. Diggs herself had worked actively in the Women's Christian Temperance Union in Kansas and as a lay preacher in the Unitarian Church when, in the mid-eighties, she journeyed east to become Boston correspondent for several Kansas papers. She returned to Kansas, worked with the Alliance, wrote on suffrage and temperance and Alliance issues despite a public disavowal by her Republican editor, and then joined Stephen McLallin, a leading Populist editor, as associ-

The Populist movement in Kansas attracted a number of talented professional women. "Women who never dreamed of becoming public speakers," said Annie Diggs, "grew eloquent in their zeal and fervor." Diggs, Fanny McCormick, Sarah Emery — all became noted women leaders. But it was Mary Lease, shown above, who attracted the most attention. One of the first female lawyers in the country, Lease was a mesmerizing lecturer for the People's Party of Kansas. "What you farmers need to do," she told agrarian audiences, "is to raise less corn and more Hell!" (Kansas State Historical Society)

ate editor of the Topeka *Advocate*. Together they shaped it into the leading reform paper in the state.

There were other noted women leaders: Fanny McCormick, assistant state lecturer who ran for state superintendent of public instruction; Sarah Emery, author of the widely read *Seven Financial Conspiracies* and a spellbinding orator; Kansas-born Fanny Vickrey, another gifted orator. But attracting most attention of all was the indomitable Mary Lease.

Lease was born in Pennsylvania of parents who were Irish political exiles and grew up in a family devastated by the Civil War; her two brothers died in the fighting, her father in Andersonville prison. She

moved to Kansas in the early 1870s, taught parochial school, raised a family, tried and failed at farming, studied law — "pinning sheets of notes above her wash tub" — became one of the first woman lawyers of Kansas, and began a tempestuous career as a speaker for Irish nationalism, temperance, woman's suffrage, union labor, and the Alliance. A tall, stately woman, she had "a golden voice," in [journalist] William Allen White's recollection, "a deep, rich contralto, a singing voice that had hypnotic qualities." But she could also hurl "sentences like Jove hurled thunderbolts," Diggs said, as she gave scores of speeches, some over two hours long, throughout Kansas. Pointing to the starving families of Chicago and the wasted corn piled along the railroad tracks or burned for heat, she exclaimed, "What you farmers need to do is to raise less corn and more Hell!"

Led by such women and men champions, propelled by acute needs and high hopes, the Kansas Populists roared to a sensational victory in 1890. They carried 96 of the 125 seats in the state's lower house and swept five out of seven congressional districts, sending Sockless Jerry along with the four others to Washington.

"THE PEOPLE ON TOP!" headlined the *Nonconformist*. But were they? The Populists elected only one statewide official, their candidate for attorney general. The Republicans still controlled the state administration, the holdover Senate, and the judiciary. The House passed a woman's suffrage bill but the Senate axed it. The Populists' one victory was to oust a conservative United States senator and send Populist editor William Peffer to Washington in his place. And now they had a crucial issue — Republican subversion of the will of the people. The Kansas Populists conducted a repeat crusade in 1892 with massive parades and encampments. This time they elected the entire state ticket and most of their congressional candidates again, including Simpson, and gained control of the Senate — but lost their majority in the House, amid accusations of wholesale Republican fraud.

The "first People's party government on earth"

was inaugurated in Topeka at the start of 1893. After a spectacular parade through downtown Topeka the new governor, Lorenzo Lewelling, gave a stirring address — his "incendiary Haymarket inaugural," a GOP editor called it — followed by Lease and Simpson. But the gala was shortlived. When the new legislature convened, the Populists organized the state Senate, but they and the Republicans each claimed a majority in the House. There followed a tug-of-war that would have been comic opera if the stakes had not been so high: each "majority" organized its own "House" with speaker and officers; neither side would vacate the hall, so they stayed put all night, with the two speakers sleeping, gavels in hand, facing each other behind the podium; finally Lewelling called up the militia — including a Gatling gun minus its firing pin — while the Republicans mobilized an army of deputy sheriffs, college students, and railroad workers. The GOP legislators smashed their way into the hall with a sledgehammer; and the militia commander, a loyal Republican like most of his troops, refused the governor's order to expel the invaders.

Bloodshed was narrowly averted when the Populists agreed to let the Republican-dominated Kansas Supreme Court rule on the issue, and predictably the court ruled against them. The Populists then paid the price. Their legislators fared worse than in 1891, passing two election reform measures and putting suffrage on the ballot, but not accomplishing much else. Their chief priority, railroad regulation with teeth, was a direct casualty of the conflict. Clearly, under the American and Kansan systems of checks and balances, a movement could win elections but still not win power.

Alliance cooperation and Populist politics spread through other Northern states, moving west into the mountain states toward the Pacific, north into Minnesota and the Dakotas, east into the big corn spreads. Everywhere the new movement mobilized people and encountered Republican party power and entrenched elites. Thus "in sundry ways, at different speeds, at varied levels of intensity, and at diverse

stages of political consciousness, the farmers brought the People's Party of the United States into being," in Goodwyn's summarization. "In so doing, they placed on the nation's political stage the first multi-sectional democratic mass movement since the American Revolution."

It was in the South, however, that the Alliance continued to expand most dramatically and yet to encounter the biggest obstacles. The first of these obstacles was the Southern Democracy [or Democratic Party], which continued to live off its role as defender of the Lost Cause. The second, closely connected, was race — not *simply* race, as C. Vann Woodward has explained, but "the complexities of the class economy growing out of race, the heritage of manumitted slave psychology, and the demagogic uses to which the politician was able to put race prejudice." Southern Populists reluctantly concluded that they could not achieve the subtreasury plan for credit and currency and other reforms unless they forged a biracial coalition of small landowners, tenant farmers, and sharecroppers. This meant war with the Southern Democracy and potential division within Populism.

Georgia was an even more tumultuous battleground than Kansas. There one man, backed by the mass of poor farmers, personified the entire movement: Tom Watson. Descended from prosperous slaveholders, he had seen his father lose his forty-five slaves and 1,400 acres after Appomattox and end up as a tavern owner in Augusta. Young Watson managed to spend two years at Mercer University before running out of money. After years of poverty he turned to law, prospered, and won election to the Georgia lower house at twenty-six, but quit before his term ended.

"I did not lead the Alliance," Watson recalled. "I followed the Alliance, and I am proud that I did." After taking leadership in the "jute fight," he decided to run for Congress as a Democrat with Alliance backing. The white Georgia Alliance sought to field its own candidates within the Democratic Party and back non–Alliance candidates only if they endorsed the Alliance program — the "Alliance yardstick," they called it. Alliance leaders took over the Democratic party state convention, wrote the party platform, won control of both houses of the "farmers' legislature," elected the governor and six of ten members of Congress. Watson trounced his Republican opponent almost ten to one in a fight as "hot as Nebuchadnezzar's furnace."

Coalitions embody conflicts. The lines were now drawn between Alliance members who were mainly Democrats and Democrats who were mainly Alliancers. The national Alliance had urged that its members of Congress not join any party caucus that did not endorse the Alliance platform. The whole Southern delegation but one stayed with the majority Democratic caucus and elected a Georgian, Charles Crisp, to the speakership. The exception was Watson. He and Sockless Jerry Simpson introduced the Alliance platform into Congress, fighting especially hard for the subtreasury proposal. Virtually none of the platform was even reported out of committee except the subtreasury item, which finally came to the floor after Watson used every maneuver to pry it out of committee; by then it was too late for action.

Beaten in Washington, Watson flourished politically at home. This was a time when many black tenants and sharecroppers were becoming alienated from the GOP and were turning to the new party. Watson called on blacks as well as whites to overthrow the plutocracy that had used race hatred to bolster its rule. "You are kept apart," he told black and white Georgians, "that you may be separately fleeced of your earnings." Campaigning for reelection in 1892, now as leader of the Georgia People's Party, Watson championed political equality for blacks, economic equality to a lesser extent — and social equality or "mixing" not at all. But despite both white and black Populist support, Watson was beaten for reelection in a campaign marked by massive election fraud and the killing of a score of Populists, most of them black.

Texas was having its own problems with the en-trenched white Democracy and entrenched capital. The Texas Alliance Exchange, the linchpin of cooperative efforts, had gotten off to a flying start by selling vast amounts of cotton to eastern mills and abroad and buying supplies and equipment. Still, it could not break the enslavement of tenants and sharecroppers to the crop lien system, and increasingly it suffered from lack of capital. Banks in Dallas and elsewhere turned a cold face to requests for loans. Desperately the leadership turned to the suballiances themselves for money. In a remarkable popular mobilization, thousands of farmers marched to county courthouses to pledge help. It was not enough; a year later the Texas Exchange closed its doors for good.

The ever-resourceful Charles Macune now presented his subtreasury plan, providing treasury notes to farmers, as a means of financing cooperatives with public rather than private credit and thus enlisting the government in the struggle to raise agricultural prices. The indefatigable William Lamb fashioned this economic reform into a weapon of political revolt as he launched a full-scale lecturing campaign in each congressional district. The Texas Alliance won a stunning victory through the Democratic Party in 1890, electing a governor and a legislature committed to most Alliance demands, but a host of Democratic "loyalists" opposed the subtreasury and bolted from the Alliance. Spurred by Lamb and other leaders, Alliance members decided to create the People's Party of Texas. At the founding convention in August 1891 white and black delegates forged a remarkable coalition, with a commitment to political and economic equality for blacks.

As the presidential election year of 1892 approached, Alliance leaders were concluding that a *national* People's Party was needed to consolidate the grand coalition of farmers and workers, strengthen the state parties, and seize control of the federal government. Plans were carefully laid. The Alliance organized a massive lecturing campaign, distributed vast quantities of books and pamphlets, including [Edward] Bellamy's *Looking Backward,* and formed a National Reform Press Association to coordinate the propaganda efforts of the one-hundred-strong Populist newspapers. A St. Louis conference of farm, labor, and women delegates drew up a platform and heard the Minnesota Populist orator and novelist Ignatius Donnelly give an unforgettable speech in which he charged: "Corruption dominates the ballot box, the legislatures, the Congress, and touches even the ermine of the bench. . . . The fruits of the toil of millions are boldly stolen to build up colossal fortunes, unprecedented in the history of the world, while their possessors despise the republic and endanger liberty. From the same prolific womb of governmental injustice we breed two great classes — paupers and millionaires."

Then came the national founding convention of the People's Party, Omaha, July 4, 1892. The delegates adopted a platform that harked back to the "Cleburne demands" six years earlier and indeed to decades of labor, farm, and socialist manifestos: a flexible "national currency" to be distributed by means of the subtreasury plan; free and unlimited coinage of silver and gold; a graduated income tax; government ownership and operation of the railroads, telegraph, and telephone; barring of alien land ownership and return of land held by railroads and other corporations "in excess of their actual needs"; political reforms such as the direct election of United States senators. But the platform ignored labor's most urgent needs and omitted mention of woman's suffrage. The convention also took a moderate course in nominating for president James B. Weaver of Iowa, the reform editor and ex-Union general who had led the Greenbackers in 1880, balancing him with an ex-Confederate general as his running mate.

Plunging into the election campaign, the Populists unsheathed their thousands of lecturers, their orators such as Lease and Donnelly, their tactics in some states of opportunistic coalition-building with Republicans in the South and especially with Democrats in the West. Weaver and his wife were rotten-egged in the South — Mrs. Weaver to the point that, according to

Lease, she "was made a regular walking omelet by the southern chivalry of Georgia." The results were promising for a fledgling third party: Weaver polled over one million votes, actually carrying Kansas and four western states with twenty-two electoral votes. Populist governors were elected in Kansas, Colorado, and North Dakota. But in the Northeast, parts of the Midwest, and the South the party fared poorly. In Texas the Populists lost badly to the Democrats. It was with mingled hopes and an exhilarating sense of momentum that the Populists turned to the economic and political struggles ahead.

The idea of liberty had been the animating impulse behind the Alliance. But during the century soon to come to an end that idea had also guided organized capital and labor. Each group of course meant something different by "liberty"—businessmen meant freedom from interference with property, labor meant freedom from boss control of its working life, farmers meant freedom from furnishing merchants, banks, railroads, trusts. More than the other groups, however, the Alliance had made liberty into a positive idea—realizing and fulfilling oneself by gaining broader control of one's working environment through participation in Alliance cooperatives. Along with industrial workers, Populist farmers had also preached the idea of equality—a real equality of opportunity. But the cooperators, with their denunciations of "selfish individualism," had moved even more than labor toward the third great concept in the Enlightenment trinity—*fraternity,* or *comradeship.* The idea of cooperation had grown out of, and had sustained, the practices of sisterhood and brotherhood.

And if the Populists had realized all three values to a greater extent than any other large group, it was mainly because of a conscious effort toward the intensive use of massive numbers of second-cadre activists — 35,000 or more "lecturers" — in rousing farmers to political self-consciousness. As in all deeply felt democratic movements, the great leaders were educators, and the great teachers were leaders.

Populism was short-lived as a third-party movement. In the South, Tom Watson's interracial coalition collapsed when conservative whites accused it of undermining white supremacy. On the national level, the Democrats stole much of the Populists' appeal when they nominated William Jennings Bryan, a reformer and a westerner, for president in the campaign of 1896. Amid bickering and grumbling, the Populists "fused" with the Democrats that year, and both organizations went down to defeat in an election that brought Republican William McKinley to power. For the Populists, the election was a disaster from which the party never recovered. "Never again," writes one historian, "would American farmers unite so militantly to demand economic reform. And never again would so large a group of Americans raise so forceful a protest against the nature of the industrial economy."

Even so, populism had a lasting effect on American politics. It helped usher in a new era of reform in the United States, the Progressive era, which will be treated in subsequent selections. During the Progressive era, many Populist demands became politically respectable and were enacted into law. Among these were a graduated income tax, a managed currency, a lower tariff, and the direct election of United States senators. The New Deal of the 1930s, moreover, adopted and modified Populist proposals for a crop storage system and agricultural credit.

Many historians contend that populism influenced later political movements, such as Huey Long's in the 1930s and George Wallace's in the 1960s. Even today there are politicians who call themselves populists, or who are so labeled. David Duke, Louisiana politico and former head of the Ku Klux Klan, has been called a populist. So have Jesse Jackson and Ronald Reagan. But in "The Party of the People" (American Heritage, *May/June 1992), historian Bernard Weisberger warns that the term is misused when applied indiscriminately to modern politicians and modern political attitudes. Stressing "the importance of historical context" and accuracy, Weisberger insists that the term* populism *be confined to the insurgent farmers of the 1890s, who gave the word its original meaning.*

QUESTIONS TO CONSIDER

1. What problems plagued American farmers in the late nineteenth century? How did this situation contrast with the traditional ideal of the farmer's role in the American republic? How did it compare with the conditions of American labor that you saw in selection 6?

2. Discuss the early farmers' alliances. How did they work and spread their message? What did they hope to accomplish? Where were they most successful?

3. When the farmers decided to organize politically on the state level, why did they choose to form a third party rather than join one of the two major parties? How were they treated by the Republicans and Democrats? What particular obstacles did they face in the South? How did Tom Watson appeal to southern farmers? How did he fare politically and why?

4. What were the basic principles of the national People's Party? What issues did it not address? How did the party fare in its first election in 1892?

5. What were the different conceptions of liberty held by capital, labor, and farmers? What does Burns mean when he says that more than anything else the farmers' alliance "had made liberty into a positive idea"? How does the populist movement compare with the development of the labor movement you read about in selection 6? Why do you think they were so different?

America's First Southeast Asian War: The Philippine Insurrection

DAVID R. KOHLER AND JAMES W. WENSYEL

The last quarter of the nineteenth century marked the second age of imperialism, a time when the industrial nations of Europe — Britain, Germany, France, Holland, and Russia — claimed colonies in Africa and spheres of influence in distant China. The United States, flexing its imperial muscles in the 1890s, was also alive with "aggressive, expansionistic, and jingoistic" sentiments. In 1893, with the help of 150 marines from a United States cruiser, American residents in Hawaii deposed the queen of the islands, set up a provisional government, and clamored for annexation. In 1898, the United States formally annexed Hawaii, thus expanding American territory and interests in the Pacific. In 1898–1899, the United States gained additional Pacific possessions in a controversial war with Spain, by then a second-rate power whose old empire in the Americas had all but disintegrated.

American expansionists, cheered on by a truculent yellow press, did not cause the war with Spain. But American policymakers and business leaders did use it as a means to extend American economic and political power. The war itself grew out of deplorable conditions in Cuba, caused by decades of Spanish misrule. A series of Cuban revolts and Spanish atrocities, which the American press exaggerated, aroused Americans' sympathy for the Cubans, whose cause seemed identical to that of the American patriots in 1776. In February 1898, American sentiment turned to outrage when the United States battleship Maine blew up in Havana harbor, killing 260 American sailors. The cause of the explosion was never established, but American expansionists — among them, Assistant

Secretary of the Navy Theodore Roosevelt — blamed Spain and demanded war. Over-
night a slogan caught the imagination of the country: "Remember the Maine! To hell
with Spain!"

In March, President William McKinley demanded that Spain agree to negotiations
that would grant independence to Cuba. Faced with the possibility of a disastrous war in
a distant hemisphere, Spain tried to maneuver, declaring an armistice with Cuban insur-
gents but hedging on Cuban independence. By then, both President McKinley and Con-
gress were prepared for war. When Congress adopted a resolution recognizing Cuban
independence, Spain retaliated by declaring war on the United States; the next day,
Congress responded in kind.

Less than a week later, the American Asiatic Squadron under Commodore George
Dewey won a dazzling victory in Manila Bay in the Spanish-held Philippines. As it
turned out, the navy's Roosevelt had secured the command for Dewey and had directed
him to prepare for action two months before official hostilities commenced. The United
States also invaded Cuba, where Teddy Roosevelt gained national fame as colonel of the
Rough Riders. After ten weeks of fighting, Spain capitulated, giving up control of Cuba
and surrendering Puerto Rico, Guam, and the Philippines to the United States. For
Secretary of State John Hay, it had been "a splendid little war."

Much has been written about the Spanish-American War and the United States empire
that emerged from it. Much less is known about an important offshoot of that war — an
American military campaign against Philippine insurgents that lasted three years, involved
126,000 United States troops, and resulted in 7,000 American and some 216,000
Filipino casualties. The United States learned a number of hard lessons about fighting
against nationalist insurgents in distant Asian jungles, but sixty years later another gen-
eration of Americans forgot those lessons when plunging into a similar conflict in Vietnam.
In the selection that follows, David R. Kohler, a naval special warfare officer, and James
W. Wensyel, a retired army officer and the author of several books, narrate American
involvement in the Filipino insurrection, 1898–1902, showing how it grew out of the
Spanish-American War and the American bid for empire. The authors point out the
influence of the Indian wars on American tactics in the Philippines, and they draw several
significant parallels between the Philippine conflict and America's involvement in Viet-
nam. It was the Philippine conflict that generated strategic hamlets, free-fire zones,
and search-and-destroy *missions — terms that were later seared into the history of*
American involvement in Vietnam. You will find it instructive to read and discuss this
selection in connection with George C. Herring's account of Vietnam (selection 24). In
what ways were the two conflicts alike and in what ways did they differ? As experienced
military men, Kohler and Wensyel contend that future American leaders should ponder the
lessons of the Philippine and Vietnamese conflicts before embarking on similar adventures.

GLOSSARY

AGUINALDO Y FAMY, GENERALISSIMO EMILIO   Commander of the Filipino nationalists who fought the Spaniards and then the Americans in an effort to achieve Philippine independence.

BOLO KNIFE   This sharp-edged instrument was the Filipino revolutionary's main weapon.

DEWEY, COMMODORE GEORGE   Commander of the American Asiatic Squadron, which sank the Spanish fleet in the Battle of Manila Bay.

GRAYSON, WILLIAM "WILLIE" WALTER   The Philippine insurrection began when he and his fellow soldiers seized Filipino nationalists within their picket line and firing broke out between the American and Filipino camps.

GUERRILLA WARFARE   Like the Vietcong and North Vietnamese sixty years later, the Filipinos eschewed conventional, Western-style warfare of pitched battles and dispersed throughout the countryside conducting "hit-and-run operations by small bands."

MACABEBES   Filipino mercenaries from Luzon province who fought for Spain and the United States against their own countrymen.

MacARTHUR, GENERAL ARTHUR   Assuming command of United States forces in 1900, he initiated new tactics designed to isolate the Filipino guerrillas from the villages that supported them; his tactics gave rise to strategic hamlets, free-fire zones, and search-and-destroy operations.

MAHAN, ADMIRAL ALFRED THAYER   United States naval strategist who contended that sea power and overseas colonies were the keys to national power; his writings greatly influenced American imperialists such as Teddy Roosevelt and Henry Cabot Lodge.

MERRITT, MAJOR GENERAL WESLEY   Commanded the United States Philippine Expeditionary Force, sent to oust the Spaniards from the islands.

SANTAYANA, GEORGE   Spanish-born philosopher, poet, and educator who observed that those who do not learn from the mistakes of the past are doomed to repeat them.

SMITH, BRIGADIER GENERAL JACOB W. "HELL ROARING JAKE"   Veteran of the Wounded Knee Sioux massacre of 1890; when the insurgents on Samar Island massacred fifty-nine American soldiers, "Hell Roaring" Smith ordered his men to burn and kill their way across the island in retaliation.

TAFT, WILLIAM HOWARD   Headed a United States civilian commission that took over the Philippine colonial government in 1901.

USS MAINE   The mysterious sinking of this American battleship was the catalyst of the Spanish-American War.

"WATER CURE"   American method of torture devised in retaliation for Filipino acts of terrorism (booby traps and assassination); a bamboo reed was placed in an insurgent's mouth, and water, often salted or dirty, was poured down his throat until he was so painfully bloated that he talked.

"WHITE MAN'S BURDEN"   Racist concept, popular among American imperialists, that whites had a "moral responsibility" to uplift and civilize supposedly inferior dark-skinned people such as the Filipinos.

Guerrilla warfare . . . jungle terrain . . . search and destroy missions . . . benevolent pacification . . . strategic hamlets . . . terrorism . . . ambushes . . . free-fire zones . . . booby traps . . . waning support from civilians at home. These words call forth from the national consciousness uncomfortable images of a war Americans fought and died in not long ago in Southeast Asia. But while the phrases may first bring to mind America's painful experience in Vietnam during the 1960s and '70s, they also aptly describe a much earlier conflict — the Philippine Insurrection — that foreshadowed this and other insurgent wars in Asia.

The Philippine-American War of 1898–1902 is one of our nation's most obscure and least-understood campaigns. Sometimes called the "Bolo War" because of the Filipino insurgents' lethally effective use of razor-sharp bolo knives or machetes against the American expeditionary force occupying the islands, it is often viewed as a mere appendage of the one-hundred-day Spanish-American War. But suppressing the guerrilla warfare waged by Philippine nationalists seeking self-rule proved far more difficult, protracted, and costly for American forces than the conventional war with Spain that had preceded it.

America's campaign to smash the Philippine Insurrection was, ironically, a direct consequence of U.S. efforts to secure independence for other *insurrectos* halfway around the world in Cuba. On May 1, 1898, less than a week after Congress declared war against Spain, a naval squadron commanded by Commodore George Dewey steamed into Manila Bay to engage the Spanish warships defending that nation's Pacific possession. In a brief action Dewey achieved a stunning victory, sinking all of the enemy vessels with no significant American losses. Destroying the Spanish fleet, however, did not ensure U.S. possession of the Philippines. An estimated 15,000 Spanish soldiers still occupied Manila and the surrounding region. Those forces would have to be rooted out by infantry.

President William McKinley had already ordered a Philippine Expeditionary Force of volunteer and regular army infantry, artillery, and cavalry units (nearly seven thousand men), under the command of Major General Wesley Merritt, to "reduce Spanish power in that quarter [Philippine Islands] and give order and security to the islands while in the possession of the United States."

Sent to the Philippines in the summer of 1898, this limited force was committed without fully considering the operation's potential length and cost. American military and government leaders also failed to anticipate the consequences of ignoring the Filipino rebels who, under Generalissimo Don Emilio Aguinaldo y Famy, had been waging a war for independence against Spain for the past two years. And when American insensitivity toward Aguinaldo eventually led to open warfare with the rebels, the American leaders grossly underestimated the determination of the seemingly ill-trained and poorly armed insurgents. They additionally failed to perceive the difficulties involved in conducting military operations in a tropical environment and among a hostile native population, and they did not recognize the burden of fighting at the end of a seven-thousand-mile-long logistics trail.

Asian engagements, the Americans learned for the first time, are costly. The enterprise, so modestly begun, eventually saw more than 126,000 American officers and men deployed to the Philippines. Four times as many soldiers served in this undeclared war in the Pacific as had been sent to the Caribbean during the Spanish-American War. During the three-year conflict, American troops and Filipino insurgents fought in more than 2,800 engagements. American casualties ultimately totaled 4,234 killed and 2,818 wounded, and the insurgents lost about 16,000 men.

From David R. Kohler and James W. Wensyel, "Our First Southeast Asian War," *American History Illustrated* (January/February 1990), 19–30. Reprinted through the courtesy of Cowles Magazines, publisher of *American History*.

The civilian population suffered even more; as many as 200,000 Filipinos died from famine, pestilence, or the unfortunate happenstance of being too close to the fighting. The Philippine war cost the United States $600 million before the insurgents were subdued.

The costly experience offered valuable and timeless lessons about guerrilla warfare in Asia; unfortunately, those lessons had to be relearned sixty years later in another war that, despite the modern technology involved, bore surprising parallels to America's first Southeast Asian campaign.

☆

ORIGINS

America's war with Spain, formally declared by the United States on April 25, 1898, had been several years in the making. During that time the American "yellow press," led by Joseph Pulitzer's *New York World* and William Randolph Hearst's *New York Journal,* trumpeted reports of heroic Cuban *insurrectos* revolting against their cruel Spanish rulers. Journalists vividly described harsh measures taken by Spanish officials to quell the Cuban revolution. The sensational accounts, often exaggerated, reminded Americans of their own uphill fight for independence and nourished the feeling that America was destined to intervene so that the Cuban people might also taste freedom.

Furthermore, expansionists suggested that the revolt against a European power, taking place less than one hundred miles from American shores, offered a splendid opportunity to turn the Caribbean into an American sea. Businessmen pointed out that $50 million in American capital was invested in the Cuban sugar and mining industries. Revolutions resulting in burned cane fields jeopardized that investment. As 1898 opened, American relations with Spain quickly declined.

In January 1898 the U.S. battleship *Maine* was sent to Cuba, ostensibly on a courtesy visit. On February 15 the warship was destroyed by a mysterious explosion while at anchor in Havana harbor, killing 262 of her 350-man crew. The navy's formal inquiry, completed on March 28, suggested that the explosion was due to an external force — a mine.

On March 29, the Spanish government received an ultimatum from Washington, D.C.: Spain's army in Cuba was to lay down its arms while the United States negotiated between the rebels and the Spaniards. The Spanish forces were also told to abolish all *reconcentrado* camps (tightly controlled areas, similar to the strategic hamlets later tried in Vietnam, where peasants were regrouped to deny food and intelligence to insurgents and to promote tighter security). Spain initially rejected the humiliation of surrendering its arms in the field but then capitulated on all points. The Americans were not satisfied.

On April 11, declaring that Spanish responses were inadequate, President McKinley told a joint session of Congress that "I have exhausted every effort to relieve the intolerable condition . . . at our doors. I now ask the Congress to empower the president to take measures to secure a full and final termination of hostilities in Cuba, to secure . . . the establishment of a stable government, and to use the military and naval forces of the United States . . . for these purposes. . . ."

Congress adopted the proposed resolution on April 19. Learning this, Spain declared war on the 24th. The following day, the United States responded with its own declaration of war.

The bulk of the American navy quickly gathered on the Atlantic coast. McKinley called for 125,000 volunteers to bolster the less than eighty-thousand-man regular army. His call was quickly oversubscribed; volunteers fought to be the first to land on Cuba's beaches.

The first major battle of the war, however, was fought not in Cuba but seven thousand miles to the west — in Manila Bay. Dewey's victory over Spanish

Admiral Patricio Montojo y Pasarón (a rather hollow victory as Montojo's fleet consisted of seven unarmored ships, three of which had wooden hulls and one that had to be towed to the battle area) was wildly acclaimed in America.

American leaders, believing that the Philippines would now fall into America's grasp like a ripe plum, had to decide what to do with their prize. They could not return the islands to Spain, nor could they allow them to pass to France or Germany, America's commercial rivals in the Orient. The American press rejected the idea of a British protectorate. And, after four hundred years of despotic Spanish rule in which Filipinos had little or no chance to practice self-government, native leaders seemed unlikely candidates for managing their own affairs. McKinley faced a grand opportunity for imperialistic expansion that could not be ignored.

The debate sharply divided his cabinet — and the country. American public opinion over acquisition of the Philippines divided into two basic factions: imperialists versus anti-imperialists.

The imperialists, mostly Republicans, included such figures as Theodore Roosevelt (then assistant secretary of the navy), Henry Cabot Lodge (Massachusetts senator), and Albert Beveridge (Indiana senator). These individuals were, for the most part, disciples of Alfred Thayer Mahan, a naval strategist who touted theories of national power and prestige through sea power and acquisition of overseas colonies for trade purposes and naval coaling stations.

The anti-imperialists, staunchly against American annexation of the Philippines, were mainly Democrats. Such men as former presidents Grover Cleveland and Rutherford B. Hayes, steel magnate Andrew Carnegie, William Jennings Bryan, union leader Samuel Gompers, and Mark Twain warned that by taking the Philippines the United States would march the road to ruin earlier traveled by the Roman Empire. Furthermore, they argued, America would be denying Filipinos the right of self-determination guaran-

teed by our own Constitution. The more practical-minded also pointed out that imperialistic policy would require maintaining an expensive army and navy there.

Racism, though demonstrated in different ways, pervaded the arguments of both sides. Imperialists spoke of the "white man's burden" and moral responsibility to "uplift the child races everywhere" and to provide "orderly development for the unfortunate and less able races." They spoke of America's "civilizing mission" of pacifying Filipinos by "benevolent assimilation" and saw the opening of the overseas frontier much as their forefathers had viewed the western frontier. The "subjugation of the Injun" (wherever he might be found) was a concept grasped by American youth — the war's most enthusiastic supporters (in contrast to young America's opposition to the war in Vietnam many years later).

The anti-imperialists extolled the sacredness of independence and self-determination for the Filipinos. Racism, however, also crept into their argument, for they believed that "protection against race mingling" was a historic American policy that would be reversed by imperialism. To them, annexation of the Philippines would admit "alien, inferior, and mongrel races to our nationality."

As the debate raged, Dewey continued to hold Manila Bay, and the Philippines seemed to await America's pleasure. President McKinley would ultimately cast the deciding vote in determining America's role in that country. McKinley, a genial, rather laid-back, former congressman from Ohio and one-time major in the Union army, remains a rather ambiguous figure during this period. In his Inaugural Address he had affirmed that "We want no wars of conquest; we must avoid the temptation of territorial aggression." Thereafter, however, he made few comments on pacifism, and, fourteen weeks after becoming president, signed the bill annexing Hawaii.

Speaking of Cuba in December 1897, McKinley said, "I speak not of forcible annexation, for that cannot be thought of. That, by our code of morality, would be criminal aggression." Nevertheless, he constantly pressured Madrid to end Spanish rule in Cuba, leading four months later to America's war with Spain.

McKinley described experiencing extreme turmoil, soul-searching, and prayer over the Philippine annexation issue until, he declared, one night in a dream the Lord revealed to him that "there was nothing left for us to do but to take them all [the Philippine Islands] and to educate the Filipinos, and uplift, and civilize, and Christianize them." He apparently didn't realize that the Philippines had been staunchly Roman Catholic for more than 350 years under Spanish colonialism. Nor could he anticipate the difficulties that, having cast its fortune with the expansionists, America would now face in the Philippines.

☆

PROSECUTING THE WAR

Meanwhile, in the Philippine Islands, Major General Wesley Merritt's Philippine Expeditionary Force went about its job. In late June, General Thomas Anderson led an advance party ashore at Cavite. He then established Camp Merritt, visited General Aguinaldo's rebel forces entrenched around Manila, and made plans for seizing that city once Merritt arrived with the main body of armed forces.

Anderson quickly learned that military operations in the Philippines could be difficult. His soldiers, hastily assembled and dispatched with limited prior training, were poorly disciplined and inadequately equipped. Many still wore woolen uniforms despite the tropical climate. A staff officer described the army's baptism at Manila: " . . . the heat was oppressive and the rain kept falling. At times the trenches were filled with two feet of water, and soon the men's shoes were ruined. Their heavy khaki uniforms were a nuisance; they perspired constantly, the loss of body salts inducing chronic fatigue. Prickly heat broke out,

inflamed by scratching and rubbing. Within a week the first cases of dysentery, malaria, cholera, and dengue fever showed up at sick call."

During his first meeting with Dewey, Anderson remarked that some American leaders were considering annexation of the Philippines. "If the United States intends to hold the Philippine Islands," Dewey responded, "it will make things awkward, because just a week ago Aguinaldo proclaimed the independence of the Philippine Islands from Spain and seems intent on establishing his own government."

A Filipino independence movement led by Aguinaldo had been active in the islands since 1896 and, within weeks of Dewey's victory, Aguinaldo's revolutionaries controlled most of the archipelago.

Aguinaldo, twenty-nine years old in 1898, had taken over his father's position as mayor of his hometown of Kawit before becoming a revolutionary. In a minor skirmish with Spanish soldiers, he had rallied the Filipinos to victory. Thereafter, his popularity grew as did his ragtag but determined army. Aguinaldo was slight of build, shy, and soft-spoken, but a strict disciplinarian.

As his rebel force besieged Manila, Aguinaldo declared a formal government for the Philippines with himself as president and generalissimo. He proclaimed his "nation's" independence and called for Filipinos to rally to his army and to the Americans, declaring that "the Americans . . . extend their protecting mantle to our beloved country . . . When you see the American flag flying, assemble in numbers: they are our redeemers!" But his enthusiasm for the United States later waned.

Merritt put off Aguinaldo's increasingly strident demands that America recognize his government and guarantee the Filipinos' independence. Aguinaldo perceived the American general's attitude as condescending and demeaning.

On August 13, Merritt's forces occupied Manila almost without firing a shot; in a face-saving maneuver the Spanish defenders had agreed to surrender to the Americans to avoid being captured — and perhaps massacred — by the Filipino insurgents. Merritt's troops physically blocked Aguinaldo's rebels, who had spent weeks in the trenches around the city, from participating in the assault. The Filipino general and his followers felt betrayed at being denied a share in the victory.

Further disenchanted, Aguinaldo would later find his revolutionary government unrepresented at the Paris peace talks determining his country's fate. He would learn that Spain had ceded the Philippines to the United States for $20 million.

Officers at Merritt's headquarters had little faith in the Filipinos' ability to govern themselves. "Should our power . . . be withdrawn," an early report declared, "the Philippines would speedily lapse into anarchy, which would excuse . . . the intervention of other powers and the division of the islands among them."

Meanwhile, friction between American soldiers and the Filipinos increased. Much of the Americans' conduct betrayed their racial bias. Soldiers referred to the natives as "niggers" and "gugus," epithets whose meanings were clear to the Filipinos. In retaliation, the island inhabitants refused to give way on sidewalks and muscled American officers into the streets. Men of the expeditionary force in turn escalated tensions by stopping Filipinos at gun point, searching them without cause, "confiscating" shopkeepers' goods, and beating those who resisted.

On the night of February 4, 1899, the simmering pot finally boiled over. Private William "Willie" Walter Grayson and several other soldiers of Company D, 1st Nebraska Volunteer Infantry, apprehended a group of armed insurgents within their regimental picket line. Shots were exchanged, and three Filipino *insurrectos* fell dead. Heavy firing erupted between the two camps.

In the bloody battle that followed, the Filipinos suffered tremendous casualties (an estimated two thousand to five thousand dead, contrasted with fifty-nine Americans killed) and were forced to withdraw. The Philippine Insurrection had begun.

☆

GUERRILLA WARFARE

The Americans, hampered by a shortage of troops and the oncoming rainy season, could initially do little more than extend their defensive perimeter beyond Manila and establish a toehold on several islands to the south. By the end of March, however, American forces seized Malolos, the seat of Aguinaldo's revolutionary government. But Aguinaldo escaped, simply melting into the jungle. In the fall, using conventional methods of warfare, the Americans first struck south, then north of Manila across the central Luzon plain. After hard marching and tough fighting, the expeditionary force occupied northern Luzon, dispersed the rebel army, and barely missed capturing Aguinaldo.

Believing that occupying the remainder of the Philippines would be easy, the Americans wrongly concluded that the war was virtually ended. But when the troops attempted to control the territory they had seized, they found that the Filipino revolutionaries were not defeated but had merely changed strategies. Abandoning western-style conventional warfare, Aguinaldo had decided to adopt guerrilla tactics.

Aguinaldo moved to a secret mountain headquarters at Palanan in northern Luzon, ordering his troops to disperse and avoid pitched battles in favor of hit-and-run operations by small bands. Ambushing parties of Americans and applying terror to coerce support from other Filipinos, the insurrectionists now blended into the countryside, where they enjoyed superior intelligence information, ample supplies, and tight security. The guerrillas moved freely between the scattered American units, cutting telegraph lines, attacking supply trains, and assaulting straggling infantrymen. When the Americans pursued their tormentors, they fell into well planned ambushes. The insurgents' barbarity and ruthlessness during these attacks were notorious.

The guerrilla tactics helped to offset the inequities

U.S. troops sent to the Philippines found the tropical climate and terrain "almost as deadly as combat." The first contingent of soldiers arrived wearing woolen uniforms. Thousands of Americans fell victim to dysentery and malaria. (Keystone-Mast Collection, California Museum of Photography, University of California, Riverside)

that existed between the two armies. The American troops were far better armed, for example, carrying .45-caliber Springfield single-shot rifles, Mausers, and then-modern .30-caliber repeating Krag-Jorgensen rifles. They also had field artillery and machine guns. The revolutionaries, on the other hand, were limited to a miscellaneous assortment of handguns, a few Mauser repeating rifles taken from the Spanish, and antique muzzle-loaders. The sharp-edged bolo knife was the revolutionary's primary weapon, and he used it well. Probably more American soldiers were hacked to death by bolos than were killed by Mauser bullets.

As would later be the case in Vietnam, the guerrillas had some clear advantages. They knew the terrain, were inured to the climate, and could generally count on a friendly population. As in Vietnam, villages controlled by the insurgents provided havens from which the guerrillas could attack, then fade back into hiding.

Americans soon began to feel that they were under siege in a land of enemies, and their fears were heightened because they never could be sure who among the population was hostile. A seemingly friendly peasant might actually be a murderer. Lieutenant Colonel J. T. Wickham, commanding the 26th Infantry Reg-

119

iment, recorded that "a large flag of truce enticed officers into ambushes . . . Privates Dugan, Hayes, and Tracy were murdered by town authorities . . . Private Nolan [was] tied up by ladies while in a stupor; the insurgents cut his throat . . . The body of Corporal Doneley was dug up, burned, and mutilated . . . Private O'Hearn, captured by apparently friendly people was tied to a tree, burned over a slow fire, and slashed up . . . Lieutenant Max Wagner was assassinated by insurgents disguised in American uniforms."

As in later guerrilla movements, such terrorism became a standard tactic for the insurgents. Both Filipinos and Americans were their victims. In preying on their countrymen, the guerrillas had a dual purpose: to discourage any Filipinos disposed to cooperate with the Americans, and to demonstrate to people in a particular region that they ruled that area and could destroy inhabitants and villages not supporting the revolution. The most favored terroristic weapon was assassination of local leaders, who were usually executed in a manner (such as beheading or burying alive) calculated to horrify everyone.

By the spring of 1900 the war was going badly for the Americans. Their task forces, sent out to search and destroy, found little and destroyed less.

The monsoon rains, jungle terrain, hostile native population, and a determined guerrilla force made the American soldiers' marches long and miserable. One described a five-week-long infantry operation: " . . . our troops had been on half rations for two weeks. Wallowing through hip-deep muck, lugging a ten-pound rifle and a belt . . . with 200 rounds of ammunition, drenched to the skin and with their feet becoming heavier with mud at every step, the infantry became discouraged. Some men simply cried, others slipped down in the mud and refused to rise. Threats and appeals by the officers were of no avail. Only a promise of food in the next town and the threat that if they remained behind they would be butchered by marauding bands of insurgents forced some to their feet to struggle on."

News reports of the army's difficulties began to erode the American public's support for the war. "To chase barefooted insurgents with water buffalo carts as a wagon train may be simply ridiculous," charged one correspondent, "but to load volunteers down with 200 rounds of ammunition and one day's rations, and to put on their heads felt hats used by no other army in the tropics . . . to trot these same soldiers in the boiling sun over a country without roads, is positively criminal. . . . There are over five thousand men in the general hospital."

Another reported that the American outlook "is blacker now than it has been since the beginning of the war . . . the whole population . . . sympathizes with the insurgents. The insurgents came to Pasig [a local area whose government cooperated with the Americans] and their first act was to hang the 'Presidente' for treason in surrendering to Americans. 'Presidentes' do not surrender to us anymore."

☆

NEW STRATEGIES

Early in the war U.S. military commanders had realized that, unlike the American Indians who had been herded onto reservations, eight million Filipinos (many of them hostile) would have to be governed in place. The Americans chose to emphasize pacification through good works rather than by harsh measures, hoping to convince Filipinos that the American colonial government had a sincere interest in their welfare and could be trusted.

As the army expanded its control across the islands, it reorganized local municipal governments and trained Filipinos to take over civil functions in the democratic political structure the Americans planned to establish. American soldiers performed police duties, distributed food, established and taught at schools, and built roads and telegraph lines.

As the war progressed, however, the U.S. commanders saw that the terrorism practiced by

Aguinaldo's guerrillas was far more effective in controlling the populace than was their own benevolent approach. Although the Americans did not abandon pacification through good works, it was thereafter subordinated to the "civilize 'em with a Krag" (Krag-Jorgensen rifle) philosophy. From December 1900 onward, captured revolutionaries faced deportation, imprisonment, or execution.

The American army also changed its combat strategy to counter that of its enemy. As in the insurgents' army, the new tactics emphasized mobility and surprise. Breaking into small units — the battalion became the largest maneuver force — the Americans gradually spread over the islands until each of the larger towns was occupied by one or two rifle companies. From these bases American troops began platoon- and company-size operations to pressure local guerrilla bands.

Because of the difficult terrain, limited visibility, and requirement for mobility, artillery now saw limited use except as a defensive weapon. The infantry became the main offensive arm, with mounted riflemen used to pursue the fleeing enemy. Cavalry patrols were so valued for their mobility that American military leaders hired trusted Filipinos as mounted scouts and cavalrymen.

The Americans made other efforts to "Filipinize" the war — letting Asians fight Asians. (A similar tactic had been used in the American Indian campaigns twenty years before; it would resurface in Vietnam sixty years later as "Vietnamization.") In the Philippines the Americans recruited five thousand Macabebes, mercenaries from the central Luzon province of Pampanga, to form the American officered Philippine Scouts. The Macabebes had for centuries fought in native battalions under the Spanish flag — even against their own countrymen when the revolution began in 1896.

Just as a later generation of American soldiers would react to the guerrilla war in Vietnam, American soldiers in the Philippines responded to insurgent terrorism in kind, matching cruelty with cruelty. Such actions vented their frustration at being unable to find and destroy the enemy. An increasing number of Americans viewed all Filipinos as enemies.

"We make everyone get into his house by 7 P.M. and we only tell a man once," Corporal Sam Gillis of the 1st California Volunteer Regiment wrote to his family. "If he refuses, we shoot him. We killed over 300 natives the first night. . . . If they fire a shot from a house, we burn the house and every house near it."

Another infantryman frankly admitted that "with an enemy like this to fight, it is not surprising that the boys should soon adopt 'no quarter' as a motto and fill the blacks full of lead before finding out whether they are friends or enemies."

That attitude should not have been too surprising. The army's campaigns against the Plains Indians were reference points for the generation of Americans that took the Philippines. Many of the senior officers and noncommissioned officers — often veterans of the Indian wars — considered Filipinos to be "as full of treachery as our Arizona Apache." "The country won't be pacified," one soldier told a reporter, "until the niggers are killed off like the Indians." A popular soldiers' refrain, sung to the tune of "Tramp, tramp, tramp, the boys are marching," began, "Damn, damn, damn the Filipinos," and again spoke of "civilizing 'em with a Krag."

Reprisals against civilians by Americans as well as insurgents became common. General Lloyd Wheaton, leading a U.S. offensive southeast of Manila, found his men impaled on the bamboo prongs of booby traps and with throats slit while they slept. After two of his companies were ambushed, Wheaton ordered that every town and village within twelve miles be burned.

The Americans developed their own terrorist methods, many of which would be used in later Southeast Asian wars. One was torturing suspected guerrillas or insurgent sympathizers to force them to reveal locations of other guerrillas and their supplies. An often-utilized form of persuasion was the "water cure," placing a bamboo reed in the victim's mouth and pouring water (some used salt water or dirty water) down his throat, thus painfully distending the victim's stomach. The subject, allowed to void this, would, under threat of repetition, usually talk freely. Another method of torture, the "rope cure," consisted of wrapping a rope around the victim's neck and torso until it formed a sort of girdle. A stick (or Krag rifle), placed between the ropes and twisted, then effectively created a combination of smothering and garroting.

The anti-imperialist press reported such American brutality in lurid detail. As a result, a number of officers and soldiers were court-martialed for torturing and other cruelties. Their punishments, however, seemed remarkably lenient. Of ten officers tried for "looting, torture, and murder," three were acquitted; of the seven convicted, five were reprimanded, one was reprimanded and fined $300, and one lost thirty-five places in the army's seniority list and forfeited half his pay for nine months.

Officers and soldiers, fighting a cruel, determined, and dangerous enemy, could not understand public condemnation of the brutality they felt was necessary to win. They had not experienced such criticism during the Indian wars, where total extermination of the enemy was condoned by the press and the American public, and they failed to grasp the difference now. Press reports, loss of public support, and the soldiers' feeling of betrayal — features of an insurgent war — would resurface decades later during the Vietnam conflict.

☆

SUCCESS

Although U.S. military leaders were frustrated by the guerrillas' determination on the one hand and by eroding American support for the war on the other, most believed that the insurgents could be subdued. Especially optimistic was General Arthur MacArthur, who in 1900 assumed command of the seventy thou-sand American troops in the Philippines. MacArthur adopted a strategy like that successfully used by General Zachary Taylor in the Second Seminole War in 1835; he believed that success depended upon the Americans' ability to isolate the guerrillas from their support in the villages. Thus were born "strategic hamlets," "free-fire zones," and "search and destroy" missions, concepts the American army would revive decades later in Vietnam.

MacArthur strengthened the more than five hundred small strong points held by Americans throughout the Philippine Islands. Each post was garrisoned by at least one company of American infantrymen. The natives around each base were driven from their homes, which were then destroyed. Soldiers herded the displaced natives into *reconcentrado* camps, where they could be "protected" by the nearby garrisons. Crops, food stores, and houses outside the camps were destroyed to deny them to the guerrillas. Surrounding each camp was a "dead line," within which anyone appearing would be shot on sight.

Operating from these small garrisons, the Americans pressured the guerrillas, allowing them no rest. Kept off balance, short of supplies, and constantly pursued by the American army, the Filipino guerrillas, suffering from sickness, hunger, and dwindling popular support, began to lose their will to fight. Many insurgent leaders surrendered, signaling that the tide at last had turned in the Americans' favor.

In March 1901, a group of Macabebe Scouts, commanded by American Colonel Frederick "Fighting Fred" Funston, captured Aguinaldo. Aguinaldo's subsequent proclamation that he would fight no more, and his pledge of loyalty to the United States, sped the collapse of the insurrection.

As in the past, and as would happen again during the Vietnam conflict of the 1960s and '70s, American optimism was premature. Although a civilian commission headed by William H. Taft took control of the colonial government from the American army in July 1901, the army faced more bitter fighting in its "pacification" of the islands.

As the war sputtered, the insurgents' massacre of fifty-nine American soldiers at Balangiga on the island of Samar caused Brigadier General Jacob W. "Hell-Roaring Jake" Smith, veteran of the Wounded Knee massacre of the Sioux in 1890, to order his officers to turn Samar into a "howling wilderness." His orders to a battalion of three hundred Marines headed for Samar were precise: "I want no prisoners. I wish you to kill and burn, the more you kill and burn the better it will please me. I want all persons killed who are capable of bearing arms against the United States." Fortunately, the Marines did not take Smith's orders literally and, later, Smith would be court-martialed.

On July 4, 1902, the Philippine Insurrection officially ended. Although it took the American army another eleven years to crush the fierce Moros of the southern Philippines, the civil government's security force (the Philippine Constabulary), aided by the army's Philippine Scouts, maintained a fitful peace throughout the islands. The army's campaign to secure the Philippines as an American colony had succeeded.

American commanders would have experienced vastly greater difficulties except for two distinct advantages: 1) the enemy had to operate in a restricted area, in isolated islands, and was prevented by the U.S. Navy from importing weapons and other needed supplies; and 2) though the insurgents attempted to enlist help from Japan, no outside power intervened. These conditions would not prevail in some subsequent guerrilla conflicts in Asia.

In addition to the many tactical lessons the army learned from fighting a guerrilla war in a tropical climate, other problems experienced during this campaign validated the need for several military reforms that were subsequently carried out, including improved logistics, tropical medicine, and communications.

The combination of harsh and unrelenting military force against the guerrillas, complemented by the exercise of fair and equitable civil government and civic action toward those who cooperated,

proved to be the Americans' most effective tactic for dealing with the insurgency. This probably was the most significant lesson to be learned from the Philippine Insurrection.

☆

LESSONS FOR THE FUTURE

Vietnam veterans reading this account might nod in recollection of a personal, perhaps painful experience from their own war.

Many similarities exist between America's three-year struggle with the Filipino *insurrectos* and the decade-long campaign against the Communists in Vietnam. Both wars, modestly begun, went far beyond what anyone had foreseen in time, money, equipment, manpower, casualties, and suffering.

Both wars featured small-unit infantry actions. Young infantrymen, if they had any initial enthusiasm, usually lost it once they saw the war's true nature; they nevertheless learned to endure their allotted time while adopting personal self-survival measures as months "in-country" lengthened and casualty lists grew.

Both wars were harsh, brutal, cruel. Both had their Samar Islands and their My Lais. Human nature being what it is, both conflicts also included acts of great heroism, kindness, compassion, and self-sacrifice.

Both wars saw an increasingly disenchanted American public withdrawing its support (and even disavowing its servicemen) as the campaigns dragged on, casualties mounted, and news accounts vividly described the horror of the battlefields.

Some useful lessons might be gleaned from a comparison of the two conflicts. Human nature really does not change — war will bring out the best and the worst in the tired, wet, hungry, and fearful men who are doing the fighting. Guerrilla campaigns — particularly where local military and civic reforms cannot be effected to separate the guerrilla from his base of popular support — will be long and difficult, and will demand tremendous commitments in resources and national will. Finally, before America commits its armed forces to similar ventures in the future, it would do well to recall the lessons learned from previous campaigns. For, as the Spanish-born American educator, poet, and philosopher George Santayana reminded us, those who do not learn from the past are doomed to repeat it.

QUESTIONS TO CONSIDER

1. How and why did the United States initially become involved in the Philippines? What, according to the authors, were the fundamental mistakes committed by the Americans in making that decision?

2. Why did the Americans decide to take over the Philippines? What were the different categories of American public opinion in reaction to this development? How were they different, and what attitudes did they share?

3. What military advantages did the Philippine insurgents have? What were American military tactics and goals, and how did they change in response to the conditions of the Philippine conflict?

4. How does the conflict in the Philippines compare with the Indian wars that preceded it and with the later war in Vietnam? In particular, how did the American public and American soldiers differ in comparing the Philippine conflict with the Indian wars, and what were the results and significance of this difference?

5. What, according to the authors, are the lessons to be learned from our involvement in the Philippines? Have they been learned?

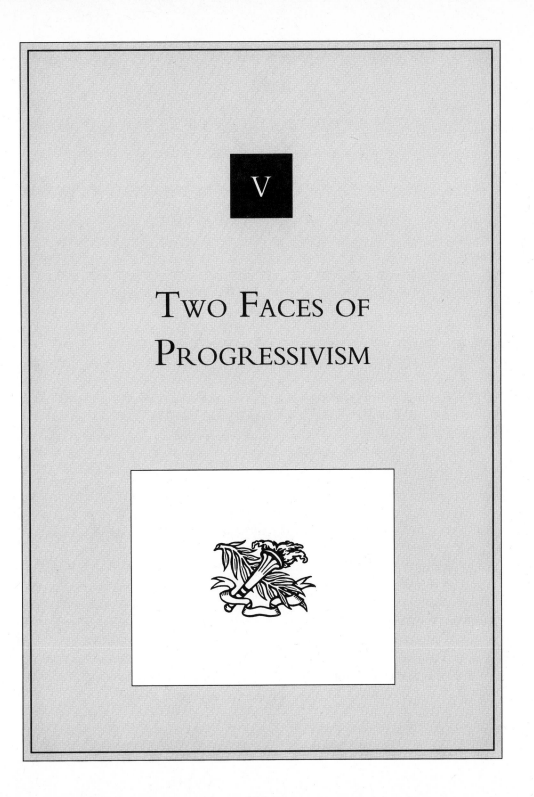

V

TWO FACES OF PROGRESSIVISM

10

Theodore Roosevelt:
Cyclone in the White House

EDMUND MORRIS

Despite a long, enervating depression, American industry continued to expand and con-solidate throughout the 1890s, and the rate of expansion was even faster in the first decade of the twentieth century. By then, economic concentration had resulted in a handful of giant combinations that were dominating each area of industrial activity. In 1909, 1 percent of American business enterprises produced 44 percent of the nation's manufactured goods. Money and property were so maldistributed that 1 percent of the United States population — the corporate magnates and their families — owned seven-eighths of the country's wealth. Middle-class families were getting by, although precariously. And the rest — industrial workers in America's teeming, dilapidated cities and debtor farmers in the South and West—lived in poverty.

The Populist movement, as we have seen, posed the first serious challenge to the new industrial order and the corporate bosses who controlled it. The Populist insurgents made thousands aware of the need for reform — the need to correct the abuses of industrial monopolies and to protect the mass of the nation's people. So did liberal intellectuals and crusading journalists — the celebrated muckrakers who exposed glaring malpractices in business and in municipal governments. Thanks to these men and women, thanks to tensions caused by rapid and unmanaged industrial growth, and thanks to a genuine desire to revive humanitarian democracy, there emerged the complex Progressive movement, which lasted from the late 1890s through the First World War. For the most part, those who joined the ranks of progressivism were victims of monopolies and were anxious to dismantle the biggest of them and control the rest.

Progressivism transcended party labels, as Democrats and Republicans alike took up the banners of reform. In the Democratic party, William Jennings Bryan crusaded against the conservative Republican–big business alliance that ran the country; later Bryan passed the leadership of Democratic progressivism to Woodrow Wilson, the subject of a subsequent selection. In the Republican party, "Fighting Bob" La Folette, governor of Wisconsin, made his state a model of progressivism. But the best-known Progressive Republican was the man who found himself elevated to the White House when an assassin murdered William McKinley in 1901. "Now look!" exclaimed a horrified Republican. "That damned cowboy is president of the United States."

That damned cowboy, of course, was Theodore Roosevelt, a whirlwind of a man whose motto was "Get action, do things; be sane, don't fritter away your time; create, act, take a place wherever you are and be somebody: get action." Get action he did, as he hunted big game on three continents, sparred with prizefighters, rode with cowboys, dashed off voluminous histories, knocked down a tough in a western saloon, led the celebrated Rough Riders during the Spanish-American War, terrorized a police force, ran the Empire State as governor, and rose to the nation's highest office. Never mind that he was an accidental president. Once in the presidency, he put on a performance — for surely that is the word for it — that held the nation spellbound.

What president since the Civil War had had such uninhibited gusto, such a sense of the dramatic? He conducted a vigorous foreign policy that made the United States a major presence in the world. He dispatched a fleet of white battleships around the globe and won a Nobel Peace Prize for mediating the Russo-Japanese War. In this hemisphere, he rattled the Monroe Doctrine, ordered American troops to Santo Domingo, stationed marines in Cuba, encouraged a revolution against the Republic of Colombia that established the new nation of Panama, and then acquired the rights to build a canal there that would furnish America with a lifeline to the Pacific. Roosevelt's actions in Panama were provocative, even unethical, but he didn't care. As he said later, "If I had followed traditional conservative methods I would have submitted a dignified state paper of probably two hundred pages to the Congress and the debate would be going on yet, but I took the Canal Zone and let the Congress debate, and while the debate goes on, the canal does also."

He was just as vigorous in his domestic policy. He trumpeted the cause of conservation, sent troops to protect strikers in the Pennsylvania coal mines, and thundered so violently against "the malefactors of great wealth" and "the criminal rich" that conservative Republicans were appalled. The first post–Civil War president to recognize the threat of monopolies and trusts to America's economic life, TR shook his fist in the face of banker J. Pierpont Morgan, and his attorney general initiated more antitrust suits than all previous *attorneys general combined. As a result, TR won a reputation as a crusading "trust buster." In point of fact, he accepted business consolidation as an economic reality in America and, instead of crushing all business combinations, established a policy of government scrutiny and control. Thus, he attacked only "bad" or "evil" trusts and left the "good" ones alone. Indeed, as one scholar put it, "the first great wave of business consolidation" actually came to a climax during Roosevelt's presidency.*

Behind Roosevelt's actions was a volatile personality that kept his legions of followers enthralled. And that personality, full of contradiction, of great charm and physical exuberance, of egotistical moralizing and militarism, fairly explodes off the pages that follow. In them, TR's Pulitzer Prize–winning biographer, Edmund Morris, makes us aware of the importance of personal qualities in shaping the conduct and careers of historical figures. As you read this spirited portrait, you may not always like Theodore Roosevelt, but you will never find him boring.

GLOSSARY

HANNA, MARK   Chairman of the Republican National Committee who aspired to take over the White House after TR had finished his "caretaker" term.

LIVINGSTONE, ROBERT   Journalist who praised TR's great "gift of personal magnetism."

ROOSEVELT, ALICE LEE   TR's first wife who died of Bright's disease (kidney inflammation) on the same day that TR's mother died of typhoid fever.

ROOSEVELT, MARTHA BULLOCH "MITTIE"   TR's mother.

TEEDIE   TR's boyhood nickname.

WASHINGTON, BOOKER T.   The Head of Alabama's all-black Tuskegee Institute whom TR invited to dine at the White House; "it was the first time that a president had ever entertained a black man in the first house of the land," and it enraged southern white supremacists.

L et us dispose, in short order, with Theodore Roosevelt's faults. He was an incorrigible preacher of platitudes. . . . He significantly reduced the wildlife population of some three continents. He piled his dessert plate with so many peaches that the cream spilled over the sides. And he used to make rude faces out of the presidential carriage at small boys in the streets of Washington.

Now those last two faults are forgivable if we accept British diplomat Cecil Spring-Rice's advice, "You must always remember the President is about six." The first fault — his preachiness — is excused by the fact that the American electorate dearly loves a moralist. As to the second and most significant fault — Theodore Roosevelt's genuine blood-lust and desire to destroy his adversaries, whether they be rhinoceroses or members of the United States Senate — it is paradoxically so much a part of his virtues, both as a man and a politician, that I will come back to it in more detail later.

One of the minor irritations I have to contend with as a biographer is that whenever I go to the library to look for books about Roosevelt, Theodore, they infallibly are mixed up with books about Roosevelt, Franklin — and I guess FDR scholars have the same problem in reverse. Time was when the single word "Roosevelt" meant only Theodore; FDR himself frequently had to insist, in the early thirties, that he was not TR's son. He was merely a fifth cousin, and what was even more distant, a Democrat to boot. In time, of course, Franklin succeeded in preempting the early meaning of the word "Roosevelt," to the point that TR's public image, which once loomed as large as Washington's and Lincoln's, began to fade like a Cheshire cat from popular memory. By the time of FDR's own death in 1945, little was left but the ghost of a toothy grin.

Only a few veterans of the earlier Roosevelt era survived to testify that if Franklin was the greater politician, it was only by a hairsbreadth, and as far as sheer personality was concerned, Theodore's superiority could be measured in spades. They pointed out that FDR himself declared, late in life, that his "cousin Ted" was the greatest man he ever knew.

Presently the veterans too died. But that ghostly grin continued to float in the national consciousness, as if to indicate that its owner was meditating a reappearance. I first became aware of the power behind the grin in Washington, in February of 1976. The National Theater was trying out an ill-fated musical by Alan Lerner and Leonard Bernstein, *1600 Pennsylvania Avenue.* For two and a half hours Ken Howard worked his way through a chronological series of impersonations of historic Presidents. The audience sat on its hands, stiff with boredom, until the very end, when Mr. Howard clamped on a pair of pince-nez and a false mustache, and bared all his teeth in a grin. The entire theater burst into delighted applause.

From Edmund Morris, "Theodore Roosevelt, President," *American Heritage,* June/July 1981, Vol. 32, No. 4 © 1981 by Forbes Inc. Reprinted by permission of *American Heritage* Magazine, a division of Forbes, Inc.

What intrigued me was the fact that few people there could have known much about TR beyond the obvious clichés of San Juan Hill and the Big Stick. Yet somehow, subconsciously, they realized that here for once was a positive President, warm and tough and authoritative and funny, who believed in America and who, to quote Owen Wister, "grasped his optimism tight lest it escape him."

In [recent times] Theodore Roosevelt has made his long-promised comeback. He has been the subject of a *Newsweek* cover story on American heroes; Russell Baker has called him a cinch to carry all fifty states if he were running for the White House today; he's starring on Broadway in *Tintypes,* on television in *Bully,* and you'll . . . see him on the big screen in *Ragtime.* Every season brings a new crop of reassessments in the university presses, and as for the pulp mills, he figures largely in the latest installment of John Jakes's Kent Chronicles. No time like the present, therefore, to study that giant personality in color and fine detail.

When referring to Theodore Roosevelt I do not use the word "giant" loosely. "Every inch of him," said William Allen White, "was overengined." Lyman Gage likened him, mentally and physically, to two strong men combined; Gifford Pinchot said that his normal appetite was enough for four people, Charles J. Bonaparte estimated that his mind moved ten times faster than average, and TR himself, not wanting to get into double figures, modestly remarked, "I have enjoyed as much of life as any nine men I know." John Morley made a famous comparison in 1904 between Theodore Roosevelt and the Niagara Falls, "both great wonders of nature." John Burroughs wrote that TR's mere proximity made him nervous. "There was always something imminent about him, like an avalanche that the sound of your voice might loosen." Ida Tarbell, sitting next to him at a musicale, had a sudden hallucination that the President was about to burst. "I felt his clothes might not contain him, he was so steamed up, so ready to go, to attack anything, anywhere."

Reading all these remarks it comes as a surprise to discover that TR's chest measured a normal forty-two inches, and that he stood only five feet nine in his size seven shoes. Yet unquestionably his initial impact was physical, and it was overwhelming. I have amused myself over the years with collecting the metaphors that contemporaries used to describe this Rooseveltian "presence." Here's a random selection. [Novelist] Edith Wharton thought him radioactive; Archie Butt and others used phrases to do with electricity, high-voltage wires, generators, and dynamos; Lawrence Abbott compared him to an electromagnetic nimbus; John Burroughs to "a kind of electric bombshell, if there can be such a thing"; James E. Watson was reminded of TNT; and Senator Joseph Foraker, in an excess of imagination, called TR "a steam-engine in trousers." There are countless other steam-engine metaphors, from Henry Adams' "swift and awful Chicago express" to Henry James's "verily, a wonderful little machine: destined to be overstrained, perhaps, but not as yet, truly, betraying the least creak." Lastly we have [western writer] Owen Wister comparing TR to a solar conflagration that cast no shadow, only radiance.

These metaphors sound fulsome, but they refer only to TR's physical effect, which was felt with equal power by friends and enemies. People actually tingled in his company; there was something sensually stimulating about it. They came out of the presidential office flushed, short-breathed, energized, as if they had been treated to a sniff of white powder. He had, as Oscar Straus once said, "the quality of vitalizing things." His youthfulness (he was not yet forty-three at the beginning of his first term, and barely fifty at the end of his second), his air of glossy good health, his powerful handshake — all these things combined to give an impression of irresistible force and personal impetus.

But TR was not just a physical phenomenon. In many ways the quality of his personality was more remarkable than its quantity. Here again, I have discov-

ered recurrences of the same words in contemporary descriptions. One of the more frequent images is that of sweetness. "He was as sweet a man," wrote Henry Watterson, "as ever scuttled a ship or cut a throat." But most comments are kinder than that. "There is a sweetness about him that is very compelling," sighed Woodrow Wilson. "You can't resist the man." Robert Livingstone, a journalist, wrote after TR's death: "He had the double gifts of a sweet nature that came out in every handtouch and tone . . . and a sincerely powerful personality that left the uneffaceable impression that whatever he said was right. Such a combination was simply irresistible." Livingstone's final verdict was that Theodore Roosevelt had "unquestionably the greatest gift of personal magnetism ever possessed by an American."

That may or may not be true, but certainly there are very few recorded examples of anybody, even TR's bitterest political critics, being able to resist him in person. Brand Whitlock, Mark Twain, John Jay Chapman, William Jennings Bryan, and Henry James were all seduced by his charm, if only temporarily. Peevish little Henry Adams spent much of the period from 1901 to 1909 penning a series of magnificent insults to the President's reputation. But this did not prevent him from accepting frequent invitations to dine at the White House and basking gloomily in TR's effulgence. By the time the Roosevelt era came to an end, Adams was inconsolable. "My last vision of fun and gaiety will vanish when my Theodore goes . . . never can we replace him."

It's a pity that the two men never had a public slanging match over the table, because when it came to personal invective, TR could give as good as he got. There was the rather slow British ambassador whom he accused of having "a mind that functions at six guinea-pig power." There was the State Supreme Court Justice he called "an amiable old fuzzy-wuzzy with sweetbread brains." There was that "unspeakable villainous little monkey," President Castro of Venezuela, and President Marroquin of Colombia, whom he described in one word as a "Pithecan-thropoid." Woodrow Wilson was "a Byzantine logothete" (even Wilson had to go to the dictionary for that one); [retail magnate] John Wanamaker was "an ill-constitutioned creature, oily, with bristles sticking up through the oil," and poor Senator Warren Pfeffer never quite recovered from being called "a pin-headed anarchistic crank, of hirsute and slabsided aspect." TR did not use bad language — the nearest to it I've found is his description of [jurist and statesman] Charles Evans Hughes as "a psalm-singing son of a bitch," but then Charles Evans Hughes tended to invite such descriptions. Moreover, TR usually took the sting out of his insults by collapsing into laughter as he uttered them. Booth Tarkington detected "an undertone of Homeric chuckling" even when Roosevelt seemed to be seriously castigating someone — "as if, after all, he loved the fun of hating, rather than the hating itself."

Humor, indeed, was always TR's saving grace. A reporter who spent a week with him in the White House calculated that he laughed, on average, a hundred times a day — and what was more, laughed heartily. "He laughs like an irresponsible schoolboy on a lark, his face flushing ruddy, his eyes nearly closed, his utterance choked with merriment, his speech abandoned for a weird falsetto. . . . The President is a joker, and (what many jokers are not) a humorist as well."

If there were nothing more to Theodore Roosevelt's personality than physical exuberance, humor, and charm, he would indeed have been what he sometimes is misperceived to be: a simple-minded, amiable bully. Actually he was an exceedingly complex man, a polygon (to use Brander Matthews' word) of so many political, intellectual, and social facets that the closer one gets to him, the less one is able to see him in the round. Consider merely this random list of attributes and achievements:

He graduated *magna cum laude* from Harvard University. He was the author of a four-volume history of the winning of the West which was considered definitive in his lifetime, and a history of the naval war of 1812 which remains definitive to this day. He also wrote biographies of Thomas Hart Benton, Gouverneur Morris, and Oliver Cromwell, and some fourteen other volumes of history, natural history, literary criticism, autobiography, political philosophy, and military memoirs, not to mention countless articles and approximately seventy-five thousand letters. He spent nearly three years of his life in Europe and the Levant, and had a wide circle of intellectual correspondents on both sides of the Atlantic. He habitually read one to three books a day, on subjects ranging from architecture to zoology, averaging two or three pages a minute and effortlessly memorizing the paragraphs that interested him. He could recite poetry by the hour in English, German, and French. He married two women and fathered six children. He was a boxing championship finalist, a Fifth Avenue socialite, a New York State Assemblyman, a Dakota cowboy, a deputy sheriff, a president of the Little Missouri Stockmen's Association, United States Civil Service Commissioner, Police Commissioner of New York City, Assistant Secretary of the Navy, Colonel of the Rough Riders, Governor of New York, Vice-President, and finally President of the United States. He was a founding member of the National Institute of Arts and Letters and a fellow of the American Historical Society. He was accepted by Washington's scientific community as a skilled ornithologist, paleontologist, and taxidermist (during the White House years, specimens that confused experts at the Smithsonian were occasionally sent to TR for identification), and he was recognized as the world authority on the big-game mammals of North America.

Now all these achievements *predate* his assumption of the Presidency — in other words, he packed them into his first forty-three years. I will spare you another list of the things he packed into his last ten, after leaving the White House in 1909, except to say that the total of books rose to thirty-eight, the total of letters to 150,000, and the catalogue of careers expanded to include world statesman, big game collector for the Smithsonian, magazine columnist, and South American explorer.

If it were possible to take a cross section of TR's personality, as geologists, say, ponder a chunk of continent, you would be presented with a picture of seismic richness and confusion. The most order I have been able to make of it is to isolate four major character seams. They might be traced back to childhood. Each seam stood out bright and clear in youth and early middle age, but they began to merge about the time he was forty. Indeed the white heat of the Presidency soon fused them all into solid metal. But so long as they were distinct they may be identified as aggression, righteousness, pride, and militarism. Before suggesting how they affected his performance as President, I'd like to explain how they originated.

The most fundamental characteristic of Theodore Roosevelt was his aggression — conquest being, to him, synonymous with growth. From the moment he first dragged breath into his asthmatic lungs, the sickly little boy fought for a larger share of the world. He could never get enough air; disease had to be destroyed; he had to fight his way through big, heavy books to gain a man's knowledge. Just as the struggle for wind made him stretch his chest, so did the difficulty of relating to abnormally contrasting parents extend his imagination. Theodore Senior was the epitome of hard, thrusting Northern manhood; Mittie Roosevelt was the quintessence of soft, yielding Southern femininity. The Civil War — the first political phenomenon little Teedie was ever aware of — symbolically opposed one to the other. There was no question as to which side, and which parent, the child preferred. He naughtily prayed God, in Mittie's presence, to "grind the Southern troops to powder," and the victory of Union arms reinforced his belief in the superiority of Strength over Weakness, Right over Wrong, Realism over Romance.

Teedie's youthful "ofserv-a-tions" in natural history gave him further proof of the laws of natural selection, long before he fully understood [Charles] Darwin and Herbert Spencer. For weeks he watched in fascination while a tiny shrew successively devoured a mass of beetles, then a mouse twice her size, then a snake so large it whipped her from side to side of the cage as she was gnawing through its neck. From then on the rule of tooth and claw, aided by superior intelligence, was a persistent theme in Theodore Roosevelt's writings.

Blood sports, which he took up as a result of his shooting for specimens, enabled him to feel the "strong eager pleasure" of the shrew in vanquishing ever larger foes; his exuberant dancing and whooping after killing a particulary dangerous animal struck more than one observer as macabre. From among his own kind, at college, he selected the fairest and most unobtainable mate — "See that girl? I'm going to marry her. She won't have me, but I am going to have *her!*" — and he ferociously hunted her down. That was Alice Lee Roosevelt, mother of the late Alice Longworth.

During his first years in politics, in the New York State Assembly, he won power through constant attack. The death of Alice Lee, coming as it did just after the birth of his first child — at the moment of fruition of his manhood — only intensified his will to fight. He hurried West, to where the battle for life was fiercest. The West did not welcome him; it had to be won, like everything else he lusted for. Win it he did, by dint of the greatest physical and mental stretchings-out he had yet made. In doing so he built up the magnificent body that became such an inspiration to the American people (one frail little boy who vowed to follow the President's example was the future world heavyweight champion, Gene Tunney). And by living on equal terms with the likes of Hashknife Simpson, Bat Masterson, Modesty Carter,

had ever entertained a black man in the first house of the land. The public outcry was deafening — horror in the South, acclamation in the North — but overnight 9,000,000 Negroes, hitherto loyal to Senator Hanna, trooped into the Rooseveltian camp. TR never felt the need to dine a black man again.

Although we may have no doubt he had the redistribution of Southern patronage in mind when he sent his invitation to Washington, another motive was simply to stamp a bright, clear, first impression of himself upon the public imagination. "I," he seemed to be saying, "am a man *aggressive* enough to challenge a hundred-year prejudice, *righteous* enough to do so for moral reasons, and *proud* enough to advertise the fact."

Again and again during the next seven years, he reinforced these perceptions of his personality. He aggressively prosecuted J. P. Morgan, Edward H. Harriman, and John D. Rockefeller (the holy trinity of American capitalism) in the Northern Securities antitrust case, threw the Monroe Doctrine at Kaiser Wilhelm's feet like a token of war in the Caribbean, rooted out corruption in his own administration, and crushed Hanna's 1904 presidential challenge by publicly humiliating the Senator when he was running for reelection in 1903. He righteously took the side of the American worker and the American consumer against big business in the great anthracite [coal] strike [in Pennsylvania], proclaimed the vanity of muckrake journalists, forced higher ethical standards upon the food and drug industry, ordered the dishonorable discharge of 160 Negro soldiers [charged with rioting and shooting in "the Brownsville Affair" in Texas], and to quote Mark Twain, "dug so many tunnels under the Constitution that the transportation facilities enjoyed by that document are rivalled only by the City of New York."

For example, when the anthracite strike began to drag into the freezing fall of 1902, TR's obvious sympathy for the miners, and for millions of Americans who could not afford the rise in fuel prices, began to worry conservative members of Congress. One day

Representative James E. Watson was horrified to hear that the President had decided to send federal troops in to reopen the anthracite mines on grounds of general hardship. Watson rushed round to the White House. "What about the Constitution of the United States?" he pleaded. "What about seizing private property for public purposes without the due processes of law?"

TR wheeled around, shook Watson by the shoulder, and roared, "*To hell with the Constitution when the people want coal!*" Remarks like that caused old Joe Cannon to sigh, "Roosevelt's got no more respect for the Constitution than a tomcat has for a marriage license."

Pride, both in himself and his office, was particularly noticeable in TR's second term, the so-called imperial years, when Henry James complained, "Theodore Rex is distinctly tending — or trying to make a court." But this accusation was not true. Although the Roosevelts entertained much more elaborately than any of their predecessors, they confined their pomp and protocol to occasions of state. At times, indeed, they were remarkable for the all-American variety of their guests. On any given day one might find a Rough Rider, a poet, a British viscount, a wolf hunter, and a Roman Catholic cardinal at the White House table, each being treated with the gentlemanly naturalness which was one of TR's most endearing traits. His pride manifested itself in things like his refusal to address foreign monarchs as "Your Majesty," in his offer to mediate the Russo-Japanese War (no American President had yet had such global presumptions), and, when he won the Nobel Peace Prize for successfully bringing the war to a conclusion, in refusing to keep a penny of the forty-thousand-dollar prize money. This was by no means an easy decision, because TR could have used the funds: he spent all his presidential salary on official functions and was not himself a wealthy man. He confessed he was tempted to put the Nobel money into a trust for his children, but decided it belonged to the United States.

Pride and patriotism were inseparable in Theodore Roosevelt's character; indeed, if we accept Lord Morely's axiom that he "was" America, they may be considered as complementary characteristics. And neither of them was false. Just as he was always willing to lose a political battle in order to win a political war, so in diplomatic negotiations was he sedulous to allow his opponents the chance to save face — take all the glory of settlement if need be — as long as the essential victory was his.

As I have noted earlier, TR's militarism did not loom large during his Presidency. The organizational structure of the U.S. Army was revamped in such a way as to strengthen the powers of the Commander in Chief, but Secretary of war Elihu Root takes credit for that. TR can certainly take the credit for expanding the American Navy from fifth to second place in the world during his seven and a half years of power — an amazing achievement, but quite in keeping with his policy, inherited from Washington, that "to be prepared for war is the most effectual means to promote peace." The gunboat TR sent to Panama in 1903 was the only example of him shaking a naked mailed fist in the face of a weaker power; for the rest of the time he kept that fist sheathed in a velvet glove. The metaphor of velvet on iron, incidentally, was TR's own; it makes a refreshing change from the Big Stick.

If I may be permitted a final metaphor of my own, I would like to quote one from *The Rise of Theodore Roosevelt* in an attempt to explain why, on the whole, TR's character shows to better advantage as President than in his years out of power. "The man's personality was cyclonic, in that he tended to become unstable in times of low pressure." The slightest rise in the barometer outside, and his turbulence smoothed into a whir of coordinated activity, while a core of stillness developed within. Under maximum pressure Roosevelt was sunny, calm, and unnaturally clear. This explains why the first Roosevelt era was a period of fair weather. Power became Theodore Roosevelt, and

absolute power became him best of all. He loved being President and was so good at his job that the American people loved him for loving it. TR genuinely dreaded having to leave the White House, and let us remember that a third term was his for the asking in 1908. But his knowledge that power corrupts even the man who most deserves it, his reverence for the Washingtonian principle that power must punctually revert to those whose gift it is, persuaded him to make this supreme sacrifice in his prime. The time would come, not many years hence, when fatal insolence tempted him to renege on his decision. That is another story. But the self denial that he exercised in 1908 gives us one more reason to admire Old Fiftyseven varieties.

QUESTIONS TO CONSIDER

1. How would you describe Theodore Roosevelt's character and personality? To what extent was he shaped by the era in which he lived? What is your impression of his intellectual capabilities?

2. Morris suggests that TR's presidency was stamped by his four most salient character traits or governing impulses: aggression, self-righteousness, pride, and militarism. What does Morris see as the sources of each of these characteristics? How did each characteristic affect TR's presidency? How much did TR's charm influence his presidency and his effect on Americans?

3. What does Morris mean when he says that Theodore Roosevelt's presidency was a performance? Do you think it was a successful or unsuccessful show, by and large? Was TR any the less sincere for all his showmanship?

4. In what ways do you think TR's was a potentially dangerous or risky personality for a president? How, for example, did he regard the Constitution when it got in the way of things he thought were important?

5. Can you think of any presidents to compare with Theodore Roosevelt? Could a Theodore Roosevelt be elected in the political climate of the late twentieth century? How would a modern-day electorate feel about a president with such an impenetrable ego or one who behaved with such highhandedness as Roosevelt exhibited in his gunboat diplomacy off Colombia? You may want to keep Teddy Roosevelt in mind when you read about Ronald Reagan in selection 31.

11

Wilson and the League

Thomas A. Bailey

The League of Nations was linked to the Progressive idealism of Woodrow Wilson, one of America's most complex and paradoxical statesmen. A college professor with a doctoral degree in political economy, he served as president of Princeton University from 1902 to 1910, when his attempt to control the graduate school and to institute social reforms brought about his forced resignation. Thereupon he left academe to pursue a career in politics and promptly won the governorship of New Jersey. A conservative Democrat before he took office as president, he became a Progressive reformer who embraced women's political rights (to be treated in a subsequent selection) and engineered the most sweeping legislative program since the days of Alexander Hamilton. Designed to regulate competition and protect those struggling to get "a foothold in the world of endeavor," the Wilson program lowered tariff duties that protected the products of monopolies, prohibited interlocking directorships, created the Federal Trade Commission to guard against unlawful suppression of competition, and installed the Federal Reserve System to stabilize America's banking and money system. A humane, sensitive, lonely man who wanted "the people to love me," Wilson felt a powerful need to guard his emotions "from painful overflow." Although his intellectual tradition was British (he extolled the British system of government and extolled English conservatives such as Edmund Burke and William Gladstone), his politics were rooted in his southern heritage. A learned, eloquent champion of democracy, he nevertheless shared the racial prejudice that prevailed among white Americans of his generation, and as president he began a policy of discrimination against African Americans in federal government.

In many ways, his foreign policy was even more paradoxical. He had a horror of vio-

lence, but he was inclined to use moralistic, gunboat diplomacy in dealing with Latin America: he transformed Nicaragua into a veritable United States protectorate, twice sent United States forces into Mexico, and ordered full-scale military occupation of Haiti and the Dominican Republic. Although Wilson convinced himself that high moral purpose justified such intervention, it left a legacy of bitterness and distrust in Latin America.

Finally, despite the pacific liberalism he had learned from British intellectuals, Wilson led the United States into the First World War on a messianic crusade to make that conflict "a war to end all wars." To achieve that goal, he devised the League of Nations, a kind of world parliament, which was the sanest blueprint for world peace anyone had yet contrived. But Wilson's noble dream ended in a crushing defeat when the United States Senate rejected the League of Nations and America turned away from the idealism that had produced it. In this selection, diplomatic historian Thomas A. Bailey deftly describes how the clash of Wilson and his adversaries, combined with the sentiment of the times, brought about America's rejection of the League. In the end, Americans were not prepared for the responsibilities of world leadership that Wilson had thrust upon them.

GLOSSARY

BORAH, SENATOR WILLIAM E.   An isolationist Republican from Idaho who vowed to kill Wilson's treaty in the Senate.

CLEMENCEAU, GEORGES   The "French realist" at the Versailles peace conference; like Lloyd George and Vittorio Orlando, he was "more interested in imperialism" than in Wilsonian idealism.

FOURTEEN POINTS   Wilson's blueprint for world peace and "the noblest expression" of his idealism; the last and most important point called for a league of nations, a kind of parliament of humankind, to resolve conflicts among nations and avoid future wars.

GEORGE, LLOYD   British delegate to the Versailles peace conference.

JINGOISM   Bellicose patriotism.

JOHNSON, SENATOR HIRAM W.   An isolationist Republican from California who joined the Senate opposition to Wilson's treaty.

LODGE, SENATOR HENRY CABOT Republican and Boston Brahmin who "broke the back" of Wilson's treaty by getting a series of crippling reservations added to it in the Senate.

MONROE DOCTRINE   Promulgated by President James Monroe in 1823, it warned that the Western Hemisphere was closed to colonization by European powers and stated that America would stay out of Europe's wars.

ORLANDO, VITTORIO   Italian delegate to the Versailles peace conference (Italy had fought on the side of France and Great Britain in the First World War).

TREATY OF VERSAILLES   Formally ended the First World War; only about four of the Fourteen Points found their way into the treaty, as "the iron hand of circumstance had forced Wilson to compromise away many of his points in order to salvage his fourteenth point, the League of Nations."

The story of America's rejection of the League of Nations revolves largely around the personality and character of Thomas Woodrow Wilson, the twenty-eighth President of the United States. Born in Virginia and reared in Yankee-gutted Georgia and the Carolinas, Wilson early developed a burning hatred of war and a passionate attachment to the Confederate-embraced principle of self-determination for minority peoples. From the writings of Thomas Jefferson he derived much of his democratic idealism and his invincible faith in the judgment of the masses, if properly informed. From his stiff-backed Scotch Presbyterian forebears, he inherited a high degree of inflexibility; from his father, a dedicated Presbyterian minister, he learned a stern moral code that would tolerate no compromise with wrong, as defined by Woodrow Wilson.

As a leading academician who had first failed at law, he betrayed a contempt for "money-grubbing" lawyers, many of whom sat in the Senate, and an arrogance toward lesser intellects, including those of the "pygmy-minded" senators. As a devout Christian keenly aware of the wickedness of this world, he emerged as a fighting reformer, whether as president of Princeton, governor of New Jersey, or President of the United States.

As a war leader, Wilson was superb. Holding aloft the torch of idealism in one hand and the flaming sword of righteousness in the other, he aroused the masses to a holy crusade. We would fight a war to end wars; we would make the world safe for democracy. The phrase was not a mockery then. The American people, with an amazing display of self-sacrifice, supported the war effort unswervingly.

The noblest expression of Wilson's idealism was his Fourteen Points address to Congress in January, 1918.

From T. A. Bailey, "Wilson and the League," *American Heritage,* June/July 1957, Vol. 8, No. 4. © 1981 by Forbes Inc. Reprinted by permission of *American Heritage* Magazine, a division of Forbes Inc.

It compressed his war aims into punchy, placard-like paragraphs, expressly designed for propaganda purposes. It appealed tremendously to oppressed peoples everywhere by promising such goals as the end of secret treaties, freedom of the seas, the removal of economic barriers, a reduction of arms burdens, a fair adjustment of colonial claims, and self-determination for oppressed minorities. In Poland university men would meet on the streets of Warsaw, clasp hands, and soulfully utter one word, "Wilson." In remote regions of Italy peasants burned candles before poster portraits of the mighty new prophet arisen in the West.

The fourteenth and capstone point was a league of nations, designed to avert future wars. The basic idea was not original with Wilson; numerous thinkers, including Frenchmen and Britons, had been working on the concept long before he embraced it. Even Henry Cabot Lodge, the Republican senator from Massachusetts, had already spoken publicly in favor of *a* league of nations. But the more he heard about the Wilsonian League of Nations, the more critical of it he became.

A knowledge of the Wilson-Lodge feud is basic to an understanding of the tragedy that unfolded. Tall, slender, aristocratically bewhiskered, Dr. Henry Cabot Lodge (Ph.D., Harvard), had published a number of books and had been known as the scholar in politics before the appearance of Dr. Woodrow Wilson (Ph.D., Johns Hopkins). The Presbyterian professor had gone further in both scholarship and politics than the Boston Brahmin, whose mind was once described as resembling the soil of his native New England: "naturally barren but highly cultivated." Wilson and Lodge, two icy men, developed a mutual antipathy, which soon turned into freezing hatred.

The German armies, reeling under the blows of the Allies, were ready to give in by November, 1918. The formal armistice terms stipulated that Germany was to be guaranteed a peace based on the Fourteen Points, with two reservations concerning freedom of the seas and reparations.

Meanwhile the American people had keyed themselves up to the long-awaited march on Berlin; eager voices clamored to hang the Kaiser. Thus the sudden end of the shooting left inflamed patriots with a sense of frustration and letdown that boded ill for Wilson's policies. The red-faced Theodore Roosevelt, Lodge's intimate of long standing, cried that peace should be dictated by the chatter of machine guns and not the clicking of typewriters.

Wilson now towered at the dizzy pinnacle of his popularity and power. He had emerged as the moral arbiter of the world and the hope of all peoples for a better tomorrow. But regrettably his wartime sureness of touch began to desert him, and he made a series of costly fumbles. He was so preoccupied with reordering the world, someone has said, that he reminded one of the baseball player who knocks the ball into the bleachers and then forgets to touch home plate.

First came his brutally direct appeal for a Democratic Congress in October, 1918. The voters trooped to the polls the next month and, by a narrow margin, returned a Republican Congress. Wilson had not only goaded his partisan foes to fresh outbursts of fury, but he had unnecessarily staked his prestige on the outcome — and lost. When the Allied leaders met at the Paris peace table, he was the only one not entitled to be there, at least on the European basis of a parliamentary majority.

Wilson next announced that he was sailing for France, presumably to use his still enormous prestige to fashion an enduring peace. At this time no President had ever gone abroad, and Republicans condemned the decision as evidence of a dangerous Messiah complex — of a desire, as former President Taft put it, "to hog the whole show."

The naming of the remaining five men to the peace delegation caused partisans further anguish. Only one, Henry White, was a Republican, and he was a minor figure at that. The Republicans, now the majority party, complained that they had been good enough to die on the battlefield; they ought to have at least an equal voice at the peace table. Nor were any United States senators included, even though they would have a final whack at the treaty. Wilson did not have much respect for the "bungalow-minded" senators, and if he took one, the logical choice would be Henry Cabot Lodge. There were already enough feuds brewing at Paris without taking one along.

Doubtless some of the Big Business Republicans were out to "get" the President who had been responsible for the hated reformist legislation of 1913–14. If he managed to put over the League of Nations, his prestige would soar to new heights. He might even arrange — unspeakable thought! — to be elected again and again and again. Much of the partisan smog that finally suffocated the League would have been cleared away if Wilson had publicly declared, as he was urged to do, that in no circumstances would he run again. But he spurned such counsel, partly because he was actually receptive to the idea of a third term.

The American President, hysterically hailed by European crowds as "Voovro Veelson," came to the Paris peace table in January, 1919, to meet with Lloyd George of Britain, Clemenceau of France, and Orlando of Italy. To his dismay, he soon discovered that they were far more interested in imperialism than in idealism. When they sought to carve up the territorial booty without regard for the colonials, contrary to the Fourteen Points, the stern-jawed Presbyterian moralist interposed a ringing veto. The end result was the mandate system — a compromise between idealism and imperialism that turned out to be more imperialistic than idealistic.

Wilson's overriding concern was the League of Nations. He feared that if he did not get it completed and embedded in the treaty, the imperialistic powers might sidetrack it. Working at an incredible pace after hours, Wilson headed the commission that drafted the League Covenant in ten meetings and some thirty hours. He then persuaded the conference not only to approve the hastily constructed Covenant but to incorporate it bodily in the peace treaty. In support of his adopted brain child he spoke so movingly on one occasion that even the hard-boiled reporters forgot to take notes.

Wilson now had to return hurriedly to the United States to sign bills and take care of other pressing business. Shortly after his arrival the mounting Republican opposition in the Senate flared up angrily. On March 4, 1919, 39 senators or senators-elect — more than enough to defeat the treaty — published a round robin to the effect that they would not approve the League in its existing form. This meant that Wilson had to return to Paris, hat in hand, and there weaken his position by having to seek modifications.

Stung to the quick, he struck back at his senatorial foes in an indiscreet speech in New York just before his departure. He boasted that when he brought the treaty back from Paris, the League Covenant would not only be tied in but so thoroughly tied in that it could not be cut out without killing the entire pact. The Senate, he assumed, would not dare to kill the treaty of peace outright.

At Paris the battle was now joined in deadly earnest. Clemenceau, the French realist, had little use for Wilson, the American idealist. "God gave us the ten commandments and we broke them," he reportedly sneered. "Wilson gave us the Fourteen Points — we shall see." Clemenceau's most disruptive demand was for the German Rhineland; but Wilson, the champion of self-determination, would never consent to handing several million Germans over to the tender mercies of the French. After a furious struggle, during which Wilson was stricken with influenza, Clemenceau was finally persuaded to yield the Rhineland and other demands in return for a security treaty. Under it, Britain and America agreed to come to the aid of France in the event of another unprovoked aggression. The United States Senate shortsightedly pigeonholed the pact, and France was left with neither the Rhineland nor security.

Two other deadlocks almost broke up the conference. Italy claimed the Adriatic port of Fiume, an area inhabited chiefly by Yugoslavs. In his battle for self-determination, Wilson dramatically appealed over the head of the Italian delegation to the Italian people, whereupon the delegates went home in a huff to receive popular endorsement. The final adjustment was a hollow victory for self-determination.

The politely bowing Japanese now stepped forward to press their economic claims to China's Shantung [province], which they had captured from the Germans early in the war. But to submit 30,000,000 Chinese to the influence of the Japanese would be another glaring violation of self-determination. The Japanese threatened to bolt the conference, as the Italians had already done, with consequent jeopardy to the League. In the end, Wilson reluctantly consented to a compromise that left the Japanese temporarily in possession of Shantung.

The Treaty of Versailles, as finally signed in June, 1919, included only about four of the original Fourteen Points. The Germans, with considerable justification, gave vent to loud cries of betrayal. But the iron hand of circumstance had forced Wilson to compromise away many of his points in order to salvage his fourteenth point, the League of Nations, which he hoped would iron out the injustices that had crept into the treaty. He was like the mother who throws her younger children to the pursuing wolves in order to save her sturdy first-born son.

Bitter opposition to the completed treaty had already begun to form in America. Tens of thousands of homesick and disillusioned soldiers were pouring home, determined to let Europe "stew in its own juice." The wartime idealism, inevitably doomed to slump, was now plunging to alarming depths. The beloved Allies had apparently turned out to be greedy imperialists. The war to make the world safe for democracy had obviously fallen dismally short of the goal. And at the end of the war to end wars there were about twenty conflicts of varying intensity being waged all over the globe.

The critics increased their clamor. Various foreign groups, including the Irish-Americans and the Italian-Americans, were complaining that the interests of the old country had been neglected. Professional liberals,

This contemporary cartoon suggests that President Wilson's cherished hopes for a world League of Nations were as fragile and ephemeral as a soap bubble. In the end, a weak League of Nations took shape in Europe without the membership of the United States, whose people and their elected representatives, clinging to isolationism and suffering from postwar disillusionment, could not agree to adopt the charter. (Historical Picture Service — Chicago)

for example the editors of the *New Republic*, were denouncing the treaty as too harsh. The illiberals, far more numerous, were denouncing it as not harsh enough. The Britain-haters, like the buzz-saw Senator James Reed of Missouri and the acid-penned [journalist] William R. Hearst, were proclaiming that England had emerged with undue influence. Such ultranationalists as the isolationist Senator William E. Borah of Idaho were insisting that the flag of no superstate should be hoisted above the glorious Stars and Stripes.

When the treaty came back from Paris, with the league firmly riveted in, Senator Lodge despaired of stopping it.

"What are you going to do? It's hopeless," he complained to Borah. "All the newspapers in my state are

for it." The best that he could hope for was to add a few reservations. The Republicans had been given little opportunity to help write the treaty in Paris; they now felt that they were entitled to do a little rewriting in Washington.

Lodge deliberately adopted the technique of delay. As chairman of the powerful Senate Committee on Foreign Relations, he consumed two weeks by reading aloud the entire pact of 264 pages, even though it had already been printed. He then held time-consuming public hearings, during which persons with unpronounceable foreign names aired their grievances against the pact.

Lodge finally adopted the strategy of tacking reservations onto the treaty, and he was able to achieve his goal because of the peculiar composition of the Senate. There were 49 Republicans and 47 Democrats. The Republicans consisted of about twenty "strong reservationists" like Lodge, about twelve "mild reservationists" like future Secretary of State Kellogg, and about a dozen "irreconcilables." This last group was headed by Senator Borah and the no less isolationist Senator Hiram Johnson of California, a fiery spellbinder.

The Lodge reservations finally broke the back of the treaty. They were all added by a simple majority vote, even though the entire pact would have to be approved by a two-thirds vote. The dozen or so Republican mild reservationists were not happy over the strong Lodge reservations, and if Wilson had deferred sufficiently to these men, he might have persuaded them to vote with the Democrats. Had they done so, the Lodge reservations could have all been voted down, and a milder version, perhaps acceptable to Wilson, could have been substituted.

As the hot summer of 1919 wore on, Wilson became increasingly impatient with the deadlock in the Senate. Finally he decided to take his case to the country, as he had so often done in response to his ingrained "appeal habit." He had never been robust, and his friends urged him not to risk breaking himself down in a strenuous barnstorming campaign. But

Wilson, having made up his mind, was unyielding. He had sent American boys into battle in a war to end wars; why should he not risk his life in battle for a League to end wars?

Wilson's spectacular tour met with limited enthusiasm in the Middle West, the home of several million German-Americans. After him, like baying bloodhounds, trailed Senators Borah and Johnson, sometimes speaking in the same halls a day or so later, to the accompaniment of cries of "Impeach him, impeach him!" But on the Pacific Coast and in the Rocky Mountain area the enthusiasm for Wilson and the League was overwhelming. The high point — and the breaking point — of the trip came at Pueblo, Colorado, where Wilson, with tears streaming down his cheeks, pleaded for his beloved Leagues of Nations.

That night Wilson's weary body rebelled. He was whisked back to Washington, where he suffered a stroke that paralyzed the left side of his body. For weeks he lay in bed, a desperately sick man. The Democrats, who had no first-rate leader in the Senate, were left rudderless. With the wisdom of hindsight, we may say that Wilson might better have stayed in Washington, providing the necessary leadership and compromising with the opposition, insofar as compromise was possible. A good deal of compromise had already gone into the treaty, and a little more might have saved it.

Senator Lodge, cold and decisive, was now in the driver's seat. His Fourteen Reservations, a sardonic parallel to Wilson's Fourteen Points, had been whipped into shape. Most of them now seem either irrelevant, inconsequential, or unnecessary; some of them merely reaffirmed principles and policies, including the Monroe Doctrine, already guaranteed by the treaty or by the Constitution.

But Wilson, who hated the sound of Lodge's name, would have no part of the Lodge reservations. They would, he insisted, emasculate the entire treaty. Yet the curious fact is that he had privately worked out his own set of reservations with the Democratic leader in the Senate, Gilbert M. Hitchcock, and these differed only in slight degree from those of Senator Lodge.

As the hour approached for the crucial vote in the Senate, it appeared that public opinion had veered a little. Although confused by the angry debate, it still favored the treaty — but with some safeguarding reservations. A stubborn Wilson was unwilling to accept this disheartening fact, or perhaps he was not made aware of it. Mrs. Wilson, backed by the President's personal physician, Dr. Cary Grayson, kept vigil at his bedside to warn the few visitors that disagreeable news might shock the invalid into a relapse.

In this highly unfavorable atmosphere, Senator Hitchcock had two conferences with Wilson on the eve of the Senate voting. He suggested compromise on a certain point, but Wilson shot back, "Let Lodge compromise!" Hitchcock conceded that the Senator would have to give ground but suggested that the White House might also hold out the olive branch. "Let Lodge hold out the olive branch," came the stern reply. On this inflexible note, and with Mrs. Wilson's anxiety mounting, the interview ended.

The Senate was ready for final action on November 19, 1919. At the critical moment Wilson sent a fateful letter to the Democratic minority in the Senate, urging them to vote down the treaty with the hated Lodge reservations so that a true ratification could be achieved. The Democrats, with more than the necessary one-third veto, heeded the voice of their crippled leader and rejected the treaty with reservations. The Republicans, with more than the necessary one-third veto, rejected the treaty without reservations.

The country was shocked by this exhibition of legislative paralysis. About four fifths of the senators professed to favor the treaty in some form, yet they were unable to agree on anything. An aroused public opinion forced the Senate to reconsider, and Lodge secretly entered into negotiations with the Democrats in an effort to work out acceptable reservations. He was making promising progress when Senator Borah got wind of his maneuvers through an anonymous telephone call. The leading irreconcilables hastily summoned a council of war, hauled Lodge before them, and bluntly accused him of treachery. Deeply disturbed, the Massachusetts Senator said: "Well, I suppose I'll have to resign as majority leader."

"No, by God!" burst out Borah. "You won't have a chance to resign! On Monday, I'll move for the election of a new majority leader and give the reasons for my action." Faced with an upheaval within his party such as had insured Wilson's election in 1912, Lodge agreed to drop his backstage negotiations.

The second-chance vote in the Senate came on March 19, 1920. Wilson again directed his loyal Democratic following to reject the treaty, disfigured as it was by the hateful Lodge reservations. But by this time there was no other form in which the pact could possibly be ratified. Twenty-one realistic Democrats turned their backs on Wilson and voted Yea; 23 loyal Democrats, mostly from the rock-ribbed South, joined with the irreconcilables to do the bidding of the White House. The treaty, though commanding a simple majority this time of 49 Yeas to 35 Nays, failed of the necessary two-thirds vote.

Wilson, struggling desperately against the Lodge reservation trap, had already summoned the nation in "solemn referendum" to give him a vote in favor of the League in the forthcoming presidential election of 1920. His hope was that he could then get the treaty approved without reservations. But this course was plainly futile. Even if all the anti-League senators up for re-election in 1920 had been replaced by the pro-League senators, Wilson would still have lacked the necessary two-thirds majority for an unreserved treaty.

The American people were never given a chance to express their views directly on the League of Nations. All they could do was vote either for the weak Democratic candidate, [James M.] Cox, who stood for the League, and the stuffed-shirt Republican candidate, [Warren G.] Harding, who wobbled all over the map of the League arguments. If the electorate had been given an opportunity to express itself, a powerful majority probably would have favored the world organization, with at least some reservations. But wearied of Wilsonism, idealism, and self-denial, and confused by the wordy fight over the treaty, the voters rose up and swept Harding into the White House. The winner had been more anti-League than pro-League, and his prodigious plurality of 7,000,000 votes condemned the League to death in America.

What caused this costly failure of American statesmanship?

Wilson's physical collapse intensifed his native stubbornness. A judicious compromise here and there no doubt would have secured Senate approval of the treaty, though of course with modifications. Wilson believed that in any event the Allies would reject the Lodge reservations. The probabilities are that the Allies would have worked out some kind of acceptance, so dire was their need of America's economic support, but Wilson never gave them a chance to act.

Senator Lodge was also inflexible, but prior to the second rejection he was evidently trying to get the treaty through — on his own terms. As majority leader of the Republicans, his primary task was to avoid another fatal split in his party. Wilson's primary task was to get the pact approved. From a purely political point of view, the Republicans had little to gain by engineering ratification of a Democratic treaty.

The two-thirds rule in the Senate, often singled out as the culprit, is of little relevance. Wilson almost certainly would have pigeonholed the treaty if it had passed with the Lodge reservations appended.

Wilson's insistence that the League be wedded to the treaty actually contributed to the final defeat of both. Either would have had a better chance if it had not been burdened by the enemies of the other. The United Nations, one should note, was set up in 1945 independently of any peace treaty.

Finally, American public opinion in 1919–20 was not yet ready for the onerous new world responsibilities that had suddenly been forced upon it. The isolationist tradition was still potent, and it was fortified by postwar disillusionment. If the sovereign voters had spoken out for the League with one voice, they almost certainly would have had their way. A treaty without reservations, or with a few reservations acceptable to Wilson, doubtless would have slipped through the Senate. But the American people were one war short of accepting leadership in a world organization for peace.

QUESTIONS TO CONSIDER

1. Woodrow Wilson's personal popularity was at an all-time high when he went to Paris in 1919. How had he achieved his vast international prestige? What happened to diminish it?

2. What prevailing sentiment did Wilson, the idealist, find among the representatives of European countries at the negotiating table in Versailles? What had happened to the "war to end all wars," the goal of which was to "make the world safe for democracy"? How did the Allied powers eventually compromise between imperialism and idealism?

3. Outline the process by which partisan politics, petty squabbles, and back-room maneuvering eventually led Congress to vote down the 1919 peace treaty and with it the League of Nations. What role did Henry Cabot Lodge play in the American rejection of the League? What does historian Thomas A. Bailey think Wilson's illness, coupled with his poor judgment on several occasions, contributed to the debacle in Congress over the treaty?

4. What does Bailey think would have happened if the American people had been given a chance to vote for the League? What specific conclusions does he reach about the collapse of the treaty and the failure of Wilsonian idealism in America and Europe?

5. Discuss the ambivalence of Americans in regard to the world leadership role that became available to them just after the First World War. What became of the vociferous jingoistic spirit that had brought about the Spanish-American War and the annexation of territories in the Pacific? What does Bailey mean when he says that "the American people were one war short of accepting leadership in a world organization for peace"? Imagine a world in which the young and powerful United States had joined the League of Nations in 1921. How might twentieth century history have been rewritten?

CURRENTS OF STRUGGLE

12

Not Wards of the Nation:
The Struggle for Women's Suffrage

WILLIAM H. CHAFE

We have seen how progressivism won over both Republicans and Democrats, enlisting the likes of Theodore Roosevelt and Woodrow Wilson in the cause of reform. In this selection, we turn to another side of progressivism — the long and arduous struggle for women's political rights. Actually, as feminist scholar William H. Chafe makes clear, the movement for women's suffrage began back in the Jacksonian period, when American women first organized to break the shackles of strict domesticity and to expand their rights and opportunities. Led by eloquent and irrepressible Elizabeth Cady Stanton, the early feminists rejected the notion of female inferiority and advocated full sexual equality with men. They demanded equal access to education, the trades, and the professions and an end to the sexual double standard. They wanted the right to vote, too, not as an end in itself but as a means of achieving their broader aim — to make women self-sufficient, equal partners with men in all areas of human enterprise.

After the Civil War, American feminists organized the Equal Rights Association, but the movement soon split over the timing of women's suffrage demands. The debate focused on the proposed Fifteenth Amendment, discussed in an earlier selection, which sought to protect the former slaves by enfranchising African American men. The amendment did not include women, black or white. One women's rights group, led by Julia Ward Howe, author of "The Battle Hymn of the Republic," endorsed the amendment, agreeing with its Republican framers that African American suffrage was already controversial enough and would go down to defeat if women's suffrage were linked to it. Better, they believed, to get African American men enfranchised first. Another feminist group, led by Stanton and by Susan B. Anthony, opposed the amendment as "an open, deliberate insult to American womanhood." Anthony and Stanton considered it extremely unfair that uneducated African American men should gain the elective franchise while educated white women were denied it. The struggle between the two women's groups reached a turning point at the 1869 convention of the Equal Rights Association, where Anthony and Stanton tried but failed to unite the delegates behind a projected Sixteenth Amendment that would enfranchise women. Shortly after that, the Anthony-Stanton faction formed the National Woman's Suffrage Association, the leaders and members of which were mostly women and the goal of which was to rally national support for a women's suffrage amendment. The rival group, with the endorsement of such well-known Republicans and reformers as the African American leader Frederick Douglass, then founded the American Woman's Suffrage Association, which made a point of seeking men's support. The group pledged itself mainly to women's suffrage and "to a genteel and philanthropic concern for women's rights," as historian Linda Evans put it.

The Anthony-Stanton group, on the other hand, embarked (in Evans's words) "on a wide-ranging exploration of women's condition." In 1872, the National Woman's Suffrage Association endorsed Victoria Woodhull for president of the United States. A radical feminist who championed free love and licensed prostitution, Woodhull enraged the enemies of the movement, who charged that feminists were members of the lunatic fringe, out to destroy the nuclear family and the moral fiber of America. As the nineteenth century drew to a close, most feminists rejected radical ideas such as Woodhull's and became conspicuously conservative, placing renewed emphasis on feminine virtue, motherhood, and community service.

By 1900, as Chafe points out, a new generation of feminists had narrowed the vision of their pre–Civil War predecessors to one goal: the winning of the elective franchise. In that year, the rival women's suffrage groups set aside their differences and formed a joint organization called the National American Woman's Suffrage Association. Chafe goes on to recount the struggles of the indefatigable suffragists, who identified their movement with progressivism and won Woodrow Wilson and the entire nation to their cause.

GLOSSARY

ADDAMS, JANE Second-generation feminist who contended that a woman's principal duty was "to preserve the health of her children and the cleanliness of her home" but that she needed the vote and political involvement to do so; this argument broadened the appeal of women's suffrage.

BULL MOOSE PARTY In the election of 1912, Theodore Roosevelt and a group of Progressive Republicans broke away from the regular Republicans and formed this independent reform party, which ran TR for president; TR and Republican nominee William Howard Taft both lost to Wilson.

CATT, CARRIE CHAPMAN Second-generation feminist leader who sought to minimize controversy; in 1915, she assumed overall charge of the suffrage campaign and devised the winning plan that won federal and state political leaders and Wilson himself to the suffrage cause.

GENERAL FEDERATION OF WOMEN'S CLUBS (GFWC) Begun as a means of fostering women's intellectual development, the clubs "caught the contagious spirit of reform" and in 1914 endorsed the women's suffrage campaign.

NATIONAL AMERICAN WOMAN'S SUFFRAGE ASSOCIATION (NAWSA) Formed by the merger of the "liberal" National Woman's Suffrage Association and the "conservative" American Woman's Suffrage Association in 1890, NAWSA focused primarily on winning women's suffrage.

NINETEENTH AMENDMENT Ratified in 1920, it stated that "the right of citizens of the United States to vote shall not be denied or abridged by the United States or by any State on account of sex."

WOMEN'S CHRISTIAN TEMPERANCE UNION Organized in 1874, the WCTU sought to close down the saloons and expand women's political participation; men were excluded from membership.

I N THE FALL OF 1918 Woodrow Wilson journeyed to Capitol Hill to address the Senate of the United States. The nation was engaged in a crusade "to make the world safe for democracy," and he had come to seek help. "The executive tasks of this war rest upon me," he told the lawmakers. "I ask that you lighten them and place in my hands instruments . . . which I do not now have, which I sorely need, and which I have daily to apologize for not being able to employ." The subject of Wilson's appeal was not guns or airplanes but woman suffrage. Its enactment, the Commander in Chief declared, "was vital to the winning of the war" and essential to implementing democracy. The President's plea added one more voice to the rising chorus of support for the suffrage, and within a year, Congress voted overwhelmingly to send the Nineteenth Amendment to the states for ratification.

The woman's movement had not always enjoyed such legitimacy or support. The feminists who gathered at Seneca Falls, New York, in 1848 were far removed from the mainstream of American life. Many had participated in the abolitionist struggle, demonstrating by their actions there the extent to which they deviated from prevailing norms of female behavior. When women abolitionists sought to speak in public or circulate petitions, they were castigated for departing from their proper place. Even male abolitionists were critical of their activities, and in 1840 women were excluded from a world anti-slavery conference in London. In response to such treatment, many of the women determined to seek freedom for themselves as well as for the slave. Bridling at the tradition that men and women should occupy totally separate spheres of activity, they demanded a drastic revision of the values and laws governing relationships

From *The American Woman: Her Changing Social, Economic, and Political Roles, 1920–1970* by William Henry Chafe. Copyright © 1972 by Oxford University Press, Inc. Reprinted by permission. Footnotes omitted.

between the sexes, and forthrightly attacked all forms of discrimination. Their efforts were greeted with derision and contempt. The Worcester *Telegram* denounced the Seneca Falls convention as an attempt at "insurrection," and a Buffalo paper referred to it as "revolutionary." Women's rights advocates were generally dismissed as a "class of wild enthusiasts and visionaries" and received little popular backing.

The contrast between 1848 and 1918 dramatized, albeit in exaggerated form, the changes which had occurred within feminism during the intervening years. In effect, the woman's movement developed from an isolated fringe group into a moderate reform coalition. Although the change could be traced in part to external forces, it also reflected shifts within the movement itself. The early feminists took an uncompromising stand on almost all issues and set out to eliminate the rigid division of labor between men and women. Suffrage constituted only one of a long series of demands. By the first decade of the twentieth century, on the other hand, the franchise had been elevated to a position of primary importance, and other more far-reaching ideas were de-emphasized. Unfortunately, most historians have defined the feminist struggle primarily as a quest for the vote and, with the Nineteenth Amendment as a reference point, have concentrated on those events and personalities most directly associated with the suffrage. But if we are to understand the suffragists themselves and the fate of the woman's movement, it is imperative that we start with the broad vision of equality which inspired the founders of feminism in the nineteenth century.

The radical nature of the early feminist movement was revealed in the Declaration of Sentiments and Resolutions passed by the women at Seneca Falls. In the nineteenth century, females were not allowed to testify in court, hold title to property, establish businesses, or sign papers as witnesses. The feminists addressed themselves both to the specifics of such discrimination and the assumptions underlying it. Beginning with the assertion that "all men and women are created equal," the Declaration proceeded

to indict mankind for its "history of repeated injuries and usurpations" toward women. The delegates charged that men had denied them political representation, made them "civilly dead," refused them the right to own their own property, and "oppressed them on all sides." In marriage, a wife was compelled to pledge obedience and to give her husband "power to deprive her of her liberty." In business, man "monopolized nearly all the profitable employments." And in morals, woman suffered from an iniquitous double standard dictated by men who claimed it as their right to "assign for her a sphere of action, when that belongs to her conscience and to her God." Hardly an area existed, the feminists concluded, where man had not consciously endeavored to "destroy woman's confidence in her own powers, to lessen her self-respect, and to make her willing to lead a dependent and abject life."

To counter the oppression which they perceived, women's rights leaders proposed the elimination of all barriers separating the activities of the two sexes. Henceforth, they declared, any law which restricted woman's freedom or placed her in a position inferior to men had "no force or authority." Proclaiming the "identity of the race in capabilities and responsibilities," they demanded the "overthrow of the monopoly of the pulpit," equal access to education, the trades, and professions, an end to the double standard, and the right to move in "the enlarged sphere" which their Creator had assigned them. God had made men and women equal, the feminists asserted, and the treatment of one sex as different from and less equal than the other ran "contrary to the great precept of nature."

The Declaration boldly challenged every social convention concerning woman's proper "place." Although the feminists sought redress of a whole series of specific grievances, the most impressive part of their document was its assault on the framework of assumptions responsible for woman's position. Implicit throughout the Declaration was the view that, as long as society prescribed separate areas of responsibility for each sex, women could never be free. By insisting that men and women were identical in "capacities and responsibilities," the feminists attacked the fundamental premise underlying relations between the sexes — the notion of distinct male and female spheres. Once it was established that the two sexes were alike in the eyes of God, there was no longer any basis for treating women as separate and inferior and the demands for equality in the church, state, and family logically followed. Instead of concentrating just on the suffrage, then, the early feminists advocated a complete transformation in society's thinking about women.

For much of the remainder of the nineteenth century, women's rights leaders continued to press for sweeping social change. The suffrage became a more prominent issue after Congress failed to recognize women's right to vote in the Fourteenth and Fifteenth amendments, but many feminists persisted in tracing female inequality to the sexual division of labor in society and warned against thinking of the franchise as a panacea. Speaking through a journal entitled *The Revolution*, Elizabeth Cady Stanton, a founder of the women's rights movement, dismissed the suffrage as a "superficial and fragmentary" question. "The ballot touches only those interests, either of men or women, which take their roots in political questions," Stanton and her followers declared in 1869. "But woman's chief discontent is not with her political, but with her social, and particularly her marital bondage." Stanton and her allies attacked economic discrimination, urged reform of the divorce laws, and in the 1890's organized a monumental effort to write a *Woman's Bible* to counteract the widespread theological assumption that females were the weak and inferior sex. Perhaps the most signficant figure in the woman's movement during the nineteenth century, Stanton supported acquisition of the vote as a partial step toward achieving freedom, but her broader aim remained "to make woman a self-supporting equal partner with man in the state, the church and the home." . . .

The depth of antagonism which the feminists provoked was disclosed in an 1866 Congressional debate on extending the franchise to the women of Washington, D.C. Women's rights advocates demanded the vote on the basis that women were individuals who had the same inalienable right as male human beings to determine their own destinies. As the historian Aileen Kraditor has pointed out, however, most Americans believed that the family, not the individual, constituted the basic unit of society. Each home existed as a "state in miniature." It had only one head — the husband — and he alone represented it in the world outside. Anyone who challenged that structure could logically be charged with attempting to subvert the family and destroy the state. "When God married our first parents in the garden," one senator declared, "they were made 'bone of one bone and flesh of one flesh'; and the whole theory of government and society proceeds upon the assumption that their interests are one . . . that whatever is for the benefit of one is for the benefit of the other." Those who urged freedom for women, he asserted, would "put her . . . in an adversary position to man and convert all the now harmonious elements of society into a state of war, and make every home a hell on earth." Pursuing the same line of argument, Senator Peter Frelinghuysen of New Jersey insisted that women had a "higher and holier" function than to engage in the turmoil of public life. "Their mission is at home," he said, "by their blandishments and their love to assuage the passions of men."

The feminists did not help their cause when they allowed themselves to be identified with proposals to liberalize sexual morality. In the 1870's Victoria Woodhull, a friend of Susan B. Anthony and Elizabeth Cady Stanton, endorsed free love and licensed prostitution in her weekly newspaper. Advocacy of sexual freedom was bad enough, but Woodhull then went on to create a public furor by charging that the respectable reformer Henry Ward Beecher was having a love affair with Elizabeth Tilton. Beecher instituted a libel suit, prolonging the public uproar, and prominent feminists rushed to Woodhull's defense. [Editor and political leader] Horace Greeley, among others, had previously stated that he could not support the feminists because they were too closely tied to the cause of free love. Now, Woodhull's pronouncements, and her widely publicized association with feminists, appeared to confirm Greeley's allegations, and added one more weapon to the anti-feminist arsenal.

Such episodes inevitably took their toll. As the century wore on, it became increasingly obvious that if the woman's movement continued to advocate serious change in marriage and the family, it would be dismissed as a radical fringe and charged with trying to destroy the moral fiber of the nation. Every social movement contains some people who insist on the need for total change and others who are willing to compromise in order to achieve tangible gains. Ordinarily, the two exist side by side — often in the same person — but usually one or the other approach is dominant. In the woman's movement, the forces of compromise gradually gained increased strength. In the years after the Civil War, feminism divided into different camps — the "conservative" American Woman's Suffrage Association, which was concerned almost exclusively with winning the ballot, and the "liberal" National Woman's Suffrage Association, which was committed to more far-reaching institutional change. By the end of the century, the degree of opposition to more radical feminist demands had made the liberal position untenable, and in 1890 the two wings of the movement reunited as the National American Woman's Suffrage Association (NAWSA) concerned primarily with the goal of winning the suffrage — the most respectable and limited feminist demand.

At the same time, women's rights leaders shifted from what Aileen Kraditor has called an "argument from justice" to an "argument from expediency." Again, there was no clear-cut gap between those espousing the different strategies. At various times, Elizabeth Cady Stanton had used the expediency argu-

ment, and later women's rights advocates never abandoned the argument from justice. But by the turn of the century there was a shift in the balance between the two positions. Instead of emphasizing the inalienable rights of females as individuals, the feminists tended to emphasize the utility of the ballot as an agent for reforming society. And rather than base their appeal on the similarity of men and women as human beings, they underlined the immutable differences which distinguished the sexes and gave to each a unique role to play in politics.

In large part, the shift developed as a natural response to a hostile political climate. As long as feminists focused on women's right to be free of social constraints, they invited association of their own movement with such issues as divorce and free love. In an age scarred by fear of anarchism and social disorder, it made sense for women leaders to de-emphasize those positions which were most likely to incur public disapproval. At the same time a different generation of leaders took over direction of the woman's movement. By the turn of the century, most of the early feminists had either died or retired from active participation in the movement. Their places were taken by people like Carrie Chapman Catt and Jane Addams — women who shared many of the same ideals as the first generation but who inevitably operated within a different frame of reference. The new leaders evolved a set of tactics designed to minimize controversy, and in the tradition of the American Suffrage Association they maintained a low level of rhetoric. As a result, the woman's movement more and more frequently accepted the opposition's premise on the sanctity of the home and pursued the fight for the vote within the context of conventional ideas on woman's place. The new direction of the movement emerged gradually. It was not marked by any special event, nor did it reflect a Machiavellian plot by any faction or group of leaders. But with the passage of time, the feminist appeal clearly took on a different tone.

The suffragists' acceptance of female distinctiveness

represented the departure point for the new strategy. In the past feminist leaders had championed the principle that the two sexes had exactly identical rights to engage in worldly activity. Now, they frequently argued that women deserved the vote precisely because they were different. The suffragists brilliantly exploited traditional assumptions about woman's unique place. Females were primarily spiritual creatures, they claimed. Hence their participation in politics would elevate the moral level of government. Men possessed special talents to cope with material problems based on their experience in the business world. But women had special abilities to cope with human problems based on their experience in the home. Each sex occupied its own particular sphere, but the two were complementary rather than incompatible. Just as the creation of a good family required the contribution of both husband and wife, so the establishment of effective government depended upon the equal participation of male and female citizens. Politics dominated by men alone constituted a half-finished social instrument. Involvement by women was essential to complete it.

The new line of argument was epitomized by the suffragists' claim that the nation was simply a macrocosm of the home. Frances Willard of the Women's Christian Temperance Union had first described politics as "enlarged housekeeping," and suffragists like Jane Addams adopted the phrase to package their appeal to the public. Woman's primary duty, Addams argued in a widely circulated magazine article, was to preserve the health of her children and the cleanliness of her home. In an urban, industrial environment, the fulfillment of her responsibilities depended on the sanitation policies, fire regulations, and housing standards of municipal government. If dirt were to be controlled, garbage collection had to be prompt. If the meat a mother bought for her family was to be free of germs, stringent government inspection was required. And if the clothes her children wore were not to be carriers of disease, government regulation of sweatshops was essential. In short, Addams declared,

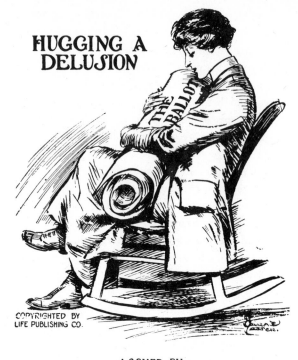

HUGGING A DELUSION

COPYRIGHTED BY LIFE PUBLISHING CO.

ISSUED BY
THE NEW YORK STATE ASSOCIATION
OPPOSED TO WOMAN SUFFRAGE

Even as late as 1917 antisuffragists, many of them women, actively opposed votes for women. This cartoon comes from an antisuffrage pamphlet issued by the New York State Association Opposed to Women's Suffrage. By this time, however, women's suffrage had become allied with progressivism and had received the support of a number of prominent male leaders, including Theodore Roosevelt. Within three years, the "delusion" of votes for women would become a reality. (Courtesy of the League of Women Voters of the United States)

"if woman would keep on with her old business of caring for her house and rearing her children, she will have to have some conscience in regard to public affairs lying outside her immediate household." Women could preserve the home and remain good mothers only if they acquired the vote and through political involvement protected the family.

By such reasoning the woman's movement broadened its appeal and neutralized the opposition's charge that it sought to destroy the home. The allegation was still made. In the 1917 suffrage debate a Southern congressman declared that giving the vote to women would "disrupt the family, which is the unit of society; and when you disrupt the family, you destroy the home, which is the foundation stone of the Republic." But such arguments no longer contained the power they once had. By avoiding issues which might alienate potential supporters while emphasizing traditional conceptions of women's proper role, the suffragists acquired growing respectability. More and more, they occupied the moderate center of the political spectrum and mirrored the views of the society around them.

The positions the suffragists took on such issues as immigration, race, and religion reflected the extent to which they shared prevailing public opinion. In 1894 Carrie Chapman Catt joined those protesting the influx of foreigners and warned against the effort of undesirables to despoil the nation's wealth. "There is but one way to avert the danger," Mrs. Catt declared: "Cut off the vote of the slums and give it to women. . . . " A year earlier the suffrage convention had blatantly appealed to nativist fears by calling attention to the fact that "there are more white women who can read and write than all negro voters; more American women who can read and write than all foreign voters." Woman suffrage, the convention suggested, "would settle the vexed question of rule by illiteracy" and ensure the perpetuation of the American way of life. Even former leaders could not escape the movement's quest for respectability. In 1895 Elizabeth Cady Stanton published the first volume of the *Woman's Bible,* an attack on established religion's responsibility for woman's subject status. The suffrage convention explicitly disassociated itself from the publication, and, in effect, disavowed Stanton's leadership.

With the advent of Progressivism, the strategy of consensus bore fruit. The suffragists had already defined the vote for women as a means of humanizing government, and in a period of generalized commitment to "reform," they were able to identify their own cause with the larger effort to extend democracy and eliminate social injustice. Progressivism meant a great many things to different people, but in large part it represented an effort to clean up the most obvious causes of corruption, disease, and poverty. Within such a context, the suffragists argued convincingly that extension of the franchise to females would help in the task of improving society. Both the rhetoric and substance of the suffrage program meshed with the ethos of reform. Women, one suffragist declared, were engaged in "a fight of the home against the saloon; . . . a struggle of justice with greed and prejudice; . . . a long strong battle between the selfish citizens and the patriotic ones." To a remarkable extent, the society at large defined the goals of Progressivism in the same way, and as a result, the suffragists succeeded in making the vote for women a prominent item on the agenda of reform.

Female reformers, of course, played a decisive part in shaping Progressivism through their involvement in the social welfare movement. Women like Jane Addams, Lillian Wald, and Florence Kelley started the settlement houses which sprouted up in urban America during the 1890's, and then carried their ideas and experience into national organizations dedicated to securing legislative change. For such women, suffrage and the cause of social welfare were inextricably tied together. Committed to building better neighborhoods and improving the conditions of workers in sweatshops and factories, they realized that they could accomplish little without political power. The construction of new parks and sewers required the approval of city officials, and wages and hours could not be regulated without state legislation. Woman suffrage thus became a natural concern of reformers who hoped to mobilize an independent political constituency which would force party bosses into action. The vote for females, the reformers believed, would add a sympathetic bloc to the electorate and provide the leverage necessary to secure social-welfare legislation. The men and women who founded Hull House and the National Consumers League were powerful figures, and their support substantially strengthened the "reform" appeal of the woman's movement.

Progressivism also provided a vehicle by which millions of hitherto uninvolved middle-class women became politicized. . . . Founded in 1890 with some 500,000 members, the General Federation of Women's Clubs (GFWC) grew to over 2 million members twenty years later. In the tradition of earlier reading and literary societies, the GFWC's original purpose was to encourage women's intellectual development and provide an opportunity for recreation. By the turn of the century, however, the club movement had caught the contagious spirit of reform. . . . In 1914 the GFWC formally endorsed the suffrage campaign, and for the first time in its history, the woman's movement had a strong base of support among women themselves.

The close ties between suffragists and reformers became increasingly obvious as the Progressive period moved on. At an early stage, the women's rights movement joined in the cry for social welfare improvements. The number of articles in the *Woman's Journal* advocating reform legislation doubled between 1895 and 1915. More important, an interlocking directorate linked the woman's movement to other groups in the Progressive coalition. . . .

The common denominator which united most of these groups was the belief that the vote for women represented an essential step toward a better society. In the tradition of Progressivism, each interpreted the value of the suffrage differently. Civic reformers believed that female voters would help oust corrupt political bosses. Devotees of democratization viewed woman suffrage as a logical extension of the initiative, referendum, and recall. And social-welfare organizations considered it a powerful new weapon in the fight for minimum-wage and child-labor legislation. All agreed, however, that, whatever one's particular definition of "reform," extending the franchise to women would enhance the possibility of achieving it.

By the second decade of the twentieth century, the suffrage movement had succeeded in establishing itself as an important part of the Progressive coalition. Significantly, nine of the eleven states which enacted woman suffrage by 1914 also had adopted the initiative and referendum. Suffrage supporters actively supported most pieces of reform legislation, and reformers reciprocated by pressuring political leaders to join the struggle for the franchise. Both major parties responded by moving closer to endorsement of the suffrage, and when the insurgent "Bull Moose" party headed by Theodore Roosevelt met in convention in 1912, it issued an unequivocal call for a constitutional amendment granting women the right to vote. In the past, the woman's movement had suffered from a lack of allies and a dearth of popular support. Now, after repeated rebuffs, it had achieved legitimacy as an entrenched part of a broad-based reform movement. No longer a deviant fringe, it had become, in the words of the *Woman's Journal,* "bourgeois," "middle class," and "middle-of-the-road."

With the support of leading reformers as an impetus, women activists revived flagging suffrage campaigns in states across the country. In 1910, the state of Washington broke a fourteen-year streak of defeats when its voters approved a suffrage amendment in a popular referendum. Victories followed in Illinois and California, proving for the first time that the vote for women had appeal in areas with large industrial and urban concentrations. In the nation's capital, meanwhile, the militant Congressional Union injected new life into the struggle for a federal amendment. Headed by Alice Paul, a Quaker and veteran of the English suffrage campaign, the Union was formed in 1913 as the Congressional Committee of NAWSA and within two months organized a tumultuous parade of 5,000 women to mark the arrival of Woodrow Wilson for the presidential inauguration ceremonies. The Congressional Union insisted that the party in power be made to answer for the failure to approve the suffrage amendment and in 1914 and 1916 mounted a

After 1915, the National American Woman's Suffrage Association, under the leadership of Carrie Chapman Catt, concentrated on influencing local and state elections, lobbying Congress, and converting President Wilson. This banner-carrying woman was photographed at the gates of the White House in 1917. Later that year forty-one women from fifteen states were arrested outside the White House for suffragist demonstrations. In 1919, after women had rallied to the support of his war policies, Wilson himself took up their cause. (UPI/Bettman Newsphotos)

national campaign to defeat Democratic candidates. Both in spirit and tactics, Alice Paul's organization offended the more conservative bent of NAWSA, and in 1915 the two groups split, but the energy, excitement, and publicity which the Congressional Union generated played a key role in focusing renewed suffragist attention on the necessity for a national constitutional amendment.

Responding to the challenge posed by the Congressional Union, NAWSA reorganized its national office in 1915 and placed Carrie Chapman Catt in charge of the over-all suffrage campaign. Catt immediately formulated a "Winning Plan" based on the concept that state and federal efforts should reinforce each other. For every victory won on a local level, she reasoned, additional congressmen and senators could be persuaded to vote for a suffrage amendment. It was especially important, she felt, for suffrage forces to break the solid front of opposition in the Northeast and South. "If New York wins in 1917," she declared, "the backbone of the opposition will be largely bent if not broken." Catt viewed herself as a field commander and brought to the suffrage movement an unprecedented amount of discipline and efficiency. While crucial local affiliates mobilized their energies to achieve state victories, a carefully selected staff of lobbyists cultivated support on Capitol Hill. Catt herself concentrated on President Wilson. Instead of denouncing him as the Congressional Union had done, she solicited his advice, invited him to address suffrage conventions, and in every way possible associated him with the suffrage cause.

Piece by piece the elements of Catt's "Winning Plan" fell into place. In 1917 the voters of New York passed a suffrage referendum, reversing their decision of two years earlier. A year later Michigan, South Dakota, and Oklahoma joined the suffrage ranks. Fourteen state legislatures in 1917 and twenty-six in 1919 petitioned Congress to enact a federal amendment. The President himself entered the fray after women had rallied to the support of his war policies. "The services of women during the supreme crisis have been of the most signal usefulness and distinction," he wrote Mrs. Catt. "It is high time that part of our debt should be acknowledged and paid." When a new Congress convened in 1919, it was as if no controversy had ever existed. The suffrage amendment passed the House by a vote of 304 to 90, the Senate by a vote of 56 to 25. Fourteen months later, Tennessee became the thirty-sixth state to ratify [and so to make it law]. Nearly three quarters of a century after Seneca Falls, the women's rights movement had reached a benchmark. "How much time and patience . . . how much hope, how much despair went into the battle," Carrie Chapman Catt reflected. "It leaves its mark on one, such a struggle. It fills the days and it rides the nights." And now the fight was over. Women had won the vote.

To a large extent, the suffrage victory represented a triumph for the strategy of compromise. By tempering those ideas most likely to offend public sensibilities and playing up the social utility of the ballot, leaders like Carrie Chapman Catt made substantial inroads into the opposition's strength and succeeded in building a political consensus on behalf of the Nineteenth Amendment. The suffragists themselves, on the other hand, were not necessarily aware of the changes which had taken place. When the Nineteenth Amendment was enacted, female leaders believed that they had carried out the mission begun at Seneca Falls and did not perceive the extent to which the vision of the earlier feminists had been narrowed. The woman's movement, Carrie Chapman Catt wrote in 1917, was engaged in a "world-wide revolt against all artificial barriers which laws and customs interpose between women and human freedom." The same purpose had inspired the founders of the women's rights movement. Thus if the nature of feminism had altered, the suffragists did not consciously recognize or acknowledge the change.

At least in part, the contradiction reflected the perspective from which the suffragists viewed the past. "The participants in a historical situation," David Potter has observed, "tend to see the alternatives in that situation as less clear cut, less sharply focused" than historians do. Potter's comments were made in a different context, but they speak directly to the suffragists' perception of their own accomplishments. Although a change in style and tone had certainly taken place within the woman's movement, it occurred over such a long period of time that it was not immediately visible to contemporary observers. There were "conservatives" in the movement in 1848 and "radicals" in 1918, and while the balance be-

tween the different points of view altered, there was no overt reversal of direction. The vote had always constituted an important plank in the feminist platform, and simply grew in prominence with the passage of time. Even the "argument from expediency" evolved gradually, never totally dominating the "argument from justice." Since the woman's movement did not split over either issue, there was no reason for suffrage leaders to perceive a discontinuity between the past and present. Indeed, if they had envisioned their goal as anything less than that of the early feminists, they would have found it difficult to justify the dedication and energy they expended in the struggle.

At the same time, the value ascribed to the vote by contemporaries reinforced women's rights leaders in their belief that they were involved in a battle of revolutionary significance. In the Progressive era, it was not unusual for different groups to define reform measures as panaceas. Prohibitionists asserted that the Eighteenth Amendment would purify the nation's morals. Trustbusters pledged that dismantling large corporations would guarantee economic freedom. And social welfare reformers contended that woman suffrage would usher in a new age of protection for workers and customers, while putting an end to graft and indifference in government. The fact that financiers, railroads, and liquor interests went to such great lengths to bankroll the fight against the Nineteenth Amendment encouraged women leaders in their belief that the suffrage would transform society.

Finally, the progress which had taken place from 1848 to 1920 provided some justification for the conviction that extending the franchise would demolish one of the last barriers to equality. Common law restrictions had largely been removed. Educational opportunity was available in a variety of private colleges and public universities. And during World War I, thousands of women had moved into jobs formerly held by men, causing many observers to assert that a revolution in the economic role of women had occurred. If not all the demands of 1848 had been met, enough had received some attention to create a basis in reality for the suffragists' hope that acquisition of the vote would place women on a par with men in society.

Thus when the last state ratified the Nineteenth Amendment, the suffragists had good reason to believe that they had scored a decisive victory in the battle for women's rights. In effect, the ballot had come to symbolize the entire struggle for equality and to embody all the demands of the woman's movement. The question was whether the suffrage could carry the heavy burden assigned to it, whether the right to vote also meant progress toward eliminating the deeper causes of inequality which had concerned the feminists at Seneca Falls. Carrie Chapman Catt told a victory celebration in New York in 1920 that she had lived to realize the greatest dream of her life. "We are no longer petitioners," she said, "we are not wards of the nation, but free and equal citizens." Only the experience of the next generation could prove whether such optimism represented wishful thinking or hard reality.

QUESTIONS TO CONSIDER

1. How did the women's rights movement, the early leaders of which had pressed for sweeping social, economic, and political changes in women's status, come to focus its energies on a single issue: the right to vote?

2. Hindsight shows that the winning of the elective franchise by women brought no revolutionary changes to American society. Explain then why the demand for women's suffrage raised such vehement opposition.

3. Why did feminists at the turn of the century shift their strategy for winning the vote from what historian Aileen Kraditor calls an "argument from justice" to an "argument from expediency"?

4. How was the second generation of feminists able to use conventional ideas about women's place to gain widespread support for women's suffrage? What price did they pay for such "respectability"?

5. How were twentieth-century feminists able to link their demand for women's suffrage with the Progressive movement? What role did women play in shaping progressivism, and how did the Progressive movement win new allies for women's rights?

A New River of Black Protest

LERONE BENNETT, JR.

There was another river of struggle in the Progressive era, an African American struggle against legally enforced segregation and the whole philosophy of white supremacy and black inferiority that underlay it. Segregation was worse in the South, because that was where most African Americans lived. Indeed, by the beginning of the twentieth century, southern whites had turned their region into a bastion of white supremacy and racial discrimination. A farrago of state constitutional amendments, Jim Crow laws, and local ordinances shackled African Americans to the bottom of the South's racist social order. African Americans could not vote or run for political office; they had to attend separate and inferior "colored" schools, sit in segregated waiting rooms in southern depots, ride in segregated trains and streetcars, drink from separate water fountains, lodge only in "colored" hotels, and face humiliating "Whites Only" signs at public swimming pools, golf courses, and libraries. In Jackson, Mississippi, they were even buried in a separate cemetery. Woe to African Americans who tried to cross the color line: they could expect a gunshot or a lynching. Indeed, lynchings multiplied at an alarming rate in the Deep South. Meanwhile, in Plessy v. Ferguson (1896), the United States Supreme Court upheld "separate but equal" accommodations in Dixie. Never mind that facilities for African Americans were almost never equal to those for whites; the Court ruled that no discrimination was involved. Justice John Marshall Harlan, however, issued a ringing dissent, arguing that "our Constitution is color-blind, and neither knows nor tolerates classes among citizens."

African Americans in the South not only faced racial barriers at every turn, they also suffered from grinding poverty — the result, in part, of being left a propertyless, laboring class during Reconstruction. In search of the Promised Land, they started migrating to the

North in ever-increasing numbers, in what amounted to a rebellion against white-controlled Dixie. By the scores, then by the hundreds, they streamed into such industrial cities as Chicago, Cleveland, and New York. To their dismay, however, the North was not the Promised Land either, and migrants found themselves herded into city ghettos and kept there by a host of real estate and municipal codes. Thereafter when African Americans went north, as writer James Baldwin observed, they did not go to New York City, they went to Harlem; they did not go to Chicago, they went to the South Side; they did not go to Los Angeles, they went to Watts. As Lerone Bennett says, "Real estate became the principal dynamic in the ensemble of northern race relations," and the walls of segregation erected across the urban North in turn produced a new anger and militancy, indeed "a new and different black world." Malcolm X, the subject of a later selection, would be a furious product of the northern black ghetto.

Initially, especially in the South, African Americans submitted to living as third-class citizens in a white-dominated country. In that period of reaction, there was little else they could do. Most followed the advice of Booker T. Washington, the head of all-black Tuskegee Institute in Alabama, who had been born a slave. In 1895, in Atlanta, Washington urged African Americans to forget about political and social equality for now and to learn skills and trades to support themselves. By imitating white standards and values, perhaps they could earn white people's friendship and preserve racial peace. But as Martin Luther Ling, Jr., noted later, it was "an obnoxious negative peace" in which "the Negro's mind and soul were enslaved."

This sets the stage for the next selection, written by African American historian Lerone Bennett, Jr., which traces the beginnings of the modern African American protest movement. That movement, as Bennett points out, began in 1905, when William Trotter, a Boston businessman, rebelled against Booker T. Washington's policy of accommodation. Trotter's rebellion in turn inspired W. E. B. Du Bois, a brilliant scholar whose militancy and racial pride were reminiscent of Frederick Douglass's. Du Bois exhorted the blacks' "Talented Tenth" to take the lead and find solutions to the misery of the masses. In 1905, against a backdrop of spiraling racial violence, Du Bois met with a small band of well-educated, bold, and unhappy African American professionals and businessmen in the city of Niagara Falls, Canada. They drafted a blazing manifesto demanding justice and equality for African Americans. The Niagara platform became a blueprint for the National Association for the Advancement of Colored People (NAACP), established in 1909 in the centennial of Abraham Lincoln's birth. Du Bois and seven other Niagara leaders joined nineteen white racial progressives on the NAACP's original board (the racial imbalance reflected the paternalistic attitudes of the white founders). The first nationwide organization dedicated to gaining African Americans their rights as citizens, the NAACP concentrated on legal action and court battles. It won its first victory in 1915 — the same year the twentieth-century Ku Klux Klan was founded on Stone Mountain in

Georgia — when the United States Supreme Court outlawed the grandfather clause in the state constitutions of Oklahoma and Maryland. Those clauses had prohibited African Americans from voting unless their grandfathers had voted in 1860.

In Bennett's stirring pages, you will meet Du Bois, Trotter, and several other significant figures — blacks and whites, men and women — who launched "the Negro rebellion" in Progressive America. As we will see in selection 25, that rebellion would profoundly change the history of American race relations. Yet, as Bennett observes, the early African American protest movement was not without its problems. Note his insightful discussion of the movement's internal ideological and racial struggles. Note, too, that the first generation of African American leaders belonged to the "black elite" and tended to speak to other literate, educated black professionals about the problems of their race. In the early years of the movement, the mass of African Americans was locked in rural enclaves in the South, where they had never heard of Du Bois or the NAACP. Even so, between 1909 and 1915, the "balance of power" among African American leaders shifted from accommodators such as Booker T. Washington to the militants and moderates in the NAACP. In 1916, at the first "black summit conference" in Amenia, New York, NAACP leaders and the followers of Washington (who had died the year before) joined forces and forged a compromise program for struggle and uplift. The NAACP itself would continue to grow until it became the biggest and most powerful civil rights organization in the country.

As you read Bennett's narrative, compare the protest and organizational techniques of the northern militants with those of the women's suffrage movement discussed in the previous selection. Also compare the Woodrow Wilson of Bennett's story with the Woodrow Wilson in the account of the women's suffrage movement. Why would Wilson endorse the latter movement and yet initiate a policy of federal discrimination against African Americans?

GLOSSARY

ABBOTT, ROBERT Launched an African American newspaper in a friend's kitchen in Chicago and helped refocus "the passion of the Negro press" by attacking every form of segregation.

BUCHANAN V. WARLEY (1917) Supreme Court decision which nullified a local ordinance imposing residential segregation on the basis of color.

DU BOIS, W. E. B. Reclusive professor of economics and sociology at Atlanta University who emerged as the leader of the African American elite, created the "myth of the Talented Tenth," helped found the NAACP, and served as first editor of the NAACP's official publication, *Crisis;* by his own reckoning, he was "the main factor in revolutionizing the attitude of the American Negro toward caste" between 1910 and 1930.

"IDEOLOGY OF NEGRO DEBASEMENT" Created by white Realtors and property owners' associations to justify segregated schools and "recreational outlets" in northern cities; "the ideology was based on the myth of the Negro's innate inferiority and his alleged propensity for lowering community standards."

JOHNSON, JAMES WELDON   The NAACP's first African American secretary.

OVINGTON, MARY WHITE   Wealthy young white social worker and associate member of the Niagara movement who played a key role in the foundation of the NAACP.

SHILLADY, JOHN   The NAACP's last white secretary, who resigned after a white mob beat him in the streets of Dallas.

THE SOULS OF BLACK FOLK (1903)   Du Bois's collection of essays, in which "restrained passion that burned like ice," summoned African Americans to resist Booker T. Washington's doctrine of accommodation; the book affected the African American community much as Uncle Tom's Cabin had a half century earlier.

SPINGARN, JOEL E.   Chairman of the NAACP board who hosted the first African American summit meeting that merged the approaches of Du Bois and Booker T. Washington.

TROTTER, WILLIAM MONROE   Boston real estate broker who in 1901 founded the Boston Guardian and "dedicated his life to the destruction of Booker T. Washington."

URBAN LEAGUE   Biracial organization founded in 1910 to focus on "the socioeconomic woes of urban Negroes."

VILLARD, OSWALD GARRISON   Grandson of William Lloyd Garrison, the great nineteenth-century abolitionist, Villard was a white journalist and pacifist who helped found the NAACP and served as chairman of its board; he resigned in protest when the board refused to censor Du Bois's "acid" editorials in Crisis.

WALLING, WILLIAM ENGLISH   Radical white Kentuckian who called for action after the race riot in Springfield, Illinois, in 1908 and who helped found the NAACP the following year.

WASHINGTON, BOOKER T.   Between 1903 and 1915, the champion of accommodation, who had once dined with President Theodore Roosevelt, found himself under a zealous ideological attack by Du Bois, Trotter, and other members of the radical African American elite.

WELLS, IDA B.   An African American newspaper editor who fought against bigotry in Memphis, Tennessee, walking the streets, as Bennett says elsewhere, "with two guns strapped to her waist"; run out of Memphis, she settled in Chicago and founded the Antilynching League, the first effective opposition to the lynching and beating of African Americans.

The Negro rebellion began not in Montgomery in 1955, not in Greensboro in 1960, not in Birmingham in 1963, but in Boston in 1905. It began with an impertinent question, a batch of red pepper, and a riot in a church.

It began, as Emerson cogently noted, where all revolts begin: in the mind of one man.

William Monroe Trotter, who started it all, was the last abolitionist and the first modern rebel. Pudgy, black, and pugnacious, with quick, darting eyes and a whole-hearted commitment to integration and revolt, Trotter was the advance man of a new breed of black rebels who fleshed out the renaissance of the Negro soul.

An authentic radical, cast in the mould of the New England dissidents, Trotter was born in 1872 and raised in a Boston suburb saturated with abolitionist memories. After graduating from Harvard with honors and a Phi Beta Kappa key, the Boston rebel married into a socially prominent family and settled down to a promising career as a real estate broker. There stretched out before him then a bright vista of achievement and service in the echelons of the black elite. But this vision seemed somehow mean to Trotter who was haunted by the creeping misery of the Negro masses and the surging tide of accommodation. With scarcely a backward glance, Trotter repudiated the elite and became an activist. Aided by George Forbes, another well-educated member of the Boston elite, Trotter founded the Boston *Guardian* in 1901 and dedicated his life to the destruction of Booker T. Washington and the idea he represented.

Washington was quick to pick up the gage flung down by the young Boston activist. The Tuskegee president made a desperate and pathetic attempt to silence Trotter, subsidizing another Boston paper, and engineering costly and time-consuming suits against

From Lerone Bennett, Jr., *Confrontation: Black and White* (New York: Penguin Books, 1968, by arrangement with Johnson Publishing Company, Chicago), extracts from 95–118.

the rebellious editor. But nothing worked; the Boston Cato went his lonely way, thundering: Booker T. Washington must be destroyed. Worse, he followed Washington from city to city in an unsuccessful effort to question him about his equivocal words. This peripatetic campaign probably would have come to naught had not Washington made an uncharacteristic mistake. Overconfident, sure of himself and his power, he accepted an invitation to speak in Boston, the citadel of Negro radicalism. When the Great Accommodator rose to speak on July 30, 1905, at Boston's AME Zion Church, the Trotterites were ready. Ignoring the chairman, they leaped to their feet and shouted questions and insults from the floor. Trotter posed several loaded questions, asking: "In view of the fact that you are understood to be unwilling to insist upon the Negro having his every right (both civil and political) would it not be a calamity at this juncture to make you our leader? . . . Is the rope and the torch all the race is to get under your leadership?"

The restive audience exploded at this point, and policemen were called to restore order. When Washington resumed his speech, he unwisely told an equivocal anecdote about an old mule and the hall heaved in thunderous screams, shouts, and hisses. In the confusion someone threw a batch of red pepper and the crowd panicked, men and women trampling each other in a frantic attempt to reach the nearest exit.

Reports of the Boston "riot" and the "insult to the Negro's greatest leader" startled America — which was, I suppose, Trotter's aim. It had not been possible, up to that point, to get prime coverage of the seething ideological dispute in the Negro world. Having selected Washington as the Negro leader, the white power structure protected him from the enfilading fire of white and Negro malcontents; but it was impossible to suppress the Boston riot, and word went out that some Negroes were displeased with "their" leader.

The heavy-handed handling of the Boston riot

(Trotter served a one-month jail sentence) was a catastrophic mistake. People who loathed Trotter began to sympathize with him. More ominously, for Booker T. Washington and the power structures, people on the perimeter began to move to the center of the arena.

The Boston riot, like the abolitionist demonstrations of the 1830's and the sit-in demonstrations of the 1960's, was more than a localized disturbance. Seen whole, within the context of forces contending for the public's ear, the riot was a plea, an appeal, and an argument. And the argument, clothed in the propaganda of a deed, was much more irresistible than mere words. Sixty-six years before, Wendell Phillips had been converted by an idea fleshed by risk and pain. Now, at another decisive hour in the history of the Negro protest, a hero came down off the fence. The convert was W. E. B. Du Bois, a thirty-five-year-old professor of economics and sociology at Atlanta University. Poet, scholar, mystic, seer, prophet, Du Bois had moved for years on the edge of the controversy, courted by both Washington and anti-Washington forces. Now he came down hard on the side of the radicals. "I did not always agree with Trotter then or later," Du Bois wrote. "But he was an honest, brilliant, unselfish man, and to treat as a crime that which was at worst mistaken judgment was an outrage."

Totally committed now, Du Bois moved out into the deeps as a fisher of men. This was a decisive moment in the history of the pioneer protest movement. Du Bois had gifts Trotter lacked. He was widely admired as an ideologue who could invoke a program in an epigram and rip an opponent to shreds in seven languages. Du Bois, moreover, was a man of genius whose academic distinction impressed both Negroes and whites.

Under Du Bois the protest movement moved to a new level of strategic and tactical effectiveness. More important, in the context of current realities, was Du Bois' role in the founding of the NAACP and the articulation of the attenuated abolitionist ideology which undergirds the modern protest movement.

W. E. B. DuBois was the foremost member of a gifted group of African American leaders during the early years of the twentieth century. A "child of the black elite" and highly educated, with a bachelor's degree from Fisk and a Ph.D. from Harvard, he played a major role in the founding of the National Association for the Advancement of Colored People and raised the "black protest movement" to a new level of effectiveness. (Schomburg Center for Research in Black Culture, The New York Public Library; Astor, Lenox and Tilden Foundations)

Thirty-one years later, the NAACP said Du Bois' ideas had "transformed the Negro world as well as a large portion of the liberal white world, so that the whole problem of the relation of black and white races has ever since had a completely new orientation. He created, what never existed before, a Negro intelligentsia, and many who have never read a word of his writings are his spiritual disciples and descendants. Without him the [NAACP] could never have been what it was and is."

In a typically immodest and yet truthful statement, Du Bois agreed. "I think I may say," he wrote, "without boasting that in the period from 1910 to 1930 I was a main factor in revolutionizing the attitude of the American Negro toward caste. My stinging hammer blows made Negroes aware of themselves, confident of their possibilities and determined self-assertion. So much so that today common slogans among the Negro people are taken bodily from the words of my mouth."

Who was this man who spoke with such frankness, such immodesty — and such truth? . . .

Du Bois' life was a history in miniature of the death and rebirth of the Negro psyche. Born three years after Appomattox, one of a handful of black pebbles in the white sea of Great Barrington, Massachusetts, Du Bois was steeped from birth in the mute pains of violated black flesh. He was three when Grant was elected, eight when Queen Victoria became Empress of India, nine when Hayes betrayed the Negro, and ninety-one when the sit-in age began.

Like Trotter, like Walter White, like almost every protest leader, Du Bois was a child of the black elite; and his deficiencies, a certain snobbishness and disdain for the masses, were deficiencies of that structure. His family was among the oldest inhabitants of Great Barrington, and they tended, Du Bois remembered, to look down on Negro newcomers and Irish and German laborers. "A knowledge of family history," he said, "was counted as highly important."

Du Bois came early to indignation. As one of the few Negro students in the school system, he took great delight in besting his companions in letters and ideas. "The sky was bluest," he said, "when I could beat my mates at examination-time, or beat them at a foot-race, or even beat their stringy heads." At an early age, the future Negro leader decided that he was destined for greatness. How he learned this is a mystery. But we catch him at the age of fifteen in an extraordinary and, considering the circumstances, somewhat immodest act: collecting and annotating his papers for posterity.

With the help of scholarships, Du Bois graduated from Fisk and Harvard and went abroad to study at the University of Berlin. There, on his twenty-fifth birthday, the young mystic decided that he would become the Moses of the Negroes of America and Africa. Alone in his room, he made a "sacrifice to the Zeitgeist" of God and Work, performing a strange ceremony with Greek wine, oil, and candles. Then he made an entry in his diary.

I am glad I am living, I rejoice as a strong man to run a race, and I am strong — is it egotism, is it assurance — or is it the silent call of the world spirit that makes me feel that I am royal and that beneath my sceptre a world of kings shall bow. The hot dark blood of that black forefather born king of men — is beating at my heart, and I know that I am either a genius or a fool . . . this I do know: be the Truth what it may I will seek it on the pure assumption that it is worth seeking — and Heaven nor Hell, God nor Devil shall turn me from my purpose till I die. I will in this second quarter century of my life, enter the dark forest of the unknown world for which I have so many years served my apprenticeship — the chart and compass the world furnishes me I have little faith in — yet, I have none better — I will seek till I find — and die. . . .

These are my plans: to make a name in science, to make a name in literature and thus to raise my race. Or perhaps to raise a visible empire in Africa thro' England, France, or Germany.

I wonder what will be the outcome? Who knows?

I will go unto the King, which is not according to the scripture, and if I perish, I perish.

Returning to America in 1894 at the age of twenty-six, Du Bois entered "the dark forest of the unknown world." He became a professor of economics and sociology and turned out a series of monographs and books on the race problem. He believed then that truth, dispassionately presented, would set men free. But he soon changed his mind. There were, he recalled later, seventeen hundred Negroes lynched between 1885 and 1894 and "each death [was] a scar on my soul." No less distressing were the daily pinpricks he suffered as a resident of Atlanta, Georgia.

Proud and sensitive, Du Bois became a virtual recluse, confining himself to the Atlanta University campus, never entering a Jim Crow streetcar or a Jim Crow theater. Those who knew him then could never forget the looks of him: thin, aristocratic, aloof — a lonely man of terrible pride who was never seen without gloves and a cane.

Somewhere in this dark age it came to Du Bois that truth will only set men free if they have been actively seeking it. And more: that truth, unsupported by organization and energy, is powerless among men running pell mell into darkness. With Du Bois, analysis was always a prelude to action. Having decided that knowledge was not enough, he began his slow descent from the olympian heights of his ivory tower.

His first act was the publication in 1903 of a book of essays, *The Souls of Black Folk,* which had an impact on its age not unlike the publication of Baldwin's *The Fire Next Time* sixty years later. With restrained passion that burned like ice, Du Bois addressed himself to the issue of the day — freedom. To speak of Negro freedom in that day was to speak of Booker T. Washington; and Du Bois, who had tried to maintain a middle course, did not shrink from the task. In an essay, "On Mr. Booker T. Washington and Others," he aligned himself with Negro militants who opposed Washington, writing: "We have no right to sit silently by while the inevitable seeds are sown for a harvest of disaster to our children, black and white." Black men of America, he said, had a duty to perform, "a duty stern and delicate, — a forward movement to oppose a part of the work of their greatest leader."

And of what did this duty consist? "So far as Mr. Washington preaches thrift, patience, and industrial training for the masses, we must hold up his hands and strive with him, rejoicing in his honors and glorying in the strength of this Joshua called of God and of man to lead the headless host. But so far as Mr. Washington apologizes for injustices, North or South, does not rightly value the privileges and duty of voting, belittles the emasculating effects of caste distinctions, and

opposes the higher training and ambition of our brighter minds, — so far as he, the South, or the nation, does this, — we must unceasingly and firmly oppose them."

So writing, Du Bois marked off the field of battles and divided the Negro community into "sheep" or "goats." According to James Weldon Johnson, Du Bois' little book had a sharper impact on the Negro community than any other book published since *Uncle Tom's Cabin.*

Two parties arose in the ghetto now, and every literate Negro had to take a stand on the respective programs of Du Bois and Washington. Between these two parties, Johnson wrote, "there were incessant attacks and counterattacks; the [accommodators] declaring that the [militants] were visionaries, doctrinaires, and incendiaries; the [militants] charging the [accommodators] with minifying political and civil rights, with encouraging opposition to higher training and higher opportunities for Negro youth, with giving sanction to certain prejudiced practices and attitudes toward the Negro, thus yielding up in fundamental principles more than could be balanced by any immediate gains. One not familiar with this phase of Negro life in the twelve- or fourteen-year period following 1903 . . . cannot imagine the bitterness of the antagonism between these two wings." The struggle continued until Washington's death.

The roots of this controversy lay deep. The surface disagreement over industrial vs. higher education obscured a fundamental disagreement over modes of being. The whole controversy turned on leadership, not trades; on power, not education. To Washington's program of submission, Du Bois proposed a strategy of "ceaseless agitation and insistent demand for equality [involving] the use of force of every sort: moral suasion, propaganda and where possible even physical resistance." Du Bois' primary interest was in the education of "the group leader, the man who sets the ideals of the community where he lives, directs its thoughts and heads its social movements." He therefore opposed Washington's stress on education of the hand and heart because without a "knowledge of modern culture" the Negro would have "to accept white leadership, and . . . such leadership could not always be trusted to guide the Negro group into self-realization and to its highest cultural possibilities."

To drive this point home, Du Bois created the myth of the Talented Tenth, the ideological substructure of the modern protest movement. "The Negro race," he said, "like all races, is going to be saved by its exceptional men. The problem of education, then, among Negroes must first of all deal with the Talented Tenth; it is the problem of developing the Best of this race that they may guide the Mass away from the contamination and death of the Worst, in their own and other races."

The important thing to note about this archetypal Negro myth is its neutrality. The myth forms the base of the leadership principle of organizations as diverse as the Roman Catholic church and the Communist party. Everything depends, in the final analysis, on the definition of the tasks of the Talented Tenth. In theory, members of the Talented Tenth were to awaken the masses, guide them, inspire them, and lead them. In fact, the early Talented Tenth consisted of talented men leading other talented men and issuing manifestoes, from afar, for the edification and instruction of masses who had never heard of Du Bois, Washington, or the Talented Tenth. . . .

. . . In the years between 1903 and 1915, when the Du Bois-Washington controversy was at its height, most Negroes lived in back-country enclaves and were not available as constituents for either Washington or Du Bois, both of whom appealed, by necessity, to educated elites. The issue was joined in 1905 with the organization of the Niagara movement, the first sustained instrument of indignation since the Reconstruction debacle. From Atlanta, in June, 1905, Du Bois issued a call "for organized determination and aggressive action on the part of men who believe in Negro freedom and growth." In July, twenty-nine business and professional men met secretly at Niagara Falls, Ontario, and organized the germinal Niagara

movement. Du Bois and Trotter were the leading lights of the movement which demanded immediate and total integration.

In 1906, the same year that Gandhi began his passive resistance campaign in South Africa, the Niagara militants abandoned caution and held an open meeting at Harpers Ferry, the scene of John Brown's martyrdom. This meeting, Du Bois said, was "in significance if not in numbers one of the greatest meetings that American Negroes have ever held . . . and we talked some of the plainest English that has been given voice to by black men in America." Raising demands that are still burning issues, the Niagara militants said:

We will not be satisfied to take one jot or tittle less than our full manhood rights. We claim for ourselves every single right that belongs to a freeborn American, political, civil, and social; and until we get these rights we will never cease to protest and assail the ears of America. . . .

In details, our demands are clear and unequivocal. First, we would vote; with the right to vote goes everything: freedom, manhood, the honor of our wives, the chastity of our daughters, the right to work, and the chance to rise. . . . We want full manhood suffrage, and we want it now, henceforth and forever.

Second. We want discrimination in public accommodation to cease. Separation in railway and streetcars, based simply on race and color, is un-American, un-Democratic, and silly.

Third. We claim the right of freemen to walk, talk, and be with them that wish to be with us. No man has a right to choose another man's friends, and to attempt to do so is an impudent interference with the most fundamental human privilege.

Fourth. We want the laws enforced against rich as well as poor; against capitalists as well as laborers; against white as well as black. We are not more lawless than the white race, we are more often arrested, convicted and mobbed. We want justice even for criminals and outlaws. We want the Constitution of the country enforced. We want Congress to take charge of the Congressional elections. We want the

Fourteenth Amendment carried out to the letter and every state disfranchised in Congress which attempts to disfranchise its rightful voters. We want the Fifteenth Amendment enforced and no state allowed to base its franchise simply on color.

Fifth. We want our children educated. The school system in the country districts of the South is a disgrace and in few towns and cities are the Negro schools what they ought to be. . . .

These are some of the chief things we want. How shall we get them? By voting where we may vote; by persistent, unceasing agitation; by hammering at the truth; by sacrifice and work.

These were fine words if the Niagara militants could make them stick, but the odds were against them. Booker T. Washington controlled the power lines between the Negro and white communities and he counterattacked with devastating thoroughness, using his considerable resources to isolate the militants from white liberals and the Negro press. The movement was also hampered by internal problems. Du Bois and Trotter were not, by any means, organization men; the presence of both in one organization guaranteed strife and dissension. Between 1905 and 1907, the young movement was racked by a series of internal ideological explosions. Finally, in 1908, Trotter broke with his associates and founded his own organization, the National Equal Rights League.

Another factor in the eventual demise of the Niagara movement was its narrow base of membership. The membership consisted of a select group of ministers, educators, and professionals, a fact which pleased Du Bois who said he only wanted to attract "the very best class of Negroes." Full membership in the organization was confined to Negroes, but whites were eligible for associate membership. Among the white associate members was Mary White Ovington, a wealthy social worker who played a key role in the founding of the National Association for the Advancement of Colored People.

By 1907, the organization had 236 members and 144 associate members.

The elite tone of this pioneer Talented Tenth organization disturbed some Negroes and whites. The editor of the (New) *Jersey City Appeal* told Du Bois that he "would do well to get closer to the people, I mean the masses as well as the classes." Mary White Ovington expressed a similar reservation. Pointing to the psychological and social chasm between the Niagara members and the Negro masses, she asked Du Bois to let her speak on the Negro and the labor problem at the 1908 convention. "I would like," she said, "to hammer that side of things into some of the aristocrats in the membership." Despite its narrow base, the Niagara movement fashioned a national organization and established local branches in Northern cities. In program and in structure, the organization was similar to the NAACP, with an action campaign based on lobbying, legal redress, and protest propaganda.

Buffeted by critics of the left (Trotter) and right (Washington) and hampered by defects of vision and structure, the movement limped along from crisis to crisis until 1910. Although the Niagara militants failed in their larger objectives, they succeeded brilliantly on another level. By hammering away at the national conscience, the militants created a climate of dissent. More significantly, the movement educated Negroes in a strategy of contention and laid the foundations for the National Association for the Advancement of Colored People.

Even as the influence of the Niagara group diffused itself through Negro society, a pivotal era in the social life of the Negro and of America was drawing to a close. New machines were changing the face of the world and the Negro was changing with it. Blacktop roads were poking inquiring fingers into the Black Belts of the South, and improvements in communications were bringing in rays of light. Of crucial importance in this connection was the Model T Ford which freed both Negroes and whites from the tyranny of the land.

Every throb of the engine, every turn of the wheel, loosened the Negro's chains. Men traveling in the South in this period noted a new phenomenon, Negro racial consciousness; and they began to warn the South that the Negro could not be held down forever. The new Negro racial consciousness sprang from conflict, segregation, and despair. But it had deep roots in dawning hope. The sharp rise in the number of Negro college graduates and the emergence of a new [black middle-class] boosted Negro morale and stoked the fires of disaffection. Tangible proof of this new orientation was the growth of protest organizations. By 1908, the pioneer Niagara movement was sharing the national spotlight with Trotter's National Equal Rights League, Ida B. Wells's Antilynching League and the interracial Constitution League of John Milholland, a white industrialist.

Another factor in the growth of racial consciousness was the renaissance of the Negro press. As the Negro public increased in literacy, the number of Negro papers increased. As Negroes increased in militancy, the tone of the Negro press became more strident. William Monroe Trotter was, as we have seen, the father of modern protest journalism. But his contemporary, Robert Abbott, played an important role in refocusing the passion of the Negro press. Abbott was a Georgian who migrated to Chicago and started a paper in the kitchen of a friend's house. Sensing the new mood of urban Negroes, Abbott made an issue of every case of segregation and discrimination, hurling charges and recriminations in bold, red headlines which attracted the masses. In the process, he created a new tradition in the Negro press and made himself a wealthy man.

With the founding of the National Association for the Advancement of Colored People, the divergent strains of Negro militancy and white liberalism merged and the modern protest became organization. Sentiment for a national interracial organization was crystallized by a 1908 riot in Springfield, Illinois. A mob, which included, the press said, many of the town's "best citizens," took possession of Springfield for two days and surged through the streets, killing and wounding scores of Negroes and driving hundreds from the city. Shouting, "Lincoln freed you, we'll show you your place," bands of white ruffians lynched and flogged Negroes within sight of the emancipator's grave.

That this should happen in a city intimately associated with the early life of Lincoln horrified liberal America. William English Walling, a radical white Kentuckian, expressed the dawning sense of outrage in a newspaper article, "Race War in the North." It was time, Walling said, for national action. "Either the spirit of Lincoln and Lovejoy must be revived and we must come to treat the Negro on a plane of absolute political and social equality, or [white supremacists] Vardaman and Tillman will soon have transferred the race war to the North. . . . Yet who realizes the seriousness of the situation, and what large and powerful body of citizens is ready to come to their aid."

No "large and powerful body of citizens" recognized the seriousness of the situation, but one woman did; and, in the end, that made all the difference in the world. Mary White Ovington, the young white social worker of the Niagara movement, read Walling's plea and sat down "within the hour" and penned an answer. Proposals and counterproposals were made and, finally, in the first week of January, 1909, a white Southerner (Walling), a Jewish social worker (Henry Moskevitz) and a white woman (Ovington) held a meeting in a Manhattan apartment, which changed the course of Negro history. It was decided at this meeting to enlist the aid of white liberals and Negro militants in a crusade for human decency. With the help of Bishop Alexander Walters of the AME church and Dr. W. H. Bulkley, a Negro principal of a white New York public school, the white liberals issued a call "for the discussion of present evils, the voicing of protests and the renewal of the struggle for civil and political liberty." Oswald Garrison Villard, then publisher of the *New York Post,* wrote the call which was issued on February 12, 1909, the centenary of Lincoln's birth. The Negro's legal status had been declining for more than sixty years. At that point it was not markedly different from the pre-Reconstruction period. With chilling eloquence, Villard, a grandson of William Lloyd Garrison, detailed the crisis of the hour.

If Mr. Lincoln could revisit this country in the flesh, he would be disheartened and discouraged. He would learn that on January 1, 1909, Georgia had rounded out a new confederacy by disfranchising the Negro, after the manner of all the other Southern States. He would learn that the Supreme Court of the United States, supposedly a bulwark of American liberties, had refused every opportunity to pass squarely upon this disfranchisement of millions, by laws avowedly discriminatory and openly enforced in such manner that the white men may vote and black men be without a vote in their government; he would discover, therefore, that taxation without representation is the lot of millions of wealth-producing American citizens, in whose hands rests the economic progress and welfare of an entire section of the country.

He would learn that the Supreme Court, according to the official statement of one of its own judges in the Berea College case, has laid down the principle that if an individual state chooses, it may "make it a crime for white and colored persons to frequent the same market place at the same time, or appear in an assemblage of citizens convened to consider questions of a public or political nature in which all citizens, without regard to race, are equally interested."

In many states Lincoln would find justice enforced, if at all, by judges elected by one element in a community to pass upon the liberties and lives of another. He would see the black men and women, for whose freedom a hundred thousand of soldiers gave their lives, set apart in trains, in which they pay first-class fares for third-class service, and segregated in railway stations and in places of entertainment; he would observe that State after State declines to do its elementary duty in preparing the Negro through education for the best exercise of citizenship.

To right these wrongs, to call America back to the dream of the Founding Fathers, to remonstrate, to petition, to denounce — in order to do these things, hundreds of Negro and white Americans gathered in New York City in the last week of May, 1909. Some of the old abolitionists, notably Thomas Wentworth Higginson, and some of the sons of the abolitionists, notably William Lloyd Garrison, refused to attend because of the alleged "radical tone" of the conference. Among the prominent Negro participants were Niagara militants like Du Bois, Trotter, J. Max Barber and prominent women leaders like Ida B. Wells and Mary Church Terrell.

This decisive conference, on which so much depended, began with an astonishing exhibition. A Columbia University anthropologist and a Cornell University zoologist exhibited bottles containing the pickled brains of apes, Negroes, and whites. The two learned gentlemen then proved to the conferees and to the press that Negroes were human.

Having proved something, the conferees got down to the hard business of inventing a structure. It became clear almost immediately that the Negroes did not trust the white people and vice versa. Most of the white participants were moderates who did not want to offend Booker T. Washington. The Negro participants, on the other hand, were militants who doubted the good faith of white liberals.

The struggle over composition of the steering committee almost wrecked the meeting. When someone suggested Booker T. Washington's name, the meeting exploded. Villard was surprised that the "whole colored crowd" was "bitterly anti–Washington." The wrangle continued until past midnight when the nominations committee, taking "a middle course [which] suited nobody," announced its selections. Booker T. Washington was not nominated; nor were Negro radicals like Ida B. Wells and Monroe

Trotter. Ida B. Wells went immediately to the chairman and insisted that her name be placed on the list; and the chairman, Mary Ovington noted, "illegally, but wisely" complied. Trotter maintained a nebulous relation with the NAACP for a few years and then dropped out, saying the organization was "too white."

One more hurdle, the resolutions, stood before the Negro and white conferees. A long and bitter debate ensued on almost every word and comma of the resolutions. The Negro militants turned on the white liberals with a cold fury, charging that "a traitorous clique" had captured the meeting; and a woman, probably Ida B. Wells, leaped to her feet and cried out, Du Bois wrote, "in passionate, almost tearful earnestness — an earnestness born of bitter experience — 'They are betraying us again, these white friends of ours.'"

Suspicion and hostility reached such a pitch that Villard conferred with a white associate over the advisability of forming another organization with more restrained Negroes. Fortunately, for all Americans, the Negro militants and white liberals patched up their differences and worked out a compromise program. The program, in essence, was a watered-down version of the Niagara platform with stress on political and legal tactics. But there were some surprising omissions. Trotter could not persuade the liberals to support a federal antilynching bill. After an "acrimonious" debate, the conference endorsed a vague statement "opposing violence."

In compromise, then, and in caution, the NAACP [was born and] embarked on an adventure of litigation, lobbying, and persuasion. At the second national conference in May, 1910, a permanent organization was effected. Moorfield Storey, a Boston lawyer, was elected president. The only Negro officer and the only Negro incorporator was Du Bois, who resigned from Atlanta University to accept the position of director of research and publicity. The new organization opened for business at 20 Vesey Street in lower Manhattan and hired a white woman, Frances Blascoer, as the first secretary. In the summer of 1910, the organization began its legal redress work by intervening in a murder case involving Pink Franklin, a South Carolina peon who had slain a constable who burst into his home at 3:00 A.M. The organization succeeded in getting Franklin's death sentence commuted to life imprisonment. Within three months, the first NAACP branch office opened in Chicago. In the next seven years, the organization grew slowly. By 1913, there were 1,100 members in a handful of Northern branches.

In the beginning, the NAACP was a typical American reform organization based on a middle-class membership and "respectable protest." The organization made no attempt to organize the masses; nor did it assume the proportion of a crusade. In essence, the NAACP was what [Ralph] Bunche called it: "an interracial petitioning and litigating body." This fact disturbed some of the Negro members. Archibald J. Grimké observed on one occasion that it required no special courage to sit in New York and issue manifestoes. He complained, according to Mary Ovington, because the NAACP was "not revolutionary." . . .

The NAACP did not revive the abolitionist tradition, but it played an absolutely indispensable role in the renewal of the protest movement, opening the eyes of Negroes to a whole new vista of legal struggle. As editor of the *Crisis,* the NAACP's house organ, W. E. B. Du Bois played a major role in setting the tone of the organization. But it is essential to note that Du Bois never agreed with the main body of NAACP tradition. He was always one step ahead, or behind, the dominant trend. The association proceeded cautiously in the courts, but Du Bois scattered shots all over the landscape, attacking the church, the press, the white power structure, philanthropic foundations, and unions.

There was a tendency in the beginning for white liberals and moderates to patronize Negro militants. Mary White Ovington said that "few colored people were trained to take such executive positions as we had to offer" in the second decade of the twentieth century. Du Bois disagreed, saying that Negroes "must not only support but control this and similar organizations and hold them unswervingly to our objects, our aims, and our ideals."

It is at this point perhaps that we ought to pause for a moment and consider the ideals of Du Bois. The acerbic professor was the second stone in a line of leadership that started with Frederick Douglass. Douglass . . . aspired to lead Negroes and questioned the right of white people to articulate the Negro's vision. Du Bois went further: he saw Negroes not only as leaders of themselves but as leaders of all the Negroes of the world. . . .

Like Douglass, his sociological father, Du Bois championed struggle and eternal protest. Unlike Douglass, however, he placed severe limitations on his leadership. He despised, he said, "the essential demagoguery of personal leadership; of that hypnotic ascendancy over men which carries out objectives regardless of their value or validity, simply by personal loyalty and admiration." As a result, Du Bois became a leader of leaders, a leader who confined himself to "a leadership solely of ideas." Du Bois went out of his way to underscore his distaste for power. He could not be bothered by the rituals of leadership. "I could not," he said, "slap people on the back and make friends of strangers. I could not easily break down an inherited reserve; or at all times curb a biting, critical tongue."

The net result of all this was that Du Bois influenced people but never gained power. His influence, for all that, was important. As editor of the *Crisis*, Du Bois became a formidable force in the Negro world. By 1918, he was regarded as the most important Negro in the world. Many people, in fact, believed Du Bois *was* the NAACP, a belief Du Bois did nothing to contradict. Mary White Ovington said quite frankly that the *Crisis*, under Du Bois, was a "rival" of the parent organization.

This anomalous situation led to a series of internal explosions. Du Bois ran the *Crisis* as a personal fief and reserved the right to criticize the organization and other sacred cows in the organization's journal. Oswald Garrison Villard, the chairman of the board, claimed the right to "control" Du Bois and the *Crisis*. But Du Bois, who was also a board member, refused to consider himself a "subordinate" of the ruling white liberal elite. He demanded the right to articulate his own private vision, a vision that differed markedly from NAACP official policy. Things reached such a pass in the Manhattan office that Du Bois suggested, probably with tongue in cheek, the establishment of separate but equal divisions of the National Association for the Advancement of Colored People. When the board refused to curb Du Bois' acid pen, Villard resigned in protest.

After the 1913 resignation of Villard, the issue of white control simmered down. But the underlying issues were not resolved until the 1920's when Negroes achieved equality in the National Association for the Advancement of Colored People. The last white secretary was John Shillady who resigned in 1920 after he was thrashed on the streets of Dallas, Texas, by a mob which included a judge, several deputy sheriffs and other substantial citizens. Bruised in body and spirit, Shillady returned to New York City and submitted his resignation, saying: "I am less confident than heretofore of the speedy success of the Association's full program and of the probability of overcoming within a reasonable period, the forces opposed to Negro equality by the means and methods which are within the Association's power to employ." After resigning, Shillady drifted in and out of hospitals and died finally, "a victim," Walter White said, "of lynching as surely as any Negro who had been strung up to a tree or burned at the stake." Mary White Ovington added a mournful postscript: "He had believed in the way of order and law and he learned that this way did not exist when the rights of the Negro or of his friends were in question." Shillady was succeeded by James Weldon Johnson, the first Negro secretary of the organization.

The doubts that assailed Shillady were not entirely groundless. In the years between 1913 and 1920, the Negro's stock dropped to a new low. The wave of repression began, oddly enough, in 1913, the fiftieth anniversary of the Emancipation Proclamation, and grew in virulence. Laws requiring segregated residential districts were passed in Norfolk, Richmond, Roanoke, Greensboro, Atlanta, and Baltimore. North Carolinians were casting about in these years for effective ways to segregate farm land; and Chicago, Philadelphia, Columbus, and Atlantic City were considering the advisability of establishing segregated schools.

By singular circumstance, this white fury coincided with the inauguration of Woodrow Wilson, the first Southern-born President since Andrew Johnson. The Wilson Administration immediately eliminated Negroes from responsible government positions and instituted separate eating rooms and lavatories in federal buildings. In Congress, there was a similar assault on the rights of Negroes. Twenty bills proposing additional discrimination against Negroes were introduced in the first Congress of the Wilson Administration.

Until that moment, the federal government had been the repository of Negro hopes. Now the last fragile thread was broken and Negroes found themselves in a no man's land between a hostile state and a hostile white majority. "What happened in Washington in 1913," Henry Blumenthal wrote, "involved more than the growing toleration of petty prejudices. Worse than that, trust was violated, and hope was lost." Even Booker T. Washington spoke out. "I have never seen the colored people so discouraged and bitter as they are at the present time." Washington's rival, William Monroe Trotter, played a central role in a minor drama that was indicative of the spirit of the times. On November 12, 1914, Trotter stormed into the White House and had a jaw-to-jaw argument with Wilson. According to reports, he shook his finger at the Virginia-born President who dismissed him for "insulting language." The President, Trotter reported, said that segregation was in the best interest of Negroes.

Abandoned by their government and insulted by their President, Negroes transferred their allegiance and their hope to the NAACP, which organized a brilliant campaign of countermoves. On November 5, 1917, the NAACP won a Supreme Court decision [*Buchanan v. Warley*] which outlawed enforced residential segregation. The importance of this victory is seldom appreciated. If the residential segregation laws had not been struck down at that point, race relations in America probably would have settled down to the black-quarter bitterness of South Africa. The NAACP also won important legal decisions in the fields of suffrage and criminal court proceedings and initiated an antilynching campaign. By pitiless publicity and incessant agitation, the organization succeeded in reducing the number of lynchings. Although the NAACP failed in Congress, where Southerners filibustered antilynching bills to death, it played a large role at the bar of public opinion. When the NAACP campaign began, few men denounced lynchings; by the late thirties, almost no one defended the practice.

Fighting a defensive battle, with all the heavy artillery in the hands of the enemy, Negro leaders concentrated, as James Weldon Johnson graphically put it, "on saving the bodies of Negroes and the souls of white folk." Of the organizations sharing the field of battle with the NAACP, none was more important than the Urban League which was not, strictly speaking, a protest organization. Founded in 1910 by a group of whites and Negroes, the Urban League was a professional social work agency which concentrated on the socioeconomic woes of urban Negroes. Edwin R. A. Seligman was its first president and Eugene Kinckle Jones served for many years as executive director. Ruth Standish Baldwin, wife of W. H. Baldwin, an ardent Booker T. Washington supporter, was the dominant force in the formative periods of the organization which pursued a strategy of concilia-

tion, using tactics of education, persuasion, and negotiation.

To avoid duplication of effort and jurisdictional
disputes, the Urban League and the NAACP divided
the battlefield. At a meeting of Negro and white men
of power, it was decided that the Urban League
would pursue a policy of conciliation and negotiation
in the fields of social service and employment and that
the NAACP would concentrate on protest and pressure in the courts and other theaters of power. The
rationale behind this decision was explained by Mary
White Ovington who said: "We could not have
raised money for philanthropy as successfully as an organization with a less militant program, and securing
employment is a business in itself."

The NAACP was founded in 1909, the Urban
League was founded in 1910, and Booker T. Washington died in 1915. Between 1909 and 1915, the
balance of power shifted in the Negro world from accommodators to militants and moderates; and the
center of gravity shifted from Tuskegee and the South
to New York City, the home base of the Urban
League and the NAACP. During this same period,
the Negro elite became a self-conscious structure of
Negro decision making. At the policy-making
Amenia Conference of 1916, Negro and white
power-holders hewed out the boundaries, and the
limitations, of the Negro protest. The conference,
which was designed to unite the supporters of Booker
T. Washington and Du Bois, was called by Joel E.
Spingarn, then chairman of the NAACP board.
About sixty Negroes and whites attended the deliberations at Spingarn's country home near Amenia, New
York. For three days, the conferees debated the state
of the race and the respective approaches of Booker
T. Washington and W. E. B. Du Bois. They decided,
predictably, on a *via media,* endorsing Du Bois' program of "political freedom" with a proviso that recognized "the peculiar difficulties" of neo–Washington leadership in the South. All this was put in a
resolution and the power-holders went home, believing that "members [of the Amenia Conference] have

arrived at a virtual unanimity of opinion in regard to
certain principles and that a more or less definite result
may be expected from its deliberation."

The first Negro summit conference was important
and "a more or less definite" result followed, but it
had no immediate effect on the lives of the vast majority of Negroes. The defense organizations were in
New York; the masses were not. The defense organizations were middle class; the masses were not. Du
Bois was brilliant, the NAACP was militant, the
Urban League was moderate — and it made absolutely no difference at all, for Negroes in the Black
Belt had never heard of Du Bois or the Amenia Conference or the NAACP. Far from the command posts,
out of sight and sound of the manifestoes, the masses
were engaged in the struggle of Sisyphus, pushing
large stones up hills only to see them roll down again.
And yet a feeling was growing, a clear sense: that
things did not have to be that way, that somehow,
somewhere life could be lived under more tolerable
conditions. The feeling moved, became a mood and
leaped from heart to heart, from plantation to plantation. Without preamble, without plan, without leadership, the people began to move, going from the
plantations to Southern cities, going from there to the
faraway concrete ghettos in the North. There they
found jobs and wrote letters, saying to a cousin or a
sister or an aunt: come. And they came, hundreds and
hundreds of thousands in an elemental flood of people
and hopes. The first great wave came between 1916
and 1919 and the second between 1920 and 1924. By
1930, more than two million Negroes had abandoned
the plantations for the Harlems of the North.

The people moved for many reasons — because
the sheriff was mean, because life was mean, because
the white man was mean. They were pushed by
drought, boll weevils, and tyranny; and they were
pulled by the lure of employment in the burgeoning
war industries. Labor agents of Northern industrialists
stimulated the movement; so did Robert Abbott and
other editors who printed great big headlines of welcome ("GOODBYE DIXIE"). New vistas, new jobs,

new opportunities: all these were in the background of the most significant movement in the history of race relations. Seen thus, as an explosion of hopes and fears, the migration movement was a revolt, and that revolt continues today as a permanent element in the Negro protest. An idea — the idea of freedom — moved the people, sending them in ever-increasing numbers to Chicago, New York, Detroit, Pittsburgh, and Philadelphia.

In the great concrete wildernesses of the North, Negroes emancipated themselves, physically and spiritually, casting off the graveclothes of slavery and the feudal South. Under the impact of industrialization and urbanization, the Negro psyche changed, became more complex, more opaque. The Negro, in the city, became less religious, more skeptical, more knowing and more demanding. As Negroes entered new trades and new occupations, they developed new conceptions of themselves and acquired new personalities. Old patterns of behavior were shattered and new social types emerged, Babbitts and Biggers [middle class business and professional folk], Dawsons and Powells [politicians], Wrights and Baldwins [writers]. The Negro folk, in a word, became proletarians.

All this had a sharp impact on Negro leadership patterns. The Negro press took on the now-familiar militant tone, and Negro agitators came forward to challenge the *bona fides* of the black elite. As early as 1922, the white power structure of Chicago called upon "responsible" Negro leadership to curb the new Negro agitators.

As the Negro changed, the racial front broadened and assumed a national character. Confronted with the flesh and blood of Negro reality, the North began a retreat from racial reality. A Negro exclusion movement crystallized, a movement propelled by the real estate interests of the power structure, the status fears of the middle class, and the sex and bread fears of the lower class.

The entry of Negro workers into new industries terrified white workers who feared, above all else, the increasing ability of Negroes to compete for restricted values. Desperately insecure, soured by their own inability to live up to the great American Dream of Success, Happiness and Power, white ethnic groups raised demands for exclusion and separatism. Even more persuasive in the crystallization of anti-Negro sentiment were emotionally-toned fears centering around the home.

At the very beginning, the race problem in the North became mired in the power structure's deepest obsession, real estate. Before the Great Migration, Negroes lived in practically every section of Northern cities. Back there, in the beginning, the appearance of a new Negro neighbor occasioned no particular outburst. When Negroes moved into one or two apartment buildings on 134th Street east of Lenox Avenue in Harlem shortly after the turn of the century, whites paid no attention. But as the Negro population continued to grow, a panic developed. Whites began fleeing, James Weldon Johnson said, " . . . as from a plague. The presence of one colored family in a block, no matter how well bred and orderly, was sufficient to precipitate a flight. House after house and block after block was actually deserted." The hysteria infected banks and lending institutions, and a quiet war of containment began.

Here, even in its embryonic form, it is possible to see the process whereby real estate became the principal dynamic in the ensemble of Northern race relations. The development of the pattern of exclusion can be traced in Chicago where a small Negro ghetto grew up on Dearborn Street near the red-light district of the First Ward. As the Negro residents in Chicago increased, the ghetto rolled south and east along State Street with whites fighting desperately to contain the black tide and Negroes fighting just as desperately to break out of the white noose. The first tactic used by white separatists was open violence. Between July, 1917, and March, 1921, fifty-eight bombs were hurled at Negro homes in Chicago.

Open violence gave way in the twenties to a campaign of coercion and intimidation led by property owners' associations and neighborhood improvement organizations. In January, 1920, the Chicago Real Estate Board congratulated the Grand Boulevard Branch of the Kenwood and Hyde Park Property Owners Association for its success in preventing Negro occupancy of fifty-seven houses south of Thirty-ninth Street. The next year, the board voted to expel any members who sold property to a Negro on a block occupied by whites.

The quest for a nonviolent instrument of exclusion continued throughout the twenties. Finally, on March 30, 1928, the *Hyde Park Herald,* a Chicago community newspaper, reported a speech proclaiming the end of the quest:

... Judge _____ of the Chicago Real Estate Board, before the Kiwanis Club of Hyde Park at the Windermere East, in summarizing the earnest and conscientious work of the Board for the last twelve months . . . proceeded to explain the fine network of contracts [restrictive covenants] that like a marvelous delicately woven chain of armor is being raised from the northern gates of Hyde Park at 35th Street and Drexel Boulevard to Woodlawn, Park Manor, South Shore, Windsor Park, and all the far-flung white communities of the South Side. And of what does this armor consist? It consists of a contract which the owner of the property signs not to exchange with, sell to, or lease to any member of a race not Caucasian.

Within a short time, the "marvelous delicately woven chain of armor" covered most of the "far-flung white communities" of the North. The invention of this device gave the Negro exclusion movement a new twist. Coming as it did from the top and not from the bottom, the restrictive covenant made bias respectable. It became modish to live in an all-white neighborhood covered by a restrictive covenant, and poor whites hastened to adopt the prejudices of their betters. In a brilliant analysis, Robert Weaver underlined the importance of the new status symbol. Noting that "groups most recently Americanized . . . have now become most vocal in their expressions of anti-Negro and anti-Semitic attitudes,"

Weaver said that "it is common to explain this as an excess of the poorly educated or least cultured persons in the community. Such deduction is superficial. Many of those who resort to violence against Negroes entering new areas are giving a class expression to their opposition; but the opposition represents an acceptance of the standards of the higher-income groups and an attempt to emulate the 'respectable people.' . . . A generation ago, residents in the poorer sections of these cities thought little about color. But soon after instruments to effect enforced residential segregation had become prestige-laden in the more desirable areas, color consciousness and prejudice spread to the more blighted areas."

Propelled now by man's desire to have someone to look down on, the Negro exclusion movement raced across the North. San Francisco and other municipalities sent experts to the Midwest to study the techniques of Negro exclusion. Even the federal government was drawn into the web of conspiracy. The Federal Housing Administration in its underwriting manual (1938) listed "protection from adverse influences," including "inharmonious racial groups," as important factors in determining eligibility for a housing loan.

The very best people — bankers, realtors, editors, merchants, and community leaders — led the Negro exclusion movement. Although financial institutions made the largest contribution to acceptance of the idea of Negro exclusion, churches, colleges, and universities did not lag behind. Among the signers of restrictive covenants were universities, churches, and "the better class of people" of all faiths.

Real estate interests and property owners' associations gave the campaign an inflammatory twist, inventing an ideology of Negro debasement, an ideology that struck deep roots in the political, social, and educational thinking of the North. The ideology was based on the myth of the Negro's innate inferiority and his alleged propensity for lowering community standards. In Detroit, Chicago, San Francisco, and other communities, property owners' associations became open and vociferous champions of segregation in schools and recreational outlets.

In the twenties and thirties, the flames of fear, guilt, and hate leaped higher and higher. As the struggle widened, even vacant land was assigned a color. Land was either black or white, and everyone — bankers, preachers, priests, rabbis, and policemen — knew the difference.

The struggle to preserve the racial integrity of the land assumed the proportions of a miniature war. Whites spoke in military terms of Negroes "invading" and "infiltrating" a neighborhood. It was necessary for whites to "hold the line" at "the perimeter" or the neighborhood would be "lost."

Thus, a quiet war emerged in the North. And in the North, as in the South, the combatants seldom, if ever, rested on their arms.

Organized white aggression evoked counterforces in the Negro community. Conflicts over segregated housing and segregated schools intensified Negro racial consciousness and welded all Negroes into a common group with a common sense of shared resentment. Negro Main Streets blossomed in every large Northern community. Gradually, almost imperceptibly, a new and different black world came into being in the heart of the American North.

One more moment in the history of the Negro and the white American had passed — never to be called back, never to be erased.

QUESTIONS TO CONSIDER

1. What were the basic principles and ideals of W. E. B. DuBois, and how did they contrast with the program called for by Booker T. Washington? To which segments of the black and white population did each of them direct his concern and to whom did they appeal?

2. What were the fundamental goals of the Niagara movement? What did the movement accomplish, and what undermined it?

3. Lerone Bennett, Jr., describes a "wave of repression" that occurred from 1913 to 1920. Why do you think it happened then? Of what specifically did it consist, and what were its material and psychological effects?

4. How does Bennett contrast the NAACP and the abolitionist movement of the early nineteenth century? How did it compare with other organizations such as the Urban League? Where did the NAACP concentrate its efforts, and what kind of success did it have in its early years?

5. Bennett calls the great African American migrations to the North in the teens and twenties "the most significant movement in the history of race relations." What caused the exodus north, and what effect did it have on African Americans? How did the white North react, and in what way did this represent a change from previous conditions?

VII

THE PERILS OF PROSPERITY

14

Henry Ford: Symbol of an Age

RODERICK NASH

The election of Warren G. Harding as president reflected a massive popular reaction against the missionary idealism of Woodrow Wilson and the reformist zeal of the Progressive era. Harding would take the country back to "normalcy," so that Americans might continue their "normal, onward way." Essentially, this meant that federal regulation of industry would be reduced to a minimum, that the business of government, as Calvin Coolidge put it, would be big business.

The popular stereotype of the 1920s is that it was a decade of political corruption, speculative orgies, violence, and the last happy fling before the Great Depression crushed American innocence. But in reality this decade of "normalcy" was a good deal more complex than that. True, business consolidation under Republican rule continued throughout the decade. True, excessive and irresponsible speculation on the New York Stock Exchange culminated in the crash of 1929. True, organized crime was widespread, and gang wars rocked Chicago and New York. And true, a revolution in manners and morals challenged traditional standards and profoundly upset Americans who clung to the old morality.

Yet for many contemporaries, the 1920s was a time of exhilarating hope and high expectation for the United States. In fact, a number of intellectuals found much in American life to celebrate. Most optimistic of all were the businesspeople, who believed they were living in a new era — a time not only of conservative Republican leadership in Washington but of striking innovation and change in business itself. As industrial officials happily observed, corporate managers were bringing scientific procedures and efficient techniques to industry. This change, they contended, would raise production so high that poverty would soon be eliminated and the American dream of abundance for all would be attained at last. Their expectations, alas, perished in the crash of 1929 and the ensuing Depression, the worst the country had ever known.

During the 1920s, however, the United States seemed enormously prosperous, and the American businessperson enjoyed new pre-eminence in American life. One businessman became a leading figure of the decade. Indeed, his technological genius, love of country, and old-fashioned Americanism made him a folk hero to a large segment of American society. This was car maker Henry Ford, who introduced the first car built for the common person — the Model T — and whose technique of assembly-line production revolutionized American technology. What Ford wrought, as David Halberstam has said, also profoundly altered the way Americans lived: it made them far more mobile than they had been in the railroad age, and it created a culture of leisure in which people thought as much about recreation as they did about their jobs. As we shall see in a subsequent selection, the automobile dramatically changed American customs of courtship.

Ironically, Ford himself despised most of the social changes he helped bring about. A champion of the Protestant work ethic, he abhorred the very idea of leisure. "Work," he contended, "is the salvation of the race, morally, physically, socially. Work does more than get us our living; it gets us our life." He could be remarkably contradictory and unpredictable. He introduced the $5 wage for an eight-hour day (which revolutionized labor policy in industrial America) and yet opposed the union movement. He owned a fifty-six-room mansion and built the Ford Motor Company into the biggest "family-owned industrial empire in the world," accumulating a total of $1 billion in profits, and yet he claimed to care little for material things and pleasures. "I have never known," he said, "what to do with money after my expenses were paid." In the end, he donated $40 million to philanthropic enterprises. He considered himself a pacifist, so much so that in 1915 he dispatched a "peace ship" to Europe in a futile if honorable attempt to stop the First World War. Yet this same man had what Roderick Nash calls a rural, "Bible-belt morality." He expatiated on the evils of jazz (it was all "monkey talk" and "jungle squeals") and blamed it and the new dances on a Jewish conspiracy. In fact, he published anti-Semitic diatribes in his Dearborn, Michigan, newspaper (he did retract his anti-Semitic statements in 1927).

The key to Ford's contradictory mind, as Nash says in the next selection, was ambivalence. He was both "old and new." He looked backward and forward at the same time, defending technology while extolling the old rural values and attitudes of a bygone era. In this respect, he symbolized the America of his age — a changing, industrial America that longed for the security of the old days as it struggled with the complexities of the new.

GLOSSARY

ALGER, HORATIO   Gilded Age author whose heroes rose from poverty to greatness and thus fulfilled the "American dream."

FORDISMUS   German word for Ford's "revolutionary mass-production techniques."

McGUFFEY READER   Its "moral-coated language lessons" in such stories as "The Hare and the Tortoise" were the staple of Ford's "academic diet."

MODEL T   Ford's first automobile, built for the masses.

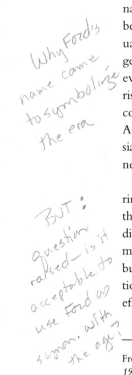

Why Ford's name came to symbolize the era

BUT: Question raised — is it acceptable to use Ford as symon. with the age?

Few names were better known to Americans from 1917 to 1930 than that of Henry Ford. Whether one read his publications,[1] or followed his headline-making public life, or merely drove the car his company manufactured, Ford was inescapable in the twenties. Indeed it is possible to think of these years as the automobile age and Henry Ford as its czar. The flivver, along with the flask and the flapper, seemed to represent the 1920s in the minds of its people as well as its historians.

Cars symbolized change. They upset familiar patterns of living, working, recreating, even thinking. Much of the roar of the twenties came from the internal combustion engine. While providing portable bedrooms in which to enjoy the decade's alleged sexual freedom, cars also assisted gangsters and bootleggers in getting away. The image of two of them in every garage helped elect a President in 1928. The rise of widespread use of the automobile, in a word, contributed significantly to setting the twenties apart. And Henry Ford, calling machinery the "new Messiah" (as he did in 1929), seemed to herald the new era.

Beneath the surface, however, such generalizations ring hollow. Neither Ford nor the twenties merited the clichés with which each has been so frequently discussed. In the case of the man, both old and new mingled in his mind. On the one hand Ford was a builder and bulwark of the modern, mechanized nation; on the other he devoted a remarkable amount of effort and expense to sustaining old-fashioned Amer-

From pp. 154–163 of *The Nervous Generation: American Thought, 1917–1930* by Roderick Nash. Published by Rand-McNally College Publishing Company, Chicago. © 1970 by Roderick Nash. Reprinted by permission of Roderick Nash.

[1] In all probability Henry Ford did not actually write the numerous books, pamphlets, and articles associated with his name and attributed to him in this chapter. He was not a literary man; his critics even alleged he could not read! But Ford could pay people to express his opinions for him, and there is no reason to think that the ideas these writers recorded were not those of their employer.

Henry Ford at the peak of his power, about 1914. As Nash observed, Henry Ford was a "plain, honest, old-fashioned billion-aire" and "technological genius" who fretted about the new morality of the jazz age, ridiculing jazz itself as "monkey talk" and "jungle squeals" and blaming illicit liquor on a Jewish conspiracy. Still, despite his rural outlook and biblical virtues, Ford was one of the most popular Americans of the roaring twenties. (Collection of Greenfield Village and Henry Ford Museum, Dearborn, Michigan)

ica. In fact, the nostalgic, backward-looking Henry Ford repeatedly deplored the very conditions that Ford the revolutionary industrialist did so much to bring about. This ambivalence did not signify a lack of values so much as a superfluity. His faith was strong if bigoted and contradictory. His prescriptions for America were clear if simple-minded. He seemed to the masses to demonstrate that there could be change without disruption, and in so doing he eased the twenties' tensions. "The average citizen," editorial-

ized the *New Republic* in 1923, "sees Ford as a sort of enlarged crayon portrait of himself; the man able to fulfill his own suppressed desires, who has achieved enormous riches, fame and power without departing from the pioneer-and-homespun tradition." In this nervous clinging to old values even while undermining them Ford was indeed a "crayon portrait" of his age.

But was Ford typical of the twenties? Can he really be said to symbolize the age? He was, after all, in his middle fifties when the decade began. However, a great many Americans were also middle-aged in the 1920s, far more in fact than the twenty-year-old collegians who have hitherto characterized these years. And at one point even a group of college students ranked Ford as the third greatest figure of all time, behind Napoleon and Jesus Christ.

The Dearborn, Michigan, into which Henry Ford was born in 1863 was a small farming community only a generation removed from the frontier. Both sides of the Ford family had agrarian backgrounds, and the children grew up on the farm. Henry's formal education began and ended in the Scotch Settlement School which he attended for eight years. The staple of his academic diet was the McGuffey reader with its moral-coated language lessons. When Ford left school to become an apprentice mechanic in Detroit, he also left the farm. But the farm never left Henry. Agrarian ideas and values shaped his thought even as he became an industrial king.

The 1880s for Ford were a time of aimlessness, his only real interest being in tinkering with watches and other engines. In 1892 he joined the Edison Company in Detroit as an engineer. During his spare time he struggled with the problem of building a gasoline engine compact enough to power a moving vehicle. By 1896 Ford had his automobile. Soon he had it doing ninety miles per hour! It required seven years more, however, for him to secure the necessary financial and administrative backing to launch the Ford Motor Company. The rest was pure Horatio Alger.

The first Model T appeared in 1908, and it soon

made good Ford's boast that he could build a car for the masses. Six thousand sold the first year. Six years later, after the introduction of assembly line production, the figure was 248,000. From May to December 1920 almost 700,000 Model Ts rolled out of the Ford plants. The total for 1921 was one million. In 1923, 57 percent of all cars manufactured in the United States were Fords. Three years later the Ford Motor Company produced its thirteen millionth car. From the perspective of efficient production the Ford organization was also something of a miracle. In 1913 it required twelve hours to make a car. The following year, after the introduction of the assembly line techniques, the figure dropped to ninety-three minutes. In 1920 Ford achieved his long-time dream of building one car for every minute of the working day. And still he was unsatisfied. On October 31, 1925, the Ford Motor Company manufactured 9,109 Model Ts, one every ten seconds. This was the high point, and competition was rising to challenge Ford's preeminence, but by the end of the twenties Henry Ford was a legend, a folk hero, and reputedly the richest man who ever lived. Transcending the role of automobile manufacturer, he had become an international symbol of the new industrialism. The Germans coined a word to describe the revolutionary mass production techniques: *Fordismus*. At home Ford's popularity reached the point where he could be seriously considered a presidential possibility for the election of 1924.

Fortunately for the historian of his thought, if not always for himself, Henry Ford had a propensity for forthrightly stating his opinions on a wide variety of subjects outside his field of competence. He also had the money to publish and otherwise implement his ideas. The resulting intellectual portrait was that of a mind steeped in traditional Americanism. For Ford agrarian simplicity, McGuffey morality, and Algerian determination were sacred objects. Nationalism was writ large over all Ford did, and America was great because of its heritage of freedom, fairness, and hard, honest work. Ford's confidence in the beneficence of old-fashioned virtues verged on the fanatical. The "spirit of '76," equal opportunity democracy, rugged individualism, the home, and motherhood were Ford's touchstones of reality. He deified pioneer ethics and values. "More men are beaten than fail," he declared in 1928. "It is not wisdom they need, or money, or brilliance, or pull, but just plain gristle and bone." A decade earlier "Mr. Ford's Page" in the *Dearborn Independent* stated that "one of the great things about the American people is that they are pioneers." This idea led easily to American messianism. "No one can contemplate the nation to which we belong," the editorial continued, "without realizing the distinctive prophetic character of its obvious mission to the world. We are pioneers. We are pathfinders. We are the roadbuilders. We are the guides, the vanguards of Humanity." Theodore Roosevelt and Woodrow Wilson had said as much, but Ford was writing *after* the war that allegedly ended the nation's innocence and mocked its mission.

Ford's intense commitment to the traditional American faith led him to suspect and ultimately to detest whatever was un-American. The same loyalties compelled him to search for explanations for the unpleasant aspects of the American 1920s that exonerated the old-time, "native" citizen. The immigrant, and particularly the Jew, were primary targets of Ford's fire. In editorial after editorial in the *Dearborn Independent* and in several books Ford argued that aliens who had no knowledge of "the principles which have made our civilization" were responsible for its "marked deterioration" in the 1920s. They were, moreover, determined to take over the country if not the world. Spurred by such fears, Ford became a subscriber to the tired legend of an international Jewish conspiracy. When he couldn't find sufficient evidence for such a plot, Ford dispatched a number of special detectives to probe the affairs of prominent Jews and collect documentation. The search resulted in the "discovery" of the so-called "Protocols of the Learned Elders of Zion," an alleged exposition of the scheme by which the Jews planned to overthrow

186

Gentile domination. Although the "Protocols" was exposed as a forgery in 1921, Ford continued to use the spurious document to substantiate his anti-Semitism until late in the decade. Everything wrong with modern American civilization, from the corruption of music to the corruption of baseball, was attributed to Jewish influence. Unable to admit that America as a whole might be blamed for its problems, unwilling to question the beneficence of time-honored ways, Ford searched for a scapegoat. He found it in the newcomers who, he believed, had no conception of or appreciation for American ideals. ~Dichotomy of farming~

The tension in Henry Ford's thought between old ~(idea)~ and new, between a belief in progress and a tendency to nostalgia, is dramatically illustrated in his attitude toward farming and farmers. On the one hand he believed farm life to be a ceaseless round of inefficient drudgery. Indeed, he had abundant personal evidence, remarking at one point, "I have traveled ten thousand miles behind a plow. I hated the grueling grind of farm work." With the incentive of sparing others this painful experience, Ford addressed himself to the problem of industrializing agriculture. The farmer, in Ford's opinion, should become a technician and a businessman. Tractors (Ford's, of course) should replace horses. Mechanization would make it possible to produce in twenty-five working days what formerly required an entire year. Fences would come down and vast economies of scale take place. Ford's modern farmer would not even need to live on his farm but instead could commute from a city home. To give substance to these ideals Ford bought and operated with astonishing success a nine-thousand-acre farm near Dearborn.

Still Ford, the "Father of Modern Agriculture," as he has been dubbed, was only part of the man. He also retained a strong streak of old-fashioned, horse-and-buggy agrarianism. Farming, from this standpoint, was more than a challenge in production; it was a moral act. Constantly in the twenties, even while he was helping make it possible, Ford branded the modern city a "pestiferous growth." He delighted in contrasting the "unnatural," "twisted," and "cooped up" lives of city-dwellers with the "wholesome" life of "independence" and "sterling honesty" that the farm environment offered. In Ford's view the importance of cities in the nation's development had been greatly exaggerated. Early in the 1920s the *Dearborn Independent* editorialized: "when we all stand up and sing, 'My Country 'Tis of Thee,' we seldom think of the cities. Indeed, in that old national hymn there are no references to the city at all. It sings of rocks and rivers and hills — the great American Out-of-Doors. And that is really The Country. That is, the country is THE Country. The real United States lies outside the cities."

As such a manifesto suggests, a bias toward nature and rural conditions was an important element in Henry Ford's thought. "What children and adults need," he told one reporter, "is a chance to breathe God's fresh air and to stretch their legs and have a little garden in the soil." This ideal led Ford to choose small towns instead of cities as the sites of his factories. "Turning back to village industry," as Ford put it in 1926, would enable people to reestablish a sense of community — with nature and with men — that urbanization had destroyed. Ford believed that cities were doomed as Americans discovered the advantages of country life.

Ford's enthusiasm for nature did not stop with ruralism. From 1914 to 1924 he sought a more complete escape from civilization on a series of camping trips with Thomas A. Edison. John Burroughs, the naturalist, and Harvey Firestone, the tire king, also participated. Although the equipment these self-styled vagabonds took into the woods was far from primitive, they apparently shared a genuine love of the outdoors. In the words of Burroughs, they "cheerfully endured wet, cold, smoke, mosquitoes, black flies, and sleepless nights, just to touch naked reality once more." Ford had a special fondness for birds. With typical exuberance he had five hundred birdhouses built on his Michigan farm, including one with seventy-six apartments which he called, appropriately, a "bird hotel." There were also electric heaters and electric brooders for Ford's fortunate birds. The whole production mixed technology and nature in a way that symbolized Ford's ambivalence. When he could not camp or visit his aviary, Ford liked to read about the natural world. Indeed he preferred the works of Emerson, Thoreau, and Burroughs to the Bible. Ford so admired Burroughs' variety of natural history that even before becoming acquainted with him he sent him a new Ford car.

Cars to roads

As for roads and automobiles, Ford saw them not as a threat to natural conditions but rather as a way for the average American to come into contact with nature. The machine and the garden were not incompatible. "I will build a motor car for the great multitude . . . ," Ford boasted, "so low in price that no man . . . will be unable to own one — and enjoy with his family the blessings of hours of pleasure in God's great open spaces." In *My Life and Work* of 1923 Ford again confronted the tension between nature and modern civilization. He declared that he did not agree with those who saw mechanization leading to a "cold, metallic sort of world in which great factories will drive away the trees, the flowers, the birds and the green fields." According to Ford, "unless we know more about machines and their use . . . we cannot have the time to enjoy the trees and the birds, and the flowers, and the green fields." Such reconciliations only partially covered Ford's nervousness about the mechanized, urbanized future. Contradictions persisted in his thinking. The same man who envisaged fenceless bonanza farms could say, "I love to walk across country and jump fences." The lover of trees could state in utmost seriousness, "better wood can be made than is grown."

history

Ford's attitude toward history has been subject to wide misunderstanding. The principal source of confusion is a statement Ford made in 1919 at the trial resulting from his libel suit against the *Chicago Tribune*. "History," he declared, "is more or less the bunk. It is tradition. We don't want tradition. We want to live in the present, and the only history that is

worth a tinker's dam is the history we make today." On another occasion he admitted that he "wouldn't give a nickel for all the history in the world." Complementing this sentiment is Ford's reputation as a forward-looking inventor and revolutionary industrialist unsatisfied with the old processes. Here seems a man fully at home in the alleged new era of the 1920s. But in fact Ford idolized the past. His "history . . . is bunk" remark came in response to a question about ancient history and Napoleon Bonaparte and had reference to written history. For history itself — what actually happened in his nation's past and its tangible evidence — Ford had only praise.

The most obvious evidence of Ford's enthusiasm for history was his collector's instinct. He began with the bastion of his own youth, the McGuffey readers. Sending agents out to scour the countryside and putting aside considerations of cost, Ford owned by 1925 one of the few complete collections of the many McGuffey editions. Hoping to share his treasures with his contemporaries, Ford had five thousand copies of *Old Favorites from the McGuffey Readers* printed in 1926. The book contained such classic stories as "Try, Try Again" and "The Hare and the Tortoise." It dispensed an ideal of individualism and self-reliance at the same time that Ford's assembly lines were making men cogs in an impersonal machine.

From books Ford turned to things, and during the 1920s amassed a remarkable collection of American antiques. He bought so widely and so aggressively that he became a major factor in prices in the antique market. Everything was fair game. Lamps and dolls, bells and grandfather clocks made their way to Dearborn. Size was no problem. Ford gathered enough machines to show the evolution of the threshing operation from 1849 to the 1920s. Another exhibit traced the development of wagons in America. Eventually the entire heterogeneous collection went into the Edison Museum at Dearborn, a pretentious building designed to resemble, simultaneously, Independence Hall, Congress Hall, and the old City Hall of Philadelphia. Ford delighted in showing visitors around the five-acre layout. Asked on one occasion why he collected, Ford replied, "so that they will not be lost to America." Later, on the same tour, Ford played a few bars on an antique organ and observed, "that takes me back to my boyhood days. They were beautiful days."

This sentiment undoubtedly figured in Ford's 1920 decision to restore his boyhood home. Everything had to be exactly as he remembered it. Furniture, china, and rugs were rehabilitated or reconstructed. Ford even used archaeological techniques to recover artifacts around the family homestead. The ground was dug to a depth of six feet and the silverware, wheels, and other equipment used by his parents in the 1860s were recovered. In 1922 Ford purchased the Wayside Inn at Sudbury, Massachusetts, to preserve it from destruction. Celebrated by the poet Henry Wadsworth Longfellow, the old inn appealed to Ford as a symbol of pioneer days. He opened it for the public's edification in 1924. But a new highway ran too near. Roaring cars disturbed the horse-and-buggy atmosphere. So, turning against the age he helped create, Ford had the state highway rerouted around the shrine at a cost of $250,000. He also bought and restored the schoolhouse in Sudbury alleged to be the site where Mary and her little lamb gamboled. Naturally the shop of the "Village Blacksmith," also in Sudbury, had to be included in Ford's antique empire.

Beginning in 1926 with the construction of Greenfield Village near Dearborn, Ford embarked on a career of large-scale historical restoration. This time not a building but a whole community was the object of his attention. Greenfield, named after the Michigan hamlet in which Ford's mother grew up, was a monument to his agrarianism as well as his reverence for the past. "I am trying in a small way," Ford explained with unwarranted modesty, "to help America take a step . . . toward the saner and sweeter idea of life that prevailed in pre-war days." Greenfield Village had gravel roads, gas street lamps, a grassy common, and an old-fashioned country store. The automobile mogul permitted only horse-drawn vehicles on the premises. The genius of assembly line mass production engaged a glass blower, blacksmith, and cobbler to practice their obsolete crafts in the traditional manner. Ford dispatched his agents to seek out, purchase, and transport to Greenfield the cottages of Walt Whitman, Noah Webster, and Patrick Henry. In time they even secured the crowning glory: the log cabin in which William Holmes McGuffey had been born and raised.

History, then, was not "bunk" to Henry Ford. The speed of change seemed to increase proportionately to his desire to retain contact with the past. As Ford declared in 1928, a year before completing Greenfield Village, "improvements have been coming so quickly that the past is being lost to the rising generation." To counter this tendency Ford labored to put history into a form "where it may be seen and felt." But values and attitudes were also on display. Ford looked back with nostalgia to the pioneer ethic. With it, he believed, the nation had been sound, wholesome, happy, and secure. "The Old Ways," as the *Dearborn Independent* declared, "Were Good."

Morals

Ford's opinion of the new morality of the jazz age was, not surprisingly, low. He deplored the use of tobacco and even went so far as to publish for mass circulation a tract, entilted *The Case Against the Little White Slaver,* which excoriated cigarettes. When Ford had the power he went beyond exhortation. "No one smokes in the Ford industries," their leader proclaimed in 1929. As for alcohol, Ford was equally unyielding. Twice he threatened to make his international labor force teetotalers at the risk of their jobs. In his American plants Ford enforced a policy of abstinence. Any workman detected drinking publicly or even keeping liquor at home was subject to dismissal. The prohibition policy of the 1920s, in Ford's estimation, was a great triumph. "There are a million boys growing up in the United States," he exulted in 1929, "who have never seen a saloon and who will never know the handicap of liquor." When confronted with evidence of widespread violation of the Eigh-

alcohol

189

teenth Amendment, Ford had a ready explanation. A Jewish conspiracy was to blame for illicit booze. The mass of real Americans, Ford believed, were, like himself, dry by moral conviction as well as by law.

sex

Sex was too delicate a matter to be addressed directly, but Ford conveyed his opinions through a discussion of music and dancing. Few aspects of the American 1920s worried him more than the evils of jazz. The new music clashed squarely with his ruralism and Bible-belt morality. In 1921 Ford struck out in anger at "the waves upon waves of musical slush that invaded decent parlors and set the young people of this generation imitating the drivel of morons." Organized Jewry, once again, was blamed for the musical degeneracy. "The mush, the slush, the sly suggestion, the abandoned sensuousness of sliding notes," declared the Dearborn Independent, "are of Jewish origin." The problem, obviously, was not only musical but sexual as well. The loosening of morals in the 1920s appalled Ford. He expressed his feelings in reference to jazz: "monkey talk, jungle squeals, grunts and squeaks and gasps suggestive of cave love are camouflaged by a few feverish notes." What Ford could only bring himself to call "the thing" appeared also in song titles such as *In Room 202* and *Sugar Baby*. Pointing to the Jewish origin of these tunes (Irving Berlin was a frequent target of attacks), Ford called on his countrymen to crush the serpent in their midst.

dance

The reform of dancing fitted nicely into Ford's campaign to elevate the nation's morals to old-time standards. His interest began with the collection of traditional folk dances. Not only the scores but the backwoods fiddlers themselves were invited to Dearborn to play *Old Zip Coon* and *Arkansas Traveler*. To Ford's delight, here was something both wholesome and historical. He also manifested concern over social dancing, publishing in 1926 a guidebook entitled *"Good Morning": After a Sleep of Twenty-five Years Old-Fashioned Dancing is Being Revived by Mr. and Mrs. Henry Ford*. The book also endeavored to revive old-fashioned morality. It began by condemning as pro-

miscuous the newer dances such as the Charleston and the whole flapper syndrome. "A gentleman," the book explained, "should be able to guide his partner through a dance without embracing her as if he were her lover." Proper deportment, according to Ford, minimized physical contact. "[The gentleman's] right hand should be placed at his partner's waist, thumb and forefinger alone touching her — that is, the hand being in the position of holding a pencil." There were also rules regarding gloves, handkerchiefs, and the way to request a partner for a dance. Ford's dance manual, in short, was a monument to the old conceptions of morality, decorum, and order, and the dances he and his wife hosted at Dearborn were implementations. Precisely at nine Ford's guests convened in evening dress in a lavish ballroom for a paean to Victorianism.

Ambivalence is the key to the mind of Henry Ford. He was both old and new; he looked both forward and backward. Confidently progressive as he was in some respects, he remained nervous about the new ways. The more conditions changed, the more the nostalgic Ford groped for the security of traditional values and institutions. He was not lost; on the contrary, he had too many gods, at least for consistency. Neither was he dissipated and roaring. And he hated jazz. But Ford was popular, indeed a national deity, in the twenties even if his senatorial and presidential bids fell short. As a plain, honest, old-fashioned billionaire, a technological genius who loved to camp out, he seemed to his contemporaries to resolve the moral dilemmas of the age. Like Charles A. Lindbergh, another god of the age, Ford testified to the nation's ability to move into the future without losing the values of the past.

QUESTIONS TO CONSIDER

1. Compare Henry Ford with "robber baron" Andrew Carnegie in selection 5. In what ways did each man symbolize the America of his age?

2.   Analyze the sources of Ford's tremendous popularity in the 1920s. Was it true, as Nash argues, that despite the revolutionary social changes Ford's cars brought to American society, Ford's commitment to old-fashioned values comforted Americans who felt anxious about the effects of modernization?

3.   Henry Ford was the symbol of the new industrial order of the 1920s, but he also reflected the urban-rural tensions of that decade, especially in his attitudes toward the "revolution in manners and morals" of the jazz age. Discuss Ford's attitudes toward alcohol, sex, music, and dancing and how they reflected the changes taking place in America in the 1920s.

4.   In addition to being a technological genius, Ford was both an anti-Semite and a Victorian prude, but the American people loved him. How much of his appeal, do you think, was based on his ability to find simplistic solutions to the moral dilemmas of his age?

15

Revolution in Manners and Morals

FREDERICK LEWIS ALLEN

The sexual revolution of the 1920s has become legendary, and by far the most famous account of the rebellion is in Frederick Lewis Allen's classic, Only Yesterday *(1931), which is excerpted here. Because Allen lived through the 1920s, he wrote about events he had witnessed. What his portrait may lack in historical perspective, however, is more than offset by its shrewd observations and colorful "you-are-there" style.*

Contrary to popular belief, the sexual revolt did not begin in the 1920s. As Allen points out, the initial attacks against the Victorian moral code started before America entered the First World War (petting parties, for example, were going on in 1918), received a boost from that conflict, and came to full flower in the 1920s. Indeed, American young people mounted what one historian calls "the first self-conscious youth revolt in American history." Attending high schools and colleges in unprecedented numbers, students of the twenties challenged the old rules about sexual conduct and used the automobile to extend the boundaries of courtship far beyond the living room. They smoked cigarettes, drank bathtub gin, did the Charleston, went on all-night automobile rides, and fornicated in closed-top cars on a scale that shocked traditionalists. Youth culture — brash and pleasure seeking — became a force in American society that it had never been before.

Still, Allen's account is misleading about the extent of the rebellion. One might infer from his narrative that sexual permissiveness was well-nigh universal in the 1920s, that almost everybody in the younger and middle generations smoked, drank, and turned their automobiles into bedrooms. Many did, of course, particularly in the cities. But a great many other Americans in both generations clung to the old Victorian code as tenaciously as did Henry Ford.

Allen is correct is asserting that the increasing independence of the American woman accelerated the revolution in manners and morals. Not only did women now have the vote but middle-class women also enjoyed greater opportunities for employment in schools, businesses, service industries, and department stores. Even middle-class women who opted for marriage and motherhood experienced dramatic changes in the home, thanks to the widespread availability of processed foods, central heating, electrical and gas appliances, hot and cold running water, and vacuum sweepers. As one historian has said, "Housework, like factory work, entered an age of mechanization."

The growing independence of middle-class women in the twenties markedly affected their manners and morals. They started smoking cigarettes in public, insisted on the right to drink with men, and wore shorter and shorter skirts, until by the late twenties the hemline was above the knee. The working woman who spurned marriage and rented her own apartment also challenged the notion of "man's economic leadership in the family." With more and more options available to them, women married later and had fewer children than had their predecessors.

According to historian Sara Evans, what was most revolutionary about the twenties was "the public acceptance of female sexuality." Ideas about that, which had once been confined to a few radicals in Greenwich Village, were now widely discussed. Indeed, as Allen points out, modern psychologists, inspired by the teachings of Sigmund Freud, assailed the old Victorian moral code as unscientific nonsense and an impediment to good health. They declared sexuality the basic force in human life and (as Evans puts it) "redefined 'normal' adulthood to include sexual expression." So long as sexual expression was heterosexual and marital, asserted the psychologists, it was normal and beneficial for everyone, women and men alike.

That idea swept through middle-class America with revolutionary force. After a century of denying women's sexuality, as Evans points out, the middle-class now acknowledged its existence. This helped create "a new ideal of marriage" in which women sought sexual happiness and emotionally rewarding companionship as well as economic security and social identity. If marriage did not afford those things, divorce was possible (in fact, the divorce rate almost doubled between the two world wars). As one historian summed it up: "The general acceptance of a new code which exalted happiness as the supreme objective of marriage, permitted divorce, and gave women and children more equality with men in family relationships signified the emergence of new social bases of American life."

The sexual revolution of the 1910s and 1920s was an important symptom of a society undergoing profound social and economic changes, and it would be instructive to discuss in that context the selection that follows. It would also be illuminating to compare the new youth culture of the period with the attitudes of Henry Ford and the rural, Bible Belt morality he represented.

GLOSSARY

BLOTTO   Slang term for drunkenness.

CLARK, DR. FRANCIS E.   President of the Christian Endeavor Society who damned modern dancing of the twenties as "an offense against womanly purity, the very fountainhead of our family and civil life."

FLAPPER   A young woman of the twenties who defied the Victorian moral code.

FITZGERALD, F. SCOTT   Novelist whose *This Side of Paradise* (1920) first reported the revolution in manners and morals.

FREUD, DR. SIGMUND   Austrian neurologist and the founder of psychoanalysis whose writings about human sexuality profoundly influenced the rebellious youth of the twenties.

HAYS, WILLIAM H.   Harding's postmaster general who became the arbiter of taste in motion pictures, laying down "moral commandments for the producers to follow."

PETTING   Twenties' term for sexual caressing and fondling.

☆ 1 ☆

A first-class revolt against the accepted American order was certainly taking place during those early years of the Post-war Decade, but it was one with which [communist leader] Nikolai Lenin had nothing whatever to do. The shock troops of the rebellion were not alien agitators, but the sons and daughters of well-to-do American families, who knew little about Bolshevism and cared distinctly less, and their defiance was expressed not in obscure radical publications or in soapbox speeches, but right across the family breakfast table into the horrified ears of conservative fathers and mothers. Men and women were still shivering at the Red Menace when they awoke to the no less alarming Problem of the Younger Generation, and realized that if the Constitution were not in danger, the moral code of the country certainly was.

This code, as it currently concerned young people, might have been roughly summarized as follows: Women were the guardians of morality; they were made of finer stuff than men and were expected to act accordingly. Young girls must look forward in innocence (tempered perhaps with a modicum of physiological instruction) to a romantic love match which would lead them to the altar and to living-happily-ever-after; and until the "right man" came along they must allow no male to kiss them. It was expected that some men would succumb to the temptations of sex, but only with a special class of outlawed women; girls of respectable families were supposed to have no such temptations. Boys and girls were permitted large freedom to work and play together, with decreasing and well-nigh nominal chaperonage, but only because the code worked so well on the whole that a sort of

Pages 88–118 from *Only Yesterday: An Informal History of the Nineteen Twenties* by Frederick Lewis Allen. Copyright 1931 by Frederick Lewis Allen. Copyright renewed 1959 by Agnes Rogers Allen. Reprinted by permission of HarperCollins Publishers, Inc.

honor system was supplanting supervision by their elders; it was taken for granted that if they had been well brought up they would never take advantage of this freedom. And although the attitude toward smoking and drinking by girls differed widely in different strata of society and different parts of the country, majority opinion held that it was morally wrong for them to smoke and could hardly imagine them showing the effects of alcohol.

The war had not long been over when cries of alarm from parents, teachers, and moral preceptors began to rend the air. For the boys and girls just growing out of adolescence were making mincemeat of this code.

The dresses that the girls — and for that matter most of the older women — were wearing seemed alarming enough. In July, 1920, a fashion-writer reported in the *New York Times* that "the American woman . . . has lifted her skirts far beyond any modest limitation," which was another way of saying that the hem was now all of nine inches above the ground. It was freely predicted that skirts would come down again in the winter of 1920–21, but instead they climbed a few scandalous inches farther. The flappers wore thin dresses, short-sleeved and occasionally (in the evening) sleeveless; some of the wilder young things rolled their stockings below their knees, revealing to the shocked eyes of virtue a fleeting glance of shin-bones and knee-cap; and many of them were visibly using cosmetics. "The intoxication of rouge," earnestly explained Dorothy Speare in *Dancers in the Dark,* "is an insidious vintage known to more girls than mere man can ever believe." Useless for frantic parents to insist that no lady did such things; the answer was that the daughters of ladies were doing it, and even retouching their masterpieces in public. Some of them, furthermore, were abandoning their corsets. "The men won't dance with you if you wear a corset," they were quoted as saying.

The current mode in dancing created still more consternation. Not the romantic violin but the barbaric saxophone now dominated the orchestra, and to its passionate crooning and wailing the fox-trotters moved in what the editor of the Hobart College *Herald* disgustedly called a "syncopated embrace." No longer did even an inch of space separate them; they danced as if glued together, body to body, cheek to cheek. Cried the *Catholic Telegraph* of Cincinnati in righteous indignation, "The music is sensuous, the embracing of partners — the female only half dressed — is absolutely indecent; and the motions — they are such as may not be described, with any respect for propriety, in a family newspaper. Suffice it to say that there are certain houses appropriate for such dances; but those houses have been closed by law."

Supposedly "nice" girls were smoking cigarettes — openly and defiantly, if often rather awkwardly and self-consciously. They were drinking — somewhat less openly but often all too efficaciously. There were stories of daughters of the most exemplary parents getting drunk — "blotto," as their companions cheerfully put it — on the contents of the hip-flasks of the new prohibition régime, and going out joyriding with men at four in the morning. And worst of all, even at well-regulated dances they were said to retire where the eye of the most sharp-sighted chaperon could not follow, and in darkened rooms or in parked cars to engage in the unspeakable practice of petting and necking.

It was not until F. Scott Fitzgerald, who had hardly graduated from Princeton and ought to know what his generation was doing, brought out *This Side of Paradise* in April, 1920, that fathers and mothers realized fully what was afoot and how long it had been going on. Apparently the "petting party" had been current as early as 1916, and was now widely established as an indoor sport. "None of the Victorian mothers — and most of the mothers were Victorian — had any idea how casually their daughters were accustomed to be kissed," wrote Mr. Fitzgerald. ". . . Amory saw girls doing things that even in his memory would have been impossible: eating three-o'clock, after-dance suppers in impossible cafés, talking of every side of life with an air half of earnestness, half of mockery, yet with a furtive excitement that Amory considered stood for a real moral let-down. But he never realized how widespread it was until he saw the cities between New York and Chicago as one vast juvenile intrigue." The book caused a shudder to run down the national spine; did not Mr. Fitzgerald represent one of his well-nurtured heroines as brazenly confessing, "I've kissed dozens of men. I suppose I'll kiss dozens more"; and another heroine as saying to a young man (*to a young man!*), "Oh, just one person in fifty has any glimmer of what sex is. I'm hipped on Freud and all that, but it's rotten that every bit of real love in the world is ninety-nine per cent passion and one little *soupçon* of jealousy"?

It was incredible. It was abominable. What did it all mean? Was every decent standard being thrown over? Mothers read the scarlet words and wondered if they themselves "had any idea how often their daughters were accustomed to be kissed." . . . But no, this must be an exaggerated account of the misconduct of some especially depraved group. Nice girls couldn't behave like that and talk openly about passion. But in due course other books appeared to substantiate the findings of Mr. Fitzgerald: *Dancers in the Dark, The Plastic Age, Flaming Youth*. Magazine articles and newspapers reiterated the scandal. To be sure, there were plenty of communities where nice girls did not, in actual fact, "behave like that"; and even in the more sophisticated urban centers there were plenty of girls who did not. Nevertheless, there was enough fire beneath the smoke of these sensational revelations to make the Problem of the Younger Generation a topic of anxious discussion from coast to coast.

The forces of morality rallied to the attack. Dr. Francis E. Clark, the founder and president of the Christian Endeavor Society, declared that the modern "indecent dance" was "an offense against womanly purity, the very fountainhead of our family and civil life." The new style of dancing was denounced in religious journals as "impure, polluting, corrupting, debasing, destroying spirituality, increasing carnality," and the mothers and sisters and church members of the land were called upon to admonish and instruct and raise the spiritual tone of these dreadful young people. President Murphy of the University of Florida cried out with true Southern warmth, "The low-cut gowns, the rolled hose and short skirts are born of the Devil and his angels, and are carrying the present and future generations to chaos and destruction." A group of Episcopal church-women in New York, speaking with the authority of wealth and social position (for they included Mrs. J. Pierpoint Morgan, Mrs. Borden Harriman, Mrs. Henry Phipps, Mrs. James Roosevelt, and Mrs. E. H. Harriman), proposed an organization to discourage fashions involving an "excess of nudity" and "improper ways of dancing." The Y.W.C.A. conducted a national campaign against immodest dress among high-school girls, supplying newspapers with printed matter carrying headlines such as "Working Girls Responsive to Modesty Appeal!" and "High Heels Losing Ground Even in France." In Philadelphia a Dress Reform Committee of prominent citizens sent a questionnaire to over a thousand clergymen to ask them what would be their idea of a proper dress, and although the gentlemen of the cloth showed a distressing variety of opinion, the committee proceeded to design a "moral gown" which was endorsed by ministers of fifteen denominations. The distinguishing characteristics of this moral gown were that it was very loose-fitting, that the sleeves reached just below the elbows, and that the hem came within seven and a half inches of the floor.

Not content with example and reproof, legislators in several states introduced bills to reform feminine dress once and for all. The *New York American* reported in 1921 that a bill was pending in Utah providing fine and imprisonment for those who wore on the streets "skirts higher than three inches above the ankle." A bill was laid before the Virginia legislature which would forbid any woman from wearing shirt-waists or evening gowns which displayed "more than three inches of her throat." In Ohio the proposed limit of decolletage was two inches; the bill introduced in the Ohio legislature aimed also to prevent the sale of any "garment which unduly displays or accentuates the lines of the female figure," and to prohibit any "female over fourteen years of age" from wearing "a skirt which does not reach to that part of the foot known as the instep."

Meanwhile innumerable familes were torn with dissension over cigarettes and gin and all-night automobile rides. Fathers and mothers lay awake asking themselves whether their children were not utterly lost; sons and daughters evaded questions, lied miserably and unhappily, or flared up to reply rudely that at least they were not dirty-minded hypocrites, that they saw no harm in what they were doing and proposed to go right on doing it. From those liberal clergymen and teachers who prided themselves on keeping step with all that was new came a chorus of reassurance: these young people were at least franker and more honest than their elders had been; having experimented for themselves, would they not soon find out which standards were outworn and which represented the accumulated moral wisdom of the race? Hearing such hopeful words, many good people took heart again. Perhaps this flareup of youthful passion was a flash in the pan, after all. Perhaps in another year or two the boys and girls would come to their senses and everything would be all right again.

They were wrong, however. For the revolt of the younger generation was only the beginning of a revolution in manners and morals that was already beginning to affect men and women of every age in every part of the country.

☆ 2 ☆

A number of forces were working together and interacting upon one another to make this revolution inevitable.

First of all was the state of mind brought about by the war and its conclusion. A whole generation had been infected by the eat-drink-and-be-merry-for-tomorrow-we-die spirit which accompanied the departure of the soldiers to the training camps and the fighting front. There had been an epidemic not only of abrupt war marriages, but of less conventional liaisons. In France, two million men had found themselves very close to filth and annihilation and very far from the American moral code and its defenders; prostitution had followed the flag and willing mademoiselles from Armentières had been plentiful; American girls sent over as nurses and war workers had come under the influence of continental manners and standards without being subject to the rigid protections thrown about their continental sisters of the respectable classes; and there had been a very widespread and very natural breakdown of traditional restraints and reticences and taboos. It was impossible for this generation to return unchanged when the ordeal was over. Some of them had acquired under the pressure of war-time conditions a new code which seemed to them quite defensible; millions of them had been provided with an emotional stimulant from which it was not easy to taper off. Their torn nerves craved the anodynes of speed, excitement, and passion. They found themselves expected to settle down into the humdrum routine of American life as if nothing had happened, to accept the moral dicta of elders who seemed to them still to be living in a Pollyanna land of rosy ideals which the war had killed for them. They couldn't do it, and they very disrespectfully said so.

"The older generation had certainly pretty well ruined this world before passing it on to us," wrote one of them (John F. Carter in the *Atlantic Monthly,* September, 1920), expressing accurately the sentiments of innumerable contemporaries. "They give us this thing, knocked to pieces, leaky, red-hot, threatening to blow up; and then they are surprised that we don't accept it with the same attitude of pretty, decorous enthusiasm with which they received it, way back in the 'eighties."

The middle generation was not so immediately affected by the war neurosis. They had had time enough, before 1917, to build up habits of conformity not easily broken down. But they, too, as the letdown of 1919 followed the war, found themselves restless and discontented, in a mood to question everything that had once seemed to them true and worthy and of good report. They too had spent themselves and wanted a good time. They saw their juniors exploring the approaches to the forbidden land of sex, and presently they began to play with the idea of doing a little experimenting of their own. The same disillusion which had defeated Woodrow Wilson and had caused strikes and riots and the Big Red Scare furnished a culture in which the germs of the new freedom could grow and multiply.

The revolution was accelerated also by the growing independence of the American woman. She won the suffrage in 1920. She seemed, it is true, to be very little interested in it once she had it; she voted, but mostly as the unregenerate men about her did, despite the efforts of women's clubs and the League of Women Voters to awaken her to womanhood's civic opportunity; feminine candidates for office were few, and some of them — such as Governor Ma Ferguson of Texas — scarcely seemed to represent the starry-eyed spiritual influence which, it had been promised, would presently ennoble public life. Few of the younger women could rouse themselves to even a passing interest in politics: to them it was a sordid and futile business, without flavor and without hope. Nevertheless, the winning of the suffrage had its effect. It consolidated woman's position as man's equal.

Even more marked was the effect of woman's growing independence of the drudgeries of house-keeping. Smaller houses were being built, and they were easier to look after. Families were moving into apartments, and these made even less claim upon the housekeeper's time and energy. Women were learning how to make lighter work of the preparation of meals. Sales of canned foods were growing, the number of delicatessen stores had increased three times as fast as the population during the decade 1910–20, the

output of bakeries increased by 60 per cent during the decade 1914–24. Much of what had once been housework was now either moving out of the home entirely or being simplified by machinery. The use of commercial laundries, for instance, increased by 57 per cent between 1914 and 1924. Electric washing-machines and electric irons were coming to the aid of those who still did their washing at home; the manager of the local electric power company at "Middletown," a typical small American city, estimated in 1924 that nearly 90 per cent of the homes in the city already had electric irons. The housewife was learning to telephone her shopping orders, to get her clothes ready-made and spare herself the rigors of dress-making, to buy a vacuum cleaner and emulate the lovely carefree girls in the magazine advertisements who banished dust with such delicate fingers. Women were slowly becoming emancipated from routine to "live their own lives."

And what were these "own lives" of theirs to be like? Well, for one thing, they could take jobs. Up to this time girls of the middle classes who had wanted to "do something" had been largely restricted to school-teaching, social-service work, nursing, stenography, and clerical work in business houses. But now they poured out of the schools and colleges into all manner of new occupations. They besieged the offices of publishers and advertisers; they went into tea-room management until there threatened to be more purveyors than consumers of chicken patties and cinnamon toast; they sold antiques, sold real estate, opened smart little shops, and finally invaded the department stores. In 1920 the department store was in the mind of the average college girl a rather bourgeois institution which employed "poor shop girls"; by the end of the decade college girls were standing in line for openings in the misses' sportswear department and even selling behind the counter in the hope that some day fortune might smile upon them and make them buyers or stylists. Small-town girls who once would have been contented to stay in Sauk Center all their days were now borrowing from father to go to New

York or Chicago to seek their fortunes — in Best's or Macy's or Marshall Field's. Married women who were encumbered with children and could not seek jobs consoled themselves with the thought that home-making and child-rearing were really "professions," after all. No topic was so furiously discussed at luncheon tables from one end of the country to the other as the question whether the married woman should take a job, and whether the mother had a right to. And as for the unmarried woman, she no longer had to explain why she worked in a shop or an office; it was idleness, nowadays, that had to be defended.

With the job — or at least the sense that the job was a possibility — came a feeling of comparative economic independence. With the feeling of economic independence came a slackening of husbandly and parental authority. Maiden aunts and unmarried daughters were leaving the shelter of the family roof to install themselves in kitchenette apartments of their own. For city-dwellers the home was steadily becoming less of a shrine, more of a dormitory — a place of casual shelter where one stopped overnight on the way from the restaurant and the movie theater to the office. Yet even the job did not provide the American woman with that complete satisfaction which the management of a mechanized home no longer furnished. She still had energies and emotions to burn; she was ready for the revolution.

Like all revolutions, this one was stimulated by foreign propaganda. It came, however, not from Moscow, but from Vienna. Sigmund Freud had published his first book on psychoanalysis at the end of the nineteenth century, and he and Jung had lectured to American psychologists as early as 1909, but it was not until after the war that the Freudian gospel began to circulate to a marked extent among the American lay public. The one great intellectual force which had not suffered disrepute as a result of the war was science; the more-or-less educated public was now absorbing a quantity of popularized information about biology and anthropology which gave a general impression that men and women were merely animals of a rather intricate variety, and the moral codes had no universal validity and were often based on curious superstitions. A fertile ground was ready for the seeds of Freudianism, and presently one began to hear even from the lips of flappers that "science taught" new and disturbing things about sex. Sex, it appeared, was the central and pervasive force which moved mankind. Almost every human motive was attributable to it: if you were patriotic or liked the violin, you were in the grip of sex — in a sublimated form. The first requirement of mental health was to have an uninhibited sex life. If you would be well and happy, you must obey your libido. Such was the Freudian gospel as it imbedded itself in the American mind after being filtered through the successive minds of interpreters and popularizers and guileless readers and people who had heard guileless readers talk about it. New words and phrases began to be bandied about the cocktail-tray and the Mah Jong table — inferiority complex, sadism, masochism, Oedipus complex. Intellectual ladies went to Europe to be analyzed; analysts plied their new trade in American cities, conscientiously transferring the affections of their fair patients to themselves; and clergymen who preached about the virtue of self-control were reminded by outspoken critics that self-control was out-of-date and really dangerous.

The principal remaining forces which accelerated the revolution in manners and morals were all 100 percent American. They were prohibition, the automobile, the confession and sex magazines, and the movies.

When the Eighteenth Amendment was ratified, prohibition seemed . . . to have an almost united country behind it. Evasion of the law began immediately, however, and strenuous and sincere opposition to it — especially in the large cities of the North and East — quickly gathered force. The results were the bootlegger, the speakeasy, and a spirit of deliberate revolt which in many communities made drinking "the thing to do." From these facts in turn flowed further results: the increased popularity of distilled as against fermented liquors, the use of the hip-flask, the cocktail party, and the general transformation of drinking from a masculine prerogative to one shared by both sexes together. The old-time saloon had been overwhelmingly masculine; the speakeasy usually catered to both men and women. As Elmer Davis put it, "The old days when father spent his evenings at Cassidy's bar with the rest of the boys are gone, and probably gone forever; Cassidy may still be in business at the old stand and father may still go down there of evenings, but since prohibition mother goes down with him." Under the new régime not only the drinks were mixed, but the company as well.

Meanwhile a new sort of freedom was being made possible by the enormous increase in the use of the automobile, and particularly of the closed car. (In 1919 hardly more than 10 percent of the cars produced in the United States were closed; by 1924 the percentage had jumped to 43, by 1927 it had reached 82.8.) The automobile offered an almost universally available means of escaping temporarily from the supervision of parents and chaperons, or from the influence of neighborhood opinion. Boys and girls now thought nothing, as the Lynds pointed out in *Middletown,* of jumping into a car and driving off at a moment's notice — without asking anybody's permission — to a dance in another town twenty miles away, where they were strangers and enjoyed a freedom impossible among their neighbors. The closed car, moreover, was in effect a room protected from the weather which could be occupied at any time of the day or night and could be moved at will into a darkened byway or a country lane. The Lynds quoted the judge of the juvenile court in "Middletown" as declaring that the automobile had become a "house of prostitution on wheels," and cited the fact that of thirty girls brought before his court in a year on charges of sex crimes, for whom the place where the offense had occurred was recorded, nineteen were listed as having committed it in an automobile.

Finally, as the revolution began, its influence fertil-

ized a bumper crop of sex magazines, confession magazines, and lurid motion pictures, and these in turn had their effect on a class of readers and movie goers who had never heard and never would hear of Freud and the libido. The publishers of the sex adventure magazines, offering stories with such titles as "What I Told My Daughter the Night Before Her Marriage," "Indolent Kisses," and "Watch Your Step-Ins," learned to a nicety the gentle art of arousing the reader without arousing the censor. The publishers of the confession magazines, while always instructing their authors to provide a moral ending and to utter pious sentiments, concentrated on the description of what they euphemistically called "missteps." Most of their fiction was faked to order by hack writers who could write one day "The Confessions of a Chorus Girl" and the next day recount, again in the first person, the temptations which made it easy for the taxidriver to go wrong. Both classes of magazines became astonishingly numerous and successful. Bernard Macfadden's *True-Story,* launched as late as 1919, had over 300,000 readers by 1923; 848,000 by 1924; over a million and a half by 1925; and almost two million by 1926 — a record of rapid growth probably unparalleled in magazine publishing.

Crowding the news stands along with the sex and confession magazines were motion-picture magazines which depicted "seven movie kisses" with such captions as "Do you recognize your little friend, Mae Busch? She's had lots of kisses, but she never seems to grow *blasé.* At least you'll agree that she's giving a good imitation of a person enjoying this one." The movies themselves, drawing millions to their doors every day and every night, played incessantly upon the same lucrative theme. The producers of one picture advertised "brilliant men, beautiful jazz babies, champagne baths, midnight revels, petting parties in the purple dawn, all ending in one terrific smashing climax that makes you gasp"; the vendors of another promised "neckers, petters, white kisses, red kisses, pleasure-mad daughters, sensation-craving mothers, . . . the truth — bold, naked, sensational." Seldom did the films offer as much as these advertise-ments promised, but there was enough in some of them to cause a sixteen-year-old girl (quoted by Alice Miller Mitchell) to testify, "Those pictures with hot lovemaking in them, they make girls and boys sitting together want to get up and walk out, go off some-where, you know. Once I walked out with a boy be-fore the picture was even over. We took a ride. But my friend, she all the time had to get up and go out with her boy friend."

A storm of criticism from church organizations led the motion-picture producers, early in the decade, to install Will H. Hays, President Harding's Postmaster-General, as their arbiter of morals and of taste, and Mr. Hays promised that all would be well. "This in-dustry must have," said he before the Los Angeles Chamber of Commerce, "toward that sacred thing, the mind of a child, toward that clean virgin thing, that unmarked slate, the same responsibility, the same care about the impressions made upon it, that the best clergyman or the most inspired teacher of youth would have." The result of Mr. Hays's labors in behalf of the unmarked slate was to make the moral ending as obligatory as in the confession magazines, to smear over sexy pictures with pious platitudes, and to black-list for motion-picture production many a fine novel and play which, because of its very honesty, might be construed as seriously or intelligently questioning the traditional sex ethics of the small town. Mr. Hays, being something of a genius, managed to keep the churchmen at bay. Whenever the threats of censor-ship began to become ominous he would promulgate a new series of moral commandments for the produc-ers to follow. Yet of the practical effects of his super-vision it is perhaps enough to say that the quotations given above all date from the period of his dictator-ship. Giving lip-service to the old code, the movies diligently and with consummate vulgarity publicized the new.

Each of these diverse influences — the post-war disillusion, the new status of women, the Freudian

gospel, the automobile, prohibition, the sex and con-fession magazines, and the movies — had its part in bringing about the revolution. Each of them, as an influence, was played upon by all the others; none of them could alone have changed to any great degree the folkways of America; together their force was irresistible.

☆ 3 ☆

The most conspicuous sign of what was taking place was the immense change in women's dress and ap-pearance.

In Professor Paul H. Nystrom's *Economics of Fash-ion,* the trend of skirt-length during the Post-war De-cade is ingeniously shown by the sort of graph with which business analysts delight to compute the ebb and flow of carloadings or of stock averages. The basis of this graph is a series of measurements of fashion-plates in the *Delineator;* the statistician painstakingly measured the relation, from month to month, of the height of the skirt hem above the ground to the total height of the figure, and plotted his curve accord-ingly. This very unusual graph shows that in 1919 the average distance of the hem above the ground was about 10 per cent of the woman's height — or to put it another way, about six or seven inches. In 1920 it curved upward from 10 to about 20 per cent. During the next three years it gradually dipped to 10 per cent again, reaching its low point in 1923. In 1924, how-ever, it rose once more to between 15 and 20 per cent, in 1925 to more than 20 per cent; and the curve continued steadily upward until by 1927 it had passed the 25 per cent mark — in other words, until the skirt had reached the knee. There it remained until late in 1929.

This graph, as Professor Nystrom explains, does not accurately indicate what really happened, for it repre-sents for any given year or month, not the average length of skirts actually worn, but the length of the skirt which the arbiters of fashion, not uninfluenced by the manufacturers of dress goods, expected and wanted women to wear. In actual fact, the dip between 1921 and 1924 was very slight. Paris dressmakers predicted the return of longer skirts, the American stylists and manufacturers followed their lead, the stores bought the longer skirts and tried to sell them, but women kept on buying the shortest skirts they could find. During the fall of 1923 and the spring of 1924, manufacturers were deluged with complaints from retailers that skirts would have to be shorter. Shorter they finally were, and still shorter. The knee-length dress proved to be exactly what women wanted. The unlucky manufacturers made valiant efforts to change the fashion. Despite all they could do, however, the knee-length skirt remained standard until the decade was approaching its end.

With the short skirt went an extraordinary change in the weight and material and amount of women's clothing. The boyishly slender figure became the aim of every woman's ambition, and the corset was so far abandoned that even in so short a period as the three years from 1924 to 1927 the combined sales of corsets and brassières in the department stores of the Cleveland Federal Reserve District fell off 11 per cent. Silk or rayon stockings and underwear supplanted cotton, to the distress of cotton manufacturers and the delight of rayon manufacturers; the production of rayon in American plants, which in 1920 had been only eight million pounds, had by 1925 reached fifty-three million pounds. The flesh-colored stocking became as standard as the short skirt. Petticoats almost vanished from the American scene; in fact, the tendency of women to drop off one layer of clothing after another became so pronounced that in 1928 the *Journal of Commerce* estimated that in 15 years the amount of material required for a woman's complete costume (exclusive of her stockings) had declined from 19 ¼ yards to 7 yards. All she could now be induced to wear, it seemed, was an overblouse (2 yards), a skirt (2 ¼ yards), vest or shirt (¾), knickers (2) and stockings — and all of them were made of silk or rayon! This

On the cover of this sheet music for a popular 1920s song sits the famous flapper in all her glory, with bobbed hair, short skirts, slim body, and bee-stung mouth. A complex amalgam of female sexuality and boyish athleticism, she was the postwar feminine ideal. "Youth was their pattern," writes Frederick Lewis Allen, "but not youthful innocence: the adolescent whom they imitated was a hard-boiled adolescent, who thought not in terms of romantic love, but in terms of sex, and who made herself desirable . . . frankly and openly." (Sheet Music Collection, the John Hay Library, Brown University)

latter statement, it is true, was a slight exaggeration; but a survey published in 1926 by the National Retail Dry Goods Association, on the basis of data from department stores all over the country, showed that only 33 per cent of the women's underwear sold was made of cotton, whereas 36 per cent was made of rayon, and 31 per cent of silk. No longer were silk stockings the mark of the rich; as the wife of a workingman with a total family income of $1,638 a year told the authors of *Middletown*, "No girl can wear cotton stockings to high school. Even in winter my children wear silk stockings with lisle or imitations underneath."

Not content with the freedom of short and skimpy clothes, women sought, too, the freedom of short hair. During the early years of the decade the bobbed head . . . became increasingly frequent among young girls, chiefly on the ground of convenience. In May, 1922, the *American Hairdresser* predicted that the bob, which persisted in being popular, "will probably last through the summer, anyway." It not only did this, it so increased in popularity that by 1924 the same journal was forced to feature bobbed styles and give its subscribers instructions in the new art, and was reporting the progress of a lively battle between the professional hairdresser and the barbers for the cream of this booming business. The ladies' hairdressers very naturally objected to women going to barbers' shops; the barbers, on the other hand, were trying to force legislation in various states which would forbid the "hairdressing profession" to cut hair unless they were licensed as barbers. Said the *Hairdresser,* putting the matter on the loftiest basis, "The effort to bring women to barber shops for hair-cutting is against the best interests of the public, the free and easy atmosphere often prevailing in barber shops being unsuitable to the high standard of American womanhood." But all that American womanhood appeared to insist upon was the best possible shingle. In the latter years of the decade bobbed hair became almost universal among girls in their twenties, very common among women in their thirties and forties, and by no means rare among women of sixty; and for a brief period the hair was not only bobbed, but in most cases cropped close to the head like a man's. Women universally adopted the small cloche hat which fitted tightly on the bobbed head, and the manufacturer of milliner's material joined the hair net manufacturer, the hairpin manufacturer, and the cotton goods and woolen goods and corset manufacturers, among the ranks of depressed industries.

For another industry, however, the decade brought new and enormous profits. The manufacturers of cosmetics and the proprietors of beauty shops had less than nothing to complain of. The vogue of rouge and lipstick, which in 1920 had so alarmed the parents of the younger generation, spread swiftly to the remotest village. Women who in 1920 would have thought the use of paint immoral were soon applying it regularly as a matter of course and making no effort to disguise the fact; beauty shops had sprung up on every street to give "facials," to apply pomade and astringents, to make war against the wrinkles and sagging chins of age, to pluck and trim and color the eyebrows, and otherwise to enhance and restore the bloom of youth; and a strange new form of surgery, "face lifting," took its place among the applied sciences of the day. Back in 1917, according to Frances Fisher Dubuc, only two persons in the beauty culture business had paid an income tax; by 1927 there were 18,000 firms and individuals in this field listed as income-tax payers. The "beautician" had arrived.

As for the total amount of money spent by American women on cosmetics and beauty culture by the end of the decade, we may probably accept as conservative the prodigious figure of three-quarters of a billion dollars set by Professor Paul H. Nystrom in 1930; other estimates, indeed, ran as high as two billion. Mrs. Christine Frederick tabulated in 1929 some other equally staggering figures: for every adult woman in the country there were being sold annually over a pound of face powder and no less than eight rouge compacts; there were 2,500 brands of perfume on the market and 1,500 face creams; and if all the lipsticks sold in a year in the United States were placed end to end, they would reach from New York to Reno — which to some would seem an altogether logical destination.

Perhaps the readiest way of measuring the change in the public attitude toward cosmetics is to compare the advertisements in a conservative periodical at the beginning of the decade with those at its end. Although the June, 1919, issue of the *Ladies' Home Journal* contained four advertisements which listed rouge among other products, only one of them commented on its inclusion, and this referred to its rouge as one that was "imperceptible if properly applied." In those days the woman who used rouge — at least in the circles in which the *Journal* was read — wished to disguise the fact. (Advertisements of talc, in 1919, commonly displayed a mother leaning affectionately over a bouncing baby.) In the June, 1929 issue, exactly ten years later, the *Journal* permitted a lipstick to be advertised with the comment, "It's comforting to know that the alluring note of scarlet will stay with you for hours." (Incidentally, the examination of those two magazines offers another contrast: In 1919 the Listerine advertisement said simply, "The prompt application of Listerine may prevent a minor accident from becoming a major infection," whereas in 1929 it began a tragic rhapsody with the words, "Spring! for everyone but her . . .")

These changes in fashion — the short skirt, the boyish form, the straight, long-waisted dresses, the frank use of paint — were signs of a real change in the American feminine ideal (as well, perhaps, as in men's idea of what was the feminine ideal). Women were bent on freedom — freedom to work and to play without the trammels that had bound them heretofore to lives of comparative inactivity. But what they sought was not the freedom from man and his desires which had put the suffragists of an earlier day into hard straw hats and mannish suits and low-heeled shoes. The woman of the nineteen-twenties wanted to be able to allure man even on the golf links and in the office; the little flapper who shingled her hair and wore a manageable little hat and put on knickerbockers for the weekends would not be parted from her silk stockings and her high-heeled shoes. Nor was the post-war feminine ideal one of fruitful maturity or ripened wisdom or practiced grace. On the contrary: the quest of slenderness, the flattening of the breasts, the vogue of short skirts (even when short skirts still suggested the appearance of a little girl), the juvenile effect of the long waist, — all were signs that, consciously or unconsciously, the women of this decade

worshiped not merely youth, but unripened youth: they wanted to be — or thought men wanted them to be — men's casual and light-hearted companions; not broad-hipped mothers of the race, but irresponsible playmates. Youth was their pattern, but not youthful innocence: the adolescent whom they imitated was a hard-boiled adolescent, who thought not in terms of romantic love, but in terms of sex, and who made herself desirable not by that sly art which conceals art, but frankly and openly. In effect, the woman of the Post-war Decade said to man, "You are tired and disillusioned, you do not want the cares of a family or the companionship of mature wisdom, you want exciting play, you want the thrills of sex without their fruition, and I will give them to you." And to herself she added, "But I will be free."

☆ 4 ☆

One indication of the revolution in manners which her headlong pursuit of freedom brought about was her rapid acceptance of the cigarette. Within a very few years millions of American women of all ages followed the lead of the flappers of 1920 and took up smoking. Custom still generally frowned upon their doing it on the street or in the office, and in the evangelical hinterlands the old taboo died hard; but in restaurants, at dinner parties and dances, in theater lobbies, and in a hundred other places they made the air blue. Here again the trend in advertising measured the trend in public opinion. At the beginning of the decade advertisers realized that it would have been suicidal to portray a woman smoking; within a few years, however, they ventured pictures of pretty girls imploring men to blow some of the smoke their way; and by the end of the decade billboards boldly displayed a smart-looking woman, cigarette in hand, and in some of the magazines, despite floods of protests from rural readers, tobacco manufacturers were announcing that "now women may enjoy a companionable smoke with their husbands and brothers." In the ten years between 1918 and 1928 the total production of cigarettes in the United States *more than doubled*. Part of this increase was doubtless due to the death of the one-time masculine prejudice against the cigarette as unmanly, for it was accompanied by somewhat of a decrease in the production of cigars and smoking tobacco, as well as — mericifully — of chewing tobacco. Part of it was attributable to the fact that the convenience of the cigarette made the masculine smoker consume more tobacco than in the days when he preferred a cigar or a pipe. But the increase could never have been so large had it not been for the women who now strewed the dinner table with their ashes, snatched a puff between the acts, invaded the masculine sanctity of the club car, and forced department stores to place ornamental ash trays between the chairs in their women's shoe departments. A formidable barrier between the sexes had broken down. The custom of separating them after formal dinners, for example, still lingered, but as an empty rite. Hosts who laid in a stock of cigars for their male guests often found them untouched; the men in the dining-room were smoking the very same brands of cigarettes that the ladies consumed in the living-room.

Of far greater social significance, however, was the fact that men and women were drinking together. Among well-to-do people the serving of cocktails before dinner became almost socially obligatory. Mixed parties swarmed up to the curtained grills of speakeasies and uttered the mystic password, and girls along with men stood at the speakeasy bar with one foot on the old brass rail. The late afternoon cocktail party became a new American institution. When dances were held in hotels, the curious and rather unsavory custom grew up of hiring hotel rooms where reliable drinks could be served in suitable privacy; guests of both sexes lounged on the beds and tossed off mixtures of high potency. As houses and apartments became smaller, the country club became the social center of the small city, the suburb, and the summer resort; and to its pretentious clubhouse, every Saturday night,

drove men and women (after a round of cocktails at somebody's house) for the weekly dinner dance. Bottles of White Rock and of ginger ale decked the tables, out of capacious masculine hip pockets came flasks of gin (once the despised and rejected of bartenders, now the most popular of all liquors), and women who a few years before would have gasped at the thought that they would ever be "under the influence of alcohol" found themselves matching the men drink for drink and enjoying the uproarious release. The next day gossip would report that the reason Mrs. So-and-so disappeared from the party at eleven was because she had had too many cocktails and had been led to the dressing-room to be sick, or that somebody would have to meet the club's levy for breakage, or that Mrs. Such-and-such really oughtn't to drink so much because three cocktails made her throw bread about the table. A passing scandal would be created by a dance at which substantial married men amused themselves by tripping up waiters, or young people bent on petting parties drove right out on the golf-links and made wheel tracks on the eighteenth green.

Such incidents were of course exceptional and in many communities they never occurred. It was altogether probable, though the professional wets denied it, that prohibition succeeded in reducing the total amount of drinking in the country as a whole and in reducing it decidedly among the workingmen of the industrial districts. The majority of experienced college administrators agreed — rather to the annoyance of some of their undergraduates — that there was less drinking among men students than there had been before prohibition and that drinking among girl students, at least while they were in residence, hardly offered a formidable problem. Yet the fact remained that among the prosperous classes which set the standards of national social behavior, alcohol flowed more freely than ever before and lubricated an unprecedented informality — to say the least — of manners.

It lubricated, too, a new outspokenness between men and women. Thanks to the spread of scientific skepticism and especially to Sigmund Freud, the dogmas of the conservative moralists were losing force and the dogma that salvation lay in facing the facts of sex was gaining. An upheaval in values was taking place. Modesty, reticence, and chivalry were going out of style; women no longer wanted to be "lady-like" or could appeal to their daughters to be "wholesome"; it was too widely suspected that the old-fashioned lady had been a sham and that the "wholesome" girl was merely inhibiting a nasty mind and would come to no good end. "Victorian" and "Puritan" were becoming terms of opprobrium: up-to-date people thought of Victorians as old ladies with bustles and inhibitions, and of Puritans as blue-nosed, ranting spoil-sports. It was better to be modern, — everybody wanted to be modern, — and sophisticated, and smart, to smash the conventions and to be devastatingly frank. And with a cocktail glass in one's hand it was easy at least to be frank.

"Listen with a detached ear to a modern conversation," wrote Mary Agnes Hamilton in 1927, "and you will be struck, first, by the restriction of the vocabulary, and second, by the higher proportion in that vocabulary of words such as, in the older jargon, 'no lady could use.'" With the taste for strong liquors went a taste for strong language. To one's lovely dinner partner, the inevitable antithesis for "grand" and "swell" had become "lousy." An unexpected "damn" or "hell" uttered on the New York stage was no longer a signal for sudden sharp laughter of shocked surprise; such words were becoming the commonplace of everyday talk. The barroom anecdote of the decade before now went the rounds of aristocratic bridge tables. Everyone wanted to be unshockable; it was delightful to be considered a little shocking; and so the competition in boldness of talk went on until for a time, as Mrs. Hamilton put it, a conversation in polite circles was like a room decorated entirely in scarlet—the result was over-emphasis, stridency, and eventual boredom.

Along with the new frankness in conversation went a new frankness in books and the theater. Consider, for example, the themes of a handful of the best plays produced in New York during the decade: *What Price Glory?*, which represented the amorous marines interlarding their talk with epithets new to the stage; *The Road to Rome,* the prime comic touch of which was the desire of a Roman matron to be despoiled by the Carthaginians; *Strange Interlude,* in which a wife who found there was insanity in her husband's family but wanted to give him a child decided to have the child by an attractive young doctor, instead of by her husband, and forthwith fell in love with the doctor; *Strictly Dishonorable,* in which a charming young girl walked blithely and open-eyed into an affair of a night with an opera singer; and *The Captive,* which revealed to thousands of innocents that fact that the world contained such a phenomenon as homosexuality. None of these plays could have been tolerated even in New York before the Post-war Decade; all of them in the nineteen-twenties were not merely popular, but genuinely admired by intelligent audiences. The effect of some of them upon these audiences is suggested by the story of the sedate old lady who, after two acts of *What Price Glory?*, reprimanded her grandson with a "God damn it, Johnny, sit down!"

The same thing was true of the novels of the decade; one after another, from *Jurgen* and *Dark Laughter* through the tales of Michael Arlen to *An American Tragedy* and *The Sun Also Rises* and *The Well of Loneliness* and *Point Counter Point,* they dealt with sex with an openness or a cynicism or an unmoral objectivity new to the English-speaking world. Bitterly the defenders of the Puritan code tried to stem the tide, but it was too strong for them. They banned *Jurgen* — and made a best seller of it and a public reputation for its author. They dragged Mary Ware Dennett into court for distributing a pamphlet for children which explained some of the mysteries of sex — only to have her upheld by a liberal judge and endorsed by intelligent public opinion. In Boston, where they were backed by an alliance between stubborn Puritanism and Roman Catholicism, they banned books wholesale, forbade the stage presentation of *Strange Interlude,* and secured the conviction of a bookseller for selling *Lady Chatterley's Lover* — only to find that the intellectuals of the whole country were laughing at them and that ultimately they were forced to allow the publication of books which they would have moved to ban ten years before. Despite all that they could do, the taste of the country demanded a new sort of reading matter.

Early in the decade a distinguished essayist wrote an article in which she contended that the physical processes of childbirth were humiliating to many women. She showed it to the editor of one of the best magazines, and he and she agreed that it should not be printed: too many readers would be repelled by the subject matter and horrified by the thesis. Only a few years later, in 1927, the editor recalled this manuscript and asked if he might see it again. He saw it — and wondered why it had ever been disqualified. Already such frankness seemed quite natural and permissible. The article was duly published, and caused only the mildest of sensations.

If in 1918 the editors of a reputable magazine had accepted a story in which one gangster said to another, "For Christ's sake, Joe, give her the gas. Some lousy bastard has killed Eddie," they would have whipped out the blue pencil and changed the passage to something like "For the love of Mike, Joe, give her the gas. Some dirty skunk has killed Eddie." In 1929 the sentence appeared in a story accepted by a magazine of the most unblemished standing, and was printed without alteration. A few readers objected, but not many. Times had changed. Even in the great popular periodicals with huge circulations and a considerable following in the strongholds of rural Methodism the change in standards was apparent. Said a short-story writer in the late nineteen-twenties, "I used to write for magazines like the *Saturday Evening Post* and the *Pictorial Review* when I had a nice innocuous tale to tell and wanted the money, and for magazines like *Harper's* and *Scribner's* when I wanted to write something searching and honest. Now I find I can sell the honest story to the big popular magazines too."

☆ 5 ☆

With the change in manners went an inevitable change in morals. Boys and girls were becoming sophisticated about sex at an earlier age; it was symptomatic that when the authors of *Middletown* asked 241 boys and 315 girls of high-school age to mark as true or false, according to their opinion, the extreme statement, "Nine out of every ten boys and girls of high-school age have petting parties," almost precisely half of them marked it as true. How much actual intercourse there was among such young people it is of course impossible to say; but the lurid stories told by Judge [Ben B.] Lindsay — of girls who carried contraceptives in their vanity cases, and of "Caroline," who told the judge that fifty-eight girls of her acquaintance had had one or more sex experiences without a single pregnancy resulting — were matched by the gossip current in many a town. Whether prostitution increased or decreased during the decade is likewise uncertain; but certain it is that the prostitute was faced for the first time with an amateur competition of formidable proportions.

As for the amount of outright infidelity among married couples, one is again without reliable data, the private relations of men and women being happily beyond the reach of the statistician. The divorce rate, however, continued its steady increase; for every 100 marriages there were 8.8 divorces in 1910, 13.4 divorces in 1920, and 16.5 divorces in 1928 — almost one divorce for every six marriages. There was a corresponding decline in the amount of disgrace accompanying divorce. In the urban communities men and women who had been divorced were now socially accepted without question; indeed, there was often about the divorced person just enough of an air of unconventionality, just enough of a touch of scarlet, to be considered rather dashing and desirable. Many young women probably felt as did the New York girl who said, toward the end of the decade, that she was thinking of marrying Henry, although she didn't care very much for him, because even if they didn't get along she could get a divorce and "it would be much more exciting to be a divorcée than to be an old maid."

The petting party, which in the first years of the decade had been limited to youngsters in their teens and twenties, soon made its appearance among older men and women: when the gin-flask was passed about the hotel bedroom during a dance, or the musicians stilled their saxophones during the Saturday-night party at the country club, men of affairs and women with half-grown children had their little taste of raw sex. One began to hear of young girls, intelligent and well born, who had spent weekends with men before marriage and had told their prospective husbands everything and had been not merely forgiven, but told that there was nothing to forgive; a little "experience," these men felt, was all to the good for any girl. Millions of people were moving toward acceptance of what a *bon-vivant* of earlier days had said was his idea of the proper state of morality — "A single standard, and that a low one."

It would be easy, of course, to match every one of these cases with contrasting cases of men and women who still thought and behaved at the end of the decade exactly as the president of the Epworth League would have wished.[1] Two women who conducted newspaper columns of advice in affairs of the heart testified that the sort of problem which was worrying young America, to judge from their bulging correspondence, was not whether to tell the boy friend about the illegitimate child, but whether it was proper to invite the boy friend up on the porch if he hadn't yet come across with an invitation to the movies, or whether the cake at a pie social should be cut with a knife. In the hinterlands there was still plenty of old-

---

[1] The Epworth League was a Methodist youth organization that promoted fellowship, Christian service, and the study of the Bible. — Ed.

fashioned sentimental thinking about sex, of the sort which expressed itself in the slogan of a federated women's club: "Men are God's trees, women are His flowers." There were frantic efforts to stay the tide of moral change by law, the most picturesque of these efforts being the ordinance actually passed in Norphelt, Arkansas, in 1925, which contained the following provisions:

"Section 1. Hereafter it shall be unlawful for any man and woman, male or female, to be guilty of committing the act of sexual intercourse between themselves at any place within the corporate limits of said town.

"Section 3. Section One of this ordinance shall not apply to married persons as between themselves, and their husband and wife, unless of a grossly improper and lascivious nature."

Nevertheless, there was an unmistakable and rapid trend away from the old American code toward a philosophy of sex relations and of marriage wholly new to the country: toward a feeling that the virtues of chastity and fidelity had been rated too highly, that there was something to be said for what Mrs. Bertrand Russell defined as "the right, equally shared by men and women, to free participation in sex experience," that it was not necessary for girls to deny themselves this right before marriage or even for husbands and wives to do so after marriage. It was in acknowledgment of the spread of this feeling that Judge Lindsay proposed, in 1927, to establish "companionate marriage" on a legal basis. He wanted to legalize birth control (which, although still outlawed, was by this time generally practiced or believed in by married couples in all but the most ignorant classes) and to permit legal marriage to be terminated at any time in divorce by mutual consent, provided there were no children. His suggestion created great consternation and was widely and vigorously denounced; but the mere fact that it was seriously debated showed how the code of an earlier day had been shaken. The revolution in morals was in full swing.

QUESTIONS TO CONSIDER

1. What factors made American society ready for a revolution in manners and morals in the 1920s?

2. According to Allen, how had changes in the home, family, and workplace made American women ripe for revolution in the 1920s?

3. Contrast the domestic code of the Victorian era, with its emphasis on female sexual purity, with the 1920s code of the flapper. Did the flapper represent the culmination of the women's movement, the sexually liberated female?

4. How, according to Allen, did changes in women's fashion indicate real changes in the American feminine ideal? What kinds of inferences and conclusions can you draw from fashion in any age?

5. *Only Yesterday,* from which this selection on the 1920s is taken, was published in 1931, so Allen was describing a "revolution in manners and morals" that he had witnessed. How do you think his proximity to his subject may have affected his interpretation of the changes he observed in American society?

VIII

FOG OVER THE LAND

16

The Cruelest Year

By the beginning of 1929, the nation seemed to have reached a permanent state of prosperity. Business and foreign trade both were expanding, the stock market was rising at a phenomenal rate, and national leadership appeared to be in expert hands. Republican Herbert Hoover had won the presidency the previous November, having easily defeated his Democratic opponent. "For the first time in our history," wrote two economists, "we have a President who, by technical training, engineering achievement, cabinet experience, and grasp of economic fundamentals, is qualified for business leadership."

"We in America today," Hoover himself had said, "are nearer to the final triumph over poverty than ever before in the history of any land. The poorhouse is vanishing from among us." Hoover was equally optimistic in his inaugural address in March 1929: "I have no fears for the future of our country," he proclaimed. "It is bright with hope."

Eight months later, the country plummeted into the most severe and protracted economic depression in American history. It started with the stock market crash in October 1929 and deepened slowly and inexorably until the entire economy and maybe the nation itself approached total collapse. It was the worst disaster the United States had faced since the Civil War, and there were voices of doubt everywhere. How had it happened? What would become of the American dream? Would the nation disintegrate? And who was to blame — President Hoover, the Republican party, or capitalism itself?

Historian William Manchester makes clear that several factors caused economic collapse — chief among them underconsumption and overproduction, as consumer buying power lagged behind the quantity of goods being turned out. As factories and other businesses found themselves overextended, they began laying off workers, which de-

creased consumer buying power, which in turn caused more layoffs and resulted in a vicious cycle.

The prosperity of the 1920s had turned into a nightmare. Unemployed men roamed the country in search of work, succumbing to feelings of guilt and worthlessness when they found nothing at all. In this selection, Manchester captures the fear and privation that gripped the nation in 1932, the Depression's cruelest year. By then, perhaps a quarter of the work force was unemployed. Banks and businesses everywhere were closing their doors. Government on all levels was utterly unprepared to deal with so monstrous a crisis. And luckless Herbert Hoover was becoming the most hated man in the land.

Even so, not all historians would agree with Manchester that the country was on the verge of revolution. One school of thought, in fact, stresses the extraordinary political stability of the United States when compared with economically depressed Germany and Italy, which gave way to fascist dictatorships. As you read the next two selections, bear in mind that the Depression was indeed a worldwide calamity that rocked industrial Europe and Japan as well as the United States. Historian John A. Garraty says, "While there were differences in its impact and in the way it was dealt with from one country to another, the course of events nearly everywhere ran something like this: By 1925 most countries had recovered from the economic disruptions caused by the Great War of 1914–18. There followed a few years of rapid growth, but in 1929 and 1930 the prosperity ended. Then came a precipitous plunge that lasted until early 1933. This dark period was followed by a gradual, if spotty, recovery. The revival, however, was aborted by the steep recession of 1937–38. It took a still more cataclysmic event, the outbreak of World War II, to end the Great Depression."

GLOSSARY

HARRIMAN, JOSEPH WRIGHT   Banker who tried to kill himself after his bank failed and who went to prison for misusing bank funds and falsifying records.

MELLON, ANDREW   Powerful secretary of the treasury in the administrations of Harding, Coolidge, and Hoover; with the onset of the Depression, Mellon's conservative economic policy came under bitter attack; he also stirred up controversy when he exhorted Americans to pay their taxes and yet cheated on his own.

NEW ERA PROSPERITY   Political and business leaders alike referred to the twenties as "a New Era" — an age of seemingly endless prosperity when America came of age as a modern nation.

RENO, MILO   Led a farmers' revolt in Sioux City, Iowa, to protest an economic system that favored distributors at the farmers' expense.

ROGERS, WILL   Entertainer whose homespun humor and ridicule of politicians made him immensely popular in Depression America.

That August [of 1932] a writer for the *Saturday Evening Post* asked John Maynard Keynes, the great British economist, whether there had been anything like the Depression before. "Yes," he replied. "It was called the Dark Ages, and it lasted four hundred years." This was calamity howling on a cosmic scale, but on at least one point the resemblance seems valid. In each case the people were victims of forces they could not understand.

Some vaguely blamed "conditions," Hoover's euphemism. Others confused the Depression with the stock market Crash of 1929 — "We haven't been to the city since the Depression," they would say, or "I used to, but that was before the Depression." A remarkable number of sufferers stoically accepted the implicit charge of malingering made by President John E. Edgerton of the National Association of Manufacturers: "Many of those who are most boisterous now in clamor for work have either struck on the jobs they had or don't want to work at all, and are utilizing the occasion to swell the communistic chorus." An explanation lies in the strength of the Protestant ethic forty years ago in America. Although millions were trapped in a great tragedy for which there could plainly be no individual responsibility, social workers repeatedly observed that the jobless were suffering from feelings of guilt. "I haven't had a steady job in more than two years," a man facing eviction told a *New York Daily News* reporter in February 1932. "Sometimes I feel like a murderer. What's wrong with me, that I can't protect my children?"

Such men had been raised to believe that if you worked diligently, you would succeed. Now failure was dragging down the diligent and the shiftless alike. Men were demoralized, and "a demoralized people," as Walter Lippmann wrote then, "is one in which the individual has become isolated. He trusts nobody and

nothing, not even himself." Seventeen years later, in *The Lonely Crowd,* Riesman explained the plight of the inner-directed man caught in such a crisis: "If repeated failures destroy his hope of future accomplishment, then it is likely that his internal strengths can no longer hold the fort against the external evidence. Overwhelmed with guilt, he will despise himself for his failures and inadequacies." Newspapers of that period are crowded with accounts of men who took their own lives rather than go on relief. Emile Durkheim had created a special category, "altruistic suicides," for men who killed themselves rather than become a burden to the community.

The real blame lay in the false underpinnings of the Coolidge-Hoover "New Era" prosperity. Seen in perspective, the Depression appears to have been the last convulsion of the industrial revolution, creating a hiatus before the technological revolution. In the aftermath of the World War, the techniques of mass production combined to increase the efficiency per man-hour by over 40 percent. This enormous output of goods clearly required a corresponding increase of consumer buying power — that is, higher wages. But the worker's income in the 1920s didn't rise with his productivity. In the golden year of 1929, Brookings economists calculated that to supply the barest necessities a family would need an income of $2,000 a year — more than 60 percent of what American families were earning. In short, the ability to buy did not keep abreast of the volume of goods being turned out. It was part of the foolishness of the time to argue that the surge in production was no problem, that "a good salesman can sell anything." In practice this meant that while the rich (and many who weren't rich) were speculating in stocks, zealous salesmen were encouraging a kind of mass speculation. Customers of limited means were being persuaded to take products anyhow, the exchange being accomplished by an overextension of credit.

The stock market, honeycombed with credit in the form of brokers' loans, crashed of its own weight, calling to account the millions of little deals consummated by commercial travelers who had sold anything

From *The Glory and the Dream: A Narrative History of America 1932–1972* by William Manchester. Copyright © 1973, 1974, by William Manchester. By permission of Little, Brown and Company and reprinted by permission of Don Congdon Associates, Inc.

and everything to people lacking the means to pay for it. Thus ended the New Era prosperity. The panic followed, and the country couldn't cope with it. The last extended economic crisis had been in 1893; since then America had become so industrialized that a massive return to the farm was impossible. There was a certain rough justice in Herbert Hoover's ascent to the Presidency on the eve of the catastrophe, for as Secretary of Commerce he had been fascinated with productivity and indifferent to the dangerous lack of buying power. Long after he left the White House, he realized what had happened and wrote: "A margin of some thousands . . . got too much of the productive pie for the services they performed. . . . Another margin of some 20 percent got too little."

Between the Crash and 1932, the cruelest year of the Depression, the economy's downward spiral was accelerated by measures which, according to all accepted canons, ought to have brought recovery, and which in practice did the opposite. To protect investments, prices had to be maintained. Sales ebbed, so costs were cut by laying off men. The unemployed could not buy the goods of other industries. Therefore sales dropped further, leading to more layoffs and a general shrinkage of purchasing power, until farmers were pauperized by the poverty of industrial workers, who in turn were pauperized by the poverty of the farmers. "Neither has the money to buy the product of the other," an Oklahoma witness testified before a congressional subcommittee, explaining the vicious circle. "Hence we have overproduction and underconsumption at the same time and in the same country."

In June 1932, Ivy League seniors joined 21,974 other alumni hunting for jobs. By then New York department stores were requiring bachelor degrees for all elevator operators, and that was the best many of them could do, but twenty-year-old Sylvia Field Porter, Hunter '32, was an exception. She switched her major from English to economics because of what she later called "an overwhelming curiosity to know why everything was crashing around me and why people were losing their jobs" and talked her way into an investment counsel firm. At the same time she began a systematic study of the financial world, with the thought that one day she might write a column about it. She then discovered that she was in the middle of a crisis without historical precedent.

. . . By the time of Miss Porter's commencement, United States Steel and General Motors had dropped to 8 percent of their pre-Crash prices. Overall, stocks listed on the Big Board were worth 11 percent of their 1929 value. Investors had lost 74 billion dollars, three times the cost of the World War. More than 5,000 American banks had failed — in Iowa City, just across the county line from Hoover's native West Branch, all five banks were shut — and 86,000 businesses had closed their doors. The country's Gross National Product had fallen from 104 billion dollars to 41 billion (in 1973 it would be 2,177 billion). In 1932, 273,000 families were evicted from their homes, and the average weekly wage of those who had jobs was $16.21.

Some enterprises flourished. The contraceptive business was netting a quarter-billion dollars a year, a fact which the youth of that day conveniently forgot after they had become parents. Over half the population was going to the movies once a week (admission was a quarter for adults, a dime for children), and each year saw an increase in the number of cigarette smokers, none of them aware that the habit might be harmful. Kelvinator refrigerators and Atwater Kent radios were moving briskly. Miniature golf courses and circulation libraries were booming. Alfred C. Fuller was doing very nicely with his corps of door-to-door brush salesmen; in the grim month of August 1932 his sales leaped from $15,000 to $50,000 and grew thereafter at the rate of a million dollars a year. A prodigy named J. Paul Getty was quietly picking up cheap petroleum wells; that February he gained control of 520,000 of the Pacific Oil Corporation's one million shares. Here and there a venture was lucky. In Quincy, Massachusetts, the owner of a curious restaurant with a bright orange roof and pseudo Colonial architecture was almost bankrupt when a stock company opened across the street. Its first play was Eugene O'Neill's nine-act *Strange Interlude*. Every evening there was an 8:30 intermission for supper, and the restaurateur, Howard Johnson, survived.

But these were exceptions. U.S. Steel, the key to heavy industry, was operating at 19.1 percent of capacity. The American Locomotive Company didn't need much steel. During the 1920s it had sold an average of 600 locomotives a year; in 1932 it sold one. Nor was the automotive industry the big steel customer it had been. Month by month its fine names were vanishing: the Stutz Motor Company, the Auburn, the Cord, the Edward Peerless, the Pierce Arrow, the Duesenberg, the Franklin, the Durant, the Locomobile. One rash man decided to challenge Ford with another low-priced car. He called it the Rockne, lost 21 million dollars, and killed himself. In January an inventive bacteriologist named Arthur G. Sherman had become the sensation of the Detroit Auto Show by exhibiting the first crude, hand-carpentered, wooden trailer. In 1932 he sold just eighty of them. Air transport nose-dived. Airliners then had twelve seats, of which, the Department of Commerce reported, an average of seven were flying empty. And with the exception of the new talkies, most entertainers were foundering. In four years the jazz musician Eddie Condon landed four recording sessions; the phonograph recording industry had dwindled from 50 million dollars a year to a quarter-million. Sally Rand was making a precarious living with her celebrated fans; to a reporter who asked why she did it, she replied, "I never made any money till I took off my pants."

Because poverty was considered shameful, people tried to conceal destitution from neighbors, often with considerable success. One could never be sure about the family across the street. The smartly dressed young lawyer who always left home at the same time each morning may have been off to sell cheap neckties, magazines, vacuum cleaners, pressure cookers, or Two-in-One shoe polish door-to-door in a remote neighborhood. He may have changed his clothes and gone to another part of the city to beg. Or he may have been one of the millions who looked for work day after day, year after year, watching his children grow thinner and fighting despair in the night. There were certain skills developed by men who spent their days in the streets. You learned to pay for a nickel cup of coffee, to ask for another cup of hot water free, and, by mixing the hot water with the ketchup on the counter, to make a kind of tomato soup. In winter you stuffed newspapers under your shirt to ward off the cold; if you knew you would be standing for hours outside an employment office, you wrapped burlap bags around your legs and tied them in place. Shoes were a special problem. Pasteboard could be used for inner soles, and some favored cotton in the heels to absorb the pounding of the concrete. But if a shoe was really gone, nothing worked. The pavement destroyed the cardboard and then the patch of sock next to it, snow leaked in and accumulated around your toes, and shoe nails stabbed your heels until you learned to walk with a peculiar gait.

It was remarkable how ingenious an impoverished, thrift-minded family could be. Men resharpened and reused old razor blades, rolled their own cigarettes or smoked Wings (ten cents a pack), and used twenty-five-watt light bulbs to save electricity. Children returned pop bottles for two cents or stood in line for day-old bread at the bakery. Women cut sheets lengthwise and resewed them to equalize wear, retailored their clothes for their daughters, and kept up a brave front with the wife next door — who may have been doing the same thing on the same meager budget. Families sorted Christmas cards so they could be sent to different friends next year. Sometimes a man would disappear for weeks. All the neighborhood knew was that he had gone on a "business trip." It was a considerate husband who withheld the details of such trips from his wife, for they were often more terrible than anything she could imagine.

He was, of course, looking for work. The legends

of job hunting had become folklore by 1932, and some of the unbelievable stories were true. Men *did* wait all night outside Detroit employment offices so they would be first in line next morning. An Arkansas man *did* walk nine hundred miles looking for work. People *did* buy jobs. In Manhattan a Sixth Avenue employment agency *did* have five thousand applicants for three hundred jobs. It is a matter of record that a labor subcommittee of the 72nd Congress heard testimony about men setting forest fires in the state of Washington so they would be hired to put them out. *Business Week* verified the fact that a great many people who no longer loved America either left it or attempted to. Throughout the early Thirties the country's emigration exceeded its immigration. Amtorg, the Russian trading agency in New York, was getting 350 applications a day from Americans who wanted to settle in Russia. On one memorable occasion Amtorg advertised for six thousand skilled workers and a hundred thousand showed up, including plumbers, painters, mechanics, cooks, engineers, carpenters, electricians, salesmen, printers, chemists, shoemakers, librarians, teachers, dentists, a cleaner and dyer, an aviator, and an undertaker.

New York drew countless job seekers from surrounding states, though the city had a million jobless men of its own. A few strangers joined Manhattan's seven thousand nickel shoeshine "boys" or found furtive roles in the bootleg coal racket — 10 percent of the city's coal was being sneaked in by unemployed Pennsylvania miners — but most outsiders wound up on one of New York's eighty-two breadlines. If a man had a dime he could sleep in a flophouse reeking of sweat and Lysol. If he was broke he salvaged some newspapers and headed for Central Park, or the steps of a subway entrance, or the municipal incinerator. The incinerator's warmth drew hundreds of men on winter nights, even though they had to sleep on great dunes of garbage.

Returning from such an expedition in or under an empty freight car, a husband would review family assets with his wife and estimate how long they could keep going. Wedding rings would be sold, furniture pawned, life insurance borrowed upon, money begged from relatives. Often the next step was an attempt at a home business, with its implicit confession to the neighborhood that the pretense of solvency had been a hoax. The yard might be converted to a Tom Thumb miniature golf course. The husband might open a "parlor grocery." The wife might offer other wives a wash, set, and manicure for a dollar. In Massachusetts, idle textile workers erected looms in their living rooms; in Connecticut, households strung safety pins on wires, toiling long hours and earning a total of five dollars a week for an entire family.

These last-ditch efforts rarely succeeded; there were so few potential customers with money. Finally hope was abandoned. The father went to the city hall, declared himself penniless, and became a statistic. Because those figures were poorly kept, the precise extent of poverty is unknown. Somewhere between 15 million and 17 million men were unemployed, with most of them representing a family in want. *Fortune,* in September 1932, estimated that 34 million men, women, and children were without any income whatever. That was nearly 28 percent of the population, and like all other studies it omitted America's 11 million farm families, who were suffering in a rural gethsemane of their own.

During the Nixon Presidency, when America's farm population had shrunk to 5.2 percent of the population, it was hard to realize that only forty years earlier 25.1 percent had been living, or trying to live, on the land. They had not shared in New Era prosperity; the Crash merely worsened a situation which had already become a national scandal. By 1932 U.S. farmers had come to remind one reporter of Mongolian peasants seen in the rotogravure sections of Sunday newspapers, and the shadow of imminent famine fell across the plains. Agricultural prices hadn't been so low since the reign of Queen Elizabeth. Farmers were getting less than twenty-five cents for a bushel of wheat, seven cents for a bushel of corn, a dime for a bushel of oats, a nickel for a pound of cotton or wool. Sugar was bringing three cents a pound, hogs and beef two and a half cents a pound, and apples — provided they were flawless — forty cents for a box of two hundred.

Translated into the bitter sweat of rural life, this meant that a wagon of oats wouldn't buy a pair of four-dollar Thom McAn shoes. A wagon of wheat would just do it, but with mortgage interest running at $3.60 an acre, plus another $1.90 in taxes, the wheat farmer was losing $1.50 on every acre he reaped. In cotton fields the strongest and most agile man would toil from "can see" to "can't see" — fourteen hours of daylight — and receive sixty cents for the 300 pounds he had picked. It was cheaper to burn corn than sell it and buy coal. With meat bringing such ruinous prices, a man would spend $1.10 to ship a sheep to market, where it would return him less than $1.00. In Montana a rancher bought bullets on credit, spent two hours slaughtering a herd of livestock, and left it rotting in a canyon. It wasn't worth its feed. Turning away, he muttered to a reporter, "One way to beat the Depression, huh?"

As farm prices caved in, tens of thousands of mortgage foreclosure notices went up on gateposts and county courthouses. It has been estimated that one-fourth of the state of Mississippi was auctioned off. William Allen White, the Republican country editor who had pleaded with Hoover to come and see what was happening to the Middle West, wrote, "Every farmer, whether his farm is under mortgage or not, knows that with farm products priced as they are today, sooner or later he must go down." When the farmer did fail, unable even to pay the small costs of binder twine, tool repair, and seed, the bank would take title as absentee landlord, and he would rent from it the land his family had owned for generations. Meantime, while ranchers fed mutton to buzzards and warmed their hands over corn fires, millions in the cities could not afford the low prices which were destroying farmers (butter at 39 cents a pound, prime rib roast at 21 cents, two dozen eggs for 41 cents) because

so many were idle and those who had jobs were often earning what could only be called starvation wages.

There was no one to protect them. [President Hoover] disapproved of wage cuts and said so, but he was equally opposed to wage-hour legislation, so that when U.S. Steel made its second big wage slash in the spring of 1932, the workers were helpless. The labor movement was almost extinct; AFL membership had dwindled from 4.1 million in 1920 to 2.2 million, about 6 percent of the work force. There were strikes of desperation in 1932. All were lost. Miners were paid $10.88 a month, were at the mercy of check-weight men, and were required to buy groceries at inflated prices in the company store; when they rebelled the protest was bloodily suppressed by armed strikebreakers backed by the National Guard. The United Mine Workers were too weak to offer the victims anything but sympathy.

In such New England mill towns as Lynn and Lowell, where only one worker in three was employed, men were treated like serfs; one of them left Manchester, New Hampshire, to apply for a job in New Haven, was arrested, brought before a judge on a charge of vagrancy, and ordered back to his Manchester mill. The immense pool of job seekers tempted employers to slash their wage bills again and again. Department stores paid clerks as little as five dollars a week. An investigation in Chicago disclosed that the majority of working girls were getting less than twenty-five cents an hour; for a fourth of them, it was less than a dime. In 1932 hourly rates had shrunk to ten cents in lumbering, seven and-a-half cents in general contracting, six cents in brick and tile manufacturing, and five cents in sawmills. Before the Depression, Massachusetts textile mills rarely required skilled operators to be responsible for more than twenty looms eight hours a day. Then the mills introduced speedups and stretch-outs, and Louis Adamic saw teenaged girls running thirty wide looms from before dawn until after sunset.

In the sweatshops of Brooklyn fifteen-year-olds were paid $2.78 a week. Women received as little as

$2.39 for a fifty-hour week. In the summer of 1932 the Connecticut Commissioner of Labor reported that there were over a hundred shops in the state paying as little as sixty cents for a fifty-five hour week. New York City was the worst sweat spot in that state, and its garment industry, employing fifty thousand women, was the most sweated trade. "Unscrupulous employers," *Time* reported, had "battered wages down to the Chinese coolie level." Hat makers crocheted hats for forty cents a dozen; in a week a worker could make two dozen. Apron girls were paid two-and-a-half cents an apron; they earned twenty cents a day. A slipper liner received twenty-one cents for lining seventy-two pairs; if she completed one slipper every forty five seconds, she took home $1.05 after a nine-hour day. Girl cleaners in a pants factory were paid a half-cent for each garment they threaded and sponged. It was a five-minute operation; their income was six cents an hour. Honest employers could not survive that kind of competition. Welfare rolls grew longer and longer, the President continued to withhold federal help, and as the fourth Depression winter loomed the relief structure began to disintegrate.

When a senator declared the workers simply could not survive on one or two days' wages a week, President J. E. Edgerton of the National Association of Manufacturers said, "Why, I've never thought of paying men on the basis of what they need. I pay for efficiency. Personally, I attend to all those other things, social welfare stuff, in my church work." Doubtless he thought he did. As *Fortune* explained it, the theory was that now, as in the past, private charity and semipublic welfare groups could care for the old, the sick, and the indigent.

It wasn't working. The Depression, while multiplying the demands upon charities, had dried up their sources of contributions. By 1932, private help had dwindled to 6 percent of the money spent upon the needy, leaving some thirty million people to public welfare. Unfortunately, local governments couldn't handle the burden. State and city budgets had been in the red since 1930. About nine-tenths of municipal income came from taxation on real estate, which in terms of the Depression dollar was ludicrously overappraised. Landlords were liable to taxation if they held title to buildings; their inability to realize income from their houses was legally irrelevant, even when their tenants were on municipal relief, which never paid rentals. The landlords tried desperately to get their money. At first, in exasperation, they turned penniless occupants out. In New York there was hardly a block without a daily dispossession, and in Philadelphia so many families were put on the street that little girls invented a doll game called Eviction.

But empty tenements solved nothing; they merely contributed to the unpopularity of men of property while leaving tax bills unpaid. Eventually, as Professor Sumner H. Slichter of the Harvard Business School explained to the Senate Committee on Manufactures, there was "a more or less national moratorium on rents, insofar as the unemployed are concerned." Delinquent tax ratios hovered between 20 and 30 percent in metropolitan areas, and the cities, lacking this revenue, cut services. Roads were unpaved, sidewalks crumbled, streets blocked by winter snow were left unplowed. Chicago, deprived of two years' receipts by a taxpayers' strike, borrowed from the banks — and agonized over its unemployed population of 600,000.

Given the bankruptcy of public treasuries, and the widespread feeling that the poor were somehow responsible for their fate, it was inevitable that admittance to relief rolls would be made extremely difficult. Before applications were even considered, homes and possessions had to be sold, insurance canceled, credit exhausted, and evidence produced that all known relatives were broke. Even then, in many cities no assistance was granted to unmarried people or people without young chidren. Every possible stigma was attached to aid. In September 1932 Lewiston, Maine, voted to bar all welfare recipients from the polls, a goal already achieved by property requirements in the constitutions of ten states from Massachusetts to Oregon. West Virginia hospitals refused to admit patients unless payment for services was guaranteed; a referring physician suggested to one surgeon that he delay operating upon a child until the parents promised to pay $1,000. Two doctors in Royce City, Texas, put the following advertisement in the local paper:

TO WHOM IT MAY CONCERN: If you are expecting the stork to visit your home this year and he has to come by way of Royce City, he will have to bring a checkbook to pay his bill before delivery.

In some communities taxpayer associations tried to prevent welfare children from attending schools, and families receiving assistance were known to have been excluded from churches.

Even those who surmounted all barriers found that the approval of a welfare application was exceptional. In mill towns, mining communities, and on sharecropper farms, *Fortune* reported, "relief is merely a name." In the cities only 25 percent of qualified families were getting some form of help. The mayor of Toledo said in 1932: "I have seen thousands of these defeated, discouraged, hopeless men and women, cringing and fawning as they come to ask for public aid. It is a spectacle of national degradation." Admittance to the rolls did not end the defeat, discouragement, and hopelessness. In Philadelphia a family of four was given $5.50 a week, which hardly encouraged the debauchery predicted by those who objected to the dole, and Philadelphia was munificent compared to New York ($2.39), Mississippi ($1.50) and Detroit ($0.60). At the most, assistance covered only food and fuel. Since welfare families had often been inadequately clothed before the Crash, their rags three winters later sometimes defied description. It was not uncommon to see the head of a family dressed like a vaudeville tramp, wearing a buttonless suit coat out at one elbow, a pair of trousers out at the knee and in the seat, an old summer cap that had hung for years in some furnace room, worn tennis

shoes covered by patched rubbers, a pair of mismatched canvas gloves; the whole covered by a filthy old sheepskin. . . .

By 1932, a third of a million children were out of school because of lack of funds. Teachers in Mississippi, northern Minnesota, Idaho, South Dakota, and Alabama managed to eat only by "boarding around" at the homes of parents. In Dayton, Ohio, schools were open only three days a week; in Arkansas over three hundred schools were closed ten months or more. In Kansas, twenty-five-cent wheat meant rural teachers were being paid $35 a month for an eight month year — $280 a year. In Iowa they were receiving $40 a month, half the income Washington had said was necessary for industrial workers to exist. Akron owed its teachers $300,000, Youngstown $500,000, Detroit $800,000, and Chicago's debts to its teachers were more than 20 million dollars.

The story of the Chicago schools was a great Depression epic. Rather than see 500,000 children remain on the streets, the teachers hitchhiked to work, endured "payless paydays" — by 1932 they had received checks in only five of the last thirteen months —and accepted city script to be redeemed after the Depression, even though Chicago bankers would not accept it. Somehow the city found money to invest in its forthcoming World's Fair of 1933, when Sally Rand would gross $6,000 a week, but it turned a deaf ear to the Board of Education. A thousand teachers were dismissed outright. Those who remained taught on at immense personal sacrifice. Collectively the 1,400 teachers lost 759 homes. They borrowed $1,128,000 on their insurance policies and another $232,000 from loan sharks at annual interest rates of 42 percent, and although hungry themselves, they fed 11,000 pupils out of their thin pocketbooks.

Teachers, welfare workers, and policemen saw hardship at close range. Nobody called cops pigs in the early 1930s. Even when they were used to break strikes, it was widely acknowledged that they were as exploited as the workers. In New York, men on the

17

FDR and the New Deal:
The Foundation of a New Political Tradition

ALONZO L. HAMBY

Franklin Roosevelt swept to power in 1932, carrying every state but six in the electoral college and gathering 23 million popular votes in contrast to Hoover's 16 million. It was a bitter defeat for the Republicans. But the election was even more disappointing for Norman Thomas and William Z. Foster, candidates for the Socialist and Communist parties, respectively. In this year of distress, with some 16 million people unemployed, Thomas collected 882,000 votes and Foster only 103,000.

Roosevelt was perhaps the most controversial president the United States ever had. For millions of Americans, he was a folk hero: a courageous statesman who saved a crippled nation from almost certain collapse and whose New Deal salvaged the best features of democratic capitalism while establishing unprecedented welfare programs for the nation. For others, he was a tyrant, a demagogue who used the Depression to consolidate his political power, whereupon he dragged the country zealously down the road to socialism. In spite of his immense popular appeal, Roosevelt became the hated enemy of much of the nation's business and political community. Conservatives denounced him as a Communist. Liberals said he was too conservative. Communists castigated him as a tool of Wall Street. And Socialists dismissed him as a reactionary. "He caught hell from all sides," recorded one observer, because few knew how to classify his political philosophy or his approach to reform. Where, after all, did he fit ideologically? Was he for capitalism or against it? Was his New Deal revolutionary or reactionary? Was it "creeping socialism" or a bulwark against socialism? Did it lift the country out of the Depression, or did it make the disaster worse?

In the next selection, Alonzo L. Hamby argues that the key to understanding Roosevelt is the Progressive tradition in which he grew up and participated. Roosevelt came to office, Hamby believes, with an ideological commitment to Progressive reform. Yet there were two brands of progressivism. The New Nationalism of Theodore Roosevelt and Herbert Croly, offered to the American electorate in 1912, had accepted business consolidation — monopolies and trusts — but had insisted that the federal government should regulate and control them. The New Freedom of Woodrow Wilson and Louis Brandeis, put forth in the same election, had held that competition must be preserved and that the best approach to monopolies was to destroy them by federal action (by his second year in office, however, Wilson had abandoned the New Freedom and embraced TR's New Nationalism). Both brands of progressivism had emerged in a period of overall prosperity in the United States; hence neither provided guidelines for dealing with an economic calamity such as the Great Depression. Franklin Roosevelt, says Hamby, preferred the ideas of the New Nationalism but found little in its doctrines to guide him in handling "the worst crisis of capitalism in American history." Therefore, flexible politician that he was, Roosevelt opted for a strategy of action: he borrowed what he could from Progressive doctrines, added some experimentation, tossed in some Keynesian economics (government spending to "prime" the stricken economy), and packaged his New Deal as a liberal reform program that appealed to many interest groups.

How successful was the New Deal? Hamby gives it a mixed score. Like many other scholars, he believes that it probably saved capitalism in America, although most corporate bosses hated Roosevelt with a passion. And while it provided relief for millions of Americans, protected the organization and bargaining rights of American labor, and saved the average farmer through a system of price supports and acreage allotments, the New Deal failed to end the Depression — World War II would finally do that. The problem lay with the inability of the New Dealers to devise a coherent strategy for dealing with the structure of the American economy and particularly with restoring consumer purchasing power — the key to successful recovery. Hamby attributes this to the influence of progressivism, which had "sought humanitarian social programs, advocated a more equitable distribution of American abundance for all social groups, decried unregulated corporate power, and possessed some impulses toward social engineering." The New Dealers tried to realize these old aspirations, but because none of them addressed an economic disaster, the efforts of the New Dealers often impeded recovery. Hamby also argues that Roosevelt's increasingly hostile rhetoric against the business elite, however understandable, "probably did more to prolong the Depression than to solve it."

Yet Hamby gives FDR high marks for balancing the conflicting groups of labor, agriculture, and business and for establishing big government as the arbiter. In the process, FDR created "a political economy of counter-veiling powers," which, with the institution of welfare measures, guarded against future depressions and helped maintain the prosperity

of the postwar years. But Roosevelt's "final legacy" to the United States, Hamby believes, was his creation of a new political tradition, which defined American politics as pluralistic, liberal, and international and to which the majority of Americans subscribed.

GLOSSARY

AGRICULTURAL ADJUSTMENT ADMINISTRATION (AAA) New Deal agency designed to relieve Depression-wracked farmers, who suffered from falling prices and mounting crop surpluses; the AAA, established in 1933, subsidized farm prices until they reached a point of "parity" and sought to reduce farm surpluses by telling farmers how much to plant (acreage allotments) and paying them for what they did not raise. Declared unconstitutional by the Supreme Court in 1935, the AAA was superceded by the Soil Conservation and Domestic Allotment Act, which authorized the federal government to pay farmers to reduce their crop production to prevent erosion and "preserve soil."

BRAINS TRUST FDR's special group of advisers led by eminent political economists Raymond Moley, Rexford G. Tugwell, and Adolph A. Berle, Jr.

HOPKINS, HARRY FDR's close friend and adviser who headed the Civil Works Administration, 1933–1934, and the Works Progress Administration, 1935–1938; he was secretary of commerce, 1938–1940.

JOHNSON, HUGH Director of the National Recovery Administration who devised voluntary codes of fair competition and used public relations and propaganda to persuade employers to adhere to them.

McADOO, WILLIAM GIBBS Wilson's secretary of the treasury who battled Alfred E. Smith for the Democratic presidential nomination in 1924; McAdoo's chief support came from the Democratic party's rural, prohibitionist wing.

MARXISM Economic-political doctrine, espoused by Karl Marx and Friedrich Engels, that holds that the structural weaknesses and contradictions of capitalism doom it to failure, that ultimately the working class (proletariat) will revolt against the capitalist class and take control of the means of production, and that the result will be a classless society in which "rational economic cooperation" replaces "the coercive state."

NATIONAL RECOVERY ADMINISTRATION (NRA) New Deal agency established in 1933 to promote industrial recovery and end unemployment by devising and promoting hundreds of "industrial fair practice codes"; in practice, it often impeded competition by sanctioning production quotas and price fixing; in 1935, the Supreme Court invalidated the act that had chartered the NRA.

PERKINS, FRANCES The first woman to serve in a presidential cabinet, she was FDR's secretary of labor, 1933–1945; she mediated bitter labor disputes and helped write the Social Security Act of 1935, the National Labor Relations Act of 1935, and other important New Deal legislation.

RESETTLEMENT ADMINISTRATION (1935) AND FARM SECURITY ADMINISTRATION (1937) Offered marginal farmers short- and long-term loans so that they could relocate on better land.

RURAL ELECTRIFICATION ADMINISTRATION (1935) Established utility cooperatives that provided electrical power to farmers.

SMITH, ALFRED E. Democratic nominee for president, 1928; the first Roman Catholic to be chosen as a party candidate for the presidency.

SOCIAL SECURITY ACT (1935)   Provided federal welfare assistance (up to $15 per month) for destitute elderly Americans and established a pension system for those working; the program, however, excluded domestic servants and agricultural workers, many of them women and African American.

TAMMANY HALL   New York's Irish-Catholic political machine; corrupt though it was, it did support welfare programs for the poor.

TENNESSEE VALLEY AUTHORITY (TVA) Public corporation created by Congress in 1933 and "an unprecedented experiment in regional planning"; the TVA completed a dam at Muscle Shoals, Alabama, on the Tennessee River, and improved or built many others, which all but ended flooding in the region; the TVA also generated and sold inexpensive electricity to thousands of rural Americans who had never had it before.

WAGNER ACT (1935)   Guaranteed labor the right to organize and set up the National Labor Relations Board (NLRB), a policing agency with the power to coerce employers into recognizing and bargaining with bonafide unions.

WORKS PROGRESS ADMINISTRATION (WPA)   New Deal agency, established in 1935, that launched numerous improvement and building projects to furnish jobs for the unemployed; the agency's name was changed in 1939 to the *Work Projects Administration*.

G overnor Roosevelt, wrote the eminent columnist Walter Lippmann in January 1932, was not to be taken seriously: "An amiable man with many philanthropic impulses, but . . . not the dangerous enemy of anything . . . no crusader . . . no tribune of the people . . . no enemy of entrenched privilege . . . a pleasant man who, without any important qualifications for the office, would very much like to be President." Lippmann's evaluation was to become the most frequently quoted example of the perils of punditry in the history of American journalism. But when it appeared it was just another expression of a widely held assessment of Franklin D. Roosevelt, written at a time when it was still possible to assume that his determined optimism and issue-straddling were the marks of a lightweight who by some accident had twice been elected governor of the nation's largest state.

By the time of FDR's death, four presidential election victories later, Lippmann's condescending dismissal was an object of ridicule. Roosevelt had become the focus of intense emotions, united in agreement only on his standing as a moving force in history. To his enemies, he represented evil incarnate — socialism and communism, dictatorship, war. To his admirers, he was an object of worship — the champion of the underprivileged, the symbol of the world struggle of democratic, humanist civilization against the darkness of fascism. Millions wept at his passing.

Roosevelt had in fact profoundly changed the nature of American politics. Although he failed to achieve many of his most important immediate objectives, although he was notoriously eclectic and non-systematic in his approach to the enormous problems of his era, FDR was the founder of a distinctively new

From Alonzo L. Hamby, *Liberalism and Its Challengers: FDR to Reagan* (Oxford: Oxford University, 1985), extracts from 12–36, 50–51.

tradition which was to preempt the mainstream of American politics after his death.

Like all great departures in American politics, the Rooseveltian political tradition had deep roots in the past, specifically in the progressivism of Theodore Roosevelt and Woodrow Wilson, and generally in the optimism of a more innocent epoch. It was Roosevelt who achieved the actual implementation of what had been in many instances little more than abstract concepts formulated by earlier progressives, added to them — however unwittingly — Keynesian economics, and encased the whole package within a framework of "pluralist" or interest-group liberalism. And it was Roosevelt who fused the diplomatic realism of his cousin Theodore with the idealism of his old leader Woodrow Wilson in such a way that the American nation was irreversibly committed to active participation in a world it had largely shunned.

To all this, he added a new *style* of political leadership scarcely less important than the substantive changes he achieved. After Roosevelt, the most consistently successful American politicians were not those who relied upon the increasingly decrepit political machines or employed old-fashioned press agentry. They were those who mastered mid-twentieth-century mass communications to impart a sense of direct contact with the people. Like many political leaders of the highest historical rank, Roosevelt was great both because of what he did and how he did it.

☆

The Man Behind the Masks

To be born and raised a Roosevelt in the penultimate decade of the nineteenth century was to discover the world in an environment of remarkable privilege and security. It was the quaint world of an American patrician aristocracy, a setting of Hudson River mansions, European vacations, private tutors, ponies, and loving, attentive parents. Moderately wealthy, possessing blood lines running back to the *Mayflower,* esteemed by the arbiters of society, still prominent in business and finance, the Roosevelts and the class they represented were on the whole free from the taints of greed, irresponsibility, vulgarity, and conspicuous consumption that the popular mind attributed to the *nouveaux riches* of the period.

Perhaps no other segment of American society so fully accepted and synthesized the dominant values and hopes of Western civilization at the high noon of the Victorian era. The young Franklin Roosevelt absorbed a climate of opinion characterized by belief in the near-inevitability of progress; the unquestioned superiority of Anglo-American liberalism; the imperative of duty to one's friends, family, church, and country; and the unimpeachable character of traditional moral standards. The Victorian world view imparted to those who accepted it an ebullient confidence and an unquenchable optimism.

The close, attentive world in which Roosevelt lived as a child provided little of the experience that one usually associates with the building of leadership. His vigorous, domineering mother both doted on him and attempted to make all his decisions up through the early years of his marriage. From a very young age, however, he managed to establish his individuality in a smothering atmosphere. He developed a calculating other-directedness based on an understanding that he could secure his own autonomy and achieve his own objectives only by seeming to be the type of person that others — his mother, his schoolmates, his political associates — wanted him to be.

At the exclusive Groton preparatory school, at Harvard, and at Columbia Law School, he was never more than a respectable scholar. He preferred instead to concentrate on the nonacademic activities that he knew would win him the recognition of his peers. He stayed on as a nominal graduate student at Harvard only to be eligible to assume the editorship of the *Crimson* and never bothered to complete his M.A. A marginal law student, he dropped out of Columbia after passing the state bar examinations although he was but a few months away from his degree. His in-

FDR at Warm Springs, Georgia, in December 1933. Roosevelt "added a new style of political leadership," writes Alonzo Hamby. "After Roosevelt, the most consistently successful American politicians . . . were those who mastered mid-twentieth-century mass communications to impart a sense of direct contact with the people." FDR "was great both because of what he did and how he did it." (UPI/Bettman Newsphotos)

telligence was keen and his interests wide-ranging, but he felt a certain amiable contempt for the world of academic scholarship and indeed for almost any sustained, disciplined intellectual effort. The appearance he presented to the world was that of a young man conventionally handsome, somewhat overeager for popularity, and determined to suppress the cerebral aspects of his personality. Girls who knew him as a college student called him "feather duster" and "the handkerchief-box young man." Many of his male acquaintances found him unimpressive. Indeed, Porcellian, the elite Harvard club of his father and of Theodore Roosevelt, rejected his candidacy for membership.

Largely because of his name and social position, young Roosevelt was taken into a prestigious Wall Street law firm. Establishing himself as a competent young attorney, he faced a secure, well-defined future in which he would move up from clerk to junior partner to senior partner, earning an increasingly lucrative income and spending his weekends as a country gentleman. Yet he possessed little interest in so confined and comfortable a life. In a rare moment of open introspection, he told some of his fellow clerks that he intended to go into politics and that he would follow precisely in the footsteps of his distant cousin, Theodore Roosevelt — from the state assembly to the assistant secretaryship of the navy to the governor-

ship of New York to the presidency. It is hard to say how serious he was, and it is uncertain whether he actually had acquired the toughness and ambition that would eventually take him to the top. It is safe to say that he had been caught up in the idealism of early-twentieth-century reform.

The progressive movement that dominated American life in the first and second decades of the century was actually several reform movements representing different social groups, drawing upon diverse political philosophies, and pursuing divergent objectives. At its heart, however, was a rejection of the unfettered industrial capitalism of the late nineteenth century and a sense of concern for the victims of its abuses. As such, it had a special appeal to the somewhat displaced younger members of older socially prominent families such as the Roosevelts. Assuming that the American system would respond to pressures for gradual change, progressivism appealed to the Victorian optimism on which Roosevelt had been nurtured. . . .

FDR's early political career followed a progression along the lines he had projected to his fellow law clerks; it moved also from a shallow amateurism to a deep professionalism. Nominated for the state assembly in 1910 by a local Democratic organization that did not take him seriously, he campaigned intensively, frequently speaking to small groups from an open touring car. His nervousness and inexperience displayed themselves in awkward pauses as he tried to remember his lines or groped for something to say to the farmers who came to hear him. Roosevelt's district was strongly Republican, but he capitalized on a national surge of discontent with the inept administration of William Howard Taft. He had the advantage of the Roosevelt name, and he employed incessant denunciations of "bossism" to identify himself with the GOP insurgent movement that looked to Theodore Roosevelt for inspiration. His victory was one of many Democratic upsets around the country.

In Albany, Roosevelt quickly made himself the leader of a small group of Democratic dissenters de-

termined to block the election of a Tammany senatorial candidate. He held the quixotic movement together for two months, using his name and his already considerable talent for drawing attention to himself to garner national recognition. He made an ultimate defeat seem somehow a victory for political virtue, but he and his followers had exemplified only the shallow side of progressivism.

To many upper-middle-class Yankee reformers, Tammany Hall was simply a corrupt, Irish-Catholic political machine engaging in every manner of boodle and sustaining its power by buying the votes, one way or another, of illiterate immigrants. This attitude was true enough as far as it went, but incomplete and a shade bigoted. It showed little awareness of the social conditions to which the machine addressed itself through an informal but well-organized system of assistance to the poor and through increasing support of social welfare legislation. Moreover, Tammany produced men of substance (among them Roosevelt's legislative colleagues Robert F. Wagner and Alfred E. Smith) — honest, creative, and equipped by their own experience to understand the problems of the urban masses far more vividly than could an upstate neophyte. For the next two years, Roosevelt played the role of gadfly to Tammany, delighting his own district but needlessly making enemies of the powers within the Democratic party.

Had this been the sum of his politics, he doubtless would have gone the way of many a good government reformer of the time, enjoying a brief period of influence and attention followed by a long exile on the fringes of American public life. He was, however, capable of growth. Some of his "good government" causes, such as a bill to establish an honest, efficient state highway commission, were more soundly based. His progressivism gradually moved in other directions also: women's suffrage, conservation, public control of electrical power, workmen's compensation, and regulation of hours and working conditions in mines and factories. By the end of his second year in the legislature, Roosevelt had loosely identified himself with a style of progressivism that moved across the spectrum of reform causes. In doing so, he had paralleled the evolution of his revered kinsman, TR. Established as a noted, it not powerful, New York Democrat, he needed only the right bit of good fortune to move onto the national scene.

Remarkably, his advancement stemmed from the ostentatious insurgency that normally would have made him unelectable to any statewide office. Displaying sound instinct, he attached himself to a new national progressive figure destined to eclipse Theodore Roosevelt — Woodrow Wilson. Although he could deliver no votes, FDR served as an attractive spokesman for the New Jersey governor and became identified as one of his major New York supporters. Wilson's victory would bring the isolated young insurgent to Washington.

It was far from coincidental that he took the post of assistant secretary of the navy. He might have obtained other powerful positions — collector of the Port of New York or assistant secretary of the treasury, for example — but the navy position was yet another step along TR's old path. Moreover, it gave Roosevelt a chance to wield power and influence on a large scale. It was an extraordinary opportunity for a man who loved ships and the sea and who from his student days had been a disciple of the great advocate of naval power, Admiral Alfred Thayer Mahan.

As assistant secretary of the navy, young FDR functioned as the second-ranking official in the department and was primarily responsible for its day-to-day administration. Like his cousin before him, Roosevelt was the official who actually managed the navy: his chief, Josephus Daniels, was a small-town North Carolina progressive chosen for his devotion to the ideals of the New Freedom and for his influence with Southern congressmen rather than for any knowledge of military matters.

In most respects, Roosevelt's performance was excellent. The coming of World War I made his office even more important than he could have anticipated, and he contributed significantly to the American mil-

itary victory. Possessing more knowledge of technical naval matters and better read in the strategy of sea power than perhaps any other high civilian official in Washington, he was also a strong and effective administrator, audacious in the exercise of his authority, receptive to new ideas, daring in his own strategic concepts. He delighted in cutting red tape to facilitate one procurement operation after another; almost single-handedly, he overcame the opposition of both the entire British Admiralty and many of his own officers to secure the laying of a massive anti-submarine mine barrage across the North Sea.

He learned much, too. He established relationships with the ranking naval officials of the Allied powers, with important business executives, and with labor union leaders in the shipyards. He gained a sense of the contours of international diplomacy and developed the art of dealing with powerful interest groups. A key figure in a federal bureaucracy attempting to manage a national crisis, he received firsthand training in the use of governmental power to create a feeling of national purpose.

He also absorbed lessons of another sort. Still playing the role of insurgent, he had allowed his name to be entered in the 1914 New York Democratic senatorial primary as the anti-Tammany candidate. The machine had countered masterfully, backing President Wilson's widely respected ambassador to Germany, James W. Gerard, who won by a margin approaching 3 to 1. FDR quickly moved toward a rapprochement; by 1917, he was the featured speaker at the Tammany Fourth of July celebration, posing amiably with Boss Murphy for the photographers. Soon the organization indicated its willingness to accept him as a unity candidate for governor.

Instead, he was an attractive vice-presidential candidate in 1920 — young, able, nationally known, a resident of the largest state in the union. Among the Democratic rank and file, and especially among young intellectuals and activists, his nomination was popular. Handsome, vigorous, and by this time a skilled public speaker, he toured the country, delivering perhaps a thousand speeches. He attracted about as much attention as his running mate, James Cox, and made hundreds of personal contacts with the state and local leadership of the Democratic party from Massachusetts to California. When he and Cox went under in the Harding landslide, few would ever again tender Cox serious attention. But somehow Roosevelt seemed to speak for the future of the party. He alone had emerged from the debacle in a position of strength, possessing greater public recognition than ever and having obtained a first-hand knowledge of the structure of the Democratic party.

In such circumstances, it seemed especially tragic that in 1921, at the age of thirty-nine, he incurred a crippling attack of polio that promised to end his active political career. It is unquestionable that Roosevelt's suffering — both physical and psychological — was enormous. The ordeal may have deepened his character, giving him a greater sense of identification with the unfortunate of the world and strengthening his resolve. It was an existential challenge from which he emerged triumphant in spirit if not in body. Despite intensive physical therapy over a period of several years, he never regained the use of his legs. But he achieved a feat of self-definition against the will of his mother, who expected him to settle down under her wing to the life of an invalid country gentleman, and against that current of American political culture that expects political leaders to be specimens of perfect health. He quickly decided to stay in politics and to continue to pursue his ultimate goal, the presidency. From the perspective of that decision, his personal tragedy was political good fortune.

Polio removed Roosevelt from active political competition in an era in which the Democratic party was in a state of disintegration, effectively subdued by the economic successes of Republican normalcy and torn by bitter dissension between urban and rural factions led by Alfred E. Smith and William Gibbs McAdoo. Engaging instead in numerous charitable and civic activities, ostentatiously maintaining an interest in the future of his party, and carefully keeping lines open to both its wings, he remained a public figure and functioned, in Frank Freidel's phrase, as a "young elder statesman." The most elementary dictates of political loyalty required him to align himself with his fellow New Yorker Smith, but he did so in a way that could have antagonized only the most fanatical McAdoo supporter. His 1924 nominating speech for Smith was an attention-getting formal return to politics and the most universally praised event of an intensely bitter Democratic convention. He steadfastly avoided name-calling and, after the disastrous Democratic defeat in November, he sent out a letter to every convention delegate asking for suggestions on the regeneration of the party. In this and other ways, he reminded the rank and file of his probable eventual availability as the man who could unify them, and yet he could bide his time. . . .

[In 1928] Roosevelt benefited from another stroke of unlikely political luck — he was drafted for the Democratic gubernatorial nomination in what seemed certain to be a Republican year. Pressed into the race by the presidential candidate, Al Smith, who realized that Roosevelt's name on the ticket would be a great help in upstate New York, he eked out a narrow victory. Smith, nonetheless, lost the state badly to Hoover. Roosevelt had established himself as New York's senior Democrat, and his new office was generally considered in those days to be the best jumping-off position for a presidential nomination. At the end of his first year as governor, with the national economy dropping sharply downward, that jumping-off position began to look much more valuable than either he or Smith could have imagined in mid-1928.

Roosevelt was a strong and effective governor, although his tenure, inhibited by constant political warfare with a Republican legislature, was more important for what it attempted than for what it accomplished. Under the pressures of political responsibility and economic distress, Roosevelt's vague progressivism began to take on a more definite shape. He pushed strongly for conservation, public development of hydroelectric facilities on the St. Lawrence

River, rural electrification, help for the hard-pressed farmer, and work relief projects for the unemployed. He surrounded himself with able, liberal-minded aides — Samuel I. Rosenman, Harry Hopkins, Frances Perkins. He developed his strongest grasp yet of public relations. Press releases and news handouts spewed from his office and got his viewpoint into many Republican papers. He took highly visible inspection trips that carried him around the state from one institution or project to another. Most importantly, he made superb use of the newest and most important medium of mass communication since the invention of the printing press — the radio. Undertaking a series of "fireside chats," he established himself as one of the few public figures of the era who instinctively knew how to project his personality over the airwaves. Roosevelt swept to a resounding reelection victory in 1930, establishing himself as the dominant contender for the Democratic presidential nomination in 1932.

The nomination was nonetheless a near thing. Facing the then hallowed rule of the Democratic party that a nominee required a two-thirds majority of the convention votes, he nearly fell to a "stop Roosevelt" alliance of candidates ranging from his former ally Smith to the one-time Wilsonian Newton D. Baker to the crusty old Southern conservative John Nance Garner of Texas. His opponents had only one thing in common: they all lacked the ideological flexibility to deal with the economic crisis America faced by 1932. Roosevelt went over the top, just as his support was on the verge of disintegration, by making a deal to give Garner the vice-presidency.

Victory in November was certain, and he took no chances in the campaign. He made it clear that his presidency would depart sharply from the policies of Herbert Hoover, that he had no respect for outmoded tradition, that he would, as he put it, give the nation "a New Deal." He ostentatiously put together a "Brains Trust" of advisers headed by three of the country's foremost political economists — Raymond Moley, Adolf A. Berle, Jr., and Rexford G. Tugwell. Still, he presented no coherent platform. His pronouncements hit both sides of some issues and approached others in the most general terms. Faced with two sharply opposing drafts of what was to be a major address on tariff policy, he was capable of telling his speechwriters to "weave the two together." He defeated Hoover by seven million votes.

☆

The New Dealer

Like most politicians, Roosevelt had followed a path to success based upon an appealing style and a mastery of political techniques. Any effort to stake out a fixed, precise ideological position probably would have been politically counterproductive. But the American political and economic systems faced an unprecedented situation that seemed to demand rigorous analysis and reevaluation. The collapse of the economy during the Hoover years, the quantum increases in the unemployment rolls, the mortgage foreclosures that afflicted small-scale farmers and middle-class homeowners alike, the crops that went unharvested for lack of a market, the collapse of the banking system, the rapidly spreading misery and deprivation that attended the lack of any decent government aid for the unfortunate — all added up to the worst crisis of capitalism in American history.

Marxist solutions were unacceptable in America, even during the worst part of the Depression. The other reform alternative, the American progressive tradition to which Roosevelt loosely subscribed, had been forged during a time of general prosperity and was torn between conflicting economic visions of competition and concentration. Intellectually, progressives were almost as unprepared for the appalling disaster as Hoover had been. It is hardly surprising that Roosevelt and those around him met the challenge of depression with a curious blend of halfway measures, irrelevant reforms, and inconsistent attitudes.

Roosevelt sensed that the American people in 1933 wanted action above all, backed by displays of confidence and optimism. In his inaugural address, he exhorted America to fear nothing but fear itself. Invariably, he maintained a buoyant appearance, exemplified by his calculated cheerfulness or by the jaunty angle of his cigarette holder. Comparing himself to a quarterback who would call the next play only after the present one had been run, he made no pretense of working from a fixed design. Instead, he simply announced that his objectives would be relief, reform, and recovery. He pursued them with a bewildering cluster of programs that left no doubt of the government's concern for the plight of its citizens and of the administration's activism.

Relief was the easiest goal to pursue. By the time Roosevelt took office, poverty seemed on the way to becoming the normal condition of life for a majority of Americans. Facing a sea of human misery, untroubled by ideological inhibitions against federal aid to the needy, the Roosevelt administration swiftly instituted public works jobs, mortgage relief legislation, farm price supports, and federal insurance for bank deposits — programs aimed directly at the plight of the individual who had been hit in one way or another by the Depression.

By contemporary standards, it is true, these efforts were relatively modest. Moreover, Roosevelt fretted constantly about their cost, and, while accepting them as a necessity, he never allowed them to be expanded sufficiently to provide jobs for the majority of the unemployed. All the same, most people who received some sort of help — a WPA job, a refinanced mortgage, a AAA acreage allotment check — were grateful in a direct personal way.

Reform posed a more difficult problem. In his own experience as an admirer of TR's New Nationalism and a participant in Wilson's New Freedom, Roosevelt embodied the two conflicting main lines of progressive thought, neither of which had been formulated to address the problem of recovery from an economic depression. The debate at bottom was between the TR–Herbert Croly vision of a political economy that accepted the dominance of the large corporation and sought to regulate it in the public interest and the Wilson–Louis Brandeis faith in an atomistic, intensely competitive economic society. The New Deal's resolution of the argument would in the end amount to little more than an evasion of choice.

The most permanent and successful items of the New Deal reform agenda were not specifically directed at Depression-created problems but had some of the appearance of relief acts. During the Progressive Era, reformers had reached a substantial consensus on the need for social legislation to provide ongoing protection to the working classes and the disadvantaged. The Social Security Act of 1935 established a national system of old-age insurance and committed the federal government to extensive subsidies for state welfare programs. The act marked a revolution in federal responsibility for the welfare of the needy. It quickly became politically unassailable, and over the next generation its coverage and benefits grew steadily.

Much the same process occurred with regard to agriculture. With the immediate objective of fighting the Depression, the New Deal introduced an extensive and quasi-permanent system of benefits and subsidies for rural America. For the cash-crop farmer and the agrarian middle class, the administration produced a series of devices aimed at achieving profitable market prices (most important among them acreage allotments and federal purchase of surpluses). Roosevelt seems to have considered the price support program a temporary expedient, but his hopes that agriculture could become self-sufficient ran up against reality. By his second term, Secretary of Agriculture Henry A. Wallace was justifying long-term [government] buying of [farm] surpluses by proclaiming the goal of an "ever-normal granary."

Price supports were only the centerpiece of the

Through the Works Progress Administration (later called the Work Projects Administration), the New Deal put unemployed men like these to work on a variety of projects, from building bridges in the cities to blazing nature trails in the wilderness. These WPA workers are engaged in a street-widening project. (The Bettmann Archive)

New Deal agricultural program. Other aspects, such as rural electrification and soil conservation, were largely successful attempts to enhance the quality of life on the land. Through the Resettlement Administration and the Farm Security Administration, the New Deal undertook the first important attack in American history on the structure of rural poverty. The agencies delivered assistance of one variety or another to the forgotten classes of the agricultural community — the impoverished dirt farmers, the sharecroppers, the migrant laborers. Their aid and rehabilitation programs sought to transform an agrarian *lumpenproletariat* [marginal underclass] into a self-sufficient yeomanry.

The results were mixed. Price support programs probably saved the average farmer from liquidation but failed to produce real prosperity; electrification and conservation brought firm gains to individuals and the land; the antipoverty efforts, underfunded stepchildren, were less successful. But in the guise of fighting the Depression, the New Deal had put the federal government into agriculture on a vast scale and a permanent basis.

The same was true of the labor programs. From the beginning, the New Deal endorsed the right of collective bargaining, and from 1933 on, union leaders told prospective recruits, "President Roosevelt wants you to join the union." Roosevelt actually had little personal enthusiasm for militant unionism. It was nonetheless a force that drew special sustenance from the New Deal's general endorsement of social change and fair play for the underdog. The Wagner Act of

1935 was not introduced at Roosevelt's behest, but it won his endorsement as it moved through Congress. The new law projected the federal government into labor-management relations in ways that would have been unimaginable just a few years earlier. It established procedures by which unions could win recognition from management, prohibited certain anti-union practices by employers, and set up a strong, permanent bureaucracy (the National Labor Relations Board) to provide continuing enforcement. For workers at the lowest, usually nonunionized levels of American business, the Fair Labor Standards Act of 1938 established nationwide wage and hour standards, prohibited child labor, and provided strict rules for the employment of teenagers.

In providing help to a blue-collar work force that had been hit hard by the Depression, the New Deal had effected long-term changes whose significance could barely be grasped as the thirties came to an end. Organized labor had emerged as a major force within the Democratic party, providing the campaign support Roosevelt and his followers needed to stay in power. The members of its unions would constitute the bulk of the additions to the post–World War II middle class.

Reform of the banking system, accompanied as it was by federal deposit insurance, was both relief for the "little people" who had lost their savings in bank failures and retribution against the bankers. Regulation of the securities markets, long overdue, was widely accepted as a form of discipline against the financiers who had encouraged irresponsible stock market practices during the twenties and thereby, it was widely (if erroneously) believed, brought on the Depression. An effort at establishing a more steeply graduated tax system, the so-called Wealth Tax Act of 1935, could achieve broad support as a way of striking at a class that had exhibited indifference to economic suffering.

The Tennessee Valley Authority [TVA], the most unique and in many ways the most radical of New Deal innovations, was an expression of Roosevelt's fullest progressive aspirations. Combining flood control, conservation, and public ownership of electrical power, it functioned in the short run as another work relief project but in the long run it was the most ambitious effort at regional economic planning ever undertaken in the United States. By almost any standard, the TVA was a resounding success. It tamed the destructive Tennessee River, encouraged sound land use practices, generated inexpensive power for homes and industries, and contributed greatly to the prosperity of the Tennessee Basin area. Yet it was never duplicated in any other region of the United States, nor did it become a model for the New Deal's approach to the American economy. These nonevents were indicative both of the American political system's resistance to sweeping change and of a split within the progressive mind over what may have been the central problem posed by the Great Depression — the organization of the American economy.

Roosevelt himself had always been primarily attracted to the New Nationalism of his kinsman, and the experience of World War I had reinforced this inclination. His natural impulse upon coming to power was to mobilize the nation in a great crusade against the Depression, much as the country had been mobilized against Germany in 1917. The economic corollary of such an effort was central management of the economy, and the New Deal's first mechanism for industrial recovery, the National Recovery Administration (NRA), was patterned closely upon the experience of the World War I War Industries Board. Quite in line with that experience, the NRA did much more than impose responsibilities upon the business community; it recognized business management as a legitimate and responsible sector of the American political economy and extended substantial benefits to it. NRA regulations, purposely mislabeled "codes of fair competition," actually stifled competition and in many instances sanctioned such cartel practices as production quotas, allocation of marketing territories, and price-fixing. The NRA represented in its way both the New Nationalism and a style of broker politics with which Roosevelt began his presidency. Had it been successful in overcoming the Depression, the words *New Deal* might today conjure up the image of a relatively moderate reform movement at war with no segment of American society.

The NRA failed for a host of reasons, some of them conceptual, some of them political. It failed to address what now appears to have been the central malady of the Depression, the liquidation of consumer spending power; in fact, its price-fixing approach actually made that problem worse. It was not sufficiently coordinated with the work relief programs, which could have injected much more money into the economy had they been managed less cautiously. It collapsed to some extent of its own weight as its frenetic head, Hugh Johnson, traveled about the country attempting to organize every mom-and-pop enterprise in sight and wildly overpromising what his agency could accomplish. By late 1934, Johnson had suffered a nervous breakdown, and the agency was washed up. Liberals decried its concessions to business; yet the business community displayed little support for it. In the spring of 1935, the Supreme Court ruled the NRA unconstitutional, dredging up a seldom-invoked sanction against excessive delegation of legislative authority by the Congress and reverting to a hyper-restrictive interpretation of the government's authority to regulate interstate commerce. Economically, politically, and constitutionally, the NRA had reached a dead end — and so had the idea of central management of the economy.

Roosevelt and those who now became the dominant economic thinkers of his administration turned to the other ready-made alternative the progressive tradition had created for them — antitrustism. It was a natural move for an administration that had become bitter over persistent hostility from the business establishment. The Wheeler-Rayburn Public Utility Holding Company Act of 1935 struck an important blow at private consolidation in a key American industry. The Antitrust Division of the Department of Justice . . . became larger and more active than ever. In Congress, administration supporters secured the establishment of a special Temporary National Economic Committee (TNEC), which over several years undertook a massive study of the problem of consolidation and anticompetitive activities in the American economy.

Yet antitrustism, while it might be a valuable component of a program designed primarily to restore consumer purchasing power, did not directly address the urgent problem of the Depression. Moreover, it was not consistently applied. Here and there, in the railroad and coal industries, for example, centralized regulation continued dominant. And in order to protect small retailers, "fair trade laws" sanctioned price-fixing for many consumer items. The antitrust effort was directed more against specific abuses than against the fundamental structure of American big business. The TNEC became an academic enterprise that produced a shelf of scholarly monographs but no meaningful legislation. Far from resolving the conflict that existed in the progressive mind, the New Deal had simply acted it out. In part, this reflected Roosevelt's own uncertainty; but it also exemplified the mood of a nation that since the beginnings of modern American industrialism had feared the growth of the large corporation while lusting after its supposed economic benefits.

This ultimate inability to arrive at a coherent strategy for dealing with the structure of the American economy leads one finally to the most conspicuous failure of the New Deal — it never achieved a full economic recovery. It is easy today to pick out some of the reasons; any above-average undergraduate economics student can recite what might be called the Keynesian critique of Roosevelt's leadership. The fundamental task of the New Deal, so the argument runs, had to be the reconstruction of consumer purchasing power. The surest and most direct way of accomplishing this objective was through massive government spending. Because the unemployment problem was so horrendous, the amount of federal economic stimulus would have to be enormous and the federal budget deficits unprecedented. But once most Americans were back at work, paying off old debts and spending money on all manner of consumer goods, a prosperous economy would be able to maintain itself, federal tax revenues would roll in, and the budget deficits would become surpluses.

In addition to its economic merits, the Keynesian approach promised the political dividends that would accrue from even higher levels of relief spending. Yet Roosevelt disregarded the Keynesian argument. He did not fully understand it, and it was incompatible with his personality. "A Keynesian solution," James MacGregor Burns has written, "involved an almost absolute commitment, and Roosevelt was not one to commit himself absolutely to any political or economic method." The result was a halfway Keynesianism that failed to provide a full cure for a desperately sick economy and yet outraged conservative sentiment. And even this policy was inconsistent. In 1937, with economic recovery having reached at best an intermediate stage far short of prosperity, Roosevelt ordered cutbacks in government spending and attempted to balance the budget. A disastrous recession ensued; there were months of hesitation, then a return to the old halfway spending levels. . . .

The failure to achieve economic recovery may be more fairly traced to the nature of the American progressive experience. Theodore Roosevelt and Woodrow Wilson had faced only sporadic economic difficulties. Roosevelt had coped with the panic of 1907 by cooperating fully with the financial establishment, led by J. P. Morgan; Wilson had all but ignored the economic problems arising from World War I. The older Populist tradition had grown out of economic distress, but its inflationary panaceas could hardly be taken seriously. (Some New Deal monetary tinkering — abandonment of the gold standard, devaluation of the dollar, a lavish silver purchase program — exhilarated populist-style politicians but failed utterly to have a positive effect on the economy.) The mainstream of American reformism, having come out of

an era of prosperity, sought humanitarian social programs, advocated a more equitable distribution of American abundance for all social groups, decried unregulated corporate power, and possessed some impulses toward social engineering. Proceeding from this frame of reference, the New Deal seized upon an opportunity to realize old reformist aspirations, doing so at times with little regard for their impact upon the economy.

The Social Security Act, for example, financed by a system of payroll taxes on employers and employees, sucked millions of dollars out of the private economy and constituted a drag on the drive for recovery. While Roosevelt fully understood this, he nonetheless insisted upon payroll contributions, which he saw as a way of guaranteeing the program's fiscal integrity and providing political insurance for it. "With those taxes in there," he remarked privately, "no damn politician can ever scrap my social security program." The NRA likewise had great appeal to Roosevelt, representing as it did a culmination of the New Nationalism and something of a recreation of the World War I effort at industrial mobilization. In practice, however, it probably had a contractionist effect on the economy, by sanctioning cartel practices based on assumptions of oversupply and depressed consumer demand.

In general, moreover, Roosevelt's increasingly vehement antibusiness attitude after 1935 probably did more to prolong the Depression than to solve it. Business confidence can be a critical determinant in investment decisions if the economy is unprosperous, and it was terribly unprosperous even at the peak of the partial recovery the New Deal did achieve. During the recession of 1937–38, Roosevelt fumed that business was deliberately refusing to help recovery along by investing in new facilities. However, in an economic environment characterized by unemployment levels of around 15 percent, only a business community that had achieved a sense of identification with the New Deal could have seriously contemplated expansion. Instead, of course, the leaders of

American corporate enterprise were overwhelmingly irrational and unenlightened in their attitudes toward Roosevelt and the New Deal. Discredited by the Depression, they had been psychologically declassed. Yet although they were hard to deal with, although it was easy and politically profitable to return their hostility in kind, there were no economic benefits in doing so.

Throughout Roosevelt's public rhetoric, beginning with his inaugural address, one finds a steadily increasing hostility toward the business elite. The money changers, he declared after taking the oath of office in 1933, had been driven at last from the temple of government. (In fact, as Arthur Schlesinger, Jr., has observed, they were helping the New Dealers draw up the Emergency Banking Act of 1933.) By 1936, he had declared open warfare, characterizing his opponents as "economic royalists" and delighting in inflammatory rhetoric. "We had to struggle with the old enemies of peace — business and financial monopoly, speculation, reckless banking, class antagonism, sectionalism, war profiteering," he declared in his final big campaign speech. "They are unanimous in their *hate* for *me — and I welcome their hatred.*"

Roosevelt was, of course, responding to a campaign of abuse that was equally bitter from his opposition. He suffered routine denunciation in the clubs and corporate boardrooms of America in the most irrational and scurrilous fashion — as a Communist, as a sinister tool of some imagined Jewish conspiracy (his "real name," so the story went, was Rosenfeld), as a syphilitic (the "actual cause" of his crippling paralysis). He derived emotional satisfaction from striking back, but he might have been better advised to do what many other great political leaders have done from time to time — to absorb criticism like a sponge and seek to coopt his enemies.

Nevertheless, Roosevelt was essentially correct in responding to conservative critics with a famous story in which he depicted himself as having rescued an aged and wealthy capitalist from drowning only to be attacked for having failed to retrieve the old man's silk hat. Roosevelt indeed probably had saved American capitalism, even if he was not appreciated by the capitalists. Although the New Deal never solved the Depression, it did bring forth some moderate reform legislation that strengthened the structure of the capitalist system. In particular, banking and securities legislation brought a new degree of responsibility and safety to the American financial world.

In a broad sense also, the New Deal strengthened American capitalism by changing its structure in a largely unplanned way. Throughout the 1930s, Roosevelt and his associates sought to balance conflicting groups within the American political economy. The New Deal farm programs had the effect of organizing agriculture; the Wagner Act permitted the self-organization of labor with federal encouragement; the once-dominant position of business was whittled down to some extent; and big government functioned as an arbiter between these forces. Half-consciously, Roosevelt created a political economy of countervailing powers.

Despite an economic record that might be charitably described as spotty, Roosevelt was remarkably successful in making himself the nation's dominant political figure and in rebuilding the structure of American politics. The intellectual and moral bankruptcy of his opposition obscured the shortcomings of the New Deal. His own charisma and his well-developed skills in the art of politics enabled him to take maximum advantage of his opportunities. Better than any other personality of his time, Roosevelt combined the two major techniques of democratic political leadership: the achievement of a sense of direct identification with the people and the construction of formidable organizational support. Neither objective required a total victory over the Depression, nor was it necessary to have a coherent vision of economic reorganization. (Here, Roosevelt's confusion may even have been politically profitable, reflecting as it did that of so many Americans.) What was required, and what Roosevelt delivered, was some progress combined with, above all, the *appearance* of caring about and attempting to alleviate the plight of the unfortunate.

Roosevelt provided the appearance with his expert use of the communications media. He regularly brought the White House reporters into the Oval Office twice a week for press conferences; a dramatic departure from past presidential aloofness, the practice won him the sympathy of most working journalists and assured his views a prominent place even in implacably Republican newspapers. His radio talks demonstrated a technical skill in the use of the medium, an ability to transmit a sense of warm concern over the airwaves, and a talent for explaining complex social-economic policies in simple but not condescending language. His entire demeanor, most fully captured by the newsreels (then shown in every movie house in America), was that of an optimistic, energetic chief executive with a sense of concern for the unfortunate.

To this, Roosevelt added the dispensing of real benefits of one sort or another to millions of people, who more often than not responded naturally enough with the feeling that he had given them a job or saved their homes or preserved their farms or secured their bank deposits. The New Deal relief programs were not evaluated by a populace employing today's expectations; rather, they were received by people who were desperate for any assistance and who could contrast FDR only with the seemingly cold and indifferent Herbert Hoover. Roosevelt encouraged the contrast and doubtless believed it valid. "Better the occasional faults of a Government that lives in a spirit of charity than the consistent omissions of a Government frozen in the ice of its own indifference," he declared in his acceptance speech at the 1936 Democratic convention. He won the uniquely personal allegiance of many individuals who had been helped in some way by the New Deal or who simply felt touched by his manifestations of sympathy with their difficulties.

At the same time, Roosevelt built organizational support broader and stronger than that of any previous Democratic leader. He was successful in bringing behind him both the traditional Democratic machines and the trade unions, the most natural representatives of the working classes and the underprivileged. He secured the support of key leaders of almost every ethnic or religious minority in the nation, ranging from such figures as Robert Vann, the most influential black newspaper editor in the country, to Joseph P. Kennedy, perhaps the wealthiest and most powerful layman in the Irish-Catholic community. The minorities were most likely to be among the underprivileged that the New Deal attempted to help, but the Roosevelt administration also took pains to give them symbolic recognition in the form of visible appointments to office.

Finally, as a fitting capstone to his coalition, Roosevelt preempted the progressive impulse for himself and his party like no Democrat before him. He actively sought and gained the backing of reformers who ran the gamut of American politics from heartland Republican mavericks to New York social democrats. Treating them almost as a minority group, he gave them important and prominent places in his administration. His secretary of the interior, Harold Ickes, and his secretary of agriculture, Henry A. Wallace, were eminent former progressive Republicans. Both embraced the Democratic party as well as the New Deal and in some respects became the rhetorical and ideological point men of the administration. . . .

Roosevelt's first reelection victory in 1936 was a landslide in which he won support from all groups. But from the beginning, his most fervent and devoted support came from the independent progressives and from those groups that might loosely be described as "working class" in the larger cities of America. (Roosevelt was not the first Democratic candidate to win over the urban working and lower classes — Alfred E. Smith had done so in 1928 — but his appeal was broader and deeper.) The liberals, the unionists, the ethnic-religious minorities, the blacks, and the urban lower classes would stay with FDR to the end.

Roosevelt and those around him interpreted the 1936 results as a mandate for an extension of the New

Deal. In his second inaugural address, the President declared, "I see one third of a nation ill-housed, ill-clad, ill-nourished." He made it clear that more help for the underprivileged was his first priority. Armed with an overwhelming popular endorsement, given a Congress with Democratic majorities of 331–89 in the House of Representatives and 76–16 in the Senate, Roosevelt appeared all but invincible. Actually, his program faced serious institutional and popular obstacles. By the end of 1938, the New Deal was dead.

The immediate precipitant was Roosevelt's push for legislation to pack a Supreme Court that had demonstrated unqualified hostility to the New Deal. He handled the effort clumsily and somewhat dishonestly (he argued that he was simply trying to invigorate an excessively aged court), and he ran squarely up against popular reverence for the judicial system and the constitutional concept of separation of powers. Any chance of success evaporated when the two "swing justices," Charles Evans Hughes and Owen Roberts, began to vote with the liberal bloc and thereby converted a pro–New Deal minority into a majority. The Court bill was killed in the Senate after a debate that split the Democratic party. Roosevelt bravely insisted that he had lost a battle but had won the war. Perhaps so, but he had sustained serious wounds. The demonstration that he could be beaten on an issue of vital importance encouraged many potential opponents who had been intimidated by his popularity.

Other events drained FDR's political strength. His identification with organized labor became something of a liability as militance increased during his second term, manifesting itself in sit-down strikes that outraged millions of property-owning Americans. The severe recession of 1937–38 graphically exposed the New Deal's failure to achieve economic recovery. Roosevelt attempted to "purge" several opponents within his own party in the 1938 Democratic primaries. Poorly conceived and executed, the purge was a near-total failure — and yet another exhibition

of the limitations inherent in the President's ad hoc approach to public policy problems.

From the Court-packing battle on, Roosevelt faced an increasingly strong opposition bloc in Congress. Made up of Republicans and anti–New Deal Democrats, the conservative coalition was composed largely of congressmen who represented safe, rural constituencies. It subscribed to the individualistic ethic of an older America shocked by the changes the New Deal had inflicted upon the nation. It benefited also from a rather general congressional resentment against FDR's "dictatorial" tactics in his dealings with Capitol Hill. Heartened by Roosevelt's post-1936 setbacks, convinced by the failure of the purge that he could not oust them from office, augmented by sizable Republican gains in the 1938 elections, the congressional conservatives became the strongest political force in Washington. From 1939 on, it would be FDR who was on the defensive, unable to enlarge the New Deal and at times forced to accept cuts in some of its peripheral programs.

Thus ended a remarkable story of success and failure in domestic reform. Roosevelt had changed American life in many ways, but he had not overcome the Depression. He had drastically altered the pattern of American politics only to create a domestic stalemate that would endure long after his death. He had made the Democratic party the country's dominant political vehicle, yet he could not control it. The new shape of American politics included a reform-oriented presidential Democratic party able to control presidential nominations and a moderate-to-conservative congressional Democratic party. Seldom in tune with the White House on domestic issues, the congressional party represented local and regional interests, was generally removed from the pressures of close electoral competition, and often willing to cooperate with the Republicans. These contours would endure for a quarter-century — until reshaped by one of FDR's most devoted followers, Lyndon B. Johnson. . . .

☆

THE ACCOMPLISHMENT

Roosevelt left a deep imprint upon his era. At his death [in 1945], he was fiercely hated by his opponents and all but worshipped by his followers. As emotions subsided over the next generation, however, the most frequent criticism of him came from liberal and radical scholars in sympathy with his aims and disenchanted by his inability to achieve all of them. In some instances, they appeared to speak little more than a lament that the New Deal failed to establish some variety of democratic socialism or to resolve all the problems of American life. Others, evaluating him by the criteria of the seminar rather than the real world of the political leader, voiced unhappiness at his lack of a systematic social and political philosophy. Some leveled the charge that after 1937 he had failed as a party leader, and there could be no arguing that mass Democratic defections had made the conservative coalition possible. They have, however, been less convincing in demonstrating the means by which FDR or any president could have whipped well-entrenched congressmen and independent local party leaders into line. His undeniable tactical mistakes seem relatively insignificant when placed against such formidable constitutional barriers to presidential control as federalism and the separation of powers.

It is legitimate to observe that Roosevelt's New Deal failed to restore the prosperity of 1929. . . . But from almost any vantage point, the nation was stronger and more secure at his death than at the time he took office. If the New Deal did not restore prosperity, it did in a number of ways lay a strong groundwork for the maintenance of prosperity after World War II. By restructuring the American political economy into a system of countervailing powers, by establishing a minimal welfare state, the New Deal smoothed out the business cycle and laid the basis for a postwar political consensus based on a widely distributed affluence. Roosevelt's role in engineering the defeat of fascism removed the most serious challenge the nation had ever faced to its security. He brought America no utopia, but he took his country through difficult times and left it able to face the future with strength and confidence.

The way in which Roosevelt gained political power and support was in some respects as important as what he did. He won the backing of established organizations actively involved in the game of political power — the machines, the unions, the various organized interests — and he achieved a sense of direct communication and empathy with the ordinary people. He employed radio as a supplement to organizational support, not as a substitute for it, and by bringing the average American into direct involvement with his personality, he called forth the intensity with which his admirers loved him and his enemies hated him.

Roosevelt created a new era in the history of American politics. His moderate liberalism, fumbling though it might seem to later critics, and his charismatic optimism, whether realistic or not, drew millions to the Democratic party and made it a vehicle of majority sentiment for the first time since the Civil War. He created a new consensus to which that majority subscribed — one that defined the objectives of American politics as pluralist and liberal and the national interests of the United States as worldwide. FDR's final legacy to the nation was no less than a new political tradition.

QUESTIONS TO CONSIDER

1. How does Alonzo Hamby portray FDR's personality and cast of mind? Describe FDR's social background and its influence on him. What effect did his time as undersecretary of the navy have on FDR? his struggle with polio? his terms as governor of New York?

2. Why does Hamby say that reform was much harder to accomplish than relief during the Depression? What were the strengths and weaknesses of the Progressive tradition, and how did FDR deal with its ambiguities throughout the 1930s?

3. Describe FDR's relationship with big business during the Depression. Why does Hamby suggest that FDR saved capitalism in America? Do you agree? How does this fit with the opinion expressed by William Manchester in selection 16?

4. Describe FDR as a politician. From whom did he get his principal support? How did ordinary Americans react to him? What effect did he have on the Democratic party? Why did he face a more determined and successful opposition after his 1936 reelection, and what did this say about the American people and their relationship to the administration and the Constitution?

5. What were some of the principal successes and failures of the New Deal? Why does Hamby think in the end it failed to bring about full economic recovery? Despite this, Hamby concludes that "FDR's legacy to the nation was no less than a new political tradition." Explain what he means. How in particular did the New Deal programs change the traditional relationship of the citizen to the federal government?

IX

A World at War

18

Day Of Infamy

OTTO FRIEDRICH

For years, detractors of Franklin Roosevelt have charged that he deliberately sent the United States Pacific Fleet to Pearl Harbor so that the Japanese could attack it and give him an excuse to involve the United States in the Second World War. There are those who still make this argument. But Gordon W. Prange's studies, At Dawn We Slept *(1981) and* Pearl Harbor: The Verdict of History *(1986), and the bulk of modern scholarship exonerate Roosevelt of such a monstrous accusation. In truth, the decisions and events that led to America's entry into the war were enormously complex, involving developments in Europe as well as Asia.*

When Nazi Germany invaded Poland in 1939 and plunged Europe into war, the United States, although theoretically neutral, was clearly sympathetic with the Allies, led by Britain and France. Indeed, Roosevelt was more preoccupied with the Nazi threat in Europe than with Japanese expansion in Asia. Time and again, he predicted that Hitler would eventually make war on the United States, and out of that belief flowed much of his European diplomacy: the destroyer-bases deal with Britain, Lend-Lease, and the At-lantic Charter. Still, through 1940 and 1941, as German planes bombed Britain and German armies swept into Russia, the Roosevelt administration often seemed adrift, as though the President and his advisers were confused, helplessly caught in a vortex of events over which they had no control.

Japanese intentions in the Pacific were especially perplexing. Since 1937, Japan had been laying waste to China, bombing its cities and capturing its coastal territory. Did Japan's aggressions against China constitute an immediate threat to United States secu-rity? Was a showdown with Japan also inevitable, as United States military leaders insisted? While the United States watched Japanese movements in Asia, Congress declared economic war against Germany with the controversial Lend-Lease Program, which gave $7 billion in military aid to embattled Britain. Soon American convoys were carrying supplies across the Atlantic. When German U-boats torpedoed several American vessels, many observers contended that war with Hitler was only a matter of time.

Meanwhile, the Japanese question had become increasingly confusing. In Tokyo, a party led by General Hideki Tojo and the military demanded that the United States be driven from the Pacific so that Japan could establish an Asian empire free of Western influence. But Prime Minister Fumimaro Konoye, a moderate, wanted to negotiate with the United States and directed his ambassador in America to present Washington with a set of proposals that might avoid war. At the same time, the war party proceeded with a top-secret plan to attack the United States Navy at Pearl Harbor if negotiations failed. By early December 1941, United States analysts knew that the Japanese were preparing to strike, but almost no one thought them capable of launching an air attack against distant Hawaii. When Japanese planes did exactly that, in a day that would "live in infamy," Americans from Pearl Harbor to Washington were caught completely by surprise.

Like the assassination of John F. Kennedy, Pearl Harbor was one of those crises that mark the people who experience them for the rest of their lives. As Otto Friedrich says, Americans of that period would recall exactly what they were doing when they first heard the news on that fateful Sunday. In this selection, Friedrich, a distinguished author, traces the dramatic events that led to the Pearl Harbor attack; he points out that if war between Japan and the United States was inevitable, it was perhaps inevitable from the time of the first contact between the two countries in 1853. Combining erudition with lucidity of expression, Friedrich describes the rise of modern, industrial Japan, the militaristic government that came to power there, and the Japanese conquest of China, which was prompted in part by the worldwide depression. From then on, Japan and the United States were on a collision course for supremacy in the Pacific. An example of narrative history at its best, Friedrich's article captures the mood, spirit, and rival perceptions of that momentous time; it shows how the interaction of people and events caused Japanese-American relations to deteriorate and finally convinced Japan to strike at Pearl Harbor, and it reconstructs in graphic detail the holocaust of destruction that virtually paralyzed American striking power in the Pacific and plunged the United States into a global conflict. On Monday, December 8, 1941, the United States formally declared war on Japan. Three days later, Germany and Italy — Japan's Axis allies — declared war on the United States. Roosevelt and Congress reciprocated at once, thus placing America on the side of the Allied powers — Great Britain, the Soviet Union, and China.

GLOSSARY

BRATTON, COLONEL RUFUS   United States Army intelligence officer who guessed from the final Japanese note that Japan would strike somewhere on Sunday, December 7, 1941.

CHIANG KAI-SHEK   Commander of the Nationalist forces — the Kuomintang — in embattled China.

FUCHIDA, MITSUO   Operational commander of the Japanese air force that struck Pearl Harbor.

GENDA, MINORU   One of Yamamoto's trusted lieutenants who played a key role in planning the Pearl Harbor attack.

HIROHITO   Emperor of Japan and "a figurehead ruler."

HULL, CORDELL   FDR's secretary of state who had "a speech difficulty" and little knowledge of Japan.

KIMMEL, ADMIRAL HUSBAND   Commander of the Pacific Fleet, with headquarters at Pearl Harbor.

MacARTHUR, GENERAL DOUGLAS   Commander of all United States Army forces in the Far East, with headquarters in the Philippines.

MAO ZEDONG (MAO TSE-TUNG)   Head of the Chinese Communists and later (1949) founder and first chairman of the People's Republic of China.

MARSHALL, GENERAL GEORGE   United States chief of staff, stationed in Washington.

NOMURA, KICHISABURO   Japanese ambassador in Washington.

SHORT, LIEUTENANT GENERAL WALTER   Commander of United States Army forces in Hawaii.

STARK, ADMIRAL HAROLD   Chief of United States Naval Operations, stationed in Washington.

TOGO, ADMIRAL HEIHACHIRO   Japanese naval hero who annihilated the Russian fleet in the battle of Tsushima (1905) during the Russo-Japanese war; his victories established Japan's naval superiority.

TOJO, GENERAL HIDEKI   Dominated Japan's militarist government and succeeded Prince Konoye as Japanese prime minister in October 1941; he approved the Pearl Harbor attack.

YAMAMOTO, ADMIRAL ISOROKU   Harvard-educated commander of Japan's Combined Fleet who devised the Pearl Harbor attack plan with the help of trusted subordinates.

he brass band on the stern of the U.S.S. *Nevada* kept on playing *The Star-Spangled Banner* for the 8 a.m. flag raising even after a Japanese bomber roared overhead and fired a torpedo at the nearby *Arizona*. The torpedo missed, but the bomber sprayed machine-gun fire at the *Nevada's* band and tore up its ensign.

"This is the best goddam drill the Army Air Force has ever put on," remarked an *Arizona* sailor standing idly at the battleship's rail.

"Air raid, Pearl Harbor, this is no drill," said the radio message that went out at 7:58 a.m. from the U.S. Navy's Ford Island command center, relayed throughout Hawaii, to Manila, to Washington. But there was an even sharper sense of imminent disaster in the words someone shouted over the public address system on another docked battleship, the *Oklahoma:* "Man your battle stations! This is no shit!" Across the lapping waters of the harbor, church bells tolled, summoning the faithful to worship.

Almost alongside the *Oklahoma,* another torpedo hurtled through the air. After releasing it, recalled Lieut. Jinichi Goto, commander of the Japanese torpedo bombers, "I saw that I was even lower than the crow's nest of the great battleship. My observer reported a huge waterspout springing up . . . '*Atarimashita!* [It hit!]' he cried."

"I felt a very heavy shock and heard a loud explosion," said the *Oklahoma's* executive officer, Commander Jesse Kenworthy Jr., "and the ship immediately began to list to port. As I attempted to get to the conning tower over decks slippery with oil and water, I felt the shock of another very heavy explosion." Kenworthy gave the order to abandon ship. He barely made it over the rising starboard side as the giant battleship began to keel over, trapping more than 400 crewmen below decks.

Just as the *Oklahoma* capsized, a tremendous explosion tore open the *Arizona*. "A spurt of flame came out of the guns in No. 2 turret, followed by an explosion of the forward magazine," said a mechanic on the nearby tanker *Ramapo*. "The foremast leaned forward, and the whole forward part of the ship was enveloped in flame and smoke and continued to burn fiercely."

In Commander Mitsuo Fuchida's bomber circling overhead, antiaircraft fire knocked a hole in the fuselage and damaged the steering gear, but Fuchida couldn't take his eyes off the fiery death throes of the *Arizona*. "A huge column of dark red smoke rose to 1,000 ft., and a stiff shock wave rocked the plane," he recalled years later, when he had become a Presbyterian missionary. "It was a hateful, mean-looking red flame, the kind that powder produces, and I knew at once that a big magazine had exploded. Terrible indeed."

As operational commander of the Japanese attackers, Fuchida watched and controlled everything. It was Fuchida who had given, exactly at 7:49 a.m. on Dec. 7, 1941, the order to attack the strongest naval base in the world: "*To!* [the first syllable of *totsugekiseyo,* meaning: Charge!] *To! To! To!*" It was Fuchida who sent back to Tokyo the triumphant signal that the attack had caught the Americans by surprise: "*Tora!* [Tiger!] *Tora! Tora!*"

Now Fuchida led the attack on the *Maryland,* another of the eight battleships berthed at the U.S. Navy's Pacific Fleet headquarters. He saw four bombs hurtling toward their target. "In perfect pattern [they] plummeted like devils of doom. They became small as poppy seeds and finally disappeared just as tiny white flashes of smoke appeared on or near the ship."

Pearl Harbor is peaceful now, blue waves in the winter sunshine, an occasional toot of harbor traffic. A concrete canopy shrouds the rusted wreckage of the *Arizona,* the remains of more than 1,000 American servicemen entombed inside. Her flag is still raised and lowered every day on the mast emerging out of the quiet water.

The [fiftieth] anniversary of the greatest U.S. mili-

Mitsubishi Reisen "Zero" Fighters prepare to launch from one of six Japanese carriers in the Pearl Harbor strike force. (U.S. Naval *Institute Photo Collection, Annapolis, MD)*

tary defeat, the day President Franklin D. Roosevelt called "a date which will live in infamy," remains a day of death and disgrace, an inglorious event, and the spirit of reconciliation still bows before gusts of rancor. When President Bush, a World War II fighter pilot, indicated that he would attend the Pearl Harbor anniversary ceremonies, White House spokesmen stiffly squelched any talk of Japanese officials' joining in. So did the Pearl Harbor Survivors Association. "We did not invite the Japanese 50 years ago, and we don't want them now," says the association's president, Gerald Glaubitz.

In American mythology, Pearl Harbor still represents, even after a half-century, a classic moment of treachery and betrayal. Certainly it was a moment of historic surprise, a moment when the impossible happened, when warfare suddenly spread, for the first and only time in history, to virtually the whole world. This was the moment that changed Americans from a nation of provincial innocents, not only ignorant of the great world but proud of their ignorance, into a nation that would often have to bear the burdens of rescuing that world. The same cataclysm also changed the Japanese from a people trying to find their place on the rim of the great world into a nation that would eventually redefine that world and place itself at the very center.

The surprise, when it first exploded over Pearl Harbor, was shattering, and everyone who experienced it can still remember what was going on when the news interrupted that quiet Sunday: the Washington Redskins playing the Philadelphia Eagles, Arthur Rubinstein as soloist in the New York Philharmonic broadcast, or just a visit with friends. Trying to explain the national sense of bewilderment, the TIME of that time reflected the kind of racism that implicitly underlay the basic American attitude. "Over the U.S. and its history," declared the weekly newsmagazine, "there was a great unanswered question: What would the people . . . say in the face of the mightiest event of their time? What they said — tens of thousands of them — was: 'Why, the yellow bastards!'"

As often happens in surprise attacks, however, the surprise of Pearl Harbor was largely a matter of national illusions. The leaders on both sides fully expected a war, indeed considered it inevitable, even to some extent desirable, but neither side really wanted to fight unless it had to. Up to the last minute, each antagonist thought the other was bluffing.

Japan's navy had already begun planning and training for the attack on Pearl Harbor when Emperor Hirohito startled his assembled advisers on Sept. 6 by asking an imperial question. In the midst of a fervent debate over when and how to go to war, the Emperor, who traditionally never spoke during such gatherings, suddenly pulled out and read in his high-pitched voice a poem by his revered grandfather Emperor Meiji:

> All the seas, in every quarter,
> are as brothers to one another.
> Why, then, do the winds and waves of strife
> rage so turbulently throughout the world?

Roosevelt, re-elected to a third term in 1940 after pledging that "your boys are not going to be sent to any foreign wars," knew that Hirohito was just a figurehead ruler over a militarist government dominated by the flinty General Hideki Tojo. Still, Roosevelt staked his hopes for peace on a last-minute message to the Emperor. "Both of us," Roosevelt said, "have a

sacred duty to restore traditional amity and prevent further death and destruction in the world."

Japanese military censors delayed that message for 10 hours, so it was almost midnight on Dec. 7 in Tokyo when U.S. Ambassador Joseph Grew sped with it to the Foreign Ministry. It was past 3 a.m. — and Fuchida's bombers were within sight of Pearl Harbor — when Foreign Minister Shigenori Togo, in full diplomatic regalia, reached the Imperial Palace. He found the Emperor listening to his shortwave radio. Togo read him the message and then the response that the government had already written for him. It said that peace was the Emperor's "cherished desire." This would "do well," Hirohito told Togo. The Foreign Minister bowed low.

If war between the U.S. and Japan was inevitable, it had probably been inevitable for a long time, perhaps as long ago as July 8, 1853. That was the day when Commodore Matthew Perry sailed his black-hulled steam frigate Susquehanna into Edo Bay (now Tokyo Bay) and "opened" Japan at gunpoint, after more than two centuries of self-imposed isolation, to American merchants and missionaries. Humiliated, the Japanese decided to modernize their feudal regime by imitating the barbarian invaders. They hired French officers to retrain their soldiers and British shipbuilders to create their navy. From the Germans they learned the secrets of modern science and from the Americans the secrets of modern commerce.

But as Japanese commerce and Japanese emigration increased, so did Western talk of a "yellow peril." In 1922 the Supreme Court ruled that Japanese immigrants were ineligible to become U.S. citizens. The following year it ruled that they could be barred from owning American land — Japanese farmers were then growing 10% of California's agricultural produce on 1% of its land. In 1924, when Congress imposed national immigration quotas, the figure for Japanese was zero.

The deepest conflict between the U.S. and Japan, though, was over the future of China, which had been in turmoil ever since the collapse of the Manchu

Empire in 1911. Though Generalissimo Chiang Kaishek claimed that his Canton-based Kuomintang represented the entire republic, local warlords ruled much of the country, notably the huge northern territory of Manchuria. The Japanese, who had blocked a number of Russian incursions into Manchuria, were moving in to gain control of the region's plentiful coal and iron, which Japan sorely lacked.

The explosive force in the midst of this ferment was Japan's fractious Kwantung Army, originally sent to the Kwantung Peninsula just east of Beijing to protect Japanese rail and shipping interests in Manchuria. After ultranationalist Kwantung officers murdered the Chinese overload of Manchuria, Tokyo installed a puppet regime in 1932 and proclaimed the independence of what it called Manchukuo. Despite calls for sanctions against Japan, outgoing President Herbert Hoover had no enthusiasm for a crisis, and the incoming President Roosevelt was preoccupied with the onrushing Great Depression.

That left Chiang and his Chinese Nationalists to fight on against the Japanese, the growing communist guerrilla forces of Mao Zedong and a clutch of surviving warlords. On the night of July 7, 1937, came the murky events that constituted the long-expected "incident." A Japanese soldier apparently wandered off to relieve himself near the Marco Polo Bridge, outside Beijing. His comrades, who later claimed they feared he had been kidnapped, got into a gunfight with a nearby Chinese Nationalist unit, and the fighting soon spread.

The worldwide depression, which partly inspired Japan's move into China, left most Americans unable to deal with anything beyond their own breadlines and Hoovervilles and, Brother, can you spare a dime? To the extent that they worried about foreign problems at all, they worried mainly about Adolf Hitler, who had seized Austria and the Czech Sudetenland in 1938, then demanded western Poland in 1939.

Americans did hear horror stories — of civilians massacred in Japanese air raids on undefended Shanghai and of the Rape of Nanking, a month of slaughter that cut down more than 200,000 civilians. Roosevelt talked of "quarantining" Japan, but American ships went on supplying Tokyo with American oil and steel. Times were hard, and business was business.

What came to dominate Japan's overall strategy was the impact of Hitler's stunning victories over the Western Allies in the spring of 1940. The Dutch army was crushed within a week, and Queen Wilhelmina fled to London, leaving the immense wealth of the Dutch East Indies (now Indonesia) in the charge of a few colonial bureaucrats. France collapsed in a month, and Marshal Pétain's feeble puppet regime, based in the French resort of Vichy, had other worries than French Indochina (Vietnam, Laos and Cambodia). Britain, threatened by a Nazi invasion, could devote little more than some Churchillian rhetoric to the defense of Singapore, Malaya, Hong Kong and Burma.

Japan's Prince Fumimaro Konoye, a serpentine conservative who had twice been Premier since 1937, realized the way was now clear "to include the British, French, Dutch and Portuguese islands of the Orient" in a Japanese commercial empire that Tokyo called the Greater East Asia Co-Prosperity Sphere. On Sept. 27, 1940, Konoye joined the Axis powers, Nazi Germany and Fascist Italy, in a formal alliance known as the Tripartite Pact. He demanded that Britain shut down the Burma Road, supply route for aid to Chiang, and that Vichy accept Japanese bases in Indochina for a southern attack on Chiang.

The U.S., the only Western power strong enough to retaliate, banned all iron and steel shipments to Japan. "It seems inevitable," said *Asahi Shimbun,* then Japan's largest daily, "that a collision should occur between Japan, determined to establish a sphere of interest in East Asia . . . and the United States, which is determined to meddle in affairs on the other side of a vast ocean." Added *Yomiuri,* another giant newspaper: "Asia is the territory of the Asiatics."

Impersonally though the tides of history may seem to flow, they now waited on one man, a remarkably squat and broad-shouldered man, no more than 5 ft.

3 in. tall. He had been born Isoroku Takano, the first name meaning 56, because that was the age at which his proud father had been presented with his sixth and last son. Later adopted, according to an old custom, into a richer family, he acquired a new name: Yamamoto.

Trained as a naval cadet, Yamamoto proudly bore the scars he got at 21, when he lost the second and third fingers on his left hand during Admiral Togo's great victory over the Russian navy at the Strait of Tsushima in 1905. Yamamoto had come to know the U.S. as a graduate student at Harvard and as naval attaché in Washington. And as executive officer of Japan's naval flight school, he had learned the new religion of air power. He loved poker, bridge and *shogi,* the Japanese version of chess. Said one of his top aides: "He had a gambler's heart."

Now 57, with a gray crew cut, Admiral Yamamoto commanded Japan's Combined Fleet, but he disliked the imperial navy's cautious strategy. In case of war, its plan was to fall back and try to lure the U.S. Pacific Fleet into the Inland Sea between the Japanese home islands of Honshu and Kyushu. But as early as spring 1940, Yamamoto remarked to one of his officers: "I wonder if an aerial attack can't be made on Pearl Harbor."

Others had suggested such a strategy but it had always been rejected as too dangerous. Pearl Harbor was too far away, too inaccessible, too well defended. Besides, the overall strategy of striking south toward Malaya and the Dutch East Indies now required all the navy's resources. Yamamoto nonetheless began in early 1941 to assemble some trusted lieutenants to make plans for Operation Hawaii, which he also named Operation *Z,* after Admiral Togo's historic banner at the battle of Tsushima.

One of Yamamoto's key planners was Commander Minoru Genda, still only 36, still a hot pilot at heart, first in his class at the Etajima naval academy, combat ace over China, leader of a daredevil stunt team called Genda's Flying Circus. Genda contributed several key ideas: that every available Japanese carrier should be assigned to the attack, that it should combine dive-bombing, high-level bombing and torpedoes, that the attackers should strike at dawn.

Not the least important of his ideas was to recruit a cadet classmate named Mitsuo Fuchida, who could train all of Yamamoto's pilots and lead them into battle. Fuchida, grandson of a famous samurai, was born in 1902, a Year of the Tiger ("Tora! Tora!"), so he was 39 when summoned to his mission. An ardent admirer of Hitler, he had grown a toothbrush mustache.

The techniques of dive-bombing and torpedo bombing were still relatively new, and aerial torpedoes were almost impossible to use in water as shallow as Pearl Harbor. Filching an idea from a recent British torpedo raid against the Italian naval base of Taranto, Genda had technicians create auxiliary wooden tail fins that would keep torpedoes closer to the surface; others converted armor-piercing shells into bombs. But drilling was Fuchida's main task, and all summer his planes staged trial runs over Kagoshima Bay in Kyushu, chosen for its physical resemblance to Pearl. Only in September did Genda tell him, "In case of war, Yamamoto plans to attack Pearl Harbor."

Ironically, Yamamoto didn't want to carry out his own plan. But if Japan was going to be forced to fight, he believed it should strike first and strike hard, in the hope that a demoralized U.S. would then accept a negotiated peace. If he was deluded in that hope, he was not deluded about U.S. power. "If I am told to fight regardless of the consequences, I shall run wild for the first six months or a year," he presciently told Prince Konoye in the fall of 1940, "but I have utterly no confidence for the second or third year."

By 1940 Japan had installed a pro-Japanese regime in Nanking, but U.S. aid enabled Chiang to fight on. Konoye began wondering about mediators to end the exasperating war that Tokyo insisted on calling the Chinese Incident. Where angels fear to tread, in rushed the missionary fathers of the Maryknoll Society, who guilelessly assured each side that the other seemed ready to talk. And so talks began in Washington in the spring of 1941.

Talks is hardly the word. Tokyo's goal was to negotiate a victory in China, Washington's goal to negotiate a Japanese withdrawal. U.S. Secretary of State Cordell Hull, nearly 70, a longtime power on Capitol Hill, was a log-cabin-born Tennessee mountaineer who knew little of the Japanese and disliked what he knew. He once referred to Tokyo's envoys as "pissants." Japan's ambassador, Kichisaburo Nomura, 64, a one-eyed retired admiral and former Foreign Minister, was considered a moderate and so was mistrusted in Tokyo. It did not help that Hull had a speech difficulty, while Nomura was partially deaf.

Hardly had the talks begun when the Japanese, having already seized a number of bases in northern Vietnam, suddenly occupied the south in July 1941. That threatened not only the back route to China but British control of Malaya and Burma (now Myanmar). Roosevelt retaliated by freezing all Japanese assets and placing an embargo on all trade in oil, steel, chemicals, machinery and other strategic goods. (The British and Dutch soon announced similar embargoes.) At the same time, he announced that General Douglas MacArthur, the retired Chief of Staff now luxuriating in the Philippines, was being recalled to active military duty and financed in mobilizing 120,000 Filipino soldiers. (Roosevelt had made another significant move that spring, when he shifted the Pacific Fleet's headquarters from San Diego to Pearl Harbor.)

Roosevelt's embargo was a devastating blow, for Japan bought more than half its imports from the U.S. The Japanese military leaders were determined to fight. When they met with the Cabinet on Sept. 3, they insisted on an October deadline for Konoye's diplomatic efforts. The Prince asked for a meeting with Roosevelt, but Hull was opposed, and Roosevelt, preoccupied with the increasing likelihood of war with Hitler, never answered. Konoye resigned on Oct. 16. Tojo, a Kwantung Army veteran who was then War Minister, became Premier.

Though Japan's military leaders had decided on war, they had not yet agreed to a surprise attack on Pearl Harbor. Yamamoto was adamant: "Japan must deal the U.S. Navy a fatal blow at the outset of the war. It is the only way she can fight with any reasonable prospect of success." But war games suggested that an attacking fleet would be spotted and badly mauled. As late as October, Yamamoto learned that the staff admirals, determined to concentrate on the drive into Southeast Asia, wanted to take away two or three of his six carriers. The First Air Fleet's own commander, Vice Admiral Chuichi Nagumo, supported that decision. "The success of our surprise attack on Pearl Harbor," Nagumo predicted dolefully, "will prove to be the Waterloo of the war to follow." Yamamoto sent an aide to inform the navy's high command that if his Pearl Harbor plan was rejected, "he will have no alternative but to resign, and with him his entire staff." Yamamoto got his way.

The military set a new target date of Dec. 8 (Dec. 7 in Hawaii), and the Emperor and his military chiefs formally approved Yamamoto's attack plan on Nov. 3. But the Foreign Ministry instructed Ambassador Nomura and Special Envoy Saburo Kurusu to make "a final effort" in Washington.

On Nov. 17, Yamamoto visited his training base in Saeki Bay to bid his men farewell. "Japan has faced many worthy opponents in her glorious history — Mongols, Chinese, Russians," Yamamoto said, "but in this operation we will meet the strongest opponent of all. I expect this operation to be a success." Genda, Fuchida and other officers joined him in eating *surume* (dried cuttlefish) for happiness and *kachiguri* (walnuts) for victory. Near portable Shinto shrines, they toasted the Emperor with sake and shouted, "Banzai!"

It took Nagumo's fleet five days to reach the rendezvous point at Hitokappu Bay in the Kuriles just north of Japan's main islands. Fog swirled over the desolate outpost, and snow fell intermittently as the fleet steamed eastward at dawn on Nov. 26.

The armada boasted six carriers, led by Nagumo's flagship, the *Akagi*, 400 warplanes, two battleships, two cruisers, nine destroyers and a dozen other surface ships. At an average 13 knots, refueling daily, the attack fleet pursued a course 3,500 miles through the empty expanse of the North Pacific. Its orders provided that "in the event an agreement is reached in the negotiations with the United States, the task force will immediately return to Japan," but nobody expected that to happen.

The envoys made their "final effort" on Nov. 20, presenting to Hull an unyielding proposal on which Foreign Minister Togo said "no further concessions" could be made. Nomura noted that this was an inauspicious day — "They call it Thanksgiving" — but he dutifully delivered the message. It said the U.S. must restore trade to pre-embargo levels, provide oil from the Dutch East Indies and not interfere with Japan's "efforts for peace" in China.

Hull's answer, just as forceful, said the U.S. oil embargo would continue, and demanded that Japan "withdraw all military, naval, air and police forces from China and from Indochina." He handed it to the envoys on Nov. 26, the day Nagumo's fleet left Hitokappu Bay for Pearl Harbor. Hull did not know that, since the fleet was under total radio silence, but he did know from intercepted messages that another Japanese war fleet had passed Formosa on its way toward Indochina or Malaya. "We must all prepare for real trouble, possibly soon," Roosevelt cabled Churchill.

The War Department then sent Hawaii and other outposts an important but significantly ambiguous "war warning." "Negotiations with Japan appear to be terminated to all practical purposes," said this Nov. 27 message over the signature of Chief of Staff George Marshall. "Japanese future action unpredictable but hostile action possible at any moment . . . You are directed to undertake such reconnaissance and other measures as you deem necessary, but these measures should be carried out so as not repeat not to alarm civil population or disclose intent. Report measures taken." Hawaii's commander, Lieut. General Walter Short, not a man of broad vision, reported back that he was taking measures to avert sabotage — parking his aircraft close together and keeping all ammunition safely locked up. Since Washington did not specify a threat to Pearl Harbor, Short felt he had done his duty, just as Marshall felt he had done his.

The Navy Department sent an even stronger message to its top commanders, specifically including the Pacific Fleet chief in Pearl Harbor, Admiral Husband Kimmel: "This dispatch is to be considered a war warning. Negotiations with Japan . . . have ceased, and an aggressive move by Japan is expected within the next few days." Kimmel, 60, a hard-driving disciplinarian who had held his command less than a year, took the warning as "no more than saying that Japan was going to attack someplace."

Kimmel and Short were only too aware that Washington was concentrating on Hitler's victories in Russia and his submarines' ravages of Atlantic shipping. Though Chief of Naval Operations Harold Stark acknowledged to Kimmel that his Pacific Fleet was weaker than the Japanese forces arrayed against it, he not only turned aside Kimmel's request for two new battleships but took away three he had, plus one of his four carriers, to help fight the Battle of the Atlantic.

Roosevelt's assertive strategy against Japan was largely a bluff, backed by inadequate armed forces and inadequate funds. Washington theoreticians saw the Philippines as a check to any Japanese move southward. MacArthur overconfidently promised that he would soon have 200,000 Filipinos ready for combat, and the War Department began in the summer of 1941 to ship him the first of a promised 128 new B-17 Flying Fortresses. By April 1942, said Marshall, that would represent "the greatest concentration of heavy-bomber strength anywhere in the world," able to interdict any Japanese assault on Southeast Asia and mount "incendiary attacks to burn up the wood and paper structures of the densely populated Japanese cities."

Perhaps the greatest single cause of American complacency in the Pacific was the fact that the U.S.

As this Japanese photograph shows, U.S. battleships anchored at Pearl Harbor were sitting ducks. Notice the torpedo plane banking over battleship row. A torpedo has just struck the Oklahoma, *kicking up a towering geyser. Struck by four additional torpedoes, the great battleship quickly capsized. (U.S. Navy Photo)*

military's Operation Magic had deciphered Japan's sophisticated Purple diplomatic code in 1940. But that triumph had its drawbacks. U.S. intelligence officials had to sift through so much trivia that they failed to react to some important messages, such as a Tokyo request to its Hawaiian consulate for the exact location of all ships in Pearl Harbor. Also, the code breaking was kept secret even from some key officials. While the British were plugged into Magic, and MacArthur too, Kimmel and Short were not.

Ironically, the Nazis warned the Japanese that their codes might have been broken, but Tokyo refused to believe the Americans were smart enough for such a feat. Just as ironically, while U.S. code breakers knew of the Japanese warships heading for Southeast Asia, Nagumo's radio silence meant that his carriers heading for Pearl Harbor simply disappeared. On Dec. 2, Kimmel's intelligence officer confessed that nothing had been heard from the Japanese carriers for about two weeks.

"What!" said Kimmel. "You don't know where [they] are?"

"No, sir, I do not. I think they are in home waters, but I do not know where they are."

"Do you mean to say that they could be rounding Diamond Head, and you wouldn't know it?"

"I hope they would be sighted before now."

And the Americans could intercept but not understand a message Yamamoto sent his fleet on Dec. 2: "Climb Mount Niitaka." That meant "Proceed with the attack."

One thing that the code breaking did tell Washington was Tokyo's answer to Hull's last proposal. Before the original even reached the Japanese envoys, a messenger brought an intercepted version to Roosevelt in his White House study after dinner on Dec. 6. The President read it carefully for about 10 minutes, then said to his closest aide, Harry Hopkins, "This means war."

Roosevelt tried to call Admiral Stark, but he was at a revival of Sigmund Romberg's *Student Prince;* the President didn't want him paged at the theater lest that cause "undue alarm." When Roosevelt did finally reach him shortly before midnight, the Navy chief said, according to his later recollection, that the message was not "something that required action." After all, Stark testified, warnings had already gone out that Japan was "likely to attack at any time in any direction."

That same Saturday night was the standard party night in Pearl Harbor, not orgiastic but convivial. Hundreds of soldiers and sailors from Schofield Barracks and Hickam and Kaneohe converged as usual on Waikiki Beach to see what was going on at Bill Leader's bar, the Two Jacks or the Mint. *Tantalizing Tootsies* was the name of the variety show at the Princess.

Kimmel attended a staid dinner party at the Halekulani Hotel and left early. He had a golf date the next morning with General Short, who went to a charity dance at the Schofield Barracks and also left early. As he rode along the coast highway, Short admired the lights of Pearl Harbor glowing below him. "Isn't that a beautiful sight?" he said. "And what a target it would make!"

Though the final Japanese note said nothing about war or Pearl Harbor, it was not quite complete — it contained 13 parts and said another would soon follow. The 14th and last part reached Washington the morning of Dec. 7. It notified the U.S. that "it is impossible to reach an agreement through further negotiations." An accompanying message instructed Nomura to deliver the note "at 1 p.m. on the 7th, your time."

Nobody in Washington knew Hirohito had asked that the warning be delivered before the attack — 1 p.m. in Washington was 7:30 a.m. in Hawaii — but an Army intelligence officer, Colonel Rufus Bratton, guessed as much. Bratton telephoned Marshall at his quarters at Fort Myers, Va., but he was out riding. More than an hour later, about 10:30 a.m., Marshall called back and said he was coming to his office shortly. About the same time, Hull was meeting with War Secretary Henry L. Stimson and Navy Secretary Frank Knox. "Hull is very certain that the Japs are planning some deviltry," Stimson recorded in his diary, "and we are all wondering when the blow will strike."

Fuchida woke at 5 a.m. As he told American military historian Gordon Prange, he put on red underwear and a red shirt so that if he was wounded, his men would not be distracted by the sight of his blood. At breakfast, one of his lieutenants said, "Honolulu sleeps."

"How do you know?" asked Fuchida.

"The Honolulu radio plays soft music. Everything is fine."

At 5:50 a.m. Nagumo's fleet reached the takeoff point, about 220 miles north of Pearl Harbor. The six carriers turned east into a brisk wind and increased speed to 24 knots. Nagumo's flagship was flying the celebrated Z pennant that Admiral Togo had flown at Tsushima in 1905. The flight decks tilted more than 10°, and the wind whipped spray over them.

"We could hear the waves splashing against the ship with a thunderous noise," Fuchida recalled later. "Under normal circumstances, no plane would be permitted to take off in such weather. . . . There were loud cheers as each plane rose into the air." Once up, the pilots circled overhead until all 183 planes assigned to the first wave were airborne. At 6:15 Fuchida gave a signal, then led the way south.

At almost that very hour — around 11:30 a.m. in Washington — Marshall arrived at his office and read the ominous words Bratton had brought him. He asked the officers assembled there what they thought it meant. All expected an imminent Japanese attack — somewhere. Marshall recalled that every major U.S. base had been warned of that more than a week earlier. Bratton and others urged a new warning. Marshall scrawled a message reporting the 1 p.m. meeting and added, "Just what significance the hour set may have we do not know, but be on alert accordingly."

Bratton rushed the message to the War Department signal center, where Marshall's scrawl had to be retyped for legibility. The message went to several points within a few minutes, but because of atmospheric difficulties, the copy for Hawaii went by commercial wireless. It reached Honolulu at 7:33 a.m. and ended in a pigeon hole, awaiting a motorcycle messenger to deliver it.

Fuchida's bombers had to fly blind over dense banks of clouds, so they homed on the Honolulu commercial radio station KGMB. Over his receiver, Fuchida heard soothing music, then a weather report: "Partly cloudy . . . over the mountains. Cloud base at 3,500 ft. Visibility good." Fuchida flew on.

To save money and fuel and manpower, the Pearl Harbor authorities had recently canceled weekend reconnaissance flights. But they had acquired some new radar equipment, though the National Park Service strongly objected to towers being installed on scenic mountaintops.

Two trainees operating a mobile radar unit at Opana, on Oahu's northern coast, were about to shut down when their watch ended at 7 a.m. Suddenly, Private Joseph Lockard noticed a large blip — "probably more than 50" planes — approaching southward from about 130 miles away. On the phone to Fort Shafter, Lockard reported to Lieut. Kermit Tyler "the largest [flight] I have ever seen on the equipment." The inexperienced Tyler figured that the planes must be a flight of the new B-17s expected from California. He told Lockard, "Don't worry about it."

As Fuchida's bombers neared Oahu, the defenders of Pearl Harbor got the last of their many warnings. Just outside the harbor, the U.S. destroyer Ward spotted an intruding submarine at 6:30 a.m. and opened fire from 50 yds. away. As the sub began diving, the Ward finished it off with depth charges. Lieut. William Outerbridge's report of his action was still ricocheting around headquarters when Fuchida arrived overhead.

"What a majestic sight," he said to himself as he counted the vessels lined up in Battleship Row in the dawn's early light. He pulled the trigger on his flare gun. That was supposed to signal the slow-moving torpedo bombers to take advantage of the surprise and strike first. But Fuchida's fighter pilots missed his signal to provide cover, so he fired again for the dive bombers to begin, and then the Japanese all attacked at once. Even when they made mistakes, it seemed that nothing could go wrong.

Within minutes, Pearl Harbor was pandemonium: explosions, screams, tearing steel, the rattle of machine guns, smoke, fire, bugles sounding, the whine of diving airplanes, more explosions, more screams. With Battleship Row afire, Fuchida's bombers circled over the maze of Pearl Harbor's docks and piers, striking again and again at the cruisers and destroyers and supply ships harbored there.

Other Japanese bombers swarmed over Hawaii's military airfields, Hickam and Wheeler, Kaneohe and Ewa. Dive-bombing and strafing the American planes neatly parked on the runways, they quickly won control of the sky. They wrecked hangars, warehouses, barracks — as well as the Hickam Field chapel and the enlisted men's new beer hall, the Snake Ranch. And in the midst of all this, a rainbow appeared over Ford Island.

To many of the Americans, the whole morning had a dreamlike unreality. Disbelief had been the overwhelming first reaction — this couldn't be happening, it was a trick, a drill, a silly rumor, a prank — disbelief and then pain and then anger, and still disbelief.

Admiral Kimmel was preparing for his golf game with General Short when an officer phoned him with the news that Japanese planes were attacking his fleet. The admiral was still buttoning his white uniform as he ran out of his house and onto the neighboring lawn of his chief of staff, Captain John Earle, which had a fine view of Battleship Row. Mrs. Earle said later that the admiral's face was "as white as the uniform he wore."

"The sky was full of the enemy," Kimmel recalled. He saw the *Arizona* "lift out of the water, then sink back down — way down." Mrs. Earle saw a battleship capsize.

"Looks like they've got the *Oklahoma,*" she said.

"Yes, I can see they have," the admiral numbly responded.

General Short, who couldn't see the explosions, bumped into an intelligence officer and asked, "What's going on out there?"

"I'm not sure, general," said Lieut. Colonel George Bicknell, "but I just saw two battleships sunk."

"That's ridiculous!" said Short.

Down on Battleship Row, Fuchida's bombers kept pounding the helpless battlewagons. The *West Virginia* took six torpedoes, then two bombs. One large piece of shrapnel smashed into the starboard side of the bridge and tore open the stomach of the skipper, Captain Mervyn Bennion. A medic patched up the dying man's wound, and a husky black mess steward, Doris Miller, who had once boxed as the ship's heavyweight champion, helped move the stricken captain to a sheltered spot.

Fire and smoke swirled around the bridge. Bennion told his men to leave him; they ignored him. He asked them how the battle was going; they told him all was well. After Bennion died, an officer told Miller

to feed ammunition into a nearby machine gun. Like other blacks in the Navy of 1941, Miller had not been trained for anything but domestic chores, but he soon took charge of the machine gun and started firing away. A young ensign recalled later that it was the first time he had seen Miller smile since he last fought in the ring.

Caught by surprise, and then often finding all ammunition neatly locked away, the defenders hacked away the locks and fought back with any weapons at hand — machine guns, rifles, pistols. This usually achieved nothing, but there were some surprises. At Kaneohe Naval Air Station on the east coast of Oahu, a flight of Mitsubishi Zeroes was strafing the hangars when a sailor named Sands darted out of an armory and fired a burst with a Browning automatic rifle.

"Hand me another BAR!" shouted Sands. "I swear I hit that yellow bastard!"

Japanese Lieut. Fusata Iida turned to strafe Sands, but the sailor fired another BAR clip, then ducked the bullets that pocked the armory's wall. As Iida's Zero climbed again, gasoline began streaming from his fuel tank. Before takeoff, Iida had said that any pilot whose engine failed should crash his plane into the enemy, so now he turned for a last attack. For one incredible minute, the two enemies faced and fired at each other, Iida from his crippled Zero, Sands with his BAR. Then the Zero nosed into a highway and smashed into pieces.

As Admiral Kimmel stood near a window, a spent machine-gun bullet smashed the glass and hit him lightly in the chest. Kimmel — who would soon, like General Short, be dismissed from his command — picked up the bullet. To an aide, he observed, "It would have been merciful had it killed me."

In Washington the disbelief was just as overwhelming. "My God, this can't be true, this must mean the Philippines," said Secretary Knox on hearing the news. "No, sir," said Admiral Stark, "this is Pearl."

Knox called Roosevelt, and Roosevelt called Hull, who was supposed to meet Nomura and Kurusu at 1 p.m. But the envoys had trouble getting the message from Tokyo decoded and retyped and asked for a delay, so it was 2:05 before they seated themselves, all unknowing, in Hull's antechamber. Hull, who had already read their message and knew about the raid on Pearl Harbor as well, made a pretense of reading the document, then lashed out at the luckless envoys. "In all my 50 years of public service," he declared, "I have never seen a document that was more crowded with infamous falsehoods and distortions." When Nomura tried to answer, Hull raised a hand to cut him off, then showed him to the door.

Fuchida's surprise attack lasted only about half an hour. Then, after a short lull, a second wave of 171 more planes roared in. By now the Americans were on the alert and firing at anything in sight. Twenty planes flying in from maneuvers with the *Enterprise* came under heavy American fire; two were shot down.

The battered *Nevada* (its band having finished *The Star-Spangled Banner*) managed to get up enough steam to proceed majestically out into the channel to the sea. Despite a gaping hole in its bow, its guns were firing, and its torn flag flew high. As it edged past the burning *Arizona,* three of that doomed ship's crewmen swam over, clambered aboard and manned a starboard gun.

"Ah, good!" the watching Fuchida said to himself as he saw the slow-moving *Nevada.* At his signal, all available bombers attacked in an effort to sink it and block the channel to the sea. Bombs ignited huge fires in the ship's bow. It escaped total destruction only by deliberately running aground.

More fortunate — indeed kissed by fortune — were Army pilots George Welch and Kenneth Taylor, who had gone from a dance at the Wheeler Officers' Club to an all-night poker game. They were still in formal dress at 8 a.m. when they saw the first Japanese planes open fire overhead. Under strafing fire, Taylor's car careened back to the P-40 fighters at Haleiwa Field. Taking off, the two went looking for Japanese planes and soon found them over Wheeler.

"I got in a string of six or eight planes," Taylor recalled. "I was on one's tail as we went over Waialua . . . and there was one following firing at me . . . Lieut. Welch, I think, shot the other man down." Welch's version: "We took off directly into them and shot some down. I shot down one right on Lieut. Taylor's tail."

Landing only for more fuel and ammunition, the two sleepless lieutenants set off for the Marine base at Barber's Point. "We went down and got in the traffic pattern and shot down several planes there," said Taylor, who suffered a severe arm wound. "I know for certain I shot down two planes or perhaps more; I don't know." Official records credited the two of them with downing seven planes, almost one-quarter of all Japanese losses.

The great attack was really fairly short. The first bombers returned to their carriers just after 10 a.m., scarcely two hours after they descended on Battleship Row. Fuchida lingered to observe and photograph the damage and was the last to return to Nagumo's fleet. It was still only noon.

Fuchida and Genda argued fiercely for renewing the attack. The oil-storage tanks had not been hit, and the raiders had not found any of Kimmel's three carriers (the *Lexington* and *Enterprise* were at sea, the *Saratoga* undergoing repairs). But Admiral Nagumo, who had mistrusted the plan from the start, felt he had accomplished his mission and saw no reason to risk his fleet any further. Back in Japan, Yamamoto strongly disapproved of Nagumo's decision to withdraw but accepted the tradition that such decisions are left to the combat commander on the scene.

Long after the Japanese had left, Pearl Harbor reverberated with reports of enemy invasions, parachute landings and other nightmares. Jittery defenders fired wildly at anything that moved. A fishing boat returning with the day's catch was shot to pieces.

On the capsized hull of the *Oklahoma,* Commander Kenworthy strode up and down for hours listening for raps and banging from the men trapped inside. Some survivors were finally pulled to safety through holes cut in the hull, but others drowned in the water rushing through the openings. Kenworthy wouldn't leave until the last of 32 survivors had been saved. By then it was Monday afternoon. Six sailors caught inside the *West Virginia* died just before Christmas — after two weeks of incarceration.

In terms of casualties and destruction, this was one of the most one-sided battles in history. The U.S. lost 2,433 killed (about half of them on the *Arizona*) and 1,178 wounded. The Japanese, who had expected to sacrifice as much as one-third of their force, lost 55 airmen, nine crewmen aboard five minisubs and approximately 65 on one sunken submarine. The U.S. lost 18 surface warships, sunk or seriously damaged; the Japanese none. The U.S. lost 188 planes destroyed and 159 damaged; the Japanese lost 29. Yet three of the five wrecked U.S. battleships (the *California, Nevada* and *West Virginia*) were eventually restored to service, and all the lost warplanes were eventually replaced — more than replaced — by the bombers that struck Tokyo and Hiroshima.

If Pearl Harbor seemed an American disaster, it proved a Japanese disaster as well. Churchill knew that when he gloated at the news: "So we had won after all!" So did Stimson, who felt "relief . . . that a crisis had come in a way which would unite all our people." So did Admiral Yamamoto, when he predicted that he would run wild for only a year. Pearl Harbor united Americans in rage and hatred, and thus united, powerful and determined, they would prove invincible.

QUESTIONS TO CONSIDER

1. In what ways was the attack on Pearl Harbor a surprise, and in what ways was it not? What does this say about American hopes, preparedness, and history?

2. Explain the main lines of the history of American-Japanese relations. What were the purpose and consequences of the manner in which they started? Describe the conflict over China. What were Japan's intentions in going into China? Why did the United States not react more? Can you see examples of racism in the reactions of both the United States and Japan?

3. Describe Admiral Yamamoto's background and personality, as well as his plan for Pearl Harbor and its purpose. How did the Japanese government react to this plan? What finally made Japanese officials adopt it?

4. How did the United States react to the possibility of an attack from Japan, and how did Hawaii respond in particular? Should or could the United States have been better prepared?

5. Why does Otto Friedrich conclude that "if Pearl Harbor seemed an American disaster, it proved a Japanese disaster as well"? Could Japan have done anything to avert this disaster? What were the longer-term effects on the positions of the United States and Japan in the world community?

19

American Women at War

SARA M. EVANS

The Second World War brought unprecedented unity at home, as Americans of all colors and conditions rallied behind a righteous crusade against Japanese, German, and Italian aggression. In the course of this terrible war, 16 million Americans, including 300,000 women and 960,000 African Americans, served in the armed forces. But compared to the destruction wrought in China, Japan, the Soviet Union, and Europe, where some 49 million people died and whole cities were flattened, the United States suffered relatively light casualties. There were no invasions of the American mainland, no bombing raids on American cities, no civilian massacres. Far fewer Americans died in the Second World War than in the Civil War. Total United States military deaths came to 408,000. By contrast, 2.2 million Chinese and about 20 million Russians — soldiers and civilians alike—perished in this, the largest and deadliest war in human history.

Despite relatively light casualties, the United States underwent profound changes during the war. With the government pumping billions of dollars into war production, full employment returned and the Great Depression finally ended. Americans savored wartime prosperity — weekly earnings of industrial workers alone rose 70 percent between 1940 and 1945 — and they endured food rationing and shortages of cigarettes and nylon stockings. In addition to producing a surge of national unity, the war crushed powerful isolationist sentiment in Congress and centralized even more power in Washington, D.C., where multiplying war agencies issued directives, devised complicated forms and schedules, and produced veritable blizzards of paper.

The war was also a crucial event for American women. In a zealous display of patriotism, they joined the Red Cross, drove ambulances, worked for the civil defense, and

enlisted in the armed services. Women were also recruited for their brains. The Navy chose select graduates of seven East Coast women's colleges to participate in military operations that were highly classified; five such women, from Goucher College, were involved in top-secret "Operation ULTRA," which broke the Germans' U-boat code. Because of labor shortages, the government in 1942 urged women to join the wartime work force, and 4.5 million did so. They flocked to Washington, D.C., to work as secretaries and typists in the government's mushrooming bureaucracy. They also donned slacks, covered their hair, and went to work in the defense plants. There they did every kind of job from clerking in toolrooms to operating cranes, welding, and riveting — in short, they performed the kind of physically demanding work once reserved for men. "Rosie the Riveter" became a famous wartime image, one that symbolized the growing importance of the female industrial worker. The story of "Rosie the Riveter" is ably documented in a film by the same name.

In this selection, historian Sara M. Evans recounts the experiences of women during the war and suggests the major role they played in the American war effort and the ultimate American victory. She examines the fears and problems created by the massive influx of women into the wartime work force — many men, for example, were afraid that women would replace them at lower pay. Despite male hostility to female blue-collar workers, the unions admitted women as members and waged an effective campaign to get them equal pay for equal work. Evans points out that working mothers had a particularly difficult time of it, because there were not nearly enough child day-care facilities. And women clerks and typists in congested Washington were obliged to double and triple up in wretched housing conditions. Nevertheless, the war was a liberating experience for American women. The government intended for them to work in the defense industry only for the duration of the war, but female workers found their jobs fulfilling and meaningful, so much so that most of them wanted to stay on when the war was over. But that was not to be. As the country reconverted to peacetime production, the media launched a propaganda campaign to return women to the home, and industry laid off women workers by the thousands. Evans concedes that one can argue that the war itself did not significantly alter the condition of American women, yet she points to long-term consequences of the war that benefited married women and anticipated the resurgence of feminism in the 1960s and 1970s.

GLOSSARY

THE DOLLMAKER Harriet Arnow's novel about a strong, creative Appalachian woman who was uprooted and thrown into economic dependency and an alien environment when her husband moved the family to Detroit, where he had taken a wartime job; "her experiences matched those of thousands of migrants moving across the United States."

PLANNED PARENTHOOD FEDERATION In 1942, Margaret Sanger's Birth Control Federation of America changed its name to Planned Parenthood and shifted its emphasis from individual freedom to family stability; as a result, the birth-control movement became "an established and accepted organization."

SELECTIVE SERVICE ACT (1940) Officially known as the *Burke-Wadsworth Act,* which (in the words of one historian) inaugurated "the first peacetime military draft in American history."

WAR LABOR BOARD Established by FDR to stabilize wages, it could rule on wage rates only in cases brought before it.

T he massive mobilization for World War II politicized daily life on a scale never before seen. Women's most mundane activities were suffused with nationalistic fervor. They saved and recycled metal toothpaste tubes and tin cans; rationed short supplies of meat, sugar, and gasoline; stretched food supplies with "victory gardens"; volunteered at the Red Cross or the Civil Defense agency; bought war bonds; deferred consumer purchases; joined the armed services; and entered the labor force in unprecedented numbers. As in previous wars, activities once viewed as inappropriate for women suddenly became patriotic duties for which women were perfectly suited.

☆

THE WAR YEARS: 1941–1945

The most powerful, immediate effects of the attack on Pearl Harbor and President Roosevelt's call for a Declaration of War were the surge of patriotism and the creation of new jobs. At the end of the 1930s, 25 percent of American workers remained unemployed, but now suddenly jobs were everywhere. Employers scrambled to find enough workers at the same time the government drafted young men into the armed services. Manpower was at a premium.

As jobs appeared in industrial centers, people flocked to them, creating overnight housing shortages and insurmountable domestic difficulties. Half the southern agricultural labor force migrated to cities. In these overcrowded and alien environments, most often women had to figure out how to set up homes in novel circumstances. Harriet Arnow in her novel *The Dollmaker* portrayed an Appalachian woman who, in her native countryside, could handle any-

Reprinted with the permission of The Free Press, a Division of MacMillan, Inc. from *Born for Liberty: A History of Women in America* by Sara M. Evans. Copyright 1989 by Sara M. Evans.

thing. Tall, strong, and creative, she planted and plowed, cooked on a wood stove, carved wooden pieces, and shared a rich fantasy life with her youngest daughter. When her husband took a job in the auto industry in Detroit, Michigan, though, she found herself uprooted, in a new landscape with different cultural and physical realities. Suddenly she had to cope with economic dependence, the cramped spaces of prefabricated housing, the purchase rather than the production of food, unfamiliar appliances that rendered her skills obsolete, school bureaucracies, and the gradual loss of her children to a new culture she did not share. Her experiences matched those of thousands of migrants moving across the United States, uprooted by national mobilization and unable to use their traditional skills.

A revived economy and wartime realities generated new patterns of marriage and childbearing. Nine months after the Selective Service Act passed in 1940 with a provision to exempt fathers from the draft, there was a sudden spurt in the birthrate. Even when the exemption was withdrawn, rates stayed high as young people married in great numbers, casting their lot with an uncertain future. The "good-bye" babies resulting from these marriages represented the first wave of a baby boom that reached new heights after the war's end.

Well-schooled in voluntary activities, women responded in massive numbers to the social needs of wartime society. Three million of them volunteered with the Red Cross. Others drove ambulances and spotted airplanes for the Civil Defense, served food and entertained soldiers at USO canteens, sold war bonds, and organized their domestic tasks around the needs of the economy for scarce materials. As men began to leave civilian life, women took up the slack, assuming responsibility for families as well as for mobilizing the community for victory.

Soon, however, the country needed women to do more than volunteer with the Red Cross or buy war bonds. By 1942 the economy had absorbed available supplies of male workers and there was widespread

War plants actively recruited women, but the average female worker made about 40% less than her male counterpart throughout the war years. This young black woman, a lathe operator in a supercharger plant, was able to take advantage of the unprecedented opportunity offered by wartime employment. Before the war even black men were seldom trained or hired to operate industrial machinery, and black women were excluded altogether from this traditional stronghold of white males. But in wartime labor-short industries began to find untouched reserves of skill and ability among those they had previously slighted. The co-worker over the young woman's shoulder, though friendly, seems rather surprised to see her working there. (Courtesy, Franklin D. Roosevelt Library)

recognition that only the employment of women could meet industrial demand. U.S. Employment Service surveys reported marked shifts that year in employers' willingness to hire women. Between January and July, employers raised their estimates of the proportion of new jobs for which women would be acceptable from 29 to 55 percent. One of the primary reasons given for refusal to hire women was the opposition of male workers who periodically walked out rather than work with, or for, a woman. However, with fewer men in the factories and increased demands for industrial output, employers saw fit to tap the pool of female workers.

By 1943 *Fortune* magazine noted, "There are practically no unmarried women left to draw upon. . . . This leaves, as the next potential source of industrial workers, the housewives." That was even more disturbing than hiring single women. As *Fortune* put it: "We are a kindly, somewhat sentimental people with strong, ingrained ideas about what women should or should not do. Many thoughtful citizens are seriously disturbed over the wisdom of bringing married women into the factories." If employers and coworkers were reluctant, so were many women. Although large numbers of women were clearly eager for well-paying jobs, many — especially those with children — faced practical obstacles. Some were unsure about the social ostracism they might encounter for crossing the boundary from acceptable female to decidedly male domains.

To entice women into the factories while allaying anxieties about the consequences of change, the government mounted a major propaganda campaign aided and abetted by the active cooperation of the media and industrial advertisers. Indeed, the mobilization of women for industrial work illustrates an extraordinary degree of governmental intervention in the economy and in molding values and attitudes achieved during the war. Through the War Production Board, the administration determined what would be produced and how scarce resources would be used. The War Manpower Commission allocated the labor supply. The War Labor Board intervened in labor disputes to prevent strikes or other disruptions. And the Office of War Information coordinated publicity and propaganda campaigns. Once the War Manpower Commission decided to recruit female workers, including married women, the War Labor Board indicated its intention to rule that women working in previously male jobs should be paid at the male rate, and the Office of War Information generated recruitment posters and pamphlets and estab-

lished guidelines for fiction, features, and advertising in the mass media. The response was immediate.

"Rosie the Riveter" became a national heroine, gracing magazine covers and ads that emphasized women's civic and patriotic duty to work in the defense industry in no way undermined their traditional femininity. In Seattle, Washington, Boeing Aircraft placed large ads urging women to come to work. They displayed "pretty girls in smart slack outfits showing how easy it is to work on a wiring board." Propaganda films such as *Glamour Girls of '43* assured women that industrial tasks and machines mimicked household work:

Instead of cutting the lines of a dress, this woman cuts the pattern of aircraft parts. Instead of baking a cake, this woman is cooking gears to reduce the tension in the gears after use. . . . After a short apprenticeship, this woman can operate a drill press just as easily as a juice extractor in her own kitchen.

Similarly, a group of 114 electric companies extolled the "modern magic" of electricity: "She's 5 feet 1 from her 4A slippers to her spun-gold hair. She loves flower-hats, veils, smooth orchestras — and being kissed by a boy who's now in North Africa. *But, man, oh man, how she can handle her huge and heavy press!*"

Labor shortages affected the military as well, and from the outset of the war women's organizations demanded that women be allowed to serve their country. The result was the creation in 1942 and 1943 of women's branches in the army (WACs), the navy (WAVES), the Coast Guard (SPARS), and the marines (MCWR) in addition to the army and navy nursing corps. Close to three hundred fifty thousand women served in these various branches and an additional thousand flew commercial and air force transport planes for the Women's Airforce Service Pilots (WASP). As in the case of women in industry, glamorized servicewomen appeared everywhere in the media, looking for all the world like Joan Crawford or Katharine Hepburn with their squared shoulders and sophisticated smiles. In another version these "girls" or "gals" peeked prettily out from under their sailor hats, looking too cute to be threatening. A Sanforized ad in 1942 epitomized the latter with a headline "Maidens in Uniform" and the following verse:

> Oh, aren't we cute and snappy
>   in our cover-alls and slacks?
> And since the tags say "Sanforized"
>   we'll stay as cute as tacks!

In retrospect, such reassurance seems excessive. The breakdown in the sexual division of labor was clearly limited to the war effort from the start. In the armed services women's work sustained the traditional values and labor force segregation of the civilian world. Most women worked in clerical and supply areas or as nurses. Each of the services avoided placing women in positions where they might give orders to men and prohibited overseas duty as long as they could (1943 for WACs and 1944 for WAVES). They also prohibited the enlistment of women with children, actively persecuted lesbians, and segregated black women.

Similarly, though women entered manufacturing industries in large numbers, many new jobs such as riveting and wiring aircraft were simply redefined from male to female work. Women were hired in far greater numbers in light industry than in heavy, and they often found themselves confined to entry-level and lower-skilled positions. In addition, many areas of growth were in jobs like clerical and teaching previously defined as female. As the numbers of female clerical workers grew by 85 percent they dominated the field more than ever, raising their proportion of all clerical workers from 50 to 70 percent. A nationwide teacher shortage induced many localities to withdraw prohibitions on the employment of married women thus increasing the numbers of female teachers as well.

Discrimination against women in traditionally male blue-collar jobs continued in spite of the crisis. Employers were reluctant to invest in training women for skilled work, as they presumed women workers were only temporary. And for the most part, they flatly refused to hire black women. When they tried to lower the wages of women workers holding formerly male jobs, however, unions protested vigorously. Even if unions were less than enthusiastic about their new female members, unions were unambiguous about protecting the wages they had fought for and they worried that lower wages for women might create an incentive for industries to retain female workers after the war. As a result they waged the first effective battles for equal pay for equal work.

Practical obstacles lay in the paths of most working women as well. Critical shortages of housing and transportation limited their options. Government agencies in Washington, D.C., for example, suddenly expanded their clerical labor force to meet wartime demands. In 1942 the Pentagon opened with office space for 35,000 workers, the largest office building in the world. Yet as thousands of young women flooded into Washington, D.C., to fill clerical jobs in the swelling federal bureaucracy, they doubled and tripled up in shabby boardinghouses and tiny rooms, unable to find decent places to live. Their conditions, however, were probably easier to bear than those of industrial workers' families crushed into prefab housing and tiny apartments in places like Detroit and Mobile. Single young women on government wages quickly learned the value of cooperative housekeeping. "The result was a whole collection of strangely-bonded female groups."

Mothers of small children found virtually no help. When the Federal Works Agency finally decided in 1943 to fund day-care centers for defense workers, their efforts met only a tiny proportion of the demand. Newspapers ran stories of infants locked in cars parked in employee lots, young children shut up in apartments most of the day, and juvenile delinquents. Local communities tried to address the problems. More than 4,400 communities had established child care and welfare committees by the summer of 1943, but their efforts paled in comparison to the need. Most women relied on family members, but a Women's Bureau survey in 1944 found that 16 percent of mothers in war industries had no child-care arrangements at all. The federal government never considered measures like those in Britain which relieved the double burdens of working mothers with time off for shopping; extended shopping hours; and restaurants offering inexpensive, take-home prepared food. As a result of these stresses, women workers' absenteeism was 50 percent higher than that of men and their turnover was twice as high.

Nevertheless, the government campaign to fill defense needs with women workers was hugely successful. Six million women who had never worked outside the home joined the labor force during the war years while millions more shifted from agricultural, domestic, or service work to industrial work. Their profile represented a marked shift toward older and married women from the traditional young and single worker, and most of them did not want their new status to be temporary. When questioned about their future intentions, women in defense industries indicated an overwhelming preference for retaining their jobs after the war. If the stresses of managing home and workplace were acute, the gains were also real. For the first time, women had access to high-paying industrial jobs requiring specialized skills and affording status. Black women, though blocked from higher-level industrial jobs, began to enter the female jobs which had previously been virtually all white, such as clerical work and nursing, and significantly reduced their reliance on domestic service. In Detroit in 1942 and 1943 black women demonstrated for jobs and housing with the support of the UAW [United Auto Workers]. Two busloads of women finally stormed a Ford plant to call attention to discriminatory hiring. Perhaps most important, half the rural black female labor force left the countryside and found employment in cities.

From the beginning, business owners and government planners worried that women might not willingly give up higher paying industrial jobs once they had access to them. Some managers consciously tried to hire the wives of the servicemen they were replacing, "reasoning that the women will not be reluctant to yield their jobs to their own husbands." Surveys of women workers confirmed planners' fears.

Shipyard worker Katherine Archibald described the constant resentment of men in the shipyard where she worked. From overt harassment in the beginning, men retreated to "a vague and emotion-charged atmosphere" in which women were always suspect of sexual improprieties. And they regaled one another with anecdotes proving that women were unsuited for the work: "'Take a look around at the women and what they're doing,' one disgruntled workman urged. 'From one end of the hull to the other they're jawing or prettying up their faces or bothering some man and keeping him from his work.'" The Minneapolis *Tribune* editorialized in August 1942, "WACS AND WAVES and women welders. . . . Where is it all going to end? . . . Is it hard to foresee, after the boys come marching home and they marry these emancipated young women, who is going to tend the babies in the next generation?"

Government and media propaganda consistently reassured Americans that while women would do their civic duty for the duration, they would certainly return to their traditional roles once the emergency was over. Ads that praised working women also emphasized the temporary nature of their positions. The Eureka Company, for example, noted women's many contributions to the war effort including filling over 70 percent of the positions on their own assembly lines "for the duration. But," the ad continued, "a day is coming when this war will be won. And on that day, like you, Mrs. America, Eureka will put aside its uniform and return to the ways of peace . . . building household appliances."

Unions reflected the prejudices of their constituents, especially fears that women would displace male workers at lower rates of pay. In the beginning, unions objected strenuously when women were

There was considerable anxiety among the nation's male leaders that women war workers might not quietly return to the home once victory was won. This advertisement was typical of a widespread effort to remind women that maintaining the family was democracy's principal foundation, and that with the return of peace, American women would be expected to return to their children and their homes. (Reprinted by permission of ADEL Fasteners; courtesy of the Trustees of the Boston Public Library)

hired, frequently to the point of going on strike. "Women don't know how to be loyal to a union," said a skilled craftsman. "They're born, and they grow up, dirty dealers. There isn't a straight one among 'em." Once the War Labor Board announced its intention to rule that women must be paid at male rates for the same work, unions expressed their willingness to support women workers and accept them as members. Because unions began to see organizing women as the key to protecting jobs and wage rates in previously all male work settings, and because the War Labor Board protected labor's right to organize, the unionization of women as well as men made enormous strides during the war. The number of organized women grew between 1940 and 1944 from eight hundred thousand to three million, and the female proportion of organized labor from 11 to 23 percent.

Even though popular culture extolled the adventures of strong female heroines, its messages were always mixed. Middle-class journals were most likely to present women as assertive, proving that they were as good as any men. In the pages of the *Saturday Evening Post,* for example, women appeared as welders, engineers, executives, and taxi drivers, heroically claiming their own capacities against the doubts and denigration of men around them. In actuality, female adventure and achievement represented little threat for middle-class men because women were being recruited either into female-dominated white-collar positions or into blue-collar industrial work. For working-class women, however, the complexities were more serious. They faced hostility from men in their own communities who were threatened by the loss of prerogatives at work as well as authority in their homes.

In pulp magazines like *True Story,* fictional female war workers' happiness rested not on their achievements but on stoic willingness to continue unrewarding work for the larger goal of victory. Boring assembly-line work, for example, took on new meaning when imbued with patriotism: "The noise of the factory [became] an articulate voice, saying: more planes, more planes, more planes — we're making them, we're building them, we're sending them out." Status in *True Story* fiction still depended on a romantic relationship with the right man. Advertisements in such magazines sustained women's consumer roles, imbuing everything with a gendered, domestic patriotism. In 1942 a columnist in *True Romance* quoted Ruth Merson, a "well-known corset designer and stylist," on the necessity of corsets in wartime: "Right now with the country embarking on its gigantic task of self-preservation it is essential that the women of America do not let down their men. Women must keep up the morale of their men and still continue to

be their guiding star. To this end they must be their trim and shapely selves."

If wartime patriotism had gendered meanings and class dimensions, it also aroused racial prejudice especially toward Japanese-Americans. In 1942 Franklin Roosevelt, responding to fears of a Japanese fifth column on American shores, signed an order removing Americans of Japanese descent from west coast states to inland relocation camps. They were allowed to bring only what they could carry, and many sold their houses and businesses at a great loss. They experienced the terror of the refugee — uprooted, deprived of control over their destiny — and the humiliation of implied disloyalty. Many were Nisei, American-born citizens. Their Japanese-born parents, the Isei, had been prohibited by law from becoming naturalized citizens. Women generally fared better than men because they were able to pursue their traditional roles in the camps and were, therefore, more resilient. Domestic tasks remained to be done while productive work outside the home did not exist. At the war's end, however, these women and their families had to begin anew to build their lives despite bitter hardship and hurt.

The war, a time of vastly expanded centralized planning and control of individual lives, witnessed the final transformation of the birth-control movement from an insurgent, feminist movement to an established and accepted organization. In 1942 the Birth Control Federation of America under the leadership of Margaret Sanger changed its name to the Planned Parenthood Federation of America. Its new reformist orientation emphasized family stability rather than individual freedom, utilizing the bureaucratic language of scientific, rational social planning and familial welfare. At a time of unprecedented governmental mobilization and control of both economic and social life, this shift seemed so logical that it went virtually unremarked.

The theme of sexual liberation, relatively submerged during the Depression years, reemerged among young people whose economic autonomy and separation from their home communities offered unprecedented opportunities for experimentation. Men in the military, urban teenagers, and women war workers discovered a new freedom that many found irresistible. "When I was sixteen I let a sailor pick me up and go all the way with me . . . mainly because I had a feeling of high adventure and because I wanted to please a member of the armed forces." For young men, such attitudes were a kind of heaven. "Where I was, a male war worker became the center of loose morality. It was a sex paradise." The intensity of wartime emotion contributed to short-term affairs, "The times were conducive for this sort of thing," as well as to sudden marriages.

Less visible to most Americans, World War II represented a turning point in the birth of a self-conscious homosexual identity among lesbians and gay men. The slow development of an urban gay subculture in the twenties and thirties had touched the lives of only a few. On the eve of the war most homosexuals remained isolated in a hostile culture. But just as heterosexual women and men found that the war diminished the authority of traditional norms and expectations, so also homosexuals discovered that World War II had "created a substantially new 'erotic situation' conducive both to the articulation of a homosexual identity and to the more rapid evolution of a gay subculture."

For lesbians the war created a dramatically different situation in two ways: First, the women's armed services recruited primarily young, unmarried women providing an all-female environment in which intimate, erotic relationships could grow despite official prohibitions. Indeed, at the height of the war the army was distinctly uninterested in losing personnel or generating unpleasant publicity. As a result, "for a time, many [homosexual] women in the military enjoyed a measure of safety that permitted their sexuality to survive relatively unharassed." Second, the fact that women visibly dominated so many public places, whether for work or recreation, provided a new safety for lesbians. They could meet each other without fearing that their presence in an all-female environment labeled them deviant. One result was that lesbian bars began to appear in cities all over the country, no longer confined only to the largest and most anonymous urban centers. In effect, specifically lesbian spaces were created that, though always threatened and vulnerable, provided the necessary conditions for group identity.

☆

RECONVERSION

At the end of the war women knew that they, as well as men, had made victory possible. The outpouring of energy and patriotic emotion had given a new dimension to citizenship and to their sense of self. Yet there was no way to institutionalize such emotions when public life itself was so thoroughly dominated by the state. The political focus of wartime activity had only one purpose — victory. There was little to debate either about means or ends. Only military and technocratic experts could know what was needed to mobilize and direct the massive resources of America. Women's duty was simply to respond, to do what was necessary "for the duration," and to maintain the family as the essential foundation for democracy. As a result, the exhilaration of wartime communal effort had neither structural nor ideological support for continuation after the war. At the same time, the changes, even if temporary, were shocking and deeply unsettling, and their consequences must be read far into the postwar era.

As men were mustered out of the army, women were mustered out of the factories; both were sent home to resume increasingly privatized lives. What the war had accomplished, with a reinvigorated economy and pent-up consumer demand, was a new expectation that most Americans could enjoy the material standard of living promised by the consumer economy in peace. The purpose of work outside the home was to procure the resources to sustain this standard of living (which now included a private house; appliances such as a refrigerator, stove, and vacuum cleaner; and a car). The female task was to oversee the quality of this private life, to purchase wisely, and to serve as an emotional center of the family and home.

The principal obstacle to this vision, however, was the possibility that women might not choose to play their publicly condoned role. Anthropologist Margaret Mead wrote at the end of the war that the media's "continuous harping on the theme: 'Will the women be willing to return to the home?'" reflected widespread anxieties. A returning serviceman was likely to wonder, "Will she have learned to be so independent that she won't want to give up her job to make a home for me?"

Articles addressed to women warned them about the care they must exercise to support the egos of returning men. One marriage counselor suggested women should "let him know you are tired of living alone, that you want him now to take charge." Others emphasized the "feminine" qualities returning vets valued including "tenderness, admiration, or at least submissiveness." Even before the war ended the pressure to quit began. "In the great factories, the ominous sound of the old saw, 'A woman's place is in the home,' is heard above the music now piped into the workrooms to make conditions more attractive for the still badly needed women workers," wrote A. G. Mezerik in the *Atlantic.*

The UAW Women's Bureau held a conference for women union leaders in April 1945 to discuss the postwar situation. Union women expressed great concern that seniority must operate in a nondiscriminatory way so that women would have equal opportunity when postwar layoffs came. Two delegates reported that their unions had surveyed women workers regarding their work needs. "In one shipyard, 98 percent of the women want to continue working in shipyards or at least continue working in those skills which they have been able to pick up there. Many of them worked in service industries be-

fore the war." Another survey in a New York manufacturing industry indicated that 82 percent of the women intended to continue working. The report of the conference noted that "several delegates proposed for labor in general a program to show that women are not just a temporary wartime group." They shared stories of struggles within unions, many successful, to win and enforce equal pay for equal work. But they earmarked for future work ongoing concerns about the wage gap between women and men due to the fact that "women work on jobs historically women's or in separate women's departments where rates are traditionally lower."

Some suggested that a job evaluation system analyze skills and experience in such a way that different job categories could be compared. Both the ideas and the techniques for "comparable worth," an issue which would not emerge full grown until the 1980s, were present in this discussion. But the principal concern expressed in this meeting and by writers, such as Lucy Greenbaum in the *New York Times Magazine,* was for women who would still need to work after the war. Greenbaum wrote in April 1945, "All organizations working with and for women in industry expect that pressure will be brought to bear on the married women to stay at home and mind the children. In war she heard promises; peacetime will be full of prohibitions."

Greenbaum was right. Even if four out of five industrial women workers preferred to keep their jobs, few had much choice. When military orders ceased, industries shut down to prepare for reconversion, laying off women workers. For a moment unemployment was high again and everyone feared the return of the depression. Plants reopened rapidly, however, and for the most part they refused to rehire women regardless of their skills or seniority rights. In the Detroit auto industry after the war, the proportion of women in the work force fell from 25 to 7.5 percent and women's share of work in durable goods industries throughout the nation dropped 50 percent.

Women who went to the U.S. Employment Service were incredulous to discover that the only jobs available to them paid only half what they had made in war industries. Skilled industrial jobs were no longer open to them. One union organizer reported that the U.S.E.S. in her area told women, "No, these jobs are for men; women can't do them." As one woman complained: "They say a woman doesn't belong behind a factory machine or in any business organization. But who will support me, I ask? And who will give my family the help they have been getting from me? No one has thought to ask me whether or not I need my job."

Women fought back, staging picket lines protesting their exclusion. But they met with little sympathy or support even from their unions, and often they found themselves blamed for their situation. Margaret Pickel, dean of women at Columbia University, said women's own shortcomings accounted for their loss of jobs. She charged that as workers they had proved to be emotionally unstable, to "lack the gift for teamwork," to "have no gift for finality," and to "lack the corporate loyalty that makes for effective unionization." While advocating the view that "marriage and sensible motherhood are probably the most useful and satisfying of all the jobs that women can do," she nevertheless characterized "marriage mortality" (i.e., women quitting work when they marry) as "women's greatest handicap." Flaying women with the cultural stereotypes their employers and male co-workers held, Pickel accused them of being "unprofessional" and displaying "a weakness for the personal." As a result, "they do not age well. By middle age, when men are at their best, a devoted woman worker is apt to degenerate into a strained fussiness or worse." The nastiness of Pickel's charges was not typical, but it was not uncommon either as women once again provided easy scapegoats in a time of anxiety and change. . . .

Millions of women left the labor force, voluntarily and involuntarily; the women who stayed represented an increase in labor force participation consistent with previous trends. In other words, one could argue that the war itself made little difference. Ideologically,

wartime propaganda justified the erosion of gender boundaries "for the duration" and no more. The intense pressure on women to return to domesticity coincided with the wishes of a younger cohort of women and men to focus on their private lives. This privatization promised a dramatically new level of isolation within the family as bulldozers began to reshape the landscape in preparation for growing suburbs.

At the same time, there were some long-term consequences of the changes in women's behavior during the war. Even though the trends the war exaggerated, toward the employment of older, married women, were clearly in place before the war, only the expanding economy created during and after the war could have allowed those trends to continue. As a result, the war removed some of the legal and cultural barriers to the employment of married women. Laws, for example, against married women teachers were removed in several states, and the equal pay for equal work standard was adopted by many unions and by eleven states. . . .

The longer-term consequence of a generation of women shaped by their wartime experiences, like that of their predecessors seared by the Great Depression, can only be inferred, but its importance should not be underestimated. The mothers of the baby boom generation experienced a moment of independence and cultural validation (whether personally or vicariously) during the war years; this may well have shaped the mixed messages they gave their daughters who loudly proclaimed the rebirth of feminism two decades later and politicized daily life once again with the slogan "the personal is political."

QUESTIONS TO CONSIDER

1. What was the effect of war on the Depression? What kinds of practical difficulties were created for women by the conversion to a wartime economy?

2. Why and how were women first recruited in large numbers into industrial work? What were the

initial responses of women? men? employers? What kinds of practical difficulties did women encounter with their new jobs? Compare the response of the American government with that of the British government. How did unions react to the new women workers and why?

3. How did the new jobs affect different groups of women — middle-class women, working-class women, African American women? How did wartime conditions affect the birth control movement and the personal lives of many working women?

4. What were the effects of the reconversion to a peacetime economy on the economy itself and on women? What role did the government play? How did the unions respond? What were the new hopes and expectations of men and women for the economy and their own lives after more than a decade of depression and war?

5. In what ways does the war seem to have made little difference in women's lives, and what may have been the long-term consequences of women's wartime working experience, according to Evans?

20

The Falling Sun: Hiroshima

Fletcher Knebel and Charles W. Bailey II

Although the country was already in a condition of semimobilization in December 1941, it took a year before the United States was ready to fight a total war. At last, in November 1942, an American expeditionary army landed in North Africa and went on to help the British whip German Panzer divisions there. After that an Anglo-American force invaded Sicily and drove on to the Italian mainland.

Then on D-Day, June 6, 1944, an Allied invasion force — the largest ever assembled — landed at Normandy, France, in what turned out to be the beginning of the end for Hitler's Third Reich. Thanks to German errors and Allied planning and execution, the invasion was a success. With a foothold in Normandy, American, British, and French armies drove a wedge into German defenses and poured inland. As the Western Allies pushed toward Germany from the west, Russian armies drove in from the east. By May 1945 — less than a year after D-Day — German resistance had collapsed and the once mighty Reich was a smoldering ruin.

Meanwhile, the United States had moved from a holding action in the Pacific to an aggressive, two-pronged island-hopping campaign. It began in November 1943, with Admiral Chester Nimitz's forces attacking at Tarawa and Kwajalein and General Douglas MacArthur's command breaking through the Japanese barrier on the Bismarck Archipelago, islands in the South Pacific. Eventually, MacArthur recaptured the Philippines and drove toward Manila, while Nimitz pushed toward Japan from the central Pacific.

Japan fought back desperately, sending out kamikaze planes to slow the American advance. They took a terrible toll: 34 American ships sunk and 288 damaged. But the "Divine Wind" vengeance that the kamikazes represented also cost the Japanese heavily:

their losses were estimated at 1,288 to 4,000 planes and pilots. Moreover, they could not stop American army and naval forces, which moved on relentlessly, capturing Iwo Jima and then Okinawa, located just south of Japan itself.

From Okinawa, the United States planned to launch an all-out invasion of the Japanese home islands, to begin sometime in November 1945. General MacArthur thought relatively light casualties would be sustained in the initial fighting but ultimately the losses would be staggering — especially if it took a year to break Japanese resistance, as some experts predicted. General George Marshall estimated that the invasion would cost the United States a half-million men.

But the invasion never took place, because the United States soon had an awesome and terrible alternative. On July 16, 1945, after three years of top-secret development and production, American scientists successfully detonated an atomic bomb in the New Mexico desert. Some scientists involved in the project urged privately that a demonstration bomb be dropped on an uninhabited island. But an advisory committee of scientists opposed any such demonstration and recommended that the bomb be used against Japan at once. Secretary of War Henry L. Stimson emphatically agreed: the bomb would kill thousands of civilians, he argued, but it would nevertheless shock Japan into surrender and save a half-million American lives.

The final decision lay with Harry Truman, who became president after Roosevelt had died of a brain hemorrhage in April 1945. "I regarded the bomb as a military weapon and never had any doubt that it should be used," Truman later wrote. "The top military advisers to the president recommended its use, and when I talked to [British Prime Minister Winston] Churchill he unhesitatingly told me that he favored the use of the atomic bomb if it might aid to end the war." On July 25, Truman ordered that atomic bombs be dropped on or about August 3, unless Japan surrendered before that date. Then the United States, Great Britain, and China sent the Japanese an ultimatum that demanded unconditional surrender. The Japanese made no official reply. When August 3 passed and Japan fought on, Truman's orders went into effect, and American B-29s unleashed two of the "superhuman fireballs of destruction" — the first on Hiroshima, the other on Nagasaki — that forced Japan to surrender. Thus, the Pacific War ended as it had begun — with a devastating air raid. You may find it profitable to compare the Pearl Harbor air raid, a sneak attack against military targets (selection 18), with the nuclear blast at Hiroshima, which annihilated civilian and military sectors alike.

Since then, many critics have questioned the wisdom of Truman's decision, contending that the bomb was not the only alternative open to him in July and August. They point out that the invasion of Japan was not scheduled until November, so Truman had plenty of time "to seek and use alternatives." He could have sought a Russian declaration of war against Japan, or he could have ignored the advisory committee of scientists and dropped a demonstration bomb to show Japan what an apocalyptic weapon it was. He had another *bomb to drop if the Japanese remained unimpressed. But Truman, in a remarkable display of "moral insensitivity," used the bomb because it was there to be used, and he never questioned his position.*

Other critics maintain that Truman employed the bomb with an eye toward postwar politics. In their view, the President wanted to end the war in a hurry, before Russia could enter the conflict against Japan, seize territory, and threaten America's role in the postwar balance of power. Still others argue that the United States could have offered the Japanese conditional surrender, or found other ways to demonstrate the bomb, and so could have ended the war before Russia entered it.

Many analysts, however, still defend Truman — still insist that his decision was a wise one that avoided a prolonged land invasion in which countless hundreds of thousands of people would have died. "Did we have to drop the bomb?" said a physicist who helped develop it. "You bet your life we did." He referred to a recent demonstration in the United States in memory of Hiroshima. "No one seems to realize," he said, "that without Pearl Harbor there wouldn't have been a Hiroshima."

For the people of Hiroshima and Nagasaki, the questions of retribution, of political motivation and grand strategy, did not matter. Nothing mattered to them but the searing flash of light that ultimately killed some 130,000 people in Hiroshima and 60,000 to 70,000 in Nagasaki, scarred and twisted thousands more, and left both cities a smoking, radioactive rubble.

Since then, a number of books have appeared about the atomic explosions at Hiroshima and Nagasaki. Among the best are John Hersey's Hiroshima, *available in a new edition, and* No High Ground *(1960), by Fletcher Knebel and Charles W. Bailey II. The latter recounts the entire history of the first atomic bomb at Hiroshima, from Truman's decision to use it to the flight of the* Enola Gay *(the B-29 that dropped "Little Boy," as the bomb was called) up to the actual explosion and its cataclysmic results. In this selection, Knebel and Bailey describe that explosion, narrating the experiences of several people who somehow lived through that "fireball of destruction." Telling the personal side of Hiroshima is what makes this such a powerful account, with implicit lessons about the horror of nuclear war that have universal resonance. We can all identify with the people here, with Mr. Nukushina, Mrs. Susukida, and Dr. Imagawa, as the atomic blast swept over their city and changed the world forever.*

GLOSSARY

ENOLA GAY   Nickname of the B-29 that dropped "Little Boy."

HIRANO, MAJOR TOSAKU   Staff officer stationed in Hiroshima, he had gone up to Tokyo and his decision to stay there a couple of extra nights saved his life; later, he persuaded Japan's leading nuclear scientist, who already suspected that the bomb dropped on Hiroshima was a nuclear weapon, to fly there and investigate.

DR. IMAGAWA   Visiting a patient's home when the bomb burst, he found himself "standing on top of a five-foot pile of rubble" with his clothes shredded; he made for his home in a suburb, helping the wounded along the way.

KINOSHITA, HIDEO   An officer at the monitoring station of the Japanese quasi-governmental news agency near Tokyo, he reported to his boss the news from America that an atomic bomb had been dropped on Hiroshima, and the boss relayed that report to the chief secretary of the Japanese cabinet.

"LITTLE BOY"   Nickname of the atomic bomb dropped on Hiroshima.

NAKAMURA, BIN   Subchief of the Hiroshima bureau of Japan's news agency, he was eating breakfast when the explosion "lifted him off the straw mat on which he was sitting and sent a wave of 'immense' heat washing over his face"; miraculously unhurt, he spent the day interviewing survivors and got a story out on a suburban radio station.

NUKUSHINA, MICHIYOSHI   Fire-truck driver at the Hiroshima Army Ordinance Supply Depot, he had just returned home when the bomb exploded, flattening his home and blowing him into a corner where two safes prevented the falling roof from crushing him; he eventually found himself at an emergency aid station on Ninoshima Island.

OPPENHEIMER, J. ROBERT   Scientist and director of the top-secret project at Los Alamos, New Mexico, that built the first atomic bomb.

SAKAMOTO, CHINAYO   A mother who was mopping her kitchen floor when the *Enola Gay* droned by overhead, she and her family escaped "the blast and fire," because their home was situated behind a high protective hill; when she learned that her husband and his entire military unit had been wiped out, she slit her throat with a razor in front of a little altar.

SUSUKIDA, HAYANO   Picking up salvaged roof tiles with other volunteers, she found herself suddenly slammed to the ground, her back severely burned, and her watch blown off; she made it to the emergency aid station on Ninoshima Island.

YAMAGUCHI, YUKO   She lived with her children in a rented farmhouse in a suburb and was just cleaning up after breakfast when the walls exploded in a black cloud of soot; unhurt, she went into the wrecked city and found her father and mother, both dying, in a Red Cross hospital; she never did find her husband's parents.

T he sounding of the all-clear signal in Hiroshima at 7:13 A.M. on August 6 made little change in the tempo of the city. Most people had been too busy, or too lazy, to pay much attention to the alert. The departure of the single, high-flying B-29 caused no more stir than its arrival over the city twenty-two minutes earlier.

As the plane flew out over the sea, Michiyoshi Nukushina, a thirty-eight-year-old fire-truck driver at the Hiroshima Army Ordinance Supply Depot, climbed onto his bicycle and headed for home. He had received special permission to quit his post half an hour before his shift ended. Wearing an official-duty armband to clear himself through the depot gates, and carrying a new pair of wooden clogs and a bag of fresh tomatoes drawn from the depot commissary, he headed home through the narrow streets of Hiroshima.

Nukushina crossed two of the seven river channels that divided the city into fingerlike islands and finally arrived at his home in Kakomachi precinct a little more than half an hour after leaving the firehouse. Propping his bicycle by an entrance to his small combination home and wineshop he walked inside and called to his wife to go get the tomatoes.

At this same instant, in a comfortable house behind the high hill that made Hijiyama Park a welcome variation in the otherwise flat terrain of Hiroshima, a mother named Chinayo Sakamoto was mopping her kitchen floor after breakfast. Her son Tsuneo, an Army captain fortunately stationed right in his home town, had left for duty with his unit. His wife Miho had gone upstairs. Tsuneo's father lay on the straw mat in the living room, reading his morning paper.

Off to the east and south of the city, a few men in air defense posts were watching the morning sky or listening to their sound-detection equipment. At the Matsunaga lookout station, in the hills east of Hiroshima, a watcher filed two reports with the air defense center. At 8:06, he sighted and reported two planes, headed northwest. At 8:09, he saw another, following some miles behind them, and corrected his report to include it.

At 8:14, the telephone talker at the Nakano searchlight battery also made a report. His sound equipment had picked up the noise of aircraft engines. Unidentified planes were coming from Saijo, about fifteen miles east of Hiroshima, and were heading toward the city.

The anti-aircraft gunners on Mukay-Shima Island in Hiroshima harbor could now see two planes, approaching the eastern edge of the city at very high altitude. As they watched, at precisely seventeen seconds after 8:15, the planes suddenly separated. The leading aircraft made a tight, diving turn to the right. The second plane performed an identical maneuver to the left, and from it fell three parachutes which opened and floated slowly down toward the city.

The few people in Hiroshima who caught sight of the two planes saw the parachutes blossom as the aircraft turned away from the city. Some cheered when they saw them, thinking the enemy planes must be in trouble and the crews were starting to bail out.

For three quarters of a minute there was nothing in the clear sky over the city except the parachutes and the diminishing whine of airplane engines as the B-29's retreated into the lovely blue morning.

Then suddenly, without a sound, there was no sky left over Hiroshima.

For those who were there and who survived to recall the moment when man first turned on himself the elemental forces of his own universe, the first instant was pure light, blinding, intense light, but light of an awesome beauty and variety.

In the pause between detonation and impact, a pause that for some was so short it could not register on the senses, but which for others was long enough for shock to give way to fear and for fear in turn to yield to instinctive efforts at self-preservation, the sole impression was visual. If there was sound, no one heard it.

To Nukushina, just inside his house, and to Mrs. Sakamoto, washing her kitchen floor, it was simply sudden and complete blackness.

For Nukushina's wife, reaching for the bag of tomatoes on her husband's bicycle, it was a blue flash streaking across her eyes.

For Dr. Imagawa, at his patient's city home, it again was darkness. For his wife, in the suburban hills to the west, it was a "rainbow-colored object," whirling horizontally across the sky over the city.

To Yuko Yamaguchi, cleaning up after breakfast in the rented farmhouse where she and her in-laws now lived, it was a sudden choking black cloud as the accumulated soot and grime of decades seemed to leap from the old walls.

Hayano Susukida, bent over to pick up a salvaged roof tile so she could pass it down the line of "volunteer" workers, did not see anything. She was merely crushed to the ground as if by some monstrous supernatural hand. But her son Junichiro, lounging outside his dormitory at Otake, saw a flash that turned from white to pink and then to blue as it rose and blossomed. Others, also at a distance of some miles, seemed to see "five or six bright colors." Some saw merely "flashes of gold" in a white light that reminded them — this was perhaps the most common description — of a huge photographic flashbulb exploding over the city.

The duration of this curiously detached spectacle varied with the distance of the viewer from the point in mid-air where the two lumps of U-235 were driven together inside the bomb. It did not last more than a few seconds at the most.

For thousands in Hiroshima it did not last even that long, if in fact there was any moment of grace at all. They were simply burned black and dead where they

This scorched watch, found in the rubble at Hiroshima, stopped at the exact moment of the atomic blast: 8:16. When the bomb exploded, thousands of people "were simply burned black and dead where they stood by the radiant heat that turned central Hiroshima into a gigantic oven." (John Launois/Black Star; Hiroshima: National Archives)

stood by the radiant heat that turned central Hiroshima into a gigantic oven. For thousands of others there was perhaps a second or two, certainly not long enough for wonder or terror or even recognition of things seen but not believed, before they were shredded by the thousands of pieces of shattered window glass that flew before the blast waves or were crushed underneath walls, beams, bricks, or any other solid object that stood in the way of the explosion.

For everyone else in history's first atomic target, the initial assault on the visual sense was followed by an instinctive assumption that a very large bomb had scored a direct hit on or near the spot where they were standing.

Old Mr. Sakamoto, who a moment before had been lounging on the living-room floor with his newspaper, found himself standing barefoot in his back yard, the paper still in his hand. Then his wife staggered out of the house, and perhaps half a minute later, his daughter-in-law Miho, who had been upstairs, groped her way out also.

Dr. Imagawa had just reached for his medical satchel to begin the examination of his patient. When the blackness lifted from his senses, he found himself standing on top of a five-foot pile of rubble that had been the sickroom. With him, surprisingly, were both the sick man and the patient's young son.

Mrs. Susukida, flat on the ground amid the pile of old roof tiles, was left all but naked, stripped of every piece of outer clothing and now wearing only her underwear, which itself was badly torn.

Mrs. Nukushina had just time to throw her hands over her eyes after she saw the blue flash. Then she was knocked insensible. When she recovered consciousness, she lay in what seemed to her to be utter darkness. All around her there was only rubble where a moment earlier there had been her home and her husband's bicycle and the bag of fresh tomatoes. She too was now without clothing except for her underwear. Her body was rapidly becoming covered with her own blood from dozens of cuts. She groped around until she found her four-year-old daughter Ikuko. She saw no trace of her husband. Dazed and terrified, she took the child's hand and fled.

But Michiyoshi Nukushina was there, and was still alive, though buried unconscious inside the wreckage of his home. His life had been saved because the blast blew him into a corner where two big, old-fashioned office safes, used in the family wine business, took the weight of the roof when it fell and thus spared him from being crushed. As he came to, raised his head and looked around, everything seemed strangely reddened. He discovered later that blood from cuts on his head had gushed down over his eyelids, forming a sort of red filter over his eyes. His first conscious thought was that the emergency water tank kept on hand for fire-bombing protection was only one-third full. As his head cleared, he called for his wife and

daughter. There was no reply. Getting painfully to his feet — his left leg was badly broken — he found a stick for a crutch and hobbled out of the rubble.

Hold out your left hand, palm down, fingers spread, and you have a rough outline of the shape of Hiroshima. The sea is beyond the fingertips. The back of the hand is where the Ota River comes down from the hills to the north. The spot where the bomb exploded is about where a wedding ring would be worn, just south of the main military headquarters and in the center of the residential-commercial districts of the city. Major Ferebee's aim was nearly perfect. Little Boy was detonated little more than two hundred yards from the aiming point on his target chart, despite the fact that it was released from a fast-moving aircraft over three miles to the east and nearly six miles up in the air.

Dropped with such precision, the bomb performed better than its makers had predicted. Several factors combined by chance to produce even more devastation than had been expected.

First was the time of the explosion. All over Hiroshima, thousands of the charcoal braziers that were the stoves in most households were still full of hot coals after being used for breakfast cooking. Almost every stove was knocked over by the massive blast wave that followed the explosion, and each became an incendiary torch to set fire to the wood-and-paper houses. In addition, where [J. Robert] Oppenheimer had estimated casualties on the assumption that most people would be inside their air-raid shelters, almost no one in Hiroshima was sheltered when the bomb actually fell. The recent all-clear, the fact that it was a time when most people were on their way to work, the mischance by which there had been no new alert when the *Enola Gay* approached the city, the fact that small formations of planes had flown over many times before without dropping bombs, all combined to leave people exposed. Thus more than seventy thousand persons instead of Oppenheimer's estimate of twenty thousand were killed outright or so badly injured that they were dead in a matter of hours.

The initial flash spawned a succession of calamities.

First came heat. It lasted only an instant but was so intense that it melted roof tiles, fused the quartz crystals in granite blocks, charred the exposed sides of telephone poles for almost two miles, and incinerated nearby humans so thoroughly that nothing remained except their shadows, burned into asphalt pavements or stone walls. Of course the heat was most intense near the "ground zero" point, but for thousands of yards it had the power to burn deeply. Bare skin was burned up to two and a half miles away.

A printed page was exposed to the heat rays a mile and a half from the point of explosion, and the black letters were burned right out of the white paper. Hundreds of women learned a more personal lesson in the varying heat-absorption qualities of different colors when darker parts of their clothing burned out while lighter shades remained unscorched, leaving skin underneath etched in precise detail with the flower patterns of their kimonos. A dress with blue polka dots printed on white material came out of the heat with dark dots completely gone but the white background barely singed. A similar phenomenon occurred in men's shirts. Dark stripes were burned out while the alternate light stripes were undamaged. Another factor that affected injury was the thickness of clothing. Many people had their skin burned except where a double-thickness seam or a folded lapel had stood between them and the fireball. Men wearing caps emerged with sharp lines etched across their temples. Below the line, exposed skin was burned, while above it, under the cap, there was no injury. Laborers working in the open with only undershirts on had the looping pattern of shoulder straps and armholes printed on their chests. Sometimes clothing protected the wearer only if it hung loosely. One man standing with his arm bent, so that the sleeve was drawn tightly over his elbow, was burned only around that joint.

The heat struck only what stood in the direct path of its straight-line radiation from the fireball. A man sitting at his desk writing a letter had his hands deeply burned because the heat rays coming through his window fell directly on them, while his face, only eighteen inches away but outside the path of the rays, was unmarked. In countless cases the human body was burned or spared by the peculiarity of its position at the moment of flash. A walking man whose arm was swinging forward at the critical instant was burned all down the side of his torso. Another, whose moving arm happened to be next to his body, was left with an unburned streak where the limb had blocked out the radiation. In scores of cases people were burned on one side of the face but not on the other because they had been standing or sitting in profile to the explosion. A shirtless laborer was burned all across his back — except for a narrow strip where the slight hollow down his spine left the skin in a "shadow" where the heat rays could not fall.

Some measure of the heat's intensity can be gained from the experience of the mayor of Kabe, a village ten miles outside the city. He was standing in his garden and even at that distance distinctly felt the heat on his face when the bomb exploded.

After the heat came the blast, sweeping outward from the fireball with the force of a five-hundred mile-an-hour wind. Only those objects that offered a minimum of surface resistance — handrails on bridges, pipes, utility poles — remained standing. The walls of a few office buildings, specially built to resist earthquakes, remained standing, but they now enclosed nothing but wreckage, as their roofs were driven down to the ground, carrying everything inside down under them. Otherwise, in a giant circle more than two miles across, everything was reduced to rubble. The blast drove all before it. The stone columns flanking the entrance to the Shima Surgical Hospital, directly underneath the explosion, were rammed straight down into the ground. Every hard object that was dislodged, every brick, every broken timber, every roof tile, became a potentially lethal missile. Every window in the city was suddenly a shower of sharp glass splinters, driven with such speed and force that in hundreds of buildings they were deeply imbedded in walls — or in people. Many people were picking tiny shards of glass from their eyes for weeks afterward as a result of the shattering of their spectacles, or trying to wash out bits of sand and grit driven under their eyelids. Even a blade of grass now became a weapon to injure the man who tended it. A group of boys working in an open field had their backs peppered with bits of grass and straw which hit them with such force that they were driven into the flesh.

Many were struck down by a combination of the heat and the blast. A group of schoolgirls was working on the roof of a building, removing tiles as the structure was being demolished for a firebreak. Thus completely exposed, they were doubly hurt, burned and then blown to the ground. So quickly did the blast follow the heat that for many they seemed to come together. One man, knocked sprawling when the blast blew in his window, looked up from the floor to see a wood-and-paper screen across the room burning briskly.

Heat and blast together started and fed fires in thousands of places within a few seconds, thus instantly rendering useless the painfully constructed firebreaks. In some spots the ground itself seemed to spout fire, so numerous were the flickering little jets of flame spontaneously ignited by the radiant heat. The city's fire stations were crushed or burned along with everything else, and two-thirds of Hiroshima's firemen were killed or wounded. Even if it had been left intact, the fire department could have done little or nothing to save the city. Not only were there too many fires, but the blast had broken open the city's water mains in seventy thousand places, so there was no pressure. Between them, blast and fire destroyed every single building within an area of almost five square miles around the zero point. Although the walls of thirty structures still stood, they were no more than empty shells.

After heat, blast, and fire, the people of Hiroshima had still other ordeals ahead of them. A few minutes after the explosion, a strange rain began to fall. The raindrops were as big as marbles — and they were black. This frightening phenomenon resulted from the vaporization of moisture in the fireball and condensation in the cloud that spouted up from it. As the cloud, carrying water vapor and the pulverized dust of Hiroshima, reached colder air at higher altitudes, the moisture condensed and fell out as rain. There was not enough to put out the fires, but there was enough of this "black rain" to heighten the bewilderment and panic of people already unnerved by what had hit them.

After the rain came a wind — the great "fire wind" — which blew back in toward the center of the catastrophe, increasing in force as the air over Hiroshima grew hotter and hotter because of the great fires. The wind blew so hard that it uprooted huge trees in the parks where survivors were collecting. It whipped up high waves on the rivers of Hiroshima and drowned many who had gone into the water in an attempt to escape from the heat and flames around them. Some of those who drowned had been pushed into the rivers when the crush of fleeing people overflowed the bridges, making fatal bottlenecks of the only escape routes from the stricken islands. Thousands of people were simply fleeing, blindly and without an objective except to get out of the city. Some in the suburbs, seeing them come, thought at first they were Negroes, not Japanese, so blackened were their skins. The refugees could not explain what had burned them. "We saw the flash," they said, "and this is what happened."

One of those who struggled toward a bridge was Nukushina, the wine seller turned fireman whose life had been saved by the big office safes in his house just over a half mile from "zero," the point over which the bomb exploded. Leaning on his stick, he limped to the Sumiyoshi bridge a few hundred yards away, where, with unusual foresight, he kept a small boat

Their homes destroyed, city dwellers huddle on the Miyuki Bridge near the heart of Hiroshima. After the heat of the explosion came the "black rain," with drops as big as marbles, and then the "fire wind." Swept with conflagration, Hiroshima grew hotter and hotter.

Many refugees, attempting to escape the heat, drowned in the rivers, and the "crush of fleeing people overflowed the bridges, making fatal bottlenecks of the only escape routes." (U.N. Photo by Yoshito Matsushige)

tied up, loaded with fresh water and a little food, ready for any possible emergency.

"I found my boat intact," he recalled later, "but it was already filled with other desperate victims. As I stood on the bridge wondering what to do next, black drops of rain began to splatter down. The river itself and the river banks were teeming with horrible specimens of humans who had survived and come seeking safety to the river."

Fortunately for Nukushina, another boat came by, operated by a friend who offered to take him on board.

"With his assistance, I climbed into the boat. At that time, they pointed out to me that my intestines were dangling from my stomach but there was nothing I could do about it. My clothes, boots and everything were blown off my person, leaving me with only my loincloth. Survivors swimming in the river shouted for help, and as we leaned down to pull them aboard, the skin from their arms and hands literally peeled off into our hands.

"A fifteen- or sixteen-year-old girl suddenly popped up alongside our boat and as we offered her our hand to pull her on board, the front of her face suddenly dropped off as though it were a mask. The nose and other facial features suddenly dropped off with the mask, leaving only a pink, peachlike face front with holes where the eyes, nose and mouth used to be. As the head dropped under the surface, the girl's black hair left a swirling black eddy. . . ."

Here Nukushina mercifully lost consciousness. He came to five hours later as he was being transferred into a launch that carried him, with other wounded, to an emergency first-aid station set up on the island of Ninoshima in the harbor. There he found safety, but no medical care. Only twenty-eight doctors were left alive and able to work in a city of a quarter million people, fully half of whom were casualties.

When Hayano Susukida tried to get up off the ground onto which she and the other members of her tile-salvaging labor gang had been thrown, she thought she was going to die. Her whole back, bared by the blast, burned and stung when she moved. But the thought of her four-year-old daughter Kazuko, who had been evacuated from the city after Hayano's husband was sent overseas and the family home had been marked for destruction in the firebreak program, made her try again. This time she got to her feet and staggered home. The blast had not leveled her house, about a mile and a quarter from the zero point, and the fire had not yet reached it. Hurriedly she stuffed a few things — a bottle of vegetable oil, some mosquito netting, two quilts, a small radio — into an old baby carriage, and started wheeling it toward the nearest bomb shelter. After going a few feet, she had to carry the carriage, for the street was choked with debris. She reached the shelter and passed the oil around to those inside, using the last of it to salve her own burns, which had not blistered or peeled but were nevertheless strangely penetrating and painful. She wondered what time it was. Her wrist watch was gone, so she walked home again to get her alarm clock. It was still running; it showed a little after ten. Back at the shelter, she just sat and waited. At noon someone handed out a few rice balls. As the survivors ate, an Army truck miraculously appeared and carried them to the water front, just beyond the edge of the bomb's destruction. Then they were ferried over to the emergency hospital on Ninoshima Island.

Dr. Imagawa, a little further from the center of the blast, was not seriously injured, although he was cut by flying glass in a number of places. His first reaction was annoyance. His clothes were in tatters, and he wondered how he would find the new pair of shoes which he had left at his patient's front door. Helping the small boy down off the five-foot rubble pile that had been the sickroom, he asked the youngster to take him to the front door. Oddly enough, they could not even find where the front of the house had been. Imagawa, much to his disgust, was out a new pair of shoes. At an artesian well with a pump that was still operating, he washed as best he could and set out for suburban Furue where his wife and children should be. He stopped frequently in response to appeals for help from the injured. One was a woman who wandered aimlessly in the street holding her bare breast, which had been split open. She pleaded with him to tell her whether she would live. The doctor, although positive she could not survive, assured her that a mere breast injury would not be fatal. Later, he drew water for a score of wounded from another well pump. Down the street, a trolley car burned briskly. Finally he got clear of the city and climbed the hill to Furue, where he found his family safe and uninjured. The walls of the house had cracked, in some places fallen, but his wife and the two little children had escaped injury, while the oldest girl had walked home from school without a scratch after the blast. The doctor ate, washed thoroughly, painted his cuts with iodine and worked till dark with his wife cleaning up their house. That evening the somewhat sybaritic physician sat down to dinner and then relaxed, as he had done the night before in Hiroshima — twenty-four hours and an age earlier — over a few cups of wine.

The doctor sipping his wine that night had one thing in common with Mrs. Susukida and Michiyoshi Nukushina, both lying injured and untended in the emergency hospital on Ninoshima Island. None of them knew what it was that had destroyed their city. Nor did they yet have either time or inclination to wonder.

But others, outside Hiroshima, were anxiously trying to find out what the *Enola Gay* had dropped on the city. The search for information was a frustrating one.

At first there had been no indication that anything unusual had happened in Hiroshima. A moment after 8:16 A.M., the Tokyo control operator of the Japanese Broadcasting Corporation noticed that his telephone line to the radio station in Hiroshima had gone dead. He tried to re-establish his connection, but found that he could not get a call through to the western city.

Twenty minutes later the men in the railroad signal center in Tokyo realized that the mainline telegraph had stopped working. The break seemed to be just north of Hiroshima. Reports began to come in from stations near Hiroshima that there had been some kind of an explosion in the city. The railroad signalmen forwarded the messages to Army General Headquarters.

It was almost ten o'clock when Ryugen Hosokawa, managing editor of the *Asahi* vernacular newspaper in Tokyo, received a telephone call at his home. It was the office, reporting that Hiroshima had "almost completely collapsed" as the result of bombing by enemy planes. Hosokawa hurried to the office and sifted through the reports collected by *Asahi's* relay room. Every one of them sounded to him like something quite different from any previous bombing. This must have been caused, he thought to himself, by very unusual bombs.

At about the same time Major Tosaku Hirano, a staff officer of the II Army Corps, was in General Headquarters in Tokyo. He had come up from Hiroshima a week earlier to report on the status of military supplies in the port city, and had been scheduled to fly back on Sunday. But he had put his departure off for a day or two and thus was still in the capital.

Now his telephone rang. It was a call from Central Command Headquarters in Osaka, an installation under the control of the II Army Corps in Hiroshima, reporting that its communications to Hiroshima and points west had failed.

Tokyo GHQ tried several times to raise the Hiroshima communications center, in the earth-and-concrete bunker next to the moat of the old castle, but could not get through. There was no explanation. The succession of reports from the radio network, from the railroad signal center, from *Asahi's* newsroom and from Osaka indicated that something serious had happened, but no one could find out what it was.

Then, shortly after 1 P.M., General Headquarters finally heard from the II Army Corps. The message was short but stunning: "Hiroshima has been annihilated by one bomb and fires are spreading."

This flash came not from Corps Headquarters but from the Army shipping depot on the Hiroshima water front, which was outside the blast area and was not reached by the fire that followed. There was considerable damage at the shipping depot, something in the neighborhood of 30 per cent, but officers there were able to get a message out as far as Kure, where the naval station relayed it to Tokyo. There was no word at all from the II Army Corps Headquarters at the old castle in the northern part of town.

Reports continued to trickle in. By the middle of the afternoon, the Army knew that only three enemy planes had been over Hiroshima when the bomb exploded. It had been told that two of these did not drop any bombs. This information supported the startling assertion in the first flash that there had been only one bomb exploded. Something very big, and very frightening, had hit Hiroshima.

In mid-afternoon the managing editors of the five

big Tokyo newspapers, plus their counterpart in the Domei news agency, were called to the office of the government Information and Intelligence Agency, which had charge of press and radio censorship. An Army press officer addressed the little group of newsmen:

"We believe that the bomb dropped on Hiroshima is different from an ordinary one. However, we have inadequate information now, and we intend to make some announcement when proper information has been obtained. Until we issue such an announcement, run the news in an obscure place in your papers and as one no different from one reporting an ordinary air raid on a city."

In other words, the lid was on. The Army already had a strong suspicion that the Hiroshima bomb might be an atomic weapon. Japanese Naval intelligence had reported U.S. work on the bomb in late 1944, noting the interest of the American government in buying up all available pitchblende (uranium ore). Thus, although the best scientists in Japan had agreed that there was no chance of the United States producing a fission bomb in less than three to five years, there was now immediate suspicion that an atomic bomb had fallen. But the Army, anxious to keep the war going so it could fight a showdown hand-to-hand battle with the Americans on Japanese soil, was determined to withhold the news from the Japanese people as long as it could.

The editors protested mildly, but the decision stood. At six o'clock that evening, the radio gave the people of Japan their first hint that Hiroshima had been chosen for a place in history as the spot where man first proved he could tear apart the basic structure of his world. A listener, however, would have been hard put to deduce the true story from the first news item as it was read:

A few B-29s hit Hiroshima city at 8:20 A.M. August 6, and fled after dropping incendiaries and bombs. The extent of the damage is now under survey.

This cryptic item was repeated several times between six and nine o'clock without further explanation. On the nine o'clock program in Osaka, the sound of the musical chime that signaled the switch from national to local news was followed by this item:

An announcement by the Osaka railway bureau in regard to changes in various transportation organs and changes in handling of passenger baggage:

First of all, the government lines. Regarding the down train, trains from Osaka will turn back from Mihara on the Sanyo line. From Mihara to Kaitichi, the trains will take the route around Kure. . . .

Mihara was about halfway from Osaka to Hiroshima. Kaitichi was on the southeastern edge of Hiroshima. Trains headed there from Osaka on the main line ordinarily ran through the Hiroshima yards and station before swinging back to the smaller community.

The morning *Asahi* in Tokyo on August 7 carried a long front-page story with a sizable headline reporting "Small and Medium Cities Attacked by 400 B-29s." At the end of this story, there was a four-line item tacked on. It read:

Hiroshima Attacked by Incendiary Bombs
Hiroshima was attacked August 6th by two B-29 planes, which dropped incendiary bombs.

The planes invaded the city around 7:50 A.M. It seems that some damage was caused to the city and its vicinity.

Those who survived in Hiroshima still did not know what it was that had struck them so viciously the day before. They did not have much time for thinking about it. Merely keeping alive was a full-time job. Some thought, as they fled the burning city, that the Americans had deluged their homes with "Molotov flower baskets," as the unhappily familiar incendiary clusters were nicknamed. Others, sniffing the air and detecting a strong "electric smell," decided that some kind of poison gas had been dropped. Another explanation was that a magnesium powder had been sprayed on the city, exploding wherever it fell on trolley wires and other exposed electrical conductors.

The prefectural government did what it could to bring order in the city. Somehow almost two hundred policemen were found for duty on August 7. They set to work, with whatever help they could commandeer, to clear the streets of bodies and debris. Police stations became emergency food depots, doling out hastily gathered supplies of rice, salt, pickled radishes, matches, canned goods, candles, straw sandals, and toilet paper.

The governor of Hiroshima prefecture, Genshin Takano, issued a proclamation:

People of Hiroshima Prefecture: Although damage is great, we must remember that this is war. We must feel absolutely no fear. Already plans are being drawn up for relief and restoration measures. . . .

We must not rest a single day in our war effort. . . . We must bear in mind that the annihilation of the stubborn enemy is our road to revenge. We must subjugate all difficulties and pain, and go forward to battle for our Emperor.

But most people in Hiroshima, if they could overcome their pain on this second day of the atomic age, were more concerned with finding their loved ones than with battling for their Emperor.

Yuko Yamaguchi, waiting out the war in the rented suburban farmhouse while her husband served overseas in the Army, was unhurt. So were her three little children. But her father-in-law, who had driven into the city Sunday for the meeting of his gas company board of directors, and her mother-in-law, who had left early Monday morning to fetch more supplies from their requisitioned city house, had not been heard from since the bomb fell. Yuko had had no word, either, from her own parents.

So at 6:30 this Tuesday morning, she left her children and set out for the city, walking the whole way because the suburban rail lines were not running. It was a long walk. By the time she reached the Red Cross Hospital, where she thought her in-laws might have been taken, it was noon.

Yuko did not find her husband's parents there. But, by sheerest chance, she found her own father, lying untended on the floor with an ugly wound in the back of his head. He begged his grief-stricken daughter for some water. When she did her best and filled a broken cup with stagnant water from a nearby pond, the delirious eye specialist was furious, insisting that ice and a slice of lemon be added to make it more palatable. Somehow, she found both in the wrecked hospital kitchen and made him as comfortable as possible. Then she started through the littered, jammed wards and halls to search for her other relatives. Again she found no trace of her in-laws, but at five o'clock she came on her own mother, lying unconscious, her face smashed almost beyond recognition and her intestines bared by a savage stomach wound.

Daughter dragged mother through the corridors to her father's side so the two could at least be together. There was little enough time. Near dusk the mother died, and Yuko had to carry the body outside, build a crude pyre and cremate it herself. At about dawn her father also died. This time, there were enough other corpses on hand so the hospital arranged a makeshift mass cremation, and Yuko left. She spent the day searching again for her husband's parents, but there was no trace of them, and she finally walked home to the hills to join her children. It was to be more than a month before she found any trace of her in-laws. Then she got only the stub of a commutation ticket bearing her mother-in-law's name, recovered from the wreckage of the train she had been riding at 8:16 A.M. Monday. A few charred bones uncovered still later in the burned-out office of the gas company president were the only trace ever found of her father-in-law.

Some who survived seemed to accept with stoicism

the death of their loved ones. Miho Sakamoto, who with her husband's parents had escaped the blast and fire because their home was protected by the city's only high hill, was told on August 7 that her husband's military unit had been completely wiped out. She shed no tears and showed no emotion. Four days later, she visited the ruins of the building in which he had died, found a bent ash tray which she recognized as his and brought it home. That night, she seemed in good spirits when she went upstairs to the room she had shared with her Tsuneo. The next morning she did not come down to breakfast. Her mother-in-law found her lying in front of a little altar, the ash tray in front of her beside a photograph of her dead husband, the razor with which she had cut her throat still clutched in her hand. She left a note of apology to "My Honorable Father and Mother":

What I am about to do, I do not do on sudden impulse; nor is it due to temporary agitation. It is a mutual vow exchanged with my husband while he still lived. This is the road to our greatest happiness and we proceed thereon. Like a bird which has lost one wing, we are crippled birds who cannot go through life without one another. There is no other way. Please, do not bewail my fate. Somewhere both of us will again be living happily together as we have in the past. . . . My honorable Tsuneo must be anxiously awaiting me and I must rush to his side.

Sixteen-year-old Junichiro Susukida, at his factory-school dormitory in Otake, sixteen miles west of Hiroshima, had seen the fireball and the great cloud that rose over the city Monday morning. When the first refugees arrived with the news that the city had been badly hit, he was one of many students who demanded permission to go to their homes, and he was one of five finally allowed to go into the city to contact authorities at the main school building and seek news of the students' families.

By the time they reached Miya-jima, on the southwestern edge of the city, the students could see the fires still burning in the bright late afternoon. As they came closer, they began to realize the full extent of the calamity. It was dark before the boys reached their home neighborhood and began their search for relatives. Junichiro, though unable to find either his mother or younger brother, did at last encounter neighbors who told him his brother had survived, though wounded, and had been taken to the home of other relatives in Fuchu. He could learn nothing about his mother, however, and finally headed back to his dormitory in Otake. Dead tired when he arrived at 2 A.M., he was nevertheless too distraught to sleep. He sat in the school auditorium and incongruously played the piano until fatigue finally subdued his nerves just before dawn on Tuesday, August 7.

Junichiro was not the only one who did not sleep that night. In Tokyo, the truth about Hiroshima was beginning to be revealed in ways that made it clear that the facts could not be kept from the people of Japan much longer.

A little before midnight on the sixth, the Tokyo office of Domei, the quasi-governmental news agency that served the whole nation, much as the Associated Press or Reuters do in the West, received a bulletin from Okayama prefecture, just east of Hiroshima. It was followed by a longer dispatch: the first eye-witness account of the bombing by a professional newsman.

Bin Nakamura, subchief of Domei's Hiroshima bureau, had been eating breakfast in his suburban garden when the bomb's explosion lifted him off the straw mat on which he was sitting and sent a wave of "immense" heat washing over his face. Once Nakamura discovered that the concussion and heat had not been caused by the nearby explosion of a "blockbuster" — his first reaction had been the typical one — he went to work as a reporter. On his bicycle and on foot, he spent the day in the city and talking to the refugees who streamed through his suburb. Then, at 10 P.M., like the experienced press-association man he was, he found communications at the suburban Haramura radio station and dictated a story to Okayama, the only point he could reach. In his dispatch, he said there was no way to tell what kind of a bomb had caused such havoc.

But before the night was much older the editors of Domei, and the leaders of Japan, had a way of telling much more about the bomb. In Saitama prefecture outside Tokyo, Domei operated a big monitoring station where nearly fifty workers, many of them Nisei girls born in the United States, listened to broadcasts from American stations. About 1 A.M. on the 7th of August (noon on the 6th in Washington, D.C.), Hideo Kinoshita, chief of the monitoring room, was awakened by the Japanese youth who had charge of the operation that night. The boy reported that U.S. stations were all broadcasting a statement by President Truman, describing the weapon that had been dropped on Hiroshima as "an atomic bomb." Kinoshita listened to the account and the boy's explanation of what "atomic bomb" might mean. Then he quickly called his own superior, Saiji Hasegawa, Domei's foreign news chief. Hasegawa was asleep in his hotel. When he was told of an "atomic bomb," he had no idea what it was, but although he was irritated at being awakened he hustled to his office. When he saw the text transcripts that were beginning to come through from the Saitama monitors, he was glad he had come to work. He reached for his telephone and called Hisatsune Sakomizu, chief secretary of the cabinet.

Sakomizu sleepily answered his bedside telephone, then came suddenly wide awake as he listened to the Domei executive. He already knew, from the first confused reports on the 6th, that the Americans had used some kind of new weapon. Now, learning that it was an atomic bomb, something the cabinet had discussed briefly almost a year earlier, he knew it meant just one thing: the war was over.

Sakomizu quickly called Prime Minister Suzuki, with whom he had been working in the effort to ar-

range a peace settlement by negotiation. They knew immediately, he said later,

. . . that if the announcement were true, no country could carry on a war. Without the atomic bomb it would be impossible for any country to defend itself against a nation which had the weapon. The chance had come to end the war. It was not necessary to blame the military side, the manufacturing people, or anyone else — just the atomic bomb. It was a good excuse.

The Army, however, was unwilling to accept this attitude, despite the urgings of the peace group that the bomb gave military leaders a chance to save face by blaming the "backwardness of scientific research" for Japan's inability to counter the new American bomb. The generals, sitting in an emergency cabinet meeting on the seventh, pointedly recalled an old Japanese legend about an Army commander who became a laughingstock because he mistook the fluttering of a flight of birds for the sound of the approaching enemy and fled. They argued that the bomb was not atomic but was merely a huge conventional projectile. They flatly refused Foreign Minister Togo's proposal to take up for immediate consideration the possibility of surrender on the terms of the Potsdam ultimatum, and insisted on keeping the Truman atomic statement from the Japanese people until the Army could conduct an "investigation" on the ground at Hiroshima.

The military had already started such a check. Major Hirano, the staff officer from the Hiroshima headquarters whose desire to spend a couple of extra nights in Tokyo had saved his life, called Yoshio Nishina, the nation's ranking nuclear scientist. He told him of the Truman claims and asked him to ride down to Hiroshima in his little liaison plane to investigate the matter. Nishina agreed to make the trip. The scientist was already pretty well convinced, on the basis of Hirano's report and further excerpts from the Truman statement given him a few minutes later by a reporter, that the bomb had indeed been the fission weapon which he and his colleagues had believed the United States could not manufacture so quickly. Truman's claim of a destructive power equal to twenty thousand tons of TNT coincided exactly with theoretical calculations made recently by one of Nishina's laboratory associates on the yield of an atomic bomb.

But the Army high command was keeping the lid on tight. When the Tokyo managing editors met again with the Information Agency censors that afternoon, they all had seen the text of Truman's statement. But they got nowhere with requests for permission to print it. The Army grudgingly allowed use of the phrase "a new-type bomb," but not the word "atomic." The editors argued hard this time, but to no avail. The end result of the wrangle was this communiqué from Imperial General Headquarters at 3:30 P.M. on Tuesday, August 7:

1   A considerable amount of damage was caused by a few B-29s which attacked Hiroshima August 6th.
2   It seems that the enemy used a new-type bomb in the raid. Investigation of the effects is under way.

By evening, the newsmen were stretching the Army embargo as far as they could. A home service broadcast at 7 P.M. amplified the cryptic communiqué by adding that "a considerable number of houses were reduced to ashes and fires broke out in various parts of the city . . . investigations are now being made with regard to the effectiveness of the bomb, which should not be regarded as light." The broadcast went on to attack the Americans for "inhuman and atrocious conduct" and to urge the Japanese not to be "misled" by "exaggerated propaganda" such as "an announcement regarding the use of a new-type bomb" by Truman.

One man who was not likely to be "misled" by any announcement that night was Major Hirano, who finally had started back to Hiroshima in his five-seater liaison plane late in the afternoon. He had arrived at the Tokyo airport with the hurriedly assembled team of investigators earlier in the day, but had been ordered to wait until afternoon to avoid the U.S. Navy fighter planes that were now operating over Japan daily. There was some top brass in the inspection group which apparently was not anxious to hasten the day of personal contact with American invaders. Thus it was almost seven in the evening when Hirano's plane came down over Hiroshima. It was still light, however, so he got the full picture with shocking suddenness:

Being a soldier, my eye had been inured to the effects of bombing by that time. But this was a different sight. *There were no roads in the wastes that spread below our eyes:* that was my first impression. In the case of a normal air raid, roads were still visible after it was over. But in Hiroshima, everything was flattened and all roads were undiscernibly covered with debris.

When Hirano stepped from his plane, the first person he saw was an Air Force officer who came out on the runway to meet the team from Tokyo. His face was marked by a sharp dividing line right down the middle. One side was smooth and unhurt. The other, the one that had been toward the explosion, was burned, blistered, blackened. The investigators picked their way through the city to the wreckage of II Army Corps headquarters. Nobody was there. They finally found what was left of the headquarters — a few officers holed up in a hillside cave. By the time they began their formal investigation the next morning, the men from Tokyo knew the truth anyway. Hirano, in fact, had known it the moment he caught sight of what was left of Hiroshima from his circling plane.

QUESTIONS TO CONSIDER

1.   What chance factors at Hiroshima added to the inherent destructiveness of the atomic bomb and pro-

duced more deaths and devastation than American scientists had expected?

2. What was the immediate reaction of the Japanese army and government to the news of what had happened at Hiroshima? Why was the true nature of the American attack kept from the Japanese people?

3. Discuss the responsibility of the Japanese high command for prolonging the war after the bombing of Hiroshima.

4. Given the present-day proliferation of atomic weapons, what lessons can we draw from the firsthand accounts of the Japanese who experienced the horrors at Hiroshima fifty years ago?

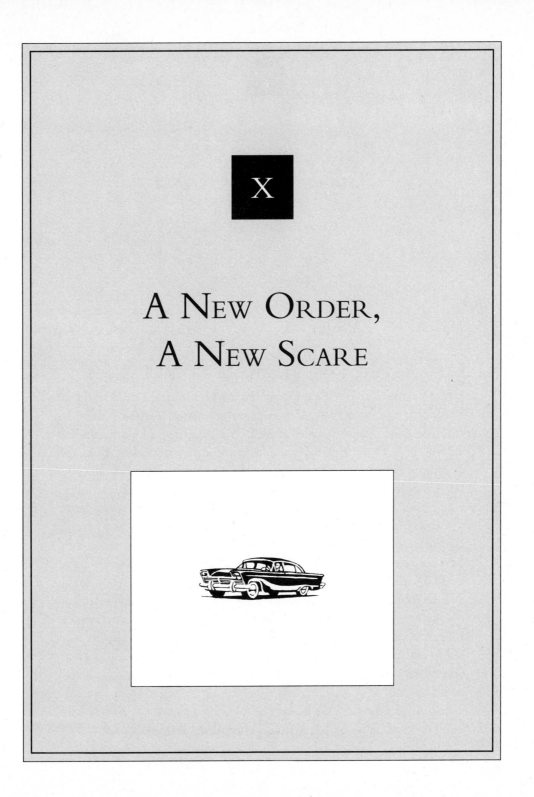

X

A New Order,
A New Scare

Truman vs. MacArthur

WALTER KARP

"We are going to win the war," Roosevelt declared after Pearl Harbor, "and we are going to win the peace that follows." The Allies won the war, but it was a victory without peace. For out of the muck and rubble of the Second World War emerged the Cold War between Russia and the West that threatened the very survival of humankind. The genesis of the Cold War (what Winston Churchill called "the Balance of Terror") went back to the early days of the Second World War and involved control of Eastern Europe. Russia and the Western Allies clashed over that area, and their rival strategies for the domination of Eastern Europe influenced most of the wartime conferences among the big three (the United States, Great Britain, and the Soviet Union). The West hoped to establish capitalistic regimes in Eastern Europe—regimes that might look to Russia for leadership but that would retain private ownership of land and factories and permit Western investment. It was an impossible program, for the massive Red Army overran Eastern Europe and Stalin vowed to maintain Soviet supremacy there. He did so not to export world communism but to ensure Russian security from the West—to make certain that no Western army could ever sweep through Poland and invade Russia as the Germans had done. The Soviet Union had lost a staggering 20 million people in the war against Germany; no other nation swept up in the war, not even Germany itself, had suffered such casualties. Dominating Eastern Europe, Soviet leaders hoped, would prevent such a catastrophe from ever happening again.

Once the Red Army occupied Eastern Europe, Roosevelt did the only thing he could do. At the Yalta Conference, held in February 1945, he acknowledged Soviet hegemony in the region but pressed Stalin to hold free elections in the countries he controlled. Mainly to hold the wartime alliance together, Stalin promised free elections for Eastern Europe. But obsessed as he was with Russian security, the Soviet boss never kept his promise, instead setting up Russian puppet states from the Baltic to the Adriatic.

The West felt betrayed. By the time Roosevelt died and Truman came to power, the United States and many of its allies increasingly saw Stalin as a mad and devious Marxist dictator out to spread communism across the globe. In the United States especially, a profound suspicion of Russia and world communism swept over Washington and the Truman White House. Unlike Roosevelt, who had tried to conciliate the Russians, Truman in 1947 adopted a get-tough containment policy designed to block Soviet expansion and save the "free world" from communism. The purpose of containment was not to overthrow the Soviet regime or invade the Soviet sphere but to prevent the Russians from expanding the influence of communism. To do that, the United States poured billions of dollars in aid into Greece, Turkey, and Western Europe and extended American military power around the world.

From 1947 on, containment formed the basis of United States foreign policy. Containment dictated that the United States get tough with China, too, after the Communists took over there in 1949 and drove Chiang Kai-shek's Nationalist Chinese into exile on Formosa (now known as Taiwan). The fall of China whipped up a storm of outrage and fears of communism in the United States. In this sinister turn of events, Americans once again saw the evil hand of Joseph Stalin. Then in 1950 came another shock. China's neighbor, Korea, was divided at the 38th parallel between a Communist regime in the north and a pro–Western government in the south. That June, North Korean forces invaded South Korea in what Washington viewed as an act of naked Communist aggression instigated by the Kremlin. Under the auspices of the United Nations, Truman sent in American troops, who in a few months drove the North Koreans back across the 38th parallel. By September, however, Truman had changed the purpose of the war: instead of simply maintaining the integrity of South Korea, he resolved to invade North Korea and liberate it from Communist rule. When the Chinese threatened to enter the war, Truman met with General Douglas MacArthur, commander of the United Nations forces, and asked the general what the chances of Chinese intervention were. "Very little," MacArthur replied, and he predicted the fighting would be over by Thanksgiving.

Extremely confident, MacArthur crossed into North Korea and drove to the Yalu River, which separated North Korea from China. That was enough for the Red Chinese: 400,000 of them crossed the Yalu and inflicted on MacArthur one of the worst military defeats in American history, sending him in pell-mell retreat back toward the 38th parallel. With that, Truman again changed the purpose of the war: he gave up fighting to liberate North Korea and fell back on the original United States goal of simply ensuring the sovereignty of South Korea.

MacArthur vehemently objected to Truman's change of policy and released public statements saying so. Obsessed with driving the Chinese out of North Korea and avenging his defeat at their hands, the general insisted that the United States must fight to win this war, even if that meant bombing Chinese bases in Manchuria—"privileged sanctuaries," he called them—and bombing and blockading China itself.

Truman and his advisers were enraged. It was rank insubordination for a general to criticize in public the policy of his commander in chief. Worse still, MacArthur was advocating all-out war with China—and in the process gaining an enormous following at home, where Truman's limited war aims were increasingly unpopular. If the United States bogged down in an unlimited Asian war, Washington feared it would encourage Soviet aggression in Europe. General Omar Bradley summed up the administration position when he asserted that a full-scale conflict with China would be "the wrong war at the wrong time with the wrong enemy."

The Truman-MacArthur imbroglio posed the severest test that civilian control of the military ever faced in this country. So argues Walter Karp in the stimulating selection that follows. In it, Karp discusses the conflict between the president and the general in the context of the domestic and foreign tensions of the Cold War. He is critical of both Truman and MacArthur, but he makes clear what would have happened if the general had successfully forced his policies on the civilian authorities.

GLOSSARY

ACHESON, DEAN   Truman's Secretary of State who helped create the North Atlantic Treaty Organizaton and implemented Truman's limited war in Korea; the Republicans accused Acheson of harboring communist sympathies, blaming him for the fall of China and the stalemate in Korea.

BRADLEY, GENERAL OMAR   World War II hero and chairman of the Joint Chiefs of Staff; summoned before a Senate hearing, he and his colleagues defended Truman's limited war in Korea and his firing of MacArthur.

MARSHALL, GENERAL GEORGE C. Secretary of State, 1947–1949, and Secretary of Defense, 1950–1951; he also told the Senate hearing that Truman was right in dismissing MacArthur and in waging a limited war in Korea.

TAFT, SENATOR ROBERT   Republican leader from Ohio who accused the Democratic party of being "soft on communism" and opposed Truman's limited-war strategy in Korea.

At 1:00 A.M. on the morning of April 11, 1951, a tense band of Washington reporters filed into the White House newsroom for an emergency press conference. Hastily summoned by the White House switchboard, they had no idea of what was to come. The Truman administration, detested by millions, had grown hesitant, timid, and unpredictable. The Korean War, so boldly begun ten months before, had degenerated into a "limited war" with no discernible limit, a bloody stalemate. Some reporters, guessing, thought they were going to hear about a declaration of war, that the administration was ready to carry the fighting into China and bring it to a swift and victorious end. That was what General Douglas MacArthur, supreme commander of U.S. and United Nations forces in the Far East, had passionately been urging for months, ever since Chinese communist troops had sent his armies reeling in retreat from the Yalu River.

President Truman did not appear in the newsroom. His press secretary merely handed out copies of three terse presidential statements. At 1:03 A.M. the great wire-service networks were carrying the news to the ends of the earth. The President had not adopted the victory plans of America's greatest living general. Instead he had relieved him of all his commands, "effective at once." The President had acted because "General of the Army Douglas MacArthur is unable to give his wholehearted support to the policies of the United States and the United Nations."

With that announcement President Truman precipitated perhaps the most convulsive popular outburst in American history and the severest test which civilian control of the military has ever had to face in this republic. On April 11 there was little reason to believe that the faltering President would triumph over his vaunting general in the clash that must ensue.

From Walter Karp "Truman vs. MacArthur," *American Heritage,* April/May, 1984, Vol. 35, No. 3 © by Forbes Inc. Reprinted by permission of *American Heritage* Magazine, a division of Forbes Inc.

Even before the news broke, the American people were upset. "A vast impatience, a turbulent bitterness, a rancor akin to revolt" coursed through the body politic, a contemporary historian observed. Dislike of communism, once a matter of course in America, had boiled into a national frenzy, devouring common prudence, common sense, and common decency. It was a time when school textbooks urged children to report suspicious neighbors to the FBI "in line with American tradition," a time when an entire city flew into a rage on learning that the geography lesson printed on children's candy wrappers dared to describe Russia as the "largest country in the world." Americans saw conspiracy in every untoward event: abroad, "Kremlin plots to conquer the world"; at home, communist plots to "take over the government." In April 1951 a substantial part of the citizenry believed that the secretary of state, Dean Acheson, was a "dupe" of the Kremlin, that the secretary of defense, George C. Marshall, a five-star general, was a "front man" for traitors in government. And now it seemed that a great general, World War II's most glamorous hero, had been mercilessly broken for daring to call for victory in Korea.

On the morning of April 11, only Western Union's rules of propriety kept Congress from being deluged with furious obscenity. "Impeach the B who calls himself President," read one telegram typical of those pouring into Washington at an unprecedented rate — 125,000 within forty-eight hours. "Impeach the little ward politician stupidity from Kansas City," read another, voicing the contempt millions now felt for the "plucky Harry" of just a few years before. The letters and telegrams, the White House admitted, were running 20 to 1 against the President. So were the telephone calls that jangled in every newsroom and radio studio. In countless towns the President was hanged in effigy. Across the country flags flew at half-mast or upside down. Angry signs blossomed on houses: "To hell with the Reds and Harry Truman."

Wherever politicians met that day, the anger in the streets was echoed and amplified. In Los Angeles the

In mid-October 1950 President Truman met with General Douglas MacArthur at Wake Island to discuss the planned assault on North Korea. The invasion was a costly failure, but six months later MacArthur was still promoting his plans for an all-out war with China, expressly contradicting the limited military aims of his commander in chief. Truman relieved him of his command. MacArthur's emotional campaign to gain support from the American people was eventually unsuccessful, and the constitutional principle of civilian command of the military was upheld. (U.S. Army, Courtesy Harry S Truman Library)

city council adjourned for the day "in sorrowful contemplation of the political assassination of General MacArthur." In Michigan the state legislature solemnly noted that "at 1:00 A.M. of this day, World Communism achieved its greatest victory of a decade in the dismissal of General MacArthur." On the Senate floor in Washington, Republicans took turns denouncing the President: "I charge that this country today is in the hands of a secret inner coterie which is directed by agents of the Soviet Union. We must cut this whole cancerous conspiracy out of our Government at once," said William Jenner of Indiana. Tru-

man had given "the Communists and their stooges . . . what they always wanted — MacArthur's scalp." So spoke the country's fastest-rising politician, Richard Nixon. Only four senators — two Democrats and two Republicans — dared defend the President.

For most Republican leaders in Congress the popular hysteria was manna in the political desert. Their best men — Ohio's Robert Taft most conspicuously — had felt doomed to perpetual impotence, spurned by an electorate that still revered the memory, and supported the policies, of the late Franklin Roosevelt. Now they saw their chance. They were determined to discredit the Democratic party and its stumbling President. At a hasty meeting on the morning of MacArthur's dismissal, Republican congressional leaders came to a decision. They intended to use every political resource at their disposal to channel popular anger over MacArthur's recall into a mass revolt against "limited war," against President Truman and the ghost of the Roosevelt New Deal.

It was a reckless decision: exalting MacArthur over the President, as Harold Ickes, the old Bull Moose Republican, was to warn a few days later, would set a "precedent" that would "develop into a monstrosity" — an uncontrollable military.

Such, in truth, were the stakes now at hazard. In the four months preceding his dismissal, General MacArthur had transgressed the fundamental rule of civilian supremacy, a rule given its classic formulation in Lincoln's stern instructions to Grant: "You are not to decide, discuss or confer with anyone or ask political questions; such questions the President holds in his own hands, and will submit them to no military conferences or conventions." What MacArthur had done was to carry out a public political campaign designed to discredit the President's policies and compel the White House to follow his own. For that the President had ordered his recall. If that recall were to end by destroying the President, if MacArthur, backed by a wave of popular support, were to force his policies on the civil authority, then for all practical purposes civilian supremacy over the military would become a dead letter. Given such a precedent, what future President would dare dismiss a popular general in wartime for publicly challenging his authority?

When the Republican meeting broke up at 10:00 A.M., the press was informed of the plan to exalt the general over the President. Republicans intended to demand a full-dress investigation of the President's war policies. That was remarkable enough considering that it was wartime. The second element in their plan, however, was more than remarkable. It had no precedent in our history. Republicans intended (if Democratic votes were forthcoming) to invite General MacArthur to address a joint session of Congress, the most august assembly the United States can provide. In the well of the House of Representatives, where only a handful of foreign statesmen and homecoming heroes had ever been allowed to speak, a rebellious, contumacious general was to be given his chance to defend his cause against the President of the United States.

What would MacArthur do? In Germany, General Eisenhower, supreme commander of Allied forces in Europe, expressed the sentiments of a good many Americans. He hoped the seventy-one-year old general, his onetime superior, would drift quietly into retirement. "I would not like to see acrimony," Eisenhower remarked somewhat wistfully to a reporter. In fact, there was no chance that MacArthur would not carry his fight to the country.

By any standard General MacArthur was an awesome and prodigious figure. He possessed an uncommonly powerful intellect, one sharpened by vast erudition, intense meditation, and an extraordinary facility with words. He was utterly fearless, unshakably self-possessed, and relentlessly willful. At the White House the President had shrunk from confronting him for months. Moreover, MacArthur's strengths were magnified by the aura surrounding him. He was dramatic, compelling, aloof, and imperious, qualities he himself had cultivated with all the theatrical arts at his command. What was to govern his conduct in the ensuing months, however, were

not his great gifts but a bitter flaw in his character — a blind, all-consuming vanity.

The general was vain in small ways; the famous MacArthur sunglasses, for example, disguised the prosaic fact of myopia. He was vain in his choice of associates; his entourage consisted of toadies and idolators. Vanity even colored his conceptions of grand strategy; the center of the world for MacArthur was always the military theater under his command. During World War II his military colleagues used to say the general had a bad case of "localitis." Vanity sometimes drove him to the borders of paranoia: a lifetime of triumphs could not efface his belief that homefront "cabals" were plotting his ruin, that "insidious forces" were stabbing him in the back. His worst enemies, MacArthur often said, had "always been behind me." Vanity led him, too, to that most perilous of convictions — an absolute faith in his own infallibility. Therein lay the crux of the matter, for that faith had been brutally assaulted five months earlier when MacArthur's armies, poised for victory near the Yalu River, had fallen into a colossal Chinese trap. On November 24, 1950, America's greatest military strategist had presided over one of the worst defeats in the history of American arms. From that day forward General MacArthur was a man thirsting for vindication and vengeance. To drive the Chinese out of North Korea had become a fixed and obsessive goal. To break the administration that stood in his way had now become, of necessity, his political object. "He did not want facts or logic," as a longtime admirer, Carlos Romulo of the Philippines, was to put it after an interview with the general. "He wanted salve for his wounded pride." That was a dangerous motive, indeed, for a general who had become, overnight, the second most powerful man in America. . . .

On Sunday, April 15, newspaper headlines told of MacArthur's "triumphant goodby" from Japan, of the crowds lining the streets, of the Japanese dignitaries on hand for the departure. The triumphal progress had now begun, its ultimate destination the nation's capital, where, at exactly 12:30 P.M. on the nineteenth, it was now announced, the general would enter the House of Representatives and throw down his gauntlet to the President. Bulletins flashing over the nation's radios marked the progress of the general's plane. At 1:00 A.M. Eastern time on Monday, the *Bataan* passed over Wake Island; first stop, Honolulu. If the general was in official disgrace, there was no sign of it: at the Hawaiian capital MacArthur and his wife and thirteen-year-old son stopped over for twenty-four hours as the guest of Admiral Arthur W. Radford, commander in chief of America's naval forces in the Pacific. At Honolulu University the general received an honorary degree in civil law, an ironic honor considering that its recipient had by now convinced himself — as he was soon to say — that American generals had the constitutional right to say whatever they pleased in public regardless of the orders of their commander in chief. Far away in New York, the city fathers announced plans to greet the general with the biggest parade in the history of that city of ticker-tape acclamations.

On the evening of April 17 General MacArthur's plane touched down at San Francisco's airport, ending the general's fourteen-year absence from his country. At the airport ten thousand people, desperate for a glimpse of their hero, surged past police barricades, mobbing the general and his entourage. It was "an indescribable scene of pandemonium," one of MacArthur's aides recalled. Tens of thousands of automobiles jammed the roads for miles around, creating the worst traffic snarl in San Francisco's history. A half-million people lined the route from the airport to MacArthur's hotel, where a powerful police cordon alone kept the general from being trampled by his admirers. Twenty-eight hours later, at Washington's National Airport, pandemonium broke loose again with surging mobs, tumultuous cheers, and a battered police cordon trying to clear a space around the general, who remained, as always, calm and unruffled, the eye of the hurricane he had created.

At the White House the President took cold comfort from his professed belief that Americans were *not* hailing an insubordinate general nor embracing his "victory" policy but merely giving a belated welcome to the last World War II hero to return to America. Like the "joint meeting" of Congress, now just hours away, it was a distinction apparent to few.

At 12:31 P.M. on April 19 a record thirty million people tuned in their radios to hear General MacArthur address Congress, his countrymen, and the world. This was the moment every supporter of the President had dreaded. Truman's case for a limited war of attrition had not yet been effectively made. Half the country was not even aware that attrition was the chosen policy of the government. Even well-informed supporters of the President were not sure what the policy meant or why it was necessary. Now General MacArthur, backed by an adoring nation and armed with high gifts of intellect and eloquence, was about to speak against it.

"I address you with neither rancor nor bitterness in the fading twilight of life," the general began in his vibrant, well-modulated voice after the wild initial ovation had subsided. MacArthur devoted the first half of his speech to a lofty and lucid disquisition on the politics and destiny of the Orient. His object, he said, was to dispel the prevailing "unreality" of American thinking on the subject. His authority established, MacArthur proceeded to praise the administration for intervening in Korea — the only time that Democrats in the audience had a chance to applaud — and for attempting to drive the communists out of North Korea. That objective had lain in his grasp when the Chinese communists intervened in the struggle. "This created a new war and an entirely new situation." Yet the administration was not fighting that new war to win. It was not attempting to "defeat this new enemy as we had defeated the old." By confining the war against Chinese aggression to Korea, it was condemning the country to "prolonged indecision."

Yet the means to achieve victory were swift and sure. Three quite moderate military measures would drive the Chinese from the Korean peninsula: bombing China's "sanctuaries" in Manchuria; blockading the Chinese coast; unleashing Chiang Kai-shek's army, holed up in Formosa, for diversionary raids on the Chinese mainland. Such was MacArthur's plan "to bring hostilities to a close with the least possible delay." What was there to be said against it? "In war, indeed, there is no substitute for victory," said MacArthur, providing his supporters with their most potent slogan. "'Why,' my soldiers asked of me, 'surrender military advantages to an enemy in the field?'" MacArthur's voice fell to a whisper: "I could not answer." Why fight Red China without attempting to drive her from Korea? This was a policy of "appeasement," said the general, hurling the deadliest epithet of the day at the Truman administration. Moreover, said MacArthur, his plan to carry the war to the Chinese mainland had been supported by "our own Joint Chiefs of Staff." With that assertion Republicans in the House gave the speaker a thunderous standing ovation, for, in fact, it was the most devastating remark in MacArthur's entire speech. In the prevailing atmosphere of derangement and conspiracy it implied that victory in Korea had been snatched from America's grasp not by the military judgment of the Pentagon but by a mere, meddlesome civilian, the President of the United States. MacArthur's assertion also posed a challenge to the Joint Chiefs themselves: he was daring them to side with the President when, as he fully believed, their purely military judgment agreed with his own.

For close observers that was the real news of the hour, the story that made the headlines. What stirred the rest of the country, however, was MacArthur's lush, emotional peroration. He recalled the old barracks ballad that "proclaimed, most proudly, that 'Old soldiers never die. They just fade away.' And like the soldier of the ballad, I now close my military career and just fade away — an old soldier who tried to do his duty as God gave him the light to see that duty." And then in a hushed voice: "Good-bye."

Generals in the audience openly wept. Legislators hurled themselves at the departing general, virtually prostrating themselves at his feet. "It's disloyal not to agree with General MacArthur!" one senator shouted from the floor. "We have heard God speak today. God in the flesh, the voice of God," shouted Rep. Dewey Short of Missouri, who had been educated at Harvard, Oxford, and Heidelberg. The normally level-headed former President Herbert Hoover hailed MacArthur as the "reincarnation of St. Paul." Fury over his dismissal boiled up anew and newspaper offices again were besieged with vehement calls condemning the "traitorous" State Department and the "bankrupt haberdasher" who was "appeasing Red China." It boiled up, too, on the floor of the House. As one senator confided to a reporter later that day: "I have never feared more for the institutions of the country. I honestly felt that if the speech had gone on much longer there might have been a march on the White House."

MacArthur's powerful speech, a magniloquent contrast to the President's pawky little lectures, "visibly and profoundly shook" the President's supporters in Congress, as *The New York Times* reported. The President's cabinet, after watching MacArthur on a White House television set, sank into gloom, convinced that the general, in a single blow, had put a finish to the Truman administration. The welcoming parade for the general in New York City confirmed their worst fears.

MacArthur flew to the city on the evening of the nineteenth, settling into what was to be his home for the remaining thirteen years of his life: a palatial ten-room suite on the thirty-seventh floor of the Waldorf-Astoria. The hotel was to be the parade's point of departure. The general would be driven in an open car — the same that had carried General Eisenhower six years before — through Central Park, down to the Battery, up through the canyons of Wall Street, and homeward along Fifth Avenue — over nineteen miles in all. The triumphal progress was to begin at 11:00 A.M., but by dawn hundreds of thousands of people had already begun pouring into the city. By the time the general's motorcade had reached the financial district, some six million flag-waving enthusiasts were jamming the sidewalks, dwarfing Eisenhower's postwar parade and Lindbergh's almost legendary reception. Overhead in the bright, cloudless sky, airplanes spelled out "Welcome Home" in mile-long streamers. Shreds of paper fell in dense blizzards, covering people's feet to the ankles and darkening television screens for minutes at a time. As the general's car approached, the crowds craned hungrily forward, then burst into cheers, deafening in their volume, startling in their intensity. Not everyone shouted his acclaim. There were people who watched the general pass by in silence, faces rapt and grim, marking a cross on their breasts. New York, as MacArthur's bodyguard was to put it, had been turned into "a band of hysterical sheep" — hardbitten, cynical New York, stronghold of the Democratic party.

Late that afternoon, while the general was passing up howling Fifth Avenue, a popular demonstration of a different sort took place at a baseball park in the nation's capital. As the President and his entourage were about to leave Griffith Stadium — Truman had thrown out the traditional first ball of the year — he was met with a storm of boos. Republicans were now saying the choice before the country was "Truman or MacArthur"; on April 20, Americans seemed already to have made it.

In his struggle with MacArthur, the President faced severe handicaps, most of them self-inflicted. The political derangement of the country was to a large extent his own doing. Determined to arouse the nation to the menace of Soviet expansion, yet convinced that he governed an obstinately "isolationist" people, Truman had never scrupled to exaggerate every danger, to sound alarms, to decry in any communist move he opposed another step in the "Kremlin plot for world conquest." Moreover, he had constantly used the great World War II generals — MacArthur included — to defend his policies and shield him

from criticism. The results were inevitable. Because Truman had glorified the wisdom of the generals, he had weakened the civilian authority he was now forced to defend. Because he justified even prudent deeds with inflammatory words, it had become difficult to justify prudent deeds with prudent arguments — the sort of argument he was now forced to make.

The President's inept handling of the Korean War was the severest handicap of all. In June 1950 Truman had intervened to repel the North Korean invasion of South Korea, an essentially defensive objective. When North Korean armies began fleeing back beyond the thirty-eighth parallel, however, Truman made a momentous and disastrous decision. He directed General MacArthur to cross the parallel and liberate North Korea from communist control too. Thus it was Truman, not MacArthur, who had first defined victory in Korea as the extirpation of communism from the entire Korean peninsula. When four hundred thousand Chinese entered the fray, however, the administration changed its mind again. Without informing the electorate, Truman decided that liberating North Korea — victory — was a prize not worth the terrible risks involved. He was now content to confine the fighting to Korea until exhausted Chinese armies eventually decided to call it a day at the thirty-eighth parallel. The administration, in short, was fighting to restore Korea to the situation it had been in on the eve of the North Korean invasion — at the cost of sixty thousand American casualties by mid-April and with no truce in sight.

Such was the policy the administration now had to defend in the court of inflamed public opinion against the clarity and emotional force of MacArthur's crisp plan for "victory." In two major radio addresses, the President's first attempts to make a case for his policy proved ineffective. His two chief arguments simply lacked conviction. First, the bombing of Chinese supply lines would, he said, lead to a general war in Asia and possibly to World War III. Here a large majority of Americans simply preferred MacArthur's military judgment to the President's. Moreover, in citing the risks involved, Truman was compelled to argue that Korea was not all that important compared with the defense of Europe. The President, in effect, was belittling his own war, which did nothing to strengthen popular confidence in his judgment.

Truman's second argument was even less convincing. The stalemated war, he insisted, was already a resounding success. It had stopped in its tracks, said the President, the Kremlin's "carefully prepared plot for conquering all of Asia." It had "slowed down the timetable of conquest," he assured the country, invoking memories of Hitler's step-by-step conquest of Europe. Since the Kremlin "timetable" was entirely supposititious, the President could offer no evidence whatever of its alleged slowdown.

Republicans had no trouble tearing the President's speeches to shreds. They simply turned Truman's own Cold War propaganda against him. Time and again the administration had argued that "punishing aggression" in Korea was preventing World War III — more echoes of the Hitler years. If so, Republicans now argued, then why was the President unwilling to punish the Chinese aggressors. It was the President's "half-war" against Red China, not MacArthur's plan for victory, that was inviting World War III. As for the President's apparent willingness to settle for a truce at the thirty-eighth parallel, it would be a "sellout," a "super Munich."

Most of all, Republicans struck at the very notion of fighting a "limited war." It was, wrote Time, "an idea unique in world history, that it is wrong and dangerous to fight the enemy in any place not of the enemy's choosing." It meant sacrificing American lives on "an altar of futility." It meant giving the enemy "privileged sanctuaries" outside Korea from which to kill American boys more effectively. It "shocks our national sense of decency," said Senator Henry Cabot Lodge, himself no friend of MacArthur's. "Psychologically, no one will stand for it," said Senator Taft, sadly abandoning his lifelong opposition to excessive overseas commitments.

Keenly aware of his fading powers of persuasion,

Truman countered with dubious blows of his own. He "leaked" to The New York Times the secret White House notes of his October 15, 1950, meeting with MacArthur at Wake Island, a meeting in which, said the notes, MacArthur had confidently assured the President that there was "very little" chance of Chinese intervention in Korea. Stung for the first time, MacArthur retorted from the Waldorf that the administration, too, had misread Chinese intentions, although it had far greater intelligence resources than a mere theater commander possessed. This was quite true. Blaming MacArthur for disastrously misleading the President was grossly unfair, but "politics isn't beanbag," as Mr. Dooley had long before observed. A few days after the "leak," MacArthur once again demonstrated his extraordinary hold on his countrymen. A flying trip to the Midwest on April 26 brought in the latest returns from the grass roots: three million acclaimed him in Chicago, one million in Milwaukee. The general had not "faded away," but five different versions of "Old Soldiers Never Die" were now blaring from America's jukeboxes.

The stage was now set for the second half of the Republican campaign to exalt the general over the President. This was the forthcoming congressional investigation of the administration's Far Eastern policies, with the general as star witness for the Republican prosecution. Nobody knew at the time that the hearings would mark the beginning of the end for MacArthur. The confident Republicans demanded public, televised hearings, the largest possible audience for their hero and their weapon. Equally convinced of the President's weakness and none too sure of the Joint Chiefs of Staff, the Democrats fought desperately to keep the hearings secret, piously citing the need to prevent high matters of state from reaching enemy ears. It took several days of bitter parliamentary strife before the ground rules of the hearings were finally laid down. They were to be conducted jointly by the Senate Armed Services and Foreign Relations Committees — fourteen Democrats and twelve Republicans in all. Press, public, and even the House of

Representatives were to be strictly excluded, but censored transcripts of the testimony would be released every hour to an avid public. In the very midst of war the military policies of the United States were to be subjected to intense and critical scrutiny as the struggle between President and general moved into the arena of a Senate caucus room. It was, as *The New York Times* put it, a "debate unprecedented in American and probably world history."

On the morning of May 3 the huge wooden doors of the caucus room banged shut on a horde of newsmen as General of the Army Douglas MacArthur took his seat as the hearing's first witness. Every major newspaper in the country planned to print his entire testimony. In the witness chair, *Time* noted, the general's "self-confidence was monumental." He carried no notes, consulted no aides, and answered every question without the slightest hesitation. While Democratic senators fumbled with their queries, he calmly puffed on a briar pipe.

As expected, he hit the administration hard. What was unexpected were his passionate outbursts. In a voice charged with emotion he accused the government again and again of wantonly squandering American lives. "I shrink — shrink with a horror that I cannot express in words — at this continuous slaughter of men. . . . Are you going to let that go by any sophistry of reasoning?" Administration arguments he dealt with skillfully. Its contention that a win-the-war policy would cost us our European allies he termed a mere pretext; the United States was already doing most of the fighting in Korea. Its contention that Russia, not China, was America's main enemy he adroitly denied by using the Truman Doctrine against Truman: the enemy was not Russia but "communism all over the world." He belittled the danger of Soviet intervention on Red China's behalf. It was the administration's policy of "appeasement" that invited aggression.

Once again MacArthur insisted that the Joint Chiefs had agreed with his plan. Their views and his

were "practically identical." He even cited an official document that seemed to prove it: a January 12 memorandum from the Chiefs "tentatively" agreeing to some of the measures against China that the general was advocating. To MacArthur the document was conclusive. On January 12, 1951, the Joint Chiefs of Staff had not been persuaded by the "sophistry of reasoning" now being woven by the "politicians," MacArthur's contemptuous — and revealing — term for the civil government of the United States.

As propaganda in a war of headlines, MacArthur's three days of testimony proved powerful indeed. Nonetheless it revealed much that would soon prove detrimental to the general and his cause. Americans acclaimed him as a great military strategist, yet as a witness he sounded like a man so obsessed with striking back at China that he seemed deliberately blind to the risks. Americans saw him as an honest soldier, yet he often sounded like a demagogue. In the Senate caucus room it was already becoming clear, like a photograph slowly developing, that MacArthur was no martyred hero but an extraordinarily ambitious and self-willed general. Whether the bulk of the electorate would come to see this was anybody's guess.

Everything depended on the next series of Senate witnesses, namely the President's principal military advisers: General George C. Marshall, secretary of defense; General Omar Bradley, chairman of the Joint Chiefs of Staff; and the three service chiefs composing that body. This was the supreme irony of the political crisis. In the spring of 1951 the fate of civilian control of the military was absolutely dependent on the military's unswerving fidelity to that principle. It was not merely a matter of swearing fealty to the rule at the hearings. It was not even enough to endorse in a general way the President's policy of limited war. MacArthur's challenge to the President was too powerful for half-measures. The military chiefs would have to do what MacArthur was certain they would never do, what he believed them too "professional" to do. They would have to appear in the caucus room, before hostile senators, and concede absolutely nothing to General MacArthur. If they harbored doubts about limited war, they would have to keep such sentiments to themselves. If they saw merit in any of MacArthur's arguments, they would have to refuse, nonetheless, to acknowledge it. To the intense relief of the President's supporters, that is exactly what they proceeded to do.

Truman's five military spokesmen spent nineteen days in the witness chair, nineteen days in which MacArthur's conduct, MacArthur's victory plan, and even MacArthur's military reputation were ceaselessly battered. Was MacArthur's dismissal warranted? It was more than warranted; it was absolutely necessary. "General MacArthur's actions were continuing to jeopardize civilian control over military affairs." His public campaign to discredit the President's policies "was against all custom and tradition for a military man." What was wrong with MacArthur's victory plan? It would not bring victory "but a larger deadlock at greater expense." Would bombing Chinese "sanctuaries" help decisively in Korea? No, but it would leave America's home air defenses "naked." What of the Joint Chiefs' now-celebrated January 12 memorandum? The military chiefs brushed it aside. It was contingent on imminent defeat in Korea, and that contingency had long since passed. Never for a single moment had the Joint Chiefs of Staff subscribed to MacArthur's plan for victory. What about "the deification of this infallible leader," asked Senator William Fulbright. Had he not blundered at the Yalu when he walked into a Chinese trap? Apparently he had — a stunning accusation. As James Reston of *The New York Times* observed: "MacArthur started as the prosecutor and is now the defendant."

It was General Bradley, a genuine World War II hero and a man untainted by political controversy, who delivered the heaviest blows and the only quotable remark the administration managed to coin. MacArthur's plan, said Bradley, would involve the United States in "the wrong war at the wrong time with the wrong enemy." That was on May 15,

Bradley's first day of testimony, with more of the same to come. Republican senators were stunned. Blindly trusting MacArthur, they simply had not expected the Pentagon to line up behind Truman's policies with such uncompromising zeal. Still less had they expected the Joint Chiefs to belittle their great colleague's military reputation or to accuse him, as General Marshall did, of undermining the morale of American combat troops by his condemnation of the war they were fighting. Republican leaders had underestimated not only the military's fidelity to "custom and tradition" but also the intense personal dislike that the imperious MacArthur had inspired in his World War II colleagues.

The testimony of the military chiefs was by no means unimpeachable. It was often glib and evasive. It was certainly no model of candor. Yet it was quite obvious to contemporaries that Republican committee members did little to discredit their testimony. Exalting MacArthur had been reckless enough. Blackening the Joint Chiefs of Staff in wartime was more than most Republicans had the heart to attempt. Already there were mutterings from the party professionals — national committeemen meeting in Tulsa — that the MacArthur affair might "boomerang" and leave Republicans looking like the "war party" for the 1952 elections. When General Bradley completed his testimony, Republicans lamely proposed that no more generals be called. The Democratic majority was not about to oblige them. Following Bradley the three service chiefs — Army, Navy, and Air Force — duly took the witness chair to hammer away in turn at MacArthur and his plan.

The testimony of the President's generals had a curious effect on public opinion. It brought no rush of support for the President — far from it. It did not personally discredit the general. It accomplished something far more significant then either; it put an end to hysteria. It compelled an inflamed citizenry to stop and think for themselves. It is to the credit of the American people that they did so and still more to their credit that they proved so open-minded, too much so for some of the President's warmer partisans — *The New York Times,* for example.

While Bradley was still offering his testimony, the *Times* canvassed newspapers around the country to determine the hearings' effect on popular opinion. Virtually every newspaper reported the same general result. Their readers were "baffled." With some consternation the *Times* reported on May 20 that "the powerful argumentation by the two sides in the dispute appears to have confused the issues instead of clarifying them." A Gallup poll taken a few days later confirmed the *Times*'s informal soundings. A mere 19 percent of the electorate explicitly supported the President's position. Thirty percent still supported the general's. Half the people polled professed themselves utterly undecided. That indecision was entirely reasonable. The President called for a war of attrition leading merely to the *status quo ante bellum.* MacArthur called for a victory that could conceivably embroil the world. There was precious little to choose between the two. The two sets of arguments canceled each other out.

What the "powerful argumentation by the two sides" had really proved was that Korea was an even worse situation than most Americans had hitherto suspected. Both sides, in effect, had belittled the war. MacArthur insisted that it was "slaughter" unless crowned with "victory." The administration insisted it was too unimportant to risk a try for victory. Then why on earth were we in Korea at all? Beneath the indecision and bafflement, the great majority of Americans were coming to a conclusion more prudent than MacArthur's and more honest than the administration's. There simply was not enough merit in the Korean War to justify anything but an end to hostilities. For bringing America into the fighting, Americans were not about to forgive President Truman. The tide was turning, nonetheless, against "victory," against "liberation," against any concern whatever for the future form of government in communist North Korea — in a word, against MacArthur.

Republicans began calling the hearings an administration "filibuster." On Memorial Day, Truman took his first holiday in months. Yet, despite the signs of returning reason, the President seemed hesitant and timid. As James Reston of the *Times* observed on June 3, limited war meant a negotiated settlement, but the administration was doing nothing to encourage negotiations. It continued to denounce Red China. It continued to speak vaguely about the ultimate "unification" of Korea. Despite the millions of words expended in defense of its limited war, the President still seemed to fear the general.

It was left to MacArthur himself to deliver the final blow to his cause. Never far from egomania, the general had by now convinced himself that opposition to his "victory" plan could not possibly be due to an honest difference of opinion. It was due, he believed, to corruption so deep and so sinister it was imperiling the nation itself. There is a hint of madness in such a conclusion, but MacArthur had nobody to gainsay him. The flunkies surrounding the general believed whatever he said. "He realized," explained General Courtney Whitney, MacArthur's factotum and spokesman, "that the dry rot that infected U.S.-Korea policy was eating away at our conduct of affairs at home. . . . He felt the compelling need to warn of the dangers he saw menacing the land and the people he loves." He would not let his countrymen down — "not to warn them was to betray them." In this dark, messianic mood MacArthur decided to launch himself on a nationwide speaking tour. He called it his "crusade" for "the spiritual recrudescence" of America.

It began on June 13 with a five-city tour of Texas. The tour, like the larger crusade, revealed few of the general's virtues and all his flaws: his vanity, his vindictiveness, his utter want of humility. He lashed out savagely against the Truman administration, condemning its "moral weakness," its disgraceful willingness to "cower before the Kremlin," its betrayal of the "Alamo spirit." He spoke darkly of the efforts being made through "propaganda to sow the seeds of fear and timidity" in America. He could be referring to nothing else but the testimony of the Joint Chiefs of Staff. He warned of "insidious forces working from within" to destroy traditional "moral precepts" and to turn the government itself into "an instrument of despotism." These same sinister forces, he hinted, had engineered his dismissal and were even using the taxing power to destroy the American soul. They "seek to make the burden of taxation so great and its progressive increases so alarming that the spirit of adventure, tireless energy and masterful initiative . . . shall become stultified and inert."

The general insisted that he harbored no presidential ambitions. Nobody believed him. He had harbored such ambitions in 1948 and he sounded like a presidential aspirant now. The electorate judged him accordingly, which is to say, with the skepticism they habitually reserve for office seekers. By wearing his uniform on the tour, MacArthur hoped to remain what he had always seemed to his countrymen — a soldier devoted to duty and country. The bemedaled uniform merely made his political ambition seem vaguely improper. By linking "victory" in Korea to the "spiritual recrudescence" of the American republic, he hoped to strengthen his cause. It merely made the electorate that much more skeptical of "victory." Overseas wars had never seemed to most Americans the true glory of their republic. Between the general and the American people lay a political chasm, and it was MacArthur's crusade, more than anything else, that revealed it to the people.

The Texas tour was only the crusade's beginning but it marked the end of MacArthur's influence over the country at large. That the general was cutting his own throat was by no means lost on the White House. On June 25, nine days after MacArthur returned from Texas to the Waldorf, President Truman finally announced his willingness to do what MacArthur and his supporters had done their utmost to prevent him from doing. He was ready, he said, to negotiate a settlement of the war at the thirty-eighth parallel. This was the "appeasement peace" against

which MacArthur had hurled his thunderbolts, against which he had pitted his enormous prestige, his lofty reputation, and, so it had seemed back in April, the entire body of the American people. He had failed to block it, and because he did, the "precedent" that would "grow into a monstrosity" had been forestalled. Civilian supremacy had beaten back its severest challenge. On July 10 American and Chinese delegates met at a Korean town named Kaesŏng to discuss terms for a truce. The crisis was over. In the end the great majority of Americans had decided against MacArthur, and though the talks would grow bitter and frustrating, that decision, once made, was never revoked.

The defeat took its toll on the general. In public his superb self-possession slowly began draining away. In speeches his beautifully modulated voice often became strident and squeaky. The polished performer developed odd mannerisms, such as jumping up and down as he spoke. His keynote address to the 1952 Republican Convention was so dull and ill-delivered that halfway through it the delegates' private chatter virtually drowned him out. Fourteen months after holding the entire nation in his thrall, General MacArthur could not even hold the attention of a Republican audience. In a mood of deep self-disgust MacArthur flew home that day to the Waldorf and out of the public life of the country.

It was the general, nonetheless, who supplied the final grace note to the great crisis of 1951. It was to come eleven years later before the corps of cadets at West Point. The general was eighty-two years old by then and he had come to his beloved military academy to deliver a last farewell. In the course of an eloquent and emotional speech, he had a word of stern advice for the future officers arrayed before him. In the high political affairs of the country, they were duty-bound not to meddle. "These great national problems," said the frail old man, "are not for your professional or military solution." An errant son of the republic had at last returned to the fold.

QUESTIONS TO CONSIDER

1. "When the President fired the general," Walter Karp says, "civilian control of the military faced its severest test in our history." Why does the United States have a civilian commander in chief of the armed forces? Why is it important to maintain this system of controls? What sometimes happens in countries where publicly or constitutionally supported civilian control of the military is not present?

2. MacArthur aroused Congress and the public with his magnificent speech before a joint session of Congress on April 19, 1951. Shortly afterward, when he undertook a nationwide speaking tour, his following began to drift away. How did MacArthur weaken his case and lose his supporters? What flaws in the general's own character contributed to his failure to find backing for a war with China?

3. Walter Karp's balanced account of the events of 1951 does not spare President Truman. What mistakes did Truman make, both in prosecuting the Korean War itself and in his attempts to gain popular support for his policies?

4. The idea of a "limited war of attrition" was new to Americans in 1951. What are the aims of such a war? Has the United States been involved in other limited wars since the Korean War? Discuss the pros and cons of "limited warfare."

22

McCarthyism: Years of Shock

ERIC GOLDMAN

A veritable anti–Communist hysteria swept over the United States in the Truman and early Eisenhower years, as Americans saw red conspiracies at home as well as abroad. It had happened before. In 1919, two years after Russia had fallen to bolshevism, American patriots warned that a Bolshevik plot was under way to overthrow the United States, too. Convinced that this was so, Attorney General A. Mitchell Palmer—"the fighting Quaker"—announced that he would round up all Bolsheviks and deport them to Russia on a special ship called the Soviet Ark. *Authorities then set about apprehending hundreds of suspicious-looking people, and newspapers ran pictures of what a Bolshevik looked like (he was bearded, bespectacled, and sinister) so that Americans might root out any such conspirators in their churches, schools, and homes. Finally the red scare subsided, but not before many innocent people had suffered.*

Now in the 1940s and 1950s—in another postwar period—it was happening again as thousands of insecure Americans began to suspect that many other citizens had suc- cumbed to communism. And out of their fears emerged a conspiracy view of history, which held that since 1932 a Communist plot had been under way to take over the United States from within and to hand the country over to Moscow. The chief agent in this plot was Franklin Roosevelt; the cast of villains also included the Brains Trusters and most of the New Dealers in the cabinet and Congress. The New Deal itself, with all its welfare measures, seemed part of a sinister world conspiracy directed by Moscow. Truman, too, in spite of his tough-guy stance toward the Russians, was linked to the Great Conspiracy. Had he not been Roosevelt's vice president? And look at his Fair Deal domestic program, the patriots said. It consisted of such "socialistic" programs as civil rights legislation for

313

African Americans, federal aid to schools, federal health insurance, and public housing. From the American right, where the patriots were clustered, came resounding accusations that the Truman administration was brimming with traitors and that all liberals were Communists.

The communist scare, however, was not confined to the American right. The fact was that Truman and the liberals were obsessed with communism, too, and out of that obsession came nuclear diplomacy and the containment policy. Furthermore, it was the liberals who went to war against communism, first in Korea and later in Vietnam. At home, moreover, Truman instituted a sweeping loyalty oath program and began extensive security checks for federal employment. In truth, the liberals' preoccupation with communism helped create a national mood in which hysterical anticommunism flourished.

And flourish it did. Thousands of conservative and moderate Americans were very much afraid that Communists had infiltrated the schools, the churches, and the federal government itself. The House Un-American Activities Committee only fanned the flames when it unearthed alleged Communists in the universities and in Hollywood. Then came the sensational trial of Alger Hiss.

Hiss had been a New Deal luminary and an official in the State Department. In 1948, Whittaker Chambers stood before the House Un-American Activities Committee and accused Hiss of being a Communist spy during the 1930s. Chambers, turning state's evidence, admitted that he had belonged to the Communist party and insisted that Hiss had given him classified State Department documents. When Hiss sued him for libel, Chambers produced microfilms of the papers. In 1949 Hiss came to trial on a charge of perjury (the statute of limitations prevented his being charged with espionage). The first trial ended in a hung jury, but the second found him guilty of perjury—and, by implication, of treason.

For many Americans, the Hiss trial was unchallengeable proof that the New Deal had been alive with Communists in government, proof that the conspiracy thesis was true, proof that the United States was in danger of being overthrown from within. Other developments in 1949—that "year of shocks"—convinced thousands of Americans (Republicans and Democrats alike) that disaster was imminent. First, China fell to communism. Then came the stunning news that Russia also had the atomic bomb. And 1950 came on. "For the frightened and embittered," writes Eric Goldman, "there was only more incitement to fright and bitterness."

GLOSSARY

BLOCK, HERBERT L.   *Washington Post* cartoonist who coined the term *McCarthyism* to describe anticommunist zealotry.

COHN, ROY   Chief counsel for McCarthy's Permanent Subcommittee on Investigations; Cohn and G. David Schine, subcommittee "consultant," ferreted out "subversion" in the State Department's overseas information program and assisted McCarthy in the Army–McCarthy hearings.

FISHER, FRED   Joseph Welch's young assistant who had once belonged to the Lawyers Guild; in the Army–McCarthy hearings, McCarthy inpugned Fisher's patriotism by labeling the Lawyers Guild "the legal bulwark of the Communist party."

FUCHS, DR. KLAUS   British atomic scientist who gave the Soviets "the inmost scientific secrets of the Western powers."

LATTIMORE, OWEN   Sometime consultant for the State Department and a noncommunist liberal; McCarthy named him "the top Russian espionage agent" in America.

PERESS, IRVING   Army dentist who was promoted and given an honorable discharge after he refused to sign a loyalty oath and to answer questions before McCarthy's subcommittee; McCarthy used the Peress case to start subcommittee hearings on the army's alleged softness on communism.

TYDINGS, SENATOR MILLARD   Senator from Maryland and militant chairman of the Senate subcommittee set up to investigate McCarthy's claim that the State Department was overrun with Communists.

WALSH, EDMUND A.   Georgetown University vice president and author of *Total Power* who alerted a young senator McCarthy to the evils of world communism.

WELCH, JOSEPH   Chief army counsel in the televised Army–McCarthy hearings, Welch received an ovation in the hearings when he challenged McCarthy's cruel accusations against Welch's young assistant, Fred Fisher.

ZWICKER, BRIGADIER GENERAL RALPH   McCarthy humiliated this esteemed army officer during the Army–McCarthy hearings; afterward, Secretary of the Army Robert Stevens and the Eisenhower administration moved to deflate the crusading senator.

On January 31, Presidential Press Secretary Charles Ross handed reporters a statement from President Truman: "It is part of my responsibility as Commander in Chief of the armed forces to see to it that our country is able to defend itself against any aggressor. Accordingly I have directed the Atomic Energy Commission to continue its work on all forms of atomic weapons, including the so-called hydrogen or superbomb." Once again a terrifying announcement had been made with all the studied toning down of a mimeographed sheet — this time the President even saw to it that he was casually lunching at Blair House when Ross met the reporters. Once again nothing could really cushion the news. . . . A hydrogen bomb [would] have one hundred to one thousand times the power of the largest atomic weapon. Twelve distinguished scientists immediately issued a joint statement which pointed out that "in the case of the fission bomb the Russians required four years to parallel our development. In the case of the hydrogen bomb they will probably need a shorter time."

Some Americans talked tough. Secretary of Defense Louis Johnson told an alumni gathering at the University of Virginia: "I want Joe Stalin to know that if he starts something at four o'clock in the morning, the fighting power and strength of America will be on the job at five o'clock in the morning." Other Americans raised harsh, portentous questions. Senator Brian McMahon, chairman of the Joint Congressional Committee on Atomic Energy, brought solemn handshakes from both sides of the chamber by a speech in which he asked: "How is it possible for free institutions to flourish or even to maintain themselves in a situation where defenses, civil and military, must be ceaselessly poised to meet an attack that might incinerate fifty million Americans — not in the space of

From *The Crucial Decade* by Eric Goldman. Copyright © 1956 by Eric G. Goldman. Reprinted by permission of Alfred A. Knopf, Inc.

an evening, but in the space of moments?" The most authoritative voice of all talked doom. Albert Einstein went on television, the simple sweater jacket, the scraggly gray hair, the childlike face with the brilliant eyes all adding to the aura of an otherworldly wisdom beyond the power of ordinary mortals. With the order of President Truman to produce an H-bomb, Einstein said, "radioactive poisoning of the atmosphere and hence annihilation of any life on earth has been brought within the range of technical possibilities. . . . General annihilation beckons."

Another four days and another jolting headline. On February 3 the British government announced the confession of Dr. Klaus Fuchs, a high-level atomic scientist. The descriptions of Fuchs sitting behind the cast-iron grill of the prisoner's dock in Bow Street police court, plainly dressed, bespectacled, quiet-mannered, gave him every inch the appearance of the dedicated scientist — "the last man in the world you would expect to be a spy," as one English reporter commented. Yet Fuchs's confession stated that from 1943 through 1947, while engaged in government atomic research in the United States and Britain, he had systematically passed over to Soviet agents the inmost scientific secrets of the Western powers. "I had complete confidence in Russian policy," he told the police, "and I had no hesitation in giving all the information I had." The knowledge Fuchs handed over, his superior, Michael Perren, stated, had been "of the highest value to a potential enemy," and no doubt speeded up the Russian production of an atom bomb "at least a year."

Senator Homer Capehart of Indiana stood up in the Senate and stormed: "How much more are we going to have to take? Fuchs and Acheson and Hiss and hydrogen bombs threatening outside and New Dealism eating away the vitals of the nation. In the name of Heaven, is this the best America can do?" The applause was loud and long, from the floor and from the galleries.

That afternoon the regular plane from Washington

to Wheeling, West Virginia, began loading. The stewardess did her duty, noted a United States Senator on the passenger list, and greeted him with a smiling, "Good afternoon, Senator McCarthy." The reply was a bit plaintive. "Why good afternoon — I'm glad somebody recognizes me."

Getting recognized was no new concern of Joseph McCarthy. The Irish settlement in northern Wisconsin where he grew up respected money and looks; the McCarthys were a struggling brood of nine and Joe was the ugly duckling, barrel-chested and short-armed with thick eyebrows and heavy lips. Mother Bridget McCarthy threw a special protective wing around the shy, sulky boy and when the rough teasing came, he sought out her big warm apron. "Don't you mind," she would console. "You be somebody. You get ahead."

Joe took heed. He would get back; he would show everybody. The shy sulkiness turned into a no-holds-barred ambition curiously mixed with a gawky, grinning likability. The boy worked so furiously on the family farm that neighbors joked he must have spent his babyhood wearing overalls instead of diapers. Starting his education late, he talked, wheedled, and shoved his way through Marquette University with so much corner-cutting that Wisconsin educators still gasp at the record.

Associates noted the fierce, blinding drive in everything McCarthy did. When he boxed and his awkwardness was getting him cut to pieces, he would keep coming in, slashed and bleeding but flailing away in the hope of striking a knockout blow. When he played poker, he played all-or-nothing. He had the "guts of a burglar," one friend remembers. "He was brutal. He'd take all the fun out of the game, because he took it so seriously." When he ran for office in college, he dropped his homework, cut school for weeks at a time, devoted night and day to buying coffees and cokes and making lavish promises. He and his opponent agreed that each would vote for the other until the election was decided. The first ballot was a tie. On the next McCarthy won by two votes.

"Joe," the defeated candidate said, "did you vote for yourself?"

McCarthy grinned his big, disarming, tail-between-the-legs grin. "Sure. You wanted me to vote for the best man, didn't you?"

Once out of Marquette, he bashed his way to a Wisconsin Circuit Judgeship and soon converted it into a political stump, knocking off divorces in five minutes or less, racing around to please people by trying as many cases as possible. After Pearl Harbor he entered the Marine Corps, turning the whole Pacific Theater of War into a headquarters of McCarthy for United States Senator, blithely giving himself the name of "Tail-gunner Joe" although most of the time he was actually serving as an intelligence officer and doing the paper work for a squadron of pilots. Elected to the Senate in 1946, he thrashed about for ways to secure his political hold. McCarthy served the interests of the Pepsi-Cola Company so faithfully he became known to fellow Senators as the "Pepsi-Cola Kid." He delighted the real-estate interests in Wisconsin by battling public housing and he pleased some of his large German-American constituency by defending the Nazis on trial for the murders of [American prisoners at] Malmédy [Belgium in 1944].

It was a great life, this being a United States Senator. "Pretty good going for a Mick from the backwoods, eh?" McCarthy would grin at the cocktail parties and the ladies thought he was awfully cute — "such an engaging primitive," as one debutante put it. But there was a problem and the engaging primitive was no more patient with a problem than he had ever been.

On January 7, 1950 McCarthy sat having a troubled dinner at the Colony Restaurant in Washington. The get-together had been arranged by Charles H. Kraus, a professor of political science at Georgetown University, and William A. Roberts, a well known Washington attorney. Kraus in particular had been seeing a good deal of the Senator and had been suggesting books for him to read — especially the potent anti-Communist volume *Total Power* by Father

Edmund A. Walsh, vice-president of Georgetown and regent of its School of Foreign Service. (McCarthy was hardly a booklover but he did like to skim hurriedly and had spoken of his desire "to read some meaty books.") The prime purpose of the dinner was to permit the Senator to meet Father Walsh, whom both Kraus and Roberts profoundly admired.

McCarthy soon brought the conversation around to what was uppermost in his mind. His situation was bad, the Senator said. Here it was already the beginning of 1950, with his term running out in two years, and he had neither the national publicity which would attract Wisconsin voters nor any specific issue likely to stir them.

Within months Kraus, Roberts, and Walsh were all to repudiate McCarthy but at this time they were well disposed toward the youthful Senator. Kraus and Roberts were also Marine veterans of World War II; everyone at the table was a Catholic; the Senator's shaggy affability could attract men as well as women. Eager to help McCarthy, the group threw out suggestions.

"How about pushing harder for the St. Lawrence seaway?" Roberts proposed.

McCarthy shook his head. "That hasn't enough appeal. No one gets excited about it."

The Senator then thought aloud about a Townsend-type pension plan for all elderly Americans. Why not start a campaign to pay one hundred dollars a month to everybody over sixty-five years of age? But the three other men agreed that the idea was economically unsound.

After dinner the group went to Roberts's office in the adjoining DeSales Building and continued the discussion. McCarthy and Roberts, both voluble men, did most of the talking but at one point Father Walsh spoke at length. He emphasized the world power of Communism and the danger that it would infiltrate any democratic government. He was sure, Walsh declared, that vigilance against Communism was of such importance that it would be an issue two years hence.

The Senator's face brightened. Communist infiltration — wasn't this what everybody was talking about? And wasn't this, after all, a *real* issue? The priest's remarks touched chords that reached far back into McCarthy's life. In the 1930's, the Irish settlement of northern Wisconsin voted for Franklin Roosevelt; the farms were in too desperate a condition for anything else. But the New Dealism had its own Midwestern, new-immigrant, Irish-Catholic coloration. It was filled with suspicion of Easterners, "radicals," "aristocrats," the British, and the "striped-pants fellows" of the State Department. McCarthy had started in politics a New Deal Democrat but as soon as the prosperity came he shifted to a more congenial Taft Republicanism. Whether a Democrat or a Republican, he had always more or less consciously assumed that the big trouble with America, as his boyhood neighbor Jim Heegan used to put it, was "those Leftists."

McCarthy cut in on Father Walsh. "The Government is full of Communists. The thing to do is to hammer at them."

Roberts, a longtime liberal attorney, spoke a sharp warning. Such a campaign would have to be based on facts; the public was weary of "Wolf! Wolf!" cries about "Reds." The Senator said offhandedly he would get the facts.

Lincoln's Birthday, the traditional time for Republican oratory, was approaching, and McCarthy — probably at his own request — was assigned by the Senate Republican Campaign Committee to speak on the topic, "Communism in the State Department." The Senator's office put together some materials drawn mostly from hearings and staff investigations of a House Appropriations subcommittee. Three weeks after Hiss was convicted, ten days after President Truman ordered work on the H-bomb, six days after the British announced the Fuchs confession, on February 9, 1950, McCarthy took the plane to deliver his speech before the Women's Republican Club in Wheeling, West Virginia. He would give it a try. He would see if he could not get someone besides polite airline stewardesses to recognize the name Joseph McCarthy.

"The reason why we find ourselves in a position of impotency [in international affairs]," the Senator told the club, "is not because our only powerful potential enemy has sent men to invade our shores, but rather because of the traitorous actions of those who have been treated too well by this Nation. . . ." Where was the situation most serious? "Glaringly" so in the State Department. And what kind of men were the offenders? "The bright young men who are born with silver spoons in their mouths are the ones who have been worst. . . . In my opinion the State Department, which is one of the most important government departments, is thoroughly infested with Communists." Most dangerous of all was Dean Acheson, that "pompous diplomat in striped pants, with a phony British accent."

McCarthy had always believed that a speaker had to get specific in order to make his points stick. Near the end of his speech he talked about a list "I hold here in my hand." Exactly what he said about the list will probably never be known with certainty. James E. Whitaker and Paul A. Myers, news editor and program director respectively of the Wheeling radio station that broadcast the speech, WWVA, later swore in an affidavit that McCarthy's words were: "I have here in my hand a list of 205 — a list of names that were known to the Secretary of State as being members of the Communist Party and who nevertheless are still working and shaping the policy in the State Department." The Senator's friends later insisted that his point was something like: "I have here in my hand 57 cases of individuals who would appear to be either card-carrying members or certainly loyal to the Communist Party, but who nevertheless are still helping to shape our foreign policy." One man who would never be sure what he had said was Joseph McCarthy. Frederick Woltman, the responsible reporter for the Scripps-Howard newspapers, has described how "on a number of occasions — mostly in my apartment at

the Congressional — I heard McCarthy and his advisors wrack their brains for some lead as to what he said in that Wheeling speech. He had no copy; he had spoken from rough notes and he could not find the notes. . . . The Senator's staff could find no one who could recall what he'd said precisely. He finally hit on the idea of appealing to ham radio operators in the area who might have made a recording of the speech. He could find none."

For the moment there was no such interesting problem. There was only another plane to catch, another polite stewardess to greet Senator McCarthy. The speech seemed to disappear; it was not even reported except in the Wheeling newspapers and in the *Chicago Tribune*. The Senator kept flailing away. On February 10, in Salt Lake City, he made a speech similar to his Wheeling talk and charged that there were "57 card-carrying members of the Communist Party" in the State Department. The next day he repeated substantially the same talk in Reno and wired President Truman demanding that the White House do something.

Things began to happen. Newspapers in many parts of the country headlined the Salt Lake City and Reno charges. President Truman and Secretary of State Acheson issued angry statements of denial. The Senate stirred, authorizing a subcommittee of the Foreign Relations Committee to investigate the Senator's statements.

But what was happening did not seem to bode well for Joseph McCarthy. The materials that he had used for his speeches were largely old and none too sturdy charges. The Senate subcommittee, chairmanned by the militantly Democratic Millard Tydings of Maryland, kept McCarthy pinned in the worst possible light. Veteran Republican Senate leaders were plainly hesitant about backing this rambunctious upstart.

Then, gradually, support came. By an instinct born of the whole climate of ideas in which he had grown up, McCarthy was attacking precisely in the way most likely to capture the groups in America who were most disturbed about foreign policy — the whole conspiracy theory of international affairs down to the last suspicion of Dean Acheson's striped pants. By the same instinct, he kept broadening the sense of conspiracy, catching more strands of the rebelliousness abroad in the country. Within a month after his Wheeling speech he was assailing as Communists the "whole group of twisted-thinking New Dealers [who] have led America near to ruin at home and abroad." Many others had been saying these things. No one had kept naming names, dozens of specific, headline-making names. And no one had attacked with such abandon — McCarthy politicking as he had done everything else, ignoring the rules, always walking in, taking his beatings, endlessly throwing wild, spectacular punches. Shortly after the Tydings subcommittee did its most telling job on the charge of fifty-seven card-carrying Communists in the State Department, the Senator closed his eyes completely and swung so hard he shook the country.

He would "stand or fall on this one," McCarthy let it be known. He was naming "the top Russian espionage agent" in the United States and a man who had long been "one of the top advisers on Far Eastern policy" — Owen Lattimore. In the ensuing uproar only the most informed Americans could make out the fact that Lattimore was a non-Communist liberal who had been called into consultation infrequently by the State Department and whose suggestions had been almost totally ignored.

By late March private contributions were pouring into the Senator's office. The awards began. The Marine Corps League of Passaic, New Jersey, announced that it had selected Joseph McCarthy to receive its 1950 citation for Americanism. Leading Taft Republicans, including Senator Taft himself, the two powerhouses, Senators Kenneth Wherry and Styles Bridges, and the chairman of the Republican National Committee, Guy Gabrielson, were giving a respectful and cooperative attention to the rambunctious upstart. Various groups which had their own special uses for McCarthy's kind of anti-Communism came to his support — including the potent manipulators who were soon known as the "China Lobby."

Now the grin was as broad as Mother Bridget's apron. The Senator was affable, endlessly affable. In the course of a discussion in McCarthy's apartment, Mrs. Frederick Woltman asked testily: "Tell me, Senator, just how long ago did you discover Communism?"

The Senator grinned. "Why, about two and a half months ago."

In the office of Herbert Block, the strongly New Dealish cartoonist of the Washington Post, there was no grinning. Herblock angrily sketched a harassed Republican elephant, being pushed and pulled by Taft, Wherry, Bridges, and Gabrielson toward a stack of buckets of tar with an extra big barrel of tar on top. The cartoonist hesitated for a moment, thinking over possible one-word labels. Then he was satisfied. On the large barrel of tar he printed the letters, MC-CARTHYISM.

Immediately, and so naturally that people promptly forgot where the term had first been used, the word McCarthyism passed into the language. The revolt that set off the shocks of 1949 had its name and the expression of its most violent, most reckless mood. . . .

The shocks of 1949 had given Senator Joseph McCarthy his start. The frustrations of 1950 and 1951 blasted wide his road to power. With America tangled in deadlocks at home and abroad, the man with the simple answer, the furious, flailing answer, had his day. In early 1951 Mickey Spillane's *One Lonely Night* started on its way to selling more than three million copies. The hero, Mike Hammer, gloated: "I killed more people tonight than I have fingers on my hands. I shot them in cold blood and enjoyed every minute of it. . . . They were Commies, Lee. They were red sons-of-bitches who should have died long ago. . . . They never thought that there were people like me in this country. They figured us all to be soft as horse manure and just as stupid." Hammer's tough-guy certainty that he was solving the world's problems by bludgeoning Communists hardly hurt the sales of *One Lonely Night*. It was a day for Mike Hammerism, in books or in politics.

Week after week Senator McCarthy became bolder and more reckless. For years General of the Army George Marshall, the over-all architect of victory in World War II, had been one of the most generally esteemed figures in the United States. But Marshall was associated with the Truman policy in the Far East and on June 14, 1951 McCarthy stood up in the Senate and delivered a sixty-thousand word speech which charged that Marshall was part of "a conspiracy so immense, an infamy so black, as to dwarf any in the history of man. . . . [a conspiracy directed] to the end that we shall be contained, frustrated and finally fall victim to Soviet intrigue from within and Russian military might from without." The more reckless McCarthy became, the more his influence mounted. Fewer and fewer Senators rose to gainsay him. Pollsters found that steadily increasing percentages of Americans were ready to answer yes to questions like, Do you in general approve of Senator McCarthy's activities?

Outside of politics, the flood of McCarthyism mounted — the people who were chasing alleged Communists, the men and the institutions who were abetting McCarthyism by acquiescing in its attitudes. Some of the furor was simply ridiculous. Monogram Pictures canceled a movie about Henry Wadsworth Longfellow. Hiawatha, the studio explained, had tried to stop wars between the Indian tribes and people might construe the picture as propaganda for the Communist "peace offensive." Wheeling, West Virginia, staged the kind of comic-opera terror that was going on in scores of cities. In Wheeling the hubbub began when a policeman announced his discovery that penny-candy machines were selling children's bonbons with little geography lessons attached to the candies. The very tininess of the messages, half the size of a postage stamp, was suspicious; most rousing of all was the revelation that some of the geography lessons bore the hammer-and-sickle Soviet flag and

the message: "U.S.S.R. Population 211,000,000. Capital Moscow. Largest country in the world." City Manager Robert L. Plummer thundered: "This is a terrible thing to expose our children to." Stern measures were taken to protect the candy-store set from the knowledge that the Soviet Union existed and that it was the biggest country in the world.

Much of the furor, far from being ridiculous, was sinister. The United States Government was tainting the names of innocent men and costing itself the services of invaluable specialists. Senator McCarthy decided that Philip Jessup, a distinguished professor of international law at Columbia and a skilled diplomat, was a man with "an unusual affinity for Communist causes"; supinely a subcommittee of the Senate Foreign Relations Committee turned down Jessup's nomination as a delegate to the UN General Assembly. Trying to fight off McCarthyism, the Truman Administration adopted loyalty procedures that were increasingly dubious. In or out of government, utterly innocent people were losing their jobs. Irene Wicker, the "Singing Lady" of television, who was soon to have an audience with the Pope and be given a special blessing for her work with children, found her TV contract canceled. The McCarthy-type magazine *Counterattack,* which was connected with the pressure to dismiss her, made everything clear. The *Daily Worker* had listed Miss Wicker as a sponsor of a Red councilmanic candidate in New York and "the *Daily Worker* is very accurate; they never make a mistake."

Everywhere in the United States, the fury against Communism was taking on — even more than it had before the Korean War — elements of a vendetta against the Half-Century of Revolution in domestic affairs, against all departures from tradition in foreign policy, against the new, the adventurous, the questing in any field. Self-confident Yale University felt it necessary to appoint a committee of distinguished alumni to protect itself against a recent undergraduate, William F. Buckley, who talked, in the same burst of indignation at the Yale faculty, about the menace of Communism and the threat of "atheists" and of men who criticized "limited government" or economic "self-reliance." For most of 1951 the best-seller lists of the country included *Washington Confidential* by two newspapermen, Jack Lait and Lee Mortimer. The book was a jumble of breathless revelations about "Communism" in Washington, quotations like the one from an unnamed Negro dope peddler who told an unnamed federal agent, "You can't arrest me. I am a friend of Mrs. Roosevelt," and such observations as "Where you find an intellectual in the District you will probably find a Red." In a number of cities, educators reported, anything "controversial" was being stripped from the schools — and more than a few times the "controversial" writing turned out to be factual information about UNESCO or New Deal legislation. A battle over a textbook in Council Bluffs, Iowa, produced the kind of statement that was commonplace. Ex-Congressman Charles Swanson opened the meeting with a roaring denunciation of "all these books. . . . They should be thrown on a bonfire — or sent to Russia. Why according to this book, Jefferson, Jackson, Wilson and Franklin Roosevelt were outstanding Presidents — what about William Howard Taft?"

In Washington, William Howard Taft's son Robert was in a new phase of his career. "The sad, worst period," his sympathetic biographer, William S. White, has called it. Certainly Senator Robert Taft was moving closer to McCarthyism. Even before the Korean War, in March, 1950, several responsible reporters asserted that Taft had remarked: "McCarthy should keep talking and if one case doesn't work out he should proceed with another." The Senator protested that this quotation misrepresented him but there can be no question about the meaning of statements he made after the Korean intervention. Taft complained that Truman had the bad habit to *"assume the innocence* of all the persons mentioned in the State Department." He also declared: "Whether Senator McCarthy has *legal evidence,* whether he has overstated or understated his case, is of lesser importance. The question is whether the Communist influence in the State Department *still exists."* (Italics added.) "This sort of thing," William White could only sadly comment, "was not the Taft one had known."

In domestic affairs the Senator's attacks became sharper and edged closer to the argument that Fair Dealism was a conspiracy of socialists. In foreign affairs, all the matters that were "open to question" in Taft's speech at the time the United States entered the Korean War were now settled and settled against the Administration. The American intervention was "an unnecessary war," an "utterly useless war," a war "begun by President Truman without the slightest authority from Congress or the people." And in explaining the international policy of the Administration the Senator was more and more using phrases that suggested a plot on the part of — to use a 1951 statement of Taft — "men who did not and do not turn their backs on the Alger Hisses."

If the Senator was going far, a large part of the GOP was moving in the same direction. In part this trend represented out-and-out McCarthyism. More of it came from the feeling — to use the phrase current then — that "I don't like some of McCarthy's methods but his goal is good." To the largest extent the development resulted from a fundamental disquietude with foreign and domestic affairs that showed itself in a violent anti-Trumanism, particularly on the issue of Far Eastern policy. . . .

General Republicans, Taftite Republicans, McCarthyite Republicans, McCarthyite Democrats, and millions of Americans who fitted none of these categories — in late 1951 and 1952 much of the nation was restlessly, irritably seeking to break through the sense of frustration. People flailed Harry Truman as a caged animal lashes at its bars. The President's Gallup rating sank to a minuscule twenty-six per cent and the personal attacks were so extreme the pro-Truman *New York Post* found itself pleading: "After all, the President of the United States is a member of the human race." Men and women were looking for some bright shining light, some road without endless roadblocks. . . .

[For a majority of Americans that "bright shining light" was Republican Dwight Eisenhower, who won the presidency in 1952 and assumed office in 1953. But the fears of Communist subversion remained, and even Eisenhower had to worry about Joe McCarthy.]

On Capitol Hill Senator Joseph McCarthy was asked his judgment of the new Administration and he smiled loftily. The Administration's record on anti-Communism, he said, was "fair."

Circumstances were hardly such as to curb the arrogance of Joseph McCarthy. The Republican capture of the Senate in 1952 had made him for the first time the chairman of his own committee — the powerful Committee on Government Operations — and he also headed its formidable subcommittee, the Permanent Subcommittee on Investigations. With a handful of exceptions the whole Senate treated him with respect or at least with care. He seemed to have proved what a politician respects most — an awesome ability to affect votes. He himself had been re-elected in 1952 by a majority of more than 140,000. No less than eight of the men in the Senate — six who had been elected in 1952 — were thought to owe their seats largely to his campaigning. Around the country his name had an increasing potency. A belligerent if small pro-McCarthy faction was making itself heard even among the group which had shown the most solid bloc resistance to him, the intellectuals of the United States.

Probably most important of all, the man in the White House had a conception of his role which very specifically ruled out openly battling McCarthy. Eisenhower not only wanted to respect the Constitutional division between the Executive and Legislative divisions. He was keenly aware that he was the head of a divided party and anxious to unite it along the lines of his own thinking. Whatever the President's own tendencies toward the right, his views were quite different from those of the right-wingers, who for the most part were bitter anti-New Dealers, all-out isolationists with respect to Europe, all-out interventionists with respect to Asia, and enthusiasts for the kind of anti-Communism represented by McCarthy. These men followed the President reluctantly when they followed him at all and Eisenhower wanted to do nothing to increase the friction. It was the President's "passion," his aide C. D. Jackson remarked, "not to offend anyone in Congress" and this attitude soon permeated most of his subordinates.

Month after month McCarthy went to further extremes and month after month the Administration sidestepped, looked the other way, or actually followed his bidding. At the beginning of the Administration McCarthy declared that he believed there were still Communists in the State Department and that [Secretary of State John Foster] Dulles could go a long way toward rooting them out by naming a good security officer. The Secretary named a good security officer — Scott McLeod, widely assumed to be a McCarthy disciple. [In] March 1953 the Senator announced that he had negotiated with Greek shipowners to stop trading at Soviet and satellite ports. Director of Mutual Security Harold Stassen angrily pointed out that this was a flagrant Senatorial interference with the functions of the Executive Branch and that by negotiating with a small group "you are in effect undermining and are harmful to our objective" of stopping the general trade with the Communists. Immediately a mollifying statement came from Frank Nash, Assistant Secretary of Defense for international affairs; and Secretary of State Dulles and McCarthy got together for a congenial lunch. At his press conference, the President did the final smoothing over by suggesting that both McCarthy and Stassen had gone a bit far. The Senator had probably made a "mistake" and the Director of Mutual Security probably meant "infringement" rather than "undermining."

All the while McCarthy was stepping up his campaign against the State Department's overseas information program. The country began to hear about the two 27-year-olds, Roy Cohn, the Subcommittee's chief counsel, and G. David Schine, an unpaid Subcommittee consultant. They left on an eighteen day whirl through western Europe to ferret out "subversion" in the overseas program. Seventeen hours in Bonn, twenty hours in Berlin, nineteen hours in Frankfurt — these and a sprinkling of other stops and McCarthy was proclaiming "appalling infiltration." The State Department reacted dutifully. It asked for resignations — including those of men like Theodore Kaghan who had probably dabbled with radicalism in the late 1930's and who now was known through central Europe as one of the most effective organizers of anti-Communist propaganda. (When the Subcommittee made its charges Leopold Figl, the ultraconservative former Chancellor of Austria, wrote Kaghan: "What goes on? After all, April Fool's day has long passed by. . . .") The State Department also issued a new directive banning from American information activities all "books, music, paintings, and the like . . . of any Communists, fellow travelers, *et cetera*" and ordering that "librarians should at once remove all books and other material by Communists, fellow travelers, *et cetera,* from their shelves and withdraw any that may be in circulation."

Many librarians, taking no chance on having a work by an *et cetera* on their shelves, removed the books of authors like Bert Andrews, chief of the Washington bureau of the Republican *New York Herald Tribune;* Walter White, head of the anti-Communist National Association for the Advancement of Colored People; Richard Lauterbach, former European correspondent of *Time;* Clarence Streit, chief figure in the strongly democratic movement for a federal union of the North Atlantic democracies; and Foster Rhea Dulles, a decidedly anti-Communist professor at Ohio State and cousin of the Secretary of State. Some librarians stored the books they removed; others burned them. . . .

McCarthy rampaged on. With the opening of 1954 he and his staff concentrated increasingly on the Department of the Army and a number of top Army officials tried hard to work with them. In January the Senator began to hammer on the case of Major Irving Peress, a New York dental officer. Peress had been

Senator McCarthy captured in a rare quiet moment at the Army-McCarthy hearings. The hearings, telecast into millions of American homes during the spring of 1954, climaxed the McCarthy era of the Cold War, an obsessional search for a wide-ranging Communist "conspiracy" that McCarthy claimed was destroying the foundations of American democracy. Before it was over, McCarthy and his minions had terrorized hundreds of Americans, both in and out of government, and ruined many reputations. (Wide World)

permitted to receive his regularly due promotion and granted an honorable discharge after he had refused to sign an Army loyalty certificate and after he had refused, on the grounds of possible self-incrimination, to answer a number of questions at a Subcommittee hearing. In a letter to McCarthy, Secretary of the Army Robert Stevens acknowledged that the Peress case had been mishandled and stated that if he found the promotion had been anything but routine he would discipline the officers involved. He also ordered that in the future Reserve officers who refused to sign a loyalty certificate were to be given an other than honorable discharge.

Unappeased, the Senator summoned Peress and a group of Army officials, including Brigadier General Ralph Zwicker, to a Subcommittee hearing. At one point, when the hearing was in executive session, McCarthy demanded that Zwicker answer questions concerning the processing of the Peress case and Zwicker replied that such information was inviolate under a Presidential order. The Senator was furious. According to Zwicker, McCarthy shouted at the General: "You are a disgrace to the uniform. You're shielding Communist conspirators. You are going to be put on public display next Tuesday. You're not fit to be an officer. You're ignorant."

Zwicker was a highly esteemed officer who was obviously simply following orders. The Army seethed with resentment. Secretary Stevens heatedly accused McCarthy of humiliating Zwicker and of undermining Army morale, and ordered two officers not to appear before the Senator's Subcommittee. McCarthy promptly replied that Stevens was an "awful dupe" and summoned the Secretary himself to testify. Stevens decided to go and prepared a strong statement which he intended to read at the hearing. But the statement was never read. Instead Stevens met with McCarthy and other members of the Subcommittee and accepted a "Memorandum of Agreement." When the memorandum was released few commentators, pro- or anti-McCarthy, interpreted it as anything but complete and abject surrender on the part of the Secretary of the Army.

That afternoon the White House was filled with glum discussions of ways to do something about the Stevens debacle. In the Capitol a reporter passed by the hearings room of the Subcommittee, noticed the door open, and looked in. He saw McCarthy and Roy Cohn sitting at the end of the table and "laughing so hard," the newsman remembered, "that the room seemed to shake." . . .

From the day of the Memorandum of Agreement

the Administration moved against McCarthy, sometimes indirectly but steadily. Secretary Stevens countered the Memorandum with a strong statement and the President made plain that he backed his Secretary "one hundred percent." On March 11, 1954 the Army attacked with the charge that Senator McCarthy, Roy Cohn, and Francis Carr, the Subcommittee staff director, had sought, separately and collectively, by improper means, to obtain preferential treatment in the Army for G. David Schine, the Subcommittee consultant who was now a private in the Army. McCarthy and "associates" promptly replied with forty-six charges against the Army, of which the key one was that Secretary Stevens and John Adams, the department counselor, had tried to stop the Subcommittee's exposure of alleged Communists at Fort Monmouth and that they used Private Schine as a "hostage" to this end. Four more days and the Subcommittee voted to investigate the Army-McCarthy clash, with TV cameras in the room and with McCarthy temporarily replaced by the next ranking Republican, Senator Karl Mundt of South Dakota. Once again a TV spectacle would transfix the country and once again television would have a major part in shaping opinion on a critical national issue.

Shortly after 10 A.M. on April 22, 1954 the red lights in the cameras went on amid the florid Corinthian columns and the brocaded curtains of the large Senate Caucus Room. Senator Mundt tapped his big pipe, leaned forward, and delivered a little speech about how everything was going to be done with "dignity, fairness, and thoroughness." The ranking Democrat, John McClellan, said a few words to the same effect.

"Thank you very much, Senator McClellan," Chairman Mundt declared. "Our counsel, Mr. Jenkins, will now call the first witness." Ray Jenkins opened his mouth but the words came from down along the table. "A point of order, Mr. Chairman," McCarthy was saying. "May I raise a point of order?"

For thirty-six days and more than 2,000,000 words

Pussyfootprints on the Sands of Time

Cartoonist Herbert Block, a long-time foe of Senator McCarthy, coined the term McCarthyism in 1950. By early 1954, many Americans, previously spellbound by the senator's namecalling and red baiting, found themselves in sympathy with "Herblock's" point of view. Many were also appalled at what they saw as the moral cowardice of the President and the Senate, who they believed had turned their backs on a dangerous phenomenon for far too long. Later that year, when Eisenhower and the Senate struck back in the Army-McCarthy hearings, McCarthy was deflated and gradually faded away. (Pussyfootprints on the Sands of Time, from Herblock's Here and Now [Simon and Schuster 1955])

of testimony the hearings went on. A thousand impressions were driven into the public mind — Senator Mundt, roly-poly and pliable and so torn between his McCarthyite sympathies and the fact that he was supposed to be an impartial chairman that someone thought to call him the "tormented mushroom"; the Subcommittee's special counsel, Ray Jenkins, the homicide lawyer from Tellico Plains, Tennessee, chin stuck forward, intoning away with his questions; Senator John McClellan of Arkansas, the real terror of the Subcommittee, cadaverous and saturnine and pursuing everyone with a rasping logic; Robert Stevens, earnest and decent but having to pour out his, the Secretary of War's, pathetic attempts to mollify the friends of buck private G. David Schine; Roy Cohn, leaning over to make a point to McCarthy with a mouth that seemed perpetually pouting, obviously tremendously attached to Schine, obviously tremendously attached to Roy Cohn; Cohn and Schine, endlessly Cohn and Schine. But with each passing day one impression was having an increasingly potent effect on the millions at their TV sets. It was Joseph McCarthy, full-life, acting precisely like Joseph McCarthy.

"Point of order, point of order, Mr. Chairman," the Senator would interrupt in his scowling, sneering way until the children of the United States were imitating him on the streets. He repaid loyalty, like that of bumbling Senator Henry Dworshak of Idaho, by riding contemptuously over what the supporter was trying to say. He seized the floor from opponents by physical force, repeating in his strong, sing-song voice until the opponent wearily gave way. McCarthy flung smears and constantly accused others of smearing; his aides tried to use a cropped photograph and he cried deceit at the Army; he sidetracked, blatantly sidetracked, and demanded the end of "diversionary tactics." Day after day he was still Joe McCarthy of the boyhood fights, ceaselessly, recklessly swinging for the knockout.

The more reckless McCarthy became, the more strongly the Administration opposed him. In mid-May the President threw the Constitution of the United States at him. McCarthy became involved in demands that were flagrant violations of the rights of the Executive and from the White House came a blunt statement of those rights, which "cannot be usurped by any individual who may seek to set himself above the laws of our land." No one, not even the President of the United States, not even a President of his own party, was immune to the Senator's standard weapon, the charge of softness toward Communism. McCarthy's answer to Eisenhower was to talk once again of "the evidence of treason that has been growing over the past twenty — " Then he paused and added darkly: "twenty-one years."

The hearings ground on. The changing national mood, the Presidential opposition, and the appearance McCarthy was making on TV were costing the Senator heavily in public support. But he was still not a ruined man. The evidence was certainly not giving either side a clear-cut victory in the issues immediately at stake. Had the McCarthy group sought preferential treatment for Schine? Clearly they had. Had the Army tried to stop McCarthy's investigation at Fort Monmouth? Equally clearly it had — though it was emphasizing that it was anxious to get "that type" of hearing ended because it demoralized the Army. Other charges and countercharges were tangled in a maze of conflicting testimony. Throughout the country a good many pro-McCarthy or anti-anti-McCarthy people were wavering but they were only wavering. The Senator could have emerged from the hearing partially intact if he had now made some moves to present himself as a reasonable, responsible person. But Joseph McCarthy was not interested in being partially intact. He went on looking for the haymaker and the right man was present to see to it that when the Senator swung his wildest, he swung himself flat on his face.

The chief Army counsel, Joseph Welch, was a senior partner of the eminent Boston law firm of Hale and Dorr and he had a well-deserved reputation as an infinitely shrewd trial lawyer. But friends emphasized more Welch's innate sense of human decency and his gift of ironic laughter. They associated him with his spacious colonial home in Walpole, where he puttered around studying his thermometers (there were twelve in the house), spending a day fishing or an evening in a game of carom or cribbage, delighting more than anything else in kindly, bantering talk about the cosmos. Mrs. Welch had a favorite story about the whimsicality of the man. She liked to tell

how she had urged him to take up gardening, which he loathed, and he countered that he would garden if she would drink beer, which she detested. So on weekends the two would alternately garden in the broiling sun and stop for a beer in the shade, both grinning through their periods of suffering.

At the hearings Welch sat questioning away, his long, drooping face quizzical, his questions softly spoken and deftly insidious, dropping a damaging little jest and looking utterly surprised when people laughed. The sessions were only eight days old when the Army counsel drew blood. Welch was driving hard at a photograph which the McCarthy forces had produced, cropped to show only Stevens and Schine together although the original photograph contained two other men. The Army counsel brought out that the original had hung on Schine's wall and he questioned James Juliana, a Subcommittee employee who had arranged the cropping, as to why he had not brought the whole picture.

JULIANA: "I wasn't asked for it. . . ."
WELCH: ". . . You were asked for something different from the thing that hung on Schine's wall?"
JULIANA: "I never knew what hung on Schine's wall. . . ."
WELCH: "Did you think this came from a pixie? Where did you think this picture that I hold in my hand came from?"
JULIANA: "I had no idea."

There was a stir of voices and McCarthy interrupted. "Will counsel for my benefit define — I think he might be an expert on that — what a pixie is?"

Welch's face was beatific. "Yes. I should say, Mr. Senator, that a pixie is a close relative of a fairy. Shall I proceed, sir? Have I enlightened you?"

The spectators roared. Roy Cohn's pouting lips hardened into angry lines. The Senator glowered.

In the world of Joseph McCarthy nothing was more alien than the deft, and the Senator's feeling about Welch steadily mounted. He denied the Army counsel, or was wary of giving him, what he considered the ordinary camaraderie. McCarthy would walk up to friends and opponents alike, hand extended and the other hand grasping an arm, but he moved a wide circle around Joseph Welch. He first-named almost everybody — Secretary Stevens was "Bob" and the obviously hostile Senator Stuart Symington was "Stu." Welch was "Mr. Welch" or "the counsel."

Eight days before the hearings ended, on June 9, the Army counsel led Roy Cohn through a mocking, destructive cross-examination and McCarthy sat fuming. Now Welch was pressing Cohn as to why, if subversion was so serious at Fort Monmouth, he had not come crying alarm to Secretary Stevens. When Welch went ahead along this line, McCarthy began to grin broadly.

The Army counsel got in another dig at Cohn: "May I add my small voice, sir, and say whenever you know about a subversive or a Communist or a spy, please hurry. Will you remember these words?"

McCarthy broke in, bashed his way to attention. "In view of Mr. Welch's request that the information be given once we know of anyone who might be performing any work for the Communist Party, I think we should tell him that he has in his law firm a young man named Fisher whom he recommended, incidentally, to do work on this committee, who has been for a number of years a member of an organization which was named, oh, years and years ago, as the legal bulwark of the Communist Party. . . ."

The Senator was grinning ever more broadly, pausing now and then to lick his lips and savor his words. Roy Cohn sat in the witness chair, his legs dangling apart, the blood drained from his face, and once his lips seemed to be forming the words, "Stop, stop." McCarthy went on: "Knowing that, Mr. Welch, I just felt that I had a duty to respond to your urgent request. . . . I have hesitated bringing that up, but I have been rather bored with your phony requests to Mr. Cohn here that he personally get every Communist out of government before sundown. . . .

"I am not asking you at this time to explain why you tried to foist him on this committee. Whether you knew he was a member of that Communist organization or not, I don't know. I assume you did not, Mr. Welch, because I get the impression that, while you are quite an actor, you play for a laugh, I don't think you have any conception of the danger of the Communist Party. I don't think you yourself would ever knowingly aid the Communist cause. I think you are unknowingly aiding it when you try to burlesque this hearing in which we are trying to bring out the facts, however."

Welch was staring at McCarthy with the look of a man who was watching the unbelievable. The puck was gone; his face was white with anger. "Senator McCarthy," Welch began, "I did not know — "

McCarthy turned away contemptuously and talked to Juliana. Twice the Army counsel demanded his attention and the Senator talked to Juliana in a still louder voice, telling him to get a newspaper clipping about Fisher so that it could be put in the record.

Welch plunged ahead. "You won't need anything in the record when I have finished telling you this.

"Until this moment, Senator, I think I never really gauged your cruelty or your recklessness. Fred Fisher is a young man who went to the Harvard Law School and came into my firm and is starting what looks to be a brilliant career with us.

"When I decided to work for this committee I asked Jim St. Clair . . . to be my first assistant. I said to Jim, 'Pick somebody in the firm who works under you that you would like.' He chose Fred Fisher and they came down on an afternoon plane. That night, when we had taken a little stab at trying to see what the case was about, Fred Fisher and Jim St. Clair and I went to dinner together. I then said to these two young men, 'Boys, I don't know anything about you except that I have always liked you, but if there is anything funny in the life of either one of you that would hurt anybody in this case you speak up quick.'

"Fred Fisher said, 'Mr. Welch, when I was in law school and for a period of months after, I belonged to the Lawyers Guild.' . . . I said, 'Fred, I just don't think I am going to ask you to work on this case. If I do, one of these days that will come out and go over national television and it will just hurt like the dickens.'

"So Senator, I asked him to go back to Boston.

"Little did I dream you could be so reckless and so cruel as to do an injury to that lad. It is true he is still with Hale & Dorr. It is true that he will continue to be with Hale & Dorr. It is, I regret to say, equally true that I fear he shall always bear a scar needlessly inflicted by you. If it were in my power to forgive you for your reckless cruelty, I would do so. I like to think I am a gentle man, but your forgiveness will have to come from someone other than me."

The Senate Caucus Room was hushed. McCarthy fumbled with some papers, began saying that Welch had no right to speak of cruelty because he had "been baiting Mr. Cohn here for hours."

Welch cut off McCarthy. "Senator, may we not drop this? We know he belonged to the Lawyers Guild, and Mr. Cohn nods his head at me." Cohn was quite plainly nodding.

WELCH: "I did you, I think, no personal injury, Mr. Cohn."
COHN: "No, sir."
WELCH: "I meant to do you no personal injury, and if I did, I beg your pardon."

Cohn nodded again. The Army counsel turned back to McCarthy and his emotion was so great that on the TV screens his eyes seemed to be filling with tears. "Let us not assassinate this lad further, Senator. You have done enough. Have you no sense of decency, sir, at long last? Have you left no sense of decency?"

McCarthy tried to ask the Army counsel a question about Fisher. Welch cut him off again. He had recovered his composure now and his voice was cold with scorn. "Mr. McCarthy, I will not discuss this with you further. You have sat within 6 feet of me, and could have asked me about Fred Fisher. You have brought it out. If there is a God in heaven, it will do neither you nor your cause any good. I will not discuss it further. I will not ask Mr. Cohn any more questions. You, Mr. Chairman, may, if you will, call the next witness."

For a long few seconds the hush in the room continued. One of the few rules Chairman Mundt had tried hard to enforce was the one against demonstrations and six policemen were present to assist him. But suddenly the room shook with applause. For the first time in the memory of Washington observers, press photographers laid aside their cameras to join in the ovation for Welch. Chairman Mundt made no effort to interfere and instead soon called for a five-minute recess.

Joseph McCarthy sat slouched in his chair, breathing heavily. Spectators and reporters avoided him. Finally he found someone to talk to. He spread out his hands in a gesture of puzzlement and asked: "What did I do wrong?"

Joseph McCarthy would never know. And that June day, 1954, millions at their TV sets learned once and for all that Joseph McCarthy would never know.

McCarthy died in 1957 and with him died the worst flames of the communist scare that had produced him. Still, McCarthyism retained a powerful hold on thousands of Americans, who regarded the late senator as "the finest American who ever lived." Nor did the country at large reject him as rapidly as many historians have contended. In fact, as Robert Griffith observes in The Politics of Fear *(1970), 36 percent of the American people still approved of McCarthy after the Army-McCarthy hearings. And in the 1960s, a national television network that reran the hearings received countless letters wanting to know where McCarthy was now that America needed him.*

QUESTIONS TO CONSIDER

1. This selection and the previous one on the Truman-MacArthur imbroglio vividly evoke the national hysteria that marked the early days of the Cold War. What were the roots of the mass fear of

Communism? Do you think that the unprecedented possibility of planetary annihilation contributed to the 1950s hysteria?

2. Americans had a difficult time adjusting to the realities of power in the postwar nuclear age. How does this difficulty help to explain the enormous appeal of Joseph McCarthy's anti-Communist crusade?

3. Is there any evidence in Joseph McCarthy's personal background that might have indicated he was capable of the ruthless opportunism he displayed during the 1950s?

4. Examine the reasons leaders of McCarthy's own party — men such as Senator Robert Taft, who should have known better — supported McCarthy's red-baiting. Why did McCarthy meet such little opposition from any quarter — politicians, intellectuals, even the Eisenhower administration?

5. When McCarthy died in 1957, the worst excesses of the communist witch hunt died with him. But the fear of a Communist conspiracy in America, with its legacy of intolerance, lingered with the continued Cold War. What lessons does McCarthyism have for Americans today?

XI

FROM EISENHOWER
TO LBJ

The Ike Age

STEPHEN E. AMBROSE

Dwight David Eisenhower, the supreme commander of Allied forces in Europe during 1944 and 1945, was America's greatest hero in the postwar years. In 1952, the Republicans chose this balding, avuncular, mild-mannered soldier to win the White House back for the GOP after twenty straight years of Democratic chief executives. No Republican had occupied the White House since Herbert Hoover, whom much of the country had blamed for the crash and Depression. In the 1952 election, Eisenhower soundly defeated liberal Democrat Adlai E. Stevenson and went on to serve two terms in the White House. He left such a mark that the 1950s became popularly known as the Eisenhower years, or "the Ike Age."

For some contemporary critics, his mark was entirely negative, for they thought him an inept president who spent more time on the golf course than in tending to affairs of state. When he did attend to his job, such critics contended, his policies only worsened Cold War tensions. He ended up adopting Truman's containment policy and even announced "the domino theory," which held that if the West allowed the Communists to take over one country, they would seize its neighbors, then their neighbors, and so on until they had conquered the world. Other contemporary critics, however, regarded Ike as a masterful statesman who ended the Korean War, opposed military intervention in the internal struggles of other nations, and presided over a period of domestic prosperity.

In the years just after his presidency, historians tended to side with Eisenhower's hostile critics and rate him a poor chief executive. But more recently, with new evidence and new perspectives, scholars took another look at Eisenhower and liked what they saw. Their "revisionist" view has had a considerable influence on the current generation, so much so *that a recent poll of historians and presidential scholars ranked Ike ninth on the list of presidents. In this selection, historian Stephen E. Ambrose, author of an authoritative two-volume biography of Eisenhower, evaluates the revisionist assessment of Ike and concludes that his record is indeed enviable. In the course of his discussion, Ambrose sheds light on the process of historical interpretation, the way historians use evidence to assess a figure and an era.*

GLOSSARY

BROWN v. *TOPEKA BOARD OF EDUCATION* (1954)   Landmark case in which the United States Supreme Court outlawed segregated public schools (see selection 25).

COOK, BLANCHE WIESEN   Eisenhower scholar who maintains that Eisenhower was a "captive hero," an instrument of the multinational corporations "to fight for the world they wanted."

DULLES, JOHN FOSTER   Eisenhower's secretary of state and a militant cold warrior who believed that threats of "massive nuclear retaliation" were the best way to deal with the Communist world.

HO CHI MINH   Leader of the Vietnamese nationalist–Communist forces, the Vietminh, that fought to liberate Vietnam from French colonial rule; Ho's forces defeated the French army at Dien Bien Phu (see selection 24).

POWERS, FRANCIS GARY   Pilot of a U-2 surveillance, or spy, plane who was shot down over the Soviet Union in 1960; furious at this invasion of Soviet air space, Nikita Khruschchev, Soviet premier and Communist party chief, canceled a scheduled summit meeting with the American president.

WARREN, EARL   Appointed chief justice of the Supreme Court by President Eisenhower in 1953, Warren wrote the opinion in the *Brown* v *Board of Education* decision and presided over the most activist Supreme Court in American history.

Since Andrew Jackson left the White House in 1837, 33 men have served as president of the United States. Of that number, only [five] have managed to serve eight consecutive years in the office — Ulysses Grant, Woodrow Wilson, Franklin Roosevelt, Dwight Eisenhower, [and Ronald Reagan]. Of these [five], only two were also world figures in a field outside politics — Grant and Eisenhower — and only two had a higher reputation and broader popularity when they left office than when they entered — Roosevelt and Eisenhower.

Given this record of success, and the relative failure of Ike's successors, it is no wonder that there is an Eisenhower revival going on. . . . Another major reason for the current Eisenhower boom is nostalgia for the 1950s — a decade of peace with prosperity, a 1.5 percent annual inflation rate, self-sufficiency in oil and other precious goods, balanced budgets, and domestic tranquility. Eisenhower "revisionism," now proceeding at full speed, gives Ike himself much of the credit for these accomplishments.

The reassessment of Eisenhower is based on a multitude of new sources, as well as new perspectives, which have become available only in the past few years. The most important of these is Ike's private diary, which he kept on a haphazard basis from the late 1930s to his death in 1969. Other sources include his extensive private correspondence with his old military and new big business friends, his telephone conversations (which he had taped or summarized by his secretary, who listened in surreptitiously), minutes of

333

meetings of the cabinet and of the National Security Council, and the extensive diary of his press secretary, the late James Hagerty. Study of these documents has changed the predominant scholarly view of Eisenhower from, in the words of the leading revisionist, political scientist Fred Greenstein of Princeton, one of "an aging hero who reigned more than he ruled and who lacked the energy, motivation, and political skill to have a significant impact on events," to a view of Ike as "politically astute and informed, actively engaged in putting his personal stamp on public policy, [a man who] applied a carefully thought-out conception of leadership to the conduct of his presidency."

The revisionist portrait of Ike contains many new features. Far from being a "part-time" president who preferred the golf course to the Oval Office, he worked an exhausting schedule, reading more and carrying on a wider correspondence than appeared at the time. Instead of the "captive hero" who was a tool of the millionaires in his cabinet, Ike made a major effort to convince the Republican right wing to accept the New Deal reforms, an internationalist foreign policy, and the need to modernize and liberalize the Republican party. Rather than ducking the controversial issue of Joseph McCarthy, Eisenhower strove to discredit the senator. Ike's failure to issue a public endorsement of *Brown* v. *Topeka* was not based on any fundamental disagreement with the Warren Court's ruling [against segregated public schools], but rather on his understanding of the separation, the balance, of powers in the US government — he agreed with the decision, it turns out, and was a Warren supporter. Nor was Ike a tongue-tied general of terrible syntax; he was a careful speaker and an excellent writer who confused his audiences only when he wanted to do so.

From Stephen E. Ambrose, "The Age of Ike," in "The Ike Age," *New Republic* (May 9, 1981). Reprinted by permission of the New Republic, © 1981, The New Republic, Inc.

Most of all, the revisionists give Eisenhower high marks for ending the Korean War, staying out of Vietnam, and keeping the peace elsewhere. They argue that these achievements were neither accidental nor lucky, but rather the result of carefully conceived policies and firm leadership at the top. The revisionists also praise Ike for holding down defense costs, a key factor in restraining inflation while maintaining prosperity.

Altogether, the "new" Ike is an appealing figure, not only for his famous grin and winning personality, but also because he wisely guided us through perilous times.

"The bland leading the bland." So the nightclub comics characterized the Eisenhower administration. Much of the blandness came from Ike's refusal to say, in public, anything negative about his fellow politicians. His lifelong rule was to refuse to discuss personalities. But in the privacy of his diary, . . . he could be sarcastic, slashing, and bitter.

In 1953, when Ike was president and his old colleague from the war, Winston Churchill, was prime minister, the two met in Bermuda. Churchill, according to Ike,

has developed an almost childlike faith that all of the answers to world problems are to be found merely in British-American partnership. . . . He is trying to relive the days of World War II. In those days he had the enjoyable feeling that he and our president were sitting on some rather Olympian platform . . . and directing world affairs. Even if this picture were an accurate one of those days, it would have no application to the present. But it was only partially true, even then, as many of us who . . . had to work out the solutions for nasty local problems are well aware.

That realistic sense of the importance of any one individual, even a Churchill or a Roosevelt, was basic to Eisenhower's thought. Back in 1942, with reference to MacArthur, Ike scribbled in his diary that in modern war, "no one person can be a Napoleon or a Caesar." What was required was teamwork and cooperation.

Although Lyndon Johnson, John F. Kennedy, Hubert Humphrey, and other Democratic senators of the 1950s catch hell from time to time in Ike's diary, he reserved his most heartfelt blasts for the Republicans (he never expected much from the Democrats anyway). Thus, Ike wrote of Senator William Knowland of California, "In his case there seems to be no final answer to the question 'How stupid can you get?'" In *Eisenhower the President* . . . William Bragg Ewald Jr., a former Eisenhower speechwriter, records that when Republicans urged Ike to convince [New York Governor] Nelson Rockefeller to take the second place on a 1960 ticket with Richard Nixon, Ike did so, rather half-heartedly, and then reported on Rockefeller: "He is no philosophical genius. It is pretty hard to get him in and tell him something of his duty. He has a personal ambition that is overwhelming." Eisenhower told Nixon that the only way to persuade Rockefeller to run for the vice presidency was for Nixon to promise to step aside in Rockefeller's favor in 1964.

Ike didn't like "politics," and he positively disliked "politicians." The behind-the-scenes compromises, the swapping of votes for pork-barrel purposes, the willingness to abandon conviction in order to be on the popular side all nearly drove him to distraction. His favorite constitutional reform was to limit congressional terms to two for the Senate and three or four for the House, in order to eliminate the professional politician from American life.

Nor did Ike much like the press. "The members of this group," he wrote in his diary, "are far from being as important as they themselves consider," but he did recognize that "they have a sufficient importance . . . in the eyes of the average Washington officeholder to insure that much government time is consumed in courting favor with them and in dressing up ideas and programs so that they look as saleable as possible." Reporters, Ike wrote, "have little sense of humor and,

because of this, they deal in negative criticism rather than in any attempt toward constructive helpfulness." (Murray Kempton, in some ways the first Eisenhower revisionist, recalled how journalists had ridiculed Ike's amiability in the 1950s, while the president actually had intelligently confused and hoodwinked them. Kempton decided that Eisenhower was a cunning politician whose purpose was "never to be seen in what he did.")

The people Ike did like, aside from his millionaire friends, were those men who in his view rose above politics, including [his brother] Milton Eisenhower, Robert Anderson, and Earl Warren. Of Milton, Ike wrote in 1953, "I believe him to be the most knowledgeable and widely informed of all the people with whom I deal. . . . So far as I am concerned, he is at this moment the most highly qualified man in the United States to be president. This most emphatically makes no exception of me. . . ." Had he not shrunk from exposing Milton to a charge of benefiting from nepotism, Ike would have made his younger brother a member of his cabinet.

In 1966, during an interview in Eisenhower's Gettysburg office, I asked him who was the most intelligent man he had ever met, expecting a long pause while he ran such names as Marshall, Roosevelt, de Gaulle, Churchill, Truman, or Khrushchev through his mind. But Ike never hesitated: "Robert Anderson," he said emphatically. Anderson, a Texan and a Democrat, served Ike in various capacities, including secretary of the navy and secretary of the treasury. Now Ewald reveals for the first time that Eisenhower offered Anderson the second spot on the Republican ticket for 1956 and wanted Anderson to be his successor. Anderson turned down the President because he thought the offer was politically unrealistic.

Which inevitably brings up the subject of Richard Nixon. Eisenhower's relations with Nixon have long been a puzzle. Ike tried to get Nixon to resign during the 1952 campaign, but Nixon saved himself with the Checkers speech [in which he announced, "I'm not a quitter," and vowed to continue fighting "crooks and Communists"]. In 1956 Ike attempted to maneuver Nixon off the ticket by offering him a high-level cabinet post, but Nixon dug in his heels and used his connections with the right wing of the party to stay in place. And in 1960, Ike's campaign speeches for Nixon were distinctly unenthusiastic. Still, Eisenhower and Nixon never severed their ties. Ike stuck with Nixon throughout his life. He often remarked that Nixon's defeat by Kennedy was one of his greatest disappointments. And, of course, his grandson married one of Nixon's daughters. Sad to say, neither the diary nor the private correspondence offers any insights into Eisenhower's gut feelings toward Nixon. The relationship between the two men remains a puzzle.

Some writers used to say the same about the Eisenhower–Earl Warren relationship, but thanks to Ike's diary, Ewald's book, and the correspondence, we now have a better understanding of Eisenhower's feelings toward Warren personally, and toward his Court. In December 1955, Jim Hagerty suggested that if Ike could not run for a second term for reasons of health, Warren might make a good nominee. "Not a chance," Ike snapped back, "and I'll tell you why. I know that the Chief Justice is very happy right where he is. He wants to go down in history as a great Chief Justice, and he certainly is becoming one. He is dedicated to the Court and is getting the Court back on its feet and back in respectable standing again."

Eisenhower and Warren were never friends; as Ewald writes, "For more than seven years they sat, each on his eminence, at opposite ends of Pennsylvania Avenue, by far the two most towering figures in Washington, each playing out a noble role, in tragic inevitable estrangement." And he quotes Attorney General Herbert Brownell as saying, "Both Eisenhower and Warren were very reserved men. If you'd try to put your arm around either of them, he'd remember it for sixty days."

336

Ike had a great deal of difficulty with *Brown* v. *Topeka,* but more because of his temperament than for any racist reasons. He was always an evolutionist who wanted to move forward through agreement and compromise, not command and force. Ike much preferred consensus to conflict. Yet Ewald argues that he privately recognized the necessity and justice of *Brown* v. *Topeka.* Even had that not been so, he would have supported the Court, because — as he carefully explained to one of his oldest and closest friends, Sweed Hazlett, in a private letter — "I hold to the basic purpose. There must be respect for the Constitution — which means the Supreme Court's interpretation of the Constitution — or we shall have chaos. This I believe with all my heart — and shall always act accordingly."

Precisely because of that feeling, Eisenhower never made a public declaration of support for the *Brown* v. *Topeka* decision, despite the pleas of liberals, intellectuals, and many members of the White House staff that he do so. He felt that once the Supreme Court had spoken, the president had no right to second guess nor any duty to support the decision. The law was the law. That Ike was always ready to uphold the law, he demonstrated decisively when he sent the U.S. Army into Little Rock in 1957 to enforce court-ordered desegregation.

Despite his respect for Warren and the Court, when I asked Eisenhower in 1965 what was his biggest mistake, he replied heatedly, "The appointment of that S.O.B. Earl Warren." Shocked, I replied, "General, I always thought that was your best appointment." "Let's not talk about it," he responded, and we did not. Now that I have seen the flattering and thoughtful references to Warren in the diary, I can only conclude that Eisenhower's anger at Warren was the result of the criminal rights case of the early 1960s, not the desegregation decisions of the 1950s.[†]

. . . Ike also refused publicly to condemn Senator McCarthy, again despite the pleas of many of his own people, including his most trusted advisor, Milton. Ike told Milton, "I will not get into a pissing contest with that skunk."

The revisionists now tell us that the president was working behind the scenes, using the "hidden hand" to encourage peaceful desegregation and to censure McCarthy. He helped Attorney General Brownell prepare a brief from the Justice Department for the Court on *Brown* v. *Topeka* that attacked the constitutionality of segregation in the schools. As for McCarthy, Greenstein writes that Eisenhower,

working most closely with Press Secretary Hagerty, conducted a virtual day-to-day campaign via the media and congressional allies to end McCarthy's political effectiveness. The overall strategy was to avoid *direct mention* of McCarthy in the president's public statements, lest McCarthy win sympathy as a spunky David battling against the presidential Goliath. Instead Eisenhower systematically condemned the *types* of actions in which McCarthy engaged.

Eisenhower revisionism is full of nostalgia for the 1950s, and it is certainly true that if you were white, male, and middle class or better, it was the best decade of the century. The 1950s saw peace and prosperity, no riots, relatively high employment, a growing GNP, virtually no inflation, no arms race, no great reforms, no great changes, low taxes, little government regulation of industry or commerce, and a president who was trusted and admired. Politics were middle-of-the-road — Eisenhower was the least partisan president of the century. In an essay entitled "Good-By to the 'Fifties — and Good Riddance," historian Eric Goldman called the Eisenhower years possibly "the dullest and dreariest in all our history." After the turmoil of the 1960s and 1970s — war, inflation, riots, higher taxes, an arms race, all accompanied by a startling growth in the size, cost, and scope of the federal government — many Americans may find the dullness and dreariness of the 1950s appealing.

Next to peace, the most appealing fact was the 1.5 percent inflation rate. The revisionists claim that Ike deserved much of the credit for that accomplishment because of his insistence on a balanced budget (which he actually achieved only twice, but he did hold down the deficits). Ike kept down the costs by refusing to expand the New Deal welfare services — to the disgruntlement of the Republican right wing, he was equally firm about refusing to dismantle the New Deal programs — and, far more important, by holding down defense spending.

This was, indeed, Ike's special triumph. He feared that an arms race with the Soviet Union would lead to uncontrollable inflation and eventually bankrupt the United States, without providing any additional security. In Ike's view, the more bombs and missiles we built, the less secure we would be, not just because of the economic impact, but because the more bombs we built, the more the Soviets would build. In short, Ike's fundamental strategy was based on his recognition that in nuclear warfare, there is no defense and can be no winner. In that situation, one did not need to be superior to the enemy in order to deter him.

The Democrats, led by Senator John F. Kennedy, criticized Ike for putting a balanced budget ahead of national defense. They accused him of allowing a "bomber gap" and, later, a "missile gap" to develop, and spoke of the need to "get America moving again." Nelson Rockefeller and Richard Nixon added to the hue and cry during the 1960 campaign, when they promised to expand defense spending. But as long as Eisenhower was president, there was no arms race. Neither the politicians nor the military-industrial complex could persuade Eisenhower to spend more money on the military. Inheriting a $50 billion defense budget from Truman, he reduced it to $40 billion and held it there for the eight years of his tenure.

Holding down defense costs was a longstanding theme of Ike's. As early as December 1945, just after he replaced George Marshall as army chief of staff, he

---

†In a series of criminal rights decisions, most notably *Miranda* v. *Arizona* (1966), the Warren Court ruled that police had to advise suspects of their right to remain silent or to have an attorney present during interrogation, and that the state had to provide suspects with counsel at state expense, if they so requested.—Ed.

jotted in his diary, "I'm astounded and appalled at the size and scope of plans the staff sees as necessary to maintain our security position now and in the future." And in 1951, before he became a candidate, he wrote in his diary that if the Congress and military could not be restrained about "this armament business, we will go broke and still have inefficient defenses."

President Eisenhower was unassailable on the subject. As one senator complained, "How in hell can I argue with Ike Eisenhower on a military matter?" But as Ike wrote in 1956 to his friend Hazlett, "Some day there is going to be a man sitting in my present chair who has not been raised in the military services and who will have little understanding of where slashes in their estimates can be made with little or no damage. If that should happen while we still have the state of tension that now exists in the world, I shudder to think of what could happen in this country."

One reason why Ike was able to reduce the military in a time of great tension was his intimate knowledge of the Soviet military situation. From 1956 on, he directed a series of flights by the U-2 spy plane over the Soviet Union. He had personally taken the lead in getting the U-2 program started, and he kept a tight personal control over the flights — he gave his approval to the individual flights only after a thorough briefing on where in the USSR the planes were going and what the CIA wanted to discover. Here too the revisionists have shown that the contemporary feeling, especially after Francis Gary Powers was shot down in 1960, that Ike was not in charge and hardly knew what was going on inside his own government is altogether wrong. He was absolutely in charge, not only of broad policy on the use of the U-2, but of implementing details as well.

The major factor in Eisenhower's ability to restrain defense spending was keeping the peace. His record here is clear and impressive — he signed an armistice in Korea less than half a year after taking office, stayed out of Vietnam, and managed to avoid war despite such crisis situations as Hungary and the Suez, Que-

moy and Matsu, Berlin and Cuba. The revisionists insist that the credit must go to Ike, and they equally insist that Eisenhower, not Secretary of State John Foster Dulles, was in command of American foreign policy in the 1950s. Dulles, says Greenstein, "was assigned the 'get tough' side of foreign-policy enunciation, thus placating the fervently anti-Communist wing of the Republican party." Ike, meanwhile, appeared to be above the battle, while actually directing it on a day-to-day basis.

"In essence, Eisenhower used Dulles." So writes Robert Divine, one of America's leading diplomatic historians, in his provocative new book, *Eisenhower and the Cold War.* . . . Divine concludes that "far from being the do-nothing President of legend, Ike was skillful and active in directing American foreign policy." All the revisionists agree that the contemporary idea that Dulles led Ike by the nose was a myth that Eisenhower himself did the most to encourage. Nevertheless, Eisenhower did have a high opinion of his secretary of state. Divine quotes Ike's comment to Emmet Hughes on Dulles: "There's only one man I know who has seen *more* of the world and talked with more people and *knows* more than he does — and that's me."

The quotation illustrates another often overlooked Eisenhower characteristic — his immense self-confidence. He had worked with some of the great men of the century — Churchill, Roosevelt, Stalin, de Gaulle, Montgomery, and many others — long before he became president. His diary entry for the day after his inauguration speaks to the point: "My first day at the president's desk. Plenty of worries and difficult problems. But such has been my portion for a long time — the result is that this just seems (today) like a continuation of all I've been doing since July 1941 — even before that."

Ike's vast experience in war and peace made him confident in crises. People naturally looked to him for leadership. No matter how serious the crisis seemed to be, Ike rarely got flustered. During a war scare in the Formosa Straits in 1955, he wrote in his diary, "I

President Eisenhower with his secretary of state, John Foster Dulles. Eisenhower was content to let Dulles take much of the credit for success in American foreign policy during the 1950s, but recent findings by historians and biographers strongly suggest that Eisenhower was really in charge. The firm, intelligent expression on Ike's face, the decisive gesture, and the energetic pose pictured here, tend to confirm the revisionist view. (UPI/Bettmann Newsphotos)

have so often been through these periods of strain that I have become accustomed to the fact that most of the calamities that we anticipate really never occur."

Ike's self-confidence was so great that, Greenstein writes, he had "neither a need nor a desire" to capture headlines. "He's employed his skills to achieve his ends by inconspicuous means." In foreign policy, this meant he did not issue strident warnings, did not — in public — threaten Russia or China with specific reprisals for specific actions. Instead, he retained his

room for maneuver by deliberately spreading confusion. He did not care if editorial writers criticized him for jumbled syntax; he wanted to keep possible opponents guessing, and he did. For example, when asked at a March 1955 press conference if he would use atomic bombs to defend [the islands of] Quemoy and Matsu [off the coast of Communist China], he replied:

Every war is going to astonish you in the way it occurred, and in the way it is carried out. So that for a man to predict, particularly if he has the responsibility for making the decision, to predict what he is going to use, how he is going to do it, would I think exhibit his ignorance of war; that is what I believe.

As he intended, the Chinese found such statements inscrutable, as they had in Korea two years earlier. When truce talks in Korea reached an impasse in mid-May 1953, Ike put the pressure on the Chinese, hinting to them that the United States might use atomic weapons if a truce could not be arranged, and backing this up by transferring atomic warheads to American bases in Okinawa. The Chinese then accepted a truce. As Divine writes, "Perhaps the best testimony to the shrewdness of the President's policy is the impossibility of telling even now whether or not he was bluffing."

Nearly all observers agree that one of Ike's greatest accomplishments was staying out of Vietnam in the face of intense pressure from his closest advisers to save the French position there or, after July 1954, to go in alone to defeat Ho Chi Minh. Ike was never tempted. As early as March 1951 he wrote in his diary, "I'm convinced that no military victory is possible in that kind of theater." And in a first draft of his memoirs, written in 1963 but not published until 1981 by Ewald, Ike wrote:

The jungles of Indochina would have swallowed up division after division of United States troops, who, unaccustomed to this kind of warfare, would have sustained heavy casualties until they had learned to live in a new environment. Furthermore, the presence of ever more numbers of white men in uniform probably would have aggravated rather than assuaged Asiatic resentments.

That was hardheaded military reasoning by General Eisenhower. But President Eisenhower stayed out of Vietnam as much for moral as for military reasons. When the Joint Chiefs suggested to him in 1954 that the United States use an atomic bomb against the Vietminh around Dien Bien Phu, the President said he would not be a party to using that "terrible thing" against Asians for the second time in less than a decade. And in another previously unpublished draft of his memoirs, he wrote:

The strongest reason of all for the United States refusal to [intervene] is that fact that among all the powerful nations of the world the United States is the only one with a tradition of anti-colonialism. . . . The standing of the United States as the most powerful of the anti-colonial powers is an asset of incalculable value to the Free World. . . . Thus it is that the moral position of the United States was more to be guarded than the Tonkin Delta, indeed than all of Indochina.

Ike's international outlook, already well known, is highlighted by the new documents. He believed that the bonds that tied Western Europe and the United States together were so tight that the fate of one was the fate of the other. In May 1947, one year before the Marshall Plan, he wrote in his diary, in reference to Western Europe:

I personally believe that the best thing we could now do would be to post 5 billion to the credit of the secretary of state and tell him to use it to support democratic movements wherever our vital interests indicate. Money should be used to promote possibilities of self-sustaining economies, not merely to prevent immediate starvation.

And, as Blanche Wiesen Cook, another of the new Eisenhower scholars (but no revisionist), points out in

The Declassified Eisenhower . . . , Ike's vision of a peaceful world . . . "involved a determination to pursue political warfare, psychological warfare, and economic warfare everywhere and at all times." Under Ike's direction, she writes, the CIA and other branches of the government "ended all pretentions about territorial integrity, national sovereignty and international law. Covert operatives were everywhere, and they were active. From bribery to assassination, no activity was unacceptable short of nuclear war."

Cook does stress the importance of Eisenhower's stance against general war and his opposition to an arms race, but insists that these positions have to be placed in context, a context that includes the CIA-inspired and -led governmental overthrows in Iran and Guatemala, covert operations of all types in Vietnam and Eastern Europe, and assassination attempts against political leaders in the Congo and Cuba. Returning to an earlier view of Ike, Cook regards him as a "captive hero," the "chosen instrument" of the leaders of the great multinational corporations "to fight for the world they wanted."

One does not have to accept Cook's "captive hero" view to realize that . . . Ike had his shortcomings and he suffered serious setbacks. For all his openness to new ideas, he was rigid and dogmatic in his anti-communism. The darker side of Eisenhower's refusal to condemn McCarthy was that Ike himself agreed with the senator on the nature, if not the extent, of the problem, and he shared the senator's goals, if not his methods. After his first year in office, Ike made a list of his major accomplishments to date. Peace in Korea was first, the new defense policy second. Third on the list: "The highest security standards are being insisted upon for those employed in government service," a bland way of saying that under his direction, the Civil Service Commission had fired 2,611 "security risks" and reported that 4,315 other government workers had resigned when they learned they were under investigation. That was the true "hidden hand" at work, and the true difference between Ike and McCarthy — Ike got rid of Communists and fellow travelers (and many liberals) quietly and effectively, while McCarthy, for all his noise, accomplished nothing.

Thus, no matter how thoroughly the revisionists document Ike's opposition to McCarthy personally or his support for Warren, it remains true that his failure to speak out directly on McCarthy encouraged the witch hunters, just as his failure to speak out directly on the *Brown* v. *Topeka* decision encouraged the segregationists. The old general never admitted that it was impossible for him to be truly above the battle, never seemed to understand that the president is inevitably a part of the battle, so much so that his inaction can have as great an impact as his action.

With McCarthy and *Brown* v. *Topeka* in mind, there is a sad quality to the following Eisenhower diary passage, written in January 1954, about a number of Republican senators whom Ike was criticizing for being more inclined to trade votes than to provide clear leadership:

They do not seem to realize when there arrives that moment at which soft speaking should be abandoned and a fight to the end undertaken. Any man who hopes to exercise leadership must be ready to meet this requirement face to face when it arises; unless he is ready to fight when necessary, people will finally begin to ignore him.

One of Ike's greatest disappointments was his failure to liberalize and modernize the Republican party, in order to make it the majority party in the United States. "The Republican party must be known as a progressive organization or it is sunk," he wrote in his diary in November 1954. "I believe this so emphatically that far from appeasing or reasoning with the dyed-in-the-wool reactionary fringe, we should completely ignore it and when necessary, repudiate it." Responding to cries of "impeach Earl Warren," Ike

wrote in his diary, "If the Republicans as a body should try to repudiate him, I shall leave the Republican Party and try to organize an intelligent group of independents, however small." He was always threatening to break with the Republican party, or at least rename it; in March 1954, he told Hagerty, "You know, what we ought to do is get a word to put ahead of Republican — something like 'new' or 'modern' or something. We just can't work with fellows like McCarthy, Bricker, Jenner and that bunch."

A favorite revisionist quotation, which is used to show Ike's political astuteness, comes from a 1954 letter to his brother Edgar:

Should any political party attempt to abolish social security and eliminate labor laws and farm programs, you would not hear of that party again in our political history. There is a tiny splinter group, of course, that believes that you can do these things. Among them are H. L. Hunt, a few other Texas oil millionaires, and an occasional politician and businessman from other areas. Their number is negligible and they are stupid.

Good enough, but a critic would be quick to point out that Ike's "tiny splinter group" managed to play a large role in the nominations of Barry Goldwater, Richard Nixon, and Ronald Reagan. In short, although Ike saw great dangers to the right in the Republican party, he did little to counter the reactionary influence in his own organization. Franklin Roosevelt did a far better job of curbing the left wing in the Democratic party, and generally in building his party, than anything Ike did for the Republicans. . . .

Shortly after Ike left office, a group of leading American historians was asked to rate the presidents. Ike came in near the bottom of the poll. That result was primarily a reflection of how enamored the professors were with FDR and Harry Truman. Today, those same historians would compare Ike with his successors rather than his predecessors and place him in the top 10, if not the top five, of all our presidents. No matter how much one qualifies that record by pointing to this or that shortcoming or failure of the Eisenhower administration, it remains an enviable record. No wonder the people like Ike.

QUESTIONS TO CONSIDER

1. Describe the picture of Ike that dominated both historical and popular thinking in the twenty years following Eisenhower's second term of office. What kind of president did most people think he had been?

2. What led historians to re-evaluate Eisenhower? In particular, what new sources came to light and what effect did they have on new scholarship?

3. Describe the "new" Ike discovered by revisionist historians in the 1970s and 1980s. Why do you think Ike's political and personal integrity, his energy, and his moderation are now seen as a deliberate policy rather than as products of apathy or lack of imagina-

tion? What motivated Eisenhower to keep his strong opinions about Chief Justice Warren, Senator McCarthy, and others to himself? Why did he allow people to think his foreign policy was being directed by Secretary of State John Foster Dulles? Why did Ike almost always work behind the scenes to achieve his aims? Why didn't he care if people thought he was a dull, golf-playing, do-nothing president?

4. Ambrose contends that Ike's major achievement was keeping the peace during the 1950s and resisting tremendous pressure from his critics and from his own party to increase military spending. Why did the old general understand the military as no one else could? Do you see a degree of prescience in Eisenhower's fears of the future effect of military spending on the American economy?

5. Were you surprised when Ambrose revised the revisionists in the last paragraphs of this selection? What does Ambrose see as Eisenhower's greatest disappointment? his most signal failures? Where would you rank Ike among all American presidents?

24

The Nightmare of Vietnam

GEORGE C. HERRING

The Vietnam War was one of the most controversial episodes in United States history. American involvement in that conflict began with Truman and persisted through Democratic and Republican administrations alike, although the largest escalation took place under Lyndon Johnson—the subject of this selection.

To place George Herring's account in proper context, let us review what had gone on in Vietnam before the Johnson escalation. For more than twenty years, war had racked that distant Asian land. Initially, Communist and nationalist forces under Ho Chi Minh had battled to liberate their homeland from French colonial rule. The United States was suspicious of Ho, who was an avowed Communist trained in Moscow. But Ho was also an intense nationalist: he was determined to create a united and independent Vietnam and never wavered from that goal. Suspicious of Ho because of his Communist connections, the United States sided with the French against Ho and the Vietnamese; by 1954, when Dwight D. Eisenhower was president, the United States was footing 70 percent of the French cost of prosecuting a war that was highly unpopular in France. When Vietnamese forces surrounded and besieged twelve thousand French troops in Dien Bien Phu, Eisenhower's closest personal advisers urged armed American intervention to save the French position. Admiral Arthur Radford, chairman of the Joint Chiefs, even recommended dropping the atomic bomb on the Vietnamese. As Stephen Ambrose points out in selection 23, Eisenhower would have none of it.

The Eisenhower administration, however, continued using American aid and influence to combat communism in Indochina. In 1955, after suffering a humiliating defeat at Dien Bien Phu, the French withdrew from Vietnam, whereupon the United States acted to prevent Ho Chi Minh from gaining complete control there. Eisenhower and his secretary of state, John Foster Dulles, ignored an international agreement in Geneva that called for free elections and helped install a repressive, anti–Communist regime in South Vietnam, supplying it with money, weapons, and military advisers. From the outset, American policymakers viewed Ho Chi Minh's government in North Vietnam as part of a world Communist conspiracy directed by Moscow and Beijing. If communism was not halted in Vietnam, they feared, then all Asia would ultimately succumb. Eisenhower himself repeated the analogy that it would be like a row of falling dominoes.

American intervention aroused Ho Chi Minh, who rushed help to nationalist guerrillas in South Vietnam and set out to unite all of Vietnam under his leadership. With civil war raging across South Vietnam, the Eisenhower administration stepped up the flow of American military aid to the government there, situated in the capital city of Saigon. Under President John F. Kennedy, an enthusiast for counterinsurgency (or counterguerrilla warfare), the number of American advisers rose from 650 to 23,000. But Kennedy became disillusioned with American involvement in Vietnam and devised a disengagement plan before he was assassinated in November 1963. Whether he would have implemented the plan cannot be stated with certainty. When Vice President Johnson succeeded Kennedy, he nullified the disengagement plan and (with the encouragement of Kennedy's own advisers) continued American assistance to South Vietnam. Then, in the Gulf of Tonkin Resolution in August 1964, Congress empowered the president to use armed force against "Communist aggression" in Vietnam. But Johnson repeatedly vowed, "We are not going to send American boys nine or ten thousand miles away from home to do what Asian boys ought to be doing for themselves."

Over the next winter, however, all that changed. In November and December 1964, South Vietnamese guerrillas of the National Liberation Front (or Vietcong) killed seven United States advisers and wounded more than a hundred others in mortar and bomb attacks. Johnson's blood was up: he wasn't going to let them "shoot our boys" out there, fire on "our flag." He talked obsessively about Communist "aggression" in Vietnam, about Munich and the lesson of appeasement, about how his enemies would call him "a coward," "an unmanly man," if he let Ho Chi Minh run through the streets of Saigon. He couldn't depend on the United Nations to act—"It couldn't pour piss out of a boot if the instructions were printed on the heel." In February 1965, the administration became convinced that the coup-plagued Saigon government was about to collapse and that the United States had to do something drastic or South Vietnam would be lost and American international prestige and influence severely damaged. Accordingly, Johnson and his advisers moved to Americanize the war, sending waves of United States warplanes roaring over North Vietnam and 3,200 marines into the South.

The Americanization of the war took place with such stealth that people at home were hardly aware of the change. As reporter David Halberstam later wrote, United States *decision makers "inched across the Rubicon without even admitting it," and the task of their press secretaries was "to misinform the public." The biggest misinformers were Johnson and his spokesmen, who lied about costs (which were staggering), casualties, victories, and build-ups. By June, more than seventy-five thousand American soldiers were in Vietnam, and combat troops were fighting Vietcong and North Vietnamese regulars in an Asian land war that Johnson had sworn to avoid. Soon troops were pouring in, and the war reeled out of control as each American escalation stiffened Vietcong and North Vietnamese resistance, which in turn led to more American escalation. By 1968, more than 500,000 American troops were fighting in that fire-scarred land. In the eyes of the administration and the Pentagon, it was unthinkable that America's awesome military power could fail to crush tiny North Vietnam and the Vietcong.*

This sets the background for "The Nightmare of Vietnam," the story of the Americanization of the war under Lyndon Johnson. Herring not only offers trenchant insight into that powerful and pungent man but also captures the inconsistencies, frustration, and horror of America's longest and costliest war. Because of the similarities between the Vietnam War and the Philippine insurrection of 1898–1902, readers might want to review Kohler and Wensyel's "America's First Southeast Asian War" (selection 9), which draws important parallels between the two conflicts. Why do you think that Johnson and his advisers did not draw on the lessons learned in the Philippine war?

GLOSSARY

ARMY OF THE REPUBLIC OF VIETNAM (ARVN) The South Vietnamese army.

BALL, GEORGE Undersecretary of State and one of a handful of dissenters within the Johnson administration, Ball opposed the bombing of North Vietnam and Johnson's entire policy of escalation and Americanization of the war.

DOVES Those who opposed the war in Vietnam.

HAWKS Those who supported the war in Vietnam.

HO CHI MINH TRAIL Communist supply route from North Vietnam to Vietcong hideouts in South Vietnam.

MCNAMARA, ROBERT Johnson's Secretary of Defense who was so closely associated with escalation that the Vietnam conflict became known as "McNamara's war"; by 1967, however, he had changed his mind about escalation and now pressed for a basic change in policy, even for some face-saving way out of Vietnam; he resigned when Johnson lost confidence in him.

NEW LEFT Radical, upper-middle-class college students who opposed the war and saw it as a means to overthrow American capitalism itself.

OPERATION ROLLING THUNDER The American bombing campaign against North Vietnam that began early in 1965 and was expanded during the next two years in a vain attempt to check North Vietnamese aid to the Vietcong and force Ho Chi Minh to negotiate for peace; the bombing would continue until 1972.

VIETCONG (NATIONAL LIBERATION FRONT) Communist guerrillas of South Vietnam who fought with the North Vietnamese regular army to unify the country.

WESTMORELAND, GENERAL WILLIAM C. United States commander in Vietnam who employed an aggressive strategy of attrition against the Vietcong and North Vietnamese.

While visiting the aircraft carrier *Ranger* off the coast of Vietnam in 1965, Robert Shaplen overheard a fellow journalist remark: "They just ought to show this ship to the Vietcong — that would make them give up." From Lyndon Johnson in the White House to the GI in the field, the United States went to war in 1965 in much this frame of mind. The President had staked everything on the casual assumption that the enemy could be quickly brought to bay by the application of American military might. The first combat troops to enter Vietnam shared similar views. When "we marched into the rice paddies on that damp March afternoon," Marine Lieutenant Philip Caputo later wrote, "we carried, along with our packs and rifles, the implicit conviction that the Viet Cong would be quickly beaten." Although by no means unique to the Vietnam War, this optimism does much to explain the form taken by American participation in that struggle. The United States never developed a strategy appropriate for the war it was fighting, in part because it was assumed that the mere application of its vast military power would be sufficient. The failure of one level of force led quickly to the next and then the next, until the war attained a degree of destructiveness no one would have thought possible in 1965. Most important, the optimism with which the nation went to war more than anything else accounts for the great frustration that subsequently developed in and out of government. Failure never comes easily, but it comes especially hard when success is anticipated at little cost.

Within two years, the optimism of 1965 had given way to deep and painful frustration. By 1967, the United States had nearly a half million combat troops in Vietnam. It had dropped more bombs than in all

From George C. Herring, *America's Longest War: The United States and Vietnam, 1950–1975* (2nd ed.), McGraw-Hill Inc. Reproduced with permission of McGraw–Hill.

theaters in World War II and was spending more than $2 billion per month on the war. Some American officials persuaded themselves that progress had been made, but the undeniable fact was that the war continued. Lyndon Johnson thus faced an agonizing dilemma. Unable to end the war by military means and unwilling to make the concessions necessary to secure a negotiated settlement, he discovered belatedly what George Ball had warned in 1964: "once on the tiger's back we cannot be sure of picking the place to dismount."

American strategy in Vietnam was improvised rather than carefully designed and contained numerous inconsistencies. The United States went to war in 1965 to prevent the collapse of South Vietnam, but it was never able to relate its tremendous military power to the fundamental task of establishing a viable government in Saigon. The administration insisted that the war must be kept limited — the Soviet Union and China must not be provoked to intervene — but the President counted on a quick and relatively painless victory to avert unrest at home. That these goals might not be compatible apparently never occurred to Johnson and his civilian advisers. The United States injected its military power directly into the struggle to cripple the Vietcong and persuade North Vietnam to stop its "aggression." The administration vastly underestimated the enemy's capacity to resist, however, and did not confront the crucial question of what would be required to achieve its goals until it was bogged down in a bloody stalemate.

While the President and his civilian advisers set limits on the conduct of the war, they did not provide firm strategic guidelines for the use of American power. Left on its own to frame a strategy, the military fought the conventional war for which it was prepared without reference to the peculiar conditions in Vietnam. . . .

The United States relied heavily on airpower. Military doctrine taught that bombing could destroy an enemy's warmaking capacity, thereby forcing him to come to terms. The limited success of airpower as ap-plied on a large scale in World War II and on a more restricted scale in Korea raised serious questions about the validity of this assumption, and the conditions prevailing in Vietnam, a primitive country with few crucial targets, might have suggested even more. The Air Force and Navy advanced unrealistic expectations about what airpower might accomplish, however, and clung to them long after experience had proven them unjustified. The civilian leadership accepted the military's arguments, at least to a point, because the bombing was cheaper in lives lost and therefore more palatable at home, and because it seemed to offer a quick and comparatively easy solution to a complex problem. Initiated in early 1965 as much from the lack of alternatives as anything else, the bombing of North Vietnam was expanded over the next two years in the vain hope that it would check infiltration into the south and force North Vietnam to the conference table.

The air war gradually assumed massive proportions. The President firmly resisted the Joint Chiefs' proposal for a knockout blow, but as each phase of the bombing failed to produce results, he expanded the list of targets and the number of strikes. Sorties against North Vietnam increased from 25,000 in 1965 to 79,000 in 1966 and 108,000 in 1967; the tonnage of bombs dropped increased from 63,000 to 136,000 to 226,000. Throughout 1965, [Operation] ROLLING THUNDER concentrated on military bases, supply depots, and infiltration routes in the southern part of the country. From early 1966 on, air strikes were increasingly directed against the North Vietnamese industrial and transportation system and moved steadily northward. In the summer of 1966, Johnson authorized massive strikes against petroleum storage facilities and transportation networks. A year later, he permitted attacks on steel factories, power plants, and other approved targets around Hanoi and Haiphong, as well as on previously restricted areas along the Chinese border.

The bombing inflicted an estimated $600 million damage on a nation still struggling to develop a viable, modern economy. The air attacks crippled North Vietnam's industrial productivity and disrupted its agriculture. Some cities were virtually leveled, others severely damaged. Giant B-52s, carrying payloads of 58,000 pounds, relentlessly attacked the areas leading to the Ho Chi Minh Trail, leaving the countryside scarred with huge craters and littered with debris. The bombing was not directed against the civilian population, and the administration publicly maintained that civilian casualties were minimal. But the CIA estimated that in 1967 total casualties ran as high as 2,800 per month and admitted that these figures were heavily weighted with civilians; [Secretary of Defense Robert] McNamara privately conceded that civilian casualties were as high as 1,000 per month during periods of intensive bombing. . . .

The manner in which airpower was used in Vietnam virtually ensured that it would not achieve its objectives, however. Whether, as the Joint Chiefs argued, a massive, unrestricted air war would have worked remains much in doubt. In fact, the United States had destroyed many major targets by 1967 with no demonstrable effect on the war. Nevertheless, the administration's gradualist approach gave Hanoi time to construct an air defense system, protect its vital resources, and develop alternative modes of transportation. Gradualism probably encouraged the North Vietnamese to persist despite the damage inflicted upon them.

North Vietnam demonstrated great ingenuity and dogged perseverance in coping with the bombing. Civilians were evacuated from the cities and dispersed across the countryside; industries and storage facilities were scattered and in many cases concealed in caves and under the ground. The government claimed to have dug over 30,000 miles of tunnels, and in heavily bombed areas the people spent much of their lives underground. An estimated 90,000 North Vietnamese, many of them women and children, worked full-time keeping transportation routes open, and piles of gravel were kept along the major roadways, enabling

"Youth Shock Brigades" to fill craters within hours after the bombs fell. Concrete and steel bridges were replaced by ferries and pontoon bridges made of bamboo stalks which were sunk during the day to avoid detection. Truck drivers covered their vehicles with palm fronds and banana leaves and traveled at night, without headlights, guided only by white markers along the roads. B-52s devastated the narrow roads through the Mu Gia Pass leading to the Ho Chi Minh Trail, but, to the amazement of the Americans, trucks moved back through the pass within several days. "Caucasians cannot really imagine what ant labor can do," one American remarked with a mixture of frustration and admiration.

Losses in military equipment, raw materials, and vehicles were more than offset by increased aid from the Soviet Union and China. Until 1965, Russia had remained detached from the conflict, but the new leaders who succeeded Khrushchev in October 1964 took much greater interest in the Vietnam conflict, and U.S. escalation presented opportunities and challenges they could not pass up. The bombing created a need for sophisticated military equipment only the Soviet Union could provide, giving Moscow a chance to wean North Vietnam away from China. At a time when the Chinese were loudly proclaiming Soviet indifference to the fate of revolutions across the world, the direct threat to a Communist state posed by the air strikes required the Russians to prove their credibility. American escalation did not force the two Communist rivals back together, as George Ball had predicted. Fearful of Soviet intrusion in Vietnam, the Chinese angrily rejected Moscow's call for "united action" (a phrase borrowed, perhaps consciously, from Dulles) and even obstructed Russian aid to North Vietnam. The increasingly heated Sino-Soviet rivalry over Vietnam did, however, enable Hanoi to play off one power against the other to get increased aid and prevent either from securing predominant influence. The Chinese continued to supply large quantities of rice, small arms and ammunition, and vehicles. Soviet aid increased dramatically after 1965, and included such modern weaponry as fighter planes, surface-to-air missiles, and tanks. Total assistance from Russia and China has been estimated in excess of $2 billion between 1965 and 1968. . . .

By 1967, the United States was paying a heavy price for no more than marginal gains. The cost of a B-52 mission ran to $30,000 per sortie in bombs. The direct cost of the air war, including operation of the aircraft, munitions, and replacement of planes lost, was estimated at more than $1.7 billion during 1965 and 1966, a period when aircraft losses exceeded 500. Overall, the United States between 1965 and 1968 lost 950 aircraft costing roughly $6 billion. According to one estimate, for each $1 of damage inflicted on North Vietnam, the United States spent $9.60. The costs cannot be measured in dollars alone, however. Captured American airmen gave Hanoi a hostage which would assume increasing importance in the stalemated war. The continued pounding of a small, backward country by the world's wealthiest and most advanced nation gave the North Vietnamese a propaganda advantage they exploited quite effectively. Opposition to the war at home increasingly focused on the bombing, which, in the eyes of many critics was at best inefficient, at worst immoral.

American ground operations in the south also escalated dramatically between 1965 and 1967. Even before he had significant numbers of combat forces at his disposal, [United States commander William C.] Westmoreland had formulated the strategy he would employ until early 1968. It was a strategy of attrition, the major objective of which was to locate and eliminate the Vietcong and North Vietnamese regular units. Westmoreland has vigorously denied that he was motivated by any "Napoleonic impulse to maneuver units and hark to the sound of cannon," but "search and destroy," as it came to be called, did reflect traditional U.S. Army doctrines of warfare. In Westmoreland's view, North Vietnam's decision to commit large units to the war left him no choice but to proceed along these lines. He did not have suffi-

cient forces to police the entire country, nor was it enough simply to contain the enemy's main units. "They had to be pounded with artillery and bombs and eventually brought to battle on the ground if they were not forever to remain a threat." Once the enemy's regulars had been destroyed, Westmoreland reasoned, the South Vietnamese government would be able to stabilize its position and pacify the countryside, and the adversary would have no choice but to negotiate on terms acceptable to the United States.

Westmoreland's aggressive strategy required steadily increasing commitments of American manpower. Even before the 1965 buildup had been completed, the General requested sufficient additional forces to bring the total to 450,000 by the end of 1966. In contrast to the air war, over which it retained tight control, the administration gave Westmoreland broad discretion in developing and executing the ground strategy, and it saw no choice but to give him most of the troops he asked for. In June 1966, the President approved a force level of 431,000 to be reached by mid-1967. While these deployments were being approved, Westmoreland was developing requests for an increase to 542,000 troops by the end of 1967.

Furnished thousands of fresh American troops and a massive arsenal of modern weaponry, Westmoreland took the war to the enemy. He accomplished what has properly been called a "logistical miracle," constructing virtually overnight the facilities to handle huge numbers of U.S. troops and enormous volumes of equipment. The Americans who fought in Vietnam were the best fed, best clothed, and best equipped army the nation had ever sent to war. In what Westmoreland described as the "most sophisticated war in history," the United States attempted to exploit its technological superiority to cope with the peculiar problems of a guerrilla war. To locate an ever elusive enemy, the military used small, portable radar units and "people sniffers" which picked up the odor of human urine. IBM 1430 computers were programmed to predict likely times and places of enemy attacks. Herbicides were used on a wide scale and

A medic treats a wounded American soldier during the Tet offensive, mounted by the North Vietnamese in late January of 1968. By that time, more than half million American men then fighting in Vietnam, and the war bogged down in a stalemate. At home protests mounted as the war became increasingly unpopular with ordinary Americans, and Lyndon Johnson, refusing to run for another term, ended his presidency in a cloud of adverse public opinion. (McCullin/Magnum Photos)

with devastating ecological consequences to deprive the Vietcong of natural cover. C-123 "RANCH-HAND" crews, with the sardonic motto "Only You Can Prevent Forests," sprayed more than 100 million pounds of chemicals such as Agent Orange over millions of acres of forests, destroying an estimated one-half of South Vietnam's timberlands and leaving human costs yet to be determined. . . .

In a war without front lines and territorial objectives, where "attriting the enemy" was the major goal, the "body count" became the index of progress. Most authorities agree that the figures were notoriously unreliable. The sheer destructiveness of combat made it difficult to produce an accurate count of enemy killed in action. It was impossible to distinguish between Vietcong and noncombatants, and in the heat of battle American "statisticians" made little effort. "If it's dead and Vietnamese, its VC, was a rule of thumb in the bush," Philip Caputo has recalled. Throughout the chain of command there was heavy pressure to produce favorable figures, and padding occurred at each level until by the time the numbers reached Washington they bore little resemblance to reality. Even with an inflated body count — and estimates of padding range as high as 30 percent — it is clear that the United States inflicted huge losses on the enemy. Official estimates placed the number as high as 220,000 by late 1967. Largely on the basis of these figures, the American military command insisted that the United States was "winning" the war.

As with the air war, the strategy of attrition had serious flaws. It assumed that the United States could inflict intolerable losses on the enemy while keeping its own losses within acceptable bounds, an assumption that flew in the face of past experience with land wars on the Asian continent and the realities in Vietnam. An estimated 200,000 North Vietnamese reached draft age each year, and Hanoi was able to replace its losses and match each American escalation. Moreover, the conditions under which the war was fought permitted the enemy to control its losses. The North Vietnamese and Vietcong remained extraordinarily elusive and were generally able to avoid contact when it suited them. They fought at times and places of their own choosing and on ground favorable to them. If losses reached unacceptable levels, they could simply melt away into the jungle or retreat into sanctuaries in North Vietnam, Laos, and Cambodia.

Thus, the United States could gain no more than a stalemate. The North Vietnamese and Vietcong had been hurt, in some cases badly, but their main forces had not been destroyed. They retained the strategic initiative, and could strike sharply and quickly when and where they chose. Westmoreland did not have sufficient forces to wage war against the enemy's regulars and control the countryside. The Vietcong political structure thus remained largely untouched, and even in areas such as the Iron Triangle, when American forces moved on to fight elsewhere, the Vietcong quietly slipped back in. It all added up to a "state of irresolution," Robert Shaplen observed in 1967. . . .

Thus, despite the impressive body count figures, it was clear to many observers by mid-1967 that the hopes of a quick and relatively inexpensive military victory had been misplaced. Each American blow "was like a sledgehammer on a floating cork," the journalist Malcolm Browne observed. "Somehow the cork refused to stay down." . . .

. . . Americanization of the war created new and equally formidable problems. Among these, the most serious — and most tragic — was that of the refugees. The expansion of American and enemy military operations drove an estimated four million South Vietnamese, roughly 25 percent of the population, from their native villages. Some drifted into the already teeming cities; others were herded into shabby refugee camps. The United States furnished the government some $30 million a year for the care of the refugees, but much of the money never reached them. Resettlement programs were initiated from time to time, but the problem was so complex that it would have taxed the ingenuity of the most imaginative officials. In any event, nothing could have compensated the refugees for the loss of their homes and lands. A large portion of South Vietnam's population was left rootless and hostile, and the refugee camps became fertile breeding grounds for Vietcong fifth columns.

The sudden infusion of half a million American troops, hundreds of civilian advisers, and billions of dollars had a profoundly disruptive effect on a weak and divided nation. The buildup was so rapid and so vast that it threatened to overwhelm South Vietnam. Saigon's ports were congested with ships and goods, and vessels awaiting unloading were backed up far out to sea. The city itself became a "thorough-going boom town," Shaplen remarked, its streets clogged with traffic, its restaurants "bursting with boisterous soldiers," its bars "as crowded as New York subway cars in the rush hour." Signs of the American presence appeared everywhere. Long strips of seedy bars and brothels sprang up overnight around base areas. In a remote village near Danang, Caputo encountered houses made of discarded beer cans: "red and white Budweiser, gold Miller, cream and brown Schlitz, blue and gold Hamm's from the land of sky-blue waters."

American spending had a devastating effect on the vulnerable South Vietnamese economy. Prices increased by as much as 170 percent during the first two years of the buildup. The United States eventually controlled the rate of inflation by paying its own soldiers in scrip and by flooding the country with consumer goods, but the corrective measures themselves had harmful side effects. Instead of using American aid to promote economic development, South Vietnamese importers bought watches, transistor radios, and Hondas to sell to people employed by the United States. The vast influx of American goods destroyed South Vietnam's few native industries and made the economy even more dependent on continued outside aid. By 1967, much of the urban population was employed providing services to the Americans.

In the bonanza atmosphere, crime and corruption flourished. Corruption was not new to South Vietnam or unusual in a nation at war, but by 1966 it operated on an incredible scale. Government officials rented land to the United States at inflated prices, required bribes for driver's licenses, passports, visas, and work permits, extorted kickbacks for contracts to build and service facilities, and took part in the illicit importation of opium. The black market in scrip, dollars, and stolen American goods became a major enterprise. On Saigon's PX Alley, an open-air market covering two city blocks and comprised of more than 100 stalls, purchasers could buy everything from hand grenades to scotch whiskey at markups as high as 300 percent. Americans and Vietnamese reaped handsome profits from the illegal exchange of currencies. International swindlers and "monetary camp followers" quickly got into the act, and the currency-manipulation racket developed into a "massive financial international network" extending from Saigon to Wall Street with connections to Swiss banks and Arab sheikdoms. The pervasive corruption undermined the U.S. aid program and severely handicapped American efforts to stabilize the economy of South Vietnam.

American officials perceived the problem, but they could not find solutions. [Prime Minister Nguyen Cao] Ky candidly admitted that "most of the generals are corrupt. Most of the senior officials in the prov-

inces are corrupt." But, he would add calmly, "corruption exists everywhere, and people can live with some of it. You live with it in Chicago and New York." The Embassy pressed the government to remove officials known to be corrupt, but with little result. "You fight like hell to get someone removed and most times you fail and you just make it worse," a frustrated American explained to David Halberstam. "And then on occasions you win, why hell, they give you someone just as bad." The United States found to its chagrin that as its commitment increased, its leverage diminished. Concern with corruption and inefficiency was always balanced by fear that tough action might alienate the government or bring about its collapse. . . .

Tensions between Americans and South Vietnamese increased as the American presence grew. Because of chronic security leaks, the United States kept Vietnamese off its major bases, and Vietcong infiltration of the ARVN's top ranks compelled U.S. officers to keep from their Vietnamese counterparts the details of major military operations. . . . The seeming indifference of many Vietnamese, while Americans were dying in the field, provoked growing resentment and hatred. The unerring ability of the villagers to avoid mines and booby traps that killed and maimed GIs led to charges of collusion with the enemy.

The Vietnamese attitude toward the foreigner was at best ambivalent. The Vietnamese undoubtedly appreciated American generosity, but they came to resent American ways of doing things. They complained that American soldiers "acted despicably" toward the villagers, tearing up roads and endangering the lives of noncombatants by reckless handling of vehicles and firearms. An ARVN major protested that Americans trusted only those Vietnamese who accepted without question their way of doing things and that they doled out their aid "in the same way as that given to beggars." The Vietnamese recognized their need for U.S. help, and some were probably quite content to let the United States assume complete responsibility for the war. On the other hand, many Vietnamese resented the domineering manner of the Americans and came to consider the U.S. "occupation" a "demoralizing scourge." Thoughtful Vietnamese recognized that Americans were not "colonialists," Shaplen observed. But, he added, "there has evolved here a colonial ambiance that can sometimes be worse than colonialism itself." . . .

The steady expansion of the war spurred strong international and domestic pressures for negotiations, but the military stalemate produced an equally firm diplomatic impasse. American officials later tallied as many as 2,000 attempts to initiate peace talks between 1965 and 1967. Neither side could afford to appear indifferent to such efforts, but neither was willing to make the concessions necessary to make negotiations a reality. Although the North Vietnamese attempted to exploit the various peace initiatives for propaganda advantage, they counted on the American people to tire of the war and they remained certain that they could achieve their goals if they persisted. Hanoi adamantly refused to negotiate without first securing major concessions from the United States. Johnson and his advisers could not ignore the various proposals for negotiations, but they doubted that anything would come of them and suspected, not without reason, that Hanoi was expressing interest merely to get the bombing stopped. Despite any firm evidence of results, the President remained confident at least until 1967 that North Vietnam would eventually bend to American pressure, and he feared that if he were too conciliatory it would undercut his strategy. To defuse international and domestic criticism, Johnson repeatedly insisted that he was ready to negotiate, but he refused to make the concessions Hanoi demanded. As each side invested more in the struggle, the likelihood of serious negotiations diminished.

The positions of the two sides left little room for compromise. The North Vietnamese denounced American involvement in Vietnam as a blatant violation of the Geneva Accords, and as a precondition to negotiations, insisted that the United States withdraw its troops, dismantle its bases, and stop all acts of war against their country. Hanoi stressed that the internal affairs of South Vietnam must be resolved by the South Vietnamese themselves "in accordance with the program of the National Liberation Front." North Vietnam was apparently flexible in regard to the timing and mechanism for political change in the south, but on the fundamental issues it was adamant. The "puppet" Saigon regime must be replaced by a government representative of the "people" in which the front would play a prominent role. Hanoi made clear, moreover, that the "unity of our country is no more a matter for negotiations than our independence." . . .

By mid–1967, Johnson was snared in a trap he had unknowingly set for himself. His hopes of a quick and relatively painless victory had been frustrated. He was desperately anxious to end the war, but he had been unable to do so by force, and in the absence of a clear-cut military advantage, or a stronger political position in South Vietnam, he could not do so by negotiations. As the conflict increased in cost, moreover, he found himself caught in the midst of an increasingly angry and divisive debate at home, a debate which by 1967 seemed capable of wrecking his presidency and tearing the country apart.

At one extreme were the "hawks," largely right-wing Republicans and conservative Democrats, who viewed the conflict in Vietnam as an essential element in the global struggle with Communism. Should the United States not hold the line, they argued, the Communists would be encouraged to further aggression, allies and neutrals would succumb to Communist pressures, and the United States would be left alone to face a powerful and merciless enemy. Strong nationalists, certain of America's invincibility, and deeply frustrated by the stalemate in Vietnam, the hawks bitterly protested the restraints imposed on the military and demanded that the administration do whatever was necessary to attain victory. . . .

At the other extreme were the "doves," a vast,

sprawling, extremely heterogeneous and fractious group, which opposed the war with increasing bitterness and force. The antiwar movement grew almost in proportion to the escalation of the conflict. It included such diverse individuals as the pediatrician Dr. Benjamin Spock, heavyweight boxing champion Muhammad Ali, actress Jane Fonda, and author Norman Mailer, old-line pacifists such as A. J. Muste and new radicals such as Tom Hayden, the black civil rights leader Dr. Martin Luther King, Jr., and Arkansas Senator J. William Fulbright. The doves comprised only a small percentage of the population, but they were an unusually visible and articulate group. Their attack on American foreign policy was vicious and unrelenting. In time, their movement became inextricably linked with the cultural revolution that swept the United States in the late 1960s and challenged the most basic of American values and institutions.

Although it defies precise categorization, the antiwar movement tended to group along three principal lines. For pacifists such as Muste, who opposed all wars as immoral, Vietnam was but another phase of a lifelong crusade. For the burgeoning radical movement of the 1960s, opposition to the war extended beyond questions of morality. Spawned by the civil rights movement, drawing its largest following among upper-middle-class youth on college campuses, the "New Left" joined older leftist organizations in viewing the war as a classic example of the way the American ruling class exploited helpless people to sustain a decadent capitalist system. Antiwar liberals far exceeded in numbers the pacifists and radicals. Although they did not generally question "the system," they increasingly questioned the war on both moral and practical grounds. Many liberal internationalists who had supported World War II, Korea, and the Cold War found Vietnam morally repugnant. By backing a corrupt, authoritarian government, they contended, the United States was betraying its own principles. In the absence of any direct threat to American security, the devastation wreaked on North and South Viet-

nam was indefensible. Many more liberals questioned the war on practical grounds. It was essentially an internal struggle, they argued, whose connection with the Cold War was at best indirect. Liberals questioned the validity of the domino theory. . . . They agreed that Vietnam was of no more than marginal significance to the security of the United States. Indeed they insisted that the huge investment there was diverting attention from more urgent problems at home and abroad, damaging America's relations with its allies, and inhibiting the development of a more constructive relationship with the Soviet Union. The liberal critique quickly broadened into an indictment of American "globalism." The United States had fallen victim to the "arrogance of power," Fulbright claimed, and was showing "signs of that fatal presumption, that over-extension of power and mission, which brought ruin to ancient Athens, to Napoleonic France and to Nazi Germany.

. . . Most liberals stopped short of advocating withdrawal from Vietnam, much less domestic revolution, proposing merely an end to the bombing, gradual deescalation, and negotiations. Disagreement on methods was even sharper. Liberals generally preferred nonviolent protest and political action within the system and sought to exclude the Communists from demonstrations. Radicals and some pacifists increasingly pressed for a shift from protest to resistance, and some openly advocated the use of violence to bring down a system that was itself violent.

Opposition to the war took many different forms. Fulbright conducted a series of nationally televised hearings, bringing before the viewing public critics of administration policies. There were hundreds of acts of individual defiance. The folk singer Joan Baez refused to pay that portion of her income tax that went to the defense budget. Muhammad Ali declared himself a conscientious objector and refused induction orders. Three army enlisted men — the Fort Hood Three — challenged the constitutionality of the conflict by refusing to fight in what they labeled an "unjust, immoral, and illegal war." Army Captain Howard Levy used the doctrine of individual responsibility set forth in the Nuremberg war crimes trials to justify his refusal to train combat teams for action in Vietnam. Thousands of young Americans exploited legal loopholes, even mutilated themselves, to evade the draft; others fled to Canada or served jail sentences rather than to go to Vietnam. A handful of Americans adopted the method of protest of South Vietnam's Buddhists, publicly immolating themselves. Antiwar rallies and demonstrations drew larger crowds in 1966 and 1967, and the participants became more outspoken in their opposition. Protesters marched daily around the White House chanting "Hey, hey, LBJ, how many kids have you killed today?" and "Ho, Ho, Ho Chi Minh, NLF is going to win." Antiwar forces attempted "lie-ins" in front of troop trains, collected blood for the Vietcong, and tried to disrupt the work of draft boards, Army recruiters, and the Dow Chemical Company, one of the makers of the napalm used in Vietnam. The most dramatic single act of protest came on October 21, 1967, when as many as 100,000 foes of the war gathered in Washington and an estimated 35,000 demonstrated at the entrance to the Pentagon, the "nerve center of American militarism."

The impact of the antiwar protests remains one of the most controversial issues raised by the war. The obvious manifestations of dissent in the United States probably encouraged Hanoi's will to hold out for victory, although there is nothing to suggest that the North Vietnamese would have been more compromising in the absence of the movement. Antiwar protest did not turn the American people against the war, as some critics have argued. The effectiveness of the movement was limited by the divisions within its own ranks. Public opinion polls make abundantly clear, moreover, that a majority of Americans found the antiwar movement, particularly its radical and "hippie" elements, more obnoxious than the war itself. In a perverse sort of way, the protest may even have strengthened support for a war that was not in itself popular. The impact of the movement was much more limited and subtle. It forced Vietnam onto the public consciousness and challenged the rationale of the war and indeed of a generation of Cold War foreign policies. It limited Johnson's military options and may have headed off any tendency toward more drastic escalation. Perhaps most important, the disturbances and divisions set off by the antiwar movement caused fatigue and anxiety among the policymakers and the public, and thus eventually encouraged efforts to find a way out of the war.

The majority of Americans appear to have rejected both the hawk and dove positions, but as the war dragged on and the debate became more divisive, public concern increased significantly. Expansion of the war in 1965 had been followed by a surge of popular support — the usual rally-round-the-flag phenomenon. But the failure of escalation to produce any discernible result and indications that more troops and higher taxes would be required to sustain a prolonged and perhaps inconclusive war combined to produce growing frustration and impatience. If any bird symbolized the growing public disenchantment with Vietnam, opinion analyst Samuel Lubell observed, it was the albatross, with many Americans sharing a "fervent desire to shake free of an unwanted burden." The public mood was probably best expressed by a housewife who told Lubell: "I want to get out but I don't want to give up."

Support for the war dropped sharply during 1967. By the summer of that year, draft calls exceeded 30,000 per month, and more than 13,000 Americans had died in Vietnam. In early August, the President recommended a 10 percent surtax to cover the steadily increasing costs of the war. Polls taken shortly after indicated that for the first time a majority of Americans felt that the United States had been mistaken in intervening in Vietnam, and a substantial majority concluded that despite a growing investment, the United States was not "doing any better." Public approval of Johnson's handling of the war plummeted to 28 percent by October. Waning public confidence was mirrored in the press and in Congress. A number of major metropolitan dailies shifted from support of the war to opposition in 1967, and the influential *Time-Life* publications, fervently hawkish at the outset, began to raise serious questions about the administration's policies. Members of Congress found it impossible to vote against funds for American forces in the field and hesitated to challenge the President directly, but many who had firmly backed him at first came out openly against him. Admitting that he had once been an "all-out hawk," Republican Senator Thruston B. Morton of Kentucky spoke for the converts when he complained that the United States had been "planted into a corner out there" and insisted that there would "have to be a change." White House aides nervously warned of further defections in Congress and major electoral setbacks in 1968 in the absence of dramatic changes in the war.

By late 1967, for many observers the war had become the most visible symbol of a malaise that had afflicted all of American society. Not all would have agreed with Fulbright's assertion that the Great Society was a "sick society," but many did feel that the United States was going through a kind of national nervous breakdown. The "credibility gap" — the difference between what the administration said and what it did — had produced a pervasive distrust of government. Rioting in the cities, a spiraling crime rate, and noisy demonstrations in the streets suggested that violence abroad had produced violence at home. Increasingly divided against itself, the nation appeared on the verge of an internal crisis as severe as the Great Depression of the 1930s. Anxiety about the war had not translated into a firm consensus for either escalation or withdrawal, but the public mood — tired, angry, and frustrated — perhaps posed a more serious threat to the administration than the anti-war movement.

The public debate on Vietnam was paralleled by increasingly sharp divisions within the government. . . . The major proponent of change by the spring of 1967 was, ironically, the Secretary of Defense, a man who had been so closely associated with escalation that the war had for a time been called "McNamara's

war." As early as the summer of 1966, McNamara began to fear that the vast expansion of the war was endangering the global security position he had labored so diligently to construct since taking office in 1961. He was troubled by the destructiveness of the war, particularly the civilian casualties, and by the growing domestic opposition, brought home to him time and again in public appearances when he had to shove his way through and shout down protesters. McNamara's reputation as a businessman and public servant had been based on his ability to attain maximum results at minimal cost. By early 1967, however, he was forced to admit that escalation of the war had not produced results in the major "end products — broken enemy morale and political effectiveness." The South Vietnamese government seemed no more stable than before; pacification had "if anything, gone backward." The air war had brought heavy costs but no results. "Ho Chi Minh is a tough old S.O.B.," McNamara conceded to his staff. "And he won't quit no matter how much bombing we do." Moreover, the Secretary of Defense admitted that the bombing had cost the United States heavily in terms of domestic and world opinion. "The picture of the world's greatest superpower killing or seriously injuring 1,000 non-combatants a week, while trying to pound a tiny, backward nation into submission on an issue whose merits are hotly disputed, is not a pretty one," he advised Johnson in early 1967. McNamara and his advisers were also disillusioned with the ground war in South Vietnam. Increases in U.S. troops had not produced correspondingly large enemy losses, and there was nothing to indicate that further expansion of the war would place any real strains on North Vietnamese manpower.

Throughout 1967, McNamara quietly and somewhat hesitantly pressed for basic changes in policy. Arguing that the major military targets in North Vietnam had already been destroyed, he proposed either an unconditional bombing halt or the restriction of the bombing to the area south of the twentieth parallel. Such a move, he added, would help to appease critics of the war at home and might lead to serious negotiations. The Secretary of Defense also advocated placing a ceiling on American troop levels, and shifting from search and destroy to a more limited ground strategy based on providing security for the population of South Vietnam. In somewhat ambiguous terms, he further proposed a scaling down of American political objectives. Inasmuch as the United States had gone to war to contain China, he argued, it had succeeded: the Communist defeat in Indonesia, as well as rampant political turmoil within China itself, suggested that trends in Asia were now running against China and in favor of the United States. The administration might therefore adopt a more flexible bargaining position. It could still hope for an independent, non-Communist South Vietnam, but it should not obligate itself to "guarantee and insist upon these conditions." Obliquely at least, McNamara appears to have been suggesting that the United States modify its military strategy and diplomatic stance in order to find a face-saving way out of its dilemma in Vietnam.

By the summer of 1967, Lyndon Johnson was a deeply troubled man, physically and emotionally exhausted, frustrated by his lack of success, torn between his advisers, uncertain which way to turn. He seems to have shared many of McNamara's reservations, and he flatly rejected the view of the military that the solution was expansion of the war. He was disenchanted by the Joint Chiefs. "Bomb, bomb, bomb, that's all you know," he is said to have complained on several occasions. He was worried by the implications of Westmoreland's ground strategy and his request for more troops. "When we add divisions, can't the enemy add divisions?" he asked the General pointedly in April. "If so, where does it all end?" He remained firmly opposed to mobilizing the reserves and expanding the war. Such measures would heighten the domestic opposition. They would not satisfy the military but would only lead to pressures for further escalation, perhaps even for the use of nuclear weapons. He continued to fear a confrontation with the Soviet Union or China. "I am not going to spit in China's face," he insisted.

Johnson could not accept McNamara's recommendations, however. He had gradually lost confidence in his Secretary of Defense, whose dovishness he incorrectly attributed to the pernicious influence of his arch-rival Robert Kennedy. The relationship between Johnson and McNamara had so soured by late 1967 that the Secretary gladly accepted an appointment to head the World Bank. Westmoreland continued to report steady progress, moreover, and the President was not ready to concede defeat. He would not consider a return to the enclave strategy — "We can't hunker down like a jackass in a hailstorm," he said — or even a ceiling on the troop level. Although he seems to have agreed that the bombing had accomplished nothing, he was not prepared to stop or even limit it. Denouncing McNamara's proposals as an "aerial Dienbienphu," the Joint Chiefs had threatened to resign en masse if Johnson approved them, and the hawkish Mississippi Senator John Stennis was planning an investigation into the conduct of the air war. The President was not prepared to risk a major confrontation with the hawks or a potentially explosive public debate on the bombing. . . .

[By the end of 1967, Vietnam was destroying Johnson's presidency.] The consensus which Johnson had so carefully woven in 1964 was in tatters, the nation more divided than at any time since the Civil War. Opposition in Congress, as well as inattention and mismanagement resulting at least partially from the administration's preoccupation with Vietnam, had brought his cherished Great Society programs to a standstill. The President himself was a man under siege in the White House, his popularity steadily waning, the target of vicious personal attacks. His top aides had to be brought surreptitiously into public forums to deliver speeches.

Johnson was alarmed by the position he found himself in, stung by his critics, and deeply hurt by the desertion of trusted aides such as McNamara. He angrily dismissed much of the criticism as unfair, and he repeatedly emphasized that his critics offered no alternatives. He had accomplished great things at home, he insisted. But the press could only whine "Veetnam, Veetnam, Veetnam, Veetnam," he would add savagely mimicking a baby crying. The harsher the criticism became, the more Johnson chose to disregard it by discrediting the source. Fulbright was a "frustrated old woman" because he had never been appointed Secretary of State. The dissent of the young sprang from ignorance. They had not lived through World War II. They would not "know a Communist if they tripped over one." . . .

. . . Johnson did not reevaluate his essential goals in Vietnam. To take such a step would have been difficult for anyone as long as there was hope of eventual success. It would have been especially difficult for Lyndon Johnson. Enormously ambitious, he had set high goals for his presidency, and he was unwilling to abandon them even in the face of frustration and massive unrest at home. It was not a matter of courage, for by persisting in the face of declining popularity Johnson displayed courage as well as stubbornness. It was primarily a matter of pride. The President had not wanted the war in Vietnam, but once committed to it he had invested his personal prestige to a degree that made it impossible for him to back off. He chose to stay the course in 1967 for the same reasons he had gone to war in the first place — because he saw no alternative that did not require him to admit failure or defeat.

While quietly contemplating a change in strategy, the President publicly made clear his determination to see the war through to a successful conclusion. "We are not going to yield," he stated repeatedly. "We are not going to shimmy. We are going to wind up with a peace with honor which all Americans seek." At a White House dinner for the Prime Minister of Singapore, the President expressed his commitment in different terms. "Mr. Prime Minister," he said, "you have a phrase in your part of the world that puts our determination very well. You call it 'riding the tiger.' You rode the tiger. We shall!"

Although Johnson continued to boast that "the enemy had been defeated in battle after battle" and that America was winning the war, the Vietcong on the last day of January 1968 launched the massive Tet offensive in South Vietnam, attacking 36 of 44 provincial capitals, 64 district towns and countless villages, 12 United States bases, and even the American embassy in Saigon. This seemed undeniable proof that Johnson's military solution was a failure and that the claims of the President and his generals could not be believed.

In 1968, the war drove Johnson from office — he refused to seek another term — and helped bring Richard Nixon to the White House, because he promised to end the conflict. Yet Nixon seemed to take up where Johnson left off. Like his predecessors, Nixon worried about "American credibility," about what would happen to American prestige if the United States sold out its South Vietnamese ally, and in 1970 he sent American troops into contiguous Cambodia to exterminate Communist hideouts there. The Cambodian invasion brought antiwar protest to a tragic climax, as Ohio national guards troops opened fire on protesting students at Kent State University and killed four of them. With the campuses in turmoil and the country divided and adrift, Nixon gradually disengaged American ground troops in Vietnam and sought détente with both Russia and China.

Although the Nixon administration continued to speak of "peace with honor" in Indochina, and although it continued to bomb Hanoi, it was clear nevertheless that American involvement in the Vietnamese civil war was a tragic and costly mistake. Indeed, the signs were unmistakable that the original premise for American intervention in Indochina was erroneous. The domino theory, based as it was on the assumption of a worldwide monolithic Communist conspiracy directed by Moscow, appeared more and more implausible. For one thing, China and Russia developed an intense and bitter ideological feud that sharply divided the Communist world, and they almost went to war over their disputed boundary. The Sino-Soviet split exploded the notion of a Communist monolith out for world dominion, and so did the fierce independence of North Vietnam itself. Although Hanoi continued to receive aid from both Russia and China, North Vietnam apparently never asked China to intervene in the struggle (and apparently China never offered to do so).

The truth was that North Vietnam was fighting to unite the country under Hanoi's leadership rather than under Beijing's or Moscow's.

At last, in top-secret negotiations in Paris, United States Secretary of State Henry Kissinger and North Vietnam's Le Duc Tho worked out a peace agreement. Eventually, the United States removed its combat forces, and in 1975 South Vietnam's regime fell to the North Vietnamese and the National Liberation Front. After almost two decades of bitter civil war and the loss of more than 1 million lives, Vietnam was united under Hanoi's Communist government, something that would probably have happened without further violence had general elections been held in 1956, according to the Geneva agreements of two years before.

QUESTIONS TO CONSIDER

1. According to Herring, what were the major problems with American military strategy in Vietnam? Why were conditions in Vietnam unsuited for conventional warfare?

2. What important social and economic consequences did Americanization of the war have for South Vietnam?

3. What repercussions did the war in Vietnam have in American society? Would you agree with Senator William Fulbright's assertion that the Great Society was a sick society?

4. Compare the prowar and antiwar arguments of American hawks and doves. How much influence did the antiwar movement have in shaping public attitudes?

5. What trait in Lyndon Johnson's personality and character made him unable to alter his course of action in Vietnam?

XIII

CULTURE SHOCK

Shattering the Feminine Mystique

MARCIA COHEN

In "Not Wards of the Nation" (selection 12), William H. Chafe described women's long, hard struggle to gain the right to vote. By 1920, they had that right. Yet it threw the women's movement into disarray. The social feminists contended that enfranchised women should enter community service and campaign for civic virtue. The more militant feminists — now organized in the Woman's party — wanted equal rights and even demanded an equal rights amendment to the Constitution. During the Great Depression, as Sara Evans has said, women "were partners in the struggle for survival." They also became involved in social and political activity; indeed, a "women's network" emerged within the New Deal and the Democratic party, allowing women for the first time to become a grassroots force. But women's achievements in the thirties proved to be short-lived, Evans says, and women as a whole "were not empowered."

During the Second World War, as we saw in selection 19, women made significant economic advances as workers in America's defense plants. But after the war, as Marcia Cohen points out in this selection, the industrial establishment tended to push women back into the home because it recognized "the housewife's valuable role as the prime consumer of household products." At the same time, women's magazines such as Red-book and McCall's, many of them published and edited by men, popularized the image of the happy housewife and stressed the old female virtues of passivity, marriage, and motherhood.

The image of the happy homemaker and contented "auxiliary" bothered Betty Friedan, who in the mid-1950s was living in the suburb of Rockland County, New York, and trying to combine marriage and motherhood with freelance journalism. Back in the 1940s, she had been a brilliant student at Smith College and had done such outstanding work in psychology that she won a fellowship from the University of California at Berkeley. There she studied with the famous analyst Erik Erikson and won an even more prestigious grant that would have carried her into a professional career. But for some incredible reason — perhaps because a young man she was dating complained about the fellowship — she turned it down. Almost at once she suffered a protracted attack of asthma. Wheezing, gasping for breath, she left academe and the young man and fled to New York, where she sought relief in psychoanalysis.

When she felt better, she secured an editorial position at a small labor newspaper, married an amusing, ambitious man named Carl Friedan, and started raising a family. When she became pregnant with her second child, her employer decided that one pregnancy leave was enough; the paper fired her, ignoring the stipulation in her contract that guaranteed her maternity leave. She protested, but the Newspaper Guild refused to support her. Meanwhile, her marriage to Carl was becoming stormy; when they argued, she said, books and sugar bowls seemed to fly. Racked again by asthma, she resumed psychoanalysis.

Now living in a suburban Victorian house, Friedan did occasional freelance writing for women's magazines. She was increasingly attracted to stories about women who wanted the same thing she did — an integrated life that used all of a woman's talents. She noted that prosperity offered the American woman an education and a living standard her grandmother would have envied, but it brought frustration too. By the 1950s, the American woman had been educated as never before, but to what end? When Friedan sent out a questionnaire for an article she was writing for McCall's, she was astounded to learn that many women felt as unhappy as she did. Worse, their discontents were hidden behind the pervasive image of the happy housewife. In 1963, after years of struggling, Friedan published a book about that image called The Feminine Mystique; it galvanized millions of female readers and rocketed Friedan to national fame. In this selection, journalist Marcia Cohen, author of The Sisterhood (1988), recounts the extraordinary story of how Friedan came to write The Feminine Mystique and to challenge a whole generation's assumptions and practices as far as women were concerned.

GLOSSARY

BROCKWAY, GEORGE   Editor at W. W. Norton who signed Friedan to write *The Feminine Mystique,* which grew out of her article, "The Togetherness Woman."

BROWN, HELEN GURLEY   Author of *Sex and the Single Girl* (1962) and editor of *Cosmopolitan* who played a "pioneering role" in the sexual liberation of women in the 1960s and 1970s.

STEIN, BOB   Editor of *Redbook* who agreed to

publish an article ("The Togetherness Woman") based on Friedan's Smith class questionnaire if she expanded it to include younger women; he rejected the completed article on the ground that it would appeal only to "the most neurotic housewife."

"THE TOGETHERNESS WOMAN"   An article Friedan wrote for *McCall's* magazine, the male editor of which refused to publish it; based on a questionnaire Friedan had sent to her Smith College classmates, the article attacked woman's "homemaking role" as dull and unrewarding.

WOMEN'S WORLD (1952)   Motion picture that stressed how much the home was a "woman's world" in which women buried their ambitions and subordinated themselves to their husbands.

It was a strange stirring, a sense of dissatisfaction, a yearning that women suffered in the middle of the twentieth century in the United States. Each suburban wife struggled with it alone. As she made the beds, shopped for groceries, matched slipcover material, ate peanut butter sandwiches with her children, chauffeured Cub Scouts and Brownies, lay beside her husband at night, she was afraid to ask even of herself the silent question — "Is this all?"

BETTY FRIEDAN, *The Feminine Mystique,* 1963

Her so-called "brilliant career"! Not much had come of that, Betty thought miserably as she trudged back to her beloved Smith College for her fifteenth reunion. The great promise her professors had seen — that eager, whirling intellectual energy — had come to nothing more than a couple of women's magazine articles. Hardly "brilliant." Hardly even worthy of the term "career"!

Betty — the class of 1942's hortatory, patriotic, tough tomato, always ready to take on an argument and, more often than not, *win* it. That same plump little girl who was so determined, way back in Peoria, to make her snooty contemporaries "respect her," who had set out, in her younger brother Harry's words, "to be somebody important . . ."

She was now, in 1957, returning to the alma mater that had been for her, such a glory, an affirmation, "that whole thing," as she would put it years later in her gruff, gravelly voice, "of the *passion* of the mind." And she was coming back not as the professional psychologist they must all have expected, but as, well, "just a housewife" with a few articles to her credit.

"It rankled me," she would remember, "because I hadn't lived up to my brilliant possibilities."

But the undergraduates on campus, she found, were

From "Shattering the Feminine Mystique" by Marcia Cohen, in Cohen's *The Sisterhood* (Simon and Schuster, 1988), 83–99. Copyright © 1988 by Marcia Cohen. Reprinted by permission of Simon & Schuster, Inc.

not the slightest bit interested in such "possibilities," and she was shocked by their distracted answers to her questions. Questions about, naturally, their scholarly interests, what ideas or professors they were "passionately excited about."

"They looked at me," she would recall, "as if I were speaking a foreign language. 'We're not excited about things like that,' they said. 'All we want to do is to get married and have children and do things with them, like go ice skating . . .'"

But it was now, of course, the quiet Eisenhower era, the gritrock pit of what would be viewed in retrospect as the heavy-duty husband-hunting years. "I chased her until she caught me," was a standard husband's joke, though the truth probably lay as much in the male youth's intent on settling down as the female's. The house in the suburbs, the station wagon bursting with kids and collie dogs, the ability to provide for a family proved manhood as much as homemaking proved femininity, and testified as well to those most important virtues of the decade: "adjustment," "maturity."

By now psychology was a preoccupation. Freud's vaunted theory of "penis envy" and [Dr. Helene] Deutsch's interpretation of the achieving, intellectual woman as "masculinized . . . her warm, intuitive knowledge . . . [having] yielded to cold unproductive thinking," hinted of maladjustments to be avoided at all costs. The idea that woman's true nature, reflecting her anatomy, was passive and could be fulfilled only through renouncing her goals and "sublimating" to a male had taken firm root in the American ethic.

The women's magazines, growing ever more powerful as advertising pages and circulations mounted, had been pounding the message home for nearly a decade. Women, as [Ferdinand] Lundberg and [Dr. Marynia F.] Farnham had written [in *Modern Woman: The Lost Sex*], needed propaganda to keep them *in* traditional homemaking tasks, such as cooking or decorating, and *out* of those "fields belonging to the male area" — that is, "law, mathematics, physics, business, industry and technology." And indeed, the

magazines invariably portrayed women as, above and beyond all else, housewives and mothers. If an interview subject happened to be an actress or dancer (two acceptably feminine undertakings), the editors quickly clarified: She was merely dabbling, taking a breather from her real work — and life — at home.

Nor was this notion purely the province of the popular press. Great citadels of learning were equally convinced and convincing. In most eastern women's schools, "gracious living" was the order of the day. This meant, on the whole, little more than learning to pour tea from a silver-plated samovar. But to carry

The idealized housewife from 1955, shown here on the cover of the Saturday Evening Post for May 21, was well dressed and fashionably coiffed, even at home. Surrounded by modern appliances in her impeccable kitchen, she looks just as discontented as Betty Freidan found her a few years later — although the problem was a great deal more complex than runny chocolate icing. (The Saturday Evening Post)

out this future mission, give or take a samovar, you had to have a life of gentility, with, of course, a husband. Most college women, even those who never stood their turn at the tea kettle, knew beyond a shadow of a doubt that marriage — not a career — was their primary goal in life. Running a close second was the psychological health of their children, who were likely to erupt into neurotic misfits, psychologists warned, should Mother attempt any serious work outside the home.

Admittedly, the female's focus on marriage had an extra edge. The birth rate was soaring and given their dependent condition, women needed to be supported financially. The status gap of the thirties — between the gracious, respected matron, cared for by her breadwinner husband, and the lonely, forlorn working girl — was revived and slickly refurbished. Rare indeed was the college counselor who, by discussing the job market, would damn a female graduate to the latter state.

Some women left college without graduating. (Might as well get on with it. What's the point of waiting, anyhow?) Most collected a "Mrs." after or with their undergraduate degrees. You understood that you were marrying not just a husband but "a life," and this wholesale effort seemed at the time to blur class distinctions. Women cooked pot roast everywhere.

That there were, in fact, differences — in both class and interests — would eventually create knotty problems for feminists of the future. Many women, not only working-class women but also those with less defined intellectual appetites, very much enjoyed their roles as homemakers, household decision makers, disciplinarians, or managers, preferences that would eventually set them at odds with the revolutionaries of the sixties.

At the moment, though, like it or not, most women were preparing for the esteemed role of "auxiliary."

If, for instance, a woman was married to a doctor, she would join the hospital "auxiliary," have dinner ready when the doctor got home, and subscribe to a magazine called *Doctor's Wife*.

It was a given, in those days, that a young woman with a burning interest in the law should marry a lawyer. She would help him develop his practice and live the life of a lawyer's wife, mother of a lawyer's children. Or an engineer's, or a writer's, or a pharmacist's, or a retailer's — or especially a corporate executive's. That the deportment of an executive's wife had a major influence on her husband's advancement was a lesson clearly delivered, not just in an announcement from Radcliffe College of an Institute for Executive Wives, but in Jean Negulesco's popular film pointedly entitled *Women's World*.

In this 1952 movie, Lauren Bacall — no longer the sultry siren of the forties — played a devoted wife who, along with two others, June Allyson and Arlene Dahl, was summoned to corporate headquarters in New York, where their husbands were about to audition for top honcho.

"The best couple for the job," the company owner frankly informed the men, "will win. Your wife is under observation. She must never compete with the company. If there is a choice between wife and work, it must be work."

As the husbands in this "women's world" proceeded with their unmemorable politicking, the motivations (and "qualifications") of the wives were quickly established. June was frightfully anxious to rush home to her kids in the Midwest. Lauren fretted that the job might exacerbate her husband's ulcer. Arlene, on the other hand, was so delighted by the prospect of life in New York that she overreached by flirting with the owner, thus proving that she had missed not just one, but several commandments dosed out in the dialogue.

I. "What's important to him is important to me."

II. "You must convince him that you're perfectly happy even if you feel like screaming."

III. "The man who gets the job must have a wife who loves him very much."

IV. (the overriding theme): "A man is working for the children, and they're your children so it's a *woman's world.*"

And if, in the end, it's Arlene's man who does win the job, this plot twist occurs only after her restrained, expressionless husband has impressed the owner by dispensing with his "handicap": his ambitious, brazen, childless (and therefore dispensable) wife.

Though heavy-handed, the movie accurately reflected a large segment of the women's world of the fifties, where back in the suburbs wives quickly buried ambitions of the sort (vicarious or not) that plagued the unfortunate Arlene.

Few could imagine, in the expanding economy of the post–Korean War years, that among these selfless wives would be many who would find themselves, twenty and thirty years hence, in the wake of defunct marriages or financial belt-tightening, pounding the pavements, or training for jobs that could bring in much-needed cash or restore flagging self-esteem.

There were, of course, exceptions. A few remarkable college graduates *did* pursue professional careers. Among them, ironically — though barely noticed at the time — was an assertive, achieving Illinois woman who, in 1952, ran for Congress. Phyllis Schlafly, who would eventually stand forth as the new feminism's most vocal enemy, who would sound the alarm for women's return to the home, was among those who were not, at the moment, at home.

For even then, in spite of the social propaganda, many women, including those from middle-income families, were quietly moving into the workforce — so many, in fact, that they soon accounted for 60 percent of its growth in that decade. Among them were many single women, including college graduates who, as they waited for Mr. Right, took jobs as "Gal Fridays" in ad agencies, or as researchers, "helping" a reporter on a news magazine. Many took speed-writ-

ing or shorthand courses so they could be secretaries and thus avoid the typing pool, jobs for which there was plenty of call under "Female" in the help-wanted columns. The men who ran America's industries knew better than to give their girls (as in "Call my girl, she'll make an appointment for you") dangerous notions about careers. "Gal Fridays," summa cum laude be damned, ran errands and made coffee. They were lucky, they were told, to be hired at all, since it was a given that they wouldn't be around for long. If they were "normal," they would soon drop out to get married, have babies.

And if they were "normal," they were known to be emotionally delicate as well, not cut out for the rough-and-tumble of the business world. . . .

If, for example, a wife was working outside the home, she retained her auxiliary, ladylike status by referring to her job as unimportant and transitory, a diversion, never a "career." She was helping out — just for the moment — with the family finances. She was subdued and modest. She strolled, seldom ran, let alone worked up a sweat. She knew better than to enter one of those rare girls' track meets, where young men guffawed to each other on the sidelines: "Nice tits" or "Some ass." She aspired, if not to June Allyson's saccharine self-sacrifice, to the controlled charm of Doris Day, the elfin poise of Audrey Hepburn, the serene aristocracy of Grace Kelly.

Any sign of ambition was disaster. What would be known in the seventies as "abrasive" in the fifties was a "castrating bitch."

Simone de Beauvoir's *The Second Sex,* a brilliant feminist polemic, was published in this country in 1953, but nobody in America talked about it much. The revolutionary Kinsey Report on *Sexual Behavior in the Human Female,* documenting the fact that women enjoyed sex both emotionally and physically pretty much the same way men did, went barely noticed in America's heartland. As the lure of television swept the country, people watched "Ozzie and Harriet" and "Father Knows Best," images of the perfect

American family. Blacks appeared on the screen almost solely as servants; women, as wives and mothers. It was the age of "conformity," or, as probably suited best, the "silent generation."

And yet . . .

Anyone with an ear to the quiet, frozen lake of the mid-fifties might have heard the rumble, the growl and surge of a riptide beneath the ice. In the late forties, Holden Caulfield, J. D. Salinger's sensitive hero of *Catcher in the Rye,* inspired thousands of young fans by limning the hypocrisy he saw around him. (No one yet used the term "drop out," but Holden seemed destined to do it.) In 1954, the Supreme Court ordered desegregation in all public schools, an act that would not only change the paper-white face of the country, but may well have precipitated the enormous upheavals to come. In 1955, the sensitive, introspective James Dean struck a chord of disaffection in *Rebel Without a Cause.* Elvis Presley had begun to heat up and transform the soul of pop music. Writers Jack Kerouac in *On the Road* and Allen Ginsberg in "Howl" were giving voice to a strange youthful ennui, a rough-timbered, off-balance sense of disillusionment.

In 1953, *Playboy* magazine — with a nude calendar photo of Marilyn Monroe — was launched. Being the "party organ," as feminist writer Barbara Ehrenreich would one day call it, of the male, hedonistic rebellion, it had nothing good to say about collie dogs, station wagons, church picnics, or the family. It was billed as Hugh Hefner's answer to conformity, to "home, family and all that jazz," as he put it, and to "togetherness" — the resoundingly successful advertising slogan of *McCall's* magazine, the symbol of the happy, glorified home with Daddy at work, Mommy in the kitchen, and 2.5 children as total fulfillment.

"The Togetherness Woman" was, in fact, the title of the article Betty had promised *McCall's.* She had taken the assignment simply to justify the months and months she had spent on a questionnaire that Smith had asked her to prepare for her class reunion.

Betty had labored mightily over the thing, even

brought a couple of her friends in to hash over the questions. She had worked so hard, in fact, that her classmates at the reunion had giggled about how *long* the form was. How involved, how detailed the questions.

"What difficulties have you found in working out your role as a woman?" "What are the chief satisfactions and frustrations of your life today?" "How do you feel about getting older?" Leave it to Betty, the psychology buff, they joked, to dream up all that stuff!

Yet all she had been trying to do was prove one little point, just a corollary to the women's home-is-all psychology of the day, a sort of reassurance to her classmates and herself.

"All I was trying to do with that questionnaire," Betty would remember, "was to show that an education wasn't *bad* for a woman, it didn't make her *maladjusted* in her role as wife and mother." That academic learning was not, in short — as so many psychologists were then implying — an actual hindrance to femininity.

"I didn't realize it at the time," she would recall, "but I was asking the questions that were beginning to concern me." For indeed, skilled as she was in social science, and guiltily restless, Betty had designed the sort of query that took dead aim at the secrets of the heart — including her own.

"How have you changed inside?" she asked. "What do you wish you had done differently?"

And when, finally, she sat down to analyze the results for *McCall's,* she discovered that the responses raised more questions than they answered. Why was it, for example, that those of her classmates who were not active outside their homes were not especially happy at all? That they seemed, in fact, just as restless as she was?

They had written about a strange sense of emptiness — how like her own! — or a gnawing guilt, or shame, an uncertainty about who, exactly, they were: Jim's wife? Sally's mother? Betty found turmoils of indecision among these stay-at-home moms, and ennui, feelings of failure, despair, depression — even, for some, alcohol and drugs. And, most striking of all, from those isolated posts in suburbia, the uneasy sense that, because they had these feelings, they were unquestionably "neurotic."

So clearly Betty was not, as she had once thought, alone with these feelings. She was not, as she had also thought, a "freak."

But was education the villain, as all the psychologists and anthropologists and social scientists and magazine writers were more or less subtly suggesting?

That was, quite simply, a premise that the intense, verbal, thirty-six-year-old sometime writer, with her longings for intellectual achievement, could not accept. And as Betty read and reread and searched and analyzed, she discovered yet another piece to the puzzle.

"I found," she would remember at a later, much calmer time of her life, "that the women who seemed the strongest were not quite living this complete image of the housewife and feminine fulfillment. And that education had made them not willing to settle. . . ."

She was on to something!

Slowly but passionately, she began to write. Words and sentences began to fill the pages, words that bore no resemblance to "Millionaire's Wife," or "Two Are an Island," or anything she had ever written before. No panaceas, no hopeful methods of adjusting to the status quo, of finding total fulfillment in the home, poured forth from her pen. Instead of praising the homemaking role, she attacked the endless, monotonous, unrewarding housework it demanded. Instead of soothing her potential readers into the "feminine role" prescribed by the magazine she was writing for, she blasted the notion of vicarious living through husband and children. Rather than touting the "togetherness" so precious to McCall's, she indicted the slogan as a fraud.

She had to be kidding.

The male editor of McCall's summarily rejected "The Togetherness Woman."

A nasty shock for Betty Friedan. Never in her life had anything she had written been turned down.

Quickly, she interviewed more women, then sent the piece to Ladies' Home Journal. There, sure enough, it was accepted, but . . .

"They rewrote it," she would remember years later, with the anger and dismay still in her voice, "to make the opposite point! That education did make women maladjusted in their role as women!"

Betty refused to allow the magazine to publish the article, retrieved it, and made one last try.

Bob Stein, then editor of Redbook, said he would indeed be interested in a piece based on Betty's Smith class questionnaire if it was greatly expanded to include younger women, and other, more extensive data.

Betty was already talking to younger married women and they weren't changing her view of the problem at all. In fact, she was beginning to think, the situation for women who graduated from college after 1942 seemed to be even worse than it was for her classmates. Given that domestic fantasy she had already seen among members of Smith's graduating class, even fewer women in their twenties and early thirties were active outside their homes; even more seemed vaguely unhappy.

She hadn't yet been paid for the article, of course, and she was violating that "enough-money-to-pay-the-maid" pact with herself. But still, since Bob Stein had asked — and since she was fascinated herself — she did more interviews. She rewrote the piece, integrating the new material, and shipped it off to the editor.

Who was, he would remember, stunned.

"I liked Betty a lot," Bob Stein would recall. "She was a solid, trustworthy writer, a bit argumentative maybe, but so were most writers worth their salt. I had been looking forward to 'The Togetherness Woman,' but when I read it, I could only wonder what in God's name had come over Betty Friedan. It was a very angry piece. I didn't think that our readers would identify with it at all."

The Redbook editor — like all successful editors of women's magazines — was fully aware of the link binding readers to *their* magazine, the great umbilical, as some called it, the trust which, if broken, could doom both magazine and its boss. And Betty was, Bob Stein would remember, "very sensitive about her writing. . . . Luckily, I'd never had to reject her work before." But this?

In years to come, Bob Stein would find himself on television and radio talk shows with Betty, defending her, if only because, as he would put it, "the opposition was so impossible," but admitting, too, that he hadn't realized "that the feelings dammed up out there were so strong." At the moment, though, he could only call Betty's agent and report regretfully: "Look, we can't print this. Only the most neurotic housewife would identify with this."

And that, perhaps, might have been the end of it.

Redbook had been Betty's last hope, and in the weeks that followed, she was very depressed. She wrote nothing and dropped out of an important writer's seminar because it met the same night of the week that she served as assistant den mother for her son's Cub Scout troop. She had already chastised herself, had an asthma attack, in fact, over missing some of those Scout meetings.

One night, though, just as a prop to her ego, just to make herself feel like a professional writer again, she made the trek in from Rockland County to hear the successful author Vance Packard talk about his book *The Hidden Persuaders,* an exposé of the sinister effects of advertising. Packard had written it, he said, after an article on the subject had been turned down by every major magazine.

And then — not long afterward, as Betty would remember it — she was riding the bus into Manhattan, taking the kids to the dentist, mulling it over . . . The juggernaut women's magazines, with their fingers on the commercial pulse, had been feeding the domestic palate to ever-rising profit margins . . .

"Damn it all," Betty suddenly realized, "I was right! Somehow what I was saying had gone against the grain of the women's magazines."

And now she knew she couldn't let it go.

In some deep place in the psyche of this impatient, demanding, worrisome, dedicated, prickly, volatile woman, a quiet vision was forming. Inside, as she would later write, she felt "this calm, strange sureness, as if in tune with something larger, more important than myself that had to be taken seriously."

It would be a book. Like *The Hidden Persuaders,* "The Togetherness Woman" could be a book. She would call that editor who had wanted her to expand "The Coming Ice Age," and this time she would tell him yes. Yes, she would write a book for W. W. Norton. But just as she had said before, it would not be about someone else's work. It would be hers. Her own research, her own social science, her own accomplishment in her field.

The Togetherness Woman.

And why not? said [Norton Editor] George Brockway, who immediately saw the potential.

The affluence of the fifties had permitted — even stimulated — critical examinations of contemporary life. *The Man in the Grey Flannel Suit, The Hucksters, Executive Suite, The View from the 40th Floor* had all been big sellers. *The Togetherness Woman,* the editor thought, would make a fine parallel to the latest sharp attack on the rage for conformity, William H. Whyte's *The Organization Man.*

And this woman had the fire in the belly.

"She was incredibly ambitious," Brockway would remember. "The most ambitious woman I had ever met. She said that she didn't know what to call the subject exactly, but that it had something to do with a lack of identity, that women weren't being told . . . they aren't being allowed . . ."

Betty talked on and on at that meeting, half her thoughts, as usual, dropping off mid-sentence, her mind going even faster than her tongue. She had been interviewing so many women. She didn't know quite how to put it, but . . .

There was *something* very wrong with the way women were feeling these days.

And, over the barrage, the furtive insights, the distress, George Brockway honed in.

"Ride it," he told Betty. "You've got the idea, now ride it, ride it!"

How long did she think it would take?

Well, she said, it took her about a month to do an article, so figure a chapter a month . . .

"A year," she said. "I'll have it done in a year." Oh, and yes, she supposed [an advance of] a thousand dollars now would be okay, with the rest of the $3,000 [advance] to come in installments.

It was years later — more research was required, a mysterious block arose — before Betty even *began* to write. She worked three days a week in the Frederick Lewis Allen Room of the New York Public Library and then, when her allotted time there ran out (and the maid quit), in her favorite spot at home, the beautiful dining room with windows on the garden.

"Neither my husband nor my publisher nor anyone else who knew about it thought I would ever finish it," she would write. "When the writing of it took me over completely . . . I wrote every day on the dining room table, while the children were in school, and after they went to bed at night. (It didn't do any good to have a desk of my own; they used it for their homework anyhow.)"

She worked against patronizing jokes about a "woman's book." Against guilt. Against fear. Given the resistance she had already encountered to her views, there must be *no* holes in her argument or her documentation, *no* room for attack.

But slowly, if not steadily, the chapters, scribbled on a legal pad, began to pile up in an old china cupboard in the corner of the dining room. In them, her thesis emerged.

At rock bottom, it was economics, if not to say greed. After World War II, women had been pushed back into the home as industrialists assessed the housewife's valuable role as the prime consumer of household products. The marketing of toasters, washing machines, cosmetics, and the like was the true purpose behind the hard sell of "femininity." Educators, sociologists, psychologists — and, of course, the

women's magazines, with their hunger for the advertising dollar — followed suit.

One by one, Betty took them all on, both the current crop and their historical forebears.

Freud and his "sexual solipsism": "It is a Freudian idea . . . hardened into apparent fact, that has trapped so many American women today." Freud and his Victorian bias had perpetrated the greatest sin in psychotherapy; he had infantilized women, denied them their ability to grow, cut them off from "the zest that is characteristic of human health."

[Anthropologist] Margaret Mead: "The role of Margaret Mead as the professional spokesman of femininity would have been less important if American women had taken the example of her own life, instead of listening to what she said in her books."

Contemporary educators: They induced women into the superficial comfort of the home, thus depriving them of their function in society, consigning millions of women "to spend their days at work an eight-year-old could do."

As for the women's magazines, which offered that fraudulent home-as-religion editorial content: "I helped create this image. I have watched American women for fifteen years try to conform to it. But I can no longer deny its terrible implications. It is not a harmless image. There may be no psychological terms for the harm it is doing."

And, of course, "togetherness": "The big lie . . . the end of the road . . . where the woman has no independent self to hide even in guilt; she exists only for and through her husband and children."

It was this vicarious existence that caused educations to "fester," caused housewife's fatigue, ennui, depression. Not neurosis. It was society — not women — that was sick!

Like Lundberg and Farnham, Betty resurrected earlier feminists, but instead of damning them as sick souls, she sang their praises as heroines. Mary Wollstonecraft, Margaret Fuller, Elizabeth Cady Stanton, Lucy Stone, Susan B. Anthony. Anatomy, she agreed, with a somewhat cursory bow to Simone de Beauvoir's evocative phrasing in *The Second Sex,* is not destiny. Women were not simply their biology. They also had *minds*. And, "as if waking from a coma," they were beginning to ask, "Where am I? What am I doing here?"

She answered the hyperbole of Lundberg and Farnham with some of her own. The isolated suburban home, she wrote, was a "comfortable concentration camp," the women trapped within them cut off, like prisoners, from past adult interests and their own identities. It was a new neurosis, this modern ache, and you could read it in the hundreds of interviews and psychological tests she had accumulated — among them, one test that must have been reassuring, since it suggested that "the high-dominance woman was more psychologically free" than one who was "timid, shy, modest, neat, tactful, quiet, introverted, retiring, more feminine, more conventional." And perhaps, Betty herself speculated, only an "ugly duckling adolescence" or an unhappy marriage could fuel the ambition to resist the deadening, conformist pressure.

For "the problem lay buried, unspoken, for many years in the minds of American women." It was a problem, she wrote, "that had no name," a problem that was caused by the pervasive social pressure relegating women to the four walls of their homes, a pressure whose weapon was an image: "the feminine mystique."

Five years from the time Betty had signed the contract, four years late, *The Feminine Mystique* was published.

It was February 1963, and the New York newspapers, including the *Times,* were on strike. With no review in the *Times,* the chances that a book — even this thunderous polemic — would reach a substantial public were practically nil. And there was plenty of competition. Morton Hunt had just published a gentle, affectionate paean to women's role *outside* as well as in the home. His book was called *Her Infinite Variety,* and it was moving off the bookstore shelves at a frighteningly rapid pace.

Betty was beside herself. And so, for that matter,

was Carl. Never had the state of their marriage been worse, never stormier than during the last year she was writing, when, Carl would complain to friends, he would come home from work and "that bitch," instead of cooking dinner, was writing away at the dining-room table. Betty, friends would whisper, was writing out the problems of her marriage, writing a book instead of leaving Carl. His one-man advertising and public relations firm was far from a booming success, and now this. Who would even hear of *The Feminine Mystique,* let alone buy it? Where, after all these years, was the payoff?

"Betty would come in with ideas to promote the book," George Brockway would recall. "You could tell Carl was behind them, saying, 'Tell 'em to do this, tell 'em to do that.'

"One day she told me that Carl wanted to know what could be done to make *The Feminine Mystique* as big a seller as *Gifts from the Sea."* (This popular book was written by Anne Morrow Lindbergh, the wife of the heroic aviator.)

" 'Tell Carl,' I told her, 'that he can fly the Atlantic solo.' "

Irascible Carl, George would call him — the low-key editor being far from charmed by what he regarded as Carl Friedan's "sharp and nasty" tongue.

But Betty thought her husband knew his business. She would always remember that it was Carl who had persuaded Norton to hire a publicist. Eventually, in fact, she would switch to another publishing house, leaving Brockway entirely.

"I remember him pleading with me," Betty would tell a reporter, "and I remember looking him right in the eye and saying, 'George, you made me feel Jewish for trying to sell that book. Go fuck yourself.' "

But, with the help of the publicist, excerpts from the book began to appear, and articles ran in major news magazines about Betty as an "angry battler for her sex." She began bouncing around the country for speaking engagements, crusaded enthusiastically on radio and that potent new vehicle, the television talk show.

After one of these appearances — outside Rocke-

The photographer has captured Betty Friedan in a moment of profound weariness. In the years after the publication of The Feminine Mystique, *Friedan worked zealously for women's rights: she organized demonstrations, lobbied for antidiscrimination legislation, and struggled to hold the women's movement together in the face of internal dissension. "In truth, she paid a high personal price for her cause." (Michael Ginsburg/Magnum Photos)*

feller Center — she met another author who had just taped a show herself. She was just about Betty's age, a former copywriter who had performed the remarkable feat of hitting the nonfiction best-seller list the year before.

The woman was Helen Gurley Brown, and her book, *Sex and the Single Girl,* aimed, obviously, at the burgeoning singles market, had actually set down in print the startling notion that it was perfectly all right to have "an affair." Even with a married man.

For those who would, in retrospect, regard the sexual revolution as either intrinsic to or actually the wellspring of the Golden Age of Feminism, it would be hard to ignore the pioneering role of Helen Brown. Most feminists, however, would manage to do just that.

It was a matter, in part, of philosophy. In even greater part, perhaps, of style.

Sex and the Single Girl was a typical how-to of the women's magazine genre. It offered advice on decorating your apartment, diet, clothes, and money — not, however, for the purpose of hooking a man into marriage, but for getting him into your bed.

Helen Brown didn't protest much of anything — least of all society's ills. She only wrote about, as she herself insisted, what was already going on anyhow. Single women having sex with men, married or not. She simply made them feel better about doing it. Like the women's magazines, and in a similarly blithe, not to say giddy style, she was reassuring and helpful. The major difference — the shocker — was that while the women's magazines were still righteously committed to the double standard, continually warning their readers of the dire consequences of sex without marriage, Helen Gurley Brown wrote that this was perfectly okay. "Nice single girls *do* have affairs and they don't necessarily die of them." *Sex and the Single Girl* — aimed, unlike underground erotica, at a mass audience — was undoubtedly something of a relief.

The single life the book touted was one of supreme independence, satisfying work, fashion and success and money — a life, in short, that most married women were bound to envy. The single woman was sexy, Helen had written, "because she lives by her wits." She was not "a parasite, a dependent, a scrounger, a sponger or a bum." And when, in 1965, Helen would take over the Hearst Corporation's ailing *Cosmopolitan,* the appeal of that view, and the skill of its pragmatic, meticulous editor, would eventually triple the magazine's circulation.

On television, Helen was, from the beginning, flirtatious, supremely tactful, frankly manipulative, an open disciple of male-flattering femininity. "Helen Gurley Girly," some viewers called her. She was a former secretary who had never gone to college and didn't plan to, a "girl" for whom *work* was the given, the man in one's life the pleasure to be sought. She had written her book at the suggestion of her husband, movie producer David Brown, and she had no hesitation about saying so.

And yet, in spite of Helen's flirtatiousness, and the focus on sex, which, Betty had written, was totally irrelevant, actually damaging to women's struggle for independence, the two women liked each other.

"We talked about business, promotion, all that," Helen would remember. "We became friends . . . and we've been friends ever since." They differed, but, in spite of her passionate nature, Betty would often differ with someone and still remain a loyal friend.

Unlike Helen Brown, however, Betty wasn't "cool"; her personality was not tailor-made for television. Often, in impatient, enthusiastic pursuit of an idea, she would talk so fast that hardly anyone could understand her. Or leave sentences dangling. Or angrily demand time. Her publicist would remember her screaming at hostess Virginia Graham on "Girl Talk": "If you don't let me have my say, I'm going to say orgasm ten times."

But Betty had been provoked.

Virginia Graham, Betty would one day explain, had coaxed the camera: "Girls, how many of us really need bylines? What better thing can we do with our lives than to do the dishes for those we love?"

"Well, I knew that her agent fought for every foot of the size of her byline on the television screen, and I wondered when the last time was she'd done the dishes for someone she loved. I turned to the camera and said, 'Women, don't listen to her. She needs you out there doing the dishes, or she wouldn't have the captive audience for this television program, whose byline she evidently doesn't want you to compete for.'"

Betty never was, never would be, any talk show host's favorite guest. She was confrontational, often tactless, and not — by any standard — a TV beauty.

But neither was she a phony. And there was something about this woman, who looked like everyone's . . . Aunt Minnie, something about what she proclaimed, in her hell-for-leather style, that made hundreds of viewers attend.

Scores of Americans, of course, including many women, were outraged. They could scarcely believe what they were hearing. A woman's career could be as important as a man's? A woman should go out in the world and compete with men? . . .

One Smith alumna, writing in *Reader's Digest* about "the feminine *mistake*," saluted the housewife's "small acts of domesticity" with the good Scout cheer: "Well, sure! That's what we signed up for!" And when the *New York Times* got around to reviewing the book — in a short blurb under "Digest" — Lucy Freeman, who had written a best-seller on her own conquest of mental illness, zapped it as "superficial. . . . The fault, dear Mrs. Friedan, is not in our culture, but in ourselves."

"*Where,*" wailed a letter writer in *Commonweal* magazine, "are all these women to go, having fled their homes? And *what* are they to do?"

In the midst of it all, Betty brought Carl and the kids back to Peoria for her twenty-fifth high school reunion. There, instead of praise, she found herself sitting alone at the banquet table. She stayed with a friend, and the next morning found the tree outside her door festooned with toilet paper.

Yet the sales of *The Feminine Mystique* were beginning to climb, and there was no stopping Betty now. Especially since hundreds of letters, expressing enormous gratitude, were starting to pour in. Letters from women who said they had no idea, until they read her book, that anyone else had such strange feelings. They had felt, they wrote, like sexual freaks, or like "appliances," insecure in their dependence, unable, much longer, to keep up the "act" of selflessness. She had given them courage, they wrote, to go back to school, to begin careers.

For threaded through the social criticism of *The Feminine Mystique* was also a message of Emersonian self-reliance and responsibility. This message was not, at bottom, altogether unlike Helen Brown's, but it was one that would set Betty at odds with many women who might have been her allies. Since, as Betty wrote, the women she was addressing were not those beset by dire poverty or disease, they were not, therefore, *completely* at the mercy of an unjust society.

"In the last analysis," Betty had written, "millions of able women in this free land choose themselves not to use the door education could have opened for them. The choice — and the responsibility — for the race back [to the] home was finally their own."

The Feminine Mystique *reached women very much like Friedan herself: white, educated wives and mothers mainly of the middle class. "Inspired and validated by finding their own truth presented as truth," as writer Marilyn French has said, "many of them changed their lives, returning to school, entering the work force." The Feminine Mystique also aroused professional and single women, both white and African American, for it exposed the attitudes and practices that blocked their own advancement. Along with Helen Gurley Brown and Gloria Steinem, Friedan helped liberate younger women, too, especially on the college campuses. Had Friedan done nothing more than write her book, she would be historically significant.*

But for her, The Feminine Mystique *was only the beginning. Thrust into national prominence as the voice of the new American woman, Friedan initiated the "second wave" of organized feminism, the first wave having ended with women's suffrage. In 1966, with the help of Dr. Kay Clarenbach, a Wisconsin women's leader, Friedan founded and became first president of the National Organization for Women (NOW), the first mainstream women's organization and the most successful in history. "It is a mystery," Betty would say later, "the whole thing — why it happened, how it started. What gave any of us the courage to make that leap?" Under NOW's banners, the new women's movement sought equality for women through political means, for the 1960s civil rights movement had shown Friedan and her colleagues how effective antidiscrimination*

legislation could be. Employing the civil rights methods of picket lines, marches, political pressure, and media exposure, NOW set out to gain full citizenship for women: it challenged federal guidelines that sanctioned discrimination against them in employment, initiated lawsuits against companies refusing to hire women in positions traditionally occupied by men, sought legal abortion, and campaigned for the Equal Rights Amendment (ERA), which had languished since 1923. NOW helped to bring about a body of laws and rulings that prohibited sexual discrimination in education and in hiring and promotion; NOW was also instrumental in gaining congressional approval of the Equal Rights Amendment. In the 1980s, however, the ERA went down to defeat when it failed to be ratified by three fourths of the states. Even so, NOW was strong enough by 1984 to pressure the Democratic presidential candidate into selecting a woman as his running mate.

Meanwhile, the women's movement had splintered into various dissenting groups; one of them even advocated lesbianism as the ultimate expression of feminism and demanded that NOW affirm this by publicly avowing, "We are all lesbians." This shocked Friedan, who with other NOW leaders argued that such a stance would alienate men and would be a tactical blunder. Feminism, she said, regarded men not as eternal foes but also as victims of a repressive, dehumanizing society.

Struggling to hold the movement together wore Friedan out. In truth, she had paid a high personal price for her cause: she had lectured and traveled everywhere in its behalf, living out of suitcases in lonely motel rooms; she had missed her children fiercely and the warmth and intimacy of family life. Too, her marriage to Carl had failed — he had beaten her more than once. In 1970, divorced and exhausted, she resigned as NOW president and turned to writing, lecturing, and teaching. She remained faithful to feminism's larger vision, a vision of "human wholeness" that liberated men as well as women. It did so by repudiating the laws and customs that prevented men from expressing their own nurturing qualities and caused them to deny women their birthright as Americans — an equal opportunity to better themselves, to realize their full potential as their talent and industry allowed.

QUESTIONS TO CONSIDER

1. Describe the American cultural ideal of womanhood in the 1950s. What does Marcia Cohen think were some of the sources of our culture's "home-is-woman's-all" psychology? Explain the role that consumerism, the press, and the American educational system played in perpetuating prevailing assumptions about women. Was anyone rebelling against all this conformity?

2. Betty Friedan did not deliberately set out to start a feminist revolution. Describe the steps she took in raising her own consciousness and the series of revelations and reversals that led her to write *The Feminine Mystique*.

3. *The Feminine Mystique* was not a political book, but just a few years after its publication Friedan found herself at the head of a reform movement and president of NOW. At what point did the yearning for self-awareness and self-fulfillment that Friedan aroused in American women become transformed into political activity? Why did women feel they needed a political movement to achieve personal gains?

4. Discuss the basic thesis of *The Feminine Mystique*. Whose ideas did Betty Friedan attack? Specifically, how did she feel about Sigmund Freud and Margaret Mead? about "togetherness"? about suburbia? about women's magazines? How did Friedan's ideas differ from those of Helen Gurley Brown? What underlying message did the two writers have in common? Did Friedan feel the sexual revolution was compatible with the new feminism?

5. Friedan's book was addressed to educated, white, upper- and middle-class women. She herself was aware that she had not tackled the problems of uneducated or poor or African American or immigrant women. Is it possible to apply all or part of Friedan's analysis to this second group? What additional complications might issues of race and social class bring to women's lives?

6. What strides has feminism made since the publication of *The Feminine Mystique*? Has true equality been achieved? What do you see as the future of the historic "women's rights" movement as we enter the last years of the twentieth century?

Heyday of the Counterculture

ALLEN J. MATUSOW

The 1960s and early 1970s were times of profound change in fashion, music, and morals on both sides of the Atlantic. In the United States, a "counterculture" revolt against established values was part of a general rebellion against the unity and conformity that had characterized American life since the Second World War and the Eisenhower years. The civil rights movement was the first major postwar assault on the old American ways, and African Americans' struggle in turn inspired many other protest movements — by rebellious youth, the New Left, Chicanos, American Indians, feminists, and groups seeking to legitimize homosexuality and to legalize drugs and abortion.

The counterculture — or "hippie culture" — did not emerge suddenly in the 1960s. As Rice University historian Allen Matusow points out, it owed much to the beat generation of the 1950s and its roots stretched back to the jazz era of the 1920s, and the black hipster of the Depression era. Although Matusow does not say so, one could argue that the counterculture rebellion was comparable to the youth rebellion of the twenties, a rebellion described by Frederick Lewis Allen in selection 15. In fact, if you read Allen's and Matusow's accounts together, you get a remarkable sense of historical continuity. For the Charleston, the saxophone, jazz, bobbed hair, short skirts, and gin and cigarettes — weapons of revolt during the 1920s — were forerunners of the twist, the electric guitar, rock 'n' roll, long hair, miniskirts, and the drugs that characterized the counterculture revolt of the 1960s. Freudian psychology, which stimulated the youth rebellion of the twenties, also figured in the hippie counterculture in a reconstructed form. While Matusow does not hazard comparisons between the two decades, he describes the heroes and happenings of the counterculture in a spirited, insightful narrative, excerpted from his

The Unraveling of America (1984), perhaps the best history of the sixties yet written. You will find a gallery of fascinating characters here, from Norman O. Brown, the intellectual prophet of the counterculture, and Timothy Leary, proselytizer of LSD and "the psychedelic revolution," to Allen Ginsberg, Ken Kesey and the Merry Pranksters, Bob Dylan, the Beatles, and the Hell's Angels, California's raunchy, violent motorcycle gang, which maintained "an uneasy alliance" with the counterculture rebels. Matusow concludes that while the hippie movement proved ephemeral, it was symptomatic of a culturewide revolt against the Protestant ethic, traditional institutions, and "the liberal values" that had long sustained American society.

Rebellious and outrageous though they often were, the youth of the 1960s were also passionately idealistic. This was the same younger generation that joined John F. Kennedy's Peace Corps and went off to live and work in countries from South America to the Far East. This was also the generation that responded to the eloquence of Martin Luther King, Jr., and marched by the thousands in the civil rights movement; young people also filled up the ranks of the peace movement and helped persuade King himself to take a public stand against the war in Vietnam. Thus they contributed to the dismantling of segregation in the South and to the end of the divisive war in Asia. These facts should be kept in mind as you ride with Matusow on a rollicking trip through the counterculture scene.

GLOSSARY

BEATLES   Irreverent British rock 'n' roll band that brought Beatlemania to America; initially, the Beatles mocked society, then, inspired by Bob Dylan, they started writing songs for "the cultural opposition."

BEATS   Cultural rebels of the 1950s who were "profoundly alienated from dominant American values"; the "beat generation" included novelist Jack Kerouac (*On the Road*) and poet Allen Ginsberg ("Howl").

BROWN, NORMAN O.   Classical scholar whose *Life Against Death* (1959) reconstructed Freud, arguing that there was no "instinctual dualism" — the sexual instinct versus the death instinct — inherent in human beings; people, he argued, could attain "eternal bodily pleasure," and he created "the Dionysian ego," which anticipated the counterculture impulse of the sixties — the

the counterculture impulse of the sixties — the search for bodily and mystic ecstasies through drugs, sex, and rock 'n' roll.

DIONYSIAN EGO   The "new ego" created by Brown, "a body ego . . . overflowing with love, knowing no limits, affirming life, reuniting male and female, Self and Other, life and death."

DYLAN, BOB   The greatest folk-rock composer of the sixties; he made rock 'n' roll an expression of "cultural radicalism"; after Dylan, rock both shaped and articulated the counterculture.

EROS   Freud's term for the sexual instinct.

GRATEFUL DEAD, THE   The "quintessential" hippie band of San Francisco, which played before packed houses of "hopelessly stoned" counterculture adherents.

HIPSTER   The "hedonistic, sensual, and sexually

uninhibited" young African American man of the 1930s; the hipster talked jive, wore a zoot suit, and showed open contempt for the white world; in 1945, a "white hipster" — Herbert Huncke — brought the "hip" underground to the rebel writers and intellectuals who would later constitute the beat generation.

KESEY, KEN   Novelist who created "the psychedelic style"; he and his Merry Pranksters established a drug commune near San Francisco, wore "weirdo" costumes and Day-Glo paint, and rode about in a hippie school bus rigged with a tape player and loudspeakers.

LSD   Diethylamide of lysergic acid, first developed as a respiratory stimulant; although Congress outlawed it, this powerful hallucinogenic drug, nicknamed *acid,* fueled the hippie revolution throughout the sixties.

LEARY, TIMOTHY   Former Harvard psychologist who dropped out and spread "the psychedelic revolution," proclaiming the mystic and sensual ecstasies attainable through marijuana and LSD.

PRESLEY, ELVIS   Led the rock 'n' roll revolution of the 1950s, which produced "a generation of cultural subversives"; although he was not the first rock 'n' roll singer, as Jimmy Guterman has noted, Presley "was the first performer to unite and then unleash all its sundry forces," earning him his legendary status as "the king of rock."

ROCK 'N' ROLL   A musical hybrid that fused black rhythm and blues with white country or hillbilly styles; "protest music" from the start, rock launched a musical revolution in the 1950s that profoundly altered American popular culture.

THANATOS   Freud's term for the death instinct.

America discovered hippies at the world's first Human Be-In, Golden Gate Park, San Francisco, January 14, 1967. The occasion was something special, even in a Bay Area underground long accustomed to spectacle. Political activists from Berkeley mingled with dropouts from Haight-Ashbury, ending their feud and initiating a "new epoch" in the history of man. "In unity we shall shower the country with waves of ecstasy and purification," sponsors of the Be-In prophesied. "Fear will be washed away; ignorance will be exposed to sunlight; profits and empire will lie drying on deserted beaches." Preparations for the Be-In were casual but appropriate. A hippie newspaper called the *Oracle* invited everyone "to bring costumes, blankets, bells, flags, symbols, cymbals, drums, beads, feathers, flowers." A local painter named Michael Bowen arranged with his guru in Mexico to exchange weather for the day. The Hell's Angels motorcycle gang agreed to guard the electronic equipment of the rock bands, which would play this gig for free. And poets Allen Ginsberg and Gary Snyder arrived two hours early to perform a "purificatory circumambulation" of the field, a ritual they had observed in 1963 in Sarnath, India, to drive out demons.

By early afternoon a crowd estimated at twenty thousand gathered in the park to enjoy the unseasonably warm sun and commune with the hip notables on the makeshift stage. Timothy Leary was there, dressed in white and wearing flowers in his hair. "Turn on to the scene, tune in to what is happening, and drop out — of high school, college, grad school, junior executive — and follow me, the hard way," said Leary, reciting his famous commercial for the synthetic hallucinogen LSD. Ginsberg, in a white Khader suit and blue rubber sandals, chanted a Buddhist mantra as Snyder blew a conchshell he had ob-

Excerpts from "Rise and Fall of a Counterculture" from *The Unraveling of America: A History of Liberalism in the 1960's* by Allen J. Matusow. Copyright © 1984 by Allen J. Matusow. Reprinted by permission of Harper Collins Publishers, Inc.

tained in Kyoto while studying Zen Buddhism. "We are primitives of an unknown culture . . ." Snyder had said on the eve of the Be-In, "with new ethics and new states of mind." Music for the occasion was acid rock, performed by Quicksilver Messenger Service, Jefferson Airplane, and the Grateful Dead. Already an underground legend, the Dead had played Ken Kesey's notorious "acid tests," which had done so much to spread LSD and the psychedelic style throughout California a year or so before. Representing the new left was Jerry Rubin, released that very morning from jail, but not yet hip enough for this occasion. "Tune-In — Drop-Out — Take-Over," Rubin had said at a press conference prior to the event. But few at the Be-In were in a mood (or condition) to take over anything.

The real show was the crowd. "The costumes were a designer's dream," wrote music critic Ralph Gleason in the San Francisco *Chronicle*, "a wild polyglot mixture of Mod, Palladin, Ringling Brothers, Cochise, and Hells Angel's Formal." Bells tinkled, balloons floated, people on the grass played harmonicas, guitars, recorders, flutes. Beautiful girls handed out sticks of incense. A young man in a paisley parachute drifted from the sky, though no plane was in sight. An old man gave away his poems. A mysterious group called the Diggers had obtained seventy-five turkeys from a drug chemist named Owsley and supplied sandwiches, homemade bread, and oranges, free, to anyone who was hungry. When a sulfur bomb exploded under the stage, people on the grass thought it was a large cloud of yellow incense and broke into appreciative applause. Finally, after poets Michael McClure, Lenore Kandell, Snyder and Ginsberg read in the silent presence of Zen Master Suzuki Roshi who was seated on the stage, and the hours of tripping, dancing, and hugging had wound down, Ginsberg turned toward the setting sun, led a chant "om gri maitreya" (Salutations to Buddha of Futurity), and asked the people to practice "a little kitchen Yoga" by picking up their trash. Officials said that no gathering had left so little litter in the park in a generation.

Newsweek was on hand to photograph the Be-In in gorgeous color and report that "it was a love feast, a psychedelic picnic, a hippie happening." Images of hip quickly began to seep into the public consciousness, provoking intense curiosity and endless analysis in the straight world. Most of the pop sociology deserved the rebuke of Bob Dylan's "Ballad of a Thin Man": "Something is happening here but you don't know what it is. Do you, Mr. Jones?" Yet understanding was imperative, for the hippie impulse that was spreading through a generation of the young challenged the traditional values of bourgeois culture, values still underpinning the liberal movement of the 1960s — reason, progress, order, achievement, social responsibility. Hippies mocked liberal politicians, scorned efforts to repair the social order, and repudiated bourgeois society. In so doing, they became cultural radicals opposed to established authority. Among the movements arrayed against him toward the end of his tenure, none baffled Lyndon Johnson more than these hippies. Somehow, in the name of liberation, they rejected everything he stood for, including his strenuous efforts to liberate the poor and the black. Clearly, liberation meant something different to liberals like him from what it meant to radicals like them.

☆ II ☆

Few hippies read much, but those who did found their purpose strikingly described and anticipated in the strange books of Norman O. Brown. A classical scholar at Wesleyan University, whose underground explorations began in middle age and never strayed beyond the library, Brown published a book in 1959 called *Life Against Death*. A manifesto of cultural radicalism, this book established Brown as a prophet of the counterculture and its preeminent intellectual. Those seeking the meaning of the hippie movement could do no better than begin with him.

Brown was a Freudian who reshaped the ideas of

Beat poet Allen Ginsberg gives a poetry reading at Indiana University, 1966, while his "sex-soul" companion, Peter Orlovsky (wearing glasses), looks on. Ginsberg's poem, "Howl," was the manifesto "for the scattered disaffiliates of fifties America" and a source of inspiration for hippies of the sixties. (AP/Wide World Photos)

the master to provide a happy ending; no mean feat, given Freud's pessimism. Man was unhappy, Freud argued, because his instincts were repressed. The realm of instinct was the id, wherein resided emotion, desire — above all, Eros, the sexual instinct, which sought bodily pleasure. But to accomplish the survival of the individual, Eros had to be controlled. Thus in childhood there emerged from the id the ego, which mediated between the individual and the outside world and attempted to repress the raging instincts. Eros could not be repressed entirely, however, and the ego was forced to admit it into consciousness —

transformed, sublimated, desexualized. Sublimated Eros provided the energy for work, art, and culture. Hence the irony and tragedy of man: he can know happiness only in gratifying his instinctual need for bodily pleasure; but to preserve life and create civilization, that need must be denied. Freud had still other grounds for pessimism. In the id he had discovered, alongside Eros and warring against it, a second instinct, which he called the death instinct, or Thanatos. As civilization advances, Eros weakens, and the death instinct gains force. Directed outward, Thanatos becomes aggression, threatening other men with harm and civilization with extinction. "Men have gained control over the forces of nature to such an extent," Freud concluded, "that with their help they would have no difficulty in exterminating one another to the last man."

Against Freud, Brown intended to show that man could achieve his infantile dream of eternal bodily pleasure. Brown began his reconstruction of Freud by denying that there existed an instinctual dualism — life and death, Eros *vs.* Thanatos — rooted in biology. The pre-Oedipal infant at his mother's breast experiences "union of the self with a whole world of love and pleasure." In this blissful state there are no dualism, no self and other, no subject-object, no life against death, only timeless experience of being one with the world, only instinctual fusion and undifferentiated unity. Bliss ends when the infant experiences separation from the mother, producing anxiety, a sense of loss, and fear of death. According to Brown's argument, it is the infant's attempt to flee death that initiates instinctual de-fusion. Eros emerges, seeking actively to reunite with the mother, the source of bodily pleasure; Thanatos emerges, seeking the peace known at her breast. The ensuing sublimations of the instincts produce the spiritual life of man and propel history, but they cannot make man happy. The flight from death, then, is the critical event in psychic life, condemning man to sickness and removing him from nature. Brown's prescription for health was simple: If man can accept death, he can accept life, achieve instinctual re-fusion, abolish repression, and find happiness through "the resurrection of the body."

There was much in *Life Against Death* that anticipated and expressed the hippie impulse. Like the hippies, Brown was resolutely nonpolitical. Man was the animal who repressed himself; his salvation lay not in social reorganization but in self-reconstruction. Like the hippies, Brown affirmed instinctual freedom against the rational, disciplined, puritanic life that had been the life of man in Western civilization. Like the hippies, Brown was in revolt against civilized sex — exclusively genital, exclusively heterosexual, exclu-

sively monogamous — affirming instead pan-sexualism, "polymorphous perversity," the union of many bodies: in short, erotic life based on the pre-Oedipal Eden. And finally Brown gave definition to the cultural project on which the hippies were soon to embark. Rejecting descent into the id as mere regression, Brown wished to make the unconscious conscious, incorporate the content of the id into the ego — to create, in other words, a new ego, a body ego, which Brown called the "Dionysian ego," overflowing with love, knowing no limits, affirming life. "Dionysus reunifies male and female, Self and Other, life and death," Brown wrote. The creation of the Dionysian ego, the ego in service of liberated Eros — this was a project millions of mothers would soon understand implicitly and fear with good reason. . . .

If Brown's books forecast the hippie projects — Dionysian ecstasies, bodily and mystic — the Human Be-In proclaimed the existence of a hippie culture, or counterculture, committed to realizing those projects through drugs, sex, and rock and roll. But just as Brown did not invent the projects, hippies did not invent their culture from scratch. Hip explorers in the realm of the Dionysian had spent a generation developing rituals and a life style from which hippies freely borrowed. Indeed, without pioneers to point the way, hippies might never have emerged to fascinate and outrage America.

☆ III ☆

The history of hip began with the black hipsters of the 1930s. Black folk had always constituted something of a counterculture in America, representing, at least in the white imagination, pure id. Migrating into northern ghettos after World War I, young black men used their new freedom to improvise a new variation on black deviance — the hipster — who was not only hedonistic, sensual, and sexually uninhibited, but openly contemptuous of the white world that contin-

Hippies of the sixties, like those shown here, sought "a life of Dionysian ecstasy" in which to synchronize themselves with the cosmos. *(Henri Cartier-Bresson/Magnum)*

ued to exclude him. The language that hipsters invented on Harlem street corners was jive, an action language honed in verbal duels and inaccessible to most whites. Some jive words that became part of the permanent hip lexicon were *cat, solid, chick, Big Apple, square, tea, gas, dip, flip. Ofay,* the jive word for white, meant foe in pig Latin. The hipster costume was the zoot suit, designed, as hip garb always would be, to defy and outrage conventional taste. For kicks, the hipster smoked marijuana, which heightened his sense of immediacy and helped him soar above his mean surroundings. The only bigger kick was sex.

Vital to the hipster experience was the uninhibited black music called jazz. In 1922 a writer in the *Atlantic Monthly* described jazz as the result of "an unloosing of instincts that nature wisely has taught us to hold in

check, but which, every now and then, for cryptic reasons, are allowed to break the bonds of civilization." Indeed, Louis Armstrong, playing his "hot," sensual, raunchy improvisations on trumpet, was the first hipster hero. As jazz changed, the hipster persona changed with it. In the early 1940s a group of rebel black jazzmen, hostile to the commercialization of the big bands, created bebop. Bebop relied on small groups and improvisation, as before, but the sound was cool, the rhythm variable, the volume low, and the technical virtuosity of its leading performers legend. The genius of bebop was Charlie "The Bird" Parker, who lived at "the level of total spontaneity," whether he was playing alto sax or getting kicks from booze, sex, or heroin. By the mid-1940s, partly because of heroin, hot was out and cool was in. Hipster dress had become more conservative; noise and brash behavior, a breach of taste; detachment, a required pose. By then, too, the hipster had ceased to be a type restricted to blacks only. In New York and other big cities, some disaffiliates among the white young found the hipster persona so expressive of their own alienation that they adopted it as their own. Thus was born, in Norman Mailer's phrase, "the white Negro," living outside the law for sex, pot, jazz, kicks — in short, for Dionysian ecstasy.

Herbert Huncke was a white hipster who first heard the language and the music on Chicago's South Side in the thirties. Before moving to New York before World War II, he had become a junkie, a habitué of the underworld, and a petty criminal so notorious that the police would name him the Creep and bar him from Times Square. An experimenter with forbidden experience, Huncke took drugs to derange the senses and expand consciousness, and he provided rich source material for Dr. Alfred Kinsey's study of American sexual mores. When wearied of the streets, he sought refuge in a detachment so complete that he was beyond feeling. Huncke had a word to describe his weariness. He said he was "beat."

One day in 1945 Huncke encountered William Burroughs, not yet a famous writer, trying to get rid of a sawed-off shotgun and some morphine. Through Burroughs, Huncke met Allen Ginsberg, Jack Kerouac, John Clellon Holmes, and others in a circle of rebel writers and intellectuals who later became known as the beat generation. Living on the fringes of Columbia University as students or dropouts, the beats engaged in obscure resistance to the "Syndrome of Shutdown" (Ginsberg's later phrase) — the movement toward a totalitarian America based on mass consumption and mass acquiescence. They were rebels too against the official culture purveyed in academic classrooms and celebrated in the lifeless literary quarterlies. In reaction they created their literature from raw experience, which they consumed with reckless and undiscriminating abandon. When Herbert Huncke introduced the proto-beats to the hipster

underground, its jive, jazz, drugs, and unconventional sex, they plunged right in. Ginsberg wrote, "As far as I know the ethos of what's charmingly Hip, and the first pronunciation of the word itself to my fellow ears first came consciously from Huncke's lips; and the first information and ritual of the emergent hip subculture passed through Huncke's person."

What the beats added to hip was the mystic quest. In the summer of 1948, living alone in East Harlem and grieving for his departed lover Neal Cassady, Allen Ginsberg had the defining experience of his life. As he lay in bed gazing at tenement roofs with a book of William Blake's *Songs of Innocence* before him, he heard the deep voice of the poet himself reciting the "Sunflower," and knew it was the voice of God. "Looking out the window, . . ." Ginsberg remembered, "suddenly it seemed that I saw into the depths of the universe, by looking simply into the ancient sky." Ginsberg had auditory experience of other poems that evening, and there were other visions in the days that followed, until, a week later, standing in the athletic field at Columbia, Ginsberg invoked the spirit and experienced the cosmos as monster. "The sky was not a blue hand anymore but like a hand of death coming down on me." It was years before Ginsberg would seek that void again, but in the meantime he did not forget those moments when the ego had overflowed the bounds of the self and illumination had been his. A year later Huncke moved in with Ginsberg, thoughtfully stashing his stolen goods elsewhere. Arrested as an accessory, Ginsberg was committed and stayed eight months in the Columbia-affiliated New York Psychiatric Institute.

After graduating from Columbia in 1949, Ginsberg worked at straight jobs and tried to master his real vocation, which was poetry. In 1954, forsaking New York, he moved to San Francisco to visit Cassady. There a brilliant circle of poets had gathered around Lawrence Ferlinghetti's City Lights Book Store in a neighborhood called North Beach. North Beach provided the cultural soil where the beat seed, originally planted in New York, took root and flowered. With its narrow streets, high walls, and cheap houses over-looking the bay, North Beach reminded Gary Snyder of "ancient terraced fertile crescent pueblos." The beats were hipsters a decade later, explorers in the realm of the Dionysian, searching for ecstasies, bodily and mystic.

For Ginsberg San Francisco was liberation. He found a psychiatrist who told him to do what he wanted, namely write poetry and love men; and he met his "life long sex-soul union" in Peter Orlovsky. Maturing rapidly, Ginsberg also found his authentic voice as a poet. One weekend in 1955 he stayed in his apartment and wrote a poem, with little revision, which one part of him believed he could not publish out of respect for his father and another part believed would change America. In September, at an artists' co-op called the Six Gallery, with his friend Jack Kerouac there to pass around the jug and shout en-couragement, Ginsberg read his astounding "Howl." Taking as its subject the life of the poet and his beat friends, "Howl" became a manifesto for the scattered disaffiliates of fifties America.

> I saw the best minds of my generation destroyed
>   by madness, starving hysterical naked,
> dragging themselves through the negro streets at
>   dawn looking for an angry fix,
> angelheaded hipsters burning for the ancient
>   heavenly connection to the starry dynamo in the
>   machinery of night
> who poverty and tatters and hollow-eyed and high
>   sat up smoking in the supernatural darkness of
>   cold-water flats floating across the tops of cities
>   contemplating jazz
> who bared their brains to Heaven under the El and
>   saw Mohammedan angels staggering on tenement
>   roofs illuminated. . . .

When the authorities brought Ferlinghetti to trial for publishing "Howl," on the grounds of obscenity, the poem attained more than literary celebrity. "Howl"

sold 100,000 copies in ten years, making it perhaps the most popular serious poem of the century. . . .

Jack Kerouac, the beat writer who shared so many of Ginsberg's adventures, also shared his mystic quest. Kerouac had gone to Columbia to play football but rebelled against the discipline, deciding instead to write novels and probe the cultural underground. Re-calling the 1940s, he wrote, "Anyway, the hipsters, whose music was bop, they looked like criminals but they kept talking about the same things I liked, long outlines of personal experience and vision, nightlong confessions full of hope that became illicit and re-pressed by War. . . . And so Huncke appeared to us and said, 'I'm beat' with radiant light shining out of his despairing eyes . . . a word perhaps brought from some midwest carnival or junk cafeteria. It was a new language, actually spade (Negro) jargon but you soon learned it."

Kerouac made his artistic breakthrough when he decided to write a semi-fictional account of his road experiences with Neal Cassady. Some people might have regarded Cassady as a bum. Reared on the streets of Denver by his wino father, in and out of jails mostly for stealing cars, Cassady possessed so much energy and lived so completely in the moment that the beat circle could not resist him. In April 1951 Kerouac fed a roll of teletype paper into a typewriter and let tales of Cassady flow spontaneously from his mind, in one paragraph 120 feet long. It took three weeks to write On the Road, six years to get it published.

On the Road portrayed Kerouac, Cassady, Ginsberg, and their hipster friends speeding across the continent in the late forties, consuming pot, jazz, and sex, envying the Negro his spontaneity, his soul, his cool. Cassady (Dean Moriarty in the book) was the natural man, the Dionysian ego, joyfully slaking his unquenchable thirst for food, sex, and life. But Kerouac saw Cassady as more than a glutton. He was "a holy con-man," "the HOLY GOOF," "Angel Dean," questing for "IT," the moment "when you know all and everything is decided forever," — that moment in jazz, Dean explained, when the man making the music "rises to his fate and has to blow equal to it." In San Francisco, deserted by Cassady and delirious from hunger, Kerouac himself (Sal Paradise) had a mystic vision, reaching "the point of ecstasy that I always wanted to reach." Eventually, as Cassady became ensnared in complication, accusation, wounds of the body, he becomes, in Kerouac's view, "BEAT — the root, the soul of Beatific." A bestseller in 1957, On the Road became a literary inspiration for the restless young even then preparing to scale the walls of American suburbia in search of Dionysus. . . .

By the late 1950s, a fully developed beat subculture had emerged not only in North Beach but also in Venice West (near Los Angeles), New York's Greenwich Village, and a few other hip resorts in between. The beats possessed deviant tastes in language, literature, music, drugs, and religion. Profoundly alienated from dominant American values, practicing voluntary poverty and spade cool, they rejected materialism, competition, the work ethic, hygiene, sexual repression, monogamy, and the Faustian quest to subdue nature. There were, to be sure, never more than a few thousand fulltime beats, but thanks to the scandalized media, images of beat penetrated and disconcerted the middle classes. Beats, like hula hoops, were a fad. Indeed, by the early 1960s the San Francisco poets had scattered, and cops and tourists had driven the rest of the beats from their old haunts in North Beach. A remnant survived, however, and found convenient shelter in another congenial San Francisco neighborhood. It was Haight-Ashbury, a racially integrated community, forty square blocks, bordering magnificant Golden Gate Park. There, beat old-timers kept alive the hip style and the Dionysian projects, until hippies moved in and appropriated both.

☆ IV ☆

In the metamorphosis from beat to hippie, hallucinogenic drugs played an indispensable part. Indians had been using peyote and magic mushrooms for sacramental purposes since before the rise of the Aztec civilization. But in industrial civilizations, knowledge of mind-altering substances had virtually disappeared. In the 1920s chemists synthesized the active ingredient in peyote, calling it mescaline, and did the same thing in 1958 for the sacred mushrooms, producing psilocybin. Science even outdid nature in 1938 when Dr. Albert Hoffman of the Sandoz Chemical Works in Switzerland fabricated a compound many times more potent than anything imbibed by the most ecstatic Indian. Searching for a respiratory stimulant, Hoffman produced the diethylamide of lysergic acid, a colorless, odorless, apparently useless substance that he called LSD. Five years later, in the course of an experiment on animals, Hoffman accidentally ingested an "unmeasurable trace" of LSD and took the world's first acid trip. (It was, incidentally, a bummer.) Hoffman kept experimenting, and Sandoz began supplying LSD to psychiatric researchers trying to cure schizophrenia. By 1960 LSD was seeping out of the laboratory into the cultural underground.

The herald of the psychedelic revolution was the British author Aldous Huxley. Swallowing some mescaline in 1953, Huxley accidentally triggered a profound mystical experience, in which he watched "a slow dance of golden lights," discovered "Eternity in a flower" and even approached the "Pure Light of the Void," before fleeing in terror from "the burning brightness of unmitigated Reality." In The Doors of Perception (1954), which recounted his journey, Huxley lamented that the rich and highly educated white people of the earth were so wedded to words and reason that they had cut themselves off from mystic knowledge. Western man, he said, should accept the "gratuitous grace" of mind-expanding drugs, thus "to be shaken out of the ruts of ordinary perception, to be shown for a few timeless hours the outer and the inner world, not as they appear to an animal obsessed with survival or to a human being obsessed with words and notions, but as they are apprehended, directly and unconditionally, by Mind at Large."

The man who purveyed Huxley's holy message to the millions was Timothy Leary. Possessor of a Ph.D. in psychology, Leary quit his job as director of the Kaiser Foundation Hospital in Oakland, California, in 1958, convinced that conventional psychiatry did not work. Accepting a post at Harvard to pursue his unorthodox ideas, Leary was on his way to a productive scientific career until, one day in Mexico, he discovered the magic mushrooms.

Leary had retreated to a villa in Cuernavaca in the summer of 1960 to write a paper that he hoped would win him points in the academic game. He had never smoked marijuana and knew nothing about mind-altering drugs. But, when a friend procured the mushrooms from a local Indian, Leary thought it might be fun to try some. On a hot afternoon sitting around a pool, Leary and a few companions choked down a bowl of filthy, foul-tasting *crudos*. The game for Leary ended right there. "Five hours after eating the mushrooms it was all changed," he wrote. "The revelation had come. The veil had been pulled back. The classic vision. The fullblown conversion experience. The prophetic call. The works. God had spoken."

Back at Harvard in the fall, Leary secured Huxley's help in designing a scientific experiment to investigate the behavioral effects of psilocybin (synthesized magic mushrooms). Soon Leary was turning on graduate students, ministers, convicts, and stray seekers showing up at his rented mansion in suburban Boston. In truth, Leary was using science to cloak his real purpose, which was to give away the keys to paradise. And he did grow in spiritual knowledge. He learned that drugs alone could not produce a state of blessedness, that they "had no specific effect on consciousness, except to expand it." God and the Devil resided together in the nervous system. Which of these was summoned depended on one's state of mind. Leary, therefore, emphasized the importance of proper "set and setting" (candles, incense, music, art, quiet) to help the seeker experience God.

In December 1960 Leary made the connection with the hip underground in the person of Allen Ginsberg. Having met him in New York, Ginsberg spent a week at Leary's home to enlist the professor in his own crusade for mind expansion. The two hit it off from the start. On Sunday, with dogs, children, and hangers-on scattered about, Leary gave Ginsberg and Peter Orlovsky the sacred mushrooms. The poets repaired to their room, stripped naked, and played Wagner on the record player. Lying in bed, Ginsberg began to succumb to hellish visions, until Leary came in, looked in his eyes, and pronounced him a great man. Ginsberg arose, and with Orlovsky padding behind, descended to the kitchen to proclaim himself the Messiah. We will go into the streets and call the people to peace and love, Leary reports him as saying. And we will get on the phone and hook up Burroughs, Kerouac, Mailer, Kennedy, and Khrushchev and "settle all this warfare bit." Hello operator, Ginsberg said. This is God. Get me Kerouac. And eventually she did. Sitting in the kitchen after the drug had worn off, Ginsberg plotted the psychedelic revolution. Everybody ought to have the mushrooms, he said, beginning with the influentials. They would not listen to him, a crazy beatnik poet, but they might listen to a Harvard professor. Leary must come to New York on weekends and turn on the likes of Kerouac, [poet] Robert Lowell, [author] LeRoi Jones, [jazz musician] Dizzy Gillespie, [jazz musician] Thelonious Monk, and other creative people in Ginsberg's personal telephone book. Leary was willing. "From this evening on," he wrote, "my energies were offered to the ancient underground society of alchemists, artists, mystics, alienated visionaries, dropouts and the disenchanted young, the sons arising."

Not until late 1961 did Leary try LSD — "the most shattering experience of my life." Taking him far beyond psilocybin, LSD enabled Leary to accomplish the projects of the counterculture — Dionysian ecstasies, mystic and bodily. He journeyed down the DNA ladder of evolution to the single cell at the beginning of life and then outward to the cosmic vibrations where he merged with pure energy, "the white light," nothingness. He also experienced the resurrection of the body. "Blow the mind and you are left with God and life — and life is sex," he said. Leary called LSD "a powerful aphrodisiac, probably the most powerful sexual releaser known to man. . . . The union was not just your body and her body but all of your racial and evolutionary entities with all of hers. It was mythic mating." *Playboy* asked Leary if it was true that women could have multiple orgasms under LSD. He replied with a straight face, "In a carefully prepared, loving LSD session, a woman can have several hundred orgasms."

Huxley had warned Leary that those in authority would oppose him. In April 1963, with LSD selling for a dollar a dose in Harvard Square, the university fired Leary, ostensibly because he cut classes, but really because his work had become an academic scandal. A month later, Richard Alpert, his colleague and collaborator, was fired too. After Mexico bounced the pair as well, a young millionaire came to Leary's rescue by renting him an estate in Millbrook, New York, complete with a musty sixty-four-room Victorian mansion and imitation Bavarian chalets. For the next two years Leary quit proselytizing and presided quietly over a religious commune based on drugs. . . .

Things began to go wrong for Leary in December 1965. On his way to Mexico with his family for a holiday, he was detained at the border and arrested with his daughter for possession of two ounces of marijuana. (Leary said he was probably the first person ever caught trying to smuggle pot *into* Mexico.) There followed more arrests, trials, convictions, appeals. The Millbrook idyll over, Leary again went public, playing to the hilt his role of unrepentant felon and high priest of the psychedelic movement. In 1966 he announced formation of a new religious organization called the League for Spiritual Discovery (LSD). That fall he conducted services in the Village Theatre in New York, where for three dollars a ticket observers could enjoy a multimedia show and a sermon by Leary. After a successful three-month run, Leary took his show on the college circuit, telling audiences to turn on, tune in, drop out. Few lines of the sixties wore so badly.

LSD was a big story in 1966. Congress outlawed it. *Newsweek, Life,* and the *Saturday Evening Post* all did cover stories on it. Sandoz stopped selling it. And the Food and Drug Administration sent a letter to two thousand colleges warning of its "widespread availability" and "profound effects on the mental processes." Years before, Leary had estimated that one million Americans would take LSD by 1967. According to *Life,* the nation had reached the million-dose mark in 1966. As for Leary himself, his reputation among heads declined rapidly after he went show biz. Many of them were already too young to know that he had once been a serious man and that at the dawn of the Aquarian Age Timothy Leary had been the Johnny Appleseed of acid.

If Leary spread the psychedelic revolution, Ken Kesey created the psychedelic style, West Coast version. In 1959, three years before publication of his modern classic *One Flew Over the Cuckoo's Nest,* Kesey took LSD as a subject in a medical experiment, and for him, then and there, the doors of perception blew wide open. In 1964, with a group of disciples called the Merry Pranksters, he established a drug commune in rural La Honda, an hour's drive from San Francisco. One of the Pranksters was Neal Cassady. On acid, Kesey and friends experienced the illusion of self, the All-in-One, the energy field of which we are all an extension. They tried to break down psychic barriers, attain intersubjectivity or group mind, and achieve synchronization with the Cosmos. And they committed themselves to a life of Dionysian ecstasy.

The Pranksters were hip, but in a new way. They were not beaten disaffiliates, warring against technology land, cursing their fate that they had not been born black. In *The Electric Kool-Aid Acid Test,* a history of Kesey in the underground, Tom Wolfe described this new hip generation, these hippies, as products of postwar affluence. Their teen years were spent driving big cars through the California suburbs, believing, like the superheroes in their Marvel comics, that anything was possible. No spade cool for them, no Zen detachment, none of Leary's "set and setting." The Pranksters used LSD to propel themselves out of their skulls toward the outer edge of Western experience. Their style was the wacko style: lurid costumes, Day-Glo paint, crazy trips in Kesey's 1939 multicolored International Harvester school bus, complete with speakers, tapes, and microphones. It was lots of kicks, of course, but it was more than kicks. For Kesey was a religious prophet whose ultimate goal was to turn America, as Michael Bowen put it, into an "electric Tibet."

Toward the end of 1965 Kesey conceived a ritual appropriate for spreading his version of cosmic consciousness. He called it the acid test. Hooking up with the rock group the Grateful Dead, he experimented with multimedia shows so noisy and frenzied that, by themselves, they menaced reason. To make sure that no one missed the point, lots of free LSD was distributed, a legal act, since California did not get around to outlawing the drug until October 1966. The purpose of the acid test was to create an experience so Dionysian that revelers would overflow the bounds of ego and plug directly into the Cosmos. After Kesey tried out the acid tests in a dozen or so road shows on the West Coast, he headed for the big time.

On January 21–23, 1966, Kesey and the Merry Pranksters produced and directed the Trips Festival at Longshoremen's Hall, San Francisco. The timing was perfect. For more than a year teenage dropouts and disillusioned campus radicals had been drifting into the beat haven of Haight-Ashbury. They were on the verge of community, but not quite there, acid freaks in search of identity. At Kesey's festival the heads of the Bay Area discovered their numbers, came out in the open, and confirmed the wacko style. The estimated twenty thousand people who attended wore every variety of wild costume, including Victorian dresses, Civil War uniforms, four-inch eyelashes, serapes, Indian headbands. Live rock propelled dancers through an electronic chaos of strobe lights, mov-

ies, tape machines, and slide projectors. High above the hall, dressed in a silver space suit, directing the whole to get the parts into sync, was Kesey himself. A few days later he took off for Mexico rather than face the consequences of a second drug bust. But Kesey's place in the history of hip was secure, no one having done more to create the hippie style that he had now to leave behind.

☆ V ☆

The Dionysian impulse in the hippie counterculture was made up in equal measures of drugs, sex, and music — not jazz music but rock and roll. When hippies moved in, the black jazz bars on Haight Street moved out. Spade jazz was now as irrelevant to hip as spade soul. Rock had once been black music too, but was so thoroughly appropriated by whites that many hip kids never knew its origins. Rock originated in the 1940s as "rhythm and blues," an urban-based blues music played with electric instruments, pounding beat, and raunchy lyrics — music by blacks for blacks. In 1952 the legendary Cleveland disc jockey Alan Freed hosted the first rhythm and blues record show for a white audience, calling the music "rock and roll." The music caught on among teenagers tired of sexless, sentimental ballads, and soon white performers fused pop and country styles with rhythm and blues to create white rock and roll. That's what Elvis Presley sang when he emerged in 1956 to become the biggest star in pop history. From the beginning, rock and roll was protest music, protest against Tin Pan Alley, protest against parental taste, protest against instinctual repression. Music of the id, fifties rock and roll helped create a generation of cultural subversives who would in time heed the siren song of hip.

In 1958, when Elvis went into the Army, rock entered a period of decline. Meanwhile, the black sound that had inspired it was being assimilated anew by other talented musicians, this time in England, and it would return to America, bigger than before, with the Beatles. During their long years of apprenticeship, playing lower-class clubs in Liverpool and Hamburg, John Lennon, Paul McCartney, and George Harrison explored the roots of rock and roll, even as they slowly fashioned a style of their own. By 1963 that style had fully matured. No longer just another scruffy group of Teddy Boys playing electronic guitars, they had become well-tailored professionals with a distinctive hair style (Eton long), immense stage presence, the best song-writing team in pop history (Lennon and McCartney), a fluid sound, contagious vitality, and, above all, the irrepressibe beat of rock and roll. That beat helped propel the Beatles to stardom in Britain in 1963 and created Beatlemania.

Within days of its release in the United States in January 1964, "I Want to Hold Your Hand" climbed to the top of the charts, to be followed quickly by "She Loves You" and "Please, Please Me." In February the Beatles themselves arrived for a tour that began with a sensational TV performance on the *Ed Sullivan Show* and continued before hysterical teen mobs in New York, Washington, and Miami. In April all five top singles in the United States were Beatles songs and the two top albums were Beatles albums. In July the first Beatles movie, *A Hard Day's Night,* amazed critics and delighted audiences with its wit and verve. Meanwhile that year Beatles merchandise — everything from dolls to dishcloths — was grossing over $50 million. Nothing comparable to Beatlemania had ever happened in the history of pop culture.

Unlike Presley or their British rivals, the Rolling Stones, the Beatles did not menace society. They mocked it. Insouciant, irreverent, flip, they took seriously no institution or person, themselves included. "What do you think of Beethoven?" a reporter asked at the Beatles' first American press conference. "I love him," replied Ringo. "Especially his poems." Treating the adult world as absurd, they told their fans to kick off their shoes, heed their hormones, and have fun. However harmless initially, the Beatles phenom-

enon contained the possibility of danger. The frenzied loyalty they inspired endowed the Fab Four with immense potential power — power to alter life styles, change values, and create a new sensibility, a new way of perceiving the world. But in the early days, as they sang their songs of teen love, that power lay dormant. When Ken Kesey attended the 1965 Beatles concert in San Francisco, he was astonished by the "concentration and power" focused on the performers. He was just as astonished by their inability to exploit them. "They could have taken this roomful of kids and snapped them," said Kesey, "and they would have left that place enlightened, mature people that would never have been quite the same again. . . . They had the power to bring off this new consciousness to people, but they couldn't do it."

The artist who first seized the power of rock and used it to change consciousness was Bob Dylan. Born Robert Zimmerman, Dylan tried on every style of teen alienation available during the fifties in Hibbing, Minnesota. Though he wanted to be a rock and roll star, he discovered on enrolling at the University of Minnesota in 1959 that folk music was the rage on campus. In 1961 Dylan arrived in Greenwich Village, the folk capital of America, determined to become the biggest folkie of them all. A little over a year later, he was. Audiences responded to his vulnerability, the nasal whine with which he delivered his songs, and lyrics so riveting they transformed the folk art. Immersing himself in the left-liberal-civil-rights ethos permeating the Village in the early 1960s, Dylan wrote folk songs as protest. He did not compose from the headlines, as other protest singers did. He used figurative language and elusive imagery to distill the political mood of his time and place. Gambling that a poet could become a star, he won big. Two weeks after Peter, Paul, and Mary recorded his song "Blowin' in the Wind," it sold more than 300,000 copies. Songs like "A Hard Rain's Gonna Fall" were hailed as true art. And his "Times They Are A-Changin'" became a generational anthem. It was no less appropriate for Dylan to sing at the 1963 March on Washington than for Martin Luther King to deliver a sermon there.

Meanwhile, the Beatles arrived and Dylan was listening. "Everybody else thought they were for the teenyboppers, that they were gonna pass right away," Dylan said. "But it was obvious to me that they had staying power. I knew they were pointing the direction of where music had to go." In July 1965 Dylan outraged the folk world by appearing at the Newport Folk Festival, no longer the ragged waif with acoustic guitar, but as a rock and roll singer, outfitted in black leather jacket and backed by an electric band. That summer his rock single, "Like a Rolling Stone," perhaps the greatest song he ever wrote, made it all the way to number one.

Dylan took rock and made it the medium for cultural statement — folk-rock, the critics quickly labeled it. As his music changed, so did the message. Moving with his generation, Dylan now abandoned liberal politics for cultural radicalism. The lyrics he sang in the mid-sixties were intensely personal and frequently obscure, but taken together, they formed a stunning mosaic of a corrupt and chaotic America. It is a fact of no small social consequence that in 1965 millions of radios and record players were daily pounding Dylan's message, subliminally or otherwise, into the skulls of a generation. There was, for example, "Highway 61," which depicted America as a junkyard road heading for war; "Maggie's Farm," a dropout's contemptuous farewell to the straight world; "Desolation Row," which portrayed an insane society, governed by insane men, teetering on the brink of apocalypse; "Ballad of a Thin Man," using homosexual imagery to describe an intellectual's confusion in a world bereft of reason; and "Gates of Eden," a mystical evocation of a realm beyond the senses, beyond ego, wherein resides the timeless Real. After Dylan, a host of other rock prophets arose to preach sex, love, peace, or revolution. After Dylan rock and roll became a music that both expressed the sixties counterculture and shaped it.

Among those acknowledging their debt to Dylan

were the Beatles. After Dylan, they too began writing songs for the cultural opposition, to which they became increasingly committed. The Beatles induced mystic ecstasies with LSD, discovered the music and religion of the East, even took an abortive pilgrimage to India to study Transcendental Meditation with the Maharishi Mahesh Yogi. In June 1967 they released *Sergeant Pepper's Lonely Hearts Club Band,* a musically innovative album placing them at the head of the psychedelic parade. ("I'd love to turn you on," John Lennon sang on the record's best cut.) Timothy Leary, after *Sergeant Pepper,* proclaimed the Beatles "evolutionary agents sent by God, endowed with a mysterious power to create a new human species."

In the view of some, this new human species had already emerged with the San Francisco hippies, who played their own brand of rock and roll. Literally hundreds of bands had formed in the Bay Area by the mid-1960s, but because no major company recorded there, they developed in isolation from the commercial mainstream. Hippie musicians were freaks who played for freaks, having no other purpose than creation of Dionysian art. They were contemptuous of the star system, top forty stations, giant concerts for idolatrous audiences, Madison Avenue hype. They played their music live in dance halls where the musicians could jam as long as they wanted, and the dancers dressed like rock stars. The songs they wrote celebrated drugs and sex, and the music they played was music to trip on. One rock critic described the San Francisco Sound as "revelatory roaring, chills of ecstasy, hallucinated wandering, mysticopsychotic wonder."

San Francisco's dance-hall craze began in the fall of 1965 when local promoters rented seedy halls to feature hippie bands like the Jefferson Airplane, Big Brother and the Holding Company, Quicksilver Messenger Service, and the Grateful Dead. After Kesey's Trips Festival in January 1966, the acid tests merged with the dances, institutionalized at weekend freakouts at the Fillmore and the Avalon Ballroom. The quintessential San Francisco band was the Grateful Dead, who had been on Kesey's trip and never got over it. "It wasn't a *gig,* it was the Acid Tests where anything was OK," the Dead's Jerry Garcia recalled. "Thousands of people, man, all helplessly stoned, all finding themselves in a roomful of other thousands of people, none of whom any of them were afraid of. It was magic, far out, beautiful magic." In June 1966 the Dead moved into a house in Haight-Ashbury, where they lived together, jammed free for the people, got stoned, got busted, and continued to seek that magic moment in their music when performers, audience, and Cosmos were One. . . .

By summer [1967] the San Francisco Sound was making the city the new rock mecca and its performers the newest rock superstars. The big song on the top forty stations that season was the Airplane's "White Rabbit," psychedelic variations on a theme from *Alice in Wonderland,* ending with the command to "feed a head, feed a head." That summer, too, thousands of teenagers took literally Scott McKenzie's musical invitation, with its implicit promise of Dionysian revels, to come to "San Francisco (Be Sure to Wear Flowers in Your Hair)." Ralph Gleason, San Francisco's hip music critic, understood well the cultural significance of rock. "At no time in American history has youth possessed the strength it possesses now," he wrote. "Trained by music and linked by music, it has the power for good to change the world." Significantly, he added, "That power for good carries the reverse, the power for evil."

☆ VI ☆

By 1967 Haight-Ashbury had attained a population large enough to merit, at last, the designation "counterculture." The question was, where was this culture tending? A few days after the famous Human Be-In, the celebrities of the movement met on Alan Watts's houseboat off Sausalito to exchange visions of utopia. [A student of Zen] Watts summed up for the others the predicament of the West: rational, technological man had lost contact with himself and nature. Fortunately, Timothy Leary said, automation could now liberate man from work and enable him to live a simpler life. Feasting off technology, dropouts from megalopolis could form tribes and move back to the land. Yes, said poet Gary Snyder. Turn Chicago into a center for cybernetic technology and the rest of America into buffalo pasture. After a while, as life got simpler, "Chicago would rust away." Man's destruction of his natural environment would cease. Nuclear families would give way to communes or tribes, whose members would share food, work, and sex. Like the Comanche and the Sioux, members of these tribes would go off alone to have visions, and all who knew them would know them as men. Already in Big Sur, Snyder continued, kids were using A. L. Kroeber's *Handbook of the California Indians* to learn the art of primitive survival, to learn how to be Indians. Fine, countered Allen Ginsberg, "but where are the people going to buy their Uher tape recorder machines?" which were being used to record the conversation.

Ginsberg's was the authentic voice of Haight-Ashbury. Addicted to electronic amenities, hippies merely played at being Indians, satisfied to wear Navaho jewelry and feathers. They communed with nature by picking Golden Gate Park bare of flowers; their notion of tribal harmony was to let everyone "do their own thing." As love had supposedly done for the Hopi, so it would do for them: it would conquer all. Armed with "flower power," hippies would overwhelm their enemies and live a life of ecstasy on the asphalt pavements of urban America. Real Indians were not much impressed. In the spring of 1967, when Ginsberg and Richard Alpert met Hopi leaders in Santa Fe to propose a Be-In in the Grand Canyon, the tribal spokesman brushed them off, saying according to the *Berkeley Barb,* "No, because you mean well but you are foolish. . . . You are a tribe of strangers to yourselves.". . .

By summer of 1967 the Haight's bizarre cast of characters was performing for a national audience.

This was the summer when *Time* described the neighborhood as "the vibrant epicenter of the hippie movement," hippies estimated their full-time population nationwide at 300,000, imitation Haight-Ashburys bloomed throughout urban America, acid rock dominated the music charts, prestigious museums exhibited psychedelic posters, and doing one's own thing became the national cliché. Once school ended, San Francisco expected one to two hundred thousand kids to flood the city for the Summer of Love. But the real story that summer, unreported by the media, was that few of the thousands who did come stayed very long. Haight-Ashbury was already dying.

Its demise, so similar to the demise of hippie ghettos elsewhere, resulted from official repression, black hostility, and media hype. In San Francisco where city fathers panicked at the prospect of runaway hordes descending upon them, police began routinely roughing up hippies, health officials harassed their communes, and narcotics agents infiltrated the neighborhood. Meanwhile, black hoods from the nearby Fillmore district cruised the streets, threatening rape and violence. Blacks did not like LSD, white kids pretending to be poor, or the fact that Haight-Ashbury was, in the words of a leftover beatnik, "the first segregated Bohemia I've ever seen." Longtime residents began staying home after dark. Finally, the beguiling images of Haight-Ashbury marketed by the media attracted not only an invasion of gawking tourists, but a floating population of the unstable, the psychotic, and the criminal. By the end of the year, *reported* crime in Haight-Ashbury included 17 murders, 100 rapes, and nearly 3,000 burglaries.

In October 1967 community leaders staged a pageant called "Death of Hippie." . . . While a country fiddler made music, a parade carried an oversized coffin, filled with hippie litter, through "Hashbury." Halting at the panhandle, mourners set the coffin on fire and danced a Dionysian dance. . . . The vision of an acid utopia based on love and flowers was already ashes.

☆ VII ☆

Though Haight-Ashbury died, the counterculture did not. If anything, in the last years of the decade the potent mix of drugs, sex, and rock and roll seduced an even larger proportion of the young. But few of these hip rebels called themselves hippies or talked of flower power any longer. Norman O. Brown had envisioned a cultural revolution in which a Dionysian ego would become the servant of Eros. But in the Freudian metaphor, Eros had to contend with Thanatos. The danger always existed that by liberating one, hip would liberate the other also. Brown himself had warned, "Not only does Dionysus without the Dionysian ego threaten us with dissolution of consciousness; he also threatens us with that 'genuine witches' brew,' 'that horrible mixture of sensuality and cruelty' (Nietzsche again), which is the result of the Dionysian against the Apollonian." After the fall from the Haight-Ashbury paradise, Thanatos, not Eros, prevailed in the counterculture. Confronted by hostile police, hysterical parents, and implacable draft boards, the freaks abandoned the rhetoric of love for the politics of rage. They became willing cannon fodder for the increasingly violent demonstrations of the new left. And they routinely threw rocks at police, rioted at rock concerts, and trashed stores. The nightmare of the Dionysian witches' brew, of Dionysus without the Dionysian ego, had become reality.

As the decade closed, it became clear that drugs, sex, and rock and roll lacked intrinsic moral content. The acid prophets had warned from the beginning that LSD did not inevitably produce the God experience. God and the Devil resided together in the nervous system, Leary had said. LSD could evoke either, depending on set and setting. The streets of Haight-Ashbury, even in the best days, had been littered with kids who deranged their senses on drugs — only to experience spiritual stupor. A fair number ended their trips in hospital emergency rooms, possessed of one or another demon. Satanic cults were not unknown in the Haight. One of them, the Process, apparently influenced Charles Manson, a hippie who lived in the neighborhood in 1967 and recruited confused young girls and a few men into his "family." Manson was an "acid fascist" who somehow found in the lyrics of the Beatles license to commit [the] ritual murder [of actress Sharon Tate and four acquaintances, whose bodies were heinously mutilated]. As violence in the counterculture mounted, LSD became chiefly a means to pierce the false rationality of the hated bourgeois world. The always tenuous link between drugs and love was broken.

Neither was sex itself necessarily the expression of Eros unalloyed with death. Sex in the counterculture did not imply love between two people, but merely gratification of the self—ecstasy through orgasm. Typical encounters in Haight-Ashbury were one-night stands. Rapists prospered, and carriers of venereal disease shared it generously. Janis Joplin, the greatest white blues singer who ever lived and the authentic voice of sexual ecstasy in Haight-Ashbury, sang Dionysian hymns to sexual climax. But for Janis the orgasm was the god that failed. How was your vacation on St. Thomas? a friend asked a year before Janis died of a heroin overdose. "It was just like anywhere else," she said. "I fucked a lot of strangers."

. . . Rock and roll was the principal art of the counterculture because of its demonstrable power to liberate the instincts. At the Woodstock Music Festival, held one weekend in August 1969 at Bethel, New York, Eros ran wild. An incredible 400,000 people gathered on a farm to hear the greatest line-up of rock talent ever assembled in one place. Overcoming conditions that could conventionally be described only as disastrous, the crowd created a loving community based on drugs, sex, and rock music. But four months later at the Altamont Raceway near San Francisco, rock revealed an equal affinity for death.

The occasion was a free concert conceived by the Rolling Stones as a fitting climax to their first American tour in three years and the documentary film that was recording it. Altamont was a calamity. Because of

a last-minute cancellation elsewhere, concert promoters had only one day to ready the site for a crush of 300,000 kids. Sanitary facilities were inadequate; the sound system, terrible; the setting, cheerless. Lots of bad dope, including inferior acid spiked with speed, circulated through the crowd. Harried medics had to fly in an emergency supply of [the tranquilizer] Thorazine to treat the epidemic of bad trips and were kept busy administering first aid to victims of the random violence. The violence originated with the Hell's Angels. On the advice of the Grateful Dead, the Stones had hired the Angels to guard the stage for $500 worth of beer. Armed with loaded pool cues sawed off to the length of billy clubs, high on bad dope washed down with Red Mountain vin rose, Angels indiscriminately clubbed people for offenses real or imagined. Vibrations of fear and paranoia spread from them outward through the crowd. And yet, when the Jefferson Airplane did their set, they called the Angels on stage to pay them homage. Once a hippie band singing acid rock, the Airplane had moved with the times, expressing in their music the anarchic rage surging through the counterculture. The song they sang to the Angels was "We Can Be Together."

> We should be together.
> All your private property is target for your enemy
> And your enemy is me.
> We are forces of chaos and anarchy.
> Everything they say we are we are.
> And we are proud of ourselves.
> Up against the wall
> Up against the wall motherfucker.

Minutes later, when the Airplane's Marty Balin tried to stop an Angel from beating a fan, he himself was knocked cold.

At nightfall, after keeping the crowd waiting in the cold for more than an hour, the Rolling Stones came on stage. Many critics regarded the Stones as the greatest rock and roll band in the world. Ever since their emergence, they had carefully cultivated an out-law image — lewd, sneering, surly — to differentiate themselves from their fellow Britons, the Beatles. Their most recent music, including, notably, "Street Fighting Man" and "Sympathy for the Devil," re-flected the growing violence of the culture of which they were superstars. Now at Altamont there was Mick Jagger, reveling in his image as rock's prince of evil, prancing on stage while the Angels flailed away with their pool cues below. It was too much even for him. Jagger stopped the music more than once to plead for order; but when the Angels ignored him, he had no choice except to sing on. Midway through "Sympathy for the Devil," only a few feet from the stage, an Angel knifed a black man named Meredith Hunter to death. The moment was captured by cam-era and made the highlight of the film *Gimme Shelter,* which as much as any counterculture document of the time revealed Thanatos unleashed.

☆ VIII ☆

For a variety of reasons, after 1970 the counterculture faded. Economic recession signaled that affluence could no longer be assumed and induced a certain caution among the young. The Vietnam War, which did so much to discredit authority, rapidly deesca-lated. And its own revels brought the hippie move-ment into disrepute. Carried to the edge of sanity by their Dionysian revels, many of the once hip retreated, some to rural communes in New Mexico or Vermont, most all the way back to the straight world.

Not least among the reasons for the waning of the impulse was the ease with which the dominant cul-ture absorbed it. Indeed, despite the generational war-fare that marked the late 1960s, hippies were only a spectacular exaggeration of tendencies transforming the larger society. The root of these tendencies, to borrow a phrase from Daniel Bell, was a "cultural

contradiction of capitalism." By solving the problems of want, industrial capitalism undermined the very virtues that made this triumph possible, virtues like hard work, self-denial, postponement of gratification, submission to social discipline, strong ego mecha-nisms to control the instincts. As early as the 1920s the system of mass production depended less on saving than consumption, not on denial but indulgence. De-pression and war retarded the implications of these changes until the 1950s.

Unprecedented affluence after World War II cre-ated a generation of teenagers who could forgo work to stay in school. Inhabiting a gilded limbo between childhood and adult responsibility, these kids had money, leisure, and unprecedented opportunity to test taboos. For them the Protestant ethic had no rel-evance, except in the lingering parental effort to en-force it. When Elvis emerged from Memphis, ham-mering out his beat and exuding sexuality, the teen breakout from jailhouse America began. The next step in the process of liberation was hip.

But middle-class teenagers were not alone in kick-ing over the traces of Puritanism. Their parents too began reckoning with the cultural implications of af-fluence. Critics had attacked the hippies as hedonistic and narcissistic. By the 1970s social discipline was eroding so rapidly that fashion condemned the whole of middle-class culture as the "culture of narcissism." Parental discipline declined, sexual promiscuity rose along with the divorce rate, worker productivity fell, ghetto obscenity insinuated itself into standard speech, marijuana became almost commonplace, sexual per-versions were no longer deemed so, and traditional institutions like the Army, the churches, and the gov-ernment lost authority. At the same time, the impulse toward ecstasy found increasing expression in Orien-tal religion, the New Consciousness Movement, and charismatic Christianity. Dionysus had been absorbed into the dominant culture and domesticated, and in the process routed the Protestant ethic.

Cultural change had political implications. While liberals earnestly sought to purge capitalism of traditional problems like unemployment and poverty, a vocal minority of American youth regarded unemployment as a blessing and chose poverty as a way of life. In the short run, hippie scorn was one more problem complicating the life of [President] Lyndon Johnson, who never could understand whatever happened to earnest youth. In the long run, though it proved ephemeral, the hippie movement was profoundly significant, portending as it did the erosion of the liberal values that had [long] sustained bourgeois society. . . .

QUESTIONS TO CONSIDER

1.   What are the historical origins of the counterculture, and how did it spread and change over time? What groups of people did it most affect? Describe the historical origins and development of counterculture music. How were the Beatles different from their predecessors and how were they similar? What does their career say about the counterculture and about the larger society at the time?

2.   Compare the image that the hippies cultivated with the actual conditions of their lives and communities. How do you account for the differences? What do you think of the psychological explanation discussed by Matusow? Is it an objective explanation or a product of the same culture?

3.   Compare the youth and the social changes of the 1960s with those of the 1920s, which you read about in selection 15. Do you see in the readings other examples of twentieth-century reactions against the traditional values of the culture?

4.   Matusow suggests that the hippies were exaggerated products of the "cultural contradiction of capitalism." How do you evaluate his using affluence to explain rebelliousness? What do you think of the possibility that noneconomic factors, political or educational, for example, might explain the rebelliousness? Why was there such a great gulf between the counterculture and liberals?

5.   What relationship does Matusow see between the hippies and cultural changes in society at large? Do you see consequences of this in today's social conditions? What implications might this have for the future?

XIV

The Seventies

29

Watergate

WALTER KARP

The early 1970s were difficult for the United States, what with the Vietnam War and the counterculture revolt still going on and still dividing the country. Then came the Watergate crisis, in which the administration of Richard M. Nixon resorted to appalling abuses of power that for a time threatened the very constitutional fabric of the Republic. Perhaps, as journalist Jonathan Schell suggested in The Time of Illusion *(1975), Vietnam and Watergate were symptomatic of the crushing burdens that a modern American president had to bear as he tried to lead a mighty nuclear power in a complex, dangerous world menaced with the specter of human extinction. Even so, there can be little doubt that Nixon brought the Watergate disaster on himself, not only by hiring dishonest assistants but by persistently lying about his own complicity in Watergate and abusing the powers of his office worse than had any other president.*

Although Nixon had promised in 1968 to "bring us together again," he and his advisers clearly viewed a great many Americans—journalists, northeastern Republicans, liberal Democrats, and protesting students—as mortal enemies of the president and therefore of the Republic itself. For Nixon and his colleagues, domestic politics became a desperate battlefield between them *and* us, *with the Nixon White House increasingly identifying* them *as traitors and* us *as the only patriots and true saviors of America. In the name of "national security," as Walter Karp points out, the Nixon administration flagrantly violated the law and the Constitution in its zeal to suppress dissent, defeat opponents, and uphold administration politics. Nixon's "campaign of subversion" produced the Watergate scandal. It began in June 1972, when five men associated with the Committee to Re-Elect the President (CREEP) broke into the Democratic National Commit-*

tee headquarters in Washington, D.C. and were arrested on a charge of burglary. For a time, Nixon successfully covered up his complicity in the break-in and the abuse of executive power it represented. When Carl Bernstein and Bob Woodward of the Washington Post, exposed the Watergate scandal, it precipitated what one historian called "the greatest constitutional crisis the country had faced since the Civil War." The crisis shook Americans of every political persuasion and eventually brought down Nixon's presidency.

Some historians have linked Watergate to the growth of an "imperial presidency," which resulted in an imbalance of power, tilted to the executive branch. Lyndon Johnson had hastened the process by waging his undeclared war in Vietnam and pressuring Congress into endorsing and funding it. In the Watergate crisis, as historian William H. Chafe observes, the country rallied against the excesses of the imperial presidency, insisting on "a government of laws rather than personal whim."

Like Vietnam, Watergate is an unhappy chapter in United States history, yet one that Americans of both political parties have tried to face openly and honestly, for they believe that the mark of a great people is an ability to admit mistakes in their leaders as well as in themselves. Here, historian and writer Walter Karp offers a frank and lucid account of the Watergate ordeal, with special emphasis on its constitutional implications.

GLOSSARY

BUTTERFIELD, ALEXANDER Former White House aide who revealed to Senator Sam Ervin that Nixon had secretly taped "his most intimate political conversations."

COX, ARCHIBALD Harvard law professor and special prosecutor who persuaded the United States Court of Appeals to order Nixon to turn over nine tape-recorded conversations.

DEAN, JOHN Nixon's legal counsel and main accuser in the Watergate scandal; Dean pleaded guilty to obstructing justice "in the investigation" of the burglary.

DOAR, JOHN Democrats' legal counsel; he and Republican counsel Albert Jenner led the House Judiciary Committee in its impeachment proceedings against Nixon.

ERVIN, SAMUEL J., JR. Chairman of the special

Senate committee that investigated the Watergate break-in and cover-up.

GRAY, L. PATRICK Director of the FBI who "burned incriminating White House documents."

MITCHELL, JOHN Nixon's attorney general who was "indicted for obstructing justice in Washington and impeding a Securities and Exchange Commission investigation in New York."

RODINO, PETER, JR. New Jersey Democrat who chaired the House Judiciary Committee, which voted to impeach Nixon for obstructing justice, "violating the constitutional rights of citizens," and "for refusing to comply with the committee's subpoenas."

ST. CLAIR, JAMES D. Nixon's lawyer who argued that he, St. Clair, represented the office of the presidency rather than Nixon individually; Nixon made a similar argument, insisting that he was protecting the presidency from forces seeking to "weaken" it.

SATURDAY NIGHT MASSACRE   Resolved to evade the court order that he turn over nine of his taped conversations, Nixon "massacred" several key players in the Watergate drama; first, he told Attorney General Elliot Richardson to fire special prosecutor Cox. Richardson refused to issue the order and resigned; when Deputy Attorney General William Ruckelshaus refused to issue the order, Nixon fired him too; finally, a third acting attorney general, Robert Bork, put forth the order that fired Cox.

In August 1974, the thirty-seventh President of the United States, facing imminent impeachment, resigned his high office and passed out of our lives. "The system worked," the nation exclaimed, heaving a sigh of relief. What had brought that relief was the happy extinction of the prolonged fear that the "system" might not work at all. But what was it that had inspired such fears? When I asked myself that question recently, I found I could scarcely remember. Although I had followed the Watergate crisis with minute attention, it had grown vague and formless in my mind, like a nightmare recollected in sunshine. It was not until I began working my way through back copies of *The New York Times* that I was able to remember clearly why I used to read my morning paper with forebodings for the country's future.

The Watergate crisis had begun in June 1972 as a "third-rate burglary" of the Democratic National Committee headquarters in Washington's Watergate building complex. By late March 1973 the burglary and subsequent efforts to obstruct its investigation had been laid at the door of the White House. By late June, Americans were asking themselves whether their President had or had not ordered the payment of "hush money" to silence a Watergate burglar. Investigated by a special Senate committee headed by Sam Ervin of North Carolina, the scandal continued to deepen and ramify during the summer of 1973. By March 1974 the third-rate burglary of 1972 had grown into an unprecedented constitutional crisis.

By then it was clear beyond doubt that President Richard M. Nixon stood at the center of a junta of henchmen without parallel in our history. One of Nixon's attorneys general, John Mitchell, was indicted for obstructing justice in Washington and for impeding a Securities and Exchange Commission

From Walter Karp, "The Hour of the Founders," *American Heritage,* June/July 1984, Vol. 35, No. 4. © 1984 by Forbes, Inc. Reprinted by permission of *American Heritage* Magazine, a division of Forbes Inc.

investigation in New York. Another, Richard Kleindienst, had criminally misled the Senate Judiciary Committee in the President's interest. The acting director of the Federal Bureau of Investigation, L. Patrick Gray, had burned incriminating White House documents at the behest of a presidential aide. Bob Haldeman, the President's chief of staff, John Ehrlichman, the President's chief domestic adviser, and Charles Colson, the President's special counsel, all had been indicted for obstructing justice in the investigation of the Watergate burglary. John Dean, the President's legal counsel and chief accuser, had already pleaded guilty to the same charge. Dwight Chapin, the President's appointments secretary, faced trial for lying to a grand jury about political sabotage carried out during the 1972 elections. Ehrlichman and two other White House aides were under indictment for conspiring to break into a psychiatrist's office and steal confidential information about one of his former patients, Daniel Ellsberg. [A former aide to Henry Kissinger, Ellsberg had leaked to the *New York Times* a file of classified Pentagon papers that exposed American policy in Vietnam up to 1968; the Nixon administration vowed to "get" Ellsberg in retaliation.] By March 1974 some twenty-eight presidential aides or election officials had been indicted for crimes carried out in the President's interest. Never before in American history had a President so signally failed to fulfill his constitutional duty to "take care that the laws be faithfully executed."

It also had been clear for many months that the thirty-seventh President of the United States did not feel bound by his constitutional duties. He insisted that the requirements of national security, as he and he alone saw fit to define it, released him from the most fundamental legal and constitutional constraints. In the name of "national security," the President had created a secret band of private detectives, paid with private funds, to carry out political espionage at the urging of the White House. In the name of "national security," the President had approved the warrantless wiretapping of news reporters. In the name of "na-

tional security," he had approved a secret plan for massive, illegal surveillance of American citizens. He had encouraged his aides' efforts to use the Internal Revenue Service to harass political "enemies" — prominent Americans who endangered "national security" by publicly criticizing the President's Vietnam War policies.

The framers of the Constitution had provided one and only one remedy for such lawless abuse of power: impeachment in the House of Representatives and trial in the Senate for "high Crimes and Misdemeanors." There was absolutely no alternative. If Congress had not held President Nixon accountable for lawless conduct of his office, then Congress would have condoned a lawless Presidency. If Congress had not struck from the President's hands the despot's cudgel of "national security," then Congress would have condoned a despotic Presidency.

Looking through the back issues of *The New York Times,* I recollected in a flood of . . . memories what it was that had filled me with such foreboding. It was the reluctance of Congress to act. I felt anew my fury when members of Congress pretended that nobody really cared about Watergate except the "media" and the "Nixon-haters." The real folks "back home," they said, cared only about inflation and the gasoline shortage. I remembered the exasperating actions of leading Democrats, such as a certain Senate leader who went around telling the country that President Nixon could not be impeached because in America a person was presumed innocent until proven guilty. Surely the senator knew that impeachment was not a verdict of guilt but a formal accusation made in the House leading to trial in the Senate. Why was he muddying the waters, I wondered, if not to protect the President?

It had taken one of the most outrageous episodes in the history of the Presidency to compel Congress to make even a pretense of action.

Back on July 16, 1973, a former White House aide named Alexander Butterfield had told the Ervin committee that President Nixon secretly tape-recorded

Caught in a web of his own making and condemned by tape-recorded words out of his own mouth, President Richard Nixon resigned on August 9, 1974, shortly before his impeachment by Congress became a certainty. At first reluctant to act on the matter,

Congress eventually fulfilled its constitutional obligation to make sure that no president could subvert the powers of the office. (Robert Pryor/John Locke Studios, Inc.)

his most intimate political conversations. On two solemn occasions that spring the President had sworn to the American people that he knew nothing of the Watergate cover-up until his counsel John Dean had told him about it on March 21, 1973. From that day forward, Nixon had said, 'I began intensive new inquiries into this whole matter." Now we learned that the President had kept evidence secret that would exonerate him completely — if he were telling the truth. Worse yet, he wanted it kept secret. Before

Butterfield had revealed the existence of the tapes, the President had grandly announced that "executive privilege will not be invoked as to any testimony [by my aides] concerning possible criminal conduct, in the matters under investigation. I want the public to learn the truth about Watergate. . . ." After the existence of the tapes was revealed, however, the President showed the most ferocious resistance to disclosing the "truth about Watergate." He now claimed that executive privilege — hitherto a somewhat shadowy presidential prerogative — gave a President "absolute power" to withhold any taped conversation he chose, even those urgently needed in the ongoing criminal investigation then being conducted by a special Watergate prosecutor. Nixon even claimed, through his lawyers, that the judicial branch of the federal government was "absolutely without power to reweigh that choice or to make a different resolution of it."

In the U.S. Court of Appeals the special prosecutor, a Harvard Law School professor named Archibald Cox, called the President's claim "intolerable." Millions of Americans found it infuriating. The court found it groundless. On October 12, 1973, it ordered the President to surrender nine taped conversations that Cox had been fighting to obtain for nearly three months.

Determined to evade the court order, the President on October 19 announced that he had devised a "compromise." Instead of handing over the recorded conversations to the court, he would submit only edited summaries. To verify their truthfulness, the President would allow Sen. John Stennis of Mississippi to listen to the tapes. As an independent verifier, the elderly senator was distinguished by his devotion to the President's own overblown conception of a "strong" Presidency. When Nixon had ordered the secret bombing of Cambodia, he had vouchsafed the fact to Senator Stennis, who thought that concealing the President's secret war from his fellow senators was a higher duty than preserving the Senate's constitutional role in the formation of United States foreign policy.

On Saturday afternoon, October 20, I and millions of other Americans sat by our television sets while the special prosecutor explained why he could not accept "what seems to me to be non-compliance with the court's order." Then the President flashed the dagger sheathed within his "compromise." At 8:31 P.M. television viewers across the country learned that he had fired the special prosecutor; that attorney general Elliot Richardson had resigned rather than issue that order to Cox; that the deputy attorney general, William Ruckelshaus, also had refused to do so and had been fired for refusing; that it was a third acting attorney general [Robert Bork] who had finally issued the order. With trembling voices, television newscasters reported that the President had abolished the office of special prosecutor and that the FBI was standing guard over its files. Never before in our history had a President, setting law at defiance, made our government seem so tawdry and gimcrack. "It's like living in a banana republic," a friend of mine remarked.

Now the question before the country was clear. "Whether ours shall continue to be a government of laws and not of men," the ex–special prosecutor said that evening, "is now for the Congress and ultimately the American people to decide."

Within ten days of the "Saturday night massacre," one million letters and telegrams rained down on Congress, almost every one of them demanding the President's impeachment. But congressional leaders dragged their feet. The House Judiciary Committee would begin an inquiry into *whether* to begin an inquiry into possible grounds for recommending impeachment to the House. With the obvious intent, it seemed to me, of waiting until the impeachment fervor had abated, the Democratic-controlled committee would consider whether to consider making a recommendation about making an accusation.

Republicans hoped to avoid upholding the rule of law by persuading the President to resign. This attempt to supply a lawless remedy for lawless power earned Republicans a memorable rebuke from one of the most venerated members of their party: eighty-one-year-old Sen. George Aiken of Vermont. The demand for Nixon's resignation, he said, "suggests that many prominent Americans, who ought to know better, find the task of holding a President accountable as just too difficult. . . . To ask the President now to resign and thus relieve Congress of its clear congressional duty amounts to a declaration of incompetence on the part of Congress."

The system was manifestly not working. But neither was the President's defense. On national television Nixon bitterly assailed the press for its "outrageous, vicious, distorted" reporting, but the popular outrage convinced him, nonetheless, to surrender the nine tapes to the court. Almost at once the White House tapes began their singular career of encompassing the President's ruin. On October 31 the White House disclosed that two of the taped conversations were missing, including one between the President and his campaign manager, John Mitchell, which had taken place the day after Nixon returned from a Florida vacation and three days after the Watergate break-in. Three weeks later the tapes dealt Nixon a more potent blow. There was an eighteen-and-a-half minute gap, the White House announced, in a taped conversation between the President and Haldeman, which had also taken place the day after he returned from Florida. The White House suggested first that the President's secretary, Rose Mary Woods, had accidentally erased part of the tape while transcribing it. When the loyal Miss Woods could not demonstrate in court how she could have pressed the "erase" button unwittingly for eighteen straight minutes, the White House attributed the gap to "some sinister force." On January 15, 1974, court-appointed experts provided a more humdrum explanation. The gap had been produced by at least five manual erasures. Someone in the White House had deliberately destroyed evidence that might have proved that President Nixon knew of the Watergate cover-up from the start.

At this point the Judiciary Committee was in its third month of considering whether to consider. But by now there was scarcely an American who did not think the President guilty, and on February 6, 1974, the House voted 410 to 4 to authorize the Judiciary Committee to begin investigating possible grounds for impeaching the President of the United States. It had taken ten consecutive months of the most damning revelations of criminal misconduct, a titanic outburst of public indignation, and an unbroken record of presidential deceit, defiance, and evasion in order to compel Congress to take its first real step. That long record of immobility and feigned indifference boded ill for the future.

The White House knew how to exploit congressional reluctance. One tactic involved a highly technical but momentous question: What constituted an impeachable offense? On February 21 the staff of the Judiciary Committee had issued a report. Led by two distinguished attorneys, John Doar, a fifty-two-year-old Wisconsin Independent, and Albert Jenner, a sixty-seven-year-old Chicago Republican, the staff had taken the broad view of impeachment for which Hamilton and Madison had contended in the *Federalist* papers. Despite the constitutional phrase "high Crimes and Misdemeanors," the staff report had argued that an impeachable offense did not have to be a crime. "Some of the most grievous offenses against our Constitutional form of government may not entail violations of the criminal law."

The White House launched a powerful counterattack. At a news conference on February 25, the President contended that only proven criminal misconduct supplied grounds for impeachment. On February 28, the White House drove home his point with a tightly argued legal paper: If a President could be impeached for anything other than a crime of "a very serious nature," it would expose the Presidency to "political impeachments."

The argument was plausible. But if Congress accepted it, the Watergate crisis could only end in disaster. Men of great power do not commit crimes. They procure crimes without having to issue incriminating orders. A word to the servile suffices. "Who will free me from this turbulent priest," asked Henry II, and four of his barons bashed in the skull of Thomas à Becket. The ease with which the powerful can arrange "deniability," to use the Watergate catchword, was one reason the criminal standard was so dangerous to liberty. Instead of having to take care that the laws be faithfully executed, a President, under that standard, would only have to take care to insulate himself from the criminal activities of his agents. Moreover, the standard could not reach the most dangerous offenses. There is no crime in the statute books called "attempted tyranny."

Yet the White House campaign to narrow the definition of impeachment met with immediate success. In March one of the members of the House of Representatives said that before voting to impeach Nixon, he would "want to know beyond a reasonable doubt that he was directly involved in the commission of a crime." To impeach the President for the grave abuse of his powers, lawmakers said, would be politically impossible. On the Judiciary Committee itself the senior Republican, Edward Hutchinson of Michigan, disavowed the staff's view of impeachment and adopted the President's. Until the final days of the crisis, the criminal definition of impeachment was to hang over the country's fate like the sword of Damocles.

The criminal standard buttressed the President's larger thesis: In defending himself he was fighting to protect the "Presidency" from sinister forces trying to "weaken" it. On March 12 the President's lawyer, James D. St. Clair, sounded this theme when he declared that he did not represent the President "individually" but rather the "office of the Presidency." There was even a National Citizens Committee for Fairness to the Presidency. It was America's global leadership, Nixon insisted, that made a "strong" Presidency so essential. Regardless of the opinion of some members of the Judiciary Committee, Nixon told a joint session of Congress, he would do nothing that "impairs the ability of the Presidents of the future to make the great decisions that are so essential to this nation and the world."

I used to listen to statements such as these with deep exasperation. Here was a President daring to tell Congress, in effect, that a lawless Presidency was necessary to America's safety, while a congressional attempt to reassert the rule of law undermined the nation's security.

Fortunately for constitutional government, however, Nixon's conception of a strong Presidency included one prerogative whose exercise was in itself an impeachable offense. Throughout the month of March the President insisted that the need for "confidentiality" allowed him to withhold forty-two tapes that the Judiciary Committee had asked of him. Nixon was claiming the right to limit the constitutional power of Congress to inquire into his impeachment. This was more than Republicans on the committee could afford to tolerate.

"Ambition must be made to counteract ambition," Madison had written in *The Federalist*. On April 11 the Judiciary Committee voted 33 to 3 to subpoena the forty-two tapes, the first subpoena ever issued to a President by a committee of the House. Ambition, at last, was counteracting ambition. This set the stage for one of the most lurid moments in the entire Watergate crisis.

As the deadline for compliance drew near, tension began mounting in the country. Comply or defy? Which would the President do? Open defiance was plainly impeachable. Frank compliance was presumably ruinous. On Monday, April 29, the President went on television to give the American people his answer. Seated in the Oval Office with the American flag behind him, President Nixon calmly announced that he was going to make over to the Judiciary Committee — and the public — "edited transcripts" of the subpoenaed tapes. These transcripts "will tell it all," said the President; there was nothing more that would need to be known for an impeachment inquiry about his conduct. To sharpen the public impression of presidential candor, the transcripts had been distributed among forty-two thick, loose-leaf binders, which were stacked in two-foot-high piles by the President's desk. As if to warn the public not to trust what the newspapers would say about the transcripts, Nixon accused the media of concocting the Watergate crisis out of "rumor, gossip, innuendo," of creating a "vague, general impression of massive wrongdoing, implicating everybody, gaining credibility by its endless repetition."

The next day's *New York Times* pronounced the President's speech "his most powerful Watergate defense since the scandal broke." By May 1 James Reston, the newspaper's most eminent columnist, thought the President had "probably gained considerable support in the country." For a few days it seemed as though the President had pulled off a coup. Republicans on the Judiciary Committee acted accordingly. On the first of May, 16 of the 17 committee Republicans voted against sending the President a note advising him that self-edited transcripts punctured by hundreds upon hundreds of suspicious "inaudibles" and "unintelligibles" were not in compliance with the committee's subpoena. The President, it was said, had succeeded in making impeachment look "partisan" and consequently discreditable.

Not even bowdlerized transcripts, however, could nullify the destructive power of those tapes. They revealed a White House steeped in more sordid conniving than Nixon's worst enemies had imagined. They showed a President advising his aides on how to "stonewall" a grand jury without committing perjury: "You can say, 'I don't remember.' You can say, 'I can't recall. I can't give any answer to that, that I can recall.'" They showed a President urging his counsel to make a "complete report" about Watergate but to "make it very incomplete." They showed a President eager for vengeance against ordinary election opponents. "I want the most comprehensive notes on all those who tried to do us in. . . . They are asking for it and they are going to get it." It showed a President discussing how "national security grounds" might be invoked to justify the Ellsberg burglary should the secret ever come out. "I think we could get by on that," replies Nixon's counsel.

On May 7 Pennsylvania's Hugh Scott, Senate Republican Minority Leader, pronounced the revelations in the transcript "disgusting, shabby, immoral performances." Joseph Alsop, who had long been friendly toward the President in his column, compared the atmosphere in the Oval Office to the "back room of a second-rate advertising agency in a suburb

of hell." A week after Nixon's seeming coup Republicans were once again vainly urging him to resign. On May 9 the House Judiciary Committee staff began presenting to the members its massive accumulation of Watergate material. Since the presentation was made behind closed doors, a suspenseful lull fell over the Watergate battleground.

Over the next two months it was obvious that the Judiciary Committee was growing increasingly impatient with the President, who continued to insist that, even in an impeachment proceeding, the "executive must remain the final arbiter of demands on its confidentiality." When Nixon refused to comply in any way with a second committee subpoena, the members voted 28 to 10 to warn him that "your refusals in and of themselves might constitute a ground for impeachment." The "partisanship" of May 1 had faded by May 30.

Undermining these signs of decisiveness was the continued insistence that only direct presidential involvement in a crime would be regarded as an impeachable offense in the House. Congressmen demanded to see the "smoking gun." They wanted to be shown the "hand in the cookie jar." Alexander Hamilton had called impeachment a "National Inquest." Congress seemed bent on restricting it to the purview of a local courthouse. Nobody spoke of the larger issues. As James Reston noted on May 26, one of the most disturbing aspects of Watergate was the silence of the prominent. Where, Reston asked, were the educators, the business leaders, and the elder statesmen to delineate and define the great constitutional issues at stake? When the White House began denouncing the Judiciary Committee as a "lynch mob," virtually nobody rose to the committee's defense.

On July 7 the Sunday edition of the *New York Times* made doleful reading. "The official investigations seem beset by semitropical torpor," the newspaper reported in its weekly news summary. White House attacks on the committee, said the *Times,* were proving effective in the country. In March, 60 percent of those polled by Gallup wanted the President tried in the Senate for his misdeeds. By June the figure had fallen to 50 percent. The movement for impeachment, said the *Times,* was losing its momentum. Nixon, it seemed, had worn out the public capacity for righteous indignation.

Then, on July 19, John Doar, the Democrats' counsel, did what nobody had done before with the enormous, confusing mass of interconnected misdeeds that we labeled "Watergate" for sheer convenience. At a meeting of the Judiciary Committee he compressed the endlessly ramified scandal into a grave and compelling case for impeaching the thirty-seventh President of the United States. He spoke of the President's "enormous crimes." He warned the committee that it dare not look indifferently upon the "terrible deed of subverting the Constitution." He urged the members to consider with favor five broad articles of impeachment, "charges with a grave historic ring," as the *Times* said of them.

In a brief statement, Albert Jenner, the Republicans' counsel, strongly endorsed Doar's recommendations. The Founding Fathers, he reminded committee members, had established a free country and a free Constitution. It was now the committee's momentous duty to determine "whether that country and that Constitution are to be preserved."

How I had yearned for those words during the long, arid months of the "smoking gun" and the "hand in the cookie jar." Members of the committee must have felt the same way, too, for Jenner's words were to leave a profound mark on their final deliberations. That I did not know yet, but what I did know was heartening. The grave maxims of liberty, once invoked, instantly took the measure of meanness and effrontery. When the President's press spokesman, Ron Ziegler, denounced the committee's proceedings as a "kangaroo court," a wave of disgust coursed through Congress. The hour of the Founders had arrived.

The final deliberations of the House Judiciary Committee began on the evening of July 24, when Chairman Peter Rodino gaveled the committee to order before some forty-five million television viewers. The committee made a curious spectacle: thirty eight strangers strung out on a two-tiered dais, a huge piece of furniture as unfamiliar as the faces of its occupants.

Chairman Rodino made the first opening remarks. His public career had been long, unblemished, and thoroughly undistinguished. Now the representative from Newark, New Jersey, linked hands with the Founding Fathers of our government. "For more than two years, there have been serious allegations, by people of good faith and sound intelligence, that the President, Richard M. Nixon, has committed grave and systematic violations of the Constitution." The framers of our Constitution, said Rodino, had provided an exact measure of a President's responsibilities. It was by the terms of the President's oath of office, prescribed in the Constitution, that the framers intended to hold Presidents "accountable and lawful."

That was to prove the keynote. That evening and over the following days, as each committee member delivered a statement, it became increasingly clear that the broad maxims of constitutional supremacy had taken command of the impeachment inquiry. "We will by this impeachment proceeding be establishing a standard of conduct for the President of the United States which will for all time be a matter of public record," Caldwell Butler, a conservative Virginia Republican, reminded his conservative constituents. "If we fail to impeach . . . we will have left condoned and unpunished an abuse of power totally without justification."

There were still White House loyalists of course: men who kept demanding to see a presidential directive ordering a crime and a documented "tie-in" between Nixon and his henchmen. Set against the great principle of constitutional supremacy, however, this common view was now exposed for what it was: reckless trifling with our ancient liberties. Can the United States permit a President "to escape account-ability because he may choose to deal behind closed doors," asked James Mann, a South Carolina conservative. "Can anyone argue," asked George Danielson, a California liberal, "that if a President breaches his oath of office, he should not be removed?" In a voice of unforgettable power and richness, Barbara Jordan, a black legislator from Texas, sounded the grand theme of the committee with particular depth of feeling. Once, she said, the Constitution had excluded people of her race, but that evil had been remedied. "My faith in the Constitution is whole, it is complete, it is total and I am not going to sit here and be an idle spectator to the diminution, the subversion, the destruction of the Constitution."

On July 27 the Judiciary Committee voted 27 to 11 (six Republicans joining all twenty-one Democrats) to impeach Richard Nixon on the grounds that he and his agents had "prevented, obstructed, and impeded the administration of justice" in "violation of his constitutional oath faithfully to execute the office of President of the United States and, to the best of his ability, preserve, protect, and defend the Constitution of the United States, and in violation of his constitutional duty to take care that the laws be faithfully executed."

On July 29 the Judiciary Committee voted 28 to 10 to impeach Richard Nixon for "violating the constitutional rights of citizens, impairing the due and proper administration of justice and the conduct of lawful inquiries, or contravening the laws governing agencies of the executive branch. . . ." Thus, the illegal wiretaps, the sinister White House spies, the attempted use of the IRS to punish political opponents, the abuse of the CIA, and the break-in at Ellsberg's psychiatrist's office — misconduct hitherto deemed too "vague" for impeachment — now became part of a President's impeachable failure to abide by his constitutional oath to carry out his constitutional duty.

Lastly, on July 30 the Judiciary Committee, hoping to protect some future impeachment inquiry from a repetition of Nixon's defiance, voted 21 to 17 to impeach him for refusing to comply with the committee's subpoenas. "This concludes the work of the committee," Rodino announced at eleven o'clock that night. Armed with the wisdom of the Founders and the authority of America's republican principles, the committee had cut through the smoke screens, the lies, and the pettifogging that had muddled the Watergate crisis for so many months. It had subjected an imperious Presidency to the rule of fundamental law. It had demonstrated by resounding majorities that holding a President accountable is neither "liberal" nor "conservative," neither "Democratic" nor "Republican," but something far more basic to the American republic.

For months the forces of evasion had claimed that impeachment would "tear the country apart." But now the country was more united than it had been in years. The impeachment inquiry had sounded the chords of deepest patriotism, and Americans responded, it seemed to me, with quiet pride in their country and themselves. On Capitol Hill, congressional leaders reported that Nixon's impeachment would command three hundred votes at a minimum. The Senate began preparing for the President's trial. Then, as countless wits remarked, a funny thing happened on the way to the forum.

Back on July 24, the day the Judiciary Committee began its televised deliberations, the Supreme Court had ordered the President to surrender sixty-four taped conversations subpoenaed by the Watergate prosecutor. At the time I had regarded the decision chiefly as an auspicious omen for the evening's proceedings. Only Richard Nixon knew that the Court had signed his death warrant. On August 5 the President announced that he was making public three tapes that "may further damage my case." In fact they destroyed what little was left of it. Recorded six days after the Watergate break-in, they showed the President discussing detailed preparations for the cover-up with his chief of staff, Bob Haldeman. They showed the President and his henchmen discussing how to use the CIA to block the FBI, which was coming dangerously close to the White House. "You call them in," says the President. "Good deal," says his aide. In short, the three tapes proved that the President had told nothing but lies about Watergate for twenty-six months. Every one of Nixon's ten Judiciary Committee defenders now announced that he favored Nixon's impeachment.

The President still had one last evasion: on the evening of August 8 he appeared on television to make his last important announcement. "I no longer have a strong enough political base in Congress," said Nixon, doing his best to imply that the resolution of a great constitutional crisis was mere maneuvering for political advantage. "Therefore, I shall resign the Presidency effective at noon tomorrow." He admitted to no wrongdoing. If he had made mistakes of judgment, "they were made in what I believed at the time to be in the best interests of the nation."

On the morning of August 9 the first President ever to resign from office boarded Air Force One and left town. The "system" had worked. But in the watches of the night, who has not asked himself now and then: How would it all have turned out had there been no White House tapes?

Nixon's only crime was not, as many Americans still contend, that he simply got caught doing what other presidents had done. Historian C. Vann Woodward observes in Responses of the Presidents to Charges of Misconduct *(1974): "Heretofore, no president has been proved to be the chief coordinator of the crime and misdemeanor charged against his own administration. . . . Heretofore, no president has been held to be the chief personal beneficiary of misconduct in his administration or of measures taken to destroy or cover up evidence of it. Heretofore, the malfeasance and misdemeanor have had no confessed ideological purpose, no constitutionally subversive ends. Heretofore, no president has been accused of extensively subverting and secretly using established government agencies to defame or discredit political opponents and critics, to obstruct justice, to conceal misconduct and protect criminals, or to deprive citizens of their* rights *and liberties. Heretofore, no president has been accused of creating secret investigative units to engage in covert and unlawful activities against private citizens and their rights."*

In "a post–Watergate backlash," as one historian termed it, American voters in 1974 gave the Democrats the second biggest congressional victory in their entire history. Two years later, they sent Democrat Jimmy Carter to the White House, ousting Republican Gerald Ford, whom Nixon had chosen as his successor.

QUESTIONS TO CONSIDER

1. According to Karp, what "high Crimes and Misdemeanors" led to impeachment proceedings against Richard Nixon?

2. Analyze the argument that erupted during Watergate over what properly constituted an impeachable offense. In Karp's view, what are the implications of insisting that a president can be impeached and removed from office only for direct criminal actions? Would this definition have the practical effect of removing impeachment as a constitutional check on the executive branch?

3. Compare Lyndon Johnson's and Richard Nixon's handling of the crises of their presidencies — Johnson with Vietnam (selection 24), Nixon with Watergate. How did each man's obsession with appearing strong contribute to his political downfall?

4. What evidence is there that Congress dragged its feet during the Watergate investigations, particularly in the matter of the president's impeachment? What does Karp think were the reasons for congressional hesitation?

5. Karp wonders whether the United States constitutional system would have worked had it not been for the revelation of White House tapes that Nixon secretly recorded. Do you think that America's experience with Watergate will make it easier or even more difficult to remove a president from office in the future?

30

How the Seventies Changed America

NICHOLAS LEMANN

To many Americans, it was the "loser" decade, a ten-year hangover from the excesses of the sixties, a time of bitter disillusionment, what with Watergate and the withdrawal from Vietnam, the only war America ever lost. It was a plastic era, to use Norman Mailer's term, that featured polyester suits and disco music. Many Americans still regard the 1970s as a vague interim between the liberal idealism and social upheaval of the sixties and the conservative individualism of the eighties. But to journalist Nicholas Lemann, looking back from today's vantage point, the seventies can no longer be dismissed as "the runt decade" in which relatively nothing significant occurred. On the contrary, he finds profound importance in terms of several "sweeping historical trends" that began or were accelerated in the seventies and that went on to shape what American society has become in our time.

First, he says, it was the decade in which geopolitics started revolving less around ideology than around oil and religion. He cites the 1973–1974 oil embargo of the oil-producing Arab-Muslim states as the "epochal event" of the decade, one that dashed the 1960s assumption of endless economic growth and prosperity for all in the United States. The oil embargo spurred the growth of the sun belt, initiated a period of staggering inflation, and marked the end, maybe forever, of "the mass upward economic mobility of American society." And that in turn fragmented the country into squabbling interest groups that cared more about looking out for themselves than about sacrificing for the national good.

Second, the presidential electorate became conservative and Republican, a trend that would last throughout the eighties, ending, for the time being, in the election of Democrat

438

Bill Clinton in 1992. In reaction to the seeming paralysis and weakness of Jimmy Carter's liberal Democratic administration, 1977–1981, American voters sent Republican Ronald Reagan to the White House, because he preached "pure strength" in foreign affairs and promised to reduce taxes at home (the Reagan presidency is treated in selection 31). Thus, Reagan capitalized on a third sweeping trend of the seventies — the middle-class tax revolt, which Lemann describes as "an aftershock" of the Arab oil embargo. For the first time, he says, the American middle class, once considered uniquely fortunate, perceived itself as an oppressed group, the victim of runaway inflation, and revolted against the use of federal funds to help the less privileged.

A reporter for the Washington Post *during the seventies, Lemann draws an arresting portrait of this oft-disparaged decade that invites comparison with Allen Matusow's discussion of the sixties (selection 28). Indeed, Lemann agrees with Matusow that the seventies witnessed "the working of the phenomena of the sixties into the mainstream of American life." Lemann contends that the sixties' obsession with self-discovery became "a mass phenomenon" in the seventies and that the ethic of individual freedom as the "highest good," converging with the end of the American economy as an "expanding pie," led Americans to look out mainly for themselves.*

GLOSSARY

DÉTENTE   Relaxing of international tensions.

EST (ERHARD SEMINARS TRAINING)
System of encounter groups designed to help people "get in touch with themselves."

ORGANIZATION OF PETROLEUM EXPORTING STATES (OPEC)   Bargaining unit for the oil-exporting states in the Middle East and Africa; OPEC's oil embargo of 1973 quadrupled the price of oil and caused soaring inflation.

PROPOSITION 13   Initiative on the California state ballot that called for a significant reduction in property taxes; it passed overwhelmingly and led to similar tax revolts across the country.

T hat's it," Daniel Patrick Moynihan, then U.S. ambassador to India, wrote to a colleague on the White House staff in 1973 on the subject of some issue of the moment. "Nothing will happen. But then nothing much is going to happen in the 1970s anyway."

Moynihan is a politician famous for his predictions, and this one seemed for a long time to be dead-on. The seventies, even while they were in progress, looked like an unimportant decade, a period of cooling down from the white-hot sixties. You had to go back to the teens to find another decade so lacking in crisp, epigrammatic definition. It only made matters worse for the seventies that the succeeding decade started with a bang. In 1980 the country elected the

---

From Nicholas Lemann, "How the Seventies Changed America," *American Heritage*, 42 (July/August 1991), 39–42, 44, 46, 48–49. Copyright © Forbes Inc., 1991. Reprinted by permission of *American Heritage* Magazine, a division of Forbes Inc.

most conservative President in its history, and it was immediately clear that a new era had dawned. (In general the eighties, unlike the seventies, had a perfect dramatic arc. They peaked in the summer of 1984, with the Los Angeles Olympics and the Republican National Convention in Dallas, and began to peter out with the Iran-contra scandal in 1986 and the stock market crash in 1987.) It is nearly impossible to engage in magazine-writerly games like discovering "the day the seventies died" or "the spirit of the seventies"; and the style of the seventies — wide ties, sideburns, synthetic fabrics, white shoes, disco — is so far interesting largely as something to make fun of.

But somehow the seventies seem to be creeping out of the loser-decade category. Their claim to importance is in the realm of sweeping historical trends, rather than memorable events, though there were some of those too. In the United States today a few basic propositions shape everything: The presidential electorate is conservative and Republican. Geopolitics revolves around a commodity (oil) and a religion (Islam) more than around an ideology (Marxism-Leninism). The national economy is no longer one in which practically every class, region, and industry is upwardly mobile. American culture is essentially individualistic, rather than communitarian, which means that notions like deferred gratification, sacrifice, and sustained national effort are a very tough sell. Anyone seeking to understand the roots of this situation has to go back to the seventies.

The underestimation of the seventies' importance, especially during the early years of the decade, is easy to forgive because the character of the seventies was substantially shaped at first by spillover from the sixties. Such sixties events as the killings of student protesters at Kent State and Orangeburg, the original Earth Day, the invasion of Cambodia, and a large portion of the war in Vietnam took place in the seventies. Although sixties radicals (cultural and political) spent the early seventies loudly bemoaning the end of the revolution, what was in fact going on was the

working of the phenomena of the sixties into the mainstream of American life. Thus the first Nixon administration, which was decried by liberals at the time for being nightmarishly right-wing, was actually more liberal than the Johnson administration in many ways — less hawkish in Vietnam, more free-spending on social programs. The reason wasn't that Richard Nixon was a liberal but that the country as a whole had continued to move steadily to the left throughout the late sixties and early seventies; the political climate of institutions like the U.S. Congress and the boards of directors of big corporations was probably more liberal in 1972 than in any year before or since, and the Democratic party nominated its most liberal presidential candidate ever. Nixon had to go along with the tide.

In New Orleans, my hometown, the hippie movement peaked in 1972 or 1973. Long hair, crash pads, head shops, psychedelic posters, underground newspapers, and other Summer of Love–inspired institutions had been unknown there during the real Summer of Love, which was in 1967. It took even longer, until the middle or late seventies, for those aspects of hippie life that have endured to catch on with the general public. All over the country the likelihood that an average citizen would wear longish hair, smoke marijuana, and openly live with a lover before marriage was probably greater in 1980 than it was in 1970. The sixties' preoccupation with self-discovery became a mass phenomenon only in the seventies, through home-brew psychological therapies like EST. In politics the impact of the black enfranchisement that took place in the 1960s barely began to be felt until the mid- to late 1970s. The tremendously influential feminist and gay-liberation movements were, at the dawn of the 1970s, barely under way in Manhattan, their headquarters, and certainly hadn't begun their spread across the whole country. The sixties took a long time for America to digest; the process went on throughout the seventies and even into the eighties.

*"Steer clear of that one. Every day
is always the first day of the rest of his life."*

*Charles Saxon's spirited sketch is good social history. In 1972 this
is what a lot of Americans looked like. (Drawing by Saxon © 1972*

The New Yorker Magazine, Inc.)

The epochal event of the seventies as an era in its own right was the Organization of Petroleum Exporting Countries' oil embargo, which lasted for six months in the fall of 1973 and the spring of 1974. Everything that happened in the sixties was predicated on the assumption of economic prosperity and growth; concerns like personal fulfillment and social justice tend to emerge in the middle class only at times when people take it for granted that they'll be able to make a living. For thirty years — ever since the effects of World War II on the economy had begun to kick in — the average American's standard of living had been rising, to a remarkable extent. As the economy grew, indices like home ownership, automobile ownership, and access to higher education got up to levels unknown anywhere else in the world, and the United States could plausibly claim to have provided a better life materially for its working class than any society ever had. That ended with the OPEC embargo.

While it was going on, the embargo didn't fully register in the national consciousness. The country was absorbed by a different story, the Watergate scandal, which was really another sixties spillover, the final series of battles in the long war between the antiwar liberals and the rough-playing anti-Communists. Richard Nixon, having engaged in dirty tricks against leftish politicians for his whole career, didn't stop doing so as President; he only found new targets, like Daniel Ellsberg and [Democratic Party chairman]

Lawrence O'Brien. This time, however, he lost the Establishment, which was now far more kindly disposed to Nixon's enemies than it had been back in the 1950s. Therefore, the big-time press, the courts, and the Congress undertook the enthralling process of cranking up the deliberate, inexorable machinery of justice, and everybody was glued to the television for a year and a half. The embargo, on the other hand, was a non-video-friendly economic story and hence difficult to get hooked on. It pertained to two subcultures that were completely mysterious to most Americans — the oil industry and the Arab world — and it seemed at first to be merely an episode in the ongoing hostilities between Israel and its neighbors. But in retrospect it changed everything, much more than Watergate did.

By causing the price of oil to double, the embargo enriched — and therefore increased the wealth, power, and confidence of — oil-producing areas like Texas, while helping speed the decline of the automobile-producing upper Midwest; the rise of OPEC and the rise of the Sunbelt as a center of population and political influence went together. The embargo ushered in a long period of inflation, the reaction to which dominated the economics and politics of the rest of the decade. It demonstrated that America could now be "pushed around" by countries most of us had always thought of as minor powers.

Most important of all, the embargo now appears to have been the pivotal moment at which the mass upward economic mobility of American society ended, perhaps forever. Average weekly earnings, adjusted for inflation, peaked in 1973. Productivity — that is, economic output per man-hour — abruptly stopped growing. The nearly universal assumption in the post–World War II United States was that children would do better than their parents. Upward mobility wasn't just a characteristic of the national culture; it was the defining characteristic. As it slowly began to sink in that everybody wasn't going to be moving for-

ward together anymore, the country became more fragmented, more internally rivalrous, and less sure of its mythology.

Richard Nixon resigned as President in August 1974, and the country settled into what appeared to be a quiet, folksy drama of national recuperation. In the White House good old Gerald Ford was succeeded by rural, sincere Jimmy Carter, who was the only President elevated to the office by the voters during the 1970s and so was the decade's emblematic political figure. In hindsight, though, it's impossible to miss a gathering conservative stridency in the politics of the late seventies. In 1976 Ronald Reagan, the retired governor of California, challenged Ford for the Republican presidential nomination. Reagan lost the opening primaries and seemed to be about to drop out of the race when, apparently to the surprise even of his own staff, he won the North Carolina primary in late March.

It is quite clear what caused the Reagan campaign to catch on: He had begun to attack Ford from the right on foreign policy matters. The night before the primary he bought a half-hour of statewide television time to press his case. Reagan's main substantive criticism was of the policy of détente with the Soviet Union, but his two most crowd-pleasing points were his promise, if elected, to fire Henry Kissinger as Secretary of State and his lusty denunciation of the elaborately negotiated treaty to turn nominal control of the Panama Canal over to the Panamanians. Less than a year earlier Communist forces had finally captured the South Vietnamese capital city of Saigon, as the staff of the American Embassy escaped in a wild scramble into helicopters. The oil embargo had ended, but the price of gasoline had not retreated. The United States appeared to have descended from the pinnacle of power and respect it had occupied at the close of World War II to a small, hounded position, and Reagan had hit on a symbolic way of expressing rage over that change. Most journalistic and academic opinion at the time was fairly cheerful about the course of American foreign policy — we were finally out of Vietnam, and we were getting over our silly Cold War phobia about dealing with China and the Soviet Union — but in the general public obviously the rage Reagan expressed was widely shared.

A couple of years later a conservative political cause even more out of the blue than opposition to the Panama Canal Treaty appeared: the tax revolt. Howard Jarvis, a seventy-five-year-old retired businessman who had been attacking taxation in California pretty much continuously since 1962, got onto the state ballot in 1978 an initiative, Proposition 13, that would substantially cut property taxes. Despite bad press and the strong opposition of most politicians, it passed by a two to one margin.

Proposition 13 was to some extent another aftershock of the OPEC embargo. Inflation causes the value of hard assets to rise. The only substantial hard asset owned by most Americans is their home. As the prices of houses soared in the mid-seventies (causing people to dig deeper to buy housing, which sent the national savings rate plummeting and made real estate prices the great conversation starter in the social life of the middle class), so did property taxes, since they are based on the values of the houses. Hence, resentment over taxation became an issue in waiting.

The influence of Proposition 13 has been so great that it is now difficult to recall that taxes weren't a major concern in national politics before it. Conservative opposition to government focused on its activities, not on its revenue base, and this put conservatism at a disadvantage, because most government programs are popular. Even before Proposition 13, conservative economic writers like Jude Wanniski and Arthur Laffer were inventing supply-side economics, based on the idea that reducing taxes would bring prosperity. With Proposition 13 it was proved — as it has been proved over and over since — that

tax cutting was one of the rare voguish policy ideas that turn out to be huge political winners. In switching from arguing against programs to arguing against taxes, conservatism had found another key element of its ascension to power.

The tax revolt wouldn't have worked if the middle class hadn't been receptive to the notion that it was oppressed. This was remarkable in itself, since it had been assumed for decades that the American middle class was, in a world-historical sense, almost uniquely lucky. The emergence of a self-pitying strain in the middle class was in a sense yet another sixties spillover. At the dawn of the sixties, the idea that *anybody* in the United States was oppressed might have seemed absurd. Then blacks, who really were oppressed, were able to make the country see the truth about their situation. But that opened Pandora's box. The eloquent language of group rights that the civil rights movement had invented proved to be quite adaptable, and eventually it was used by college students, feminists, Native Americans, Chicanos, urban blue-collar "white ethnics," and, finally, suburban homeowners.

Meanwhile, the social programs started by Lyndon Johnson gave rise to another new, or long-quiescent, idea, which was that the government was wasting vast sums of money on harebrained schemes. In some ways the Great Society accomplished its goal of binding the country together, by making the federal government a nationwide provider of such favors as medical care and access to higher education; but in others it contributed to the seventies trend of each group's looking to government to provide it with benefits and being unconcerned with the general good. Especially after the economy turned sour, the middle class began to define its interests in terms of a rollback of government programs aimed at helping other groups.

As the country was becoming more fragmented, so was its essential social unit, the family. In 1965 only 14.9 percent of the population was single; by 1979 the figure had risen to 20 percent. The divorce rate went

With fleeting success, Jimmy Carter brings moral pressure to bear on a troubled world in a 1977 cartoon by Edward Sorel. (Courtesy of Edward Sorel)

from 2.5 per thousand in 1965 to 5.3 per thousand in 1979. The percentage of births that were out of wedlock was 5.3 in 1960 and 16.3 in 1978. The likelihood that married women with young children would work doubled between the mid-sixties and the late seventies. These changes took place for a variety of reasons — feminism, improved birth control, the legalization of abortion, the spread across the country of the sixties youth culture's rejection of traditional mores — but what they added up to was that the nu-

clear family, consisting of a working husband and a nonworking wife, both in their first marriage, and their children, ceased to be the dominant type of American household during the seventies. Also, people became more likely to organize themselves into communities based on their family status, so that the unmarried often lived in singles apartment complexes and retirees in senior citizens' developments. The overall effect was one of much greater personal freedom, which meant, as it always does, less social cohesion. Tom Wolfe's moniker for the seventies, the Me Decade, caught on because it was probably true that the country had placed relatively more emphasis on individual happiness and relatively less on loyalty to family and nation.

Like a symphony, the seventies finally built up in a crescendo that pulled together all its main themes. This occurred during the second half of 1979. First OPEC engineered the "second oil shock," in which, by holding down production, it got the price for its crude oil (and the price of gasoline at American service stations) to rise by more than 50 percent during the first six months of that year. With the onset of the summer vacation season, the automotive equivalent of the Depression's bank runs began. Everybody considered the possibility of not being able to get gas, panicked, and went off to fill the tank; the result was hours-long lines at gas stations all over the country.

It was a small inconvenience compared with what people in the Communist world and Latin America live through all the time, but the psychological effect was enormous. The summer of 1979 was the only time I can remember when, at the level of ordinary life as opposed to public affairs, things seemed to be out of control. Inflation was well above 10 percent and rising, and suddenly what seemed like a quarter of every day was spent on getting gasoline or thinking about getting gasoline — a task that previously had been completely routine, as it is again now. Black markets sprang up; rumors flew about well-connected people who had secret sources. One day that summer, after an hour's desperate and fruitless search, I ran out of gas on the Central Expressway in Dallas. I left my car sitting primly in the right lane and walked away in the hundred-degree heat; the people driving by looked at me without surprise, no doubt thinking, "Poor bastard, it could have happened to me just as easily."

In July President Carter scheduled a speech on the gas lines, then abruptly canceled it and repaired to Camp David to think deeply for ten days, which seemed like a pale substitute for somehow setting things aright. Aides, cabinet secretaries, intellectuals, religious leaders, tycoons, and other leading citizens were summoned to Carter's aerie to discuss with him what was wrong with the country's soul. On July 15 he made a television address to the nation, which has been enshrined in memory as the "malaise speech," although it didn't use that word. (Carter did, however, talk about "a crisis of confidence . . . that strikes at the very heart and soul and spirit of our national will.")

To reread the speech today is to be struck by its spectacular political ineptitude. Didn't Carter realize that Presidents are not supposed to express doubts publicly or to lecture the American people about their shortcomings? Why couldn't he have just temporarily imposed gas rationing, which would have ended the lines overnight, instead of outlining a vague and immediately forgotten six-point program to promote energy conservation?

His describing the country's loss of confidence did not cause the country to gain confidence, needless to say. And it didn't help matters that upon his return to Washington he demanded letters of resignation from all members of his cabinet and accepted five of them. Carter seemed to be anything but an FDR-like reassuring, ebullient presence; he communicated a sense of wild flailing about as he tried (unsuccessfully) to get the situation under control.

I remember being enormously impressed by Carter's speech at the time because it was a painfully honest and much thought-over attempt to grapple with the main problem of the decade. The American economy had ceased being an expanding pie, and by unfortunate coincidence this had happened just when an ethic of individual freedom as the highest good was spreading throughout the society, which meant people would respond to the changing economic conditions by looking out for themselves. Like most other members of the word-manipulating class whose leading figures had advised Carter at Camp David, I thought there *was* a malaise. What I didn't realize, and Carter obviously didn't either, was that there was a smarter way to play the situation politically. A President could maintain there was nothing wrong with America at all — that it hadn't become less powerful in the world, hadn't reached some kind of hard economic limit, and wasn't in crisis — and, instead of trying to reverse the powerful tide of individualism, ride along with it. At the same time, he could act more forcefully than Carter, especially against inflation, so that he didn't seem weak and ineffectual. All this is exactly what Carter's successor, Ronald Reagan, did.

Actually, Carter himself set in motion the process by which inflation was conquered a few months later, when he gave the chairmanship of the Federal Reserve Board to Paul Volcker, a man willing to put the economy into a severe recession to bring back price stability. But in November fate delivered the *coup de grâce* to Carter in the form of the taking hostage of the staff of the American Embassy in Teheran, as a protest against the United States' harboring of Iran's former shah.

As with the malaise speech, what is most difficult to convey today about the hostage crisis is why Carter made what now looks like a huge, obvious error: playing up the crisis so much that it became a national obsession for more than a year. The fundamental problem with hostage taking is that the one sure remedy — refusing to negotiate and thus allowing the hostages to be killed — is politically unacceptable in the democratic media society we live in, at least when the hostages are middle-class sympathetic figures, as they were in Iran.

There isn't any good solution to this problem, but Carter's two successors in the White House demonstrated that it is possible at least to negotiate for the release of hostages in a low-profile way that will cause the press to lose interest and prevent the course of the hostage negotiations from completely defining the

Presidency. During the last year of the Carter administration, by contrast, the hostage story absolutely dominated the television news (recall that the ABC show *Nightline* began as a half-hour five-times-a-week update on the hostage situation), and several of the hostages and their families became temporary celebrities. In Carter's defense, even among the many voices criticizing him for appearing weak and vacillating, there was none that I remember willing to say, "Just cut off negotiations and walk away." It was a situation that everyone regarded as terrible but in which there was a strong national consensus supporting the course Carter had chosen.

So ended the seventies. There was still enough of the sixties spillover phenomenon going on so that Carter, who is now regarded (with some affection) as having been too much the good-hearted liberal to maintain a hold on the presidential electorate, could be challenged for renomination by Ted Kennedy on the grounds that he was too conservative. Inflation was raging on; the consumer price index rose by 14.4 percent between May 1979 and May 1980. We were being humiliated by fanatically bitter, premodern Muslims whom we had expected to regard us with gratitude because we had helped ease out their dictator even though he was reliably pro–United States. The Soviet empire appeared (probably for the last time ever) to be on the march, having invaded Afghanistan to Carter's evident surprise and disillusionment. We had lost our most recent war. We couldn't pull together as a people. The puissant, unified, prospering America of the late 1940s seemed to be just a fading memory.

I was a reporter for the *Washington Post* during the 1980 presidential campaign, and even on the *Post's* national desk, that legendary nerve center of politics, the idea that the campaign might end with Reagan's being elected President seemed fantastic, right up to the weekend before the election. At first Kennedy looked like a real threat to Carter; remember that

Brian Basset saw Carter lying helpless while the 1980 election bore down; the polls never did let him loose. (Reprinted courtesy of Dennis Ryan)

up to that point no Kennedy had ever lost a campaign. While the Carter people were disposing of Kennedy, they were rooting for Reagan to win the Republican nomination because he would be such an easy mark.

He was too old, too unserious, and, most of all, too conservative. Look what had happened to Barry Goldwater (a sitting officeholder, at least) only sixteen years earlier, and Reagan was so divisive that a moderate from his own party, John Anderson, was running for President as a third-party candidate. It was not at all clear how much the related issues of inflation and national helplessness were dominating the public's mind. Kennedy, Carter, and Anderson were all, in their own way, selling national healing, that great post-sixties obsession; Reagan, and only Reagan, was selling pure strength.

In a sense Reagan's election represents the country's rejection of the idea of a sixties-style solution to the great problems of the seventies — economic stagnation, social fragmentation, and the need for a new world order revolving around relations between the oil-producing Arab world and the West.

The idea of a scaled-back America — husbanding its resources, living more modestly, renouncing its restless mobility, withdrawing from full engagement with the politics of every spot on the globe, focusing on issues of internal comity — evidently didn't appeal. Reagan, and the country, had in effect found a satisfying pose to strike in response to the problems of the seventies, but that's different from finding a solution.

Today some of the issues that dominated the seventies have faded away. Reagan and Volcker did beat inflation. The "crisis of confidence" now seems a long-ago memory. But it is striking how early we still seem to be in the process of working out the implications of the oil embargo. We have just fought and won [the Gulf War] against the twin evils of Middle East despotism and interruptions in the oil supply, which began to trouble us in the seventies. We still have not really even begun to figure out how to deal with the cessation of across-the-board income gains, and as a result our domestic politics are still dominated by squabbling over the proper distribution of government's benefits and burdens. During the seventies themselves the new issues that were arising seemed nowhere near as important as those sixties legacies, minority rights and Vietnam and Watergate. But the runt of decades has wound up casting a much longer shadow than anyone imagined.

QUESTIONS TO CONSIDER

1. What does Nicholas Lemann see as the long-term influence of the 1960s on American politics and culture? In what way were "the phenomena of the sixties" worked into the cultural mainstream? How does this view compare with Matusow's in selection 28?

2. Lemann sees the OPEC oil embargo of 1973–1974 as "the epochal event" of the 1970s. What were its economic and practical effects? What were the psychological effects on Americans' confidence in their country and their culture? How did the cultural trends of the 1970s make this reaction even more critical at the end of the decade?

3. According to Lemann, the 1970s were characterized by a "gathering conservative stridency." Discuss the events and developments in which this shows up. In what ways was it fed by trends from the 1960s, and in what ways was it a reaction against the sixties?

4. What is Lemann's judgment of Jimmy Carter and Ronald Reagan as men and as politicians? Does he find Reagan's presidency more successful than Carter's?

5. What does Lemann see as the long-term importance of the 1970s and their influence today? Do you see any signs of change, or do you think we are still working out the legacy of the 1970s?

XV

TOWARD THE TWENTY-FIRST CENTURY

31

Summing Up the Reagan Era

KARL ZINSMEISTER

As we saw in the previous selection, the late 1970s witnessed a regeneration of American conservatism, an inevitable reaction to the soaring rate of inflation, ever-expanding big government, the libertine impulses set loose in the 1960s, and two decades of ferment and self-doubt. The new conservatism appeared in many guises: middle-class disillusionment with political liberalism and social permissiveness, a zealous anti-abortion movement, refurbished fundamentalism and evangelical influences in politics, revived national pride, and renewed hostility toward communism and the Soviet Union. The New Right even took root on college campuses, often sanctuaries of liberal sentiment, as conservative student organizations and student newspapers emerged to challenge the alleged left-wing biases of professors and established student groups.

But it was in presidential politics that the resurgent right seemed to find its most dramatic expression. In the 1980 election, Ronald Reagan, former governor of California, a one-time movie actor and New Deal Democrat turned Republican, rode the conservative trend into the White House, defeating Democratic incumbent Jimmy Carter, not to mention independent John Anderson, by capturing 50.7 percent of the popular votes. Reagan not only capitalized on Carter's lackluster record — his inability to check double-digit inflation, his impotence in the Iranian hostage crisis — but captured the country with his personal charm and resounding promise to change the direction of America. Analysts were quick to label Reagan's the most decisive victory since that of Franklin Roosevelt in 1932. Yet, as historian Richard C. Wade has pointed out, the 1980 election "drew the smallest voter turnout in modern history," as slightly more than half of the registered voters bothered to go to the polls. Why the decline in registration and voting? Wade believes the decline occurred because television has converted politics into "a spectator sport," with most people content to watch the candidates on the screen and not bother to vote.

Even so, Reagan appeared to be the dream president of the American right, an unabashed patriot and stern Christian who advocated a return to the old morality. Reagan not only opposed abortion and favored prayer in public schools but also vowed to end big government, slash federal spending, balance the budget, restore individual enterprise, beef up the military, get tough with the Russians, and revive America's sagging influence in the world. In short, the Great Communicator, with an easy smile and a cheerful contempt for his critics, stood prepared to inaugurate a new era of conservative rule.

According to his liberal critics, that was precisely what he did. As his first term progressed, liberals denounced him as a prisoner of atavistic politics and obsolete economics; they damned his stance on school prayer and abortion and condemned him for his insensitivity to environmental issues, women's rights, African Americans, and the poor; they blamed him for a staggering federal debt, accused him of accelerating the arms race, called him obtuse if not senile (he was in his early seventies), and summoned American voters to throw the doddering relic out of office in 1984. Instead, the ever-shrinking American electorate sent him back to the White House by a considerable margin in popular votes — and not without reason. Thanks to Reagan, the rate of inflation slowed dramatically, interest rates plummeted, and the country as a whole was prosperous and proud. His second term brought an even more impressive accomplishment: the president who had once called Russia "the evil empire" contributed to a significant thaw in United States–Soviet relations and negotiated with Russian leader Mikhail Gorbachev the pioneering Intermediate Nuclear Forces Treaty to jettison intermediate-range missiles.

Yet there were conspicuous failures too. Under Reagan, the federal debt soared higher still (to $2.3 trillion) and the drug problem, particularly in the crime-racked inner cities, became worse than ever. Moreover, Reagan sounded like the most militant of cold warriors in his stance on Nicaragua, where he supported the "Contra" guerrillas in their intermittent war against the Marxist Sandinistas who ruled the country. It was in connection with the Contras that the administration committed its worst fiasco. Congressional investigations, carried around the world on television, revealed that the administration was involved in a secret deal in which the Central Intelligence Agency sold arms to Iran through go-betweens; profits from the arms sale were to be funneled to the Contra rebels. In the wake of the Iran-Contra revelations, Reagan's approval rating in the polls took a plunge. Yet Reagan survived the scandal. Indeed, when he stepped down in January 1989, his presidential approval ratings were among the highest end-of-term levels in polling history. Still grinning, the Great Communicator left Washington more popular than he had been when he arrived.

In this selection, Karl Zinsmeister, a distinguished statistical analyst at the American Enterprise Institute for Public Policy Research, tells us what the statistics suggest about the

"Reagan Revolution" and the Reagan record. Not to fear: Zinsmeister's essay is not a boring, overly technical analysis. It offers a sprightly, lucid portrait of the Reagan era through a creative use of numbers. According to the numbers, the Reagan "revolution" was "a clear underachiever," because government spending continued unabated, taxes rose, and big government grew bigger than ever. Yet the Reagan decade was also a time of healthy economic growth and a rising standard of living. And it was a time when religion enjoyed a popular comeback and buildings, books, and television shows displayed a "pronounced turn toward traditionalism." According to Zinsmeister, the true significance of Reagan himself lay not so much in his actions as in the "altered picture" he presented to the country during the eighties, an idealized picture of a proud, patriotic, and moral citizenry no longer torn by internal dissent and by doubt and despair in foreign affairs. Other experts would challenge Zinsmeister's argument that Reagan's was "the most important presidency since World War II" and that in popular culture "hairy-chested masculinity" came roaring back as "an American ideal." But Zinsmeister's statistical portrait affords a stimulating view of a complex and controversial decade.

GLOSSARY

BLOOM, ALLAN His best-selling book, *The Closing of the American Mind,* savaged modern education.

"THE COSBY SHOW" This family situation comedy was the most popular TV show during the Reagan era.

DEFICIT The discrepancy between tax revenue and spending.

GROSS NATIONAL PRODUCT (GNP) A country's total output of goods and services in a given year.

MOYNIHAN, DANIEL PATRICK Democratic senator from New York who engineered welfare reform during the Reagan years.

SCHULTZ, GEORGE Reagan's second secretary of state.

For all the academic ink devoted to the subject of revolution, history is rarely discontinuous, rarely an affair of dramatic leaps or breaks. While rhetoric and the emotional environment can shift quickly, the actual workings of a society usually change at about the same rate as the proverbial freight train. Just the same, there are occasional turning points in any nation's life, when the engine crests a hill or enters a deep curve. The train remains a train — momentum intact — but thanks to a thousand small changes in pressure and direction among its moving parts a different hum rises from the tracks.

Since we now find ourselves at the end of a decade, the question naturally presents itself: Were the 1980s such a time for America?

Viewed presidentially, the '80s were one part Jimmy Carter, eight parts Ronald Reagan and one

From Karl Zinsmeister, "Summing Up the Reagan Era," *Wilson Quarterly* (Winter 1990), 110–117. Reprinted by permission of Karl Zinsmeister, an Ithaca, NY writer and a fellow of the American Enterprise Institute for Public Policy Research.

part George Bush. The decade seems destined to be known, however, as the era of the "Reagan Revolution." Just how revolutionary a time it was depends upon where you set your gaze, but the range of sub-possibilities extends from "More than you might think," to "A lot less than you've been told."

At its self-proclaimed core, the revolution was a clear underachiever. For an epoch supposedly characterized by its backlash against government spending, government intrusion, and government presence in national life, there was far less action than fanfare. Not a single public housing project was privatized. The sagebrush rebellion didn't pry any western lands out of Uncle Sam's grasp [Reagan had proposed that 80 million acres of public wilderness be opened to developers by the end of the century]. Zooming farm subsidies and protections cost a total of $200 billion during the 1980s, by far the highest figure in our history. Enterprise zones, school prayers, and "the anti-communist resistance" in Nicaragua were so real to White House staffers as to have earned their own function keys on the speechwriting computers. But to average Americans they remained just slogans. Not a single tuition or social-service voucher was ever handed to a poor person over the head of a bureaucrat. And not only is there still a Department of Education, it spent one-and-a-half times as much in 1989 as it did ten years earlier.

In fiscal year 1980 the federal budget totaled 22.1 percent of U.S. GNP. By 1989, the figure had dropped all the way to 22.2 percent. No axe job! Not even any whittling! No decrease at all! (For ancient history buffs, the figure was 16.0 percent in 1950.) That's the revenge of the Neanderthal conservatives?

Even on the narrower front of federal taxes, where it is constantly claimed that the Reagan administration made cuts of "irresponsible" proportions, the changes were distinctly mouse-like: Over the decade, the proportion of national output channeled into the federal till went from 19.4 to 19.3 percent (compared with 14.8 percent in 1950). And if state and local taxes are taken into consideration, one can only conclude that during the 1980s the American people took a little more government onto their backs.

Mathematicians in the audience will detect a mismatch between the taxes-in and spending-out figures cited above. That discrepancy is called "the deficit," a definite growth sector and the favorite subject of the policy class during most of the last decade. The federal deficit stood at $74 billion in 1980, peaked at $221 billion in 1986, and weighed in at $115 billion by decade's end. So much for fiscal prudence and other pinched Republican concepts.

Accumulated and metamorphosed over the years like so much sea-bottom silt, federal deficits eventually become federal debt, an increasingly plentiful quantity in America during the 1980s. On New Year's Eve 1979 the national debt stood at $834 billion. Ten Auld Lang Syne's later it hit $2.3 trillion. These figures inspired rare harmonic caterwauls from both the right and the left.

Recent U.S. binging, however, appears only routine when viewed against the behavior of other big-spending national governments. The U.S. deficit [in late 1989] amounted to a little over 3 percent of GNP. The Japanese — they of the mystical discipline, the sober frugality — were running up tabs half again as large, as of 1987. The Canadians, Austrians, and Spanish were also overspending their allowances by a larger portion than the United States, and the Italians, Irish, and Belgians, heaven help them, actually had double-digit deficit/GNP ratios.

If we sharpen our focus on U.S. budget figures even further and look toward the supposed heart of the Reagan hit list — social welfare spending — we still see little evidence of any adherence to an anti-bloat diet. Federal spending on Social Security, Aid to Families with Dependent Children, health, housing, education, and anti-poverty measures totaled 4.9 percent of GNP in 1960, 7.8 percent in 1970, 11.3 percent in 1980, and 11.3 percent in 1987. Much

President Reagan sometimes had trouble explaining his budgets to the nation. During his budget speech of April 29, 1982, he couldn't get his red marker to work on his charts. (A/P Wide World Photos)

ballyhooed overhauls of the Social Security and welfare systems, replete with "blue-ribbon" commissions, presidential task forces, and "shadow committee" proposals resulted in the end in two distinct "Poofs!" that could be heard hundreds of miles from the nation's capital. Both reform efforts ultimately carried far more fingerprints of steady-as-she-goes Democratic Senator Daniel Patrick Moynihan than of the would-be earthquake inducers in the Reagan administration.

The Reagan presidency was not without its effect on the budget, however. Raising spending is a lot easier than reducing it, naturally, and in the area of national defense a notable expansion was accomplished. From its 1980 level of just under $200 billion, defense spending was increased to slightly more than $300 bil-

lion in the late 1980s (both figures in 1989 dollars). Here too, though, ephemerality was the byword. Defense outlays, which had represented 9.5 percent of GNP in 1960, 8.3 percent in 1970, and 5.0 percent in 1980, bobbed up to a peak of 6.5 percent of GNP in 1986 before dribbling back under six percent again by the decade's end.

People who understand physics claim that entropy is the law of the universe, but in Washington, D.C., inertia dominates. Truth is, the alleged "political realignment" of the 1980s produced relatively minor alterations of policy, and it resulted in almost no lasting change of casts. Following the relatively short-lived dominance of Republicans in the Senate (1981–87), the iron rule of the incumbents (which in Congress means Democrats) reasserted itself. In . . . elections, incumbents in the House of Representatives have been victorious in literally 99 percent of their races. (Early in this century it was common for half of all Congressional incumbents to be replaced in an election year. As recently as the late 1940s, about one-fifth got dumped.) Competition has effectively disappeared from national representational politics.

The two lasting political effects of Reaganism are disparate: Party identification has taken a so-far enduring swing toward the GOP, with self-described Republicans even becoming a majority among some young voting cohorts. Among 18- to 29-year-olds, for instance, 52 percent inclined to Republicanism in the first quarter of 1989, versus 33 percent in 1980. (While young voters tend to be comparatively liberal on issues like race and gender, they toe a more conservative line on economics, crime, and foreign policy.) And the Supreme Court, with five reasonably solid right-leaning justices, has been transformed from a clearly liberal institution of more than 20 years' standing to what most observers describe as a "moderately conservative" one. (The same is true for the federal judiciary generally.) Again, however, the transmogrifying jump was distinctly un-quantum like.

But the federal fisc and Washington are not the nation. In the myriad private universes of America, movement during the last 10 years was much more rapid. Indeed, change ranging between gradual and dizzying was virtually the rule.

For one thing, the place of technical innovation — which accelerates largely without regard to ditherings beyond the laboratory — continues to defy most people's expectations. Scientific advances initiated in the 1980s include the first higher-temperature superconductivity, the first anomalous indications that nuclear fusion may be possible at sub-stellar temperatures, creation of the first genetically altered animals, and the first field tests of genetically engineered plants.

It must be remembered that personal computers and workstations — of which there were nearly 60 million in operation [in late 1989] — were only invented in the 1980s. Likewise cellular phones (a couple million in motion), laser printers (more than 3 million), any number of new drugs, and a host of other daily-life-changing products. Undoubtedly, though their significance is often hard to grasp at the moment of breakthrough, the advances now sweeping electronics, biotechnology, chemistry and other hard sciences will eventually cause our era to be thought of as an epochal one in human civilization.

The results of these quiet marches can be seen in fundamental indicators like life expectancy. Average life expectation for a child born in the United States was 70.8 years in 1970, 73.7 in 1980, and 75.0 in 1987. With each passing year during the 1980s, average life spans increased 67 days. (To lay a prominent Reagan-attack to rest, infant mortality rates also continued to improve steadily during this period, falling from 12.6 deaths per 1,000 births to 9.9 in the first eight years of the decade.)

To put improvements of this magnitude in perspective, consider that when my still-living grandmother was born in 1900, U.S. life expectancy at birth was 47.3 years (10 years *below* the current level in India). The nearly 28-year improvement in longevity in her lifetime is more than occurred during the previous 10,000 years of human history.

It takes serious exertion to achieve progress like that, and the United States has spared no expense. In 1980, health expenditures represented 9.2 percent of our Gross Domestic Product. By 1986, they had jumped up to 11.1 percent and are still climbing. We spent $1,926 on health for every man, woman, and child in the country in 1986 — far more than, for instance, the $831 invested by the Japanese, or the $1,031 per capita expended in West Germany.

We also poured a lot of money into our education system during the 1980s. Spending per elementary and secondary school student zoomed up 26 percent from 1980 to 1988, and the average salary of public-school teachers rose 23 percent (both figures in constant dollars). Our high-school drop-out rate edged down a couple of percentage points — among blacks it was down about a third from 1980 to 1987. And college attendance continued to increase to an all-time high of 55 percent of all high-school graduates in 1986.

It's not clear, however, that all the extra effort improved the quality of education. During the 1980s, employment in school administrative bureaucracies grew two-and-a-half times as fast as employment of instructors. Barely half of all school employees today are full-time teachers. And judging by test results, not all of those teachers are teaching that well. The national average combined Scholastic Aptitude Test score bottomed out at 890 (out of 1600) in 1980. When the figure rebounded to 906 by the mid-1980s, backs were thumped everywhere. But average scores commenced to fall again after 1987. Our best assessment of nationwide educational competence stood at 903 as the decade ended, compared to an average score of 958 in 1968.

To return for a moment to the subject of life and limb, there is one very troubling 1980s retrogression that must be noted. Life expectancy for black Americans has actually *fallen* since 1984, an unprecedented occurrence. Given the health-care spending surge and all the countervailing technological factors regularly pushing life spans up, only a serious breakdown in the social arena could drag the figure lower. Unfortunately, such a breakdown exists today, in the form of the drug abuse and homicide epidemics which are tragically sweeping black communities across the nation. Jesse Jackson has taken to saying that dope is doing more damage to African-Americans than KKK ropes ever did, and on this critical statistical axis he is literally correct.

But the crime and drug waves which so damaged underclass communities during the 1980s went against society-wide trends. U.S. overall crime victimization crested in about 1979, and fell 14 percent for violent crime, 23 percent for personal thefts, and 28 percent for household thefts in the nine years following. The national trendlines on drug use by high school students peaked at about the same time. The fraction of high school seniors reporting use of an illicit substance within the previous 12 months declined 29 percent from the class of '79 to the class of '88.

Tougher law enforcement during the 1980s may have had something to do with these shifts. There were 29,000 criminal defendants convicted in U.S. District Courts in 1980 (about the same number as in 1970). By 1988 the number had jumped to 43,000. Likewise, the number of federal and state convicts behind bars increased from 316,000 in 1980 to 674,000 eight-and-a-half years later.

If gradual progress was ironically accompanied by a public sense of worsening crisis in the areas of crime and drugs, in another area almost the opposite phenomenon took place. The 1980s were the decade when the family arrived as a political issue. The public saw infant strollers clogging neighborhoods full of baby boomers and concluded that the return to traditional family values the president was calling for had actually taken place. Not so. The divorce rate did finally level off in the early 1980s, but that is mostly because the marriage rate had fallen so low. And divorce has stabilized at a level more than double the pre-1970s norm. (Current rates, extrapolated into the future, suggest that half of today's marriages will eventually break up.)

As for the birthrate, it has not risen from the low, less-than-population-replacement level it hit in the mid-1970s. All those strollers you are seeing are just a consequence of the aging of the baby boomers. An entire, large generation has hit the swollen-belly stage, but per couple they are having relatively few offspring (an average of 1.8 per woman, which doesn't even fill the places of mom and dad). Since the mid-1980s, for the first time in our history, the number of childless households in the United States has exceeded the number containing children.

Live from Heritage Village Church near Charlotte, N.C. Scandals have shaken "televangelism," but religious TV viewers increased *from 42 percent of Americans in 1980 to 49 percent in 1989. (Steve McCurry/Magnum Photos)*

And traditionalism is hardly on a roll. During the first seven years of the 1980s, right in the midst of a supposedly calm and conservatizing era, the number of births out of wedlock soared 40 percent. The astonishing result is that by the end of the decade one-quarter of all children born in America arrived without benefit of married parents. Literally a majority of them will depend upon welfare payments instead of a contributing father.

The combined result of 1980s divorce and illegitimacy patterns is that 27 percent of all children in this country now live apart from one or both of their par-

ents. (In Japan, 96 percent of all children live in two-parent families. Could broken homes, with known negative effects on "human capital," be part of our competitiveness problem?) An even more frightening fact is this: At *some* point in their childhood, at least 60 percent of all American youngsters born in the 1980s will spend time in a single-parent home.

If family salvation and shrunken government were Reaganisms that just didn't happen, a few other battle cries translated more successfully into reality. While critics worried that greed and self-interest would

457

overwhelm the voluntarism and individual account-ability called for by the president, Americans re-mained very generous during the 1980s. Private giv-ing for philanthropic purposes increased from $49 billion to $104 billion in the first eight years of the decade. More than four-fifths of that was comprised of individual donations. Corporate giving also jumped, by 66 percent in seven years. Mutual aid and fraternal cooperation are alive and well in the United States, as further indicated by the jump in national non-profit associations, from 14,726 in 1980 to 21,911 in 1989.

The Reaganites always insisted that the best aid program in the world was economic growth, and of that there was a surprisingly large measure during the 1980s. As this is being written in the waning weeks of 1989 the United States is entering its 85th straight month of economic growth, the second longest ex-pansion since record-keeping began in 1854, and one that economist Herbert Stein characterizes as "the longest and strongest *noninflationary* expansion in our history."

In addition to confounding economists of varying hues, this long expansion did nice things to the pock-etbooks of American citizens. Median family income, in constant 1988 dollars, stood at $29,919 in 1980. The decade-opening recession pushed it down to $28,708 by 1982. Then over the next six years it zipped up to $32,191. Income per capita, in many ways a purer indicator because it is not distorted by changes in family configuration over time, grew even more strongly: up a total of 17 percent from 1980 to 1988, or an annual rate of 2 percent since the expan-sion began.

Two percent annual growth sounds unexceptional, until you realize that it would *double* your standard of living in 35 years. For most of human history, an in-crease in life quality of that magnitude would have taken many generations. Today it is the legacy of a single presidential term.

Growth like that also has a way of eating up surplus labor. Early in the decade the air was full of talk of

long-term "structural" unemployment. By late 1989 unemployment was just a bit over 5 percent, and a record 63 percent of all Americans 16 and over were in harness. The raw aggregates too are quite impres-sive: As of 1979, 100 million Americans were earning a paycheck. In 1989 it was up to 119 million. There has been a whole lot of shaking going on in the world of job creation.

Perhaps the best indicator of the progress made on this front is the fact that unemployment stories almost never show up on news programs anymore. Which is not to say we don't have a serious employment prob-lem in this country. We do. As one Vermont state labor official puts it, "You've heard of the discour-aged worker effect; what we're seeing is the discour-aged employer effect."

New England, with 13 million residents, had a late-1980s unemployment rate of 3.1 percent. In the Maryland/D.C./Virginia region (home to 11 mil-lion), the figure was 3.5 percent. In many areas, grave labor *shortages* exist. . . . The minimum wage has be-come a fiction in many places (pizza deliverers for the Domino's chain are now paid between $8 and $12 an hour in the nation's capital), and employers through-out the land are finding it hard to fill positions with qualified workers.

Evidence of the rising prosperity of American pri-vate lives in the later 1980s could be seen in every-thing from skyrocketing housing demand (median sales prices of existing homes up 25 percent from 1985 to 1989) to record moviehouse admissions ($4.5 billion in 1988 versus $2.7 billion in 1980) to all-time highs in the fraction of American meals eaten out at restaurants (38 cents of every food dollar in 1987, up from 32 cents in 1980). Forty percent of Americans now attend an art event in the course of a year, 49 percent partake of live sports, 48 percent visit amuse-ment parks. (We now spend the same amount attend-ing cultural events as we do on athletic events. Twenty years ago it was only half as much.) The number of painters, authors and dancers has increased more than 80 percent over the last decade. The number of U.S. opera companies rose from 986 to 1,224 in just the first seven years of the 1980s.

Book purchases are up, national park visits and trips abroad have soared, cable TV hook-ups are climbing, wine sales have jumped, big-ticket athletic shoes are huge sellers. Nearly one out of every five houses now standing in the U.S. was built since 1980. Numbers of motor vehicles and numbers of phones have risen toward saturation (more than one of each for every adult in the country), and video cameras, microwave ovens, personal computers, food processors and other gadgets have come out of nowhere since 1980 to take their places right next to the toaster and other "necessities."

Expanded choices and new services confront even the reluctant consumer. Anyone spinning the FM radio dial in 1989 encountered a great many more stations than he or she did in 1980 (a thousand more nationwide, up 30 percent). New regional and specialty magazines fill every niche from *Organic Farmer* to *PC World*. Just about any item that a person desires can now be purchased from catalogs which slip conveniently through our mailslots every day.

One example of the increasingly riotous variety that bubbled through American life in the 1980s: The number of different fresh fruits and vegetables stocked by the average supermarket tripled in ten years. Visiting Soviet legislator Boris Yeltsin went home raving that the Americans HAVE 30,000 ITEMS IN THEIR GROCERY STORES! The fact that before returning he converted all his lecture fees into hypodermic needles — one of thousands of vital low-tech commodities that Mother Russia has found it impossible to produce in adequate supply — indicates how grotesquely fantastical these material riches must seem to people in countries of low economic creativity.

Perhaps out of frustration, many talented residents of those less creative nations decided to vote with their feet during the 1980s. Nearly 6 million legal immigrants came to our shores during the decade, a little less than half from Asia, somewhat under 40 percent from Latin America and the Caribbean, and most of the rest from Europe. The number of people of Hispanic origin in the United States rose from 15 million in 1980 to 20 million in 1989, and the ranks of Asian-Americans grew from 4 million to about twice that. Measures to draw immigrants from various continents in somewhat fairer relation to the existing make-up of the U.S. population were wending their way through Congress as the '80s drew to a close.

One of the biggest statistical "dud" stories of the 1980s concerned our supposed invasion by illegal aliens. After years of hearing alarmist guessers make alarming guesses, the Census Bureau in 1986 finally undertook an official calculation of the extent of illegal immigration to the United States. Their best estimate: about 200,000 per year. (This was prior to passage of the Simpson-Rodino bill in 1986, which tightened things up. Presumably there are fewer these days.)

The Census Bureau also attempted to quantify *out*-migration from the country (most of it by foreign-born Americans returning to the country of their birth) and came up with a figure of around 160,000 annually. When the Immigration and Naturalization Service conducted its amnesty program for illegals in the later 1980s, just 1.8 million individuals applied for permanent legal status, confirming that the "undocumented" population in this country is much smaller than the 5 to 20 million figure sometimes bandied about.

A factual survey like this necessarily concentrates on subjects that can be measured and expressed statistically. But many of the most important shifts of the 1980s fell in softer categories, loosely organizable under the topic "cultural attitudes." In the long run, the new cultural thinking that coincided with the Reagan era (I do not wish to make a case here concerning cause and effect) may be more significant to the life of the nation than anything that happened in, say, the governmental or financial realms.

There was, for instance, a pronounced religious revival, with most of the action taking place within evangelical and theologically conservative churches. Even though the total percentage of Americans who attend church weekly is about the same today as it was in 1939 — 40 percent — the number of persons reporting they watch religious television rose from 42 percent in 1980 to 49 percent in 1989. A network of thousands of religious book stores has spread across the country. Twenty-five hundred retail stores were members of the Christian Booksellers Association in 1980, versus 3,000 in 1989. If sales figures from such shops were included by the tabulators, religious books by authors like James Dobson, Charles Swindoll, Frank Peretti, Jeanette Olsen, Robert Schuller, and Rabbi Harold Kushner would have appeared prominently on U.S. best-seller lists during the 1980s (with around 30 million books sold among them).

In other corners of American culture there has been a pronounced turn toward traditionalism. Our buildings, for instance, are once again being built with · columns, ornaments, and gold leaf. On our stages, screens, political podiums, and playing fields, hairy-chested masculinity has roared back as an American ideal. In the music industry, classical recordings began to sell like rock recordings for the first time during the 1980s. Luciano Pavarotti's "Oh, Silent Night" went Platinum (one million or more sales), the Mozart soundtrack for *Amadeus* hit Gold (500,000 or more sales), and other pressings like "Horowitz in Moscow," RCA's "Pachelbel Canon," and Leonard Bernstein's "West Side Story" on Deutsche Gramophone are all approaching bullion status. Many of the most influential new pop artists were dubbed "New Traditionalists" because of their affinities for both older musical styles (acoustic instruments have made a big comeback, for example) and older lyrical themes. Love of family and flag, expressions of faith, and praise for independence and hard work were among the favorite songwriting topics of the 1980s.

Conservatism played well in the nation's bookstores as well. Allan Bloom sold around 850,000 copies of *The Closing of the American Mind,* a book which

may best be described as a declamation against the 20th century. The two most influential public-policy books of the decade were a defense of supply-side economics by George Gilder and an attack on the Great Society by Charles Murray (the former, *Wealth and Poverty,* sold 114,000 copies in hardbound alone; the latter, *Losing Ground,* 56,000 copies). After 52 weeks on the fiction best-seller lists, *The Bonfire of the Vanities,* Tom Wolfe's conservative critique of urban collapse, continues to sell briskly. Even writers of a usually leftish inclination started behaving uncharacteristically. In 1986, at a Poets, Essayists, and Novelists (PEN) conference in New York, none other than Norman Mailer surprised his audience with a defense of Reagan's Secretary of State, George Shultz.

On television and in film, too, new values — or at least a new wistfulness for old values — became apparent. Among the movies that American audiences consumed most hungrily during the 1980s were ones like "Chariots of Fire," "Top Gun," "Hoosiers," and "Trading Places" — films that treated religion sympathetically, that frankly admired military values, that celebrated small-town virtue, that were anti-communist, that were pro-entrepreneurial and anti-bureaucratic. Among the most popular television fare was "The Bill Cosby Show," with its full embrace of the traditional bourgeois family values (top rated for four of its five full seasons to date), and the attacks on liberalism in criminal justice on "Hill Street Blues" (winner of 25 Emmy awards).

The currents and crosscurrents of the 1980s had their cumulative effect in subtle but significant ways. Toward the end of the decade an extremely average American woman named Anita Folmar, one of many conservative Democrats whom Ronald Reagan had induced to become a Republican, was quoted in an unimportant little newspaper piece praising the president for bringing a "return to morality . . . wearing jeans where jeans should be worn, not all the time." That is about as good a summary of the most important presidency since World War II as we are likely to get. Ronald Reagan — himself more a cultural icon, an embodied idea, than an actual motive force — was important mostly because he presented an *altered picture* to America in the 1980s.

In his own daffy way, Reagan characterized the decade perfectly. He wasn't quite the man he claimed to be, and he, like us, didn't carry through on a lot of his boldest resolutions. Few molds got broken during the 1980s. But Reagan projected an idealized image that was rather different from what we had become used to, and he quite sincerely aspired to fill it. He, and we, deeply wanted us to be the old shining city on the hill. . . .

QUESTIONS TO CONSIDER

1.   Karl Zinsmeister calls the "Reagan Revolution" a "clear underachiever." What were the stated goals of President Reagan's policies, and how did they fail? What role did the government play in the changes of the 1980s? What does Zinsmeister point to as the lasting political effects of the Reagan era?

2.   Describe what Zinsmeister sees as the big changes of the 1980s in Americans' daily lives, both for the better and the worse. How have these changes developed since the 1980s? Do you see any hopeful or alarming trends?

3.   In particular, what developments occurred in the 1980s in American families and what was their significance? How would you answer Zinsmeister's question: "Could broken homes, with known negative effects on 'human capital,' be part of our competitiveness problem?"

4.   What are Zinsmeister's observations and conclusions about prosperity in the 1980s? How have these trends developed since 1989 when Zinsmeister wrote his article?

5.   What were the dominant "cultural attitudes" and trends of the 1980s, according to the author, and what does he see as the significance of Ronald Reagan? Why do you think Zinsmeister says that Reagan's is "the most important presidency since World War II"? Do you agree? Compare the developments of the 1980s with those of other decades you have read about — for example, the 1920s (selection 15), the 1960s (selection 28), and the 1970s (selection 30).

32

Some Lessons from the Cold War

ARTHUR M. SCHLESINGER, JR.

The demise of the Soviet empire and the end of the Cold War — if indeed it has ended — came with such speed and surprise that the pace of events was almost too much to comprehend. It began in 1985 when Mikhail Gorbachev acceded to power as Soviet boss. To the utter astonishment of the West, he became "the most revolutionary figure in world politics in at least four decades," as one historian puts it. Gorbachev not only launched glasnost, which ended many of the Soviet Union's most repressive practices, but started perestroika, or the restructuring of the Soviet Union, in order to end decades of economic stagnation and backwardness under communism. Gorbachev sought to remake the Soviet economy by introducing such elements of capitalism as the profit motive and private ownership of property. Gorbachev's policies set the Soviet Union down the road toward a market economy; sped the doom of the Soviet Communist party, which lost its monopoly of political power in 1990; brought about détente and the Intermediate Nuclear Force (INF) Treaty with the United States; and ignited nationalist movements within the Soviet empire that finally tore the Soviet Union apart.

In 1989, meanwhile, world communism itself appeared to collapse. Our television sets brought us the stunning spectacle of Eastern Europeans, subjected to decades of violent repression, demonstrating in the streets in favor of individual freedom and democratic government. Every nation in the Eastern bloc — East Germany, Bulgaria, Romania, Hungary, Czechoslovakia, and Poland — overthrew its Communist regime or made that regime reform itself into a noncommunist government. Most dramatic of all was the dismantling of the Berlin Wall, long the preeminent symbol of the Cold War between East and West, and the reunification of Germany itself. At long last, the troubled legacy of

World War II seemed to be over, leaving the world a safer place. For those of us who lived through World War II and the entire length of the Cold War, the events of the late 1980s and early 1990s defied belief. Few thought we would ever live to see the collapse of the Soviet Communist state and the end of the Cold War at the same time.

It is too soon, of course, to know what all this means for the future of humankind. But it is not too soon to reflect on some lessons of the Cold War, which on at least one occasion — the Cuban missile crisis of October 1962 — almost exploded into a nuclear holocaust and the end of the world as we know it. How did humankind survive the Cold War? What caused and sustained it? The experts do not agree. Some see the Cold War as fundamentally an ideological struggle between the forces of freedom and the forces of autocracy. Still others view the Cold War as a geopolitical and military contest that involved not just a Soviet–United States confrontation but a Western Europe–Soviet confrontation as well. While some specialists maintain that the Cold War strengthened hard liners in the Soviet Union and sustained Communist rule there, others, such as Ronald Steel, believe that American policymakers exaggerated the military capacity of the Soviet Union throughout the Cold War, thus creating a bogus enemy that justified huge American defense build-ups.

In the selection that follows, Arthur M. Schlesinger, Jr., one of our greatest historians, argues that it is irrelevant to allocate blame for the Cold War. It emerged, he says, from the efforts of the United States and the Soviet Union to fill the "power vacuum" left by World War II, and it developed into "a holy war" because of very real ideological differences between the two new superpowers and their allies. At bottom, Schlesinger believes, the Cold War was a "fundamental debate" between communism and liberalism, including democratic socialism, and that debate charged the Cold War with its religious intensity.

Now that the holy war is over, Schlesinger suggests six fallacies that helped make it so long, so dark, and so dangerous. These fallacies, Schlesinger suggests, resulted from the perception of events by both sides. Yes, the perception of reality is the crucial element in understanding the past. How people perceive events and the motives of an alleged enemy determine how they act, and how they act in turn affects the course of subsequent events. When it comes to the Cold War, human error, exaggeration, misunderstanding, over-interpretation — all played a key role in shaping and sustaining tensions between East and West. Schlesinger hopes that his six fallacies, or errors of perception, judgment, and action, will benefit future policymakers, so that the world can avoid another Cold War, another "intimate brush with collective suicide." In the end, he argues, "Democracy won the political argument between East and West" and "the market won the economic argument." Yet in retrospect, Schlesinger says, the Cold War can only remind us "of the ultimate interdependence of nations and of peoples."

GLOSSARY

STALIN, JOSEPH   Soviet dictator from the 1920s until his death in 1953, he ruled the Soviet Union with a brutal hand, resorting to massive purges in the 1930s and again in the post–World War II years; he viewed the West as a devious menace (several times in its history Russia had been invaded by Western European powers) and clamped an iron hand on Eastern Europe, using it as a bulwark against Western "aggression."

WALLACE, HENRY A.   FDR's vice president, 1941–1945, and Truman's secretary of commerce, 1945–1946; Wallace was forced to resign as commerce secretary after he publicly attacked Truman's "get tough" policy toward the Soviets; in 1948, Wallace made an unsuccessful bid for the presidency as the candidate of the Progressive party.

ZERO-SUM GAME   Cold War notion that "a gain for one side was by definition a defeat for the other."

In those faraway days when the Cold War was young, the English historian Sir Herbert Butterfield lectured at Notre Dame on "The Tragic Element in Modern International Conflict." Historians writing about modern wars, Butterfield said, characteristically start off with a "heroic" vision of things. They portray good men struggling against bad, virtue resisting evil. In this embattled mood, they see only the sins of the enemy and ignore the underlying structural dilemmas that so often provoke international clashes.

As time passes and emotions subside, history enters the "academic" phase. Now historians see "a terrible human predicament" at the heart of the story, "a certain situation that contains the element of conflict irrespective of any special wickedness in any of the parties concerned." Wickedness may deepen the predicament, but conflict would be there anyway. Perspective, Butterfield proposed, teaches us "to be a little more sorry for both parties than they knew how to be for one another." History moves on from melodrama to tragedy.

Butterfield made a pretty good forecast of the way Cold War historiography has evolved in the more than forty years since he spoke. In the United States the "heroic" phase took two forms: the orthodox in the 1940s and 1950s, with the Russians cast as the villains, and the revisionist in the 1960s, with the Americans as the villains. By the 1980s, American Cold War historians discerned what one of the best of them, John Lewis Gaddis, called an "emerging post-revisionist synthesis." History began to pass from a weapon in the battle into a more analytical effort to define structural dilemmas and to understand adversary concerns. *Glasnost* permitted comparable historiographical evolution in the former Soviet Union.

From Arthur M. Schlesinger, Jr., "Some Lessons from the Cold War," in Michael J. Hogan (ed.), *The End of the Cold War: Its Meaning and Implications* (Cambridge: Cambridge University Press, 1992), 53–62. Reprinted by permission of the author.

In late 1988, Gorbachev announced that he would reduce Soviet military presence in the Eastern bloc nations. Five months later, the first of the military units scheduled for withdrawal — thirty-one Soviet T.64 tanks — pulled out of Hungary and returned to the U.S.S.R. (Jean Gaumy/Magnum)

ideological conviction, and the political will to fill these vacuums.

But why did this old-fashioned geopolitical rivalry billow up into a holy war so intense and obsessive as to threaten the very existence of human life on the planet? The two nations were constructed on opposite and profoundly antagonistic principles. They were divided by the most significant and fundamental disagreements over human rights, individual liberties, cultural freedom, the role of civil society, the direction of history, and the destiny of man. Each state saw the other as irrevocably hostile to its own essence. Given the ideological conflict on top of the geopolitical confrontation, no one should be surprised at what ensued. Conspiratorial explanations are hardly required. The real surprise would have been if there had been no Cold War.

And why has humanity survived the Cold War? The reason that the Cold War never exploded into hot war was surely (and by providential irony) the invention of nuclear weapons. One is inclined to support the suggestion (Elspeth Rostow's, I think) that the Nobel Peace Prize should have gone to the atomic bomb.

At last this curious episode in modern history is over, and we must ask what lessons we may hope to learn from a long, costly, dark, dreary, and dangerous affair; what precautions humanity should take to prevent comparable episodes in the future. I would suggest half a dozen fallacies that the world might well forego in years to come.

The first might be called the fallacy of over-interpreting the enemy. In the glory days of the Cold War, each side attributed to the other a master plan for world domination joined with diabolical efficiency in executing the plan. Such melodramatic imagining of brilliant and demonic enemies was truer to, say, Sax Rohmer, the creator of Dr. Fu Manchu, than to shuffling historical reality.

No doubt Soviet leaders believed that the dialectic of history would one day bring about the victory of communism. No doubt Western leaders believed that

Quite right: The more one contemplates the Cold War, the more irrelevant the allocation of blame seems. The Second World War left the international order in acute derangement. With the Axis states vanquished, the Western European allies spent, the colonial empires in tumult and dissolution, great gaping holes appeared in the structure of world power. Only two nations — the United States and the Soviet Union — had the military strength, the

465

the nature of man and markets would one day bring about the victory of free society. But such generalized hopes were far removed from operational master plans.

"The superpowers," as Henry Kissinger well put it,

often behave like two heavily armed blind men feeling their way around a room, each believing himself in mortal peril from the other whom he assumes to have perfect vision. Each side should know that frequently uncertainty, compromise, and incoherence are the essence of policymaking. Yet each tends to ascribe to the other a consistency, foresight, and coherence that its own experience belies. Of course, over time, even two blind men can do enormous damage to each other, not to speak of the room.

The room has happily survived. But the blind men meanwhile escalated the geopolitical/ideological confrontation into a compulsively interlocked heightening of tension, spurred on by authentic differences in principle, by real and supposed clashes of interest, and by a wide range of misperception, misunderstanding, and demagoguery. Each superpower undertook for what it honestly saw as defensive reasons actions that the other honestly saw as unacceptably threatening and requiring stern countermeasures. Each persevered in corroborating the fears of the other. Each succumbed to the propensity to perceive local conflicts in global terms, political conflicts in moral terms, and relative differences in absolute terms. Together, in lockstep, they expanded the Cold War.

In overinterpreting the motives and actions of the other, each side forgot Emerson's invaluable precept: "In analysing history, do not be too profound, for often the causes are quite simple." Both superpowers should have known from their own experience that governments mostly live from day to day responding to events as they come, that decisions are more often the result of improvisation, ignorance, accident, fatigue, chance, blunder, and sometimes plain stupidity than of orchestrated master plans. One lesson to be drawn from the Cold War is that more things in life

are to be explained by cock-up, to use the British term, than by conspiracy.

An accompanying phenomenon, at first a consequence and later a reinforcing cause of overinterpretation, was the embodiment of the Cold War in government institutions. Thus our second fallacy: The fallacy of overinstitutionalizing the policy. The Soviet Union, a police state committed to dogmas of class war and capitalist conspiracy and denied countervailing checks of free speech and press, had institutionalized the Cold War from the day Lenin arrived at the Finland Station. In later years the Cold War became for Stalin a convenient means of justifying his own arbitrary power and the awful sacrifices he demanded from the Soviet peoples. "Stalin needed the Cold War," observed Earl Browder, whom Stalin purged as chief of the American Communist party, "to keep up the sharp international tensions by which he alone could maintain such a regime in Russia."

In Washington by the 1950s the State Department, the Defense Department, the Central Intelligence Agency, the Federal Bureau of Investigation, and the National Security Council developed vested bureaucratic interests in the theory of a militarily expansionist Soviet Union. The Cold War conferred power, money, prestige, and public influence on these agencies and on the people who ran them. By the natural law of bureaucracies, their stake in the conflict steadily grew. Outside of government, arms manufacturers, politicians, professors, publicists, pontificators, and demagogues invested careers and fortunes in the Cold War.

In time, the adversary Cold War agencies evolved a sort of tacit collusion across the Iron Curtain. Probably the greatest racket in the Cold War was the charade periodically enacted by generals and admirals announcing the superiority of the other side in order to get bigger budgets for themselves. As President John F. Kennedy remarked to Norman Cousins, the editor of the *Saturday Review,* in the spring of 1963, "The hard-liners in the Soviet Union and the United States feed on one another."

Institutions, alas, do not fold their tents and silently steal away. Ideas crystallized in bureaucracies resist change. With the Cold War at last at an end, each side faces the problem of deconstructing entrenched Cold War agencies spawned and fortified by nearly half a century of mutually profitable competition. One has only to reflect on the forces behind the anti-Gorbachev conspiracy of August 1991 [which sought in vain to overthrow him].

A third fallacy may be called the fallacy of arrogant prediction. As a devotee of a cyclical approach to American political history, I would not wish to deny that history exhibits uniformities and recurrences. But it is essential to distinguish between those phenomena that are predictable and those that are not. Useful historical generalizations are mostly statements about broad, deep-running, long-term changes: the life-cycle of revolutions, for example, or the impact of industrialization and urbanization, or the influence of climate or sea power or the frontier. The short term, however, contains too many variables, depends too much on accident and fortuity and personality, to permit exact and specific forecasts.

We have been living through extraordinary changes in the former Soviet Union and in Eastern Europe, in South Africa and in the Middle East. What is equally extraordinary is that *no one foresaw these changes*. All the statesmen, all the sages, all the savants, all the professors, all the prophets, all those bearded chaps on "Nightline" — all were caught unaware and taken by surprise; all were befuddled and impotent before the perpetual astonishments of the future. History has an abiding capacity to outwit our certitudes.

Just a few years back some among us were so absolutely sure of the consequences if we did not smash the Reds at once that they called for preventive nuclear war. Had they been able to persuade the U.S. government to drop the bomb on the Soviet Union in the 1950s or on China in the 1960s . . . but, thank heaven, they never did; and no one today, including those quondam preventive warriors themselves, regrets the American failure to do so.

The Almighty no doubt does know the future. But He has declined to confide such foresight to frail and erring mortals. In the early years of the Cold War, [theologian] Reinhold Niebuhr warned of "the depth of evil to which individuals and communities may sink . . . when they try to play the role of God to history." Let us not fall for people who tell us that we must take drastic action today because of their conjectures as to what some other fellow or nation may do five or ten or twenty years from now.

Playing God to history is the dangerous consequence of our fourth fallacy — the fallacy of national self-righteousness. "No government or social system is so evil," President Kennedy said in his American University speech in 1963, "that its people must be condemned as lacking in virtue," and he called on Americans as well as Russians to reexamine attitudes toward the Cold War, "for our attitude is as essential as theirs." This thought came as rather a shock to those who assumed that the American side was so manifestly right that self-examination was unnecessary.

Kennedy liked to quote a maxim from the British military pundit Liddell Hart: "Never corner an opponent, and always assist him to save his face. Put yourself in his shoes — so as to see things through his eyes. Avoid self-righteousness like the devil — nothing is so self-blinding." Perhaps Kennedy did not always live up to those standards himself, but he did on great occasions, like the Cuban missile crisis, and he retained a capacity for ironical objectivity that is rare among political leaders.

Objectivity — seeing ourselves as others see us — is a valuable adjunct to statesmanship. Can we be so sure that our emotional judgments of the moment represent the last word and the final truth? The angry ideological conflicts that so recently obsessed us may not greatly interest our posterity. Our great-grand-children may well wonder what in heaven's name those disagreements could have been that drove the Soviet Union and the United States to the brink of blowing up the planet.

467

Men and women a century from now will very likely find the Cold War as obscure and incomprehensible as we today find the Thirty Years War — the terrible conflict that devastated much of Europe not too long ago. Looking back at the twentieth century, our descendants will very likely be astonished at the disproportion between the causes of the Cold War, which may well seem trivial, and the consequences, which could have meant the veritable end of history.

Russians and Americans alike came to see the Cold War as a duel between two superpowers, a Soviet-American duopoly. But the reduction of the Cold War to a bilateral game played by the Soviet Union and the United States is a fifth fallacy. The nations of Europe were not spectators at someone else's match. They were players too.

Revisionist historians, determined to blame the Cold War on an American drive for world economic hegemony, have studiously ignored the role of Europe. Washington, they contend, was compelled to demand an "open door" for American trade and investment everywhere on the planet because American capitalism had to expand in order to survive. The Soviet Union was the main obstacle to a world market controlled by the United States. So, by revisionist dogma, American leaders whipped up an unnecessary Cold War in order to save the capitalist system.

No matter that some fervent open door advocates, like Henry A. Wallace, were also fervent opponents of the Cold War. No matter that the republics of the former Soviet Union now want nothing more than American trade and investment and full integration into the world market. And no matter that most Western European nations in the 1940s had Socialist governments and that the democratic socialist leaders — Clement Attlee and Ernest Bevin in Britain, Leon Blum and Paul Ramadier in France, Paul-Henri Spaak in Belgium, Kurt Schumacher, Ernst Reuter, and Willy Brandt in West Germany — had powerful reasons of their own to fear the spread of Stalinist influence and Soviet power.

Such men could not have cared less about an open door for American capitalism. They cared deeply, however, about the future of democratic socialism. When I used to see Aneurin Bevan, the leader of the left wing of the British Labour party, in London in 1944, he doubted that the wartime alliance would last and saw the struggle for postwar Europe as between the democratic socialists and the Communists. "The Communist party," Bevan wrote in 1951, "is the sworn and inveterate enemy of the Socialist and Democratic parties. When it associates with them it does so as a preliminary to destroying them." Many in the Truman administration in the 1940s espoused this view and, dubbing themselves (in private) NCL, favored American support for the non-Communist Left.

The democratic socialists, moreover, were in advance of official Washington in organizing against the Stalinist threat. Despite his above-the-battle stance at Notre Dame, Herbert Butterfield himself wrote in 1969, "A new generation often does not know (and does not credit the fact when informed) that Western Europe once wondered whether the United States could ever be awakened to the danger from Russia." The subsequent opening of British Foreign Office papers voluminously documents Sir Herbert's point.

Far from seeing President Truman in the revisionist mode as an anti-Soviet zealot hustling a reluctant Europe into a gratuitous Cold War, the Foreign Office saw him for a considerable period as an irresolute waffler distracted by the delusion that the United States could play mediator between Britain and the Soviet Union. Ernest Bevin, Britain's Socialist foreign secretary, thought Truman's policy was "to withdraw from Europe and in effect leave the British to get on with the Russians as best they could." A true history of the Cold War must add European actors to the cast and broaden both research nets and analytical perspectives.

The theory of the Cold War as a Soviet-American duopoly is sometimes defended on the ground that, after all, the United States and the Soviet Union were in full command of their respective alliances. But nationalism, the most potent political emotion of the

The Berlin Wall, a symbol of the Cold War for nearly three decades, separated Communist East Berlin from West Berlin. With the easing of Cold War tensions, "the wall" was torn down in 1989 and Germany itself was reunited under Western rule. (Guy Le Querrec/Magnum)

age, challenged the reign of the superpowers almost from the start: Tito [of Yugoslavia], Mao, and others vs. Moscow; De Gaulle, Eden and others vs. Washington. Experience has adequately demonstrated how limited superpowers are in their ability to order their allies around and even to control client governments wholly dependent on them for economic and military support. Far from clients being the prisoners of the superpower, superpowers often end as prisoners of their clients.

These are lessons Washington has painfully learned (or at least was painfully taught; has the government finally learned them?) in Vietnam, El Salvador, Israel, Saudi Arabia, Kuwait. As for the Soviet Union, its brutal interventions and wretched Quislings in East-

ern Europe only produced bitterness and hatred. The impact of clients on principals is another part of the unwritten history of the Cold War. The Cold War was *not* a bilateral game.

Nor was it — our sixth and final fallacy — a zero-sum game. For many years, Cold War theology decreed that a gain for one side was by definition a defeat for the other. This notion led logically not to an interest in negotiation but to a demand for capitulation. In retrospect the Cold War, humanity's most intimate brush with collective suicide, can only remind us of the ultimate interdependence of nations and of peoples.

After President Kennedy and Premier Khrushchev stared down the nuclear abyss together in October

1962, they came away determined to move as fast as they could toward détente. Had Kennedy lived, Khrushchev might have held on to power a little longer, and together they would have further subdued the excesses of the Cold War. They rejected the zero-sum approach and understood that intelligent negotiation brings mutual benefit. I am not an unlimited admirer of Ronald Reagan, but he deserves his share of credit for taking Mikhail Gorbachev seriously, abandoning the zero-sum fallacy he had embraced for so long, and moving the Cold War toward its end.

And why indeed has it ended? If the ideological confrontation gave the geopolitical rivalry its religious intensity, so the collapse of the ideological debate took any apocalyptic point out of the Cold War. The proponents of liberal society were proven right. After seventy years of trial, communism turned out — by the confession of its own leaders — to be an economic, political, and moral disaster. Democracy won the political argument between East and West. The market won the economic argument. Difficulties lie ahead, but the fundamental debate that created the Cold War is finished.

QUESTIONS TO CONSIDER

1.   What are the six fallacies of judgment and action that aggravated the tensions between East and West after World War II, according to Arthur Schlesinger, and why did the two sides fall into them? What are the overarching lessons Schlesinger would like nations and peoples to learn from the mistakes of the Cold War?

2.   Schlesinger says that democracy and the market economy won the Cold War, but do we know for certain what the future holds for the former Soviet Union and for Eastern Europe? What do you think are the lasting effects of the Cold War on the United States and how might they affect our future?

3.   What have been the general trends in Cold War historiography? How are historians influenced by the traditions from which they come and the times in which they live, and do you think they may in turn influence those times?

4.   As you think about Schlesinger's selection and all the readings in this book, what do you think is the relative importance of general social and political factors and the actions of individuals on the course of history? Where have you seen examples of the influence of people's perceptions on subsequent events?

5.   Arthur Schlesinger calls himself a "devotee of a cyclical approach to American political history." As you look back over the readings in this book and your general experience in American history, do you see certain recurring themes or trends or concerns in that story? What might these tell you about the basic principles and character of the American experience?

An Invitation to Respond

We would like to find out a little about your background and about your reactions to the sixth edition of *Portrait of America*. Your evaluation of the book will help us to meet the interests and needs of students in future editions. We invite you to share your reactions by completing the questionnaire below and returning it to *College Marketing. Houghton Mifflin Company, 222 Berkeley Street, Boston, MA 02116.*

1. How do you rate this textbook in the following areas?

	Excellent	*Good*	*Adequate*	*Poor*
a. Understandable style of writing	_____	_____	_____	____
b. Physical appearance/ readability	_____	_____	_____	____
c. Fair coverage of topics	_____	_____	_____	____
d. Comprehensiveness (covered major issues and time periods)	_____	_____	_____	____

2. Can you comment on or illustate your above ratings? _____
   _____
   _____
   _____

3. What chapters or features did you particularly like? _____
   _____
   _____
   _____

4. What chapters or features did you dislike or think should be changed?
   _____
   _____
   _____

5. What material would you suggest adding or deleting? _____
   _____
   _____
   _____

6. Are you a student at a community college or a four-year school? _____
   _____

7. Do you intend to major in history? _____

8. We would appreciate any other comments or reactions you are willing to share. _____
   _____
   _____